17th International Conference on Spoken Language Translation (IWSLT 2020)

Online
9-10 July 2020

ISBN: 978-1-7138-1388-0

17th International Conference on Spoken Language Translation (IWSLT 2020)

Online
9-10 July 2020

IWSLT 2020

The 17th International Conference on Spoken Language Translation

Proceedings of the Conference

July 9 - 10, 2020

Preface

The International Conference on Spoken Language Translation (IWSLT) is the premiere annual scientific conference for the study, development and evaluation of spoken language translation technology. Launched in 2004 and spun out from the C-STAR speech translation consortium before it (1992-2003), IWSLT is the main venue for scientific exchange on all topics related to speech-to-text translation, speech-to- speech translation, simultaneous and consecutive translation, speech dubbing, cross-lingual communication including all multimodal, emotional, paralinguistic, and stylistic aspects and their applications in the field. The conference organizes evaluations and workshop sessions around challenge areas, and presents scientific work and system descriptions.

In 2020, IWSLT joins ACL as the first ACL speech translation conference. It features six challenge tracks: 1.) Simultaneous speech translation, 2.) Video speech translation, 3.) Offline speech translation, 4.) Conversational speech translation, 5.) Open domain translation, and 6.) Non-native speech translation. These topics represent open problems toward effective cross-lingual communication and we expect the community effort and discussion will greatly advance the state of the field. Each track was coordinated by a chair. The resulting evaluation campaigns attracted a total of 30 teams, from academy and industry. System submissions resulted in system papers that will be presented at the conference.

The great turnout this year demonstrates the growing academic and commercial interest in spoken language translation. It has been empowered by growing availability of data resources also facilitated by the conference over the years. The versatility of neural network models and broad availability of training frameworks further support this trend as even smaller groups can now tackle complex problems, like speech translation, directly. Given the growing interest and international demand, we invite researchers and potential organizers to propose new IWSLT challenges for the future.

Following our call for papers this year, 43 submissions were received. In a blind review process, 9 research papers were selected out of 19 for oral presentation (47%) in addition to 24 system papers. The program committee is excited about the quality of the accepted papers and expects lively discussion and exchange at the conference.

The conference chairs and organizers would like to express their gratitude to everyone who contributed and supported IWSLT. Our IWSLT-20 program exceeds all our expectations in quality and breath, particularly when considering the challenges during a pandemic under lock-downs and health and travel restrictions. We thank the challenge track chairs, organizers, and participants, the program chairs and committee members, as well as all the authors that went the extra mile to submit system and research papers to IWSLT, and make this year's conference our most vibrant than ever. We also wish to express our sincere gratitude to ACL for hosting our conference and for arranging the logistics and infrastructure that allow us to hold IWSLT 2020 as a virtual online conference.

Welcome to IWSLT 2020, in Seattle, Mountain View or wherever you may be hiding out!

Marcello Federico and Alex Waibel
Conference Chairs

Organizers:

Marcello Federico, Amazon, USA (Chair)
Alex Waibel, CMU, USA (Chair)
Kevin Knight, DiDi Labs, USA
Satoshi Nakamura, NAIST, Japan
Hermann Ney, RWTH, Germany
Jan Niehues, Maastricht University, Netherlands
Sebastian Stüker, KIT, Germany
Dekai Wu, HKUST Hong Kong, China
Joseph Mariani, LIMSI/CNRS, France
Francois Yvon, LIMSI/CNRS, France

Challenge Track Organizers:

Simultaneous Speech Translation
Jiatao Gu, Facebook, USA (Chair)
Juan Pino, Facebook, USA
Changhan Wang, Facebook, USA
Xutai Ma, JHU, USA
Fahim Dalvi, QCRI, Qatar
Nadir Durrani, QCRI, Qatar
Video Speech Translation
Fei Huang, Alibaba, USA (Chair)
Nguyen Bach, Alibaba, USA
Wei Luo, Alibaba, USA
Boxing Chen, Alibaba, USA
Fei Huang, Alibaba, USA
Offline Speech Translation
Marco Turchi, FBK, Italy (Chair)
Matteo Negri, FBK, Italy
Roldano Cattoni, FBK, Italy
Sebastian Stüker, KIT, Germany
Jan Niehues, Maastricht University, Netherland
Conversational Speech Translation
Elizabeth Salesky, JHU, USA (Chair)
Open Domain Translation
Ajay Nagesh, Didi Labs, USA (Chair)
Amittai Axelrod, Didi Labs, USA
Arkady Arkhangorodsky, Didi Labs, USA
Boliang Zhang, Didi Labs, USA
Xing Shi, Didi Labs, USA
Non-Native Speech Translation
Ondrej Bojar, Charles University, Czech Republic (Chair)
Ebrahim Ansari, Charles University, Czech Republic

Program Committee:

Christian Federmann, Microsoft Research, USA (Chair)
Will Lewis, Microsoft Research, USA (Chair)
Akiko Eriguchi, Microsoft, USA
Antonio Toral, U. Groningen, Netherlands
Boxing Chen, Alibaba, China
Christian Hardmeier, Uppsala U., Sweden
David Vilar, Amazon, Germany
Dongdong Zhang, Microsoft, USA
Duygu Ataman, U. Zurich, Switzerland
Elizabeth Salesky, JHU, USA
Evgeny Matusov, AppTek, Germany
Frank Seide, Microsoft, USA
Hieu Hoang, U. Edinburgh, USA
Hoang Cuong, Amazon, USA
José G. C. de Souza, eBay, Germany
Juan Pino, Facebook, USA
Julian Salazar, Amazon, USA
Katsuhito Sudoh, NAIST, Japan
Keisuke Sakaguchi, AI2 Seattle, USA
Krzysztof Wolk, PJA, Poland
Laurent Besacier, IMAG, France
Marcin Junczys-Dowmunt, Microsoft, USA
Marco Turchi, FBK, Italy
Markus Freitag, Google, USA
Matteo Negri, FBK, Italy
Matthias Huck, LMU, Germany
Mattia di Gangi, FBK/U. Trento, Italy
Nguyen Bach, Alibaba, USA
Nicholas Ruiz, Interaction, USA
Preslav Nakov, QCRI, Qatar
Roman Grundkiewicz, U. Edinburgh, UK
Surafel Melaku Lakew, FBK/U. Trento, Italy
Thanh-Le Ha, KIT, Germany
Vincent Vandeghinste, KU Leuven, Belgium
Young Jin Kim, Microsoft, USA
Yves Lepage, U. Waseda, Japan

Table of Contents

Conference Program

Day 1

Evaluation Overview

Day 1-2

System Papers: Simultaneous Speech Translation

System Papers: Conversational Speech Translation

FINDINGS OF THE IWSLT 2020 EVALUATION CAMPAIGN

Ebrahim Ansari
Charles U./IASBS

Amittai Axelrod
DiDi Labs

Nguyen Bach
Alibaba

Ondřej Bojar
Charles U.

Roldano Cattoni
FBK

Fahim Dalvi
QCRI

Nadir Durrani
QCRI

Marcello Federico
Amazon AI

Christian Federmann
Microsoft Research

Jiatao Gu
Facebook AI

Fei Huang
Alibaba

Kevin Knight
DiDi Labs

Xutai Ma
JHU/Facebook AI

Ajay Nagesh
DiDi Labs

Matteo Negri
FBK

Jan Niehues
Maastricht U.

Juan Pino
Facebook AI

Elizabeth Salesky
JHU

Xing Shi
DiDi Labs

Sebastian Stüker
KIT

Marco Turchi
FBK

Alex Waibel
CMU/KIT

Changhan Wang
Facebook AI

Abstract

The evaluation campaign of the International Conference on Spoken Language Translation (IWSLT 2020) featured this year six challenge tracks: (i) Simultaneous speech translation, (ii) Video speech translation, (iii) Offline speech translation, (iv) Conversational speech translation, (v) Open domain translation, and (vi) Non-native speech translation. A total of 30 teams participated in at least one of the tracks. This paper introduces each track's goal, data and evaluation metrics, and reports the results of the received submissions.

1 Introduction [Marcello]

The International Conference on Spoken Language Translation (IWSLT) is an annual scientific conference (Akiba et al., 2004; Eck and Hori, 2005; Paul, 2006; Fordyce, 2007; Paul, 2008, 2009; Paul et al., 2010; Federico et al., 2011, 2012; Cettolo et al., 2013, 2014, 2015, 2016, 2017; Niehues et al., 2018, 2019) for the study, development and evaluation of spoken language translation technology, including: speech-to-text, speech-to-speech translation, simultaneous and consecutive translation, speech dubbing, cross-lingual communication including all multi-modal, emotional, para-linguistic, and stylistic aspects and their applications in the field. The goal of the conference is to organize evaluations and sessions around challenge areas, and to present scientific work and system descriptions. This paper reports on the evaluation campaign organized by IWSLT 2020, which features six challenge tracks:

- **Simultaneous speech translation**, addressing low latency translation of talks, from English to German, either from a speech file into text, or from a ground-truth transcript into text;

- **Video speech translation**, targeting multi-modal speech translation of video clips into text, either from Chinese into English or from English into Russian

- **Offline speech translation**, proposing speech translation of talks from English into German, using either cascade architectures or end-to-end models, able to directly translate source speech into target text;

- **Conversational speech translation**, targeting the translation of highly disfluent conver-

Proceedings of the 17th International Conference on Spoken Language Translation (IWSLT), pages 1–34
July 9-10, 2020. ©2020 Association for Computational Linguistics
https://doi.org/10.18653/v1/P17

sations into fluent text, from Spanish to English, starting either from audio or from a verbatim transcript;

- **Open domain translation**, addressing Japanese-Chinese translation of unknown mixed-genre test data by leveraging heterogeneous and noisy web training data.

- **Non-native speech translation**, considering speech translation of English-to-Czech and English-to-German speech in a realistic setting of non-native spontaneous speech, in somewhat noisy conditions.

The challenge tracks were attended by 30 participants (see Table 1), including both academic and industrial teams. This correspond to a significant increment with respect to the last year's evaluation campaign, which saw the participation of 12 teams. The following sections report on each challenge track in detail, in particular: the goal and automatic metrics adopted for the challenge, the data used for training and testing data, the received submissions and the summary results. A detailed account of the results for each challenge is instead reported in a corresponding appendix.

2 Simultaneous Speech Translation

Simultaneous machine translation has become an increasingly popular topic in recent years. In particular, simultaneous speech translation enables interesting applications such as subtitle translations for a live event or real-time video-call translations. The goal of this challenge is to examine systems for translating text or audio in a source language into text in a target language from the perspective of both translation quality and latency.

2.1 Challenge

Participants were given two parallel tracks to enter and encouraged to enter both tracks:

- text-to-text: translating ground-truth transcripts in real-time.

- speech-to-text: translating speech into text in real-time.

For the speech-to-text track, participants were able to submit systems either based on cascaded or end-to-end approaches. Participants were required to implement a provided API to read the input and write the translation, and upload their system as a

Docker image so that it could be evaluated by the organizers. We also provided an example implementation and a baseline system[1].

Systems were evaluated with respect to quality and latency. Quality was evaluated with the standard metrics BLEU (Papineni et al., 2002a), TER (Snover et al., 2006b) and METEOR (Lavie and Agarwal, 2007). Latency was evaluated with the recently developed metrics for simultaneous machine translation including average proportion (AP), average lagging (AL) and differentiable average lagging (DAL) (Cherry and Foster, 2019). These metrics measure latency from an algorithmic perspective and assume systems with infinite speed. For the first edition of this task, we report wall-clock times only for informational purposes. In the future, we will also take wall-clock time into account for the official latency metric.

Three regimes, low, medium and high, were evaluated. Each regime was determined by a maximum latency threshold. The thresholds were measured with AL, which represents the delay to a perfect real-time system (milliseconds for speech and number of words for text). The thresholds were set to 3, 6 and 15 for the text track and to 1000, 2000 and 4000 for the speech track, and were calibrated by the baseline system. Participants were asked to submit at least one system per latency regime and were encouraged to submit multiple systems for each regime in order to provide more data points for latency-quality trade-off analyses.

2.2 Data

Participants were allowed to use the same training and development data as in the Offline Speech Translation track. More details are available in §4.2.

2.3 Submissions

The simultaneous task received submissions from 4 teams: 3 teams entered both the text and the speech tracks while 1 team entered the text track only. Teams followed the suggestion to submit multiple systems per regime, which resulted in a total of 56 systems overall.

ON-TRAC (Elbayad et al., 2020) participated in both the speech and text tracks. The authors used a hybrid pipeline for simultaneous speech

---

[1] `https://github.com/pytorch/fairseq/tree/simulastsharedtask/examples/simultaneous_translation`

Team	Organization
AFRL	Air Force Research Laboratory, USA (Ore et al., 2020)
AppTek/RWTH	AppTek and RWTH Aachen University, Germany (Bahar et al., 2020a)
BHANSS	Samsung Research, South Korea (Lakumarapu et al., 2020)
BUT	Brno University of Technology, Czech Republic (no system paper)
CASIA	Inst. of Automation, Chinese Academy of Sciences, China (Wang et al., 2020b)
CUNI	Charles University, Czech Republic (Polák et al., 2020)
DBS	Deep Bleu Sonics, China (Su and Ren, 2020)
DiDi Labs	DiDi Labs, USA (Arkhangorodsky et al., 2020)
ELITR	CUNI + KIT + UEdin (Macháček et al., 2020)
FBK	Fondazione Bruno Kessler, Italy (Gaido et al., 2020)
HY	University of Helsinki, Finland (Vázquez et al., 2020)
HW-TSC	Huawei Co. Ltd, China (Wang et al., 2020a)
IITB	Indian Institute of Technology Bombay, India (Saini et al., 2020)
ISTIC	Inst. of Scientific and Technical Inf. of China (Wei et al., 2020)
Kingsoft	Kingsoft, China. (no system paper)
KIT	Karlsruhe Institute of Technology, Germany (Pham et al., 2020)
KSAI	Kingsoft AI Lab, China (no system paper)
NAIST	Nara Institute of Science and Technology, Japan (Fukuda et al., 2020)
NICT	National Institute of Comm. Techn., Japan (no system paper)
Octanove	Octanove Labs LLC, USA (Hagiwara, 2020)
ON-TRAC	ONTRAC Consortium, France (Elbayad et al., 2020)
OPPO	Beijing OPPO Telecommunications Co., Ltd., China (Zhang et al., 2020)
SJTU	Shanghai Jiao Tong University, China (no system paper)
SRC-B	Samsung Research, China (Zhuang et al., 2020)
SRPOL	Samsung Research , Poland (Potapczyk and Przybysz, 2020)
SRSK	Samsung Research, South Korea (Han et al., 2020)
Tamkang	Tamkang University, Taiwan (no system paper)
Tsukuba	University of Tsukuba, Japan (Cui et al., 2020)
UEdin	University of Edinburgh, UK(Chen et al., 2020)
Xiaomi	Xiaomi AI Lab, China (Sun et al., 2020)

Table 1: List of Participants

translation track, with a Kaldi-based speech recognition cascaded with transformer-based machine translation with wait-k strategy (Ma et al., 2019). In order to save the cost of encoding every time an input word is streamed, a uni-directional encoder is used. Multiple wait-k paths are jointly optimized in the loss function. This approach was found to be competitive with the original wait-k approach without needing to retrain for a specific k.

SRSK (Han et al., 2020) participated in the speech and text tracks. This is the only submission to use an end-to-end approach for the speech track. The authors use transformer-based models combining the wait-k strategy (Ma et al., 2019) with a modality-agnostic meta learning approach (Indurthi et al., 2020) to address data sparsity. They

also use the ST task along with ASR and MT as the source task, a minor variation explored compared to the original paper. In the text-to-text task, the authors also explored English-German and French-German as source tasks. This training setup is facilitated using a universal vocabulary. They analyzed models with different values in wait-k during training and inference and found the meta learning approach to be effective when the data is limited.

AppTek/RWTH (Bahar et al., 2020a) participated in the speech and text tracks. The authors proposed a novel method to simultaneous translation, by training an additional binary output to predict chunk boundaries in the streaming input. This module serves as an agent to decide when the contextual information is sufficient for the decoder to write output. The training examples for chunk prediction are generated using word alignments. On the recognition side, they fixate the ASR system to the output hypothesis that does not change when further context is added. The model chooses chunk boundaries dynamically.

KIT (Pham et al., 2020) participated in the text track only. The authors used a novel read-write strategy called Adaptive Computation Time (ACT) (Graves, 2016). Instead of learning an agent, a probability distribution derived from encoder timesteps, along with the attention mechanism from (Arivazhagan et al., 2019b) is used for training. The ponder loss (Graves, 2016) was added to the cross-entropy loss in order to encourage the model towards shorter delays. Different latency can be achieved by adjusting the weight of the ponder loss.

2.4 Results

We discuss results for the text and speech tracks. More details are available in Appendix A.1.

2.4.1 Text Track

Results for the text track are summarized in the first table of Appendix A.1. Only the ON-TRAC system was able to provide a low latency model. The ranking of the systems is consistent throughout the latency regimes. The results for all systems are identical between the high latency regime and the unconstrained regime except for SRSK who submitted a system above the maximum latency threshold of 15.

In the table, only the models with the best BLEU score for a given latency regime are reported. In order to obtain a broader sense of latency-quality thresholds, we plot in Figure 1 all the systems submitted to the text track. The ON-TRAC models present competitive trade-offs across a wide latency range. The APPTEK/RWTH system obtains competitive performance for medium latency, but its characteristics in low and high latency regimes are unclear.

2.4.2 Speech Track

Results for the speech track are summarized in the second table of Appendix A.1. We also report latency-quality trade-off curves in Figure 2. The ON-TRAC system presents better trade-offs across a wide latency range. We also note that the APPTEK/RWTH systems are all above the highest

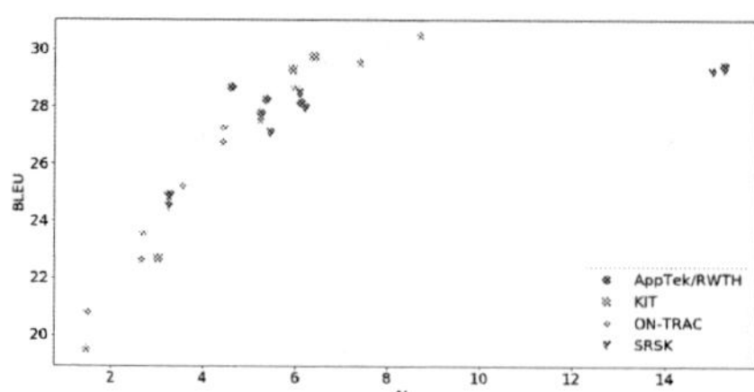

Figure 1: Latency-quality trade-off curves, measured by AL and BLEU, for the systems submitted to the text track.

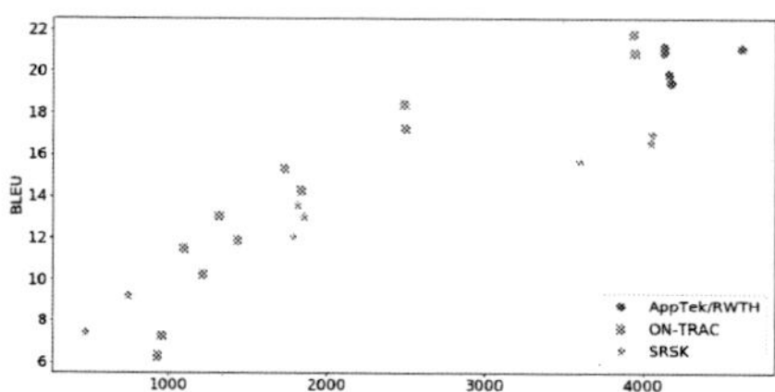

Figure 2: Latency-quality trade-off curves, measured by AL and BLEU, for the systems submitted to the speech track.

latency threshold of 4000, which makes it difficult to compare its trade-offs to other systems.

2.5 Future Editions

In future editions, we will include wall-clock time information as part of the official latency metric. This implies that the evaluation will be run in a more controlled environment, for example, the hardware will be defined in advance. We will also encourage participants to contrast cascade and end-to-end approaches for the simultaneous speech track.

3 Video Speech Translation

We are living the multiple modalities world in which we see objects, hear sounds, feel texture, smell odors, and so on. The purpose of this shared task is to ignite possibilities of multimodal machine translation. This shared task examines methods for combining video and audio sources as input of translation models.

3.1 Challenge

In this year's evaluation campaign, we added the video translation track to ignite possibilities of multimodal machine translation. This track examines methods for combining video and audio sources as input of translation models. We offer two evaluation tasks. The first one is the constrained track in which systems are required to only use the datasets we provided in the data section. The second one was unconstrained systems in which additional datasets are allowed. Both tasks are available for Chinese-English and English-Russian language pairs.

3.2 Data

We are focusing on e-Commerce domain, particularly on the live video shows similar to the ones on e-Commerce websites such as AliExpress, Amazon, and Taobao. A typical live show has at least one seller in a wide range of recording environments. The live show contents cover product description, review, coupon information, chitchat between speakers, interactive chat with audiences, commercial ads, and breaks. We planned to collect videos from Taobao for Chinese-English, and videos from AliExpess for English-Russian.

We have experienced data collection and annotation challenges during these unprecedented times. Our English-Russian plan could not be carried out smoothly. Therefore, instead of collecting and annotating e-Commerce videos, we use the How2 dataset[2] and translate the dev and test sets from English to Russian.

For Chinese-English, we collected ten Taobao full live shows which last between fifteen minutes and four hours. After quality check, we keep seven live shows for annotation. For each live show we sampled video snippets ranging from 1 to 25 minutes relatively to the length of the original show. Audio files are extracted from video snippets. Each audio file is further split into smaller audios based on the silence and voice activities. We ask native Chinese speakers to provide human transcriptions. For human translation, we encourage annotators to watch video snippets before translating. There are 2 English translation references for a total of 104 minutes of Chinese live shows. All data is available on GitHub[3].

3.3 Submissions

We received 4 registrations, however, due to the pandemic we received only 1 submissions from team HW-TSC. We also used the cascaded speech translation cloud services from 2 providers which will be named as Online A and Online B.

Team HW-TSC participated in the Chinese-English unconstrained sub-task. HW-TSC submission is a cascaded system of a speech recognition system, a disfluency detection system, and a machine translation system. They simply extract the sound tracks from videos, then feed them to their proprietary ASR system and proceed transcripts to downstream modules. ASR outputs are piped into a BERT-based disfluency detection system which performs repeat spoken words removal, detect insertion and deletion noise. For the machine translation part, a transformer-big has been employed. They experimented multi-task learning with NMT decoding and domain classification, back translation and noise data augmentation. For the details of their approach, please refer to their paper (Table 1).

3.4 Results

We use vizseq[4] as our main scoring tool. We evaluate ASR systems in CER without punctuations. The final translation outputs are evaluated with lower-cased BLEU, METEOR, and chrF. We also break down the translation performances by the CER error buckets with sentence-level BLEU scores. HW-TSC has a better corpus-level performance than other online cloud services. All systems are sensitive to speech recognition errors.

4 Offline Speech Translation

In continuity with last year (Niehues et al., 2019), the offline speech translation task required participants to translate English audio data extracted from TED talks[5] into German. Participants could submit translations produced by either *cascade* architectures (built on a pipeline of ASR and MT components) or *end-to-end* models (neural solutions for the direct translation of the input audio), and were asked to specify, at submission time, which of the two architectural choices was made for their system.

Similar to last year, valid end-to-end submissions had to be obtained by models that:

- Do not exploit intermediate discrete representations (e.g., source language transcrip-

---

tion or hypotheses fusion in the target language);

- Rely on parameters that are all jointly trained on the end-to-end task

4.1 Challenge

While the cascade approach has been the dominant one for years, the end-to-end paradigm has recently attracted increasing attention as a way to overcome some of the pipeline systems' problems, such as higher architectural complexity and error propagation. In terms of performance, however, the results of the IWSLT 2019 ST task still showed a gap between the two approaches that, though gradually decreasing, was still of about 1.5 BLEU points. In light of this, the main question we wanted to answer this year is: *is the cascaded solution still the dominant technology in spoken language translation?* To take stock of the situation, besides being allowed to submit systems based on both the technologies, participants were asked to translate also the 2019 test set, which last year was kept undisclosed to enable future comparisons.

This year's evaluation also focused on a key issue in ST, which is *the importance of a proper segmentation of the input audio.* One of the findings of last year's campaign, which was carried out on unsegmented data, was indeed the key role of automatically segmenting the test data in way that is close to the sentence-level one present in the training corpora. To shed light on this aspect, the last novelty introduced this year is the possibility given to participants to process the same test data released in two versions, namely with and without pre-computed audio segmentation. The submission instructions included the request to specify, together with the type of architecture (cascade/end-to-end) and the data condition (constrained/unconstrained – see §4.2) also the chosen segmentation type (own/given).

Systems' performance is evaluated with respect to their capability to produce translations similar to the target-language references. To enable performance analyses from different perspectives, such similarity is measured in terms of multiple automatic metrics: case-sensitive/insensitive BLEU (Papineni et al., 2002b), case-sensitive/insensitive TER (Snover et al., 2006a), BEER (Stanojevic and Sima'an, 2014), and CharacTER (Wang et al., 2016). Simi-

lar to last year, the submitted runs are ranked based on the case-sensitive BLEU calculated on the test set by using automatic re-segmentation of the hypotheses based on the reference translations by mwerSegmenter.[6]

4.2 Data

Training and development data. Also this year, participants had the possibility to train their systems using several resources available for ST, ASR and MT. The training corpora allowed to satisfy the "constrained" data condition include:

- MuST-C (Di Gangi et al., 2019a)

- WIT[3] (Cettolo et al., 2012)

- Speech-Translation TED corpus[7]

- How2 (Sanabria et al., 2018)[8]

- LibriVoxDeEn (Beilharz and Sun, 2019)[9]

- Europarl-ST (Iranzo-Sánchez et al., 2020)

- TED LIUM v2 (Rousseau et al., 2014) and v3 (Hernandez et al., 2018)

- all the data provided by WMT 2019[10]

- OpenSubtitles 2018 (Lison et al., 2018)

- Augmented LibriSpeech (Kocabiyikoglu et al., 2018)[11]

- Mozilla Common Voice[12]

- LibriSpeech ASR corpus (Panayotov et al., 2015)

The list of allowed development data includes the dev set from IWSLT 2010, as well as the test sets used for the 2010, 2013, 2014, 2015 and 2018 IWSLT campaigns. Using other training/development resources was allowed but, in this case, participants were asked to mark their submission as an "unconstrained" one.

---

[6] https://www-i6.informatik.rwth-aachen.de/web/Software/mwerSegmenter.tar.gz

[7] http://i13pc106.ira.uka.de/~mmueller/iwslt-corpus.zip

[8] only English - Portuguese

[9] only German - English

[10] http://www.statmt.org/wmt19/

[11] only English - French

[12] https://voice.mozilla.org/en/datasets – English version en_1488h_2019-12-10

Test data. A new test set was released by processing, with the same pipeline used to build MuST-C (Di Gangi et al., 2019a), a new set of 22 talks that are not included yet in the public release of the corpus. To measure technology progress with respect to last year's round, participants were asked to process also the undisclosed 2019 test set. Both test corpora were released with and without sentence-like automatic segmentation. For the segmented versions, the resulting number of segments is 2,263 (corresponding to about 4.1 hours of translated speech from 22 talks) for the 2020 test set and 2,813 (about 5.1 hours from 25 talks) for the 2019 test set.

4.3 Submissions

We received submissions from 10 participants (twice as much compared to last year's number) coming from the industry, the academia and other research institutions. Eight teams submitted at least one run obtained with end-to-end technology, showing a steady increase of interest towards this emerging paradigm. In detail:

- 5 teams (DiDiLabs, FBK, ON-TRAC, BHANSS, SRPOL) participated only with end-to-end systems;

- 3 teams (AppTek/RWTH, KIT, HY) submitted runs obtained from both cascade and end-to-end systems;

- 2 teams (AFRL, BUT) participated only with cascade systems.

As far as input segmentation is concerned, participants are equally distributed between the two possible types, with half of the total submitting only runs obtained with the given segmentation and the other half submitting at least one run with in-house solutions. In detail:

- 5 teams (BHANSS, BUT, DiDiLabs, FBK, HY) participated only with the given segmentation of the test data;

- 2 teams (AFRL, ON-TRAC) participated only with their own segmentation;

- 3 teams (AppTek/RWTH, KIT, SRPOL) submitted runs for both segmentation types.

Finally, regarding the data usage possibilities, all teams opted for constrained submissions exploiting only the allowed training corpora listed in §4.2.

In the following, we provide a bird's-eye description of each participant's approach.

AFRL (Ore et al., 2020) participated with a cascade system that included the following steps: (1) speech activity detection using a neural network trained on TED-LIUM, (2) speech recognition using a Kaldi system (Povey et al., 2011) trained on TED-LIUM, (3) sentence segmentation using an automatic punctuator (a bidirectional RNN with attention trained on TED data using Ottokar Tilk[13]), and (4) machine translation using OpenNMT (Klein et al., 2017). The contrastive system differs from the primary one in two aspects: Step 3 was not applied, and the translation results were obtained using Marian (Junczys-Dowmunt et al., 2018) instead of openNMT.

AppTek/RWTH (Bahar et al., 2020b) participated with both cascade and end-to-end speech translation systems, paying attention to careful data selection (based on sentence embedding similarity) and weighting. In the cascaded approach, they combined: (1) high-quality hybrid automatic speech recognition (based on hybrid LSTM/HMM model and attention models trained on data augmented with a variant SpecAugment (Park et al., 2019), layer-wise pretraining and CTC loss (Graves et al., 2006) as additional loss), with (2) the Transformer-based neural machine translation. The end-to-end direct speech translation systems benefit from: (1) pre-training of adapted LSTM-based encoder and Transformer-based decoder components, (2) an adapter component in-between, and (3) synthetic data and fine-tuning. All these elements make the end-to-end models able to compete with the cascade ones in terms of MT quality.

BHANSS (Lakumarapu et al., 2020) built their end-to-end system adopting the Transformer architecture (Vaswani et al., 2017a) coupled with the meta-learning approach proposed in (Indurthi et al., 2020). Meta-learning is used mitigate the issue of over-fitting when the training data is limited, as in the ST case, and allows their system to take advantage of the available ASR and MT data. Along with meta-learning, the submitted system also exploits training on synthetic data created with different techniques. These include automatic English to German translation to generate artificial text data, and speech perturbation with

---

[13]https://pypi.org/project/punctuator/

the Sox audio manipulation tool[14] to generate artificial audio data similar to (Potapczyk et al., 2019).

BUT (unpublished report) participated with cascade systems based on (Vydana et al., 2020). They rely on ASR-MT Transformer models connected through neural hidden representations and jointly trained with ASR objective as an auxiliary loss. At inference time, both models are connected through n-best hypotheses and the hidden representation that correspond to the n-best hypotheses. The n-best hypothesis from the ASR model are processed in parallel by the MT model. The likelihoods of the final MT decoder are conditioned on the likelihoods of the ASR model. The discrete symbol token sequence, which is obtained as the intermediate representation in the joint model, is used as an input to an independent text-based MT model, whose outputs are ensembled with the joint model. Similarly, the ASR module of the joint model is ensembled from a separately trained ASR model.

DiDiLabs (Arkhangorodsky et al., 2020) participated with an end-to-end system based on the S-Transformer architecture proposed in (Di Gangi et al., 2019b,c). The base model trained on MuST-C was extended in several directions by: (1) encoder pre-training on English ASR data, (2) decoder-pre-training on German ASR data, (3) using wav2vec (Schneider et al., 2019) features as inputs (instead of Mel-Filterbank features), and (4) pre-training on English to German text translation with an MT system sharing the decoder with S-Transformer, so to improve the decoder's translation ability.

FBK (Gaido et al., 2020) participated with an end-to-end-system adapting the S-Transformer model (Di Gangi et al., 2019b,c). Its training is based on: *i)* transfer learning (via ASR pre-training and – word/sequence – knowledge distillation), *ii)* data augmentation (with SpecAugment (Park et al., 2019), time stretch (Nguyen et al., 2020a) and synthetically-created data), *iii)* combining synthetic and real data marked as different "domains" as in (Di Gangi et al., 2019d), and *iv)* multitask learning using the CTC loss (Graves et al., 2006). Once the training with word-level knowledge distillation is complete the model is fine-tuned using label smoothed cross entropy (Szegedy et al., 2016).

HY (Vázquez et al., 2020) participated with both cascade and end-to-end systems. For the end-to-end system, they used a multimodal approach (with audio and text as the two modalities treated as different languages) trained in a multi-task fashion, which maps the internal representations of different encoders into a shared space before decoding. To this aim, they incorporated the inner-attention based architecture proposed by (Vázquez et al., 2020) within Transformer-based encoders (inspired by (Tu et al., 2019; Di Gangi et al., 2019c)) and decoders. For the cascade approach, they used a pipeline of three stages: (1) ASR (trained with S-Transformer (Di Gangi et al., 2019c)), (2) re-punctuation and letter case restoration (based on Marian's implementation (Junczys-Dowmunt et al., 2018) of Transformer), and (3) MT (also based on Marian).

KIT (Pham et al., 2020) participated with both end-to-end and cascade systems. For the end-to-end system they applied a deep Transformer with stochastic layers (Pham et al., 2019b). Position encoding (Dai et al., 2019) is incorporated to mitigate issues due to processing long audio inputs, and SpecAugment (Park et al., 2019) is applied to the speech inputs for data augmentation. The cascade architecture has three components: (1) ASR (both LSTM (Nguyen et al., 2020b) and Transformer-based (Pham et al., 2019a)) (2) Segmentation (with a monolingual NMT system (Sperber et al., 2018) that adds sentence boundaries and case, also inserting proper punctuation), and (3) MT (a Transformer-based encoder-decoder model implementing Relative Attention following (Dai et al., 2019) adapted via fine-tuning on data incorporating artificially-injected noise). The WerRTCVAD toolkit[15] is used to process the unsegmented test set.

ON-TRAC (Elbayad et al., 2020) participated with end-to-end systems, focusing on speech segmentation, data augmentation and the ensembling of multiple models. They experimented with several attention-based encoder-decoder models sharing the general backbone architecture described in (Nguyen et al., 2019), which comprises an encoder with two VGG-like (Simonyan and Zisserman, 2015) CNN blocks followed by five stacked BLSTM layers. All the systems were developed using the ESPnet end-to-end speech processing toolkit (Watanabe et al., 2018). An ASR

---

[14] `http://sox.sourceforge.net/`

[15] `https://github.com/wiseman/py-webrtcvad`

model trained on Kaldi (Povey et al., 2011) was used to process the unsegmented test set, training the acoustic model on the TED-LIUM 3 corpus. Speech segments based on the recognized words with timecodes were obtained with rules, whose thresholds were optimised to get a segment duration distribution in the development and evaluation data that is similar to the one observed in the training data. Data augmentation was performed with SpecAugment (Park et al., 2019), speed perturbation, and by automatically translating into German the English transcription of MuST-C and How2. The two synthetic corpora were combined in different ways producing different models that were eventually used in isolation and ensembled at decoding time.

SRPOL (Potapczyk and Przybysz, 2020) participated with end-to-end systems based on the one (Potapczyk et al., 2019) submitted to the IWSLT 2019 ST task. The improvements over last year's submission include: (1) the use of additional training data (synthetically created, both by translating with a Transformer model as in (Jia et al., 2019) and via speed perturbation with the Sox audio manipulation tool); (2) training data filtration (applied to WIT^3 and TED LIUM v2); (3) the use of SpecAugment (Park et al., 2019); (4) the introduction of a second decoder for the ASR task, obtaining a multitask setup similar to (Anastasopoulos and Chiang, 2018); (5) the increase of the encoder layer depth; (6) the replacement of simpler convolutions with Resnet-like convolutional layers; and (7) the increase of the embedding size. To process the unsegmented test set, the same segmentation technique used last year was applied. It relies on iteratively joining, up to a maximal length of 15s, the fragments obtained by dividing the audio input with a silence detection tool.

4.4 Results

Detailed results for the offline ST task are provided in Appendix A.3. For each test set (i.e. this year's *tst2020* and last year's *tst2019*), the scores computed on unsegmented and segmented data (i.e. *own* vs *given* segmentation) are reported separately. Background colours are used to differentiate between cascade (white background) and end-to-end architectures (grey).

Cascade vs end-to-end. Looking at the results computed with case-sensitive BLEU (our primary evaluation metric), the first interesting thing to

remark is that the highest score (25.3 BLEU) is achieved by an end-to-end system, which outperforms the best cascade result by 0.24 BLEU points. Although the performance difference between the two paradigms is small, it can be considered as an indicator of the steady progress done by end-to-end approaches to ST. Back to our initial question *"is the cascaded solution still the dominant technology in ST?"*, we can argue that, at least in this year's evaluation conditions, the two paradigms are now close (if not on par) in terms of final performance.

The importance of input segmentation. Another important aspect to consider is the key role played by a proper segmentation of the input speech. Indeed, the top five submitted runs are all obtained by systems operating under the "unsegmented" condition, that is with own segmentation strategies. This is not surprising considering the mismatch between the provided training material (often "clean" corpora split into sentence-like segments, as in the case of MuST-C) and the supplied test data, whose automatic segmentation can be far from being optimal (i.e. sentence-like) and, in turn, difficult to handle. The importance of a good segmentation becomes evident looking at the scores of those teams that participated with both segmentation types (i.e. AppTek/RWTH, KIT, SRPOL): in all cases, their best runs are obtained with own segmentations. Looking at these systems through the lens of our initial question about the distance between cascade and end-to-end approaches, it's interesting to observe that, although the two approaches are close when participants applied their own segmentation, the cascade is still better when results are computed on presegmented data.^{16} Specifically, on unsegmented data, AppTek/RWTH's best cascade score (22.49 BLEU) is 2 points better than their best end-to-end score (20.5). For KIT's submissions the distance is slightly larger (22.06 - 19.82 = 2.24). In light of this consideration, as of today it is still difficult to draw conclusive evidence about the real distance between cascade and end-to-end ST since the effectiveness of the latter seems to highly depend a critical pre-processing step.

Progress wrt 2019. Comparing participants' results on *tst2020* and *tst2019*, the progress made by

---

[16]This is only possible for the submissions by AppTek/RWTH and KIT, since SRPOL participated only with their own segmentation.

the ST community is quite visible. Before considering the actual systems' scores, it's worth observing that the overall ranking is almost identical on the two test sets. This indicates that the top-ranked approaches on this year's evaluation set are consistently better on different new test data coming from the TED Talks domain. Three systems, two of which end-to-end, were able to outperform last year's top result (21.55 BLEU), which was obtained by a cascade system. Moreover, two out of the three systems that also took part in the IWSLT 2019 campaign (FBK, KIT and SRPOL) managed to improve their previous scores on the same dataset. In both cases, they did it with a large margin: from 3.85 BLEU points for FBK to 4.0 BLEU points for SRPOL. As the 2019 test set was kept undisclosed, this is another confirmation of the progress made in one year by ST technology in general, and by the end-to-end approach in particular.

5 Conversational Speech Translation

In conversational speech, there are many phenomena which aren't present in well-formed text, such as disfluencies. Disfluencies comprise e.g., filler words, repetitions, corrections, hesitations, or incomplete sentences. This differs strongly from typical machine translation training data. This mismatch needs to be accounted for when translating conversational speech both for domain mismatch as well as generating well-formed, fluent translations. While previously handled with intermediate processing steps, with the rise of end-to-end models, how and when to incorporate such a pre- or post-processing steps between speech processing and machine translation is an open question.

Disfluency removal typically requires token-level annotations for that language. However, most languages and translation corpora do not such annotations. Using recently collected fluent references (Salesky et al., 2018) for the common Fisher Spanish-English dataset, this task poses several potential questions: how should disfluency removal be incorporated into current conversational speech translation models where translation may not be done in a pipeline, and can this be accomplished without training on explicit annotations?

5.1 Challenge

The goal of this task is to provide fluent, English translations given disfluent Spanish speech or text. We provide three ways in which submissions may differ and would be scored separately:

- Systems which translate from speech, or from text-only

- Systems may be *unconstrained* (use additional data beyond what is provided) or *constrained* (use only the Fisher data provided)

- Systems which do and do not use the fluent references to train

Submissions were scored against the fluent English translation references for the challenge test sets, using the automatic metric BLEU (Papineni et al., 2002a) to assess fluent translations and METEOR (Lavie and Agarwal, 2007) to assess meaning preservation from the original disfluent data. By convention to compare with previous published work on the Fisher translation datasets (Post et al., 2013), we score using lowercased, detokenized output with all punctuation except apostrophes removed. At test time, submissions could only be provided with the evaluation data for their track. We compare submissions to the baseline models described in Salesky et al. (2019).

5.2 Data

This task uses the LDC Fisher Spanish speech (disfluent) (Graff et al.) with new target translations (fluent) Salesky et al. (2018). This dataset has 160 hours of speech (138k utterances): this is a smaller dataset than other tasks, designed to be approachable. We provide multi-way parallel data for training:

- disfluent Spanish speech

- disfluent Spanish transcripts (gold)

- disfluent Spanish transcripts (ASR output)

- disfluent English translations

- fluent English translations

Each of these are parallel at level of the training data, such that the disfluent and fluent translation references have the same number of utterances. Additional details for the fluent translations can be found here: Salesky et al. (2018). We arranged an evaluation license agreement with the LDC where all participants could receive this data without cost for the purposes of this task.

The `cslt-test` set is originally Fisher dev2 (for which the fluent translations are released for this first time with this task). We provided participants with two conditions for each test set for the text-only track: gold Spanish transcriptions, and ASR output using the baseline's ASR model.

5.3 Submissions

We received two submissions, both for the text-only track, as described below.

Both teams described both constrained and unconstrained systems. While NAIST submitted multiple (6) systems, IIT Bombay submitted ultimately only their unconstrained system. Both teams submitted at least one model without fluent translations used in training – rising to the challenge goal of this task to generalize beyond available annotations.

NAIST (Fukuda et al., 2020) used a two-pronged approach: first, to leverage both a larger dataset which is out-of-domain (UN Corpus: i.e. both fluent and also out-of-domain for conversational speech) they utilize an unsupervised style transfer model, and second, to adapt between fluent and disfluent parallel corpora for NMT they pretrain on the original disfluent-disfluent translations and fine-tune to the target disfluent-fluent case. They find that their style transfer domain adaptation was necessary to make the most effective use of style-transfer, as without it, the domain mismatch was such that meaning was lost during disfluent-fluent translation.

IIT Bombay (Saini et al., 2020) submit both unconstrained and constrained systems, both without use of the parallel fluent translations. They use data augmentation through noise induction to create disfluent–fluent English references from English NewsCommentary. Their translation model uses multiple encoders and decoders with shared layers to balance shared modeling capabilities while separating domain-specific modeling of e.g. disfluencies within noised data.

5.4 Results

This task proved challenging but was met by very inventive and different solutions from each team. Results are shown in Appendix A.4.

In their respective description papers, the two teams scored their systems differently, leading to different trends between the two papers than may be observed in our evaluation.

The unconstrained submissions from each site utilized external data in very different ways, though with the same underlying motivation. Under the matched condition — unconstrained but no fluent references used during training — given gold source Spanish transcripts, The submissions from NAIST (Fukuda et al., 2020) were superior by up to 2.6 BLEU. We see that this is not the case, however, when ASR output is the source, where the IITB submission performs ≈3.4 better on BLEU; this submission, in fact, outperforms all submitted under any condition, though it has not been trained on the parallel fluent references. This may suggest perhaps that the multi-encoder and multi-decoder machine translation model from IITB transferred better to the noise seen in ASR output. Interestingly, we see a slight improvement in BLEU for both sites with ASR output as source under this matched conditions (e.g. for those models where the fluent data is not used).

Turning to our second metric, METEOR, where we assess meaning preservation with the original disfluent references, we see that the IITB submission from ASR output preserves much more of the content contained in the disfluent references, resulting in a much higher METEOR score than all other submissions. The utterances in these outputs are also 10% longer than those of NAIST-e. Qualitatively, these segments also appear to have more repetitions than the equivalents translated from gold transcripts. This suggests perhaps that NAIST's noised training using the additional unconstrained data may have transferred better to the noise seen in ASR output, causing less of a change given this challenge condition. This may not reflected by BLEU computed against fluent references, because in addition to removing disfluent content, other tokens have been changed. This reminds us this metric may not capture all aspects of producing fluent translations.

NAIST submitted 6 models, allowing us to see additional trends though there are no additional submissions with matched conditions. The unconstrained setting where they leveraged noising of UN Corpus data gave significant improvements of ≈ 5 BLEU. Surprisingly to us, their submissions which do not leverage fluent references in training are not far behind those which do — the respective gap between otherwise matched submissions is typically ≈ 2 BLEU.

Overall, we are very encouraged to see submissions which did not use the fluent parallel data, and encourage further development in this area!

6 Open Domain Translation

The goals of this task were to further promote research on translation between Asian languages, the exploitation of noisy parallel web corpora for MT, and thoughtful handling of data provenance.

6.1 Challenge

The open domain translation task focused on machine translation between Chinese and Japanese, with one track in each direction. We encouraged participation in both tracks.

We provided two bilingual parallel Chinese-Japanese corpora, and two additional bilingual Zh-Ja corpora. The first was a large, noisy set of segment pairs assembled from web data. Section 6.2 describes the data, with further details in Appendix A.5. The second set was a compilation of existing Japanese-Chinese parallel corpora from public sources. These include both freely-downloadable resources and ones released as part of previous Chinese-Japanese MT efforts. We encouraged participants to use only these provided corpora. The use of other data was allowed, as long as it was disclosed.

The submitted systems were evaluated on a held-out, mixed-genre, test set curated to contain high-quality segment pairs. The official evaluation metric was 4-gram character BLEU (Papineni et al., 2002c). The scoring script[17] was shared with participants before the evaluation phase.

6.2 Parallel Training Data

We collected all the publicly available, parallel Chinese-Japanese corpora we could find, and made it available to participants as the `existing_parallel`. These include Global Voices, News Commentary, and Ubuntu corpora from OPUS Tiedemann (2012); OpenSubtitles (Lison and Tiedemann, 2016); TED talks (Dabre and Kurohashi, 2017); Wikipedia (Chu et al.,

---

[17] https://github.com/didi/iwslt2020_
open_domain_translation/blob/master/
eval/bleu.py

2014, 2015); Wiktionary.org; and WikiMatrix (Schwenk et al., 2019). We also collected parallel sentences from Tatoeba.org, released under a CC-BY License. Table 2 lists the size of each of these existing corpora. In total, we found fewer than 2 million publicly available Chinese-Japanese parallel segments.

Corpus	Segments	ZH Chars
Crawled (pipeline)	18,966,595	493,902,539
Ubuntu	92,250	1,549,964
Open Subtitles	914,355	10,932,722
TED	376,441	5,345,867
Global Voices	16,848	337,194
Wikipedia	228,565	5,067,489
Wiktionary	62,557	222,562
News Commentary	570	65,038
Tatoeba	4,243	50,846
WikiMatrix	267,409	9,950,657
Total	**20,929,833**	**527,424,878**

Table 2: Provided Chinese-Japanese parallel data.

We therefore built a data-harvesting pipeline to crawl the web for more parallel text. The data collection details can be found in Appendix A.5. The result was the `webcrawled_parallel_filtered` dataset, containing nearly 19M hopefully-parallel segment pairs (494M Zh chars) with provenance information. This crawled data combined with the existing corpora provide 20.9M parallel segments with 527M Chinese characters. We included provenance information for each segment pair.

6.3 Unaligned and Unfiltered Data

In addition to the aligned and filtered output of the pipeline, we released two other variations on the pipeline output. We hoped these larger yet noisier versions of the data would be of use for working on upstream data processing.

We provided a larger aligned, but unfiltered, version of the web-crawled data produced by the pipeline after Stage 5 (`webcrawled_parallel_unfiltered`). This corpus contains 161.5M segment pairs, and is very noisy (e.g. it includes languages other than Chinese and Japanese). Our expectation is that more sophisticated filtering of this noisy data will increase the quantity of good parallel data.

We also released the parallel document contents, with boundaries, from Step 4 in the pipeline shown in Appendix A.5. These documents are the contents of the webpages paired by URL (e.g. `gotokyo.org/jp/foo` and `gotokyo.org/zh/foo`), and processed with `BeautifulSoup`, but before using Hunalign (Varga et al., 2005) to extract parallel sentence pairs. We released 15.6M document pairs as `webcrawled_unaligned`. Sentence aligner improvements (and their downstream effects) could be explored using this provided data.

6.4 Dev and Test Sets

The provided development set consisted of 5304 basic expressions in Japanese and Chinese, from the Kurohashi-Kawahara Lab at Kyoto University.[18] The held-out test set was intended to cover a variety of topics not known to the participants in advance. We selected test data from high-quality (human translated) parallel web content, authored between January and March 2020. The test set curation process can be found in Appendix A.5.

This curation produced 1750 parallel segments, which we divided randomly in half: 875 lines for the Chinese-to-Japanese translation test set, and 875 lines for the other direction. The Japanese segments have an average length of 47 characters, and the Chinese ones have an average length of 35.

6.5 Submissions

Twelve teams submitted systems for both translation directions, and three more submitted only for Japanese-to-Chinese. Of the 15 participants, 6 were from academia and 9 were from industry.

We built a baseline system before the competition began, based on Tensor2Tensor (Vaswani et al., 2018), and provided participants with the baseline BLEU scores to benchmark against. We also provided the source code for training the baseline, as a potential starting point for experimentation and development. Our source code for the baseline system is now publicly available.[19]

The following summarizes some key points of the participating teams that submitted system descriptions; broad trends first, and then the individual systems in reverse-alphabetical order. Further details for these systems can be found in the relevant system description papers in the full workshop proceedings.

Architecture: All participants used either the Transformer architecture (Vaswani et al., 2017b) or a variant, such as dynamic linear combination of layers, or transformer-evolved with neural architecture search. Most participants submitted ensemble models, showing consistent improvement over the component models on the dev set.

Data Filtering: As anticipated, all teams invested significant effort in data cleaning, normalization and filtering of the provided noisy corpora. A non-exhaustive list of the techniques used includes length ratios, language id, converting traditional Chinese characters to simplified, sentence deduplication, punctuation normalization, and removing html markup.

XIAOMI (Sun et al., 2020) submitted a large ensemble, exploring the performance of a variety of Transformer-based architectures. They also incorporated domain adaptation, knowledge distillation, and reranking.

TSUKUBA (Cui et al., 2020) used the unfiltered data for backtranslation, augmented with synthetic noise. This was done in conjunction with n-best list reranking.

SRC-B (Samsung Beijing) (Zhuang et al., 2020) mined the provided unaligned corpus for parallel data and for backtranslation. They also implemented relative position representation for their Transformer.

OPPO (Zhang et al., 2020) used detailed rule-based preprocessing and multiple rounds of backtranslation. They also explored using both the unfiltered parallel dataset (after filtering) and the unaligned corpus (after alignment). Their contrastive system shows the effect of character widths on the BLEU score.

OCTANOVE (Hagiwara, 2020) augmented the dev set with high-quality pairs mined from the training set. This reduced the size of the webcrawled data by 90% before using. Each half of the discarded pairs was reused for backtranslation.

ISTIC (Wei et al., 2020) used the provided unfiltered webcrawl data after significant filtering. They also used adaptation, using elasticsearch to find sentence pairs similar to the test set, and optimizing the system on them.

DBS Deep Blue Sonics (Su and Ren, 2020) successfully added noise to generate augmented data for backtranslation. They also experimented with

---

[18]`http://nlp.ist.i.kyoto-u.ac.jp/EN/index.php?JEC%20Basic%20Sentence%20Data`

[19]DiDi baseline source code available at: github.com/didi/iwslt2020_open_domain_translation

language model fusion techniques.

CASIA (Wang et al., 2020b) ensembled many models into their submission. They used the unfiltered data for backtranslation, used a domain classifier based on segment provenance, and also performed knowledge-distillation. They also used 13k parallel sentences from external data; see the "External data" note in Section 6.6.

6.6 Results and Discussion

Appendix A.5 contains the results of the Japanese-to-Chinese and Chinese-to-Japanese open-domain translation tasks. Some comments follow below.

Data filtering was unsurprisingly helpful. We released 4 corpora as part of the shared task. All participants used `existing_parallel` and `webcrawled_parallel_filtered`. Overall, participants filtered out 15%-90% of the data, and system performance increased by around 2-5 BLEU points. The `webcrawled_parallel_unfiltered` corpus was also used successfully, but required even more aggressive filtering. The `webcrawled_unaligned` data was even harder to use, and we were pleased to see some teams rise to the challenge. *Data augmentation* via backtranslation also consistently helped. However, there was interesting variation in how participants selected the data to be translated. *Provenance* information is not common in MT evaluations; we were curious how it would be used. Hagiwara (2020) tried filtering `web_crawled_parallel_filtered` using a provenance indicator, but found it was too aggressive. Wang et al. (2020b) instead trained a domain classifier, and used it at decoding time to reweight the domain-specific translation models in the ensemble.

External data was explicitly allowed, potentially allowing the sharing of external resources that were unknown to us. Hagiwara (2020) improved on their submitted system, in a separate experiment, by gathering 80k external parallel question-answer pairs from HiNative and incorporating them into the training set. Wang et al. (2020b) also improved their system by adding 13k external sentence pairs from hujiangjp. However, this inadvertently included data from one of the websites from which the task's blind test set was drawn, resulting in 383/875 and 421/875 exact matching segments on the Chinese side and Japanese side respectively.

Overall, we are heartened by the participation in this first edition of the open-domain Chinese-Japanese shared task, and encourage participation in the next one.

7 Non-Native Speech Translation

The non-native speech translation task has been added to IWSLT this year. The task focuses on the very frequent setting of non-native spontaneous speech in somewhat noisy conditions, one of the test files even contained speech transmitted through a remote conferencing platform. We were interested in submissions of both types: the standard two-stage pipeline (ASR+MT, denoted "Cascaded") as well as end-to-end ("E2E") solutions.

This first year, we had English as the only source language and Czech and German as the target languages. Participants were allowed to submit just one of the target languages.

The training data sets permitted for "constrained" submissions were agreed upon the training data with the Offline Translation Task (Section 4) so that task participants could reuse their systems in both tasks. Participants were however also allowed to use any other training data, rendering their submissions "unconstrained".

7.1 Challenge

The main evaluation measure is translation quality but we invited participants to report time-stamped outputs if possible, so that we could assess their systems also using metrics related to *simultaneous* speech translation.

In practice, the translation quality is severely limited by the speech recognition quality. Indeed, the nature of our test set recordings is extremely challenging, see below. For that reason, we also asked the participants with cascaded submissions to provide their intermediate ASR outputs (again with exact timing information, if possible) and score it against our golden transcripts.

A further critical complication is the lack of input sound segmentation to sentence-like units. The Offline Speech Translation Task (Section 4) this year allowed the participants to come up either with their own segmentation, or to rely upon the provided sound segments. In the Non-Native task, no sound segmentation was available. In some cases, this could have caused even a computational challenge, because our longest test document is

25:55 long, well beyond the common length of segments in the training corpora. The reference translations in our test set do come in segments and we acknowledge the risk of automatic scores being affected by the (mis-)match of candidate and reference segmentation, see below.

7.1.1 SLT Evaluation Measures

The SLT evaluation measures were calculated by SLTev,[20] a comprehensive tool for evaluation of (on-line) spoken language translation.

SLT Quality ($BLEU_1$ and $BLEU_{mw}$) As said, we primarily focus on *translation quality* and we approximate it with BLEU (Papineni et al., 2002a) for simplicity, despite all the known shortcomings of the metric, e.g. Bojar et al. (2010).

BLEU was designed for text translation with a clear correspondence between source and target segments (sentences) of the text. We have explored multiple ways of aligning the segments produced by the participating SLT systems with the reference segments. For systems reporting timestamps of individual source-language words, the segment-level alignment can be based on the exact timing. Unfortunately, only one system provided this detailed information, so we decided to report only two simpler variants of BLEU-based metrics:

$BLEU_1$ The whole text is concatenated and treated as *one* segment for BLEU. Note that this is rather inappropriate for longer recordings where many n-grams could be matched far from their correct location.

$BLEU_{mw}$ (mwerSegmenter + standard BLEU). For this, first we concatenate the whole document and segment it using the mwerSegmenter tool (Matusov et al., 2005). Then we calculate the BLEU score for each document in the test set and report the average.

Since the BLEU implementations differ in many details, we rely on a stable one, namely sacreBLEU (Post, 2018).[21]

SLT Simultaneity In online speech translation, one can trade translation quality for delay and vice versa. Waiting for more input generally allows the

system to produce a better translation. A compromise is sought by systems that quickly produce first candidate outputs and *update* them later, at the cost of potentially increasing cognitive load for the user by showing output that will become irrelevant.

The key properties of this trade-off are captured by observing some form of *delay*, i.e. how long the user has to wait for the translation of the various pieces of the message compared to directly following the source, and *flicker*, i.e. how much "the output changes". We considered several possible definitions of delay and flicker, including or ignoring information on timing, segmentation, word reordering etc., and calculated each of them for each submission. For simplicity, report only the following ones:

Flicker is inspired by Arivazhagan et al. (2019a). We report a normalized revision score calculated by dividing the total number of words produced by the true output length, i.e. by the number of words in the completed sentences. We report the average score across all documents in the test set.

$Delay_{ts}$ relies on timing information provided by the participants for individual *segments*. Each produced word is assumed to have appeared at the time that corresponds proportionally to its (character) position in the segment. The same strategy is used for the reference words. Note that the candidate segmentation does not need to match the reference one, but in both cases, we get an estimated time span for each word.

$Delay_{mw}$ uses mwerSegmenter to first find correspondences between candidate and reference segments based on the actual words. Then the same strategy of estimating the timing of each word is used.

The Delay is summed over all words and divided by the total number of words considered in the calculation to show the average delay per word.

Note that we use a simple exact match of the candidate and reference word; a better strategy would be to use some form of monolingual word alignment which could handle e.g. synonyms. In our case, non-matched words are ignored and do not contribute to the calculation of the delay at all,

---

[20]https://github.com/ELITR/SLTev

[21]We use the default settings, i.e. the signature BLEU+case.mixed+numrefs.1+smooth.exp+ +tok.13a+version.1.4.6.

Domain	Files	Overall Duration	Segments	EN Words	CS Words	DE Words
Antrecorp	28	0h38m	427	5040	4071	4660
Khan Academy	5	0h18m	346	2886	2272	2660
SAO	6	1h39m	654	11928	9395	10613
Total	39	2h35m	1427	19854	15738	17933

Table 3: Non-Native Speech Translation Task test data composition. Words are estimated simply by splitting at whitespace without tokenization.

reducing the reliability of the estimate. To provide an indication of how reliable the reported Delays are, we list also the percentage of reference words matched, i.e. successfully found in the candidate translation. This percentage ranges from 20% to up to 90% across various submissions.

Note that only one team provided us with timing details. In order to examine the empirical relations between these conflicting measures, we focus on the several contrastive runs submitted by this them in Section 7.4.1.

7.1.2 ASR Evaluation Measures

The ASR-related scores were also calculated by SLTev, using the script ASRev which assumes that the "translation" is just an identity operation.

We decided to calculate WER using two different strategies:

WER_1 concatenating all segments into one long sequence of tokens, and

WER_{mw} first concatenating all segments provided by task participants and then using mwerSegmenter to reconstruct the segmentation that best matches the reference.

In both cases, we pre-process both the candidate and reference by lower casing and removing punctuation.

7.2 Data

7.2.1 Training Data for Constrained Submissions

The training data was aligned with the Offline Speech Translation Task (Section 4) to allow cross-submission in English-to-German SLT. English-to-Czech was unique to the Non-Native Task.

The permitted data for constrained submissions were:

For English ASR:

- LibriSpeech ASR corpus (Panayotov et al., 2015),

- Mozilla Common Voice,[22]

- Speech-Translation TED corpus.[23]

For English→Czech Translation:

- MuST-C (Di Gangi et al., 2019a), release 1.1 contains English-Czech pair,

- CzEng 1.7 (Bojar et al., 2016).[24] Note that CzEng overlaps with English-German test data of the Offline Speech Translation Task so it was not allowed to use this English-Czech corpus to train English-German (multi-lingual) systems.

For English→Czech Translation:

- All the data for English-German track by WMT 2019[25] News Translation Task, i.e.:

  - English-German parallel data,
  - German monolingual data,

- MuST-C (Di Gangi et al., 2019a), release 1.0 contains English-German pair,

- Speech-Translation TED corpus,[26] the English-German texts,

- WIT[3] (Cettolo et al., 2012).

---

[22]https://voice.mozilla.org/en/datasets – English version en_1488h_2019-12-10

[23]http://i13pc106.ira.uka.de/~mmueller/iwslt-corpus.zip

[24]https://ufal.mff.cuni.cz/czeng/czeng17

[25]http://www.statmt.org/wmt19/

[26]http://i13pc106.ira.uka.de/~mmueller/iwslt-corpus.zip

7.2.2 Test Data

The test set was prepared by the EU project ELITR[27] which aims at automatic simultaneous translation of speech into subtitles in the particular domain of conference speeches on auditing.

The overall size of the test set is in Table 3. The details about the preparation of test set components are in Appendix A.6.

7.3 Submissions

Five teams from three institutions took part in the task. Each team provided one "primary" submission and some teams provided several further "contrastive" submissions. The primary submissions are briefly described in Table 4. Note that two teams (APPTEK/RWTH and BUT) took the opportunity to reuse their systems from Offline Translation Task (Section 4) also in our task.

For the purposes of comparison, we also included freely available ASR services and MT services by two companies and denote the cascaded run for each of them as PUBLIC-A and PUBLIC-B. The ASR was run at the task submission deadline, the MT was added only later, on May 25, 2020.

7.4 Results

Appendix A.6 presents the results of the Non-Native Speech Translation Task for English→German and English→Czech, resp.

Note that the primary choice of most teams does not agree with which of their runs received the best scores in our evaluation. This can be easily explained by the partial domain mismatch between the development set and the test set.

The scores in both German and Czech results indicate considerable differences among the systems both in ASR quality as well as in BLEU scores. Before drawing strong conclusions from these scores, one has to consider that the results are heavily affected by the lack of reliable segmentation. If MT systems receive sequences of words not well matching sentence boundaries, they tend to reconstruct the sentence structure, causing serious translation errors.

The lack of golden sound segmentation also affects the evaluation: mwerSegmenter used in preprocessing of WER_{mw} and $BLEU_{mw}$ optimizes WER score but it operates on a slightly different tokenization and casing. While the instability will be small in WER evaluation, it could cause

more problems in $BLEU_{mw}$. Our BLEU calculation comes from sacreBLEU it its default setting. Furthermore, it needs to be considered that this is the first instance of the Non-Native shared task and not all peculiarities of the used evaluation measures and tools are quite known.[28] A manual evaluation would be desirable but even that would be inevitably biased depending on the exact way of presenting system outputs to the annotators. A procedure for a reliable manual evaluation of spoken language translation without pre-defined segmentation is yet to be sought.

The ASR quality scores[29] WER_1 and WER_{mw} are consistent with each other (Pearson .99), ranging from 14 (best submission by APPTEK/RWTH) to 33 WER_1. WER_{mw} is always 1–3.5 points absolute higher.

Translation quality scores $BLEU_1$ and $BLEU_{mw}$ show a similarly high correlation (Pearson .987) and reach up to 16. For English-to-German, the best translation was achieved by the secondary submissions of APPTEK/RWTH, followed by the primary ELITR-OFFLINE and one of the secondary submissions of CUNI-NN. The public services seem to score worse, PUBLIC-B follows very closely and PUBLIC-A seems to seriously underperform, but it is quite possible that our cascaded application of their APIs was suboptimal. The only on-line set of submissions (ELITR) score between the two public systems.

The situation for English-to-Czech is similar, except that APPTEK/RWTH did not take part in this, so ELITR-OFFLINE provided the best ASR as well as translations (one of their secondary submissions).

Often, there is a big variance of BLEU scores across all the submissions of one team. This indicates that the test set was hard to prepare for and that for a practical deployment, testing on the real input data is critical.

As expected, the ASR quality limits the trans-

---

[28] In our analysis, we also used BLEU as implemented in NLTK (Bird et al., 2009), observing substantial score differences. For instance, BUT1 received NLTK-BLEU of 12.68 instead of 0.63 reported in Appendix A.6 $BLEU_{mw}$. For other submissions, NLTK-BLEU dropped to zero without a clear reason, possibly some unexpected character in the output. The explanation of why NLTK can inflate scores is still pending but it should be performed to be sure that sacreBLEU does not unduly penalize BUT submissions.

[29] Note that the same ASR system was often used as the basis for translation into both Czech and German so the same ASR scores appear on multiple lines in Tables in Appendix A.6.

Team	Paper	Training Data	Off/On-Line	Cascaded
APPTEK/RWTH	Bahar et al. (2020a)†	Unconstrained	Off-Line	Cascaded
BUT	(unpublished draft)	Unconstrained	Off-Line	Ensemble E2E+Cascaded
CUNI	Polák et al. (2020)	Unconstrained	Off-Line	Cascaded
ELITR	Macháček et al. (2020)	Unconstrained	On-Line	Cascaded
ELITR-OFFLINE	Macháček et al. (2020)	Unconstrained	Off-Line	Cascaded
PUBLIC-A	– (public service)	Unconstrained	Off-Line	Cascaded
PUBLIC-B	– (public service)	Unconstrained	Off-Line	Cascaded

† The paper describes the basis of the systems but does not explicitly refer to non-native translation task.

Table 4: Primary submissions to Non-Native Speech Translation Task. The public web-based services were added by task organizers for comparison, no details are known about the underlying systems.

lation quality. WER_1 and $BLEU_1$ correlate negatively (Pearson -.82 for translation to German and -.66 for translation to Czech). Same correlations were observed for WER_{mw} and $BLEU_{mw}$.

The test set as well as the system outputs will be made available at the task web page[30] for future deep inspection.

7.4.1 Trade-Offs in Simultaneous SLT

The trade-offs in simultaneity of the translation can be studied only on submissions of ELITR, see Appendix A.6. We see that the Delay ranges between 1 and up to 2.5 seconds, with $Delay_{mw}$ giving sligthly lower scores on average, correlated reasonably well with $Delay_{ts}$ (Pearson .989). Delay into German seems higher for this particular set of MT systems.

The best score observed for Flicker is 5.18 and the worst is 7.51. At the same time, Flicker is not really negatively correlated with the Delays, e.g. $Delay_{ts}$ vs. Flicker have the Pearson correlation of -.20.

Unfortunately, our current scoring does not allow to study the relationship between the translation quality and simultaneity, because our BLEU scores are calculated only on the final segments. Any intermediate changes to the translation text are not reflected in the scores.

Note that the timing information on when each output was produced was provided by the participants themselves. A fully reliable evaluation would require participants installing their systems on our hardware to avoid effects of network traffic, which is clearly beyond the goals of this task.

8 Conclusions

The evaluation campaign of the IWSLT 2020 conference offered six challenge tracks which attracted a total of 30 teams, both from academy and industry. The increasing number of participants witnesses the growing interest towards research on spoken language translation by the NLP community, which we believe has been partly driven by the availability of suitable training resources as well as the versatility of neural network models, which now permit to directly tackle complex tasks, such as speech-to-text translation, which formerly required building very complex system. We hope that this trend will continue and invite researchers interested in proposing new challenges for the next edition to get in touch with us. Finally, results of the human evaluation, which was still ongoing at the time of writing the overview paper, will be reported at the conference and will be included in an updated version of this paper.

9 Acknowledgements

The offline Speech Translation task has been partially supported by the "End-to-end Spoken Language Translation in Rich Data Conditions" Amazon AWS ML Grant. The Non-Native Speech Translation Task was supported by the grants 19-26934X (NEUREM3) of the Czech Science Foundation, and H2020-ICT-2018-2-825460 (ELITR) of the EU. We are also grateful to Mohammad Mahmoudi for the assistance in the task evaluation and to Jonáš Kratochvíl for processing the input with public web ASR and MT services by two well-known companies.
The Open Domain Translation Task acknowledges the contributions of Yiqi Huang, Boliang Zhang and Arkady Arkhangorodsky, colleagues at DiDi Labs, for their help with the organization and sincerely thank Anqi Huang, a bilingual speaker, for validating the quality of the collected evaluation dataset.

---

[30] http://iwslt.org/doku.php?id=non_native_speech_translation

References

Yasuhiro Akiba, Marcello Federico, Noriko Kando, Hiromi Nakaiwa, Michael Paul, and Jun'ichi Tsujii. 2004. Overview of the IWSLT04 Evaluation Campaign. In *Proceedings of the International Workshop on Spoken Language Translation*, pages 1–12, Kyoto, Japan.

Antonios Anastasopoulos and David Chiang. 2018. Tied Multitask Learning for Neural Speech Translation. In *Proceedings of the 2018 Conference of the North American Chapter of the Association for Computational Linguistics: Human Language Technologies, Volume 1 (Long Papers)*, pages 82–91, New Orleans, Louisiana. Association for Computational Linguistics.

Naveen Arivazhagan, Colin Cherry, Te I, Wolfgang Macherey, Pallavi Baljekar, and George Foster. 2019a. Re-translation strategies for long form, simultaneous, spoken language translation.

Naveen Arivazhagan, Colin Cherry, Wolfgang Macherey, Chung-Cheng Chiu, Semih Yavuz, Ruoming Pang, Wei Li, and Colin Raffel. 2019b. Monotonic infinite lookback attention for simultaneous machine translation. In *Proceedings of the 57th Annual Meeting of the Association for Computational Linguistics*, pages 1313–1323, Florence, Italy. Association for Computational Linguistics.

Arkady Arkhangorodsky, Yiqi Huang, and Amittai Axelrod. 2020. DiDi Labs' End-to-End System for the IWSLT 2020 Offline Speech Translation Task. In *Proceedings of the 17th International Conference on Spoken Language Translation (IWSLT)*.

Parnia Bahar, Patrick Wilken, Tamer Alkhouli, Andreas Guta, Pavel Golik, Evgeny Matusov, and Christian Herold. 2020a. Start-Before-End and End-to-End: Neural Speech Translation by AppTek and RWTH Aachen University. In *Proceedings of the 17th International Conference on Spoken Language Translation (IWSLT)*.

Parnia Bahar, Patrick Wilken, Tamer Alkhouli, Andreas Guta, Pavel Golik, Evgeny Matusov, and Christian Herold. 2020b. Start-Before-End and End-to-End: Neural Speech Translation by AppTek and RWTH Aachen University. In *Proceedings of the 17th International Conference on Spoken Language Translation (IWSLT)*.

Benjamin Beilharz and Xin Sun. 2019. LibriVoxDeEn - A Corpus for German-to-English Speech Translation and Speech Recognition.

Steven Bird, Ewan Klein, and Edward Loper. 2009. *Natural Language Processing with Python*, 1st edition. O'Reilly Media, Inc.

Ondřej Bojar, Ondřej Dušek, Tom Kocmi, Jindřich Libovický, Michal Novák, Martin Popel, Roman Sudarikov, and Dušan Variš. 2016. CzEng 1.6: Enlarged Czech-English Parallel Corpus with Processing Tools Dockered. In *Text, Speech, and Dialogue: 19th International Conference, TSD 2016*, number 9924 in Lecture Notes in Computer Science, pages 231–238, Cham / Heidelberg / New York / Dordrecht / London. Masaryk University, Springer International Publishing.

Ondřej Bojar, Kamil Kos, and David Mareček. 2010. Tackling Sparse Data Issue in Machine Translation Evaluation. In *Proceedings of the ACL 2010 Conference Short Papers*, pages 86–91, Uppsala, Sweden. Association for Computational Linguistics.

Mauro Cettolo, Marcello Federico, Luisa Bentivogli, Jan Niehues, Sebastian Stüker, K. Sudoh, K. Yoshino, and Christian Federmann. 2017. Overview of the IWSLT 2017 Evaluation Campaign. In *Proceedings of the 14th International Workshop on Spoken Language Translation (IWSLT 2017)*, pages 2–14, Tokyo, Japan.

Mauro Cettolo, Christian Girardi, and Marcello Federico. 2012. WIT[3]: Web Inventory of Transcribed and Translated Talks. In *Proceedings of the Annual Conference of the European Association for Machine Translation (EAMT)*, Trento, Italy.

Mauro Cettolo, Jan Niehues, Sebastian Stüker, Luisa Bentivogli, Roldano Cattoni, and Marcello Federico. 2015. The IWSLT 2015 Evaluation Campaign. In *Proceedings of the 12th International Workshop on Spoken Language Translation (IWSLT 2015)*, Da Nang, Vietnam.

Mauro Cettolo, Jan Niehues, Sebastian Stüker, Luisa Bentivogli, and Marcello Federico. 2013. Report on the 10th IWSLT Evaluation Campaign. In *Proceedings of the Tenth International Workshop on Spoken Language Translation (IWSLT 2013)*, Heidelberg, Germany.

Mauro Cettolo, Jan Niehues, Sebastian Stüker, Luisa Bentivogli, and Marcello Federico. 2014. Report on the 11th IWSLT Evaluation Campaign, IWSLT 2014. In *Proceedings of the Eleventh International Workshop on Spoken Language Translation (IWSLT 2014)*, Lake Tahoe, USA.

Mauro Cettolo, Jan Niehues, Sebastian Stüker, Luisa Bentivogli, and Marcello Federico. 2016. The IWSLT 2016 Evaluation Campaign. In *Proceedings of the 13th International Workshop on Spoken Language Translation (IWSLT 2016)*, Seattle, USA.

Pinzhen Chen, Nikolay Bogoychev, and Ulrich Germann. 2020. Character Mapping and Ad-hoc Adaptation: Edinburgh's IWSLT 2020 Open Domain Translation System. In *Proceedings of the 17th International Conference on Spoken Language Translation (IWSLT)*.

Colin Cherry and George Foster. 2019. Thinking slow about latency evaluation for simultaneous machine translation. *arXiv preprint arXiv:1906.00048*.

Chenhui Chu, Toshiaki Nakazawa, and Sadao Kurohashi. 2014. Constructing a Chinese-Japanese Parallel Corpus from Wikipedia. *LREC (International Conference on Language Resources and Evaluation)*.

Chenhui Chu, Toshiaki Nakazawa, and Sadao Kurohashi. 2015. Integrated Parallel Sentence and Fragment Extraction from Comparable Corpora: A Case Study on Chinese–Japanese Wikipedia. *ACM Transactions on Asian and Low-Resource Language Information Processing*.

Hongyi Cui, Yizhen Wei, Shohei Iida, Masaaki Nagata, and Takehito Utsuro. 2020. University of Tsukuba's Machine Translation System for IWSLT20 Open Domain Translation Task. In *Proceedings of the 17th International Conference on Spoken Language Translation (IWSLT)*.

Raj Dabre and Sadao Kurohashi. 2017. MMCR4NLP: multilingual multiway corpora repository for natural language processing. *CoRR*, abs/1710.01025.

Zihang Dai, Zhilin Yang, Yiming Yang, Jaime Carbonell, Quoc Le, and Ruslan Salakhutdinov. 2019. Transformer-XL: Attentive Language Models beyond a Fixed-Length Context. In *Proceedings of the 57th Annual Meeting of the Association for Computational Linguistics*, pages 2978–2988, Florence, Italy. Association for Computational Linguistics.

Mattia A. Di Gangi, Roldano Cattoni, Luisa Bentivogli, Matteo Negri, and Marco Turchi. 2019a. MuST-C: a Multilingual Speech Translation Corpus. In *Proceedings of the 2019 Conference of the North American Chapter of the Association for Computational Linguistics: Human Language Technologies, Volume 1 (Long and Short Papers)*, pages 2012–2017, Minneapolis, Minnesota.

Mattia A. Di Gangi, Matteo Negri, Roldano Cattoni, Roberto Dessì, and Marco Turchi. 2019b. Enhancing Transformer for End-to-end Speech-to-Text Translation. In *Proceedings of Machine Translation Summit XVII Volume 1: Research Track*, pages 21–31, Dublin, Ireland. European Association for Machine Translation.

Mattia A. Di Gangi, Matteo Negri, and Marco Turchi. 2019c. Adapting Transformer to End-to-End Spoken Language Translation. In *Interspeech 2019, 20th Annual Conference of the International Speech Communication Association, Graz, Austria, 15-19 September 2019*, pages 1133–1137. ISCA.

Mattia A. Di Gangi, Matteo Negri, and Marco Turchi. 2019d. One-To-Many Multilingual End-to-end Speech Translation. In *Proceedings of the 2019 IEEE Automatic Speech Recognition and Understanding Workshop (ASRU)*, pages 585–592, Sentosa, Singapore.

Matthias Eck and Chiori Hori. 2005. Overview of the IWSLT 2005 evaluation campaign. In *Proceedings of the International Workshop on Spoken Language Translation*, pages 1–22, Pittsburgh, PA.

Maha Elbayad, Ha Nguyen, Fethi Bougares, Natalia Tomashenko, Antoine Caubrière, Benjamin Lecouteux, Yannick Estève, and Laurent Besacier. 2020. ON-TRAC Consortium for End-to-End and Simultanouus Speech Translation Challenge Tasks at IWSLT 2020. In *Proceedings of the 17th International Conference on Spoken Language Translation (IWSLT)*.

Marcello Federico, Luisa Bentivogli, Michael Paul, and Sebastian Stüker. 2011. Overview of the IWSLT 2011 Evaluation Campaign. In *Proceedings of the International Workshop on Spoken Language Translation*, pages 11–27, San Francisco, USA.

Marcello Federico, Mauro Cettolo, Luisa Bentivogli, Michael Paul, and Sebastian Stüker. 2012. Overview of the IWSLT 2012 Evaluation Campaign. In *Proceedings of the International Workshop on Spoken Language Translation*, pages 11–27, Hong Kong, HK.

Cameron Shaw Fordyce. 2007. Overview of the IWSLT 2007 evaluation campaign. In *Proceedings of the International Workshop on Spoken Language Translation*, pages 1–12, Trento, Italy.

Ryo Fukuda, Katsuhito Sudoh, and Satoshi Nakamura. 2020. NAIST's Machine Translation Systems for IWSLT 2020 Conversational Speech Translation Task. In *Proceedings of the 17th International Conference on Spoken Language Translation (IWSLT)*.

Marco Gaido, Mattia Antonio Di Gangi, Matteo Negri, and Marco Turchi. 2020. End-to-End Speech-Translation with Knowledge Distillation: FBK@IWSLT2020. In *Proceedings of the 17th International Conference on Spoken Language Translation (IWSLT)*.

David Graff, Shudong Huang, Ingrid Cartagena, Kevin Walker, and Christopher Cieri. Fisher spanish speech (LDC2010S01). Https://catalog.ldc.upenn.edu/ ldc2010s01.

Alex Graves. 2016. Adaptive computation time for recurrent neural networks. *arXiv preprint arXiv:1603.08983*.

Alex Graves, Santiago Fernández, Faustino J. Gomez, and Jürgen Schmidhuber. 2006. Connectionist Temporal Classification: Labelling Unsegmented Sequence Data with Recurrent Neural Networks. In *Proceedings of the 23rd international conference on Machine learning (ICML)*, pages 369–376, Pittsburgh, Pennsylvania.

Masato Hagiwara. 2020. Octanove Labs' Japanese-Chinese Open Domain Translation System. In *Proceedings of the 17th International Conference on Spoken Language Translation (IWSLT)*.

Houjeung Han, Mohd Abbas Zaidi, Sathish Indurthi, Nikhil Kumar Lakumarapu, Beomseok Lee, and Sangha Kim. 2020. End-to-End Simultaneous Translation System for the IWSLT2020 using Modality Agnostic Meta-Learning. In *Proceedings of the 17th International Conference on Spoken Language Translation (IWSLT)*.

François Hernandez, Vincent Nguyen, Sahar Ghannay, Natalia A. Tomashenko, and Yannick Estève. 2018. TED-LIUM 3: twice as much data and corpus repartition for experiments on speaker adaptation. *CoRR*, abs/1805.04699.

S. Indurthi, H. Han, N. K. Lakumarapu, B. Lee, I. Chung, S. Kim, and C. Kim. 2020. End-end speech-to-text translation with modality agnostic meta-learning. In *ICASSP 2020 - 2020 IEEE International Conference on Acoustics, Speech and Signal Processing (ICASSP)*, pages 7904–7908.

Javier Iranzo-Sánchez, Joan Albert Silvestre-Cerdà, Javier Jorge, Nahuel Roselló, Adrià Giménez, Albert Sanchis, Jorge Civera, and Alfons Juan. 2020. Europarl-st: A multilingual corpus for speech translation of parliamentary debates. In *Proc. of 45th Intl. Conf. on Acoustics, Speech, and Signal Processing (ICASSP 2020)*, pages 8229–8233, Barcelona (Spain).

Ye Jia, Melvin Johnson, Wolfgang Macherey, Ron J. Weiss, Yuan Cao, Chung-Cheng Chiu, Naveen Ari, Stella Laurenzo, and Yonghui Wu. 2019. Leveraging weakly supervised data to improve end-to-end speech-to-text translation. *ICASSP 2019 - 2019 IEEE International Conference on Acoustics, Speech and Signal Processing (ICASSP)*.

Marcin Junczys-Dowmunt, Roman Grundkiewicz, Tomasz Dwojak, Hieu Hoang, Kenneth Heafield, Tom Neckermann, Frank Seide, Ulrich Germann, Alham Fikri Aji, Nikolay Bogoychev, André F. T. Martins, and Alexandra Birch. 2018. Marian: Fast neural machine translation in C++. In *Proceedings of ACL 2018, System Demonstrations*, pages 116–121, Melbourne, Australia. Association for Computational Linguistics.

Guillaume Klein, Yoon Kim, Yuntian Deng, Jean Senellart, and Alexander Rush. 2017. OpenNMT: Open-source toolkit for neural machine translation. In *Proceedings of ACL 2017, System Demonstrations*, pages 67–72, Vancouver, Canada. Association for Computational Linguistics.

Ali Can Kocabiyikoglu, Laurent Besacier, and Olivier Kraif. 2018. Augmenting Librispeech with French Translations: A Multimodal Corpus for Direct Speech Translation Evaluation. In *Proceedings of LREC 2018*, Miyazaki, Japan.

Nikhil Kumar Lakumarapu, Beomseok Lee, Sathish Indurthi, Houjeung Han, Mohd Abbas Zaidi, and Sangha Kim. 2020. End-to-End Offline Speech Translation System for IWSLT 2020 using Modality Agnostic Meta-Learning. In *Proceedings of the*

17th International Conference on Spoken Language Translation (IWSLT).

Alon Lavie and Abhaya Agarwal. 2007. METEOR: An Automatic Metric for MT Evaluation with High Levels of Correlation with Human Judgments. In *Proceedings of the Second Workshop on Statistical Machine Translation (WMT)*, pages 228–231, Prague, Czech Republic.

Jason Li, Vitaly Lavrukhin, Boris Ginsburg, Ryan Leary, Oleksii Kuchaiev, Jonathan M Cohen, Huyen Nguyen, and Ravi Teja Gadde. 2019. Jasper: An end-to-end convolutional neural acoustic model. *arXiv preprint arXiv:1904.03288*.

Pierre Lison and Jörg Tiedemann. 2016. OpenSubtitles2016: Extracting Large Parallel Corpora from Movie and TV Subtitles. *LREC (International Conference on Language Resources and Evaluation)*.

Pierre Lison, Jörg Tiedemann, and Milen Kouylekov. 2018. OpenSubtitles2018: Statistical rescoring of sentence alignments in large, noisy parallel corpora. In *Proceedings of the Eleventh International Conference on Language Resources and Evaluation (LREC 2018)*, Miyazaki, Japan. European Language Resources Association (ELRA).

Mingbo Ma, Liang Huang, Hao Xiong, Renjie Zheng, Kaibo Liu, Baigong Zheng, Chuanqiang Zhang, Zhongjun He, Hairong Liu, Xing Li, Hua Wu, and Haifeng Wang. 2019. STACL: Simultaneous translation with implicit anticipation and controllable latency using prefix-to-prefix framework. In *Proceedings of the 57th Annual Meeting of the Association for Computational Linguistics*, pages 3025–3036, Florence, Italy. Association for Computational Linguistics.

Dominik Macháček, Jonáš Kratochvíl, Tereza Vojtěchová, and Ondřej Bojar. 2019. A speech test set of practice business presentations with additional relevant texts. In *Statistical Language and Speech Processing*, pages 151–161, Cham, Switzerland. Springer Nature Switzerland AG.

Dominik Macháček, Jonáš Kratochvíl, Sangeet Sagar, Matús Žilinec, Ondřej Bojar, Thai-Son Nguyen, Felix Schneider, Philip Williams, and Yuekun Yao. 2020. ELITR Non-Native Speech Translation at IWSLT 2020. In *Proceedings of the 17th International Conference on Spoken Language Translation (IWSLT)*.

E. Matusov, G. Leusch, O. Bender, , and H. Ney. 2005. Evaluating Machine Translation Output with Automatic Sentence Segmentation. In *Proceedings of the 2nd International Workshop on Spoken Language Translation (IWSLT)*, Pittsburgh, USA.

I. Mccowan, G. Lathoud, M. Lincoln, A. Lisowska, W. Post, D. Reidsma, and P. Wellner. 2005. The ami meeting corpus. In *In: Proceedings Measuring Behavior 2005, 5th International Conference on Methods and Techniques in Behavioral Research. L.P.J.J.*

Noldus, F. Grieco, L.W.S. Loijens and P.H. Zimmerman (Eds.), Wageningen: Noldus Information Technology.

Ha Nguyen, Natalia, Marcely Zanon Boito, Antoine Caubriere, Fethi Bougares, Mickael Rouvier, Laurent Besacier, and Esteve Yannick. 2019. ON-TRAC consortium end-to-end speech translation systems for the IWSLT 2019 shared task. In *Proceedings of 16th International Workshop on Spoken Language Translation (IWSLT)*, Hong Kong.

Thai-Son Nguyen, Sebastian Stueker, Jan Niehues, and Alex Waibel. 2020a. Improving Sequence-to-sequence Speech Recognition Training with On-the-fly Data Augmentation. In *Proceedings of the 2020 International Conference on Acoustics, Speech, and Signal Processing – IEEE-ICASSP-2020*, Barcelona, Spain.

Thai-Son Nguyen, Sebastian Stuker, Jan Niehues, and Alex Waibel. 2020b. Improving sequence-to-sequence speech recognition training with on-the-fly data augmentation. In *ICASSP 2020 - 2020 IEEE International Conference on Acoustics, Speech and Signal Processing (ICASSP)*. IEEE.

J. Niehues, R. Cattoni, S. Stüker, M. Negri, M. Turchi, T. Ha, E. Salesky, R. Sanabria, L. Barrault, L. Specia, and M. Federico. 2019. The IWSLT 2019 Evaluation Campaign. In *Proceedings of the 16th International Workshop on Spoken Language Translation (IWSLT 2019)*, Hong Kong, China.

Jan Niehues, Roldano Cattoni, Sebastian Stüker, Mauro Cettolo, Marco Turchi, and Marcello Federico. 2018. The IWSLT 2018 Evaluation Campaign. In *Proceedings of the 15th International Workshop on Spoken Language Translation (IWSLT 2018)*, pages 2–6, Bruges, Belgium.

Brian Ore, Eric Hansen, Timothy Anderson, and Jeremy Gwinnup. 2020. The AFRL IWSLT 2020 Systems: Work-From-Home Edition. In *Proceedings of the 17th International Conference on Spoken Language Translation (IWSLT)*.

Vassil Panayotov, Guoguo Chen, Daniel Povey, and Sanjeev Khudanpur. 2015. Librispeech: An asr corpus based on public domain audio books. *2015 IEEE International Conference on Acoustics, Speech and Signal Processing (ICASSP)*, pages 5206–5210.

Kishore Papineni, Salim Roukos, Todd Ward, and Wei-Jing Zhu. 2002a. Bleu: a method for automatic evaluation of machine translation. In *Proceedings of the 40th annual meeting on association for computational linguistics*. Association for Computational Linguistics.

Kishore Papineni, Salim Roukos, Todd Ward, and Wei-Jing Zhu. 2002b. BLEU: a Method for Automatic Evaluation of Machine Translation. In *Proceedings of the 40th Annual Meeting of the Association for*

Computational Linguistics (ACL), pages 311–318, Philadelphia, USA.

Kishore Papineni, Salim Roukos, Todd Ward, and Wei-jing Zhu. 2002c. BLEU: A Method for Automatic Evaluation of Machine Translation. *ACL (Association for Computational Linguistics)*.

Daniel S. Park, William Chan, Yu Zhang, Chung-Cheng Chiu, Barret Zoph, Ekin D. Cubuk, and Quoc V. Le. 2019. SpecAugment: A Simple Data Augmentation Method for Automatic Speech Recognition. *Interspeech 2019*.

Michael Paul. 2006. Overview of the IWSLT 2006 Evaluation Campaign. In *Proceedings of the International Workshop on Spoken Language Translation*, pages 1–15, Kyoto, Japan.

Michael Paul. 2008. Overview of the IWSLT 2008 Evaluation Campaign. In *Proceedings of the International Workshop on Spoken Language Translation*, pages 1–17, Waikiki, Hawaii.

Michael Paul. 2009. Overview of the IWSLT 2009 Evaluation Campaign. In *Proceedings of the International Workshop on Spoken Language Translation*, pages 1–18, Tokyo, Japan.

Michael Paul, Marcello Federico, and Sebastian Stüker. 2010. Overview of the IWSLT 2010 Evaluation Campaign. In *Proceedings of the International Workshop on Spoken Language Translation*, pages 3–27, Paris, France.

Ngoc-Quan Pham, Thai-Son Nguyen, Thanh-Le Ha, Juan Hussain, Felix Schneider, Jan Niehues, Sebastian Stuker, and Alexander Waibel. 2019a. The IWSLT 2019 KIT Speech Translation System. In *Proceedings of 16th International Workshop on Spoken Language Translation (IWSLT)*, Hong Kong.

Ngoc-Quan Pham, Thai-Son Nguyen, Jan Niehues, Markus Müller, Sebastian Stüker, and Alexander Waibel. 2019b. Very deep self-attention networks for end-to-end speech recognition.

Ngoc-Quan Pham, Felix Schneider, Tuan-Nam Nguyen, Thanh-Le Ha, Thai-Son Nguyen, Maximilian Awiszus, Sebastian Stüker, and Alexander Waibel. 2020. KIT's IWSLT 2020 SLT Translation System. In *Proceedings of the 17th International Conference on Spoken Language Translation (IWSLT)*.

Peter Polák, Sangeet Sagar, Dominik Macháček, and Ondřej Bojar. 2020. Neural ASR with Phoneme-Level Intermediate Step — A Non-Native Speech Translation Task Submission to IWSLT 2020. In *Proceedings of the 17th International Conference on Spoken Language Translation (IWSLT)*.

Matt Post. 2018. A call for clarity in reporting BLEU scores. In *Proceedings of the Third Conference on Machine Translation: Research Papers*, pages 186–191, Belgium, Brussels. Association for Computational Linguistics.

Matt Post, Gaurav Kumar, Adam Lopez, Damianos Karakos, Chris Callison-Burch, and Sanjeev Khudanpur. 2013. Improved speech-to-text translation with the fisher and callhome spanish–english speech translation corpus.

Tomasz Potapczyk and Pawel Przybysz. 2020. SR-POL's System for the IWSLT 2020 End-to-End Speech Translation Task. In *Proceedings of the 17th International Conference on Spoken Language Translation (IWSLT)*.

Tomasz Potapczyk, Pawel Przybysz, Marcin Chochowski, and Artur; Szumaczuk. 2019. Samsung's System for the IWSLT 2019 End-to-End Speech Translation Task. In *Proceedings of 16th International Workshop on Spoken Language Translation (IWSLT)*, Hong Kong.

Daniel Povey, Arnab Ghoshal, Gilles Boulianne, et al. 2011. The kaldi speech recognition toolkit. In *IEEE 2011 Workshop on Automatic Speech Recognition and Understanding*. IEEE Signal Processing Society. IEEE Catalog No.: CFP11SRW-USB.

Anthony Rousseau, Paul Deléglise, and Yannick Esteve. 2014. Enhancing the ted-lium corpus with selected data for language modeling and more ted talks. In *LREC*.

Nikhil Saini, Jyotsana Khatri, Preethi Jyothi, and Pushpak Bhattacharyya. 2020. Generating Fluent Translations from Disfluent Text Without Access To Fluent References. In *Proceedings of the 17th International Conference on Spoken Language Translation (IWSLT)*.

Elizabeth Salesky, Susanne Burger, Jan Niehues, and Alex Waibel. 2018. Towards fluent translations from disfluent speech. In *2018 IEEE Spoken Language Technology Workshop (SLT)*, pages 921–926. IEEE.

Elizabeth Salesky, Matthias Sperber, and Alex Waibel. 2019. Fluent translations from disfluent speech in end-to-end speech translation. In *Proceedings of the 2019 Conference of the North American Chapter of the Association for Computational Linguistics: Human Language Technologies, Volume 1 (Long and Short Papers)*, pages 2786–2792.

Ramon Sanabria, Ozan Caglayan, Shruti Palaskar, Desmond Elliott, Loïc Barrault, Lucia Specia, and Florian Metze. 2018. How2: a large-scale dataset for multimodal language understanding. In *Proceedings of the Workshop on Visually Grounded Interaction and Language (ViGIL)*. NeurIPS.

Steffen Schneider, Alexei Baevski, Ronan Collobert, and Michael Auli. 2019. wav2vec: Unsupervised pre-training for speech recognition. In *INTERSPEECH*.

Holger Schwenk, Vishrav Chaudhary, Shuo Sun, Hongyu Gong, and Francisco Guzmán. 2019. Wikimatrix: Mining 135m Parallel Sentences in 1620 Language Pairs from Wikipedia. *arXiv preprint arXiv:1907.05791*.

Karen Simonyan and Andrew Zisserman. 2015. Very Deep Convolutional Networks for Large-Scale Image Recognition. In *3rd International Conference on Learning Representations, ICLR 2015, San Diego, CA, USA, May 7-9, 2015, Conference Track Proceedings*.

Matthew Snover, Bonnie Dorr, Richard Schwartz, Linnea Micciulla, and John Makhoul. 2006a. A Study of Translation Edit Rate with Targeted Human Annotation. In *Proceedings of the The Seventh Conference of the Association for Machine Translation in the Americas (AMTA)*, pages 223–231, Cambridge, USA.

Matthew Snover, Bonnie Dorr, Richard Schwartz, Linnea Micciulla, and John Makhoul. 2006b. A study of translation edit rate with targeted human annotation. In *Proceedings of association for machine translation in the Americas*.

Matthias Sperber, Ngoc Quan Pham, Thai Son Nguyen, Jan Niehues, Markus Muller, Thanh-Le Ha, Sebastian Stuker, and Alex Waibel. 2018. KIT's IWSLT 2018 SLT Translation System. In *15th International Workshop on Spoken Language Translation (IWSLT 2018)*, Bruges, Belgium.

Milos Stanojevic and Khalil Sima'an. 2014. BEER: BEtter evaluation as ranking. In *Proceedings of the Ninth Workshop on Statistical Machine Translation*. Association for Computational Linguistics.

Enmin Su and Yi Ren. 2020. Deep Blue Sonics' Submission to IWSLT 2020 Open Domain Translation Task. In *Proceedings of the 17th International Conference on Spoken Language Translation (IWSLT)*.

Yuhui Sun, Mengxue Guo, Xiang Li, Jianwei Cui, and Bin Wang. 2020. Xiaomi's Submissions for IWSLT 2020 Open Domain Translation Task. In *Proceedings of the 17th International Conference on Spoken Language Translation (IWSLT)*.

Christian Szegedy, Vincent Vanhoucke, Sergey Ioffe, Jon Shlens, and Zbigniew Wojna. 2016. Rethinking the Inception Architecture for Computer Vision. In *Proceedings of 2016 IEEE Conference on Computer Vision and Pattern Recognition (CVPR)*, pages 2818–2826, Las Vegas, Nevada, United States.

Jörg Tiedemann. 2012. Parallel Data, Tools and Interfaces in OPUS. *LREC (International Conference on Language Resources and Evaluation)*.

Mei Tu, Wei Liu, Lijie Wang, Xiao Chen, and Xue Wen. 2019. End-to-end speech translation system description of LIT for IWSLT 2019. In *Proceedings of 16th International Workshop on Spoken Language Translation (IWSLT)*, Hong Kong.

Dániel Varga, Péter Halácsy, András Kornai, Viktor Nagy, László Németh, and Viktor Trón. 2005. Parallel Corpora for Medium Density Languages. *RANLP (Recent Advances in Natural Language Processing)*.

Ashish Vaswani, Samy Bengio, Eugene Brevdo, Francois Chollet, Aidan N. Gomez, Stephan Gouws, Llion Jones, Łukasz Kaiser, Nal Kalchbrenner, Niki Parmar, Ryan Sepassi, Noam Shazeer, and Jakob Uszkoreit. 2018. Tensor2Tensor for Neural Machine Translation. *arXiv preprint arXiv:1803.07416*.

Ashish Vaswani, Noam Shazeer, Niki Parmar, Jakob Uszkoreit, Llion Jones, Aidan N Gomez, Łukasz Kaiser, and Illia Polosukhin. 2017a. Attention is All You Need. In *Proceedings of NIPS 2017*.

Ashish Vaswani, Noam Shazeer, Niki Parmar, Jakob Uszkoreit, Llion Jones, Aidan N Gomez, Łukasz Kaiser, and Illia Polosukhin. 2017b. Attention Is All You Need. *NeurIPS (Neural Information Processing Systems)*.

Raúl Vázquez, Mikko Aulamo, Umut Sulubacak, and Jörg Tiedemann. 2020. The University of Helsinki submission to the IWSLT2020 Offline Speech Translation Task. In *Proceedings of the 17th International Conference on Spoken Language Translation (IWSLT)*.

Raúl Vázquez, Alessandro Raganato, Mathias Creutz, and Jorg Tiedemann. 2020. A systematic study of inner-attention-based sentence representations in multilingual neural machine translation. *Computational Linguistics*, 0((ja)):1–53.

Pavel Vondricka. 2014. Aligning Parallel Texts with InterText. *LREC (International Conference on Language Resources and Evaluation)*.

Hari Krishna Vydana, Martin Karafi'at, Katerina Zmolikova, Luk'as Burget, and Honza Cernocky. 2020. Jointly trained transformers models for spoken language translation.

Minghan Wang, Hao Yang, Yao Deng, Ying Qin, Lizhi Lei, Daimeng Wei, Hengchao Shang, Jiaxin Guo, Ning Xie, and Xiaochun Li. 2020a. The HW-TSC Video Speech Translation system at IWSLT 2020. In *Proceedings of the 17th International Conference on Spoken Language Translation (IWSLT)*.

Qian Wang, Yuchen Liu, Cong Ma, Yu Lu, Yining Wang, Long Zhou, Yang Zhao, Jiajun Zhang, and Chengqing Zong. 2020b. CASIA's Submission for IWSLT 2020 Open Domain Translation. In *Proceedings of the 17th International Conference on Spoken Language Translation (IWSLT)*.

Weiyue Wang, Jan-Thorsten Peter, Hendrik Rosendahl, and Hermann Ney. 2016. CharacTer: Translation edit rate on character level. In *Proceedings of the First Conference on Machine Translation: Volume 2, Shared Task Papers*. Association for Computational Linguistics.

Shinji Watanabe, Takaaki Hori, Shigeki Karita, Tomoki Hayashi, Jiro Nishitoba, Yuya Unno, Nelson Enrique Yalta Soplin, Jahn Heymann, Matthew Wiesner, Nanxin Chen, Adithya Renduchintala, and Tsubasa Ochiai. 2018. Espnet: End-to-end speech processing toolkit. *Proceedings of the Annual Conference of the International Speech Communication Association, INTERSPEECH*, 2018-September:2207–2211.

Jiaze Wei, Wenbin Liu, Zhenfeng Wu, You Pan, and Yanqing He. 2020. ISTIC's Neural Machine Translation System for IWSLT'2020. In *Proceedings of the 17th International Conference on Spoken Language Translation (IWSLT)*.

Qian Zhang, Tingxun Shi, Xiaopu Li, Dawei Dang, Di Ai, Zhengshan Xue, and Jie Hao. 2020. OPPO's Machine Translation System for the IWSLT 2020 Open Domain Translation Task. In *Proceedings of the 17th International Conference on Spoken Language Translation (IWSLT)*.

Yimeng Zhuang, Yuan Zhang, and Lijie Wang. 2020. LIT Team's System Description for Japanese-Chinese Machine Translation Task in IWSLT 2020. In *Proceedings of the 17th International Conference on Spoken Language Translation (IWSLT)*.

Appendix A. Evaluation Results and Details

A.1. Simultaneous Speech Translation

· Summary of the results of the simultaneous speech translation **text track.**
· Results are reported on the blind test set and systems are grouped by latency regime.
· Tabulated raw data will also be provided on the task web site[31] and the repository[32].

Team	BLEU	AP	AL	DAL
Low Latency				
ON-TRAC	23.59	0.77	2.71	3.92
Medium Latency				
ON-TRAC	29.38	0.65	5.95	6.94
KIT	29.31	0.63	5.93	6.84
AppTek/RWTH	28.69	0.65	4.61	7.26
SRSK	27.10	0.91	5.44	6.44
High Latency				
ON-TRAC	30.51	0.63	8.71	9.63
KIT	29.76	0.63	6.38	7.32
AppTek/RWTH	28.69	0.65	4.61	7.26
SRSK	28.49	0.91	6.09	7.13
Unconstrained				
ON-TRAC	30.51	0.63	8.71	9.63
KIT	29.76	0.63	6.38	7.32
SRSK	29.41	0.90	15.28	15.68
AppTek/RWTH	28.69	0.65	4.61	7.26

· Summary of the results of the simultaneous speech translation **speech track.**
· Results are reported on the blind test set and systems are grouped by latency regime.
· Tabulated raw data will also be provided on the task web site[33] and the repository[34].

Team	BLEU	AP	AL	DAL
Low Latency				
SRSK	9.25	1.17	738.75	1102.96
ON-TRAC	7.27	0.97	955.11	1833.27
Medium Latency				
ON-TRAC	15.31	0.86	1727.49	3280.03
SRSK	13.58	1.07	1815.93	2243.25
High Latency				
ON-TRAC	21.80	0.74	3932.21	5029.31
SRSK	15.70	1.07	3602.02	4677.22
Unconstrained				
ON-TRAC	21.80	0.74	3932.21	5029.31
AppTek/RWTH	21.19	0.74	4123.67	4750.24
SRSK	16.99	1.03	4054.18	4799.37

A.2. Video Speech Translation

· Systems are ordered according to the *CER* metrics.
· *BLEU* and *METEOR* scores are given as percent figures (%).

Video Translation: Chinese-English

System	CER	BLEU	METEOR	chrF
HW_TSC	36.54	14.96	30.4	35.2
Online A	37.65	11.97	26.3	32.4
Online B	47.89	13.19	26.0	30.4

**Chinese-English: Average sentence-level
BLEU score within CER ranges**

CER	HW_TSC	Online A	Online B
< 15.0	14.55	11.61	20.75
(15.0, 20.0]	15.72	14.78	17.17
(20.0, 25.0]	13.94	15.18	21.21
(25.0, 30.0]	13.10	7.84	16.38
(30.0, 35.0]	9.58	5.54	15.48
(35.0, 40.0]	5.85	5.77	15.82
> 40.0	7.65	3.32	4.71

A.3. Offline Speech Translation

· Systems are ordered according to the *BLEU* metrics.
· *BLEU* and *TER* scores are given as percent figures (%).
· End-to-end systems are indicated by gray background.

Speech Translation : TED English-German tst 2020 (own segmentation)

System	BLEU	TER	BEER	characTER	BLEU(CI)	TER(CI)
SRPOL	25.3	59.45	53.16	49.35	26.4	57.60
AppTek/RWTH	25.06	61.43	53.51	48.24	26.29	59.20
AFRL	23.33	62.12	52.46	50.05	24.53	59.96
AppTek/RWTH	23.29	64.77	52.31	49.12	24.67	62.42
KIT	22.56	65.56	50.04	53.15	23.71	63.42
ON-TRAC	22.12	63.87	51.20	51.46	23.25	61.85
KIT	21.81	66.50	50.99	51.30	24.21	63.06

Speech Translation : TED English-German tst 2020 (given segmentation)

System	BLEU	TER	BEER	characTER	BLEU(CI)	TER(CI)
AppTek/RWTH	22.49	65.20	51.40	52.75	23.73	62.93
KIT	22.06	65.38	51.22	51.26	23.24	63.10
SRPOL	21.49	65.74	49.81	56.20	22.7	63.82
FBK	20.75	68.11	49.87	55.31	21.88	66.04
AppTek/RWTH	20.5	70.08	49.65	54.85	21.84	67.95
KIT	19.82	70.51	48.62	56.91	22	67.36
BHANSS	18.09	71.78	47.09	60.96	19	70.06
HY	17.02	76.37	47.03	58.32	18.07	74.23
DiDi Labs	10.14	101.56	41.95	62.60	10.83	99.60
HY	6.77	86.31	36.81	76.30	7.26	84.91

Speech Translation : TED English-German tst 2019 (own segmentation)

System	BLEU	TER	BEER	characTER	BLEU(CI)	TER(CI)
SRPOL	23.96	60.79	51.45	51.16	24.94	59.12
AppTek/RWTH	23.4	63.53	52.13	49.23	24.6	61.27
AppTek/RWTH	21.58	66.15	50.87	50.54	22.85	63.79
AFRL	21.28	64.96	51.11	51.88	22.5	62.66
KIT	21.07	66.59	49.88	52.74	22.33	64.32
KIT	20.43	66.29	50.99	50.26	22.99	62.46
ON-TRAC	20.19	66.38	49.89	52.51	21.23	64.26

Speech Translation : TED English-German tst 2019 (given segmentation)

System	BLEU	TER	BEER	characTER	BLEU(CI)	TER(CI)
SRPOL	20.1	67.73	47.76	59.08	21.17	65.92
FBK	19.52	68.93	48.07	58.26	20.65	66.87
AppTek/RWTH	19.23	71.22	47.94	57.96	20.53	68.97
KIT	18.83	70.08	47.83	57.88	21.2	66.66
BHANSS	17.85	70.32	46.63	61.01	18.85	68.55
HY	16.44	76.26	46.06	60.42	17.46	74.17
DiDi Labs	10.22	97.01	42.13	62.77	10.95	94.93
HY	7.64	83.85	37.48	75.74	8.25	82.47

A.4. Conversational Speech Translation

· MT systems are ordered according to the *BLEU* metric.
· BLEU scores utilize 2 **fluent** English references to assess fluent translation.
· METEOR scores utilize 4 **disfluent** English references to test meaning preservation from the original disfluent data.

** = submitted with an off-by-one error on L2077; corrected by the organizers*

Text Translation : `test, gold transcript`

System	Constrained?	No Fluent Data?	BLEU	METEOR
NAIST-b			**25.6**	28.5
NAIST-c			25.4	28.1
NAIST-a	✓		**20.8**	25.7
NAIST-f		✓	**23.6**	33.8
NAIST-e		✓	23.1	34.1
IITB		✓	21.0	33.0
NAIST-d	✓	✓	**18.5**	30.8

Text Translation : `test, ASR output`

System	Constrained?	No Fluent Data?	BLEU	METEOR
NAIST-b			**23.9**	23.5
NAIST-c			22.0	22.0
NAIST-a	✓		**17.0**	21.6
IITB		✓	**28.1***	39.1
NAIST-e		✓	24.7	31.3
NAIST-f		✓	24.7	30.9
NAIST-d	✓	✓	**13.7**	22.3

A.5. Open Domain Translation

Shared translation task overall results for all participants, evaluated with 4-gram character BLEU.
** = collected external parallel training data that inadvertently overlapped with the blind test set.*

JA → ZH		ZH → JA	
Baseline	22.0	Baseline	26.3
CASIA	55.8*	CASIA	43.0*
SRC-B	34.0	XIAOMI	34.3
OPPO	32.9	TSUKUBA	33.0
XIAOMI	32.5	OCTANOVE	31.7
TSUKUBA	32.3	DBS	31.2
UEDIN	30.9	OPPO	30.1
KSAI	29.4	UEDIN	29.9
ISTIC	28.2	SRC-B	28.4
DBS	26.9	ISTIC	27.7
OCTANOVE	26.2	NICT	26.3
KINGSOFT	25.3	KSAI	25.9
NICT	22.6	HW-TSC	7.1
HW-TSC	11.6		
TAMKANG	1.8		
SJTU	0.1		

Pipeline for crawling parallel Chinese-Japanese data

The pipeline's stages, diagrammed in Figure 3, are:

1. Deep-crawl the target URL list. We skipped this step in the first run, and instead started with 5 billion entries from CommonCrawl.[35]

2. Identify potentially-parallel Chinese-Japanese webpage pairs using URL structure. For example, `https://www.gotokyo.org/jp/` and `https://www.gotokyo.org/cn/` only differ by the country codes `jp` and `cn`.

3. Download the potentially parallel page pairs.

4. Strip HTML and markup metadata with the `BeautifulSoup` Python module. Split each page into sentence segments.

5. Align segments to be parallel, using Hunalign (Varga et al., 2005).

6. Filter pairs by language ID and length ratio.

The first pipeline run produced 227k URL pairs (1.4m segment pairs) of parallel data containing 28.7m characters on the Chinese side. We used the 227k URL pairs to trace which domains yielded the most parallel data. We then re-ran the pipeline on each of the 6000 most-promising domains, but now deep-crawling the domain using `scrapy` in Step 1 to produce the URL list examined in Step 2.

We concatenated the parallel output from all the runs, keeping track of the provenance URL of each segment. Finally, we applied a filter to remove objectionable content. The result was `webcrawled_parallel_filtered` dataset, containing nearly 19m hopefully-parallel segment pairs (494m Zh chars) with provenance information.

---

[35] `https://commoncrawl.org/`

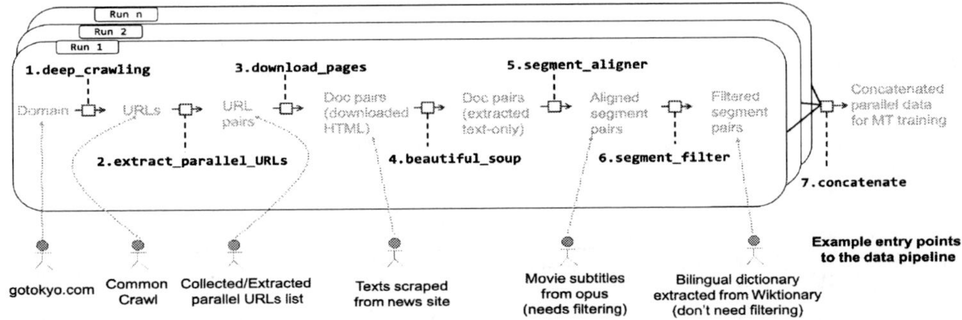

Figure 3: Pipeline to harvest parallel zh-jp text. The modules are numbered in black, with inputs/outputs in orange. The examples at the bottom show how the pipeline can be entered at intermediate stages.

Test Set Provenance

The held-out test set was intended to cover a variety of topics not known to the participants in advance. We selected test data from high-quality (human translated) parallel web content, authored between January and March 2020. Because of this timeframe, COVID19 is a frequent topic in the test set. We collected bilingual material from 104 webpages, detailed in the Appendix. Table 5.

Pages	Source
54	jp.hjenglish.com : Chinese website with Japanese learning material.
38	j.people.com.cn : the Japanese version of the People's Daily newspaper.
4	china-embassy.or.jp : the Embassy of China in Japan
4	people.com.cn : the People's Daily newspaper, in Chinese.
3	emb-japan.go.jp : the Embassy of Japan in China
1	kantei.go.jp : the Prime Minister of Japan's office

Table 5: Provenance of the Chinese-Japanese test set.

To build the test set, we first identified articles on these sites with translations, and copied their contents into separate files. All segments were then manually aligned by a native Chinese speaker with basic knowledge of Japanese, using the InterText tool (Vondricka, 2014). Lastly, a bilingual speaker filtered the aligned pairs, excluding pairs that were not parallel. This produced 1750 parallel segments, which we divided randomly in half: 875 lines for the Chinese-to-Japanese translation test set, and 875 lines for the other direction. The Japanese segments have an average length of 47 characters, and the Chinese ones have an average length of 35.

A.6. Non-Native Speech Translation

English→German

· Complete result for English-German SLT systems followed by public systems PUBLIC-A and PUBLIC-B for comparison.
· Primary submissions are indicated by gray background. Best results in bold.

| | | | SLT | | | | ASR | |
| | Quality | | | Simultaneity | | | Quality | |
System	BLEU$_1$	BLEU$_{mw}$	Flicker	Delay$_{ts}$[Match%]	Delay$_{mw}$[Match%]		WER$_1$	WER$_{mw}$
APPTEK/RWTH1	14.70	13.28	-	-	-		**14.27**	**16.26**
APPTEK/RWTH2	**16.14**	**15.00**	-	-	-		**14.27**	**16.26**
APPTEK/RWTH3	15.92	14.50	-	-	-		**14.27**	**16.26**
BUT1	2.25	0.63	-	-	-		32.33	34.09
BUT2	2.25	0.67	-	-	-		32.91	34.46
BUT3	1.93	0.59	-	-	-		32.91	34.46
BUT4	2.29	0.72		-	-		32.91	34.46
CUNI-NN11	6.37	5.86	-	-	-		28.68	32.10
CUNI-NN12	14.08	12.38	-	-	-		17.39	20.46
CUNI-NN13	14.32	12.73	-	-	-		17.02	19.98
CUNI-NN14	6.65	6.20	-	-	-		28.75	32.23
CUNI-NN15	12.51	10.88	-	-	-		16.54	18.19
CUNI-NN16	13.15	11.50	-	-	-		16.33	17.95
ELITR31	9.72	7.22	6.71	**1.901 [50.91%]**	1.926 [30.01%]		23.77	25.15
ELITR32	9.18	7.32	7.48	1.926 [30.01%]	1.944 [30.42%]		22.91	24.26
ELITR33	9.18	7.32	7.48	1.972 [52.61%]	1.945 [30.43%]		22.91	24.26
ELITR34	9.18	7.32	7.43	1.951 [52.53%]	1.923 [30.41%]		22.91	24.26
ELITR35	9.18	7.32	6.48	2.038 [52.84%]	2.024 [30.76%]		22.91	24.26
ELITR36	9.18	7.32	5.97	2.034 [52.66%]	2.029 [30.79%]		22.91	24.26
ELITR37	9.39	7.05	6.33	2.471 [34.14%]	**1.828 [31.81%]**		23.81	25.25
ELITR38	9.40	7.06	6.35	2.461 [34.24%]	1.846 [31.85%]		23.81	25.25
ELITR39	9.40	7.06	6.33	2.380 [33.37%]	**1.810 [31.63%]**		23.81	25.25
ELITR40	9.39	7.05	5.66	2.544 [34.28%]	1.964 [32.28%]		23.81	25.25
ELITR41	9.39	7.06	**5.30**	2.391 [34.09%]	1.957 [32.28%]		23.81	25.25
ELITR-OFFLINE21	14.83	12.67	-	-	-		15.29	17.67
ELITR-OFFLINE22	13.31	11.35	-	-	-		15.29	17.67
ELITR-OFFLINE23	14.08	12.33	-	-	-		15.29	17.67
ELITR-OFFLINE24	13.03	10.76	-	-	-		15.29	17.67
ELITR-OFFLINE25	12.88	10.83	-	-	-		15.29	17.67
ELITR-OFFLINE26	10.45	8.32	-	-	-		15.29	17.67
ELITR-OFFLINE27	11.58	9.87	-	-	-		16.33	17.95
ELITR-OFFLINE28	11.76	9.83	-	-	-		16.33	17.95
ELITR-OFFLINE29	12.51	10.88	-	-	-		16.33	17.95
ELITR-OFFLINE30	11.34	9.42	-	-	-		16.33	17.95
ELITR-OFFLINE31	12.51	10.53	-	-	-		16.33	17.95
ELITR-OFFLINE32	7.89	5.72	-	-	-		16.33	17.95
CUNI-KALDI01	-	-	-	-	-		22.88	24.53
CUNI-KALDI02	-	-	-	-	-		30.42	31.17
CUNI-KALDI03	-	-	-	-	-		21.25	23.40
PUBLIC-A	4.29	3.02	-	-	-		30.10	31.09
PUBLIC-B	13.75	12.35	-	-	-		21.54	23.59

English→Czech

· Complete result for English-Czech SLT systems followed by public systems PUBLIC-A and PUBLIC-B for comparison.
· Primary submissions are indicated by gray background. Best results in bold.

| System | Quality | | SLT | Simultaneity | | ASR | Quality |
	BLEU$_1$	BLEU$_{mw}$	Flicker	Delay$_{ts}$[Match%]	Delay$_{mw}$[Match%]	WER$_1$	WER$_{mw}$
CUNI-NN01	10.57	10.34	-	-	-	28.68	32.10
CUNI-NN02	10.89	11.50	-	-	-	17.39	20.46
CUNI-NN03	12.74	11.38	-	-	-	17.02	19.98
CUNI-NN04	10.24	10.21	-	-	-	28.75	32.23
CUNI-NN05	11.85	10.57	-	-	-	16.54	18.19
CUNI-NN06	12.27	11.00	-	-	-	16.33	17.95
ELITR01	7.87	6.22	7.00	1.530 [42.45%]	1.575 [23.93%]	23.77	25.15
ELITR02	7.56	5.95	6.46	1.696 [22.01%]	1.561 [25.25%]	23.81	25.25
ELITR03	7.56	5.95	6.38	1.744 [22.26%]	1.618 [25.34%]	23.81	25.25
ELITR04	7.54	5.93	6.38	1.725 [22.09%]	1.603 [25.32%]	23.81	25.25
ELITR05	8.93	7.67	7.51	1.605 [44.80%]	1.623 [92.49%]	23.81	25.25
ELITR06	8.79	7.54	7.00	**1.198 [52.55%]**	**1.082 [32.18%]**	23.81	25.25
ELITR07	8.93	7.67	6.97	1.596 [44.79%]	1.630 [24.86%]	23.81	25.25
ELITR08	8.93	7.67	6.54	1.586 [44.64%]	1.629 [24.91%]	23.81	25.25
ELITR09	8.93	7.65	7.38	1.520 [42.80%]	1.503 [23.23%]	23.81	25.25
ELITR10	8.93	7.67	7.41	1.630 [44.77%]	1.667 [24.96%]	23.81	25.25
ELITR11	6.50	4.94	6.00	1.677 [20.99%]	1.595 [24.58%]	23.81	25.25
ELITR12	6.50	4.94	6.26	1.610 [20.87%]	1.504 [24.35%]	23.81	25.25
ELITR13	6.50	4.94	6.26	1.495 [19.47%]	1.399 [23.30%]	23.81	25.25
ELITR14	6.52	4.95	5.69	1.650 [20.88%]	1.597 [24.63%]	23.81	25.25
ELITR15	6.50	4.94	**5.18**	1.541 [20.71%]	1.594 [24.59%]	23.81	25.25
ELITR16	7.40	5.74	6.64	1.633 [21.89%]	1.468 [24.43%]	23.81	25.25
ELITR17	8.45	7.32	6.56	1.597 [44.85%]	1.728 [25.35%]	22.91	24.26
ELITR18	8.36	7.17	6.00	1.514 [45.58%]	1.629 [26.54%]	22.91	24.26
ELITR19	8.56	7.45	5.31	1.600 [46.81%]	1.713 [27.94%]	22.91	24.26
ELITR20	8.55	7.41	6.31	1.557 [45.78%]	1.704 [26.51%]	22.91	24.26
ELITR-OFFLINE01	13.33	11.75	-	-	-	**15.29**	**17.67**
ELITR-OFFLINE02	13.44	11.64	-	-	-	**15.29**	**17.67**
ELITR-OFFLINE03	13.56	11.79	-	-	-	**15.29**	**17.67**
ELITR-OFFLINE04	**14.08**	**12.57**	-	-	-	**15.29**	**17.67**
ELITR-OFFLINE05	10.07	8.23	-	-	-	**15.29**	**17.67**
ELITR-OFFLINE06	8.42	6.99	-	-	-	**15.29**	**17.67**
ELITR-OFFLINE07	9.62	8.16	-	-	-	**15.29**	**17.67**
ELITR-OFFLINE08	11.88	10.26	-	-	-	16.33	17.95
ELITR-OFFLINE09	11.52	9.83	-	-	-	16.33	17.95
ELITR-OFFLINE10	11.43	9.99	-	-	-	16.33	17.95
ELITR-OFFLINE11	11.85	10.57	-	-	-	16.33	17.95
ELITR-OFFLINE12	9.29	7.76	-	-	-	16.33	17.95
ELITR-OFFLINE13	7.76	6.35	-	-	-	16.33	17.95
ELITR-OFFLINE14	7.37	6.54	-	-	-	16.33	17.95
PUBLIC-A	3.30	2.47	-	-	-	30.10	31.09
PUBLIC-B	10.79	9.85	-	-	-	21.54	23.59

Test Set Provenance

Only a limited amount of resources could have been invested in the preparations of the test set and the test set thus build upon some existing datasets. The components of the test sets are:

Antrecorp[36] (Macháček et al., 2019), a test set of up to 90-second mock business presentations given by high school students in very noisy conditions. None of the speakers is a native speaker of English (see the paper for the composition of nationalities) and their English contains many lexical, grammatical and pronunciation errors as well as disfluencies due to the spontaneous nature of the speech.

For the purposes of this task, we equipped Antrecorp with manual translations into Czech and German. No MT system was used to pre-translate the text to avoid bias in automatic evaluation.

---

[36] http://hdl.handle.net/11234/1-3023

Because the presentations are very informal and their translation can vary considerably, we created two independent translations into Czech. In the end, only the first one of them was used as the reference, to keep BLEU scores across test set parts somewhat comparable.

Khan Academy[37] is a large collection of educational videos. The speaker is not a native speaker of English but his accent is generally rather good. The difficulty in this part of the test lies in the domain and also the generally missing natural segmentation into sentences.

SAO is a test set created by ELITR particularly for this shared task, to satisfy the need of the Supreme Audit Office of the Czech Republic. The test sets consists of 6 presentations given in English by officers of several supreme audit institutions (SAI) in Europe and by the Europan Court of Auditors. The speakers nationality (Austrian, Belgian, Dutch, Polish, Romanian and Spanish) affects their accent. The Dutch file is a recording of a remote conference call with further distorted sound quality.

The development set contained 2 other files from Antrecorp, one other file from the SAO domain and it also included 4 files from the AMI corpus (Mccowan et al., 2005) to illustrate non-native accents. We did not include data from AMI corpus in the test set because we found out that some participants trained their (non-constrained) submissions on it.

For SAO and Antrecorp, our test set was created in the most straightforward way: starting with the original sound, manual transcription was obtained (with the help of ASR) as a line-oriented plaintext. The transcribers were instructed to preserve all words uttered[38] and break the sequence of words into sentences in as natural way as possible. Correct punctuation and casing was introduced at this stage, too. Finally, the documents were translated in Czech and German, preserving the segmentation into "sentences".

For the evaluation of SLT simultaneity, we force-aligned words from the transcript to the sound using a model trained with Jasper (Li et al., 2019) and resorted to fully manual identification of word boundaries in the few files where forced alignment failed.

Despite a careful curation of the dataset, we are aware of the following limitations. None of them are too frequent or too serious but they still deserve to be mentioned:

- Khan Academy subtitles never had proper segmentation into sentences and manual correction of punctuation and casing. The subtitles were supposedly manually refined but the focus was on their presentation in the running video lecture, not on style and typesetting.

- Khan Academy contains many numbers (written mostly as numbers). For small numbers, both digits and words are often equally suitable but automatic metrics treat this difference as a mistranslation and no straightforward reliable normalization is possible either, so we did not apply any.

- Minor translation errors into German were seen in Khan Academy videos and in the "Belgian" SAO file.

---

[37] http://www.khanacademy.org/

[38] This decision is possibly less common in the ASR community but it is motivated by the subsequent translation step which has the capacity to recover from disfluences as needed.

ON-TRAC Consortium for End-to-End and Simultaneous Speech Translation Challenge Tasks at IWSLT 2020

Maha Elbayad[1,4]*, **Ha Nguyen**[1,2]*, **Fethi Bougares**[3], **Natalia Tomashenko**[2],
Antoine Caubrière[3], **Benjamin Lecouteux**[1], **Yannick Estève**[2], **Laurent Besacier**[1]

[1]LIG - Université Grenoble Alpes, France
[2]LIA - Avignon Université, France
[3]LIUM - Le Mans Université, France
[4]Inria - Grenoble, France

Abstract

This paper describes the ON-TRAC Consortium translation systems developed for two challenge tracks featured in the Evaluation Campaign of IWSLT 2020, offline speech translation and simultaneous speech translation. ON-TRAC Consortium is composed of researchers from three French academic laboratories: LIA (Avignon Université), LIG (Université Grenoble Alpes), and LIUM (Le Mans Université). Attention-based encoder-decoder models, trained end-to-end, were used for our submissions to the offline speech translation track. Our contributions focused on data augmentation and ensembling of multiple models. In the simultaneous speech translation track, we build on Transformer-based *wait-k* models for the text-to-text subtask. For speech-to-text simultaneous translation, we attach a *wait-k* MT system to a hybrid ASR system. We propose an algorithm to control the latency of the ASR+MT cascade and achieve a good latency-quality trade-off on both subtasks.

1 Introduction

While cascaded speech-to-text translation (AST) systems (combining source language speech recognition (ASR) and source-to-target text translation (MT)) remain state-of-the-art, recent works have attempted to build end-to-end AST with very encouraging results (Bérard et al., 2016; Weiss et al., 2017; Bérard et al., 2018; Jia et al., 2019; Sperber et al., 2019). This year, IWSLT 2020 *offline translation track* attempts to evaluate if end-to-end AST will close the gap with cascaded AST for the English-to-German language pair.

Another increasingly popular topic is simultaneous (online) machine translation which consists in generating an output hypothesis before the entire input sequence is available. To deal with this low latency constraint, several strategies were proposed for neural machine translation with input text (Ma et al., 2019; Arivazhagan et al., 2019; Ma et al., 2020). Only a few works investigated low latency neural speech translation (Niehues et al., 2018). This year, IWSLT 2020 *simultaneous translation track* attempts to stimulate research on this challenging task.This paper describes the ON-TRAC consortium automatic speech translation (AST) systems for the IWSLT 2020 Shared Task (Ansari et al., 2020). ON-TRAC Consortium is composed of researchers from three French academic laboratories: LIA (Avignon Université), LIG (Université Grenoble Alpes), and LIUM (Le Mans Université).

We participated in:

- IWSLT 2020 *offline translation track* with end-to-end models for the English-German language pair,

- IWSLT 2020 *simultaneous translation track* with a cascade of an ASR system trained using Kaldi (Povey et al., 2011) and an online MT system with *wait-k* policies (Dalvi et al., 2018; Ma et al., 2019).

This paper goes as follows: we review the systems built for the offline speech translation track in §2. Then, we present our approaches to the simultaneous track for both text-to-text and speech-to-text subtasks in §3. We ultimately conclude this work in §4.

2 Offline Speech translation Track

In this work, we developed several end-to-end speech translation systems, using a similar architecture as last year (Nguyen et al., 2019) and adapting it for translating English speech into German text (En-De). All the systems were developed using the

---

*Equal contribution.

35

Proceedings of the 17th International Conference on Spoken Language Translation (IWSLT), pages 35–43
July 9-10, 2020. ©2020 Association for Computational Linguistics
https://doi.org/10.18653/v1/P17

Name	#segments	Total length (in hours)
MuST-C train	229.703	400
MuST-C dev	1.423	2.5
MuST-C tst-COMMON	2.641	4.1
MuST-C tst-HE	600	1.2
Europarl train	32.628	77
Europarl dev	1.320	3.1
How2 synthetic	176.564	285.5
tst2019	2.813	5.1
tst2020	2.263	4.1

Table 1: Statistics of training and evaluation data. The statistics of tst2019 and tst2020 are measured on the segmented version provided by IWSLT2020 organizers.

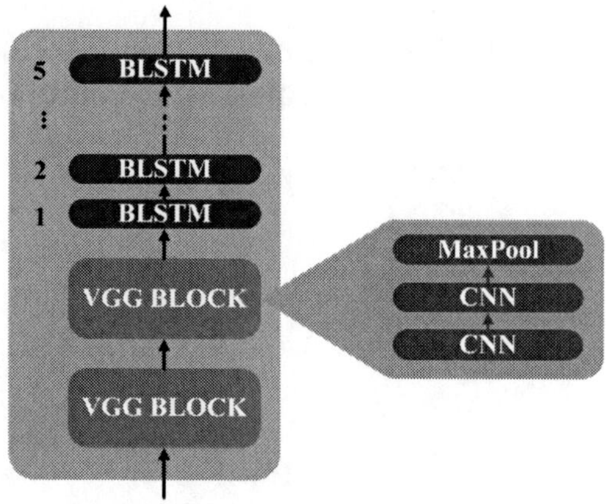

Figure 1: Architecture of the speech encoder: a stack of two VGG blocks followed by 5 BLSTM layers.

ESPnet (Watanabe et al., 2018) end-to-end speech processing toolkit.

2.1 Data and pre-processing

Data. We relied on MuST-C (Di Gangi et al., 2019) English-to-German (hereafter called MuST-C original), and Europarl (Iranzo-Sánchez et al., 2020) English-to-German as our main corpora. Besides, we automatically translated (into German) the English transcription of MuST-C and How2 (Sanabria et al., 2018) in order to augment training data. This resulted in two synthetic corpora, which are called *MuST-C synthetic* and *How2 synthetic* respectively. The statistics of these corpora, along with the provided evaluation data, can be found in Table 1. We experimented with different ways of combining those corpora. The details of these experiments are presented later in this section.

Speech features and data augmentation. 80-dimensional Mel filter-bank features, concatenated with 3-dimensional pitch features[1] are extracted from windows of $25ms$ with a frame shift of $10ms$. We computed mean and variance normalization on these raw features of the training set, then applied it on all the data. Beside speed perturbation with factors of 0.9, 1.0, and 1.1, SpecAugment (Park et al., 2019) is applied to the training data (Ko et al.,

---

[1]Pitch-features are computed using the Kaldi toolkit (Povey et al., 2011) and consist of the following values (Ghahremani et al., 2014): (1) probability of voicing (POV-feature), (2) pitch-feature and (3) delta-pitch feature. For details, see `http://kaldi-asr.org/doc/process-kaldi-pitch-feats_8cc.html`

2015). All three SpecAugment methods were used, including time warping ($W = 5$), frequency masking ($F = 30$), and time masking ($T = 40$).

Text preprocessing. The same as last year, we normalize punctuation, and tokenize all the German text using Moses.[2] Texts are case-sensitive and contain punctuation. Moreover, the texts of the MuST-C corpus contain multiple non speech events (*i.e 'Laughter'*, *'Applause'* etc.). All these marks are removed from the texts before training our models. This results in a vocabulary of 201 characters. We find that some of these characters should not appear in the German text, for example, ♪, 你, 葱, 送, etc. Therefore, we manually exclude them from the vocabulary. In the end, we settle with an output vocabulary of 182 characters.

2.2 Architecture

We reuse our last year attention-based encoder-decoder architecture. As illustrated in Figure 1, the encoder has two VGG-like (Simonyan and Zisserman, 2015) CNN blocks followed by five stacked 1024-dimensional BLSTM layers. Each VGG block is a stack of two 2D-convolution layers followed by a 2D-maxpooling layer aiming to reduce both time (T) and frequency (D) dimensions of the input speech features by a factor of 2. After these two VGG blocks, input speech features' shape is transformed from ($T \times D$) to ($T/4 \times D/4$). We used Bahdanau's attention mechanism (Bahdanau et al., 2015) in all our experiments. The decoder is a stack of two LSTM layers 1024 dimensional memory cells. We would like to men-

---

[2]`http://www.statmt.org/moses/`

No.	Experiment	MuST-C tst-COMMON	MuST-C tst-HE	tst2015 (iwslt seg)	tst2015 (ASR seg)
1	MuST-C original + EuroParl	20.18	19.82	12.59	14.85
2	MuST-C original + Europarl + How2 synthetic	20.51	20.10	12.10	13.66
3*	MuST-C original + Europarl + How2 synthetic	23.55	22.35	13.00	15.30
4*	MuST-C original + Europarl + How2 synthetic + MuST-C synthetic	22.75	21.31	14.00	16.45
5*	Finetune 3* on MuST-C original	23.60	22.26	13.71	15.30
6*	Finetune 3* on MuST-C original+ MuST-C synthetic	23.64	22.23	13.67	15.29
7	**Ensemble (1 to 6)**	**25.22**	**23.80**	**15.20**	**16.53**

Table 2: Detokenized case-sensitive BLEU scores for different experiments - * represents experiments that apply SpecAugment.

Model	iwslt seg	ASR seg
3*	constrastive5	constrastive3
4*	constrastive4	constrastive2
Ensemble	constrastive1	**primary**

Table 3: The ranking of out submitted systems. Model 3* and 4* are respectively corresponding to No.3* and No.4* of Table 2.

tion that Transformer based models have also been tested using the default ESPnet architecure and showed weaker results compared to the LSTM-based encoder-decoder architecture.

Hyperparameters' details. All of our models are trained in maximum 20 epochs, with early stopping after 3 epochs if the accuracy on the development set does not improve. Dropout is set to 0.3 on the encoder part, and Adadelta is chosen as our optimizer. During decoding time, the beam size is set to 10. We prevent the models from generating too long sentences by setting a $maxlenratio^3 = 1.0$. All our end-to-end models are similar in terms of architecture. They are different mainly in the following aspects: (1) training corpus; (2) type of tokenization units;[4] (3) fine-tuning and pretraining strategies. Description of different models and evaluation results are given in Section 2.4.

2.3 Speech segmentation

Two types of segmentation of evaluation and development data were used for experiments and submitted systems: segmentation provided by the IWSLT organizers and automatic segmentation based on the output of an ASR system.

The ASR system, used to obtain automatic segmentation, was trained with the Kaldi speech recognition toolkit (Povey et al., 2011). An acoustic model was trained using the TED-LIUM 3 corpus (Hernandez et al., 2018).[5] This ASR system produces recognized words with timecodes (start time and duration for each word). Then we form the speech segments based on this output following the rules: (1) if silence duration between two words is longer than a given threshold $\Theta = 0.65$ seconds, we split the audio file; (2) if the number of words in the current speech segment exceeds 40, then Θ is reduced to 0.15 seconds in order to avoid too long segments. These thresholds have been optimised to get segment duration distribu-

---

$$^3 maxlenratio = \frac{maximum\_output\_length}{encoder\_hidden\_state\_length}$$

[4] All systems use 182 caracter output tokens except system 1 which has 201

[5] The off-limit TED talks from IWSLT-2019 were excluded from the training subset

No.	Set	BLEU	TER	BEER	CharacTER	BLEU(ci)	TER(ci)
1	2019.contrastive1	17.57	71.68	47.24	58.03	18.64	69.66
2	2019.contrastive2	17.83	71.60	48.66	53.49	18.9	69.26
3	2019.contrastive3	19.03	66.96	49.12	54.10	19.97	65.01
4	2019.contrastive4	15.08	78.79	45.87	59.06	16.06	76.62
5	2019.contrastive5	15.87	74.17	46.18	59.96	16.86	72.15
6	**2019.primary**	**20.19**	**66.38**	**49.89**	**52.51**	**21.23**	**64.26**
7	2020.contrastive1	18.47	71.85	48.92	55.83	19.46	69.88
8	2020.contrastive2	19.31	69.30	49.55	52.68	20.36	67.14
9	2020.contrastive3	20.51	64.88	50.19	53.06	21.5	62.99
10	2020.contrastive4	15.48	83.45	46.68	57.56	16.42	81.33
11	2020.contrastive5	16.5	75.15	47.23	57.90	17.42	73.22
12	**2020.primary**	**22.12**	**63.87**	**51.20**	**51.46**	**23.25**	**61.85**

Table 4: IWSLT 2020 official results (offline track) on tst2019 and tst2020.

tion in the development and evaluation data that is similar to the one observed in the training data. It will be shown in next subsection that this ASR segmentation improves results over the provided segmentation when the latter is noisy (see experimental results on iwslt/tst2015).

2.4 Experiments and results

After witnessing the benefit of merging different corpora from our submission last year (Nguyen et al., 2019), we continue exploring different combinations of corpora in this submission. As shown in the first two rows of Table 2, merging How2 synthetic with the baseline (MuST-C original + Europarl) does not bring significant improvement. It is noticeable that this pool is worse than the baseline on both tst2015 (iwslt seg) and tst2015 (ASR seg). However, we find that applying data augmentation (SpecAugment) on this same combination helps outperform the baseline on every investigated testset, most significantly on MuST-C tst-COMMON, and MuST-C tst-HE. Therefore, SpecAugment is consistently applied to all the experiments that follow. Adding MuST-C synthetic to this pool surprisingly decreases BLEU scores on both MuST-C testsets, while significantly increases the scores on both tst2015 (iwslt seg) and tst2015 (ASR seg). Not being able to investigate further on this matter due to time constraint, instead of fine-tuning 4*, we decided to fine-tune 3*, which performs reasonably well among all the testsets, on MuST-C original and MuST-C original+synthetic. We witness that the impact of fine tuning is very limited. One can also see once again that adding MuST-C synthetic does not make much difference. Finally, the last

row of the table shows the results of ensembling all six models at decoding time. It is clear from the table that ensembling yields the best BLEU scores across all the testsets.

2.5 Overview of systems submitted

Two conclusions that can be drawn from Table 2 are (1) ensembling all six models is the most promising among all presented models, (2) our own segmentation (tst2015 ASR segmentation) is better than the default one. Therefore, we choose as our primary submission the translations of the ASR segmentations generated by the ensemble of all six models. Model 3* and 4* (Table 2) are also used to translate our contrastive submission runs, whose ranks are shown in Table 3. The official results for all our submitted systems can be found in Table 4. They confirm that our segmentation approach proposed is beneficial.

3 Simultaneous Speech Translation Track

In this section, we describe our submission to the Simultaneous Speech Translation (SST) track. Our pipeline consists of an automatic speech recognition (ASR) system followed by an online machine translation (MT) system. We first define our online ASR and MT models in §3.1 and §3.2 respectively. Then, we outline in §3.3 how we arrange the two systems for the speech-to-text subtask. We detail our experimental setup and report our results on the text-to-text subtask in §3.4 and on the speech-to-text in §3.5.

3.1 Online ASR

Our ASR system is a hybrid HMM/DNN system trained with lattice-free MMI (Povey et al., 2016), using the Kaldi speech recognition toolkit (Povey et al., 2011). The acoustic model (AM) topology consists of a Time Delay Neural Network (TDNN) followed by a stack of 16 factorized TDNNs (Povey et al., 2018). The acoustic feature vector is a concatenation of 40-dimensional MFCCs without cepstral truncation (MFCC-40) and 100-dimensional i-vectors for speaker adaptation (Dehak et al., 2010). Audio samples were randomly perturbed in speed and amplitude during the training process. This approach is commonly called audio augmentation and is known to be beneficial for speech recognition (Ko et al., 2015).

Online decoding with Kaldi. The online ASR system decodes under a set of rules to decide when to stop decoding and output a transcription. An endpoint is detected if either of the following conditions is satisfied:

(a) After t seconds of silence even if nothing was decoded.

(b) After t seconds of silence after decoding something, if the final-state was reached with $\text{cost}_{\text{relative}} < c$.

(c) After t seconds of silence after decoding something, even if no final-state was reached.

(d) After the utterance is t seconds long regardless of anything else.

Each rule has an independent characteristic time t and condition (b) can be duplicated with different times and thresholds (t, c). The value of $\text{cost}_{\text{relative}}$ reflects the quality of the output, it is *null* if a final-state of the decoding graph had the best cost at the final frame, and *infinite* if no final-state was active.

3.2 Online MT

Our MT systems are Transformer-based (Vaswani et al., 2017) wait-k decoders with unidirectional encoders. Wait-k decoding starts by reading k source tokens, then alternates between reading and writing a single token at a time, until the source is depleted, or the target generation is terminated. With a source-target pair $(\boldsymbol{x}, \boldsymbol{y})$, the number of source tokens read when decoding y_t following a *wait-k* policy is $z_t^k = \min(k + t - 1, |\boldsymbol{x}|)$. To stop leaking signal from future source tokens, the energies of the encoder-decoder multihead-attention are masked to only include the z_t tokens read so far.

Unlike Transformer *wait-k* models introduced in Ma et al. (2019) where the source is processed with a bidirectional encoder, we opt for a unidirectional encoding of the source. In fact, this change alleviates the cost of re-encoding the source sequence after each read operation. Contrary to offline task, where bidirectional encoders are superior, unidirectional encoder achieve better quality-lagging trade-offs in online MT.

Ma et al. (2019) optimize their models with maximum likelihood estimation w.r.t. a single wait-k decoding path $\boldsymbol{z}^k$:

$$\log p(\boldsymbol{y} \mid \boldsymbol{x}, \boldsymbol{z}^k) = \sum_{t=1}^{|\boldsymbol{y}|} \log p_\theta(y_t | \boldsymbol{y}_{<t}, \boldsymbol{x}_{\le z_t^k}). \quad (1)$$

Instead of optimizing a single decoding path, we jointly optimize across multiple wait-k paths. The additional loss terms provide a richer training signal, and potentially yield models that could perform well under different lagging constraints. Formally, we consider an exhaustive set of wait-k paths and in each training epoch we encode the source sequence then uniformly sample a path to decode with. As such, we optimize:

$$Z = \left\{ \boldsymbol{z}^k \mid k \in \{1, \ldots, |\boldsymbol{x}|\} \right\}, \quad (2)$$

$$\mathbb{E}_{\boldsymbol{z}}[\log p(\boldsymbol{y}|\boldsymbol{x}, \boldsymbol{z})] \approx \sum_{\boldsymbol{z} \sim \in Z} \log p_\theta(\boldsymbol{y}|\boldsymbol{x}, \boldsymbol{z}). \quad (3)$$

We will refer to this training with *multi-path*.

3.3 Cascaded ASR+MT

For speech-to-text online translation we pair an ASR system with our online MT system and decode following the algorithm described in Algorithm 1.

In this setup, the lagging is controlled by the endpointing of the ASR system. The online MT system follows the lead of the ASR and translates prefix-to-prefix. Since the MT system is not trained to detect end of segments and can only halt the translation by emitting </s>, we constrain it to decode $\alpha |\boldsymbol{x}^{\text{asr}}| + \beta$ tokens, where $\boldsymbol{x}^{\text{asr}}$ is the partial transcription and (α, β) two hyper-parameters.

Along with the hyper-parameters of the ASR's endpointing rules, we tune (α, β) on a development set to achieve good latency-quality trade-offs.

3.4 Text-to-text translation subtask

Training MT. We train our online MT systems on English-to-German MuST-C (Di Gangi et al., 2019)

Algorithm 1 ASR+MT decoding algorithm

Input: source audio blocks x.
Output: translation hypothesis y.
Initialization: action=READ, $z=0$, $t=1$,
$$x^{\text{asr}}=(),\ y=(<s>)$$
Hyper-parameters sz, α, β.
while $y_t \neq </s>$ **do**
  while action = READ $\wedge\ z < |x|$ **do**
    Read sz elements from x. $z\ +=\ sz$
    Feed the new audio blocks to the ASR system.
    if Endpoint detected $\vee\ z = |x|$ **then**
      Output transcription and append it to x^{asr}.
      action = WRITE
    end if
  end while
  if $|y| < \alpha|x^{\text{asr}}| + \beta$ **then**
    Given y and x^{asr}, predict the next token y_{t+1}
    $t\ +=\ 1$
  else
    action = READ
  end if
end while

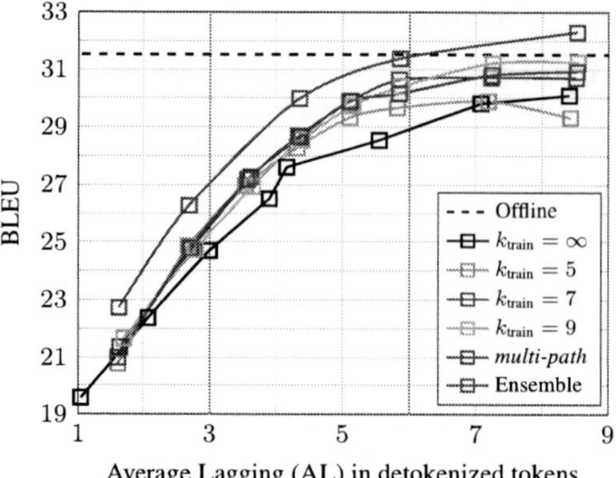

Figure 2: [Text-to-Text] Latency-quality trade-offs evaluated on MuST-C tst-COMMON with greedy decoding. Offline systems have an AL of 18.55 words. The red vertical bars correspond to the AL evaluation thresholds.

	Pairs	English words	German words
Europarl	1,730K	43,7M	41,1M
Common Crawl	1,543K	31,0M	30,0M
News Commentary	320K	7,0M	7,2M
MuST-C	214K	3,9M	3,7M

Table 5: Parallel training data for the MT systems.

and WMT'19 data,[6] namely, Europarl (Koehn, 2005), News Commentary (Tiedemann, 2012) and Common Crawl (Smith et al., 2013). We remove pairs with a length-ratio exceeding 1.3 from Common Crawl and pairs exceeding a length-ratio of 1.5 from the rest. We develop on MuST-C dev and report results on MuST-C tst-COMMON. For open-vocabulary translation, we use *SentencePiece* (Kudo and Richardson, 2018) to segment the bitexts with byte pair encoding (Sennrich et al., 2016). This results in a joint vocabulary of 32K types. Details of the training data are provided in Table 5.

We train Transformer *big* architectures and tie the embeddings of the encoder with the decoder's input and output embeddings. We optimize our models with label-smoothed maximum likelihood (Szegedy et al., 2016) with a smoothing rate $\epsilon = 0.1$. The parameters are updated using

Adam (Kingma and Ba, 2015) ($\beta_1, \beta_2 = 0.9, 0.98$) with a learning rate that follows an inverse square-root schedule. We train for a total of 50K updates and evaluate with the check-pointed weights corresponding to the lowest (best) loss on the development set. Our models are implemented with Fairseq (Ott et al., 2019). We generate translation hypotheses with greedy decoding and evaluate the latency-quality trade-off by measuring case-sensitive detokenized BLEU (Papineni et al., 2002) and word-level Average Lagging (AL) (Ma et al., 2019).

Results. We show in Figure 2 the performance of our systems on the test set (MuST tst-COMMON) measured with the provided evaluation server.[7] We denote with $k_{\text{train}}=\infty$ a unidirectional model trained for wait-until-end decoding *i.e.* reading the full source before writing the target. We evaluate four *wait-k* systems each trained with a value of k_{train} in $\{5, 7, 9, \infty\}$ and decoded with k_{eval} ranging from 2 to 11. We then ensemble the aforementioned *wait-k* models and evaluate a *multi-path* model that jointly optimizes a large set of *wait-k* paths. The results demonstrate that *multi-path* is competetive with *wait-k* without the need to select which path to optimize (some values of k, *e.g.* 5, underperform in comparison). Ensembling the *wait-k* models gives a boost of 1.43 BLEU points on average.

---

[6] http://www.statmt.org/wmt19/

[7] https://github.com/pytorch/fairseq/ blob/simulastsharedtask/examples/ simultaneous_translation

Corpus	#hours	#words	#speakers
TED-LIUM 3	452	5.05M	2,028
How2	365	3.31M	13,147
Europarl	94	0.75M	171

Table 6: Corpora used for the acoustic model.

Decoding	Corpus	WER
Offline	TED-LIUM 3 dev	7.65
Offline	TED-LIUM 3 test	7.84
Offline	MuST-C tst-COMMON	14.2
Online	MuST-C tst-COMMON	16.3

Table 7: WERs for the ASR system with offline and online decoding (AL=5s for online)

3.5 Speech-to-text translation subtask

Training ASR. We train our system following the *tedlium* recipe[8] while adapting it for the IWSLT task. The TDNN layers have a hidden dimension of 1536 with a linear bottleneck dimension of 160 in the factorized layers. The i-vector extractor is trained on all acoustic data (speech perturbed + speech) using a 10s window. The acoustic training data includes TED-LIUM 3, How2 and Europarl. These corpora are detailed in Table 6 and represent about 900 hours of audio.

As a language model, we use the 4-grams *small* model provided with TED-LIUM 3. The vocabulary size is 152K, with 1.2 million of 2-grams, 622K 3-grams and 70K 4-grams.

The final system is tuned on TED-LIUM 3 dev and tested with TED-LIUM 3 test and MuST-C tst-COMMON. Results are shown in Table 7.

Training MT. To train the MT system for the ASR+MT cascade we process source-side data (English) to match transcriptions of the ASR. This consists of lower-casing, removing punctuation and converting numbers into letters. For this task we use two distinct English and German vocabularies of 32K BPE tokens each. We train Transformer *big* architectures with tied input-output decoder embeddings following the setup described in §3.4.

Results. Similar to the text-to-text subtask, we show our results in a plot of BLEU-to-AL in Figure 3. The systems are evaluated on the test via the provided evaluation server where MuST-

[8]https://github.com/kaldi-asr/kaldi/tree/master/egs/tedlium

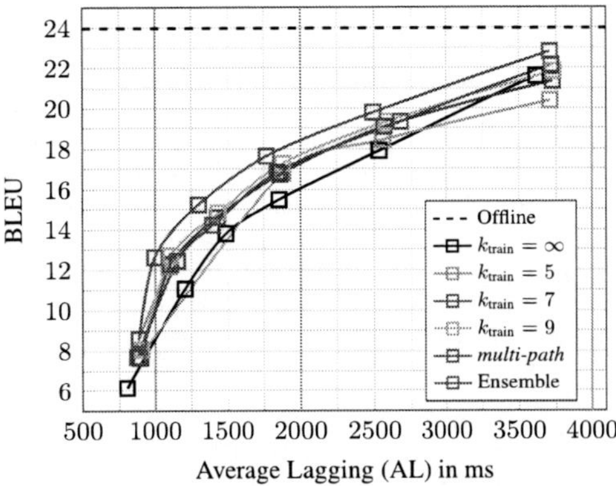

Figure 3: [Speech-to-Text] Latency-quality trade-offs evaluated on MuST-C tst-COMMON with greedy decoding. Offline systems have an AL of 5806 ms. The red vertical bars correspond to the AL evaluation thresholds.

C's sentence-level aligned segments are streamed and decoded online and the lagging is measured in milliseconds. Note that in this task we use a single ASR model and only ensemble the MT *wait-k* models. The cascade of an online ASR with *wait-k* MT follows the same trends as the text-to-text models. In particular, *multi-path* is competitive with specialized *wait-k* models and ensembling boosts the BLEU scores by 0.67 points on average.

4 Conclusion

This paper described the ON-TRAC consortium submission to the IWSLT 2020 shared task. In the continuity of our 2019 participation, we have submitted several end-to-end systems to the offline speech translation track. A significant part of our efforts was also dedicated to the new simultaneous translation track: we improved *wait-k* models with unidirectional encoders and multi-path training and cascaded them with a strong ASR system. Future work will be dedicated to simultaneous speech translation using end-to-end models.

5 Acknowledgements

This work was funded by the French Research Agency (ANR) through the ON-TRAC project under contract number ANR-18-CE23-0021.

References

Ebrahim Ansari, Amittai Axelrod, Nguyen Bach, Ondrej Bojar, Roldano Cattoni, Fahim Dalvi, Nadir Durrani, Marcello Federico, Christian Federmann, Jiatao Gu, Fei Huang, Kevin Knight, Xutai Ma, Ajay Nagesh, Matteo Negri, Jan Niehues, Juan Pino, Elizabeth Salesky, Xing Shi, Sebastian Stüker, Marco Turchi, and Changhan Wang. 2020. Findings of the IWSLT 2020 Evaluation Campaign. In *Proceedings of the 17th International Conference on Spoken Language Translation (IWSLT 2020)*, Seattle, USA.

Naveen Arivazhagan, Colin Cherry, Wolfgang Macherey, Chung-Cheng Chiu, Semih Yavuz, Ruoming Pang, Wei Li, and Colin Raffel. 2019. Monotonic infinite lookback attention for simultaneous machine translation. In *Proc. of ACL*.

Dzmitry Bahdanau, Kyunghyun Cho, and Yoshua Bengio. 2015. Neural Machine Translation by Jointly Learning to Align and Translate. In *Proc. of ICLR*.

Alexandre Bérard, Laurent Besacier, Ali Can Kocabiyikoglu, and Olivier Pietquin. 2018. End-to-End Automatic Speech Translation of Audiobooks. In *Proc. of ICASSP*.

Alexandre Bérard, Olivier Pietquin, Christophe Servan, and Laurent Besacier. 2016. Listen and translate: A proof of concept for end-to-end speech-to-text translation. In *NIPS Workshop on End-to-end Learning for Speech and Audio Processing*.

Fahim Dalvi, Nadir Durrani, Hassan Sajjad, and Stephan Vogel. 2018. Incremental decoding and training methods for simultaneous translation in neural machine translation. In *Proc. of NAACL-HLT*.

Najim Dehak, Patrick J Kenny, Réda Dehak, Pierre Dumouchel, and Pierre Ouellet. 2010. Front-end factor analysis for speaker verification. *IEEE Transactions on Audio, Speech, and Language Processing*.

Mattia Antonino Di Gangi, Roldano Cattoni, Luisa Bentivogli, Matteo Negri, and Marco Turchi. 2019. Must-c: a multilingual speech translation corpus. In *Proc. of NAACL-HLT*.

Pegah Ghahremani, Bagher BabaAli, Daniel Povey, Korbinian Riedhammer, Jan Trmal, and Sanjeev Khudanpur. 2014. A pitch extraction algorithm tuned for automatic speech recognition. In *Proc. of ICASSP*.

François Hernandez, Vincent Nguyen, Sahar Ghannay, Natalia Tomashenko, and Yannick Estève. 2018. TED-LIUM 3: twice as much data and corpus repartition for experiments on speaker adaptation. In *International Conference on Speech and Computer*.

Javier Iranzo-Sánchez, Joan Albert Silvestre-Cerdà, Javier Jorge, Nahuel Roselló, Adrià Giménez, Albert Sanchis, Jorge Civera, and Alfons Juan. 2020. Europarl-ST: A multilingual corpus for speech translation of parliamentary debates. In *Proc. of ICASSP*.

Ye Jia, Melvin Johnson, Wolfgang Macherey, Ron J. Weiss, Yuan Cao, Chung-Cheng Chiu, Naveen Ari, Stella Laurenzo, and Yonghui Wu. 2019. Leveraging weakly supervised data to improve end-to-end speech-to-text translation. In *Proc. of ICASSP*.

Diederik P. Kingma and Jimmy Ba. 2015. Adam: A method for stochastic optimization. In *Proc. of ICLR*.

Tom Ko, Vijayaditya Peddinti, Daniel Povey, and Sanjeev Khudanpur. 2015. Audio augmentation for speech recognition. In *Proc. of INTERSPEECH*.

Philipp Koehn. 2005. Europarl: A parallel corpus for statistical machine translation. In *MT summit*.

Taku Kudo and John Richardson. 2018. SentencePiece: A simple and language independent subword tokenizer and detokenizer for neural text processing. In *Proc. of EMNLP: System Demonstrations*.

Mingbo Ma, Liang Huang, Hao Xiong, Renjie Zheng, Kaibo Liu, Baigong Zheng, Chuanqiang Zhang, Zhongjun He, Hairong Liu, Xing Li, Hua Wu, and Haifeng Wang. 2019. STACL: Simultaneous translation with implicit anticipation and controllable latency using prefix-to-prefix framework. In *Proc. of ACL*.

Xutai Ma, Juan Pino, James Cross, Liezl Puzon, and Jiatao Gu. 2020. Monotonic multihead attention. In *Proc. of ICLR*.

Ha Nguyen, Natalia Tomashenko, Marcely Zanon Boito, Antoine Caubriere, Fethi Bougares, Mickael Rouvier, Laurent Besacier, and Yannick Esteve. 2019. ON-TRAC consortium end-to-end speech translation systems for the IWSLT 2019 shared task. In *Proc. of IWSLT*.

Jan Niehues, Ngoc-Quan Pham, Thanh-Le Ha, Matthias Sperber, and Alex Waibel. 2018. Low-latency neural speech translation. In *Proc. of INTERSPEECH*.

Myle Ott, Sergey Edunov, Alexei Baevski, Angela Fan, Sam Gross, Nathan Ng, David Grangier, and Michael Auli. 2019. fairseq: A fast, extensible toolkit for sequence modeling. In *Proc. of NAACL-HLT: Demonstrations*.

Kishore Papineni, Salim Roukos, Todd Ard, and Wei-Jing Zhu. 2002. Bleu: a method for automatic evaluation of machine translation. In *Proc. of ACL*.

Daniel S Park, William Chan, Yu Zhang, Chung-Cheng Chiu, Barret Zoph, Ekin D Cubuk, and Quoc V Le. 2019. Specaugment: A simple data augmentation method for automatic speech recognition. In *Proc. of INTERSPEECH*.

Daniel Povey, Gaofeng Cheng, Yiming Wang, Ke Li, Hainan Xu, Mahsa Yarmohammadi, and Sanjeev Khudanpur. 2018. Semi-orthogonal low-rank matrix factorization for deep neural networks. In *Proc. of INTERSPEECH*.

Daniel Povey, Arnab Ghoshal, Gilles Boulianne, Nagendra Goel, Mirko Hannemann, Yanmin Qian, Petr Schwarz, Georg Stemmer, et al. 2011. The Kaldi speech recognition toolkit. In *In IEEE 2011 workshop*.

Daniel Povey, Vijayaditya Peddinti, Daniel Galvez, Pegah Ghahremani, Vimal Manohar, Xingyu Na, Yiming Wang, and Sanjeev Khudanpur. 2016. Purely sequence-trained neural networks for ASR based on lattice-free MMI. In *Proc. of INTERSPEECH*.

Ramon Sanabria, Ozan Caglayan, Shruti Palaskar, Desmond Elliott, Loïc Barrault, Lucia Specia, and Florian Metze. 2018. How2: a large-scale dataset for multimodal language understanding. In *ViGIL Workshop, NeurIPS*.

Rico Sennrich, Barry Haddow, and Alexandra Birch. 2016. Neural machine translation of rare words with subword units. In *Proc. of ACL*.

Karen Simonyan and Andrew Zisserman. 2015. Very deep convolutional networks for large-scale image recognition. In *Proc. of ICLR*.

Jason Smith, Herve Saint-Amand, Magdalena Plamadă, Philipp Koehn, Chris Callison-Burch, and Adam Lopez. 2013. Dirt cheap web-ccale parallel text from the common crawl. In *Proc. of ACL*.

Matthias Sperber, Graham Neubig, Jan Niehues, and Alex Waibel. 2019. Attention-passing models for robust and data-efficient end-to-end speech translation. *TACL*.

Christian Szegedy, Vincent Vanhoucke, Sergey Ioffe, Jon Shlens, and Zbigniew Wojna. 2016. Rethinking the inception architecture for computer vision. In *Proc. of CVPR*.

Jörg Tiedemann. 2012. Parallel data, tools and interfaces in OPUS. In *Proc. of LREC*.

Ashish Vaswani, Noam Shazeer, Niki Parmar, Jakob Uszkoreit, Llion Jones, Aidan N. Gomez, Łukasz Kaiser, and Illia Polosukhin. 2017. Attention is all you need. In *Proc. of NeurIPS*.

Shinji Watanabe, Takaaki Hori, Shigeki Karita, Tomoki Hayashi, Jiro Nishitoba, Yuya Unno, Nelson Enrique Yalta Soplin, Jahn Heymann, Matthew Wiesner, Nanxin Chen, et al. 2018. Espnet: End-to-end speech processing toolkit. In *Proc. of INTERSPEECH*.

Ron J Weiss, Jan Chorowski, Navdeep Jaitly, Yonghui Wu, and Zhifeng Chen. 2017. Sequence-to-sequence models can directly transcribe foreign speech. In *Proc. of INTERSPEECH*.

Start-Before-End and End-to-End: Neural Speech Translation by AppTek and RWTH Aachen University

Parnia Bahar[*], **Patrick Wilken, Tamer Alkhouli, Andreas Guta,**
Pavel Golik, Evgeny Matusov, Christian Herold[*]

Applications Technology (AppTek), Aachen, Germany

{pbahar,pwilken,talkhouli,aguta,pgolik,ematusov,cherold}@apptek.com

[*] Also RWTH Aachen University, Germany

Abstract

AppTek and RWTH Aachen University team together to participate in the offline and simultaneous speech translation tracks of IWSLT 2020. For the offline task, we create both cascaded and end-to-end speech translation systems, paying attention to careful data selection and weighting. In the cascaded approach, we combine high-quality hybrid automatic speech recognition (ASR) with the Transformer-based neural machine translation (NMT). Our end-to-end direct speech translation systems benefit from pretraining of adapted encoder and decoder components, as well as synthetic data and fine-tuning and thus are able to compete with cascaded systems in terms of MT quality. For simultaneous translation, we utilize a novel architecture that makes dynamic decisions, learned from parallel data, to determine when to continue feeding on input or generate output words. Experiments with speech and text input show that even at low latency this architecture leads to superior translation results.

1 Introduction

When developing English→German speech translation systems for the IWSLT 2020 evaluation, we had the following goals:

- To obtain the best possible translation quality with the baseline cascaded approach. This includes data filtering, weighting, and domain adaptation for the MT component, hybrid ASR (Section 2.1) with a strong recurrent language model (LM) for the ASR component, and a preprocessing scheme that converts the written English source text into spoken forms with hand-crafted rules for numbers, dates, abbreviations, etc. (Section 2.2).
- Starting from the best cascaded system for text and speech input in terms of data composition, to design and implement an architecture that obtains the best possible transla-

tion quality for simultaneous speech translation at different levels of latency, learning a flexible read/output strategy from the underlying linguistic qualities of aligned parallel data. Our simultaneous translation approach is described in Section 3.

- For the end-to-end direct speech translation, to benefit as much as possible from the model components of the cascaded approach, including pre-training encoder/decoder parts, an adapter component, and using synthetic data at different levels (see Section 4), and try to obtain translation quality that reaches the level of our best cascaded approach.

Traditionally, RWTH/AppTek can train strong attention-based LSTM models, which still compete on-par with Transformer-based architectures on some language pairs and translation tasks. Therefore, we train both LSTM and Transformer *base* and *big* models (Vaswani et al., 2017). For the simultaneous translation task, we choose LSTM models for their simpler architecture that allows for an easier modification of the encoder and decoder process to partial input and prediction of chunk boundaries, as will be discussed in Section 3. For the offline translation tasks, our final submissions are ensembles of different encoder-decoder architectures, as well as ensembles of cascaded and end-to-end direct speech translation systems.

2 Cascaded Speech Translation

2.1 Automatic Speech Recognition

Our ASR systems are based on hybrid LSTM/HMM model (Bourlard and Wellekens, 1989; Hochreiter and Schmidhuber, 1997) and attention models (Bahdanau et al., 2015).

2.1.1 Hybrid LSTM/HMM model

The acoustic model has been trained on a total of approx. 2300 hours of transcribed speech including

Proceedings of the 17th International Conference on Spoken Language Translation (IWSLT), pages 44–54
July 9-10, 2020. ©2020 Association for Computational Linguistics
https://doi.org/10.18653/v1/P17

EuroParl, How2, MuST-C, TED-LIUM (excluding the black-listed talks), LibriSpeech, Mozilla Common Voice, and IWSLT TED corpora.

As described in (Matusov et al., 2018), we apply an automatic re-alignment process to improve the quality of the TED talk segmentations. We use the TED-LIUM pronunciation lexicon. The acoustic model takes 80-dim. MFCC features as input and estimates state posterior probabilities for 5K tied triphone states. It consists of 4 bi-directional (BiLSTM) layers with 512 units for each direction. Frame-level alignment and state tying are obtained from a bootstrap model based on a Gaussian mixture acoustic model. We train the network for 10 epochs using the Adam update rule (Kingma and Ba, 2015) with Nesterov momentum and reducing the learning rate using the Newbob scheme.

The baseline language model is a simple 4-gram count model trained with Kneser-Ney smoothing on all allowed English text data (approx. 2.8B running words). The vocabulary consists of the same 152k words from the training lexicon and the out-of-vocabulary rate is far below 1%.

In addition, we train a neural LM with noise contrastive estimation (NCE) loss (Gutmann and Hyvärinen, 2010). The model estimates the distribution over the full vocabulary given the unconstrained history starting from the sentence begin. It learns 128-dim. word embeddings that are processed by two LSTM layers with 2048 units each. The output of the second LSTM layer is projected by a linear bottleneck layer onto 512 dimensions. We use the frequency sorted log-uniform distribution to sample 1024 negative examples for NCE loss calculation. This training approach results in a self-normalized model (Gerstenberger et al., 2020), which allows for an efficient, single-pass decoding with the neural LM (Beck et al., 2019).

The streaming recognizer implements a version of chunked processing (Chen and Huo, 2016; Zeyer et al., 2016), which allows to use the same BiLSTM-based acoustic model in both offline and online speech translation applications.

2.1.2 Attention Model

Following the work of LSTM-based attention ASR models (Zeyer et al., 2019), we apply a 6-layer BiLSTM encoder of 1024 nodes with interleaved max-pooling resulting in a total time reduction factor of 6 and a 1-layer LSTM decoder with a size of 1024 equipped with a single-head additive attention. We use a variant of SpectAugment (Park et al., 2019) for data augmentation. A layer-wise pre-training strategy similar to (Zeyer et al., 2018b) is applied during training for a more stable and faster initial convergence. We start with a small encoder (small in depth and width, i.e. number of layers and hidden dimensions) and then grow it over time. It means, we add layer by layer till the 6th layer, and increase the dimension till 1024 nodes. With each pre-training epoch, we grow the network in terms of both the number of layers and the number of hidden dimensions. Moreover, connectionist temporal classification (CTC) (Graves et al., 2006) as an additional loss is used on top of the speech encoder during training.

The models are trained using the Adam optimizer, dropout probability of 0.1 and label smoothing. We employ a learning rate scheduling scheme with a decay factor in the range of 0.8 to 0.9 based on perplexity on the development set. We apply byte-pair-encoding (BPE) (Sennrich et al., 2016b) with 5k merge operations with a dropout of 0.1. The beam size of 12 is used during the search without an extra language model. To enable the pre-training of the components, the same architecture is used in the speech encoder side of our direct speech translation models.

2.2 Written-to-Spoken Text Conversion

The large majority of MT parallel data comes from text sources and thus includes punctuation marks, digits, and special symbols. We apply additional preprocessing to the English side of the data to make it look like speech transcripts produced by the ASR system. We lowercase the text, remove all punctuation marks, expand common abbreviations, especially for measurement units, and convert numbers, dates, and other entities expressed with digits into their spoken form. For the cases of multiple readings of a given number (e.g. "one oh one" and "one hundred and one"), we select one randomly, so that the system can learn to convert alternative readings in English to the same number expressed with digits in German. Because of this preprocessing, our MT systems learn to insert punctuation marks, restore word case, and convert spoken number and entity forms to digits as part of the translation process. The same preprocessing is applied to the English monolingual data that is used in language model training of the ASR system.

2.3 Data Filtering and Domain Adaptation

For NMT training, we utilize the parallel data allowed for the IWSLT 2020 evaluation. We divide it into three parts: in-domain, clean, and out-of-domain. We consider data from the TED and MuST-C corpora as in-domain and use it for subsequent fine-tuning experiments, as well as the "ground truth" for filtering the out-of-domain data based on sentence embedding similarity with the in-domain data. As "clean" we consider the News-Commentary, Europarl, and WikiTitles corpora and use their full versions in training.

To reduce the size of the training data, we apply a filtering approach based on sentence similarity. We train monolingual GloVe word embeddings (Pennington et al., 2014) both on the source and the target side of the data. Following Arora et al. (2017) we use a weighted average over the word embeddings of a sentence to generate a fixed-size sentence embedding. To obtain a sentence *pair* embedding, we concatenate the source and target sentence embedding of each bilingual sentence pair. Afterwards we employ k-Means clustering from the scikit-learn toolkit (Pedregosa et al., 2011) in the sentence pair embedding space.

After obtaining a set of clusters, we use the in-domain data to determine which clusters should be used for training. This is done by selecting all clusters which contain a non-negligible portion of the in-domain data using a fixed threshold n. We apply this technique to the noisy and out-of-domain corpora, namely ParaCrawl, CommonCrawl, rapid and OpenSubtitles. With the tuned threshold $n = 5.0\%$ we achieve a data reduction of around 45% (from 42.5M to 23.3M lines) and an improvement in the system performance of 1.6% BLEU on the development set (from 30.7% to 32.3% BLEU).

A similar approach is applied to the German monolingual data allowed by the IWSLT 2020 evaluation that we incorporate into the MT training using back-translation (Sennrich et al., 2016a). First, from the billions of words of allowed text data we extract only sentence portions of at least four words which are enclosed in quotes. Especially in the news texts, these often represent quoted speech and thus may be more suitable to be used in training of speech NMT systems. Then, we apply the monolingual variant of the sentence embedding similarity approach described above to select 7.9M sentences. To create the synthetic parallel data, we translate these sentences into English with a De-En NMT Transformer base model that is trained on the in-domain and clean parallel data.

2.4 Neural Machine Translation

We employ the *base* and *big* Transformer model with multi-head attention. The base Transformer model consists of a self-attentive encoder and decoder, each of which is composed of 6 stacked layers. Every layer consists of two sub-layers: a 8-head self-attention layer followed by a rectified linear unit (ReLU). We apply layer normalization (Ba et al., 2016) before and dropout (Srivastava et al., 2014) and residual connections (He et al., 2016) after each sub-layer. All projection and multi-head attention layers consist of 512 nodes followed by a feed-forward layer equipped with 2048 nodes.

In comparison, the architecture of the big Transformer model incorporates 16-head self-attention sub-layers. Furthermore, all projection and attention layers consist of 1024 nodes and each feed-forward layer consists of 4096 nodes.

All models are trained on a single GPU and increased the effective batch size by accumulating gradient updates before applying them with a factor of 2 and 8 for the base and big Transformer respectively. All models are trained using Adam optimizer with an initial learning rate of 0.0003 and 1M lines per checkpoint. We apply a learning rate scheduling based on the perplexity on the validation set for a few consecutive evaluation checkpoints. Label smoothing (Pereyra et al., 2017) and dropout rates of 0.1 are used. The source and target sentences are segmented into subwords using SentencePiece (SP) (Kudo and Richardson, 2018) with a vocabulary size of 20K and 30K respectively.

3 Simultaneous Translation

In simultaneous translation a stream of source words is translated into a stream of target words without relying on the context of a full sentence. In this process, the system has to make decisions on when to read further input and when to produce partial translations. Hence, there is an inherent compromise between latency and MT quality.

3.1 Alignment-based Chunking

We develop a novel model architecture, based on offline LSTM models which are similar to Bahdanau et al. (2015). The approach is described in full detail in Wilken et al. (2020). Our model consists of a multi-layer BiLSTM encoder, a unidirectional decoder and an attention mechanism. We expand the forward encoder with an additional binary output trained to predict chunk boundaries in the incoming source word stream. These chunk boundaries mark positions where enough context for translation is present to trigger a translation. We generate training examples for such chunks based on statistical word alignment, created using the Eflomal Toolkit (Östling and Tiedemann, 2016). The chunk sequence of a sentence pair is defined such that it is monotonic[1], no word in the chunk is aligned to a word outside the chunk, and chunks are of minimal size. By this, reordering happens only within the chunks, thus in terms of word alignment the source side of a chunk provides enough information to continue the partial translation monotonically.

We shift the extracted source boundaries by D positions to the right such that the first words after the actual boundary provide context for the boundary detection component. Furthermore, we improve the chunk extraction described above by removing a chunk boundary if the target word following it is important as context for translation of the last word in the candidate chunk. Details are given in (Wilken et al., 2020). The words in the chunks are converted to SP subword sequences prior to the training of the simultaneous NMT system.

3.2 Streaming ASR

For the speech-to-text condition we use the cascaded approach, integrating the streaming version of the ASR system described in Section 2.1 into the decoder. We send 1-second chunks of the incoming audio into the ASR system. We have to alter the ASR system to output the common prefix of all hypothesized transcriptions in the beam, such that words in the output are guaranteed to not change due to further evidence. For each 1-second chunk we check whether new words were generated by the ASR. If so, we pass them to the encoder of the MT system. From that point on, translation happens as described in the next section.

3.3 Online MT Decoding

For each word in the input stream, we first apply subword splitting. Then we feed the subwords into the forward encoder one by one, producing the encoding of that subword and a boundary decision. If a boundary is predicted, all source words of the current chunk are fed into the backwards encoder. After that, the decoder produces the translation attending to the forward and backwards encodings of all words of the sentence read so far. Here, we perform the beam search with a beam size of 12. For length normalization, we divide the scores by $I^{0.9}$, I being the target length. To know when to stop decoding of a chunk, we predict the target chunk

---

Training data\Running words	EN	DE
DST	7.5M	8.1M
ASR[1]	32.9M	-
MT[2]	309.8M	289.9M
SYNTH_SPEECH[3]	4.2M	5.0M
SYNTH_TRANS[4]	32.9M	37.3M
BT[5]	125.2M	117.3M

Table 1: Data size. [1]Contains the ASR portion of DST data; [2]contains the MT supervised data of DST data; [3]additional synthetic DST data by synthesizing bilingual MT data (using TTS model); [4]additional synthetic DST data by translation ASR transcriptions; [5]back-translation of German monolingual data.

boundaries via a binary translation factor (Wilken and Matusov, 2019). A hypothesis in the beam is considered final as soon as a boundary is predicted. The states of the forward encoder and the decoder are kept across chunks. The backward encoder is initialized for each chunk. In both encoder and decoder we feed an embedding of the boundary decision into the next recurrent step, analogous to label feedback of the target word.

4 End-to-End Direct Speech Translation

The direct speech translation models have been trained using direct speech translation (DST) training data including MuST-C, IWSLT TED, and EuroParl corpora, i.e. a total of approx. 420 hours of transcribed and translated speech (see Table 1). We remove all sequences longer than 75 tokens and all utterances longer than 6000 frames.

The end-to-end models are based on encoder-decoder architectures. The LSTM-based *speech encoder* uses 6 stacked BiLSTM layers with interleaved max-pooling layers in between to reduce the utterance length with a factor of 6. We apply layerwise encoder pre-training w.r.t. both the number of layers and dimensions. The CTC loss is used on top of speech encoder except in pre-training. All other parameters are similar to ASR training; thus, we also apply SpectAugment in all of our DST experiments similar to (Bahar et al., 2019b).

The *text decoder* is based on the decoder of MT models, as illustrated in Figure 1, using either the LSTM or the Transformer topology. In LSTM setups, the decoder is equipped with a 1-layer unidirectional LSTM with cell size 1024 and single-head additive attention. All tokens are mapped into a 512-dimensional embedding space. Both base and big Transformer decoders are based on the architecture explained in Section 2.4.

To solve the data sparseness problems of DST

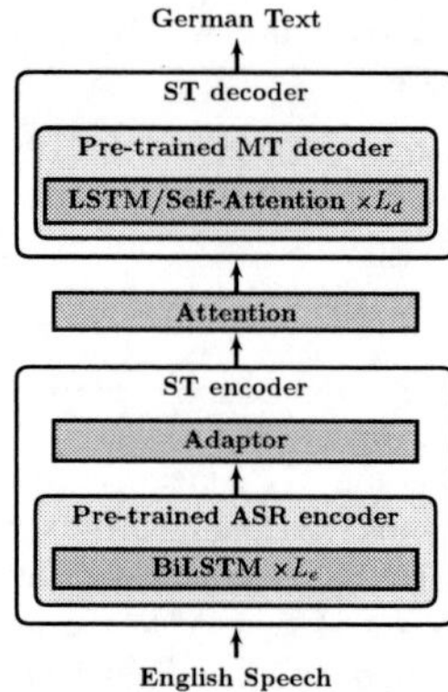

Figure 1: Overview of the DST model with pretraining and an adaptor. Shallow grey blocks correspond to pre-trained components, and dark grey blocks are fine-tuned on the DST task.

training, we explore various strategies to augment the data by leveraging weakly supervised data, i.e. ASR and MT training data. Our high-quality Transformer *big* model has been employed to generate synthetic DST training data by automatically translating the correct transcripts of ASR training data (Jia et al., 2019). SYNTH_TRANS refers to machine-translated ASR training data. As listed in Table 1, we translate the whole ASR training data (32.9M words) resulting in 37.3M German tokens and combine it with the original DST data, weighting each set equally. Similarly, we create synthetic DST training data by generating speech from the source side of an MT parallel corpus (Jia et al., 2019). We refer to it as SYNTH_SPEECH, and its statistics can be found in Table 1. Our text-to-speech synthesis (TTS) model is trained on ASR LibriSpeech dataset as described in (Rossenbach et al., 2020). Using the TTS model, we synthesize 800k random samples (total of 5M words as listed in Table 1) from the OpenSubtitles corpus pre-filtered as described in Section 2.3. Again, the generated data is uniformly mixed with the original DST data.

To further leverage the weakly supervised data, we apply pre-training of both the encoder and decoder with an adaptor layer in between. Initialization of model components using pre-trained ASR and MT models is a common transfer learning strategy to reduce dependency on scarce DST training data. We pre-train the encoder using our ASR model explained in Section 2.1, and the decoder using our MT model, either the LSTM attention or Transformer, as described in Section 2.4. After initialization with pre-trained components, we fine-tune on the DST training data. As proposed

in (Bahar et al., 2019a), in order to familiarize the pre-trained text decoder with the output of the pre-trained speech encoder, we insert an additional adaptor layer which is a BiLSTM layer between the encoder and decoder. We train the adaptor component jointly without freezing the parameters in the fine-tuning stage. An abstract overview is shown in Figure 1.

5 Experimental Results

In this section we report results for offline cascaded and direct speech translation, as well as for simultaneous NMT under various training data conditions.

Acoustic training of the baseline model and the HMM decoding have been performed with the RWTH ASR toolkit (Wiesler et al., 2014). All neural models have been built with RETURNN (Doetsch et al., 2017; Zeyer et al., 2018a) using Sisyphus framework (Peter et al., 2018).

The number of running words of all training corpora is presented in Table 1. The data used for training the NMT models is referred to as MT and contains the in-domain, clean, and filtered bilingual data as defined in Section 2.3. On the other hand, BT denotes the parallel data obtained through back-translating the filtered monolingual data (see also Section 2.3). When the concatenation of MT and BT is used for training, we over-sample the in-domain and clean part of MT 5 times. We remove transcriber comments and emulate the ASR output using the preprocessing described in Section 2.2.

As heldout tuning sets, we use the concatenation of the TED dev2010, tst2014, and MuST-C dev corpora. As heldout test data, we use TED tst2015, MuST-C tst-HE and MuST-C tst-COMMON.

We report case-sensitive BLEU (Papineni et al., 2002) and TER (Snover et al., 2006) scores. For simultaneous NMT, also the average lagging (AL) metric (Ma et al., 2019) is reported. To measure AL, we have integrated our online decoder into the server-client implementation of IWSLT 2020 within the fairseq framework (Ott et al., 2019).

5.1 ASR Quality

For training of the ASR component used in the cascaded approach, we first pool the data from all available corpora, removing utterances that can not be aligned using a baseline model trained on the IWSLT TED corpus, resulting in 2300h of aligned audio. The performance of the model trained on this data is shown in the first line of Table 2. To understand the contribution of the various data

#	Model		TED	MuST-C	MuST-C
	AM	**LM**	**tst2015**	**tst-HE**	**tst-COM**
Hybrid HMM					
1	LSTM	4-gram	8.7	10.5	13.1
2	LSTM	4-gram	11.1	9.4	11.5
3	LSTM	LSTM	9.6	7.5	9.9
Attention					
4	LSTM	None	6.9	7.7	10.6

Table 2: ASR word error rate results in [%].

sources, we train a model for each corpus. Based on the accuracy on the dev set we decide to exclude EuroParl and How2 data sets, as they appear to be the worst match for the target domain. The second line shows that fine-tuning on the "matched" subset (about 85% of the total training data) does not lead to a consistent reduction of WER. Still, we decide to proceed with this acoustic model, based on the experience with the single corpus experiments. Finally, switching to the neural LM (see Section 2.1.1) considerably improves the accuracy on the test sets shown in line 3. This final system is used in the cascaded translation approach. The attention ASR model described in Section 2.1.2 has been trained using 2300h meaning 32.9M words. As shown in Table 2, the performance of the LSTM model (line 4) is competitive to the hybrid HMM model. We use LSTM speech encoder for all of our direct ST modeling in pre-training.

5.2 ASR Output for MT Fine-Tuning

For cascaded speech translation, both offline and simultaneous, we apply fine-tuning on the DST corpora. with correct source transcripts. In addition, we augment this data with the MuST-C and TED tst2010 through tst2013 sets, the source side of which is generated using the hybrid HMM (see Table 2 line 2). All fine-tuning systems employ an initial learning rate of 0.0008. The simultaneous systems and the offline Transformer base model trained on the MT+BT data (see Table 1) are fine-tuned using 100k lines per checkpoint, whereas the other offline models use 1M lines per checkpoint.

5.3 Offline Speech Translation

The results for the offline speech translation systems are presented in Table 3. The first line shows the results obtained when translating the ground truth source text of the test sets with a Transformer base model trained on the MT data, thus eliminating potential speech recognition errors. The preprocessing on the source side emulates the ASR output by applying lower-casing, removing punctuation

marks and removing transcriber comments.

Line 2 through 8 present the results of translating the output of the hybrid HMM ASR system (see Table 2 line 3). In comparison to the first line, we see a significant loss of up to 3.5% BLEU when translating the ASR output (line 2). Fine-tuning this model as described in Section 5.2 leads to a performance gain of up to 1.9% BLEU (line 3).

Furthermore, we train models on the MT+BT data (line 4 to 8). Although the Transformer base model in line 4 outperforms the corresponding model in line 2, applying fine-tuning (line 5) does not yield better performance than the fine-tuned model in line 3, which can be traced back to the over-sampled clean data. The big Transformer models in line 6 and 7 outperform the base models in lines 4 and 5, respectively.

Overall, the fine-tuned big model (line 7) performs better on tst2015 and tst-HE, whereas the fine-tuned base model trained without oversampling and back-translated data (line 3) performs better on tst-COMMON. Our final submission (line 8) consists of the ensemble of the fine-tuned models in line 5 and 7 and yields the best performance on average. The results obtained translating the output of the attention ASR system (see Table 2 line 4) using the ensemble of the two models (line 5 and 7) are listed in line 9.

5.4 Direct Speech Translation

The fourth block of Table 3 shows the results of direct speech translation where we do not rely on intermediate transcriptions. In the first set of experiments, our DST models are based on the LSTM attention architecture where both encoder and decoder are composed of LSTM units (line 10 to 12). The LSTM attention model outperforms the Transformer model. Again, pre-training the entire network (plus a BiLSTM layer as an adaptor in between) yields improvements of 2.9% BLEU and 4.3% TER on average across all test sets indicating that pre-training is an effective strategy to leverage the supervised ASR and MT training data in practice.

Augmenting ASR data with automatic translations (SYNTH_TRANS) shows slightly worse results (line 12), which might be due to domain mismatch. In line with our pure MT and ASR experiments, we combine our strong speech LSTM encoder with our powerful text decoder, i.e. big Transformer (lines 13 to 16). As shown, this combination provides additional gain over vanilla pre-trained models. These lines differ in terms of training data

#	System	TED tst2015		MuST-C tst-HE		MuST-C tst-COMMON		Training data composition
		BLEU	TER	BLEU	TER	BLEU	TER	
Pure text MT								
1	Transformer base	**31.2**	**52.3**	**28.5**	**55.8**	**31.3**	**50.1**	MT
Cascaded hybrid ASR → MT								
2	Transformer base	29.0	56.6	26.3	58.9	27.8	54.7	MT+ASR
3	+ fine-tune	30.2	55.7	28.1	57.2	**29.7**	**53.1**	MT+ASR
4	Transformer base	29.8	56.1	27.2	57.8	28.3	54.9	(MT+BT)+ASR
5	+ fine-tune	30.1	55.7	28.2	56.7	28.8	55.7	(MT+BT)+ASR
6	Transformer big	30.5	55.2	27.9	56.7	28.7	54.6	(MT+BT)+ASR
7	+ fine-tune	**30.9**	**55.2**	**28.6**	**56.3**	28.8	55.5	(MT+BT)+ASR
8	Ensemble (5, 7)	30.9	55.2	28.7	56.4	29.7	54.5	(MT+BT)+ASR
Cascaded attention ASR → MT								
9	Ensemble (5, 7)	30.3	54.2	28.3	56.9	28.8	55.3	(MT+BT)+ASR
End2end Direct DST								
10	LSTM-attention	23.6	64.1	22.1	63.3	24.3	59.1	DST
11	+ pretraining	26.0	59.1	24.7	60.1	27.9	54.3	DST+ASR+MT
12	+ pretraining	25.0	61.0	24.3	60.3	26.7	55.7	(DST + SYNTH_TRANS)+ASR+MT
13	+ big Transformer decoder	26.4	58.2	24.6	59.3	**29.1**	**53.8**	DST+DST+MT
14	+ big Transformer decoder	26.1	58.6	**25.1**	**58.8**	28.7	53.8	DST+ASR+MT
15	+ big Transformer decoder	25.9	59.3	24.1	63.5	27.0	55.9	(DST + SYNTH_SPEECH)+ASR+MT
16	+ big Transformer decoder	**27.0**	**58.3**	25.1	61.3	27.3	55.8	(DST + SYNTH_TRANS)+ASR+MT
17	+ fine-tune	26.8	58.6	25.1	62.3	27.9	55.3	(DST + SYNTH_TRANS)+ASR+MT
18	Ensemble (13, 17)	27.2	57.9	25.5	60.7	29.4	53.3	
19	Ensemble (13, 15, 16, 17)	28.0	57.3	26.5	58.1	29.6	53.4	

Table 3: Offline speech translation results measured in BLEU [%] and TER [%].

which is used either for pre-training or for fine-tuning. For instance, in line 13, we use the ASR model trained on the DST (in-domain) data for pre-training the encoder whereas line 14 corresponds to the ASR model trained on all (in-domain and out-of-domain) ASR data. In lines 15 and 16, we use additional augmented data. In general, ASR data augmented with synthetic translations can help the model, while synthesized speech for the MT data is less effective and still performs worse than the model using DST data only (see lines 14, 15). Another aspect to consider is that the additional synthetic data we generate might be out-of-domain. Therefore, we fine-tune on top of generated data to mitigate the domain gap (line 17). This approach improves the results on the tst-COMMON set. In the end, to benefit from all data variations, we do an ensemble of models that outperforms all single ones.

With data augmentation, pre-training, fine-tuning, and careful architecture selection, a combination of LSTM encoder and big Transformer decoder, we obtain comparable results and even on par on tst-COMMON set and close the gap between the cascaded and the direct models.

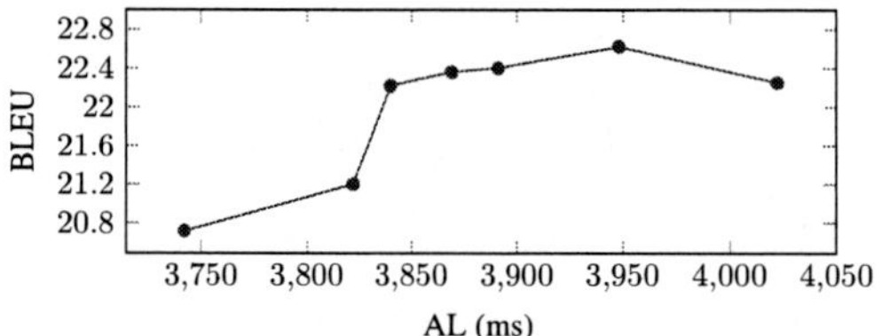

Figure 2: BLEU vs. Average Lagging latency for a unidirectional 6-encoder 2-decoder system, generated by varying the maximum chunk size using the values $C \in \{5, 6, 7, 8, 9, 10, 20\}$. The results are computed for the tst-HE dataset.

5.5 Simultaneous Speech Translation

We present results for simultaneous speech and text translation models fine-tuned on a concatenation of the MuST-C and TED training data. In the case of speech translation models, the fine-tuning is done as described in Section 5.2. All simultaneous models use 30k SP units for the source and target side.

Table 4 displays the results for the simultaneous speech translation task. In the upper part, we provide the results for the offline Transformer base system trained on the same data for reference. The results are shown for the reference transcript, and the streaming ASR output. In the middle of the table, we list multiple simultaneous NMT systems with varying settings. We enforce a maximum source-

System	TED tst2015		MuST-C tst-HE			MuST-C tst-COMMON	
	BLEU	TER	BLEU	TER	AL	BLEU	TER
Offline baseline, Transformer (MT+BT training data)							
using reference transcript	32.7	50.9	30.1	54.3		32.6	48.9
using streaming ASR	28.6	56.3	26.0	59.2		26.4	57.3
Simultaneous NMT (AL $\leq$ 4s)							
6enc, 2dec, C=10, D=2	24.3	60.8	22.6	63.1	3.95s	22.4	60.2
6enc, 4dec, C=10, D=2	25.1	59.5	22.2	63.1	3.94s	22.3	60.0
6enc, 2dec, C=6, D=3	23.3	62.1	21.9	64.7	3.98s	22.3	61.3
2x4enc, 1dec, C=6, D=3	23.8	60.9	22.3	63.1	3.99s	22.3	61.0
6enc, 2dec, C=20, D=4	24.9	61.2	23.0	63.0	4.45s	22.1	62.0

Table 4: Experimental results (in %) for simultaneous NMT of speech, IWSLT 2020 English→German. C refers to the enforced maximum chunk size, D indicates the boundary decision delay.

System	Avg. AL	TED tst2015		MuST-C tst-HE		MuST-C tst-COMMON	
		BLEU	TER	BLEU	TER	BLEU	TER
Simultaneous NMT							
6enc, 2dec, D=2	4.55	30.5	52.5	29.0	54.6	30.3	50.4
6enc, 2dec, D=3	5.21	30.5	52.6	28.9	55.4	29.8	51.0
6enc, 2dec, D=4	5.99	30.3	52.7	29.1	54.0	30.5	50.3
2x4enc, 1dec, D=3	5.33	29.9	53.4	29.0	54.9	30.7	50.4

Table 5: Experimental results (in %) for simultaneous NMT of text input, IWSLT 2020 English→German, D indicates the boundary decision delay.

side chunk size C and vary the source boundary delay D to achieve a latency below 4 seconds on tst-HE. We compare a unidirectional architecture of 6 LSTM encoder layers and 2 or 4 LSTM decoder layers to a bidirectional model. The model has two stacks of 4 forward and 4 backward LSTM encoder layers, concatenated at the top-most layer. The model uses 1 LSTM decoder layer. We observe that training with a lower delay D=2 and relaxing the maximum chunk size (C=10) produces better results than training with a larger delay (D=3), and using a smaller (C=6). The lower row shows results for a system with C=20, achieving a latency of 4.45 seconds. We note that the model makes dynamic decisions to decide on the source chunk boundaries that directly influence the latency.

Table 5 shows the results for simultaneous text translation. We compare unidirectional and bidirectional models with different latencies. All models use a fixed maximum chunk size of C=20. The models are trained with different delay values. We observe that even with a delay D=2 the model is able to learn reasonable chunk boundaries that achieve lower latency than higher-delay models and also maintain a comparable performance.

Figure 2 illustrates the performance on tst-HE against average lagging (AL) latency. The latency is varied by changing the maximum chunk size C. The model used is a unidirectional 6-encoder 2-decoder model trained with delay D=2. We observe little improvement when increasing the max-

imum chunk size beyond C=7. At C=7, AL is equal to 3.84s with a performance of 22.2% BLEU, comparable to 22.3% BLEU obtained when setting C=20 (corresponding to AL=4.02s). This is likely due to the learned chunking that is able to set the boundaries without the need for external intervention by capping the chunk size. On the other hand, reducing the maximum chunk size to 5 and 6 tokens reduces latency, but also reduces translation context and therefore hurts performance.

6 Final Results

Compared to last year's submission, the results of both cascade and direct offline speech translation models have improved. The cascade system shows an improvement of 2.0% BLEU compared to the 2018 submission. The MT quality of the direct model almost reached the one of the cascade model, obtaining a huge improvement of 12.4% BLEU. The performance on the tst2019 and tst2020 test sets is shown in Table 6, as evaluated by the IWSLT 2020 server. Our primary cascade and direct systems correspond to the lines 8 and 19 of Table 3 respectively. The contrastive systems which are single models correspond to the lines 7 and 17 of the table. We see that the provided reference segmentation negatively affects the MT quality. In contrast, the segmentation obtained by our hybrid ASR model yields segments which apparently are more sentence-like, include less noise and thus can be better translated. On the condition with automatic segmentation, the difference between our cascade and direct models ranges from 1.8 to 2.3 BLEU points. This holds both for our primary ensemble submission and the contrastive single systems, which have lower BLEU scores by 1% or less as compared to the ensembles. More results can be found in (Ansari et al., 2020).

System	TED tst2019		TED tst2020	
	BLEU	TER	BLEU	TER
reference segmentation				
cascade (primary)	21.0	67.2	22.5	65.2
direct (primary)	19.2	71.2	20.5	70.1
automatic segmentation				
cascade (primary, ensemble)	23.4	63.5	25.1	61.4
direct (primary, ensemble)	21.6	66.2	23.3	64.8
cascade (contrastive, single)	23.2	63.6	24.6	61.9
direct (contrastive, single)	20.9	67.2	22.3	66.5

Table 6: AppTek/RWTH IWSLT 2020 submission for offline speech translation, BLEU and TER scores in %.

7 Conclusions

In this paper, we summarize the results of the joint participation of AppTek and RWTH Aachen University in the IWSLT 2020 evaluation. For the first time, we present simultaneous translation results on real speech from our hybrid streaming ASR system. With a latency of 4 seconds they are only 4 BLEU points behind our strong cascaded offline NMT baseline. This baseline still exhibits the best results in the offline speech translation task, but our direct single end-to-end system, with careful architecture selection, pre-training, and data augmentation, is almost able to compete with our best cascaded system, obtaining a BLEU score of 29.1 vs 29.7% on MuST-C tst-COMMON set. On the TED tst2015 set, the ensemble of our direct end-to-end systems yields a BLEU score of 28.0%, exactly reaching AppTek's cascaded system results at IWSLT 2018, obtained one and a half years ago. At that time, our first DST prototype scored only 17.1% BLEU on the same test set. This shows the fast and tremendous progress of our direct speech translation research.

References

Ebrahim Ansari, Amittai Axelrod, Nguyen Bach, Ondrej Bojar, Roldano Cattoni, Fahim Dalvi, Nadir Durrani, Marcello Federico, Christian Federmann, Jiatao Gu, Fei Huang, Kevin Knight, Xutai Ma, Ajay Nagesh, Matteo Negri, Jan Niehues, Juan Pino, Elizabeth Salesky, Xing Shi, Sebastian Stüker, Marco Turchi, and Changhan Wang. 2020. Findings of the IWSLT 2020 Evaluation Campaign. In *Proceedings of the 17th International Conference on Spoken Language Translation (IWSLT 2020)*, Seattle, USA.

Sanjeev Arora, Yingyu Liang, and Tengyu Ma. 2017. A simple but tough-to-beat baseline for sentence embeddings. In *5th International Conference on Learning Representations, ICLR 2017, Toulon, France, April 24-26, 2017, Conference Track Proceedings*.

Jimmy Lei Ba, Jamie Ryan Kiros, and Geoffrey E Hinton. 2016. Layer normalization. *arXiv preprint arXiv:1607.06450*. Version 1.

Parnia Bahar, Tobias Bieschke, and Hermann Ney. 2019a. A comparative study on end-to-end speech to text translation. In *IEEE Automatic Speech Recognition and Understanding Workshop*, pages 792–799, Sentosa, Singapore.

Parnia Bahar, Albert Zeyer, Ralf Schlüter, and Hermann Ney. 2019b. On using specaugment for end-to-end speech translation. In *International Workshop on Spoken Language Translation*, Hong Kong, China.

Dzmitry Bahdanau, Kyunghyun Cho, and Yoshua Bengio. 2015. Neural machine translation by jointly learning to align and translate. In *Proceedings of the International Conference on Learning Representations (ICLR)*.

Eugen Beck, Wei Zhou, Ralf Schlüter, and Hermann Ney. 2019. LSTM language models for LVCSR in first-pass decoding and lattice-rescoring. Https://arxiv.org/abs/1907.01030.

Hervé Bourlard and Christian J. Wellekens. 1989. Links between Markov models and multilayer perceptrons. In D.S. Touretzky, editor, *Advances in Neural Information Processing Systems I*, pages 502–510. Morgan Kaufmann, San Mateo, CA, USA.

Kai Chen and Qiang Huo. 2016. Training deep bidirectional LSTM acoustic model for LVCSR by a context-sensitive-chunk BPTT approach. *IEEE/ACM Transactions on Audio, Speech, and Language Processing*, 24(7):1185–1193.

Patrick Doetsch, Albert Zeyer, Paul Voigtlaender, Ilia Kulikov, Ralf Schlüter, and Hermann Ney. 2017. Returnn: the rwth extensible training framework for universal recurrent neural networks. In *IEEE International Conference on Acoustics, Speech, and Signal Processing*, pages 5345–5349, New Orleans, LA, USA.

Alexander Gerstenberger, Kazuki Irie, Pavel Golik, Eugen Beck, and Hermann Ney. 2020. Domain robust, fast, and compact neural language models. In *IEEE International Conference on Acoustics, Speech, and Signal Processing*, pages 7954–7958, Barcelona, Spain.

Alex Graves, Santiago Fernández, Faustino J. Gomez, and Jürgen Schmidhuber. 2006. Connectionist temporal classification: labelling unsegmented sequence data with recurrent neural networks. In *Machine Learning, Proceedings of the Twenty-Third International Conference (ICML 2006), Pittsburgh, Pennsylvania, USA, June 25-29*, pages 369–376.

Michael Gutmann and Aapo Hyvärinen. 2010. Noise-contrastive estimation: A new estimation principle for unnormalized statistical models. In *Proceedings of the Thirteenth International Conference on Artificial Intelligence and Statistics*, volume 9, pages 297–304, Chia Laguna Resort, Sardinia, Italy.

Kaiming He, Xiangyu Zhang, Shaoqing Ren, and Jian Sun. 2016. Deep residual learning for image recognition. In *2016 IEEE Conference on Computer Vision and Pattern Recognition, CVPR 2016, Las Vegas, NV, USA, June 27-30, 2016*, pages 770–778.

Sepp Hochreiter and Jürgen Schmidhuber. 1997. Long short-term memory. *Neural Computation*, 9(8):1735–1780.

Ye Jia, Melvin Johnson, Wolfgang Macherey, Ron J. Weiss, Yuan Cao, Chung-Cheng Chiu, Naveen Ari, Stella Laurenzo, and Yonghui Wu. 2019. Leveraging weakly supervised data to improve end-to-end speech-to-text translation. In *IEEE International Conference on Acoustics, Speech and Signal Processing, ICASSP 2019, Brighton, United Kingdom, May 12-17, 2019*, pages 7180–7184. IEEE.

Diederik P. Kingma and Jimmy Ba. 2015. Adam: A method for stochastic optimization. In *Proceedings of the International Conference on Learning Representations (ICLR)*, San Diego, CA, USA.

Taku Kudo and John Richardson. 2018. Sentencepiece: A simple and language independent subword tokenizer and detokenizer for neural text processing. In *Proceedings of the 2018 Conference on Empirical Methods in Natural Language Processing: System Demonstrations*, pages 66–71.

Mingbo Ma, Liang Huang, Hao Xiong, Renjie Zheng, Kaibo Liu, Baigong Zheng, Chuanqiang Zhang, Zhongjun He, Hairong Liu, Xing Li, Hua Wu, and Haifeng Wang. 2019. STACL: Simultaneous translation with implicit anticipation and controllable latency using prefix-to-prefix framework. In *Proceedings of the 57th Annual Meeting of the Association for Computational Linguistics*, pages 3025–3036, Florence, Italy. Association for Computational Linguistics.

Evgeny Matusov, Patrick Wilken, Parnia Bahar, Julian Schamper, Pavel Golik, Albert Zeyer, Joan Albert Silvestre-Cerda, Adria Martinez-Villaronga, Hendrik Pesch, and Jan-Thorsten Peter. 2018. Neural speech translation at apptek. In *Proceedings of the 15th International Workshop on Spoken Language Translation*, pages 104–111, Bruges, Belgium.

Robert Östling and Jörg Tiedemann. 2016. Efficient word alignment with Markov Chain Monte Carlo. *Prague Bulletin of Mathematical Linguistics*, 106:125–146.

Myle Ott, Sergey Edunov, Alexei Baevski, Angela Fan, Sam Gross, Nathan Ng, David Grangier, and Michael Auli. 2019. fairseq: A fast, extensible toolkit for sequence modeling. In *Proceedings of NAACL-HLT 2019: Demonstrations*.

Kishore Papineni, Salim Roukos, Todd Ward, and Wei-Jing Zhu. 2002. BLEU: a Method for Automatic Evaluation of Machine Translation. In *Proceedings of the 41st Annual Meeting of the Association for Computational Linguistics*, pages 311–318, Philadelphia, Pennsylvania, USA.

Daniel S Park, William Chan, Yu Zhang, Chung-Cheng Chiu, Barret Zoph, Ekin D Cubuk, and Quoc V Le. 2019. SpecAugment: A simple data augmentation method for automatic speech recognition. *arXiv preprint arXiv:1904.08779*.

Fabian Pedregosa, Gaël Varoquaux, Alexandre Gramfort, Vincent Michel, Bertrand Thirion, Olivier Grisel, Mathieu Blondel, Peter Prettenhofer, Ron Weiss, Vincent Dubourg, Jake VanderPlas, Alexandre Passos, David Cournapeau, Matthieu Brucher, Matthieu Perrot, and Edouard Duchesnay. 2011. Scikit-learn: Machine learning in python. *J. Mach. Learn. Res.*, 12:2825–2830.

Jeffrey Pennington, Richard Socher, and Christopher D. Manning. 2014. Glove: Global vectors for word representation. In *Proceedings of the 2014 Conference on Empirical Methods in Natural Language Processing, EMNLP 2014, October 25-29, 2014, Doha, Qatar, A meeting of SIGDAT, a Special Interest Group of the ACL*, pages 1532–1543.

Gabriel Pereyra, George Tucker, Jan Chorowski, Lukasz Kaiser, and Geoffrey E. Hinton. 2017. Regularizing neural networks by penalizing confident output distributions. *CoRR*, abs/1701.06548.

Jan-Thorsten Peter, Eugen Beck, and Hermann Ney. 2018. Sisyphus, a workflow manager designed for machine translation and automatic speech recognition. In *Conference on Empirical Methods in Natural Language Processing*, Brussels, Belgium.

Nick Rossenbach, Albert Zeyer, Ralf Schlüter, and Hermann Ney. 2020. Generating synthetic audio data for attention-based speech recognition systems. In *IEEE International Conference on Acoustics, Speech, and Signal Processing*, Barcelona, Spain.

Rico Sennrich, Barry Haddow, and Alexandra Birch. 2016a. Improving neural machine translation models with monolingual data. pages 86–96.

Rico Sennrich, Barry Haddow, and Alexandra Birch. 2016b. Neural machine translation of rare words with subword units. In *Proceedings of the 54th Annual Meeting of the Association for Computational*

Linguistics, ACL 2016, August 7-12, 2016, Berlin, Germany, Volume 1: Long Papers.

Matthew Snover, Bonnie Dorr, Richard Schwartz, Linnea Micciulla, and John Makhoul. 2006. A Study of Translation Edit Rate with Targeted Human Annotation. In *Proceedings of the 7th Conference of the Association for Machine Translation in the Americas*, pages 223–231, Cambridge, Massachusetts, USA.

Nitish Srivastava, Geoffrey E. Hinton, Alex Krizhevsky, Ilya Sutskever, and Ruslan Salakhutdinov. 2014. Dropout: a simple way to prevent neural networks from overfitting. *Journal of Machine Learning Research*, 15(1):1929–1958.

Ashish Vaswani, Noam Shazeer, Niki Parmar, Jakob Uszkoreit, Llion Jones, Aidan N Gomez, Łukasz Kaiser, and Illia Polosukhin. 2017. Attention is all you need. In *Advances in Neural Information Processing Systems*, pages 5998–6008.

Simon Wiesler, Alexander Richard, Pavel Golik, Ralf Schlüter, and Hermann Ney. 2014. RASR/NN: The RWTH neural network toolkit for speech recognition. In *IEEE International Conference on Acoustics, Speech, and Signal Processing*, pages 3313–3317, Florence, Italy.

Patrick Wilken, Tamer Alkhouli, Evgeny Matusov, and Pavel Golik. 2020. Neural simultaneous speech translation using alignment-based chunking. In *International Workshop on Spoken Language Translation*.

Patrick Wilken and Evgeny Matusov. 2019. Novel applications of factored neural machine translation. *arXiv preprint arXiv:1910.03912*.

Albert Zeyer, Tamer Alkhouli, and Hermann Ney. 2018a. RETURNN as a generic flexible neural toolkit with application to translation and speech recognition. In *Proceedings of ACL 2018, Melbourne, Australia, July 15-20, 2018, System Demonstrations*, pages 128–133.

Albert Zeyer, Parnia Bahar, Kazuki Irie, Ralf Schlüter, and Hermann Ney. 2019. A comparison of transformer and lstm encoder decoder models for asr. In *IEEE Automatic Speech Recognition and Understanding Workshop*, pages 8–15, Sentosa, Singapore.

Albert Zeyer, Kazuki Irie, Ralf Schlüter, and Hermann Ney. 2018b. Improved training of end-to-end attention models for speech recognition. In *19th Annual Conf. Interspeech, Hyderabad, India, 2-6 Sep.*, pages 7–11.

Albert Zeyer, Ralf Schlüter, and Hermann Ney. 2016. Towards online-recognition with deep bidirectional LSTM acoustic models. In *Interspeech*, pages 3424–3428, San Francisco, CA, USA.

KIT's IWSLT 2020 SLT Translation System

Ngoc-Quan Pham, Felix Schneider, Tuan-Nam Nguyen, Thanh-Le Ha,
Thai-Son Nguyen, Maximilian Awiszus, Sebastian Stüker, Alexander Waibel
Karlsruhe Institute of Technology
`firstname.lastname@kit.edu`

Abstract

This paper describes KIT's submissions to the IWSLT2020 Speech Translation evaluation campaign. We first participate in the simultaneous translation task, in which our simultaneous models are Transformer-based and can be efficiently trained to obtain low latency with minimized compromise in quality. On the offline speech translation task, we applied our new Speech Transformer architecture to end-to-end speech translation. The obtained model can provide translation quality which is competitive to a complicated cascade. The latter still has the upper hand, thanks to the ability to transparently access to the transcription, and resegment the inputs to avoid fragmentation.

1 Introduction

The Karlsruhe Institute of Technology (KIT) participated in the IWSLT 2020 Evaluation Campaign (Ansari et al., 2020) in two main tracks: Offline Speech Translation task (SLT) and Simultaneous Text Translation. Our highlight s the proposal of a novel method for training simultaneous translation models, with the Adaptive Computation Time technique (Graves, 2016) incorporated to the Transformer models (Vaswani et al., 2017). On the other hand, the end-to-end speech translation models have observed a single deep Speech Transformer (Pham et al., 2019b) approaching the performance of a heavily powered cascade. The latter, however, is more transparent because of visible inputs and outputs to each components. It is still the dominant approach, thanks to the segmentation module that adds punctuations and sentence boundaries, so the MT models do not suffer from fragmentation.

2 Data

The overall data that the project employed can be divided into two main sections: speech and text corpora.

Speech Corpora. We gathered the allowed training data included MuST-C and Speech-Translation TED Talks containing both parallel data for audio to English and German. The TEDLIUM3 and the Mozilla Common Voice data are speech recognition-specific. Furthermore we also considered the How2 dataset (the Portuguese translation is ignored). The data is further cleaned with ASR models (the details are unveiled in Section 4.4) to obtain the training time as shown in Table 1.

Table 1: Speech Training data

Data	Segments	Total time
MuST-C	229K	408h
Speech Translation	142K	160h
TEDLIUM	264K	415h
Common Voice	854K	1490h
How2	217K	360h

Text Corpora. We collected the text parallel training data as presented in Table 2.

Table 2: Text Training Data

Dataset	Sentences
TED Talks (TED)	220K
Europarl (EPPS)	2.2MK
CommonCrawl	2.1M
Rapid	1.21M
ParaCrawl	25.1M
OpenSubtitles	12.6M
WikiTitle	423K
Back-translated News	26M

Proceedings of the 17th International Conference on Spoken Language Translation (IWSLT), pages 55–61
July 9-10, 2020. ©2020 Association for Computational Linguistics
https://doi.org/10.18653/v1/P17

3 Simultaneous Speech Translation

For simultaneous speech translation, we deploy a novel model on the text-to-text task based on Adaptive Computation Time (ACT, Graves (2016)). At each decoder step, the model makes a decision on whether to READ another input token or to WRITE an output token (c. f. Raffel et al. (2017)).

In our case, these decisions are made by a mechanism based on ACT: At each decoder step, we calculate a probability distribution over the encoder timesteps, representing the prediction where the decoder should halt and WRITE an output. Specifically, for decoder step i, we calculate:

$$p_i^n = \sigma(\text{ENERGY}(s_i^n)) \tag{1}$$

$$N(i) = \min\{n' : \sum_{n=1}^{n'} p_i^n \geq 1 - \epsilon\} \tag{2}$$

$$R(i) = 1 - \sum_{n=1}^{N(i)-1} p_i^n \tag{3}$$

$$\alpha_i^n = \begin{cases} R(i) & \text{if } n = N(i) \\ p_i^n & \text{otherwise} \end{cases} \tag{4}$$

It follows from the definition that α_i is a probability distribution. We use this distribution along with the attention mechanism from Arivazhagan et al. (2019) to calculate the encoder-decoder attention. In order to incentivise the model to keep the delays short, we employ the *ponder loss* in addition to the usual cross-entropy:

$$L(\theta) = - \sum_{(\mathbf{x},\mathbf{y})} \log p(\mathbf{y}|\mathbf{x}; \theta) + \lambda\mathcal{C}(\mathbf{n}) \tag{5}$$

$$\mathcal{C} = \sum_{i=1}^{|\mathbf{x}|} N(i) + R(i) \tag{6}$$

For more information on the ponder loss, see (Graves, 2016). By varying the parameter λ, we can produce systems with different latency regimes. However, each model produces many different latency-quality tradeoffs during training.

We use sentencepiece (Kudo and Richardson, 2018) to create a shared 37000 word BPE dictionary for source and target. We then train an offline transformer (Vaswani et al., 2017) model with relative self-attention (Dai et al., 2019). Based on this, we train several ACT models with λ varying from 0.15 to 0.7. For all models, we use the Adam optimizer (Kingma and Ba, 2015). We train the offline model for 200 000 steps, varying the learning rate from $2.5 \cdot 10^{-4}$ to 0 with a cosine schedule, then train each of the simultaneous models for 1000 steps with initializing parameters from the offline model. All models use the transformer "base" configuration (layer size 512, feed-forward size 2048, 8 attention heads, 6 layers in encoder and decoder). Because the evaluation primarily measures delay in terms of tokens, not time, we could have used a larger model, but we decided to choose our model for a more realistic scenario where evaluation time is an important factor.

4 Offline Speech Translation

We participate to the offline speech translation task using two different approaches: cascade and end-to-end. In the cascade, the audio inputs are fed into our Speech Recognition component (ASR - Section 4.1), then the outputs will go through a Segmentation module (Section 4.2) to have well-formed inputs prior to our Machine Translation module (MT - Section 4.3). The outputs of our MT are the final outputs of the cascade system. On the other hand, the end-to-end approach, as its name suggests, performs trainings for a single model from the English audio inputs to produce text outputs in German (Section 4.4).

4.1 Speech Recognition

Data preparation and Segmentation tool We used two different training data sets for this evaluation. Having collected all audios from the TED-LIUM and How2 corpora provided by the organizer, we then generated 40 features of Mel-filterbank coefficients for ASR training models using Janus Recognition Toolkit. We use Sentence-Piece toolkit (Kudo and Richardson, 2018) to train and create 4000 different byte-pair-encoding (BPE) for all models. After that, the WerRTCVAD toolkit (Wiseman, 2016) was used to segment the audio in two unsegmented datasets.

Model We only focus on sequence-to-sequence ASR models, which are based on two different network architectures: The long short-term memory (LSTM) and the Transformer. Our LSTM-based models consist of 6 bidirectional layers of 1024 units for the encoder and 2 unidirectional layers for the decoder (Nguyen et al., 2019). Our transformer-based models presented in (Pham et al., 2019b) consist of 32 blocks for the encoder and 12 blocks for the decoder. Inputs to the LSTM model are

Mel-filterbank features with 40 coefficients. For the Transformer model, we concatenated 4 consecutive features, then combined them with the position information and put them to the self-attention blocks. For LSTM regularization, we applied the dropout rate 0.35 in all LSTM layers, and the embedding dropout rate 0.35 for LSTM. For Transformer regularization, we applied dropout of rate is 0.5 and Stochastic Layers in our models (Pham et al., 2019b).

4.2 Segmentation

Automatic speech recognition (ASR) systems typically do not generate punctuation marks or reliable casing. Using the raw output of these systems as input to MT causes a performance drop due to mismatched train and test conditions. To create segments and better match typical MT training conditions, we use a monolingual NMT system to add sentence boundaries, insert proper punctuation, and add case where appropriate before translating [15]. The idea of the monolingual machine translation system is to translate from lower-cased, without-punctuation text into text with case information and punctuation.

This year, we reuse the segmentation model from (Pham et al., 2019a). We ultilize a transformer-based NMT system to to translate from an English sentence into a sequence of punctuation and casing notations. The training data for that are EPPS, NC and a filtered version of the ParaCrawl corpus. Then, we fine-tune the model on the TED corpus. For more details, please refer to (Pham et al., 2019a).

4.3 Machine Translation

Data Preparation. This year, we use an approximating of 70 millions sentence pairs, coming from TED, EPPS, NC, CommonCrawl, ParaCrawl, Rapid and OpenSubtitles corpora, including around 26 millions back-translation sentence pairs. The data are applied tokenization and smart-casing using the Moses scripts. Furthermore, we segment words into subword units using BPE method (Sennrich et al., 2016). The smartcasing and BPE model are trained on what we call clean datasets (TED, EPPS, NC and CommonCrawl), with the number of BPE merging operation of 40000, jointly learned from English and German sides.

Modeling and Training. Basically our translation system employs Transformer-based encoder-decoder model (Vaswani et al., 2017). Our model comprises of a 12-layer encoder and 12-layer decoder, in which each layer' size is 1024, while the the inner size of feed-forward network inside each layer is 4096. The notable different of our translation model compared to the original Transformer lays on the attention blocks. We implemented Relative Attention following the work of (Dai et al., 2019). The self-attention layers take into account the relative distances between the states instead of using an absolute position encoding scheme by adding the position vectors to the word embeddings. For the encoder, in order to distinguish the two directions of attention (forward and backward), we use negative distances for forward, and positive distances for backward. Each attention block is multi-head attention with 16 heads. We also employ label smoothing in order to regularize the cross-entropy loss. Since we share the vocabularies of the source and target, we are able to tie the embedding weights of the encoder and decoder layers.

Since we utilize a large amount of data, we set dropout at 0.1 and trained for 300000 steps. We use the learning rate schedule with 8000 steps of warming up before linearly scaling down afterwards. We then average five best models according to perplexity on a validation set. We denote this as *Large* configuration.

Domain Adaptation. From the *Large* model, we perform fine-tuning on the TED data, which we consider the in-domain data for the task. In addition to the original TED data, we introduce some noises into a portion of that data and mix this noised data to the original one, then do the fine-tuning. The noises are simply produced by duplicating or deleting n words in some random positions conforming to some distributions[1] and inserting or deleting a punctuation from the original sentence.

The main differences between the *Fine-tuning* configuration and the *Large* configuration is that we apply more strict regularizations, since the fine-tuning data is significantly smaller. Particularly, the dropout is now 0.3, word dropout (Gal and Ghahramani, 2016) is at 0.1 and we also implement switchout (Wang et al., 2018) with the rate of 0.95. Switchout is especially useful when we want to

---

[1] The probability of whether the noise is introduced is $p_{w\_noise} = 0.7$. The distribution of duplicating and deleting a word is $p_{w\_manipulate} = (0.6, 0.4)$. The distribution of how many words ranging from 1 to 3 ($n = 1, 2, 3$) is $p_{w\_num} = (0.6, 0.35, 0.05)$. Those distributions are deliberately chosen after we looked into the outputs of a validation set from our ASR.

simulate the noisy conditions of speech translation, in which the automatic transcripts often contain errors. We train one fine-tuned model from the original TED, and another model with the mix of TED and noised TED with the same *Fine-tuning* configuration. Both of them are trained for 2800 steps with the learning rate of 2 and the same warm-up schedule as before, then again five best models of each are averaged. Finally, we ensemble these two averaged models to be our submitted system.

4.4 End-to-End Model

Corpora The main source of parallel data comes from the MUST-C corpus (Di Gangi et al., 2019b) (only the English-German part) and the Speech Translation data provided by the organizer. The speech features are regenerated with the in-house Janus Recognition Toolkit.

In order to utilize the English audio utterances without aligned German translations, we generate the *synthetic* translations for the available TED Talks in the TEDLIUM dataset and furthermore the large Mozilla Common Voice (CV). Even though these datasets contain their aligned transcriptions, it is still challenging to generate the translations accordingly. The audio segmentation process in the data collection process does not necessarily force the utterances to be encapsulated within sentence borders, and also the transcriptions are often lower-cased and stripped off punctuations. As a result, we used the Transformer-based punctuation model (Cho et al., 2017) to generate punctuations for each utterance. The translation models are trained with the WMT 2018 dataset combined with OpenSubtitles as in (Pham et al., 2019a) (which still satisfy the "constrained" conditions for the evaluation campaign). It is notable that, even though we can generate better translations by using the window technique as in (Cho et al., 2017) to have better sentence boundaries, such method breaks the alignment with audio utterances. Therefore, the generated translation can be incomplete or noisy compared to the translation acquired from the available parallel corpora.

The data is further cleaned from the potential errors (in alignment). These errors can be detected by first training an ASR model, that we based on the Transformer-based ASR (Pham et al., 2019b), and then decoding the audio inputs. We then compute the GLEU score (Wu et al., 2016) between the generated and the annotated transcripts. With the

threshold of 0.67, we removed the utterances with the lower scores, and end up with the training SLT data as in Table 1

During training, the validation data is the Development set of the MuST-C corpus. The reason is that the SLT testsets often do not have the aligned audio and translation, while training end-to-end models often rely on perplexity for early stopping.

Modeling The main architecture is the deep Transformer (Vaswani et al., 2017) with stochastic layers (Pham et al., 2019b). Each model has 32 encoder layers and 12 decoder layers, and they are randomly dropped in training according to the linear schedule presented in the original work, with the top layer has the highest dropout rate $p = 0.5$.

In order to make training stable, we initialized the encoder of the network with the ASR model with the same configuration (so that the parameters can be transferred). We have two intermediate ASR models for this purpose, one is trained on top of TEDLIUM and MuST-C combined, and one learns from the combination of CV, TEDLIUM and MuST-C, serving two different data settings presented in the next section.

With the initialized encoder, the networks can be trained with an aggressive learning rate with 2048 warm-up rate. Label-smoothing and dropout rates are set at 0.1 and 0.25 respectively for all models. Furthermore, all speech inputs are augmented with spectral augmentation (Park et al., 2019; Bahar et al., 2019). All models are trained for 100000 steps, each consists of accumulated 12000 target tokens.

Finally, in order to alleviate the weaknesses of the Transformer models when it comes to dealing with long inputs, such as speech signals, we incorporated the relative position encoding (Dai et al., 2019) into our Transformers. The self-attention layers use the relative distance between states to compute their similarity functions, instead of relying on an absolute position encoding scheme which is vulnerable for this task.

Speech segmentation A big challenge of end-to-end speech translation is audio segmentation, which could harm the performance significantly. The model does not have the ability to re-segment the audio inputs compared to the cascade. Here we simply use the WerRTCVAD toolkit (Wiseman, 2016) to provide the translation model with segments.

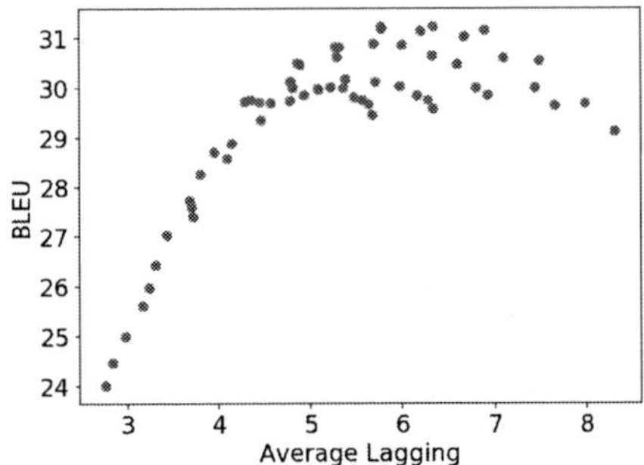

Figure 1: Quality-latency tradeoffs of various checkpoints on the *MUST-C* test set. Metrics are determined by the official evaluation script.

Model	BLEU	AL	DAL	AP
Offline	32.9	18.6	18.6	1.00
High Latency	31.5	6.3	7.2	0.81
Medium Latency	31.4	6.0	6.9	0.80
Low Latency	25.0	3.0	3.8	0.66

Table 3: Performance of our submitted models on the *MUST-C* test set.

4.5 Experimental Results

4.5.1 Simultaneous Translation

We evaluate our model on the *MUST-C* test set, `tst-COMMON`. As each model goes through many different quality-latency trade-offs during training, we evaluated a large number of checkpoints before choosing three models for the low-latency (AL $\leq$ 3), medium latency (AL $\leq$ 6) and high-latency (AL $\leq$ 12) categories. Figure 1 shows all evaluated models on a quality-latency graph. The performance peaks at around 6 Average Lagging, convenient for the medium latency category. Higher latency models can reach similar performance with longer training (the shown models are trained for 1000 steps or less), but only barely exceed the peak at 6 Average Lagging, indicating that that is this model's ideal maximum latency. Table 3 shows the performance of our models on the *MUST-C* test set.

4.5.2 Cascade Offline Speech Translation

Speech Recognition. We tested our ASR systems on two datasets, tst2015 and How2 evaluation set. The ensemble of LSTM-based and Transformer-based sequence-to-sequence model provide the best results, which are 4.1 and 10.6 WERs respectively for two evaluation sets.

Data	tst2015	How2
Transformer-based	6.5	12.5
LSTM-based	4.5	11.5
Ensemble	4.1	10.6

Table 4: WER on tst2015 and How2 sets

Machine Translation. The SLT results on tst2014 are reported in Table 5. By fine-tuning on TED and introducing noises, we are able to gain an improvements of 0.64 BLEU points from the model which is already better than the best model of last year's evaluation.

Table 5: Cascade SLT result on tst2014 (En-De)

System	tst2014 (BLEU)
Large	25.46
TED Finetune	25.90
Noised TED Finetune	26.03
Ensemble	26.10

4.5.3 End-to-end Offline Speech Translation

We tested three different data conditions. The **Small** setup uses only MuST-C as the data. The **Medium** model is trained on MuST-C, Speech-Translation and TEDLIUM. Finally the **Large** one is trained on all data we have including the Mozilla CV. This naming convention only indicates the data size, while the model size and training procedure is kept the same across all settings.

We tested the models on two different setups. The tst-COMMON is provided with the MuST-C and it is not necessary to resegment the translation afterwards to match the translation reference. On the other hand, the tst2014 set requires this step, because depending on the segmentation, the hypothesis and reference can have different alignment. All of the evaluations were performed with cased BLEU scores.

Table 6: SLT BLEU scores on MuST-C test set and tst2014 (En-De)

Data	MuST-C tst-COMMON	tst2014
Small	25.2	-
Medium	30.6	25.4
Large	28.0	23.2
Large+Adapt	28.1	23.3

We obtained the results as in 6. Our **Small** setup has achieved 25.2 BLEU scores on tst-COMMON which already outperformed the best published results on this test set (Di Gangi et al., 2019a). Adding the Speech-Translation and the TEDLIUM data helped us to further improve the result to 30.6. On the other hand, the **Large** setup suffered a 2 BLEU point loss compared to the **Medium** counterpart. This could be the result of the difference in terms of domain between the Mozilla CV and TED Talks, as well as the recording environment and the translation quality obtained with the MT models. However, even adapting these models on the MuST-C and Speech-Translation corpora cannot further improve this setup.

On the tst2014 test set, our end-to-end models achieved the best result with 25.4 BLEU scores, which is closely competitive with the best system in IWSLT 2019 (Pham et al., 2019a), which was 25.7. This indicates that a deep Transformer network can potentially reach the performance of a strong cascade pipeline with mutliple models. Simplicity is the advantage of this setup, however, when the output can be obtained directly after the feature generation step, instead of having several components which have different input and output formats.

5 Conclusion

At the IWSLT2020 evaluation campaign, we first presented a novel simultaneous model that can efficiently learn to wait and translate using ACT technique. Afterwards, we built two systems for offline speech translation, namely a cascade and an end-to-end model using Deep Transformer networks. We showed that the end-to-end model can rival even the best cascade in challenging speech translation tests.

Acknowledgments

The work leading to these results has received funding from the European Union under grant agreement n°825460 and the Federal Ministry of Education and Research (Germany)/DLR Projektträger Bereich Gesundheit under grant agreement n° 01EF1803B.

References

Ebrahim Ansari, Nguyen Bach, Ondrej Bojar, Rol dano Cattoni, Marcello Federico, Christian Federmann, Jiatao Gu, Fei Huang, Ajay Nagesh, Matteo Negri, Jan Niehues, Elizabeth Salesky, Sebastian Stüker, and Marco Turchi. 2020. Findings of the IWSLT 2020 Evaluation Campaign. In *Proceedings of the 17th International Conference on Spoken Language Translation (IWSLT 2020)*, Seattle, USA.

Naveen Arivazhagan, Colin Cherry, Wolfgang Macherey, Chung-Cheng Chiu, Semih Yavuz, Ruoming Pang, Wei Li, and Colin Raffel. 2019. Monotonic infinite lookback attention for simultaneous machine translation. In *Proceedings of the 57th Annual Meeting of the Association for Computational Linguistics*, pages 1313–1323.

Parnia Bahar, Albert Zeyer, Ralf Schlüter, and Hermann Ney. 2019. On using specaugment for end-to-end speech translation. *arXiv preprint arXiv:1911.08876*.

Eunah Cho, Jan Niehues, and Alex Waibel. 2017. NMT-based segmentation and punctuation insertion for real-time spoken language translation. In *Interspeech 2017*. ISCA.

Zihang Dai, Zhilin Yang, Yiming Yang, Jaime Carbonell, Quoc Le, and Ruslan Salakhutdinov. 2019. Transformer-XL: Attentive language models beyond a fixed-length context. In *Proceedings of the 57th Annual Meeting of the Association for Computational Linguistics (ACL)*.

M Di Gangi, Matteo Negri, Viet Nhat Nguyen, Amirhossein Tebbifakhr, and Marco Turchi. 2019a. Data augmentation for end-to-end speech translation: FBK@IWSLT'19. In *Proceedings of the 16th International Workshop on Spoken Language Translation (IWSLT)*.

Mattia A. Di Gangi, Roldano Cattoni, Luisa Bentivogli, Matteo Negri, and Marco Turchi. 2019b. MuST-C: a Multilingual Speech Translation Corpus. In *Proceedings of the Conference of the North American Chapter of the Association for Computational Linguistics (NAACL)*.

Yarin Gal and Zoubin Ghahramani. 2016. A theoretically grounded application of dropout in recurrent neural networks. In *Advances in Neural Information Processing Systems 29 (NIPS)*.

Alex Graves. 2016. Adaptive computation time for recurrent neural networks. *arXiv preprint arXiv:1603.08983*.

Diederik Kingma and Jimmy Ba. 2015. Adam: a method for stochastic optimization (2014). *arXiv preprint arXiv:1412.6980*, 15.

Taku Kudo and John Richardson. 2018. Sentencepiece: A simple and language independent subword tokenizer and detokenizer for neural text processing. In *Proceedings of the 2018 Conference on Empirical Methods in Natural Language Processing: System Demonstrations*, pages 66–71.

Thai-Son Nguyen, Sebastian Stueker, Jan Niehues, and Alex Waibel. 2019. Improving sequence-to-sequence speech recognition training with on-the-fly data augmentation. *arXiv preprint arXiv:1910.13296*.

Daniel S Park, William Chan, Yu Zhang, Chung-Cheng Chiu, Barret Zoph, Ekin D Cubuk, and Quoc V Le. 2019. Specaugment: A simple data augmentation method for automatic speech recognition. *arXiv preprint arXiv:1904.08779*.

Ngoc-Quan Pham, Thai-Son Nguyen, Thanh-Le Ha, Juan Hussain, Felix Schneider, Jan Niehues, Sebastian Stüker, and Alexander Waibel. 2019a. The iwslt 2019 kit speech translation system.

Ngoc-Quan Pham, Thai-Son Nguyen, Jan Niehues, Markus Muller, and Alex Waibel. 2019b. Very deep self-attention networks for end-to-end speech recognition. *arXiv preprint arXiv:1904.13377*.

Colin Raffel, Minh-Thang Luong, Peter J Liu, Ron J Weiss, and Douglas Eck. 2017. Online and linear-time attention by enforcing monotonic alignments. In *Proceedings of the 34th International Conference on Machine Learning-Volume 70*, pages 2837–2846. JMLR. org.

Rico Sennrich, Barry Haddow, and Alexandra Birch. 2016. Neural machine translation of rare words with subword units. *Proceedings of the 54th Annual Meeting of the Association for Computational Linguistics (Volume 1: Long Papers)*.

Ashish Vaswani, Noam Shazeer, Niki Parmar, Jakob Uszkoreit, Llion Jones, Aidan N Gomez, Łukasz Kaiser, and Illia Polosukhin. 2017. Attention is all you need. In *Advances in Neural Information Processing Systems*, pages 5998–6008.

Xinyi Wang, Hieu Pham, Zihang Dai, and Graham Neubig. 2018. SwitchOut: an efficient data augmentation algorithm for neural machine translation. In *Proceedings of the 2018 Conference on Empirical Methods in Natural Language Processing*, pages 856–861, Brussels, Belgium. Association for Computational Linguistics.

John Wiseman. 2016. python-webrtcvad. `https://github.com/wiseman/py-webrtcvad`.

Yonghui Wu, Mike Schuster, Zhifeng Chen, Quoc V Le, Mohammad Norouzi, Wolfgang Macherey, Maxim Krikun, Yuan Cao, Qin Gao, Klaus Macherey, et al. 2016. Google's neural machine translation system: Bridging the gap between human and machine translation. *arXiv preprint arXiv:1609.08144*.

End-to-End Simultaneous Translation System for the IWSLT2020 using Modality Agnostic Meta-Learning

Houjeung Han, Mohd Abbas Zaidi, Sathish Indurthi,
Nikhil Kumar Lakumarapu, Beomseok Lee, Sangha Kim
Next AI Solution Lab, Samsung Research, Seoul, South Korea
{h.j.han, abbas.zaidi, s.indurthi, n07.kumar, bsgunn.lee, sangha01.kim}@samsung.com

Abstract

In this paper, we describe end-to-end simultaneous speech-to-text and text-to-text translation systems submitted to IWSLT2020 online translation challenge. The systems are built by adding wait-k and meta-learning approaches to the Transformer architecture. The systems are evaluated on different latency regimes. The simultaneous text-to-text translation achieved a BLEU score of 26.38 compared to the competition baseline score of 14.17 on the low latency regime (Average latency $\leq$ 3). The simultaneous speech-to-text system improves the BLEU score by 7.7 points over the competition baseline for the low latency regime (Average Latency $\leq$ 1000).

1 Introduction

Simultaneous Neural Machine Translation (SNMT) addresses the problem of live interpretation in machine translation. In a traditional neural machine translation model, the encoder first reads the entire source sequence, and then the decoder generates the translated target sequence. On the other hand, a simultaneous neural machine translation model alternates between reading the source sequence and writing the target sequence using either a fixed or an adaptive policy. This would allow the model to avoid intolerable delay in live or streaming translation scenarios.

In this work, we build a simultaneous translation system for text-to-text(t2t) and speech-to-text(s2t) problems based on Transformer wait-k model (Ma et al., 2019a). We adopt the meta-learning approach presented in (Indurthi et al., 2020) to deal with the data scarcity issue in the speech-to-text translation task. The system architecture and data processing techniques are designed for the IWSLT 2020 online translation task (Ansari et al., 2020). However, these techniques can be applied to current and future SNMT models as well. We conduct several

experiments on both text-to-text and speech-to-text problems to evaluate the proposed system. Our experimental results reveal that the proposed system achieves significant performance gains over the provided competition baselines on both the translation tasks.

2 Simultaneous Translation

2.1 Base Model

The machine translation task involves converting an input sequence $\mathbf{x} = (x_1, x_2, \ldots, x_n)$, $x_i \in \mathbb{R}^{d_x}$ in the source language to the output sequence $\mathbf{y} = (y_1, y_2, \ldots, y_k)$, $y_t \in \mathbb{R}^{d_y}$ in the target language. In the simultaneous translation task, the model produces the output in an online fashion as the input is read. Hence, while producing an output y_t, the complete input sequence might not have been processed .

Our model derives from the transformer wait-k model proposed in (Ma et al., 2019a). Similar to (Ma et al., 2019b), the encoder consists of uni-directional transformer blocks unlike bi-directional transformer blocks used in the original transformer. The decoder starts producing the translation after having read the first k input units from the source sequence. It learns to anticipate the information which might be missing due to word order differences between the input and target sequences. The model also supports training and testing under different latency regimes, i.e., different k.

In the machine translation task, the input and output can have different lengths. This difference is highly prominent for language pairs such as English-Chinese. The average source to target ratio for each language pair(r) is defined as $r = \overline{|\mathbf{y}|/|\mathbf{x}|}$ and the catch-up frequency is defined as $c = r - 1$. For the speech-to-text translation task, $|\mathbf{x}|$ is set to the length of the transcript of input waveform and we define stride, s, which represents the number

Proceedings of the 17th International Conference on Spoken Language Translation (IWSLT), pages 62–68
July 9-10, 2020. ©2020 Association for Computational Linguistics
https://doi.org/10.18653/v1/P17

of frames in the source waveform to be consumed in order to produce each target text token. Usually, s is set to 1 for the text-to-text translation task. The wait-k model adjusts the reading speed of the decoder according to this ratio r and stride s. Hence, the final decoding policy of the model can be defined by the the following equation:

$$g_{wait-k,\,c,s}(t) = \min\{(k + t - 1 - \lfloor ct \rfloor) * s, |x|\},$$

where $g(t)$ is the number of input units processed in order to produce y_t.

2.2 Meta Learning

Recently, (Indurthi et al., 2020) proposed a Modality Agnostic Meta-Learning (MAML, (Finn et al., 2017)) approach to address the data scarcity issue in the speech-to-text translation task. We adopt this approach to train our simultaneous translation task. Here, we briefly describe the MAML approach used for training, for more details, please refer to (Indurthi et al., 2020).

The MAML approach involves two steps: (1) Meta-Learning Phase, (2) Fine-tuning Phase. In the meta-learning phase, we use a set of related high resource tasks as source tasks to train the model. In this phase, the model captures the general learning aspects of the tasks involved. In the fine-tuning phase, we initialize the model from the parameters learned during the meta-learning phase and train further to learn the specific target task.

Meta-Learning Phase: The set of source tasks involved in the meta-learning phase are denoted by T. For each step in this phase, we first uniformly sample one source task $\tau \in T$ and then sample two batches(D_τ and D_τ') of training examples. The D_τ is used to train the model to learn the task specific distribution, and this step is called meta-train step. In each meta-train step, we create auxiliary parameters (θ_τ^a) initialized from the original model parameters (θ^m). We update the auxiliary parameters during this step while keeping the original parameters of the model intact. The auxiliary parameters (θ^a) are updated using gradient-descent steps, which is given by,

$$\theta_\tau^a = \theta^m - \alpha \nabla_{\theta^m} \ell(D_\tau; \theta^m). \qquad (1)$$

After the meta-train step, the auxiliary parameters (θ^a) are evaluated on D_τ' . This step is called meta-test and the gradients computed during this step are used to update the original model parameters(θ^m).

$$\theta_\tau^m = \theta^m - \beta \nabla_{\theta^a} \ell(D_\tau'; \theta^a).` \qquad (2)$$

Exposing the meta-learned parameters((θ^m) to the vast data of the source tasks T during this phase makes them suitable to act as a good initialization point for the future related target tasks.

Fine-tuning Phase: During the fine-tuning phase, the model is initialized from the meta-learned parameters (θ^m) and trained on a specific target task. In this phase, the model training is carried out like a usual neural network training without involving the auxiliary parameters.

2.3 Training

We train our systems with and without using the meta-learning approach described in Section 2.2. In the meta-learning approach, we first pre-train the model on the source tasks and further fine-tune on the target task, which is represented as 'wMT'. We also train another model directly on the given target task without using the meta-learning approach, represented as 'woMT'. The meta-learning training approach helps the low resource tasks to utilize the training examples from the high resource source tasks.

The source tasks used for simultaneous speech-to-text translation are Automatic Speech Recognition (ASR), Machine Translation (MT), and Speech Translation (ST) tasks. Unlike (Indurthi et al., 2020), we also added the ST task as a source task, and this improved the performance of our system further. Even though the simultaneous text-to-text translation task has sufficient training data, we apply the meta-learning training approach to learn possible language representations across different language pairs. We use English-German and French-German language pairs as the source tasks in the meta-training for the text-to-text translation task.

The text sequences are represented as word-piece tokens, and the speech signals are represented as Log Mel 80-dimensional features. Usually, the speech sequences are a few times longer than the text sequences, therefore, we use an additional layer to compress the speech signal and exploit structural locality. The compression layer consists of 3 Convolution layers with stride 2, both on the time and frequency domain of the speech sequence. The compressed speech sequence is passed to the encoder layer for further processing. To facilitate

Pair \ Dataset	Must-C	OpenSubtitles	WMT19	All
EnDe	229k	22.5m	38m	61m
FrDe	-	-	9.8m	9.8m

Table 1: Dataset Statistics for T2T

Dataset \ Wait-k	4	7	8	15	Offline
All	25.50	28.31	28.80	29.70	-
All + BT	25.06	28.22	28.71	-	-
All_reduced	26.04	28.57	29.07	30.27	31.20

Table 2: Comparing Datasets for T2T

Task	Dataset	Hours	Sent. #
MT	Open Subtitles	-	22.5m
MT	WMT 19	-	4.6m
ASR	LibriSpeech	982	233k
ASR	IWSLT 19 ST	272	145k
ASR	MuST-C	400	229k
ASR	TED LIUM 3	452	28.6k
ST	Europarl-ST	89	97.9k
ST	IWSLT ST 19	272	726k
ST	MuST-C	400	918k
ST	TED-LIUM 3	452	537k

Table 3: Dataset Statistics for S2T

the training on multiple language pairs and tasks, we create a universal vocabulary ((Gu et al., 2018a)) for both text-to-text and speech-to-text translation systems. The universal vocabularies are created based on the source and target tasks.

For each simultaneous task, we train the system on a dataset D of parallel sequences to maximize the the log likelihood:

$$\ell(D; \theta) = \frac{1}{|D|} \sum_{i=1}^{|D|} \log p\left(\boldsymbol{y}^i | \boldsymbol{x}^i; \theta\right), \quad (3)$$

where θ denotes the parameters of the model. We train the systems for three different latency regimes based on the competition requirements.

3 Experiments

3.1 Datasets

3.1.1 Simultaneous Text-to-Text Translation

For the text-to-text translation task, we use the MuST-C, IWSLT 2020, OpenSubtitles2018, and WMT19 (presented as 'All' in the Table 2) for training. We evaluate our system on the MuST-C Dev set. Our parallel corpus of WMT19 consists of Europarl v9, ParaCrawl v3, Common Crawl, News Commentary v14, Wiki Titles v1 and Document-split Rapid for the German-English language pair. We also use the WMT19 German-French language pair as one of the source tasks during the meta-learning training phase. The statistics of the data we use for text-to-text translation are provided in the Table 1. We also use monolingual data from the News crawl corpus for data augmentation using back-translation technique. About 20M English sentences are translated by the En-De translation model, which was trained on the WMT19 corpus (presented as 'All + BT' in the Table 2). Due to the presence of noise in the OpenSubtitles2018

and ParaCrawl, we use only 10M randomly sampled examples from these corpora (presented as 'All_reduced' in the Table 2).

3.1.2 Simultaneous Speech-to-Text Translation

The speech-to-text translation models are trained on examples collected from the Must-C, IWSLT 2020, Europarl-ST, and TED-LIUM3 datasets. The statistics for the same are provided in the Table 3. The models are evaluated using the MuST-C Dev set. Due to the limited availability of training examples for the ST task, we increase the number of training examples by using data augmentation techniques. For data augmentation on the text side, we use English-to-German NMT model to generate synthetic German sequences from the English sequences. We use two NMT models and top-K beam results to generate multiple synthetic German sequences. These NMT models are based on the Transformer architecture and trained on the WMT19 dataset with different hyper-parameter settings. For speech sequence, we use the Sox library to generate the speech signal using different values of speed, echo, and tempo parameters similar to (Potapczyk et al., 2019). The parameter values are uniformly sampled using these ranges for each parameter: tempo $\in (0.85, 1.3)$, speed $\in (0.95, 1.05)$, echo_delay $\in (20, 200)$, and echo_decay $\in (0.05, 0.2)$. We increase the size of the IWSLT2020 ST dataset to five times of the original size by augmenting 4X data – four text sequences using the NMT models and four speech signals using the Sox parameter ranges. For the Europarl-ST, we augment 2X examples to triple the size. The TED-LIUM3 dataset does not contain speech-to-text translation examples originally, hence, we create 2X synthetic speech-to-text trans-

Train-k^t	4		7		8		26		27		28	
Decode-k	BLEU	AL	BLEU	AL	BLEU	AL	BLEU	AL	BLEU	AL	BLEU	AL
k^t	$26.04^\oplus$	2.84	28.57^*	5.15	29.07	5.85	30.78	14.59	30.16	14.93	30.48	15.17
$k^t - 1$	24.32	2.06	28.24	4.47	29.07^*	5.15	30.73	14.27	30.13	14.60	30.48	14.89
$k^t - 3$	17.98	0.32	$26.38^\oplus$	2.93	27.75	3.71	30.69	13.58	30.21	13.96	30.49	14.27

Table 4: Varying k during Testing for T2T: k^t denotes k used for training

Latency regimes		Low			Medium			High		
Methods	Dataset	BLEU	AL	k	BLEU	AL	k	BLEU	AL	k
Fairseq	Must-C	14.17	2.91	4	17.28	5.88	8	19.53	12.37	20
woMT	All_reduced	26.04	2.84	4	29.07	5.85	8	30.78	14.59	26
wMT	All_reduced	25.31	2.83	4	28.75	5.76	8	30.08	14.57	26

Table 5: Comparing Training Strategies for T2T

lations using speech-to-text transcripts. Finally, for the MuST-C datasest, we use synthetic speech to increase the dataset size to 4X. Overall, we created the synthetic training data of size roughly equal to two times the original data using data augmentation techniques described above.

3.2 Implementation Details

For the text-to-text translation, we use base parameter settings from the Transformer model (Vaswani et al., 2017), except that we use uni-directional encoder. Each model is trained for 500k steps with a batch size of 4096 tokens. The source tasks used in the meta-training phase are English-German and French-German language pairs. The stride s is set to 1.

For the speech-to-text translation, the number of encoder and decoder layers are 8 and 6, respectively. The compression layer consists of three Convolutional layers. Each model is trained for 300k meta steps and fine-tuned for another 300k with a text batch size of 4096 tokens and a speech batch size of 1.5M frames. The models are trained using the multi-step Adam optimizer (Saunders et al., 2018) with the gradients accumulated over 32 steps.

Our code is based on the Tensor2Tensor framework (Vaswani et al., 2018), and we use 4*NVIDIA P40 GPUs for all the experiments. We use the server-client API based evaluation code provided by the organizers of the IWSLT2020 online translation challenge. This evaluation API gives several metrics to measure the translation quality and latency, such as BLEU, METEOR, TER, Differentiable Average Lagging(DAL), Average Lagging(AL) and Average Proportion (AP). In this paper, we report the BLEU scores along with the

AL. We also report the numbers from the baselines provided by the organizing committee in the Table 5 and 7. All the results are reported on the MuST-C Dev set, unless stated otherwise. The emission rate r of German-English is set to 1.0. Moreover, we use the same parameter value for k and s during training and testing, unless stated otherwise.

4 Results

4.1 Simultaneous Text-to-Text Translation

We train our models on different dataset sizes which are created by using back translation and sampling techniques and compare the performance across these datasets. The BLEU scores with various wait-k values for models trained on different dataset sizes have been reported in the Table 2. As we can see in the Table 2, the augmented dataset ('All + BT') performs poorly compared to the model trained on the original dataset. On the contrary, the reduced dataset gives best performance among all these datasets. All these models are trained using the *woMT* training strategy.

Motivated by (Ma et al., 2019a), we decode the target text using smaller k values than the k value used during the training. As one can observe (by comparing the marked cells) in the Table 4, the result obtained from a model upon decoding using $k = 7$, when trained using $k = 8$ is better than the model which is both trained and decoded using $k = 7$. A similar trend is also observed for $k = 4$. Also, as train-k or decode-k increases, usually the BLEU and the AL also increases. However, this trend is limited to the low or medium latency regimes, since the models with larger k are less sensitive to k value and the performance degrades as k reaches towards the input sequence length. For

Train-k^t/s^t	3/300		4/350		3/400		4/800		5/800	
Decode-k/s	BLEU	AL	BLEU	AL	BLEU	AL	BLEU	AL	BLEU	AL
k^t/s^t	12.85	1136.11	14.59	1875.04	15.89	1940.67	17.95	3967.49	17.42	4318.34
k^t-1/s^t	12.24	897.79	13.88	1539.73	14.9	1653.62	17.79	3582.93	17.43	4002.83
k^t/s^t-100	7.16	45.48	10.77	715.92	12.79	1084.11	17.81	3679.68	17.14	4027.91

Table 6: Varying k/s during Testing for S2T: k^t/s^t denote k/s used during training

Latency regimes		Low				Medium				High			
Methods	Dataset	BLEU	AL	k	s	BLEU	AL	k	s	BLEU	AL	k	s
Fairseq	Must-C	4.5	792.28	1	320	9.3	1828.28	2	400	11.49	3664.19	2	800
woMT	iwslt20_aug	6.70	1061.90	3	300	9.11	1882.17	3	400	12.59	4020.97	4	800
wMT	iwslt20_aug	12.85	1136.11	3	300	15.89	1940.67	3	400	17.95	3967.49	4	800

Table 7: Comparing the Training Strategies for S2T

example, the model trained with $k = 26$ has the highest BLEU score among the models trained on k values ranging from 26 to 28. All the models reported in the Table 4 use the All_reduced dataset and the *woMT* training approach.

We compare the *wMT* and *woMT* training strategies on three latency regimes. The results have been tabulated in the Table 5. Unlike speech translation, we did not witness any improvement in the text-translation from the meta-learning approach. In the Table 5, models trained using the *woMT* strategy achieved a better results than the *wMT* strategy. A possible reason for this might be that the English-German text translation problem is not suffering from data scarcity. Moreover, the number or diversity of source tasks used for meta-learning training is limited compared to the speech-to-text translation source tasks. We also observe that English-German and French-German corpus have an overlap of over 70% German words limiting the variability of the source tasks, which hampers the model from learning any meta-aspects of the text translation tasks during the meta-learning phase. This might be the reason behind meta-training being less effective for online text-to-text task.

4.2 Simultaneous Speech-to-Text Translation

Similar to the online text-to-text task, we vary the latency parameters while decoding the simultaneous speech model as well. We vary both k and strides(s), and report the BLEU in the Table 4. We can see from the Table 6 that as k and s increase, the BLEU score increases while AL decreases. Unlike the text-to-text translation, decoding with decreased k and s does not result in any BLEU score improvement. For instance, as seen in the Table 6, the result of model trained with 5/800(where $k = 5$ and stride $s = 800$) and decoded with 4/800 shows lower performance than that of the model both trained and decoded using 4/800. Also, a similar trend can be observed between the models trained with 3/400 and 3/300. As we can see in the last two columns, the BLEU score decreases as k increases from 4 to 5 for $s = 800$. This is similar to what we observed in the text case as well, increasing k in the high latency regime leads to a drop in the performance. All the models reported in the Table 6 are trained using the augmented datasets and the *wMT* training approach.

Finally, we explore the effectiveness of the meta-learning approach for the online speech-to-text translation task for the three latency regimes. In the Table 7, we can easily see that there is a significant BLEU score gap between models trained using the *wMT* and *woMT* training strategy. The results show that our meta-learning approach improves the performance of the models in all the latency regimes. Compared to the online text-to-text translation task, the meta-learning approach in the online speech-to-text task exploits many sub-problems with a variety of source tasks such as ASR, MT and ST. Also, the speech-to-text task suffers severely from the data-scarcity issue as compared to the text-to-text task, and using the meta-learning approach helps overcome this issue.

5   Related Work

Simultaneous Translation: The earlier works in simultaneous translation such as (Cho and Esipova, 2016; Gu et al., 2016; Press and Smith, 2018; Dalvi et al., 2018) lack the ability to anticipate the words with missing source context. The wait-k model introduced by (Ma et al., 2019a) brought in many improvements by introducing a simultaneous translation module which can be easily integrated into most of the sequence to sequence models. Arivazhagan et al. (2019) introduced MILk which is capable of learning an adaptive schedule by using hierarchical attention; hence it performs better on the latency quality trade-off. Wait-k and MILk are both capable of anticipating words and achieving specified latency requirements by varying the hyper-parameters.

Speech to Text Translation: Most of the existing systems tackle the problem of simultaneous speech to text translation using a cascaded pipeline of online ASR and MT systems.

Previous works such as (Niehues et al., 2016);(Ari et al., 2020) propose re-translation strategies for simultaneous speech translation, but their use case is limited to settings where output revision is allowed.

Although there has been some work towards making an end-to-end offline speech translation modules, the paucity of training datasets remains a bottleneck. The work done by (Ma et al., 2019a) cannot simply be extended to the domain of simultaneous speech translation as we discussed earlier. Similar to our model (Gu et al., 2016) also uses a pre-trained model for the simultaneous translation task. However, they use a full-sentence model during pre-training, unlike ours. Our proposed model alleviates these issues, both our pre-training and fine-tuning training phases are done in an online fashion, hence avoiding any train-inference discrepancies. Our model has a controllable latency which can be specified by k.

Meta Learning: Meta-Learning approaches have been particularly useful with low resource problems since they inherently learn to adapt to a new problem with less training examples. Andrychowicz et al. (2016); Ha et al. (2016) focuses more on the meta policy while MAML system proposed by (Finn et al., 2017) focuses more on finding a good initialization point for the target tasks. The work done by (Indurthi et al., 2020) and (Gu et al., 2018b) employ the MAML algorithm for low resource settings in offline speech-to-text and text-to-text translation task. In this work, we adopt these strategies to the online translation tasks.

6 Conclusion

In this work, we develop an end-to-end simultaneous translation system for both text-to-text and speech-to-text tasks by using the wait-k method and the meta-learning approach. We evaluate the proposed system with different data settings and latency regimes. We explore the effectiveness of the meta-learning approach for the online translation tasks. The meta-learning approach proves to be essential in settings where the training data is scarce. Compared to the baseline provided in the competition, both online text-to-text and speech-to-text models achieved significant BLEU score improvements.

References

Marcin Andrychowicz, Misha Denil, Sergio Gomez, Matthew W Hoffman, David Pfau, Tom Schaul, Brendan Shillingford, and Nando De Freitas. 2016. Learning to learn by gradient descent by gradient descent. In *Advances in neural information processing systems*, pages 3981–3989.

Ebrahim Ansari, Amittai Axelrod, Nguyen Bach, Ondrej Bojar, Roldano Cattoni, Fahim Dalvi, Nadir Durrani, Marcello Federico, Christian Federmann, Jiatao Gu, Fei Huang, Kevin Knight, Xutai Ma, Ajay Nagesh, Matteo Negri, Jan Niehues, Juan Pino, Elizabeth Salesky, Xing Shi, Sebastian Stüker, Marco Turchi, and Changhan Wang. 2020. Findings of the IWSLT 2020 Evaluation Campaign. In *Proceedings of the 17th International Conference on Spoken Language Translation (IWSLT 2020)*, Seattle, USA.

Naveen Ari, Colin Andrew Cherry, I Te, Wolfgang Macherey, Pallavi Baljekar, and George Foster. 2020. Re-translation strategies for long form, simultaneous, spoken language translation.

Naveen Arivazhagan, Colin Cherry, Wolfgang Macherey, Chung-Cheng Chiu, Semih Yavuz, Ruoming Pang, Wei Li, and Colin Raffel. 2019. Monotonic infinite lookback attention for simultaneous machine translation. *arXiv preprint arXiv:1906.05218*.

Kyunghyun Cho and Masha Esipova. 2016. Can neural machine translation do simultaneous translation? *arXiv preprint arXiv:1606.02012*.

Fahim Dalvi, Nadir Durrani, Hassan Sajjad, and Stephan Vogel. 2018. Incremental decoding and training methods for simultaneous translation in neural machine translation. In *Proceedings of the 2018 Conference of the North American Chapter of the Association for Computational Linguistics: Human Language Technologies, Volume 2 (Short Papers)*, pages 493–499, New Orleans, Louisiana. Association for Computational Linguistics.

Chelsea Finn, Pieter Abbeel, and Sergey Levine. 2017. Model-agnostic meta-learning for fast adaptation of deep networks. In *Proceedings of the 34th International Conference on Machine Learning-Volume 70*, pages 1126–1135. JMLR. org.

Jiatao Gu, Hany Hassan, Jacob Devlin, and Victor O.K. Li. 2018a. Universal neural machine translation for extremely low resource languages. In *Proceedings of the 2018 Conference of the North American Chapter of the Association for Computational Linguistics: Human Language Technologies, Volume 1 (Long Papers)*, pages 344–354, New Orleans, Louisiana. Association for Computational Linguistics.

Jiatao Gu, Graham Neubig, Kyunghyun Cho, and Victor OK Li. 2016. Learning to translate in real-time with neural machine translation. *arXiv preprint arXiv:1610.00388*.

Jiatao Gu, Yong Wang, Yun Chen, Kyunghyun Cho, and Victor OK Li. 2018b. Meta-learning for low-resource neural machine translation. *arXiv preprint arXiv:1808.08437*.

David Ha, Andrew Dai, and Quoc V Le. 2016. Hypernetworks. *arXiv preprint arXiv:1609.09106*.

S. Indurthi, H. Han, N. K. Lakumarapu, B. Lee, I. Chung, S. Kim, and C. Kim. 2020. End-end speech-to-text translation with modality agnostic meta-learning. In *ICASSP 2020 - 2020 IEEE International Conference on Acoustics, Speech and Signal Processing (ICASSP)*, pages 7904–7908.

Mingbo Ma, Liang Huang, Hao Xiong, Renjie Zheng, Kaibo Liu, Baigong Zheng, Chuanqiang Zhang, Zhongjun He, Hairong Liu, Xing Li, Hua Wu, and Haifeng Wang. 2019a. STACL: Simultaneous translation with implicit anticipation and controllable latency using prefix-to-prefix framework. In *Proceedings of the 57th Annual Meeting of the Association for Computational Linguistics*, pages 3025–3036, Florence, Italy. Association for Computational Linguistics.

Xutai Ma, Juan Pino, James Cross, Liezl Puzon, and Jiatao Gu. 2019b. Monotonic multihead attention. *arXiv preprint arXiv:1909.12406*.

Jan Niehues, Thai Son Nguyen, Eunah Cho, Thanh-Le Ha, Kevin Kilgour, Markus Müller, Matthias Sperber, Sebastian Stüker, and Alex Waibel. 2016. Dynamic transcription for low-latency speech translation. In *Interspeech*, pages 2513–2517.

Tomasz Potapczyk, Pawel Przybysz, Marcin Chochowski, and Artur Szumaczuk. 2019. Samsung's system for the iwslt 2019 end-to-end speech translation task. Zenodo.

Ofir Press and Noah A Smith. 2018. You may not need attention. *arXiv preprint arXiv:1810.13409*.

Danielle Saunders, Felix Stahlberg, Adrià de Gispert, and Bill Byrne. 2018. Multi-representation ensembles and delayed SGD updates improve syntax-based NMT. In *Proceedings of the 56th Annual Meeting of the Association for Computational Linguistics (Volume 2: Short Papers)*, pages 319–325, Melbourne, Australia. Association for Computational Linguistics.

Ashish Vaswani, Samy Bengio, Eugene Brevdo, Francois Chollet, Aidan N. Gomez, Stephan Gouws, Llion Jones, Łukasz Kaiser, Nal Kalchbrenner, Niki Parmar, Ryan Sepassi, Noam Shazeer, and Jakob Uszkoreit. 2018. Tensor2tensor for neural machine translation. *CoRR*, abs/1803.07416.

Ashish Vaswani, Noam Shazeer, Niki Parmar, Jakob Uszkoreit, Llion Jones, Aidan N Gomez, Łukasz Kaiser, and Illia Polosukhin. 2017. Attention is all you need. In *Advances in neural information processing systems*, pages 5998–6008.

DiDi Labs' End-to-End System for the IWSLT 2020 Offline Speech Translation Task

Arkady Arkhangorodsky, Yiqi Huang, Amittai Axelrod
DiDi Labs
4640 Admiralty Way
Marina del Rey, CA 90292
{arkadyarkhangorodsky, yiqihuang, amittai}@didiglobal.com

Abstract

We describe the DiDi Labs system submitted for the IWSLT 2020 Offline Speech Translation Task (Ansari et al., 2020). We trained an end-to-end system that translates audio from English TED talks to German text, without producing intermediate English text. Our base system used the S-Transformer architecture (Di Gangi et al., 2019b), trained using the MuST-C dataset (Di Gangi et al., 2019a). We extended the system via decoder pre-training, pre-trained speech features, and text translation, but these extensions did not yield improved results.

1 Introduction

The performance of end-to-end speech translation systems at IWSLT has been approaching that of cascaded systems, with the gap shrinking to 1.5 BLEU points in 2019 (Niehues et al., 2019). With additional effort, end-to-end systems could finally surpass cascaded systems. The 2020 task required participants to translate audio from English TED talks to German text.

We trained several different end-to-end speech translation systems. We used the MuST-C dataset to train models for speech translation and speech recognition, the Europarl-ST dataset for speech recognition (Iranzo-Sánchez et al., 2019), and the WMT-19 news commentary dataset for text translation (Tiedemann, 2012). Our best performing model used an encoder that was first pre-trained for English speech recognition, and then fine-tuned for speech translation. This system scored 17.1 BLEU on the MuST-C test set.

2 Experimental Framework

Our models used the S-Transformer architecture of Di Gangi et al.. This is an adaptation of the Transformer architecture (Vaswani et al., 2017) for speech inputs. The encoder performs a 2-D convolution on the audio input before applying self-attention as in the Transformer. Another distinction is that the decoder operates at the character level, instead on the byte-pair encoding (BPE) tokenization that is typically used with transformer models for text. The system uses a 512-dimensional embedding in the self-attention layers. Each of the encoder and decoder have 8-headed attention and 6 self-attention layers. The models have 32,132,040 parameters.

Each of our models were run on a single Nvidia Tesla P-100 GPU. We used a batch size of 8, and the Adam optimizer with a learning rate of 0.005 and an inverse square root warm-up schedule starting from 0.0003 for the first 4000 training steps. Each model was trained for up to 50 epochs, stopping early when validation loss had not decreased for 10 consecutive epochs.

We trained 6 models using different methods. We used the German transcripts and German audio from Europarl-ST for decoder pre-training. We used the WMT News Commentary parallel corpus for text translation. All other experiments used the MuST-C dataset. Table 1 contains the statistics for the corpora we used.

3 Extending S-Transformer

3.1 Naïve Model

Our simplest model was the S-Transformer, trained end-to-end on the MuST-C corpus using English audio inputs and German text outputs. This model was not able to successfully learn the task, achieving a score of 0 BLEU on the MuST-C test set. This is not surprising, as the relationship between the English audio and German text is not obvious without prior knowledge, even to most humans. This model effectively learned to memorize the most common output sentence from

Proceedings of the 17th International Conference on Spoken Language Translation (IWSLT), pages 69–72
July 9-10, 2020. ©2020 Association for Computational Linguistics
https://doi.org/10.18653/v1/P17

Dataset	Segments	Input	Output
MuST-C training	229,703	EN Audio	EN, DE Text
MuST-C dev	1,423	EN Audio	EN, DE Text
MuST-C test	2,641	EN Audio	EN, DE Text
WMT news commentary	338,285	EN Text	DE Text
Europarl-ST training	12,904	DE Audio	DE Text
Europarl-ST dev	2,603	DE Audio	DE Text

Table 1: Details of the datasets we use in our experiments

the training set ("Vielen Dank"), and produced this as output every time.

3.2 Encoder Pre-Training

The task was too difficult for a naïve system to learn from scratch, so we tried training it in two stages. First, the system was trained to predict English text given the English audio inputs from the MuST-C dataset. This model successfully learned to transcribe English audio, achieving a BLEU score on the MuST-C validation set of 60.45. [1]

We then discarded the *decoder* from this English ASR system. The rest of the model was then fine-tuned to predict German text from English audio. We were thus able to train an end-to-end system in stages without having the intermediate inputs and outputs inherent to a cascaded system.

By first learning the simpler task of speech recognition, the system was able to make sense of the audio input before attempting to learn to translate it. This system was the strongest that we trained, achieving a BLEU score of 17.1 on the MuST-C test set.

3.3 Decoder Pre-Training

Pre-training the encoder using the simpler speech recognition task was successful, so we attempted to similarly pre-train just the *decoder*, except for German speech recognition instead.

We started by training a German ASR system using the same initial S-Transformer architecture as in Section 3.2. Here we trained the ASR system on German audio inputs and German text outputs from the Europarl-ST dataset. This system successfully learned to transcribe German audio, achieving a score on the Europarl-ST validation set of 36.9 BLEU.

The rest of the training was analogous to the pre-trained encoder system: the *encoder* of this

model was discarded, then the model was trained on the speech translation task. However, this model performed similarly to the naïve system.

This suggests that just learning the input audio without a corresponding text in the same language remains a key challenge. This is perhaps not surprising, as audio input and a text transcript operate at different timescales: text inputs have atomic elements, but audio inputs are not only subdivisible via faster sampling, but also overlapping in time if the stride distance is short.

3.4 Combining Pre-Trained Encoder and Pre-Trained Decoder

Although we were not able to fine-tune the pre-trained decoder system of Section 3.3 to produce a strong speech translation model, we wondered if it could still could be a useful addition to a system with a pre-trained encoder. We fine-tuned an end-to-end model that started with the encoder trained for English ASR, and the decoder trained for German ASR. However, this model was only about as good as using only the pre-trained encoder. Perhaps this approach could produce stronger results if the encoded representations of the encoder and decoder were aligned to one another, as occurs when learning seq2seq models from scratch.

4 Using wav2vec Inputs

The MuST-C corpus represents the input audio using 40-dimensional Mel-Filterbank features. Schneider et al. (2019) presented `wav2vec`: unsupervised pre-training to learn speech representations, with improved speech recognition results. We attempted to apply this same approach to speech translation, replacing the Mel-Filterbank features with `wav2vec` features as input to the system.

We use the pre-trained model released in the `fairseq` library[2] to compute features for the

---

[1] We used the BLEU score instead of standard ASR metrics to simplify our implementation. This metric was mainly used to determine whether or not the model was useful as a starting point for fine-tuning; the value of the score was less significant.

[2] `https://github.com/pytorch/fairseq/tree/master/examples/wav2vec`

MuST-C dataset. `wav2vec` features are 512-dimensional vectors, but the Mel-Filterbank features are 40-element vectors. We applied principal component analysis (PCA) to reduce the `wav2vec` vectors to 40 dimensions to match the existing architecture. To reduce the computational load, we simply computed the PCA transformation on the first segment of the training set, and then applied the same transformation matrix to each subsequent sample.

We then attempted to pre-train the encoder for English ASR using the same S-Transformer architecture as before, in Section 3.2. However, this model does not successfully learn to transcribe English audio during pre-training. After fine-tuning, it cannot translate English audio and also gets a score of 0 BLEU.

We suspected our dimensionality reduction from 512 to 40 was too crude, losing too much information. To see if this was the case, we also attempted to use the full 512-dimensional `wav2vec` features as input, and increased the system layer widths accordingly. However, computational constraints limited us to only training on 20,000 segments of the MuST-C training set. However, this model also does not successfully learn to transcribe English audio during pre-training. After fine-tuning, it still cannot translate English audio and also gets a score of 0 BLEU.

5   Text translation multi-task training

Strong text translation systems are often trained on many millions of sentences, if they are available. Transcribing audio and translating is more expensive than finding parallel sentences, so the MuST-C corpus is considerably smaller than text translation corpora. We hypothesized that additional training on translation data would improve performance.

We pre-trained an English to German MT system that shared the decoder with our S-Transformer system in Section 3.2, in order to improve the decoder's translation ability. This model used a standard transformer encoder, not the S-Transformer. Unfortunately after training, this model was not able to successfully learn to translate text, though this same corpus has been successfully used in previous work (Barrault et al., 2019). We did not conduct further experiments trying to use the shared decoder in this model for speech translation.

Model	BLEU
1. Baseline S-Transformer model	0.00
2. #1 + encoder pre-trained on English ASR	**17.1**
3. #1 + decoder pre-trained on German ASR	0.00
4. #1 + #2 + #3	16.8
5. #2 + `wav2vec` preprocessing	0.00
6. #1 + text translation multi-task training	0.00

Table 2: BLEU scores of our experiments, evaluated on the MuST-C test set

6   Results and Conclusion

Table 2 contains our experimental results. The model using an encoder pre-trained for English speech recognition performed best. Combining this model with a decoder pre-trained for German speech recognition performed roughly similarly.

We have presented several different experiments in training end-to-end speech translation system based on the S-Transformer architecture. Unfortunately, none of the experiments we presented were able to improve performance on the MuST-C test set relative to the models of Di Gangi et al. (2019c). With more work, the ideas we attempted could produce stronger systems in the future.

References

Ebrahim Ansari, Amittai Axelrod, Nguyen Bach, Ondrej Bojar, Roldano Cattoni, Fahim Dalvi, Nadir Durrani, Marcello Federico, Christian Federmann, Jiatao Gu, Fei Huang, Kevin Knight, Xutai Ma, Ajay Nagesh, Matteo Negri, Jan Niehues, Juan Pino, Elizabeth Salesky, Xing Shi, Sebastian Stüker, Marco Turchi, and Changhan Wang. 2020. Findings of the IWSLT 2020 Evaluation Campaign. *Proceedings of the 17th International Conference on Spoken Language Translation (IWSLT 2020)*.

Loïc Barrault, Ondřej Bojar, Marta R. Costa-Jussà, Christian Federmann, Mark Fishel, Yvette Graham, Barry Haddow, Matthias Huck, Philipp Koehn, Shervin Malmasi, Christof Monz, Mathias Müller, Santanu Pal, Matt Post, and Marcos Zampieri. 2019. Findings of the 2019 Conference on Machine Translation (WMT19). *WMT Conference on Machine Translation*.

Mattia A. Di Gangi, Roldano Cattoni, Luisa Bentivogli, Matteo Negri, and Marco Turchi. 2019a. MuST-C: a Multilingual Speech Translation Corpus. *NAACL (North American Association for Computational Linguistics)*.

Mattia A. Di Gangi, Matteo Negri, Roldano Cattoni, Roberto Dessi, and Marco Turchi. 2019b. Enhancing Transformer for End-to-End Speech-to-Text Translation. *MT Summit*.

Mattia A. Di Gangi, Matteo Negri, and Marco Turchi. 2019c. Adapting Transformer to End-to-End Spoken Language Translation. *INTERSPEECH*.

Javier Iranzo-Sánchez, Joan Albert Silvestre-Cerdà, Javier Jorge, Nahuel Roselló, Adrià Giménez, Albert Sanchis, Jorge Civera, and Alfons Juan. 2019. Europarl-ST: A Multilingual Corpus For Speech Translation Of Parliamentary Debates. *arXiv [cs.CL]*.

Jan Niehues, Roldano Cattoni, Sebastian Stüker, Matteo Negri, Marco Turchi, Elizabeth Salesky, R. Sanabria, Loïc Barrault, Lucia Specia, and Marcello Federico. 2019. The IWSLT 2019 Evaluation Campaign. *IWSLT (International Workshop on Spoken Language Translation)*.

Steffen Schneider, Alexei Baevski, Ronan Collobert, and Michael Auli. 2019. wav2vec: Unsupervised Pre-Training for Speech Recognition. *arXiv [cs.CL]*.

Jörg Tiedemann. 2012. Parallel data, tools and interfaces in OPUS. *LREC (International Conference on Language Resources and Evaluation)*.

Ashish Vaswani, Noam Shazeer, Niki Parmar, Jakob Uszkoreit, Llion Jones, Aidan N Gomez, Łukasz Kaiser, and Illia Polosukhin. 2017. Attention Is All You Need. *NeurIPS (Neural Information Processing Systems)*.

End-to-End Offline Speech Translation System for IWSLT 2020 using Modality Agnostic Meta-Learning

Nikhil Kumar Lakumarapu*, Beomseok Lee*, Sathish Indurthi,
Houjeung Han, Mohd Abbas Zaidi, Sangha Kim
Next AI Solution Lab, Samsung Research, Seoul, South Korea
{n07.kumar, bsgunn.lee, s.indurthi, h.j.han, abbas.zaidi, sangha01.kim}@samsung.com

Abstract

In this paper, we describe the system submitted to the IWSLT 2020 Offline Speech Translation Task. We adopt the Transformer architecture coupled with the meta-learning approach to build our end-to-end Speech-to-Text Translation (ST) system. Our meta-learning approach tackles the data scarcity of the ST task by leveraging the data available from Automatic Speech Recognition (ASR) and Machine Translation (MT) tasks. The meta-learning approach combined with synthetic data augmentation techniques improves the model performance significantly and achieves BLEU scores of 24.58, 27.51, and 27.61 on IWSLT test 2015, MuST-C test, and Europarl-ST test sets respectively.

1 Introduction

The goal of the IWSLT 2020 Offline Speech Translation challenge(Ansari et al., 2020) is to check the feasibility of end-to-end models for translating audio speech of one language into text of a different target language. The success of end-to-end neural models for ASR (Graves et al., 2013) and MT (Bahdanau et al., 2015) inspired to build end-to-end neural models for the more challenging Speech-to-Text translation (ST) task (Bérard et al., 2016). Traditionally the ST systems are built by cascading ASR and MT systems (Ney, 1999). However, the cascaded system suffers from error propagation, latency, and memory requirement issues. Although these issues can be addressed using end-to-end ST models, it is hard to collect such data for training these models.

In this work, we build an end-to-end ST system which not only addresses the issues of a cascaded system but also works with limited training data. The proposed system is fine-tuned towards

IWSLT 2020 Offline Speech-Translation Task [1]. However, the proposed training strategies and the data augmentation techniques can be adopted into existing and future ST models. We adopt the meta-learning approach proposed for ST task (Indurthi et al., 2019) to train our system. The meta-learning based training approach not only allows us to leverage huge amounts of training data available in ASR and MT tasks but also helps to find a good initialization point for the target ST task.

We conduct several experiments involving ASR, MT, and ST corpora to test our model performance on the IWSLT 2020, MuST-C, and Europarl-ST English-German (En-De) ST tasks. Our experiments reveal that the proposed model trained using the meta-learning approach achieves significant performance gains over the model which only utilizes the ST data for training. Our model achieves 4.81, 5.37, and 8.46 BLEU score improvements on IWSLT test 2015, MuST-C test, Europarl-ST test sets compared to the models trained without using the meta-learning approach for training. Our best system attains 24.58, 27.51, and 27.61 BLEU scores on IWSLT test 2015, MuST-C test, and Europarl-ST test sets, respectively.

2 Model Architecture

We use the Transformer model as a base Sequence-to-Sequence (seq2seq) model to train the ASR, MT, and ST tasks. In this section, we describe briefly about the Transformer architecture and how it is adopted to ASR and ST tasks. In Section 2.2, we describe the meta-learning algorithm used to train our seq2seq model.

2.1 Base Architecture

A general seq2seq architecture (Sutskever et al., 2014) generates a target sequence y =

---

* The two authors contributed equally to this paper

[1] The International Conference on Spoken Language Translation ACL - 17th IWSLT 2020

Proceedings of the 17th International Conference on Spoken Language Translation (IWSLT), pages 73–79
July 9-10, 2020. ©2020 Association for Computational Linguistics
https://doi.org/10.18653/v1/P17

$\{y_1, \cdots, y_n\}$ given a source sequence $x = \{x_1, \cdots, x_m\}$ by modeling the conditional probability, $p(y|x, \theta)$. The MT task is one example of seq2seq problems where x represents the input sequence in the source language and y represents the translated output sequence in the target language.

The non-recurrent Transformer network (Vaswani et al., 2017) has been extensively used to solve general seq2seq problems, especially the MT task. The Transformer is based on an encoder-decoder architecture (Cho et al., 2014). The encoder and decoder blocks of the Transformer network are composed of stacks of N, M identical layers. Each encoder layer has two sub-layers, the first being a multi-head self-attention mechanism, and the second sub-layer being a position-wise fully connected feed-forward network. Similarly, each decoder has these two sub-layers. In addition to these two sub-layers, the decoder contains an additional sub-layer for computing the encoder-decoder attention vector based on soft attention mechanism (Bahdanau et al., 2015).

2.2 MAML

Meta-Learning approach is proven to be very useful to mitigate the data scarcity issue in low resource tasks. Due to the scarcity of ST data in our task, we use the variant of meta-learning approach called Modality Agnostic Meta-Learning (MAML) (Finn et al., 2017a) to leverage high resource tasks when training on low resource tasks. Here, we briefly describe the MAML approach for the ST task. For more details about the meta-learning approach for the ST task, please refer to (Indurthi et al., 2019).

The MAML approach involves two phases: (1) Meta-Learning Phase, (2) Fine-tuning Phase. In the meta-learning phase, we use a set of related high resource tasks as source tasks to train the model. In this phase, the model captures the general learning aspects of the tasks involved. During the fine-tuning phase, we tune the model towards the specific target task after initializing the model from the parameters learned in the meta-learning phase.

Meta-Learning Phase: In this phase, we use the high resource tasks as source tasks $\{\tau^1, \cdots, \tau^s\}$ to find a good parameter initialization point θ^0 for the low resource target task τ^0. For each step in this phase, we first uniformly sample one source task τ at random from the set of

source tasks $\{\tau^1, \cdots, \tau^s\}$. We then sample two batches(D_τ and D'_τ) of training examples from this task τ. The D_τ is used to train the model to learn the task specific distribution and this step is called meta-train step. In each meta-train step, we create auxiliary parameters (θ^a_τ) initialized from the original model parameters (θ^m). We update the auxiliary parameters during this step using D_τ while keeping original parameters intact. The auxiliary parameters (θ^a) are updated using the gradient-decent step and it is given by,

$$\theta^a_\tau = \theta^m - \alpha \nabla_{\theta^m} \ell(D_\tau; \theta^m). \qquad (1)$$

After the meta-train step, the auxiliary parameters (θ^a) are evaluated on D'_τ to compute the loss. This step is called meta-test and the computed loss is used to update the original model parameters (θ^m).

$$\theta^m_\tau = \theta^m - \beta \nabla_{\theta^a} \ell(D'_\tau; \theta^a).^` \qquad (2)$$

Note that the meta-test step is performed over the model parameters (θ^m), whereas the loss is computed using the auxiliary parameters (θ^a). In effect, the meta-learning phase aims to optimize the model parameters such that a new low resource target task can be quickly learned during the fine-tuning phase.

Fine-tuning Phase: During fine-tuning phase, the model is initialized from the meta-learned parameters (θ^m) and trained on specific target task. In this phase, the model training is done like a usual neural network training without involving the auxiliary parameters.

Exposing the model parameters to vast amounts of data from high resource source tasks $\{\tau^1, \cdots, \tau^s\}$ during the meta-learning phase makes them suitable to act as a good initialization point for the target task τ^0.

2.3 Speech-to-text Translation:

We adopt the basic Transformer (Vaswani et al., 2017) architecture described in Section 2.1 to train ASR and ST tasks. We represent the speech sequence in these tasks using the Log Mel 80-dimensional features. The speech sequences are usually a few times longer than the text sequences. Thus, we add a compression layer at the beginning of the Transformer network to compress and extract structure locality from the speech sequences. This compressed signal is given as input to the Transformer encoder. The compression layer comprises of a stack of CNN layers. The text sequences in all the ASR, MT, and ST tasks are represented using word piece vocabulary.

The limited amount of training data in the ST task can result in over-fitting and leads to an inferior performance. Hence, we use the meta-learning approach described in the Section 2.2. The meta-learning approach for ST task proposed by (Indurthi et al., 2019) suggests high resource tasks such as Automatic Speech Recognition (ASR) and Machine Translation (MT) as source tasks during meta-learning phase. Unlike (Indurthi et al., 2019), we include ST task as one of the source tasks during the meta-learning phase to leverage the ST training data as well. So, the set of source tasks in our meta-learning phase are $\{ASR, MT, ST\}$ and the target task τ^0 during the fine-tuning phase is ST. We dynamically disable the compression layer whenever we sample the MT task during the meta-learning phase. This allows us to train the model on the tasks with different input-output modalities.

During the meta-learning phase, the parameters of the model (θ^m) are exposed to vast amounts of speech-to-transcripts and text-to-text translation examples via ASR and MT tasks along with the original ST tasks' speech-to-text translation examples. This allows the parameters of all the sublayers in the model such as compression, encoder, decoder, encoder-decoder attention, and output layers to learn the individual language representations and translation relations between them.

2.4 Training

The speech-to-text translation models are trained on a dataset D of parallel sequences to maximize the the the log likelihood:

$$\ell(D; \theta) = \frac{1}{|D|} \sum_{i=1}^{|D|} \log p\left(\boldsymbol{y}^i | \boldsymbol{x}^i; \theta\right) \quad (3)$$

where θ denotes the parameters of the model. To facilitate the training on multiple languages and tasks, we create a universal vocabulary by following (Gu et al., 2018). The universal vocabulary is created based on all the tasks involved in the meta-learning and fine-tuning phases.

3 Datasets

3.1 Dataset composition

Datasets used to train our model come from three different tasks, ASR, MT, and ST. All of these

Task	Corpus	# hours	# Examples
MT	Open Subtitles	N/A	22,512,639
MT	WMT 19	N/A	4,592,289
ASR	LibriSpeech	982	232,958
ASR	IWSLT 19 ST(filtered)	220	145,372
ASR	MuST-C	400	229,702
ASR	TED-LIUM 3	452	286,263
ST	Europarl-ST	89	32,628
ST	IWSLT 19 ST(filtered)	220	145,372
ST	MuST-C	400	229,703

Table 1: Number of original training examples in each dataset.

datasets are used during the meta-learning phase, while only the ST task dataset is used for fine-tuning. All the corpora we used are from the IWSLT 2020's allowed training data. The details of all the datasets are given in the Table 1.

ST Task: For ST task, we used Europarl-ST(Iranzo-Sánchez et al., 2019), IWSLT 19(filtered), and MuST-C(Di Gangi et al., 2019) datasets. The total number of examples from these three datasets is 407K, where as the size of the ASR corpora is 894K examples. To resolve the ST data scarcity issue, we augment the training data for ST with various approaches described in the Section 3.2. Thus, we increased the size of the ST training data from 407K examples to 2.2M examples.

ASR Task: We used four different datasets to train the ASR English task, IWSLT 19(filtered), LibriSpeech(Panayotov et al., 2015), MuST-C, and TED-LIUM 3(Hernandez et al., 2018), which adds a total of 894K English speech-to-text transcripts. Although, IWSLT 19(filtered), MuST-C, and TED-LIUM 3 are ST corpora, they also have the English transcripts, so we include them into ASR tasks as well. We do not augment the ASR datasets with synthetic data, unlike the ST datasets. Adding more synthetic data for ASR task may bias the model towards ASR task rather than target ST task.

MT Task: WMT 19 and Open Subtitles(Lison et al., 2019) corpora are used for the MT task. The examples used for training MT come from Common Crawls, Europarl v9, and News Commentary v14 sets of WMT 19, which amounts to 27M training examples.

3.2 Data augmentation

For the data augmentation on the text side, we use two English-to-German NMT model and top-2 beam results to generate synthetic German sequences from the corresponding English sequences.

Corpus	Use original data	Speech Augmentation	Text Augmentation	# Pairs	# Examples
Europarl-ST	Y	×2	×2	3 pairs	97,884
IWSLT 19 ST(filtered)	Y	×4	×4	5 pairs	726,380
MuST-C	Y	×3	None	4 pairs	918,812
TED-LIUM 3	N	×2	×2	2 pairs	536,526

Table 2: Data augmentation strategies for the ST task.

For speech sequence, we use the Sox library to generate the speech signal using different values of speed, echo, and tempo parameters similar to (Potapczyk et al., 2019). The parameter values are uniformly sampled using these ranges : tempo $\in (0.85, 1.3)$, speed $\in (0.95, 1.05)$, echo_delay $\in (20, 200)$, and echo_decay $\in (0.05, 0.2)$. We increase the size of the IWSLT 19(filtered) ST dataset to five times of the original size by augmenting 4X data – four text sequences using the NMT models and four speech signals using the Sox parameter ranges. For the Europarl-ST, we augment 2X examples to triple the size. The TED-LIUM 3 dataset does not contain speech-to-text translation examples originally, hence, we create 2X synthetic speech-to-text translations using speech-to-text transcripts. Finally, for the MuST-C datasest, we use synthetic speech to increase the dataset size to 4X. Overall, we created the synthetic training data of size roughly equal to four times the original data using data augmentation techniques described above. The details of these synthetic datasets are given in the Table 2. During training, we also tried SpecAugment(Park et al., 2019) to increase the speech data, but it did not help to boost overall performance.

3.3 Data processing

In order to deal with different input and output modalities, we use universal vocabulary (Gu et al., 2018) generated from all the text data, i.e. ASR transcripts, MT source and target text and ST translations. For input speech signal in ASR and ST tasks, we use Log Mel 80-dimensional features to process the input speech. Additionally, to remove noisy data in IWSLT 19 ST dataset, we use a pretrained ASR model to filter examples with word error rate (WER) ≥ 70.

Dev/Test set	# Examples
IWSLT Test 2010	1,568
IWSLT Test 2015	1,080
MuST-C Dev	1,423
MuST-C Test	2,641
Europarl-ST Dev	1,320
Europarl-ST Test	1,253

Table 3: The number of examples of dev and test sets.

4 Experiments

4.1 Implementation Details

We trained all our models on 4*NVIDIA V100 GPUs. The MAML model is implemented based on the Tensor2Tensor framework (Vaswani et al., 2018). We train the models in the meta-learning phase for 1600k steps and then finetune for 400k steps. The compression layer is composed of three CNN layers. The number of encoder and decoder layers(N and M) in the base transformer model is set to 10 and 8, respectively. In all the experiments, a dropout rate of 0.2 is used. We use a batch size of 1.5M frames for the speech sequences and a batch size of 4096 tokens for the text sequences. In order to deal with small batches due to long speech signals, we use Multistep Adam optimizer (Saunders et al., 2018) in our experiments, with the gradients accumulated over 32 steps.

4.2 Results

In this section, we report the performance of our models on different ST datasets. We report the performance of models on IWSLT tst 2010, tst 2015, MuST-C dev, MuST-C test, Europarl-ST dev, and Europarl-ST test sets. The number of examples in these test sets are reported in the Table 3.

We trained one model using only ST datasets shown in Table 2, called *woML* (without Meta-Learn) from here on. This model *woML* is trained without using the meta-learning approach. We trained another model, called *wML* (with Meta-

Model	IWSLT		MuST-C		Europarl-ST	
	tst 2010	tst 2015	Dev	Test	Dev	Test
woML (without Meta-Learn)	20.21	19.77	16.8	22.14	19.23	19.15
wML (with Meta-Learn)	25.98	24.4	22	26.77	25.8	26.8
Model Averaging	**26.43**	**24.58**	**23.59**	**27.51**	**26.88**	**27.61**

Table 4: Performance of models trained using with/without meta-learning approach on various datasets.

Learn), in which we first pre-train the model using the meta-learning approach described in the Section 2.2 using all the ASR, MT, ST tasks. We then finetune the model from the meta-learned parameters on the ST task. As we can see from the Table 4, the *wML* model achieves a better BLEU score than *woML* on all the ST datasets. We see that the *wML* model out-performs *woML* by achieving a BLEU score of 24.4 on IWSLT 2015 test set as compared to the 19.77 BLEU score achieved by *woML*. These results clearly show that the meta-learning phase helps to leverage the data from ASR, MT datasets and helps to learn the individual language representations and the relations between them.

We got further improvements on the ST BLEU score by averaging 10 checkpoints around the best model. In the Table 4, one can see that ensemble model attained an improvement of 0.18 BLEU score on IWSLT 2015 test set, 0.74 BLEU score on MuST-C test set, 0.81 BLEU score on Europarl-ST test sets. The ensemble model achieved a performance of 24.58 BLEU score on IWSLT 2015 test set by using meta-learning, data augmentation and average checkpoint techniques.

5 Related Work

End-to-end Speech Translation: Previously, speech translation leveraged the success of MT and ASR systems to build the cascade speech translation system(Post et al., 2013). The cascade models mostly suffer from problems such as propagating errors between models and high latency during decoding. In order to overcome these limitations, various attempts have been made to develop end-to-end ST models by aligning source speech signal and target text translation without using intermediate transcripts(Duong et al., 2016). However, due to the limited availability of training data unlike ASR or MT corpora, various data augmentation strategies have been proposed to leverage the data from ASR or MT tasks to improve the end-to-end ST(Jia et al., 2019; Pino et al., 2019) performance. Recently, several learning approaches such as multi-

task learning using either ASR+ST or MT+ST data pairs have been suggested and explored. However, in these approaches, the parameters of the model are updated independently based on individual task performance, which may lead to sub-optimal solutions. Indurthi et al. (2019) proposed a meta-learning approach to overcome these limitations.

Meta-Learning: Meta-learning algorithms are used to adapt quickly to new tasks with relatively few examples as the main goal of the algorithm is learning to learn. Unlike the past meta-learning approaches which focused on learning a meta policy(Ha et al., 2016; Andrychowicz et al., 2016), (Finn et al., 2017b) recently proposed a meta-learning algorithm which puts more weight on finding a good initialization point for new target tasks.

6 Conclusion

In this work, we improve the performance of end-to-end speech translation system based on the data available from the IWSLT2020 Offline Speech Translation Task. We train end-to-end models to solve the complex task of speech translation. We leverage the large out-of-domain training data from the ASR, MT tasks to improve the performance of the ST task. We adopt Model Agnostic Meta-Learning(MAML) and data augmentation techniques to achieve a performance of 24.58, 27.51, 27.61 BLEU scores on IWSLT test 2015, MuST-C test, and Europarl-ST test sets respectively.

References

Marcin Andrychowicz, Misha Denil, Sergio Gomez, Matthew W Hoffman, David Pfau, Tom Schaul, Brendan Shillingford, and Nando De Freitas. 2016. Learning to learn by gradient descent by gradient descent. In *Advances in neural information processing systems*, pages 3981–3989.

Ebrahim Ansari, Amittai Axelrod, Nguyen Bach, Ondrej Bojar, Roldano Cattoni, Fahim Dalvi, Nadir Durrani, Marcello Federico, Christian Federmann, Jiatao Gu, Fei Huang, Kevin Knight, Xutai Ma, Ajay Nagesh, Matteo Negri, Jan Niehues, Juan Pino, Elizabeth Salesky, Xing Shi, Sebastian Stüker, Marco

Turchi, and Changhan Wang. 2020. Findings of the IWSLT 2020 Evaluation Campaign. In *Proceedings of the 17th International Conference on Spoken Language Translation (IWSLT 2020)*, Seattle, USA.

Dzmitry Bahdanau, Kyunghyun Cho, and Yoshua Bengio. 2015. Neural machine translation by jointly learning to align and translate.

Alexandre Bérard, Olivier Pietquin, Christophe Servan, and Laurent Besacier. 2016. Listen and translate: A proof of concept for end-to-end speech-to-text translation. *arXiv preprint arXiv:1612.01744*.

Kyunghyun Cho, Bart Van Merriënboer, Caglar Gulcehre, Dzmitry Bahdanau, Fethi Bougares, Holger Schwenk, and Yoshua Bengio. 2014. Learning phrase representations using rnn encoder-decoder for statistical machine translation. *arXiv preprint arXiv:1406.1078*.

Mattia A. Di Gangi, Roldano Cattoni, Luisa Bentivogli, Matteo Negri, and Marco Turchi. 2019. MuST-C: a Multilingual Speech Translation Corpus. In *Proceedings of the 2019 Conference of the North American Chapter of the Association for Computational Linguistics: Human Language Technologies, Volume 1 (Long and Short Papers)*, pages 2012–2017, Minneapolis, Minnesota. Association for Computational Linguistics.

Long Duong, Antonios Anastasopoulos, David Chiang, Steven Bird, and Trevor Cohn. 2016. An attentional model for speech translation without transcription. In *Proceedings of the 2016 Conference of the North American Chapter of the Association for Computational Linguistics: Human Language Technologies*, pages 949–959.

Chelsea Finn, Pieter Abbeel, and Sergey Levine. 2017a. Model-agnostic meta-learning for fast adaptation of deep networks. In *Proceedings of the 34th International Conference on Machine Learning-Volume 70*, pages 1126–1135. JMLR. org.

Chelsea Finn, Pieter Abbeel, and Sergey Levine. 2017b. Model-agnostic meta-learning for fast adaptation of deep networks.

Alex Graves, Abdel-rahman Mohamed, and Geoffrey Hinton. 2013. Speech recognition with deep recurrent neural networks. *ICASSP, IEEE International Conference on Acoustics, Speech and Signal Processing - Proceedings*, 38.

Jiatao Gu, Hany Hassan, Jacob Devlin, and Victor O.K. Li. 2018. Universal neural machine translation for extremely low resource languages. In *Proceedings of the 2018 Conference of the North American Chapter of the Association for Computational Linguistics: Human Language Technologies, Volume 1 (Long Papers)*, pages 344–354, New Orleans, Louisiana. Association for Computational Linguistics.

David Ha, Andrew Dai, and Quoc V Le. 2016. Hypernetworks. *arXiv preprint arXiv:1609.09106*.

François Hernandez, Vincent Nguyen, Sahar Ghannay, Natalia Tomashenko, and Yannick Estève. 2018. Ted-lium 3: Twice as much data and corpus repartition for experiments on speaker adaptation. *Lecture Notes in Computer Science*, page 198–208.

Sathish Indurthi, Houjeung Han, Nikhil Kumar Lakumarapu, Beomseok Lee, Insoo Chung, Sangha Kim, and Chanwoo Kim. 2019. Data efficient direct speech-to-text translation with modality agnostic meta-learning. *arXiv preprint arXiv:1911.04283*.

Javier Iranzo-Sánchez, Joan Albert Silvestre-Cerdà, Javier Jorge, Nahuel Roselló, Adrià Giménez, Albert Sanchis, Jorge Civera, and Alfons Juan. 2019. Europarl-st: A multilingual corpus for speech translation of parliamentary debates. *arXiv preprint arXiv:1911.03167*.

Ye Jia, Melvin Johnson, Wolfgang Macherey, Ron J Weiss, Yuan Cao, Chung-Cheng Chiu, Naveen Ari, Stella Laurenzo, and Yonghui Wu. 2019. Leveraging weakly supervised data to improve end-to-end speech-to-text translation. In *ICASSP 2019-2019 IEEE International Conference on Acoustics, Speech and Signal Processing (ICASSP)*, pages 7180–7184. IEEE.

Pierre Lison, Jörg Tiedemann, Milen Kouylekov, et al. 2019. Open subtitles 2018: Statistical rescoring of sentence alignments in large, noisy parallel corpora. In *LREC 2018, Eleventh International Conference on Language Resources and Evaluation*. European Language Resources Association (ELRA).

Hermann Ney. 1999. Speech translation: Coupling of recognition and translation. In *1999 IEEE International Conference on Acoustics, Speech, and Signal Processing. Proceedings. ICASSP99 (Cat. No. 99CH36258)*, volume 1, pages 517–520. IEEE.

V. Panayotov, G. Chen, D. Povey, and S. Khudanpur. 2015. Librispeech: An asr corpus based on public domain audio books. In *2015 IEEE International Conference on Acoustics, Speech and Signal Processing (ICASSP)*, pages 5206–5210.

Daniel S. Park, William Chan, Yu Zhang, Chung-Cheng Chiu, Barret Zoph, Ekin D. Cubuk, and Quoc V. Le. 2019. Specaugment: A simple data augmentation method for automatic speech recognition. *Interspeech 2019*.

Juan Pino, Liezl Puzon, Jiatao Gu, Xutai Ma, Arya D McCarthy, and Deepak Gopinath. 2019. Harnessing indirect training data for end-to-end automatic speech translation: Tricks of the trade. In *Proceedings of the 16th International Workshop on Spoken Language Translation (IWSLT)*.

Matt Post, Gaurav Kumar, Adam Lopez, Damianos Karakos, Chris Callison-Burch, and Sanjeev Khudanpur. 2013. Improved speech-to-text translation with the fisher and callhome spanish–english speech translation corpus. In *Proc. IWSLT*.

Tomasz Potapczyk, Pawel Przybysz, Marcin Chochowski, and Artur Szumaczuk. 2019. Samsung's system for the iwslt 2019 end-to-end speech translation task. Zenodo.

Danielle Saunders, Felix Stahlberg, Adrià de Gispert, and Bill Byrne. 2018. Multi-representation ensembles and delayed SGD updates improve syntax-based NMT. In *Proceedings of the 56th Annual Meeting of the Association for Computational Linguistics (Volume 2: Short Papers)*, pages 319–325, Melbourne, Australia. Association for Computational Linguistics.

Ilya Sutskever, Oriol Vinyals, and Quoc V. Le. 2014. Sequence to sequence learning with neural networks. In *Proceedings of the 27th International Conference on Neural Information Processing Systems - Volume 2*, NIPS'14, pages 3104–3112, Cambridge, MA, USA. MIT Press.

Ashish Vaswani, Samy Bengio, Eugene Brevdo, Francois Chollet, Aidan N. Gomez, Stephan Gouws, Llion Jones, Łukasz Kaiser, Nal Kalchbrenner, Niki Parmar, Ryan Sepassi, Noam Shazeer, and Jakob Uszkoreit. 2018. Tensor2tensor for neural machine translation. *CoRR*, abs/1803.07416.

Ashish Vaswani, Noam Shazeer, Niki Parmar, Jakob Uszkoreit, Llion Jones, Aidan N Gomez, Łukasz Kaiser, and Illia Polosukhin. 2017. Attention is all you need. In *Advances in neural information processing systems*, pages 5998–6008.

End-to-End Speech-Translation with Knowledge Distillation: FBK@IWSLT2020

Marco Gaido[1,2], Mattia Antonino Di Gangi[1,2], Matteo Negri[1], Marco Turchi[1]
[1]Fondazione Bruno Kessler, Trento, Italy
[2]University of Trento, Italy
{mgaido|digangi|negri|turchi}@fbk.eu

Abstract

This paper describes FBK's participation in the IWSLT 2020 offline speech translation (ST) task. The task evaluates systems' ability to translate English TED talks audio into German texts. The test talks are provided in two versions: one contains the data already segmented with automatic tools and the other is the raw data without any segmentation. Participants can decide whether to work on custom segmentation or not. We used the provided segmentation. Our system is an end-to-end model based on an adaptation of the Transformer for speech data. Its training process is the main focus of this paper and it is based on: *i)* transfer learning (ASR pretraining and knowledge distillation), *ii)* data augmentation (SpecAugment, *time stretch* and synthetic data), *iii)* combining synthetic and real data marked as different domains, and *iv)* multi-task learning using the CTC loss. Finally, after the training with word-level knowledge distillation is complete, our ST models are fine-tuned using label smoothed cross entropy. Our best model scored 29 BLEU on the MuST-C En-De test set, which is an excellent result compared to recent papers, and 23.7 BLEU on the same data segmented with VAD, showing the need for researching solutions addressing this specific data condition.

1 Introduction

The offline speech translation task consists in generating the text translation of speech audio recordings into a different language. In particular, the IWSLT2020 task (Ansari et al., 2020) evaluates German translation of English recordings extracted from TED talks. The test dataset is provided to participants both segmented in a sentence-like format using a Voice Activity Detector (VAD) and in the original unsegmented form. Although custom segmentation of the data can provide drastic improvements in the final scores, in our work we have not addressed it, participating only with the provided segmentation.

Two main approaches are possible to face the speech translation task. The classic one is the cascade solution, which includes automatic speech recognition (ASR) and machine translation (MT) components. The other option is an end-to-end (E2E) solution, which performs ST with a single sequence-to-sequence model. Both of them are allowed for the IWSLT2020 task, but our submission is based on an E2E model.

E2E ST models gained popularity in the last few years. Their rise is due to the lack of error propagation and the reduced latency in generating the output compared to the traditional cascaded approach. Despite these appealing properties, they failed so far to reach the same results obtained by cascade systems, as shown also by last year's IWSLT campaign (Niehues et al., 2019). One reason for this is the limited amount of parallel corpora compared to those used to separately train ASR and MT components. Moreover, training an E2E ST system is more difficult because the task is more complex, since it deals with understanding the content of the input audio and translating it into a different language directly and without recurring to intermediate representations.

The above-mentioned observations have led researchers to focus on transferring knowledge from MT and ASR systems to improve the ST models. A traditional approach consists in pretraining components: the ST encoder is initialized with the ASR encoder and the ST decoder with the MT decoder. The encoder pretraining has indeed proved to be effective (Bansal et al., 2019), while the decoder pretraining has not demonstrated to be as effective, unless with the addition of adaptation layers (Bahar et al., 2019a). A more promising way to transfer knowledge from an MT model is to use the MT as

Proceedings of the 17th International Conference on Spoken Language Translation (IWSLT), pages 80–88
July 9-10, 2020. ©2020 Association for Computational Linguistics
https://doi.org/10.18653/v1/P17

a teacher to distill knowledge for the ST training (Liu et al., 2019). This is the approach we explore in the paper.

Despite its demonstrated effectiveness, ASR pretraining has been replaced in some works by multitask learning (Weiss et al., 2017). In this case, the model is jointly trained with two (or more) loss functions and usually the model is composed of 3 components: *i)* a shared encoder, *ii)* a decoder which generates the transcription, and *iii)* a decoder which generates the translation. We adopt the slightly different approach introduced by (Bahar et al., 2019a), which does not introduce an additional decoder but relies on the CTC loss in order to predict the transcriptions (Kim et al., 2017). As this multi-task learning has been proposed for speech recognition and has demonstrated to be useful in that scenario, we also include the CTC loss in ASR pretraining.

Another topic that received considerable attention is data augmentation. Many techniques have been proposed: in this work we focus on SpecAugment (Park et al., 2019), *time stretch* and subsequence sampling (Nguyen et al., 2020). Moreover, we used synthetic data generated by automatically translating the ASR datasets with our MT model. This process can also be considered as a sequence-level knowledge distillation technique, named Sequence KD (Kim and Rush, 2016).

In this paper, we explore different ways to combine synthetic and real data. We also check if the benefits of the techniques mentioned above are orthogonal and joining them leads to better results.

Our experiments show that:

- knowledge distillation, ASR pretraining, multi-task learning and data augmentation are complementary , i.e. they cooperate to produce a better model;

- combining synthetic and real data marking them with different tags (Caswell et al., 2019) leads to a model which generalizes better;

- fine-tuning a model trained with word-level knowledge distillation using the more classical label smoothed cross entropy (Szegedy et al., 2016) significantly improves the results;

- there is a huge performance gap between data segmented in sentences and data segmented with VAD. Indeed, on the same test set, the score on VAD-segmented data is lower by 5.5 BLEU.

To summarize, our submission is characterized by tagged synthetic data, multi-task with CTC loss on the transcriptions, data augmentation and word-level knowledge distillation.

2 Training data

This section describes the data used to build our models. They include: *i)* MT corpora (English-German sentence pairs), for the model used in knowledge distillation; *ii)* ASR corpora (audio and English transcriptions), for generating a pretrained encoder for the ST task; *iii)* ST corpora (audios with corresponding English transcription and German translation), for the training of our ST models. For each task, we used all the relevant datasets allowed by the evaluation campaign[1].

MT. All datasets allowed in WMT 2019 (Barrault et al., 2019) were used for the MT training, with the addition of OpenSubtitles2018 (Lison and Tiedemann, 2016). These datasets contain spurious sentence pairs: some target sentences are in a language different from German (often in English) or are unrelated to the corresponding English source or contain unexpected characters (such as ideograms). As a consequence, an initial training on them caused the model to produce some English sentences, instead of German, in the output. Hence, we cleaned our MT training data using Modern MT (Bertoldi et al., 2017)[2], in order to remove sentences whose language is not the correct one. We further filtered out sentences containing ideograms with a custom script. Overall, we removed roughly 25% of the data and the final dataset used in the training contains nearly 49 million sentence pairs.

ASR. For this task, we used both pure ASR and ST available corpora. They include TED-LIUM 3 (Hernandez et al., 2018), Librispeech (Panayotov et al., 2015), Mozilla Common Voice[3], How2 (Sanabria et al., 2018), the En-De section of MuST-C (Di Gangi et al., 2019a), the Speech-Translation TED corpus provided by the task organizers[1] and the En-De section of Europarl-ST (Iranzo-Sánchez et al., 2020). All data was lowercased and punctuation was removed.

ST. In addition to the allowed ST corpora (MuST-C, Europarl-ST and the Speech-Translation TED

---

[1] http://iwslt.org/doku.php?id=offline_speech_translation
[2] We run the CleaningPipelineMain class of MMT.
[3] https://voice.mozilla.org/

corpus), we generated synthetic data using Sequence KD (see Section 3.2) for all the ASR datasets missing the German reference. Moreover, we generated synthetic data for the En-Fr section of MuST-C. Overall, the combination of real and generated data resulted in a ST training set of 1.5 million samples.

All texts were preprocessed by tokenizing them, de-escaping special characters and normalizing punctuation with the scripts in the Moses toolkit (Koehn et al., 2007). The words in both languages were segmented using BPE with 8,000 merge rules learned jointly on the two languages of the MT training data (Sennrich et al., 2016). The audio was converted into 40 log Mel-filter banks with speaker normalization using XNMT (Neubig et al., 2018). We discarded samples with more than 2,000 filter-banks in order to prevent memory issues.

3 Models and training

3.1 Architectures

The models we trained are based on Transformer (Vaswani et al., 2017). The MT model is a plain Transformer with 6 layers for both the encoder and the decoder, 16 attention heads, 1,024 features for the attention layers and 4,096 hidden units in feed-forward layers.

2D Self-Attention	Encoder	Decoder	BLEU
2	6	6	16.50
0	8	6	**16.90**
2	9	6	17.08
2	9	4	17.06
2	12	4	**17.31**

Table 1: Results on Librispeech with Word KD varying the number of layers.

The ASR and ST models are a revisited version of the S-Transformer introduced by (Di Gangi et al., 2019c). In preliminary experiments on Librispeech (see Table 1), we observed that replacing 2D self-attention layers with additional Transformer encoder layers was beneficial to the final score. Moreover, we noticed that adding more layers in the encoder improves the results, while removing few layers of the decoder does not harm performance. Hence, the models used in this work process the input with two 2D CNNs, whose output is projected into the higher-dimensional space used by the Transformer encoder layers. The projected output is summed with positional embeddings before being fed to the Transformer encoder layers, which

use logarithmic distance penalty.

Both our ASR and ST models have 8 attention heads, 512 features for the attention layers and 2,048 hidden units in FFN layers. The ASR model has 8 encoder layers and 6 decoder layers, while the ST model has 11 encoder layers and 4 decoder layers. The ST encoder is initialized with the ASR encoder (except for the additional 3 layers that are initialized with random values). The decision of having a different number of encoder layers in the two encoders is motivated by the idea of introducing adaptation layers, which (Bahar et al., 2019a) reported to be essential when initializing the decoder with that of a pretrained MT model.

3.2 Data augmentation

One of the main problems for end-to-end ST is the scarcity of parallel corpora. In order to mitigate this issue, we explored the following data augmentation strategies in our participation.

SpecAugment. SpecAugment is a data augmentation technique originally introduced for ASR, whose effectiveness has also been demonstrated for ST (Bahar et al., 2019b). It operates on the input filterbanks and it consists in masking consecutive portions of the input both in the frequency and in the time dimensions. On every input, at each iteration, SpecAugment is applied with probability p. In case of application, it generates *frequency masking num* masks on the frequency axis and *time masking num* masks on the time axis. Each mask has a starting index, which is sampled from a uniform distribution, and a number of consecutive items to mask, which is a random number between 0 and respectively *frequency masking pars* and *time masking pars*. Masked items are set to 0. In our work, we always applied SpecAugment to both the ASR pretraining and the ST training. The configuration we used are: $p = 0.5$, *frequency masking pars* = 13, *time masking pars* = 20, *frequency masking num* = 2 and *time masking num* = 2.

Time stretch. *Time stretch* (Nguyen et al., 2020) is another technique which operates directly on the filterbanks, aiming at generating the same effect of speed perturbation. It divides the input sequence in windows of w features and re-samples each of them by a random factor s drawn by a uniform distribution between 0.8 and 1.25 (in our implementation, the lower bound is set to 1.0 in case of an input sequence with length lower than 10). In this work, we perturb an input sample using *time stretch* with probability 0.3.

Sub-sequence sampling. As mentioned in the introduction, there is a huge gap in model's performance when translating data split in well-formed sentences and data split with VAD. In order to reduce this difference, we tried to train the model on sentences which are not always well-formed by using sub-sequence sampling (Nguyen et al., 2020). Sub-sequence sampling requires the alignments between the speech and the target text at word level. As this information is not possible to obtain for the translations, we created the sub-sequences with the alignments between the audio and the transcription, and then we translated the obtained transcription with our MT model to get the target German translation. For every input sentence, we generated three segments: *i)* one starting at the beginning of the sentence and ending at a random word in the second half of the sentence, *ii)* one starting at a random word in the first half of the sentence and ending at the end of the sentence, and *iii)* one starting at a random word in the first quarter of the sentence and ending at a random word in the last quarter of the sentence.

In our experiments, this technique has not provided significant improvements (the gain was less than 0.1 BLEU on the VAD-segmented test set). Hence, it was not included in our final models.

Synthetic data. Finally, we generated synthetic translations for the data in the ASR datasets to create parallel audio-translation pairs to be included in the ST trainings. The missing target sentences were produced by translating the transcript of each audio sample with our MT model, as in (Jia et al., 2019). If the transcription of a dataset was provided with punctuation and correct casing, this was fed to the MT model; otherwise, we had to use the lowercase transcription without punctuation.

Top K	BLEU
4	16.43
8	**16.50**
64	16.37
1024	16.34

Table 2: Results on Librispeech with different K values, where K is the number of tokens considered for Word KD.

3.3 Knowledge distillation

While the ASR and MT models are optimized on label smoothed cross entropy with smoothing factor 0.1, our ST models are trained with word-level knowledge distillation (Word KD). In Word KD, the model being trained is named *student* and the goal is to teach it to produce the same output distribution of another - pretrained - model, named *teacher*. This is obtained by computing the KL divergence (Kullback and Leibler, 1951) between the distribution produced by the student and the distribution produced by the teacher. The rationale of knowledge distillation resides in providing additional information to the student, as the output probabilities produced by the teacher reflect its hidden knowledge (the so-called *dark knowledge*), and in the fact that the soft labels produced by the teacher are an easier target to match for the student than cross entropy.

In this work, we follow (Liu et al., 2019), so the teacher model is our MT model and the student is the ST model. Compared to (Liu et al., 2019), we make the training more efficient by extracting only the top 8 tokens from the teacher distribution. In this way, we can precompute and store the MT output instead of computing it at each training iteration, since its size is reduced by three orders of magnitude. Moreover, this approach does not affect negatively the final score, as shown by (Tan et al., 2019) and confirmed for ST by our experiments in Table 2).

Moreover, once the training with Word KD is terminated, we perform a fine-tuning of the ST model using the label smoothed cross entropy. Fine-tuning on a different target is an approach whose effectiveness has been shown by (Kim and Rush, 2016). Nevertheless, they applied a fine-tuning on knowledge distillation after a pretraining with the cross entropy loss, while here we do the opposite. Preliminary experiments on Librispeech showed that there is no difference in the order of the trainings (16.79 vs 16.81 BLEU, compared to 16.5 BLEU before the fine-tuning). In the fine-tuning, we train both on real and synthetic data, but we do not use the other data augmentation techniques.

3.4 Training scheme

A key aspect is the training scheme used to combine the real and synthetic datasets. In this paper, we explore two alternatives:

- **Sequence KD + Finetune**: this is the training scheme suggested in (He et al., 2020). The model is first trained with Sequence KD and Word KD on the synthetic datasets and then it is fine-tuned on the datasets with ground-truth targets using Word KD.

- **Multi-domain**: similarly to our last year submission (Di Gangi et al., 2019b), the training is executed on all data at once, but we introduce three *tokens* representing the three types of data, namely: *i)* those whose ground-truth translations are provided, *ii)* those generated from true case transcriptions with punctuation, *iii)* those generated from lowercase transcriptions without punctuation. We explore the two most promising approaches according to (Di Gangi et al., 2019d) to integrate the token with the data, i.e. summing the token to all input data and summing the token to all decoder input embeddings.

3.5 Multi-task training

We found that adding the CTC loss (Graves et al., 2006) to the training objective gives better results both in ASR and ST, although it slows down the training by nearly a factor of 2. During the ASR training, we added the CTC loss on the output of the last layer of the encoder. During the ST training, instead, the CTC loss was computed using the output of the last layer pretrained with the ASR encoder, ie. the 8th layer. In this way, the ST encoder has three additional layers which can transform the representation into features which are more convenient for the ST task, as Bahar et al. (2019a) did introducing an adaptation layer.

4 Experimental settings

For our experiments, we used the described training sets and we picked the best model according to the perplexity on MuST-C En-De validation set. We evaluated our models on three benchmarks: *i)* the MuST-C En-De test set segmented at sentence level, *ii)* the same test set segmented with a VAD (Meignier and Merlin, 2010), and *iii)* the IWSLT 2015 test set (Cettolo et al., 2015).

We trained with Adam (Kingma and Ba, 2015) (betas *(0.9, 0.98)*). Unless stated otherwise, the learning rate was set to increase linearly from 3e-4 to 5e-4 in the first 5,000 steps and then decay with an inverse square root policy. For fine-tuning, the learning rate was kept fixed at 1e-4. A 0.1 dropout was applied.

Each GPU processed mini-batches containing up to 12K tokens or 8 samples and updates were performed every 8 mini-batches. As we had 8 GPUs,

the actual batch size was about 512. In the case of multi-domain training, a batch for each domain was processed before an update: since we have three domains, the overall batch size was about 1,536. Moreover, the datasets in the different domains had different sizes, so the smaller ones were oversampled to match the size of the largest.

As the truncation of the output values of the teacher model to the top 8 leads to a more peaked distribution, we checked if contrasting this bias is beneficial or not. Hence, we tuned the value of the temperature at generation time in the interval 0.8-1.5. The temperature T is a parameter which is used to divide the *logits* before the *softmax* and determines whether to output a softer (if $T > 1$) or a sharper (if $T < 1$) distribution (Hinton et al., 2015). By default T is 1, returning an unmodified distribution. The generation of the results reported in this paper was performed using $T = 1.3$ for the models trained on Word KD. This usually provided a 0.1-0.5 BLEU increase on our benchmarks compared to $T = 1$, confirming our hypothesis that a compensation of the bias towards a sharper distribution is useful. Instead, the T was set to 1 during the generation with models trained with label smoothed cross entropy, as in this case a higher (or lower) temperature caused performance losses up to 1 BLEU point.

All experiments were executed on a single machine with 8 Tesla K80 with 11GB RAM. Our implementation is built on top of fairseq (Ott et al., 2019), an open source tool based on PyTorch (Paszke et al., 2019).

5 Results

The MT model used as teacher for Sequence KD and Word KD scored 32.09 BLEU on the MuST-C En-De test set. We trained also a smaller MT model to initialize the ST decoder with it. Moreover, we trained two ASR models. One without the multitask CTC loss and one with it. They scored respectively 14.67 and 10.21 WER. All the ST systems having CTC loss were initialized with the latter, while the others were initialized with the former.

Table 3 shows our ST models' results computed on the MuST-C En-De and IWSLT2015 test set.

Model	MuST-C sentence	MuST-C VAD	IWSLT 2015
Seq KD+FT (w/o TS)	25.80	20.94	17.18
+ FT w/o KD	27.55	19.64	16.93
Multi ENC (w/o TS)	25.79	21.37	19.07
+ FT w/o KD	27.24	20.87	19.08
Multi ENC+DEC PT	25.30	20.80	16.76
+ FT w/o KD	27.40	21.90	18.55
Multi ENC+CTC	*27.06*	*21.58*	*20.23*
+ FT w/o KD (1)	27.98	22.51	20.58
Multi ENC+CTC (5e-3)	25.44	20.41	16.36
+ FT w/o KD	**29.08**	**23.70**	20.83
+ AVG 5 (2)	28.82	23.66	**21.42**
Multi DEC+CTC (5e-3)	26.10	19.94	17.92
+ FT w/o KD	28.22	22.61	18.31
Ensemble (1) and (2)	**29.18**	**23.77**	**21.83**

Table 3: Case sensitive BLEU scores for our E2E ST models. Notes: Seq KD: Sequence KD; FT: finetuning on ground-truth datasets; TS: time stretch; Multi ENC: multi-domain model with sum of the language token to the encoder input; Multi DEC: multi-domain model with sum of the language token to the decoder input; DEC PT: pretraining of the decoder with that of an MT model; CTC: multitask training with CTC loss on the 8th encoder layer in addition to the target loss; FT w/o KD: finetuning on all data with label smoothed cross entropy; 5e-3: indicates the learning rate used; AVG 5: average 5 checkpoints around the best.

5.1 Sequence KD + Finetune VS Multi-domain

First, we compare the two training schemes examined. As shown in Table 3, *Sequence KD + Finetune* [Seq KD+FT] has the same performance as *Multi-domain* with language token summed to the input [Multi ENC] (or even slightly better) on the MuST-C test set, but it is significantly worse on the two test set segmented with VAD. This can be explained by the higher generalization capability of the *Multi-domain* model. Indeed, *Sequence KD + Finetune* seems to overfit more the training data; thus, on data coming from a different distribution, as VAD-segmented data are, its performance drops significantly. For this reason, all the following experiments use the *Multi-domain* training scheme.

5.2 Decoder pretraining and *time stretch*

The pretraining of the decoder with that of an MT model does not bring consistent and significant improvements across the test sets [Multi ENC+DEC PT]. Before the fine-tuning with label smoothed cross entropy, indeed, the model performs worse on all test sets. The fine-tuning, though, helps improving performances on all test sets, which was not the case with the previous training. This can be related to the introduction of *time stretch*, which reduces the overfitting to the training data. Therefore, we decided to discard the MT pretraining and keep *time stretch*.

5.3 CTC loss and learning rate

The multitask training with CTC loss, instead, improves the results consistently. The model trained with it [Multi ENC+CTC] outperforms all the others on all test sets by up to 1.5 BLEU points. During the fine-tuning of these models, we do not perform multitask training with the CTC loss, so the fine-tuning training is exactly the same as for previous models.

Interestingly, increasing the learning rate [Multi ENC+CTC (5e-3)], the performance before the fine-tuning is worse, but the fine-tuning of this models brings an impressive improvement over all test sets. The reason of this behavior is probably related to a better initial exploration of the solution space thanks to the higher learning rate, which, on the other side, prevents to get very close to the local optimum found. In this scenario, the fine-tuning with a lower learning rate helps getting closer to the local optimum, in addition to the usual benefits.

5.4 Token integration strategy

Finally, we tried adding the language token to the embeddings provided to the decoder, instead of the input data [Multi DEC+CTC (5e-3)]. This was motivated by the idea that propagating this information through the decoder may be more difficult due to the CTC loss, which is not dependent on that information so it may hide it to higher layers. The experiments disproved this hypothesis, as after the fine-tuning the results are lower on all benchmarks.

5.5 Submissions

We averaged our best model over 5 checkpoints, centered in the best according to the validation loss. We also created an ensemble with the resulting model and the best among the others. Both operations were not useful on the two variants of the MuST-C test set, but improved the score on the IWSLT2015 test set. We argue this means that they are more robust and generalize better.

Our *primary* submission has been obtained with the ensemble of two models, scoring 20.75 BLEU on the 2020 test set and 19.52 BLEU on the 2019 test set. Our *contrastive* submission has been generated with the 5 checkpoints average of our best model, scoring 20.25 BLEU on the 2020 test set and 18.92 BLEU on the 2019 test set.

6 Conclusions

We described FBK's participation in IWSLT2020 offline speech translation evaluation campaign (Ansari et al., 2020). Our work focused on the integration of transfer learning, data augmentation, multi-task training and the training scheme used to combine real and synthetic data. Based on the results of our experiments, our submission is characterized by a multi-domain training scheme, with additional CTC loss on the transcriptions and word-level knowledge distillation, followed by a fine-tuning on label smoothed cross entropy.

Overall, the paper demonstrates that the combination of the above-mentioned techniques can improve the performance of end-to-end ST models so that they can be competitive with cascaded solutions. Moreover, it shows that *i)* tagged synthetic data leads to more robust models than a pretraining on synthetic data followed by a fine-tuning on datasets with ground-truth targets and *ii)* fine-tuning on label smoothed cross entropy after a training with knowledge distillation brings significant improvements. The huge gap (5.5 BLEU) between data segmented in sentences and data segmented with VAD highlights the need of custom solutions for the latter. In light of these considerations, our future research will focus on techniques to improve the results when the audio segmentation is challenging for ST models.

Acknowledgments

This work is part of the "End-to-end Spoken Language Translation in Rich Data Conditions" project,[4] which is financially supported by an Amazon AWS ML Grant.

References

Ebrahim Ansari, Amittai Axelrod, Nguyen Bach, Ondrej Bojar, Roldano Cattoni, Fahim Dalvi, Nadir Durrani, Marcello Federico, Christian Federmann, Jiatao Gu, Fei Huang, Kevin Knight, Xutai Ma, Ajay Nagesh, Matteo Negri, Jan Niehues, Juan Pino, Elizabeth Salesky, Xing Shi, Sebastian Stüker, Marco Turchi, and Changhan Wang. 2020. Findings of the IWSLT 2020 Evaluation Campaign. In *Proceedings of the 17th International Conference on Spoken Language Translation (IWSLT 2020)*, Seattle, USA.

Parnia Bahar, Tobias Bieschke, and Hermann Ney. 2019a. A Comparative Study on End-to-end Speech to Text Translation. In *Proceedings of International Workshop on Automatic Speech Recognition and Understanding (ASRU)*, pages 792–799, Sentosa, Singapore.

Parnia Bahar, Albert Zeyer, Ralf Schlüter, and Hermann Ney. 2019b. On Using SpecAugment for End-to-End Speech Translation. In *Proceedings of 16th International Workshop on Spoken Language Translation (IWSLT)*, Hong Kong.

Sameer Bansal, Herman Kamper, Karen Livescu, Adam Lopez, and Sharon Goldwater. 2019. Pretraining on High-resource Speech Recognition Improves Low-resource Speech-to-text Translation. In *Proceedings of the 2019 Conference of the North American Chapter of the Association for Computational Linguistics: Human Language Technologies, Volume 1 (Long and Short Papers)*, pages 58–68, Minneapolis, Minnesota. Association for Computational Linguistics.

Loïc Barrault, Ondřej Bojar, Marta R. Costa-jussà, Christian Federmann, Mark Fishel, Yvette Graham, Barry Haddow, Matthias Huck, Philipp Koehn, Shervin Malmasi, Christof Monz, Mathias Müller, Santanu Pal, Matt Post, and Marcos Zampieri. 2019. Findings of the 2019 Conference on Machine Translation (WMT19). In *Proceedings of the Fourth Conference on Machine Translation (Volume 2: Shared Task Papers, Day 1)*, pages 1–61, Florence, Italy. Association for Computational Linguistics.

Nicola Bertoldi, Roldano Cattoni, Mauro Cettolo, Amin Farajian, Marcello Federico, Davide Caroselli, Luca Mastrostefano, Andrea Rossi, Marco Trombetti, Ulrich Germann, and David Madl. 2017. MMT: New Open Source MT for the Translation Industry. In *Proceedings of the 20th Annual Conference of the European Association for Machine Translation (EAMT)*, pages 86–91, Prague, Czech Republic.

Isaac Caswell, Ciprian Chelba, and David Grangier. 2019. Tagged Back-Translation. In *Proceedings of the Fourth Conference on Machine Translation (Volume 1: Research Papers)*, pages 53–63, Florence, Italy. Association for Computational Linguistics.

Mauro Cettolo, Jan Niehues, Sebastian Stüker, Luisa Bentivogli, Roldano Cattoni, and Marcello Federico. 2015. The IWSLT 2015 Evaluation Campaign. In *Proceedings of 12th International Workshop on Spoken Language Translation (IWSLT)*, Da Nang, Vietnam.

Mattia Di Gangi, Roldano Cattoni, Luisa Bentivogli, Matteo Negri, and Marco Turchi. 2019a. MuST-C: a Multilingual Speech Translation Corpus. In *Proceedings of the 2019 Conference of the North American Chapter of the Association for Computational Linguistics: Human Language Technologies (NAACL-HLT)*, page 2012–2017, Minneapolis, Minnesota.

---

[4] https://ict.fbk.eu/ units-hlt-mt-e2eslt/

Mattia Antonino Di Gangi, Matteo Negri, Viet Nhat Nguyen, Amirhossein Tebbifakhr, and Marco Turchi. 2019b. Data Augmentation for End-to-End Speech Translation: FBK@IWSLT '19. In *Proceedings of 16th International Workshop on Spoken Language Translation (IWSLT)*, Hong Kong.

Mattia Antonino Di Gangi, Matteo Negri, and Marco Turchi. 2019c. Adapting Transformer to End-to-End Spoken Language Translation. In *Proceedings of Interspeech 2019*, pages 1133–1137, Graz, Austria.

Mattia Antonino Di Gangi, Matteo Negri, and Marco Turchi. 2019d. One-To-Many Multilingual End-to-end Speech Translation. In *Proceedings of the 2019 IEEE Automatic Speech Recognition and Understanding Workshop (ASRU)*, pages 585–592, Sentosa, Singapore.

Alex Graves, Santiago Fernández, Faustino J. Gomez, and Jürgen Schmidhuber. 2006. Connectionist Temporal Classification: Labelling Unsegmented Sequence Data with Recurrent Neural Networks. In *Proceedings of the 23rd international conference on Machine learning (ICML)*, pages 369–376, Pittsburgh, Pennsylvania.

Junxian He, Jiatao Gu, Jiajun Shen, and Marc'Aurelio Ranzato. 2020. Revisiting Self-Training for Neural Sequence Generation. In *Proceedings of the International Conference on Learning Representations (ICLR)*, Virtual Conference.

François Hernandez, Vincent Nguyen, Sahar Ghannay, Natalia Tomashenko, and Yannick Estève. 2018. TED-LIUM 3: Twice as Much Data and Corpus Repartition for Experiments on Speaker Adaptation. In *Proceedings of the Speech and Computer - 20th International Conference (SPECOM)*, pages 198–208, Leipzig, Germany. Springer International Publishing.

Geoffrey Hinton, Oriol Vinyals, and Jeff Dean. 2015. Distilling the Knowledge in a Neural Network. In *Proceedings of NIPS Deep Learning and Representation Learning Workshop*, Montréal, Canada.

Javier Iranzo-Sánchez, Joan Albert Silvestre-Cerdà, Javier Jorge, Nahuel Roselló, Giménez. Adrià, Albert Sanchis, Jorge Civera, and Alfons Juan. 2020. Europarl-ST: A Multilingual Corpus For Speech Translation Of Parliamentary Debates. In *Proceedings of 2020 IEEE International Conference on Acoustics, Speech and Signal Processing (ICASSP)*, pages 8229–8233, Barcelona, Spain.

Ye Jia, Melvin Johnson, Wolfgang Macherey, Ron J. Weiss, Yuan Cao, Chung-Cheng Chiu, Naveen Ari, Stella Laurenzo, and Yonghui Wu. 2019. Leveraging Weakly Supervised Data to Improve End-to-End Speech-to-Text Translation. In *Proceedings of the 2019 IEEE International Conference on Acoustics, Speech and Signal Processing (ICASSP)*, pages 7180–7184, Brighton, UK.

Suyoun Kim, Takaaki Hori, and Shinji Watanabe. 2017. Joint CTC-Attention based End-to-End Speech Recognition using Multi-task Learning. In *Proceedings of the 2017 IEEE International Conference on Acoustics, Speech and Signal Processing (ICASSP)*, pages 4835–4839, New Orleans, Louisiana.

Yoon Kim and Alexander M. Rush. 2016. Sequence-Level Knowledge Distillation. In *Proceedings of the 2016 Conference on Empirical Methods in Natural Language Processing*, pages 1317–1327, Austin, Texas.

Diederik Kingma and Jimmy Ba. 2015. Adam: A Method for Stochastic Optimization. In *Proceedings of 3rd International Conference on Learning Representations (ICLR)*, San Diego, California.

Philipp Koehn, Hieu Hoang, Alexandra Birch, Chris Callison-Burch, Marcello Federico, Nicola Bertoldi, Brooke Cowan, Wade Shen, Christine Moran, Richard Zens, Chris Dyer, Ondřej Bojar, Alexandra Constantin, and Evan Herbst. 2007. Moses: Open Source Toolkit for Statistical Machine Translation. In *Proceedings of the 45th Annual Meeting of the Association for Computational Linguistics Companion Volume Proceedings of the Demo and Poster Sessions*, pages 177–180, Prague, Czech Republic. Association for Computational Linguistics.

Solomon Kullback and Richard Arthur Leibler. 1951. On information and sufficiency. *Ann. Math. Statist.*, 22(1):79–86.

Pierre Lison and Jörg Tiedemann. 2016. OpenSubtitles2016: Extracting Large Parallel Corpora from Movie and TV Subtitles. In *Proceedings of the Tenth International Language Resources and Evaluation Conference (LREC)*, pages 923–929, Portoroz, Slovenia.

Yuchen Liu, Hao Xiong, Jiajun Zhang, Zhongjun He, Hua Wu, Haifeng Wang, and Chengqing Zong. 2019. End-to-End Speech Translation with Knowledge Distillation. In *Proceedings of Interspeech 2019*, pages 1128–1132, Graz, Austria.

Sylvain Meignier and Teva Merlin. 2010. LIUM SpkDiarization: An Open Source Toolkit For Diarization. In *Proceedings of the CMU SPUD Workshop*, Dallas, Texas.

Graham Neubig, Matthias Sperber, Xinyi Wang, Matthieu Felix, Austin Matthews, Sarguna Padmanabhan, Ye Qi, Devendra Sachan, Philip Arthur, Pierre Godard, John Hewitt, Rachid Riad, and Liming Wang. 2018. XNMT: The eXtensible Neural Machine Translation Toolkit. In *Proceedings of the 13th Conference of the Association for Machine Translation in the Americas (Volume 1: Research Papers)*, pages 185–192, Boston, MA. Association for Machine Translation in the Americas.

Thai-Son Nguyen, Sebastian Stueker, Jan Niehues, and Alex Waibel. 2020. Improving Sequence-to-sequence Speech Recognition Training with On-the-fly Data Augmentation. In *Proceedings of the 2020 International Conference on Acoustics, Speech, and Signal Processing – IEEE-ICASSP-2020*, Barcelona, Spain.

Jan Niehues, Roldano Cattoni, Sebastian Stucker, Matteo Negri, Marco Turchi, Thanh-Le Ha, Elizabeth Salesky, Ramon Sanabria, Loic Barrault, Lucia Specia, and Marcello Federico. 2019. The IWSLT 2019 Evaluation Campaign. In *Proceedings of 16th International Workshop on Spoken Language Translation (IWSLT)*, Hong Kong.

Myle Ott, Sergey Edunov, Alexei Baevski, Angela Fan, Sam Gross, Nathan Ng, David Grangier, and Michael Auli. 2019. fairseq: A Fast, Extensible Toolkit for Sequence Modeling. In *Proceedings of the 2019 Conference of the North American Chapter of the Association for Computational Linguistics (Demonstrations)*, pages 48–53, Minneapolis, Minnesota. Association for Computational Linguistics.

Vassil Panayotov, Guoguo Chen, Daniel Povey, and Sanjeev Khudanpur. 2015. Librispeech: An ASR corpus based on public domain audio books. In *2015 IEEE International Conference on Acoustics, Speech and Signal Processing (ICASSP)*, pages 5206–5210, South Brisbane, Queensland, Australia.

Daniel S. Park, William Chan, Yu Zhang, Chung-Cheng Chiu, Barret Zoph, Ekin D. Cubuk, and Quoc V. Le. 2019. SpecAugment: A Simple Data Augmentation Method for Automatic Speech Recognition. In *Proceedings of Interspeech 2019*, pages 2613–2617, Graz, Austria.

Adam Paszke, Sam Gross, Francisco Massa, Adam Lerer, James Bradbury, Gregory Chanan, Trevor Killeen, Zeming Lin, Natalia Gimelshein, Luca Antiga, Alban Desmaison, Andreas Kopf, Edward Yang, Zachary DeVito, Martin Raison, Alykhan Tejani, Sasank Chilamkurthy, Benoit Steiner, Lu Fang, Junjie Bai, and Soumith Chintala. 2019. Pytorch: An imperative style, high-performance deep learning library. In H. Wallach, H. Larochelle, A. Beygelzimer, F. Alché-Buc, E. Fox, and R. Garnett, editors, *Proceedings of Advances in Neural Information Processing Systems 32 (NIPS)*, pages 8024–8035. Curran Associates, Inc.

Ramon Sanabria, Ozan Caglayan, Shruti Palaskar, Desmond Elliott, Loïc Barrault, Lucia Specia, and Florian Metze. 2018. How2: A Large-scale Dataset For Multimodal Language Understanding. In *Proceedings of Visually Grounded Interaction and Language (ViGIL)*, Montréal, Canada. Neural Information Processing Society (NeurIPS).

Rico Sennrich, Barry Haddow, and Alexandra Birch. 2016. Neural Machine Translation of Rare Words with Subword Units. In *Proceedings of the 54th Annual Meeting of the Association for Computational Linguistics (Volume 1: Long Papers)*, pages 1715–1725, Berlin, Germany. Association for Computational Linguistics.

Christian Szegedy, Vincent Vanhoucke, Sergey Ioffe, Jon Shlens, and Zbigniew Wojna. 2016. Rethinking the Inception Architecture for Computer Vision. In *Proceedings of 2016 IEEE Conference on Computer Vision and Pattern Recognition (CVPR)*, pages 2818–2826, Las Vegas, Nevada, United States.

Xu Tan, Yi Ren, Di He, Tao Qin, and Tie-Yan Liu. 2019. Multilingual Neural Machine Translation with Knowledge Distillation. In *Proceedings of International Conference on Learning Representations (ICLR)*, New Orleans, Louisiana, United States.

Ashish Vaswani, Noam Shazeer, Niki Parmar, Jakob Uszkoreit, Llion Jones, Aidan N. Gomez, Lukasz Kaiser, and Illia Polosukhin. 2017. Attention is All You Need. In *Proceedings of Advances in Neural Information Processing Systems 30 (NIPS)*, pages 5998–6008, Long Beach, California.

Ron J. Weiss, Jan Chorowski, Navdeep Jaitly, Yonghui Wu, and Zhifeng Chen. 2017. Sequence-to-Sequence Models Can Directly Translate Foreign Speech. In *Proceedings of Interspeech 2017*, pages 2625–2629, Stockholm, Sweden.

SRPOL's System for the IWSLT 2020 End-to-End Speech Translation Task

Tomasz Potapczyk, Pawel Przybysz
Samsung R&D Institute, Poland
`{t.potapczyk,p.przybysz}@samsung.com`

Abstract

This paper describes the submission to IWSLT 2020(Ansari et al., 2020) End-to-End speech translation task by Samsung R&D Institute, Poland. We took part in the offline End-to-End English to German TED lectures translation task. We based our solution on our last year's submission(Potapczyk et al., 2019). We used a slightly altered *Transformer*(Vaswani et al., 2017) architecture with ResNet-like(He et al., 2016) convolutional layer preparing the audio input to Transformer encoder. To improve the model's quality of translation we introduced two regularization techniques and trained on machine translated *Librispeech*(Panayotov et al., 2015) corpus in addition to *iwslt-corpus*, *TEDLIUM2*(Rousseau et al., 2014) and *Must_C*(Di Gangi et al., 2019) corpora. Our best model scored almost 3 *BLEU* higher than last year's model. To segment 2020 test set we used exactly the same procedure as last year.

1 Introduction

This paper describes the submission to IWSLT 2020 End-to-End Speech Translation task by Samsung R&D Institute, Poland.

We propose a few improvements to our previous system. Introducing additional training data gave us 0.7 *BLEU* improvement. Spectrogram augmentation techniques increased quality by 0.2 *BLEU*. Encoder layer depth of 12 layers gives an increase of *BLEU* by 1 point and 1.8 points when combined with additional training data and two spectrogram augmentation techniques. Replacing simpler convolutions with ResNet-like convolutional layers gave around 0.5 *BLEU* improvement. Combining all of these and increasing embedding size to 512 resulted in almost 3 *BLEU* improvement compared to our last year's model.

Document structure is as follows. Firstly we describe data preparation and augmentation. Then we provide system specification and training procedure used in our experiments. We describe data segmentation algorithm used to segment test sets TED 2019 and TED 2020. We show results of our experiments. Finally we conclude our results.

2 Training Data

To train our system we used only IWSLT 2020 permissible audio corpora - *iwslt-corpus*, *TEDLIUM2* (Rousseau et al., 2014), *Must_C* corpus(Di Gangi et al., 2019) and machine translated *Librispeech* (Panayotov et al., 2015) corpus. We did not do any further data preparation in case of iwslt-corpus and *TEDLIUM2*, we used the same data as in 2019. In case of *Must_C* corpus, this year we ran a training with half of translations being synthetic. This improved the score by 0.35 *BLEU*. We used the same text translation models as last year to generate synthetic translations. Both models scored around 33.8 and 31.1 *BLEU* on *tst2010* and *tst2015* sets respectively.

2.1 Data filtration

We trained English ASR system that was used to filter iwslt-corpus and *TEDLIUM2* corpora. We removed cases where *WER* score exceeded 75% when comparing ASR output and English reference. We decided that *Must_C* corpus does not need filtration. Additionally, we filtered iwslt-corpus with regard to quality of translation using statistical dictionary-based methods. Size of the corpora before and after filtration is shown in Table 1. We did not filter Librispeech corpus.

2.2 Synthetic target data

TEDLIUM2 corpus did not provide any German translations, therefore we generated synthetic targets using two *Transformer Big* MT systems trained with different hyperparameters on WMT data - *Paracrawl*, *Europarl* and *OpenSubtitles*.

Proceedings of the 17th International Conference on Spoken Language Translation (IWSLT), pages 89–94
July 9-10, 2020. ©2020 Association for Computational Linguistics
https://doi.org/10.18653/v1/P17

Corpora	Size	Filtered	Length
iwslt-corpus(ASR)	171121	158737	224h
+ trans. quality	158737	126817	188h
TEDLIUM2	92973	90715	197h
Must-C	229703	229703	400h
Librispeech	281241	281241	1000h

Table 1: Size (number of audio utterances) of the training corpora before and after filtration. *Iwslt-corpus* (ASR) is corpus filtered by ASR only. The last column is total audio length after filtration.

Training data for these systems has been prepared with our in-house data preparation pipeline. We also used synthetic translations as an alternative translation in *iwslt-corpus* when augmenting it. To diversify target data as much as possible, for each example created in augmentation process, we generated 4 translations, 2 per each MT model. Such a technique was described in (Jia et al., 2019). Number of training examples with synthetic data are shown in Table 6. Last year we did not examine the effectiveness of synthetic translations on our models. This year we altered our corpus and included synthetic translations of *Must_C corpus*. This corpus was augmented 3 times and in the case of 2 versions out of 4, synthetic translations were used.

Corpora	Ref.	MT-1	MT-2
iwslt-corpus	126817	2x158737	2x158737
TEDLIUM2	0	3x90715	3x90715
Must_C	229703	229703	229703
Librispeech	281241	281241	281241

Table 2: Size (number of text lines) of the training corpora with synthetic data. For each model two or three best beam results have been used.

2.3 Data Augmentation

We augmented the data by processing the audio files with three Sox's effects: *tempo*, *speed* and *echo*. We sampled the parameters with uniform distribution within ranges presented in Table 3.

For each file we repeated the process four times. *Librispeech* was augmented only once because it is the largest corpus and it is out of domain. As a result we had nearly five times larger audio corpus. The range of *speed* option is very small because we did not want our model to train on an unnaturally

Option	Min value	Max value
tempo	0.85	1.3
speed	0.95	1.05
echo delay	20	200
echo decay	5	20

Table 3: Sox parameters value ranges used in processing of audio data. Echo effect is parametrized by two values.

sounding samples. The rationale behind using *echo* option is the fact that many TED lectures have a significant echo.

Final number of training audio examples is shown in Table 4.

Corpora	Orig.&Augm.	Length
iwslt-corpus	761765	1084h
TEDLIUM2	544290	1182h
Must_C	918812	1600h
Librispeech	562482	2000h
Total	2787349	5866h

Table 4: Size of the training audio corpora with data augmentation. Number of distinct audio and text pairs.

3 E2E Speech Translation System

In this section we will describe the architecture and training techniques of our end-to-end spoken language translation system. Some of these were used in our 2019 system.

3.1 ASR Transformer for SLT

As a baseline system we used our last year's Transformer architecture implemented in TensorFlow. The *Baseline* Transformer has hidden layer of size 384, convolutional (kernel size 9) feed forward layer of size 1536, 8-head self-attention, 6 encoder layers and 4 decoder layers. Audio data is turned into log mel spectrogram with frame size of 25 ms, frame step 10 ms and 80 filters. To log mel spectrograms we apply 2D 3x3 convolution twice with stride 2x2 and 256 filters and then 3x20 convolution to reduce the spectrogram to a 384 dimentional vector, exactly like in the case of ASR. Apart from baseline, we propose changes to convolutional layer and increase number of encoder layers and embedding size. Finally, our best system has ResNet-like convolutional layer, 12 encoder layers and embedding size of 512.

3.2 Dual learning: ASR and SLT tasks

This year we also introduced a second decoder with ASR task, making it a multitask setup similar to (Anastasopoulos and Chiang, 2018). A separate dictionary of size 32k was used for this task. In such a setup loss is calculated with two targets - one in English and one in German. Two decoders with different weights are simultaneously trained on these targets; convolutional layers and encoder are shared. An early experiment on non-augmented data showed almost 2 *BLEU* increase (15.23 vs 17.15 on tst2010) compared to the same model trained on a single task. All our trainings this year used dual learning.

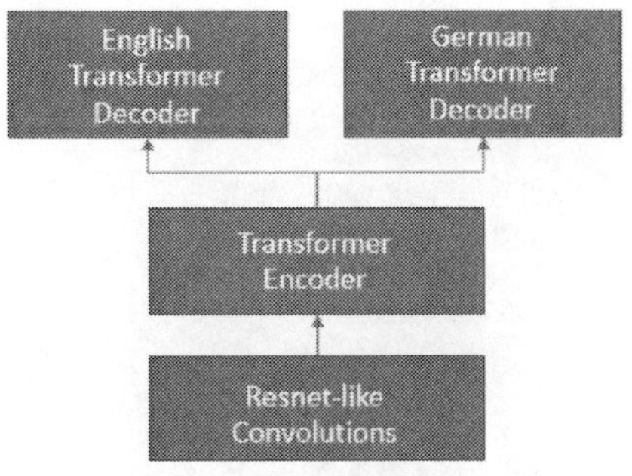

Figure 1: Dual learning architecture

3.3 Spectrogram augmentation

To augment data we implemented spectrogram masking technique described in (Park et al., 2019) This technique involves masking the spectrogram for a range of frequencies and periods of time. In our implementation we chose to introduce three such masks for frequency. The width of frequency range is selected randomly between values 5 and 10. This means that out of 80 filters 15 to 30 are masked. In time we chose one mask for every 300 time steps. Again, the length of such mask is random between 10 and 20 time steps. Apart from last year's data augmentation techniques used in 2019, we introduced additional regularization techniques - warp (Figure 2) and spectrogram noise. We implemented warping technique similar to Park et al.(Park et al., 2019). For each 10 time steps in spectrogram we delete one random time step and insert a step which is an average of two neighboring steps. The result is very similar to warp distortion - some parts of a spectrogram are shifted to the right and some are shifted to the left. We also

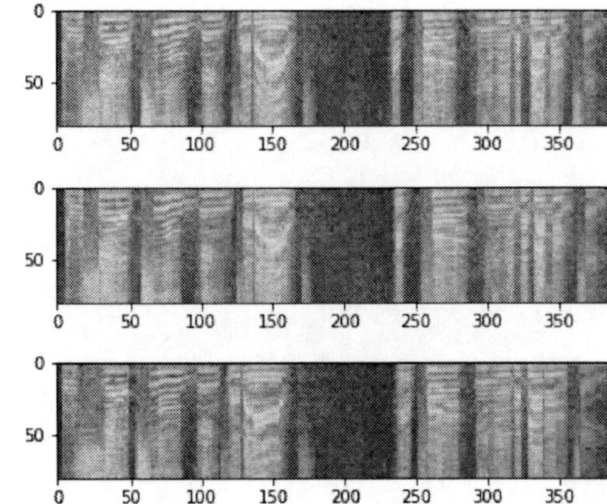

Figure 2: Original and warped spectrograms. The bottom figure is an exaggerated version of warping where much more insertions/deletions were used.

introduced a multiplicative noise on spectrogram with a value of +- 1%. Table 5 below shows the results of these techniques. We experimented with randomly varying step and window size of spectrograms during the training. Step size was varied between 8 and 12 ms and window size between 23 and 27 ms. This however gave mixed results and we did not include it in the final model. Figure 5 shows clear advantage of models with warp and spectrogram noise. The advantage of the model with varied step/window size is dubious.

Model	tst2010	tst2015	average
baseline[1]	26.5	21.87	24.15
warp	26.63	22.42	24.41
spec. noise	26.81	21.87	24.34
step/window	26.22	22.15	24.2

Table 5: Maximal BLEU scores on two tests sets. The last column is maximal average of two test sets for one checkpoint.

3.4 Synthetic Must_C and Librispeech data

Addition of synthetic *Must_C* translations improved *BLEU* score by over 0.35 *BLEU*. Addition of *Librispeech* corpus further improved *BLEU* by 0.35. Table 6 below shows the results.

---

[1] the same model as 2019 primary submission but trained for 1.2M steps which resulted with higher score than previously reported

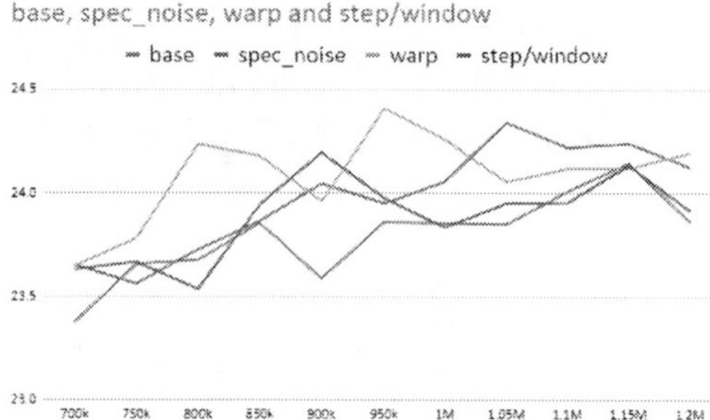

Figure 3: Comparison of warped and noised trainings to baseline. Y axis is average BLEU on tst2010 and tst2015. X axis is number of steps.

Model	tst2010	tst2015	average
base	26.5	21.87	24.15
synth_mc	27.08	22.04	24.5
+ libri	27.91	21.81	24.86

Table 6: Maximal BLEU scores on two test sets for *baseline*, additional *Must_C* synthetic targets and additional *Librispeech* data. The last column is maximal average of two tests set for one checkpoint.

3.5 12 layer encoder

Our experience with text translation suggests it is more efficient to increase number of layer in the encoder rather than decoder therefore we increased number of encoder layers to 12. Number of decoder layers stayed the same at 4 layers. This increased *BLEU* score by 1 point. Introducing warping, noise and Librispeech corpus increased *BLEU* by another 0.8 *BLEU*. Table 7 shows the results.

Model	tst2010	tst2015	average
base	26.5	21.87	24.15
12layer	27.48	22.92	25.14
12_wal	28.4	23.63	25.97

Table 7: Maximal BLEU scores on two test sets. Model *12_wal* is the model with 12 layers and trained on noised and warped data with *Librispeech* corpus. The last column is maximal average of two tests set for one checkpoint.

3.6 ResNet-like convolutional layers

Another improvement to our model is ResNet-like convolutional layers processing the spectrogram input. The idea is to make the convolutional layers deeper instead of using large number of channels. The spectrogram input is shrinked gradually

in both axis using 2x2 pooling. As the spectrogram is shrinked channel, size is increasing. We start with a smaller channel size compared to the previous solution - 64 channels instead of 256 and end the convolutional processing with 256 channels. Figure 4 shows architectural diagram of our solution. Replacing previous architecture with ResNet improved the model by around 0.5 *BLEU*. Table 8 shows the results. Note that strictly maximal scores do not show the improvement well. Figure 5 shows a plot of the results which proofs stable advantage (around 0.5) of ResNet solution. We experimented with a version without the residual connections however decided not to include it in the final model.

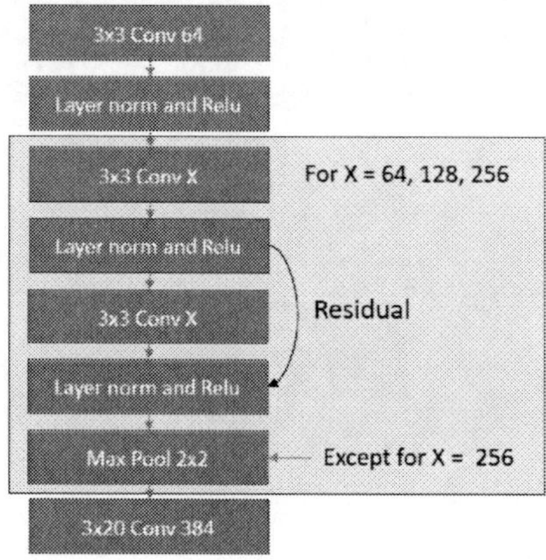

Figure 4: Convolutional layers architecture

Model	tst2010	tst2015	average
base	26.5	21.87	24.15
resnet	27.15	21.81	24.33
- residual	27.05	21.96	24.5

Table 8: Maximal BLEU scores on two test sets. The third row is same as ResNet model but without residual connections. The last column is maximal average of two tests set for one checkpoint.

3.7 Training process

We trained our models on 4 GTX 1080 Ti GPUs for about one and a half week, which resulted in 1.2M steps. *12layer* models were trained slightly longer - for 3 weeks because the training was slower. They were also trained on two NVIDIA Quadro 8000 GPUs because of its memory size. Batch size was 400000 timesteps for trainings on 1080 Ti and

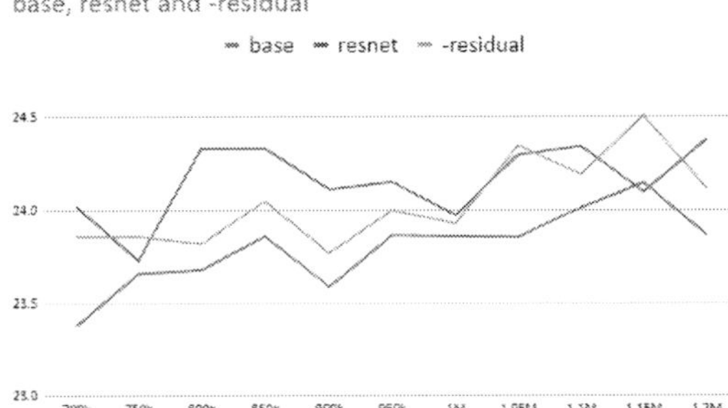

Figure 5: Comparison of Resnet trainings to baseline. Y axis is average BLEU on tst2010 and tst2015. X axis is number of steps.

3000000 timesteps on Quadro 8000. In the case of all trainings (except one) 10% dropout was applied. The final model with 12 layer and 512 embedding size used 20% dropout. Adam Multistep optimiser was used, effective batch size was increased 32 times.

3.8 Model averaging

For the final validation we averaged last 7 checkpoints of the training. Averaging checkpoints almost always resulted in higher *BLEU* scores. We experimented with continuation of training after averaging but it did not give any better results.

4 Final model

In this paper we presented improvements on simpler models. The final model uses a combination of all the promising techniques together with a larger embedding size. It would be unfeasible to perform all of these experiments on such a large model as its training took almost a month. However we are very satisfied with the end result which is 3 *BLEU* improvements compared to our baseline. The improvements from individual techniques cumulated very well.

Model	tst2010	tst2015	average
base	26.5	21.87	24.15
12_wal	28.4	23.63	25.97
+resnet[2]	28.26	23.77	26.02
+512 (final)	29.44	24.6	27.02

Table 9: Maximal BLEU scores on two test sets. The fourth row is our final submitted system. The last column is maximal average of two tests set for one checkpoint.

5 Segmentation

This year we used the same segmentation technique as last year. It relies on dividing the audio input densely using silence detection tool. These small fragments are then joined together up to a certain length depending on the length of the silence between them. Shorter distances between segments are joined earlier. This procedure is repeated until further joining results in segments longer than maximal length. Last year we determined such length should be 11s. However, for our current best model this distance turned out to be 15s. We used *tst2015* to optimize the process. We present the result in Table 10.

6 Evaluation

We have improved our score on *tst2019* by 4 *BLEU* compared to our last year's submission. It is importnat to notice the difference between given and our custom segmentation. Our method produces longer segments than the ones in the given segmentation. Our models seem to work much better on these longer segments giving around 3.9 *BLEU* higher scores.

tst2019	tst2019*	tst2020	tst2020*
20.1	23.96	21.49	25.3

Table 10: BLEU scores for our final model. * test sets use our custom segmentation

7 Conclusions

In this paper we have presented a significant improvement of translation quality of our end-to-end model. We have shown that despite limited parallel training data, end-to-end systems can compete with traditional pipeline systems. Using a longer segmentation, our model outscored the best IWSLT2019 pipeline system on *tst2019*(iws, 2019).

References

2019. *The IWSLT 2019 Evaluation Campaign*. Zenodo.

Antonios Anastasopoulos and David Chiang. 2018. Tied multitask learning for neural speech translation. *arXiv preprint arXiv:1802.06655*.

---

[2]trained for shorter time than the other two

Ebrahim Ansari, Amittai Axelrod, Nguyen Bach, Ondrej Bojar, Roldano Cattoni, Fahim Dalvi, Nadir Durrani, Marcello Federico, Christian Federmann, Jiatao Gu, Fei Huang, Kevin Knight, Xutai Ma, Ajay Nagesh, Matteo Negri, Jan Niehues, Juan Pino, Elizabeth Salesky, Xing Shi, Sebastian Stüker, Marco Turchi, and Changhan Wang. 2020. Findings of the IWSLT 2020 Evaluation Campaign. In *Proceedings of the 17th International Conference on Spoken Language Translation (IWSLT 2020)*, Seattle, USA.

Mattia A Di Gangi, Roldano Cattoni, Luisa Bentivogli, Matteo Negri, and Marco Turchi. 2019. Must-c: a multilingual speech translation corpus. In *Proceedings of the 2019 Conference of the North American Chapter of the Association for Computational Linguistics: Human Language Technologies, Volume 1 (Long and Short Papers)*, pages 2012–2017.

Kaiming He, Xiangyu Zhang, Shaoqing Ren, and Jian Sun. 2016. Deep residual learning for image recognition. In *Proceedings of the IEEE conference on computer vision and pattern recognition*, pages 770–778.

Ye Jia, Melvin Johnson, Wolfgang Macherey, Ron J Weiss, Yuan Cao, Chung-Cheng Chiu, Naveen Ari, Stella Laurenzo, and Yonghui Wu. 2019. Leveraging weakly supervised data to improve end-to-end speech-to-text translation. In *ICASSP 2019-2019 IEEE International Conference on Acoustics, Speech and Signal Processing (ICASSP)*, pages 7180–7184. IEEE.

Vassil Panayotov, Guoguo Chen, Daniel Povey, and Sanjeev Khudanpur. 2015. Librispeech: An asr corpus based on public domain audio books. *2015 IEEE International Conference on Acoustics, Speech and Signal Processing (ICASSP)*, pages 5206–5210.

Daniel S Park, William Chan, Yu Zhang, Chung-Cheng Chiu, Barret Zoph, Ekin D Cubuk, and Quoc V Le. 2019. Specaugment: A simple data augmentation method for automatic speech recognition. *arXiv preprint arXiv:1904.08779*.

Tomasz Potapczyk, Pawel Przybysz, Marcin Chochowski, and Artur Szumaczuk. 2019. Samsung's system for the iwslt 2019 end-to-end speech translation task. In *Proceedings of the 16th International Conference on Spoken Language Translation (IWSLT 2019)*.

Anthony Rousseau, Paul Deléglise, and Yannick Esteve. 2014. Enhancing the ted-lium corpus with selected data for language modeling and more ted talks. In *LREC*, pages 3935–3939.

Ashish Vaswani, Noam Shazeer, Niki Parmar, Jakob Uszkoreit, Llion Jones, Aidan N Gomez, Łukasz Kaiser, and Illia Polosukhin. 2017. Attention is all you need. In *Advances in neural information processing systems*, pages 5998–6008.

The University of Helsinki submission to the IWSLT2020 Offline Speech Translation Task

Raúl Vázquez, Mikko Aulamo, Umut Sulubacak, Jörg Tiedemann

University of Helsinki
{name.surname}@helsinki.fi

Abstract

This paper describes the University of Helsinki Language Technology group's participation in the IWSLT 2020 offline speech translation task, addressing the translation of English audio into German text. In line with this year's task objective, we train both cascade and end-to-end systems for spoken language translation. We opt for an end-to-end multitasking architecture with shared internal representations and a cascade approach that follows a standard procedure consisting of ASR, correction, and MT stages. We also describe the experiments that served as a basis for the submitted systems. Our experiments reveal that multitasking training with shared internal representations is not only possible but allows for knowledge-transfer across modalities.

1   Introduction

An effective solution for performing spoken language translation (SLT) must deal with the evident challenge of transferring the implicit semantics between audio and text modalities. An end-to-end SLT system must hence appropriately address this problem while simultaneously performing accurate machine translation (MT) (Sulubacak et al., 2018).

In last year's IWSLT challenge, both end-to-end and cascade systems yielded similar results (Niehues et al., 2019). It follows that this year's IWSLT offline speech translation challenge focuses on whether *"the cascaded solution is still the dominant technology in spoken language translation"* (Ansari et al., 2020). For our participation on this task, we train both cascade and end-to-end systems for SLT. For the end-to-end system, we use a multimodal approach trained in a multitask fashion, which maps the internal representations of different encoders into a shared space before decoding. For the cascade approach, we use a pipeline of three stages: (i) automatic speech recognition (ASR),

(ii) punctuation and letter-case restoration, and (iii) MT.

We focus on exploiting the knowledge-transfer capabilities of a multitasking architecture based on language-specific encoders-decoders (Lu et al., 2018; Schwenk and Douze, 2017; Luong et al., 2016). This idea has been proposed and studied in the multilingual scenario (Vázquez et al., 2020; Subramanian et al., 2018; Firat et al., 2017), however, we adapt it to be used in a multimodal scenario. Regarding different modalities (in this case, audio and text) as different languages when training the model, allows us to employ a cross-modal intermediate shared layer for performing SLT in an end-to-end fashion. By jointly training this layer, we aim for the the model to combine the semantic information provided in the text-to-text MT tasks with the ability to generate text from audio in the ASR tasks.

2   Proposed Systems

End-to-end SLT

We use an inner-attention based architecture proposed by Vázquez et al. (2020). In a nutshell, it follows the conventional structure of an encoder-decoder model of MT (Bahdanau et al., 2015; Luong et al., 2016) enabled with multilingual training by incorporating language-specific encoders and decoders trainable with a language-rotating scheduler (Dong et al., 2015; Schwenk and Douze, 2017), and an intermediate shared inner-attention layer (Cífka and Bojar, 2018; Lu et al., 2018). We implement our model on top of an OpenNMT-py (Klein et al., 2017) fork, which we make available for reproducibility purposes.[1]

The text encoders and the decoders (always text output) are transformers (Vaswani et al., 2017).

---

[1] `https://github.com/Helsinki-NLP/`
`OpenNMT-py/tree/iwslt2020`

Proceedings of the 17th International Conference on Spoken Language Translation (IWSLT), pages 95–102
July 9-10, 2020. ©2020 Association for Computational Linguistics
https://doi.org/10.18653/v1/P17

We implement the transformer-based audio encoders inspired by the SLT architecture with tied layer structure from Tu et al. (2019) and the R-Transformer from Di Gangi et al. (2019b). It consists of n CNN layers; the first one taking k stacked Mel filterbank features as input channels, and the following ones 32 input channels. Afterwards, a linear layer corrects the shape of the embeddings and is concatenated with the positional embeddings to be fed as input to m transformer layers.

Given the multimodal nature of the task, we modified the source-target rotating scheduler. Instead of a uniform distribution over the language pairs, we propose using a weighted sampling scheme based on the inverse of the batch size of the modalities. This modification allows us to have a more balanced training because audio inputs tend to be considerably longer than text inputs, and a transformer-based encoder could not possibly handle the 4096 tokens conventionally used as the ad-hoc choice of batch size for a text-based transformer.

Cascade approach

The ASR stage of our pipeline is trained with an S-Transformer (Di Gangi et al., 2019b); an adaptation of the transformer architecture to end-to-end SLT. The encoder in this architecture makes it possible to process audio features. It consists of two 2-dimensional CNN-blocks meant to downsample the input, followed by two 2-dimensional self-attention layers to model the long-range context, an attention layer that concatenates its output with the positional encodings of the input, and six transformer-based layers.

The output of the ASR stage is followed by the **restoration stage** for punctuation and letter case restoration. Since the training data for the ASR model mixes different training sets with different formatting, the raw output from the ASR block can have stylistic differences from the input seen during the training of the translation stage. The restoration stage involves the use of an auxiliary transformer-based MT model to perform "intralingual translation" from lowercased text without punctuation into fully-cased and punctuated text. Stripping punctuation on the ASR output, converting the text to lowercase, and processing the result through the restoration stage ensures that the output conforms to the same format that the translation stage was optimized for.

As the last step, **the translation stage** uses another transformer to translate the processed ASR output to German. Both this transformer model and the one used in the restoration stage are based on the freely available Marian NMT implementation (Junczys-Dowmunt et al., 2018). Our configuration uses a learning rate of 0.0003 with linear warmup through the first 16 000 batches, decaying afterwards. The decoder normalizes scores by translation length (normalization exponent of 1.0) during beam search. All other options use the default values.

3 Data Preprocessing

The MT, ASR and end-to-end SLT systems have been trained on different subsets of the allowed training corpora. For the cascade approach SLT system

Corpora	# utterances	Length
Europarl-ST	40,141	89 hrs
IWSLT2018	166,214	271 hrs
How2	189,366	297 hrs
MuST-C	264,036	400 hrs
Mozilla Common Voice	854,430	1,118 hrs

Table 1: Size of audio data used.

Data for the end-to-end SLT system. We use Europarl-ST (Iranzo-Sánchez et al.), IWSLT2018 (Niehues et al., 2019) and MuST-C (Di Gangi et al., 2019a), a total of 433k utterances after cleaning some corrupt files or with other problems in the sampling. We extracted 80-dimensional Mel filterbank features for each sentence-like segment using our own implementation.

Text data for the end-to-end SLT system. For the text data of the multimodal end-to-end SLT system, we use a total of ~51M sentence pairs from corpora specified in Table 2. Instead of using all of this data, we first filter out noisy translations. OpenSubtitles2018, which consists of subtitle translations, and corpora gathered by crawling the internet, Common Crawl and ParaCrawl, are especially likely to contain noisy data. For filtering the corpora, we utilize OpusFilter (Aulamo et al., 2020), a toolbox for creating clean parallel corpora.

First, we extract six feature values for each of the sentence pairs. In particular, we apply the following features: CharacterScore, CrossEntropy,

LanguageID, NonZeroNumeral, TerminalPunctuation and WordAlign, each of which is defined in Aulamo et al. (2020). Secondly, we train a logistic regression classifier based on those features. The classifier is trained only on WIT[3], MuST-C, Europarl-ST and IWSLT18, which are multimodal datasets with speech-to-text and text-to-text data. This allows the system to adapt to text translations that are associated with speech translations. Finally, we use the classifier to assign a cleanness score ranging from 0 to 1 for all sentence pairs in all corpora. The data is then ranked based on the cleanness score, after which a portion of noisy pairs is removed from the tail. Our preliminary translation experiments showed that removing up to 40% of the data improves the translation quality, leaving us ∼30.5M sentence pairs of training data, which are then used in all our end-to-end experiments.

Corpora	# sentences
WIT[3]	196,112
MuST-C train	229,703
Rapid 2019	1,480,789
Europarl v9	1,817,763
OpenSubtitles2018	11,621,073
News Commentary v14	365,340
Common Crawl	2,399,123
Europarl-ST	32,628
WikiTitles	1,305,078
IWSLT2018	171,025
ParaCrawl v3	31,360,203
Total	50,978,837
Filtered	30,540,267

Table 2: Text training data used for end-to-end systems.

Audio for the cascade system. We have extracted 40-dimensional Filterbank features with speaker normalization for each sentence-like segment of the MuST-C, How2 (Sanabria et al., 2018) and Mozilla Common Voice (Ardila et al., 2019) corpora using XNMT (Neubig et al., 2018). After getting rid of audio files that were too short (less than 0.4 seconds), corrupted, or no longer available for download from YouTube, some 1.2M clean utterances remained for training the ASR system, and 30k for validation.

On the target side, we use two contrastive preprocessing pipelines:

i) the same subword segmentation used for the MT system

```
_it _& apos ; s _a _lobster _made
_of _play d ough _that _& apos ; s
_afraid _of _the _dark _.
```

ii) character level segmentation

```
I t <space> ' s <space> a <space>
l o b s t e r <space> m a d e <space>
o f <space> p l a y d o u g h <space>
t h a t <space> ' s <space> a f r a i d
<space> o f <space> t h e <space>
d a r k <space> .
```

Text data for the cascade system. In our SLT pipeline, the data we applied for our restoration and translation models have some overlap and some differences. For training, both models use the text data from the IWSLT 2018 speech translation corpus, the MuST-C training set, News Commentary v14, Europarl v9, and Rapid 2019. The translation model also uses data from the OpenSubtitles2018 dataset, which the restoration model does not since this dataset is particularly noisy in terms of punctuation and letter cases. Conversely, the restoration model also uses data from the How2 and Mozilla Common Voice datasets, which the translation model does not use as they do not contain German text. The translation model uses the IWSLT development set from 2010 and test sets from 2011–2015 as validation data, while the restoration model uses them as supplementary training data in order to reinforce domain bias, using only the MuST-C development set for validation.

Initially, we "clean" the output of our ASR model to remove segments containing musical note characters (♫ ♪), and repeating phrases that were consistently hallucinated during silence, applause, laughter or noise in the audio (e.g. in our case, "Shake. Fold."), as well as parts of segments that designate the speaker (e.g. "Audience: ..."). Subsequently, we use the same preprocessing pipeline for the cleaned ASR output as we do for all of our text data. For this, we start by removing non-printing characters, normalizing punctuation, and retokenizing the text using the corresponding utilities from the Moses toolkit (Koehn et al., 2007). Afterwards, we apply subword segmentation via SentencePiece (Kudo and Richardson, 2018), using a joint English–German BPE model with a vocabulary size of 32 000 for all of our translation models,

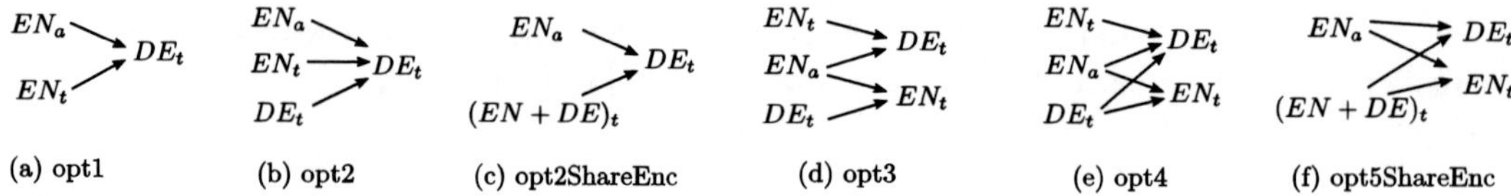

Figure 1: Configurations tested for multitask training.

and an English unigram model with a vocabulary size of 24 000 for the restoration stage of our cascade SLT, both trained on all of the data used for the translation and restoration models combined.

Before the training of the restoration model, the training data was run through a Moses truecaser model (trained on the same selection of training data as the restoration model) as an additional step before segmentation. This step removes sentence-initial capitalization for words that would not be capitalized otherwise, ensuring that differences in distributions of words appearing in sentence-initial positions does not influence case restoration for the model. Once truecased and segmented, we assign the processed data as the target for the restoration model, and continue to strip punctuation and lowercase the target to generate the source. This configuration comes with the useful side effect of the model learning to generate truecased output, which may be beneficial for MT.

4 Experiments

In this section we report on the experiments that lead up to our final submissions. The experiments on this section have been trained, validated and tested on the respective splits of the MuST-C dataset.

As a first stage, we focused on selecting the multitask training strategy that performed better. Having the three modalities EN AUDIO, EN TEXT and DE TEXT as possible inputs, and both text modalities as possible outputs, there can be up to 64 combinations where audio is an input[2] without taking into account the cases where the text encoder is shared between German and English. We considered the 5 scenarios depicted in Figure 1 and present its results in Table 3 together with the number of steps it took for them to converge.

All the models were trained using the same set of hyperparameters. At the time we ran these experiments, the final version of the audio encoder was not ready for deployment, so we used a 4-

layered pyramidal CNN+RNN encoder adaptation from Amodei et al. (2016) with 512 hidden units and pooling factors of (1,1,2,2) after each layer, respectively. For the text encoders, we applied embedding layers of 512 dimensions, four stacked bidirectional LSTM layers with 512 hidden units (256 per direction). We use attentive text decoders composed of two unidirectional LSTM layers with 512 units. Regarding the shared attention bridge layer, we used 100 *attention heads* with 1024 hidden units each. Training is performed using the Adam optimizer (Kingma and Ba, 2015) with a learning rate of 0.0002 and batch size 32 for all source-target pairs, for at most 100,000 steps per language pair[3]. At this stage, we apply a uniform language-rotating scheduler. Isolating the effect of multitasking from the effect of weighting the scheduling distribution helped us understand the importance of weighting it with respect to the batch size.

Configuration	BLEU	Steps
opt3	5.00	330K
opt5shareEnc	4.94	250K
opt2shareEnc	4.84	250K
opt4	4.50	300K
opt1	4.30	220K
opt2	3.62	190K

Table 3: Training steps and best BLEU scores obtained with end-to-end systems on the German part fo the MuST-C test set.

Our preliminary BLEU scores[4] for these models are low. We, however, justify our choice to include them given the low performance of other experiments in similar scenarios reported in the literature. Namely, Tu et al. (2019) reported 9.55 BLEU training on the same set with a transformer based architecture, the only paper that trains and tests on the same set, and thus the only truly com-

---

[2]64 is the total number of bipartite graphs that can be defined on sets of three and two vertices.

[3]Model configuration 3, for instance, has 4 language pairs was trained for at most 400K steps

[4]We use the `multi-bleu-detok.pl`+ Moses script, that uses sentence smoothing for detokenized input.

System	status	de BLEU	en BLEU	WER	Steps
end-to-end opt6	submission time	12.90	56.65	36	172K
	converged	14.38	59.22	33	294K
end-to-end opt3	submission time	9.47	44.12	48	32K
	converged	11.71	52.91	40	72K
cascade bpe37k		22.20	60.87	29	-
cascade char-level		20.90	54.49	55	-

Table 4: Scores of our primary and contrastive submissions on on the MuST-C test set.

parable results. In addition, Di Gangi et al. (2019a) reported 12.25 BLEU training MuST-C together with IWSLT18 and initialized their system with the ASR system.

The well-known sensitivity to hyperperparameter choice of the transformer architecture is also visible in our transformer-based audio encoders. We performed hyperparameter tuning on opt3 multitask training configuration (Figure 1 (d)). This resulted in a performance of a 9.53 BLEU score on German translations and 47.63 on the English, a clear increase from the untuned models that got at most 1 BLEU point in any of them. The final hyperparameter setup consists of:

- text encoders and decoders using 3 layered transformer architecture with 8 heads, 512 dimensional embeddings, 2048 feedforward hidden dimensions, and a batch size of 4096 tokens;

- audio encoders as described in Section 2 with 2 CNN layers with stride of 2 and kernel width of, the first of which takes a single input channel, three 8-headed transformer layers, positional embeddings of size 512 concatenated to the output of a linear layer for being passed to the transformer layers, a batch size of 32 utterances; and

- an attention bridge of size 100 with a hidden dimension of 1024.

Training was done with 8,000 warmup steps, using an Adam optimizer with learning rate 2 and Noam decay method, accumulation count of 8 to have an approximate effective batch size of 256 for the audio utterances, dropping utterances above the length of 5500, and a language rotating scheduler that uses the inverse of the batch size as weights [5].

We also tried other strategies such as (i) using 3, 4 and 6 stacked filterbanks as different channel inputs for the CNNs to reduce the input size instead of dropping utterances, (ii) using SpecAugment (Park et al., 2019) layers (2 frequency masks of width 20 and 2 time masks of width 50) to produce a data augmentation effect while training, (iii) including layer normalization after the attention bridge, (iv) using the positional embeddings of our transformer-based audio encoder in other places of the encoder or not using them at all. Unfortunately, none of them produced as effective improvements as what we describe above. We note that it is probable that using milder hyperparameters for SpecAugment could be beneficial.

5 Results

From the insights gained out of our experiments on the MuST-C dataset, for our submission, we train a system using the data as described in section 3 with the training configuration opt3 (see Figure 1 (d)) and the hyperparameters that yielded the best results. Further, we decided to try out an additional training configuration we had not previously tried out: ENAUDIO as input and DETEXT and ENTEXT as output, which we refer to as opt6. Configurations from Figure 1 use both modalities as input, whereas opt6 separates them by using only-audio input and only-text output. This might be the reason why opt6 outperformed them when tested on the MuST-C test set. Further experimentation would be required to make this statement conclusive. One of our main aims in participating in this task is to test our multitask architecture; for this reason we submit our best SLT system as primary system and the cascade approach with subword segmentation as contrastive baseline. We would like to

---

[5]In case of training opt3, the weights assigned to ENAU-

DIO → {DETEXT,ENTEXT} are 0.42 each and both text-to-text pairs get 0.08 because the average sentence length of MuST-C is around 24, which implies that 4096 tokens are about 170 sentences.

note that, unfortunately, at the time of submission, our end-to-end systems had not converged yet.

For the sake of consistency, these have been benchmarked with the MuST-C test set as well. The results are reported in Table 4, where we also report BLEU and WER for English, corresponding to the ASR task.

6 Conclusion

In this paper we present our work for the IWSLT2020 offline speech translation task, along with the set of experiments that led to our final systems. Our submission includes both a cascaded baseline and a multimodal system trainable in a multitask fashion. Our work shows that it is possible to train a system that shares internal representations for transferring the implicit semantics between audio and text modalities. The nature of the architecture enables end-to-end SLT, while at the same time providing a system capable of performing ASR and MT. Although this represents an important step in multimodal MT, there is still a lot of room for improvement in the proposed systems. In future work, we would like to implement more sophisticated audio encoders, such as the S-Transformer. This, along with using the same amount of data during training, will allow us to draw a truly fair comparison between both end-to-end and cascade approaches.

Acknowledgments

This work is part of the FoTran project, funded by the European Research Council (ERC) under the European Union's Horizon 2020 research and innovation programme (grant agreement № 771113), as well as the MeMAD project, funded by the European Union's Horizon 2020 Research and Innovation Programme (grant № 780069).

References

Dario Amodei, Sundaram Ananthanarayanan, Rishita Anubhai, Jingliang Bai, Eric Battenberg, Carl Case, Jared Casper, Bryan Catanzaro, Qiang Cheng, Guoliang Chen, Jie Chen, Jingdong Chen, Zhijie Chen, Mike Chrzanowski, Adam Coates, Greg Diamos, Ke Ding, Niandong Du, Erich Elsen, Jesse Engel, Weiwei Fang, Linxi Fan, Christopher Fougner, Liang Gao, Caixia Gong, Awni Hannun, Tony Han, Lappi Johannes, Bing Jiang, Cai Ju, Billy Jun, Patrick LeGresley, Libby Lin, Junjie Liu, Yang Liu, Weigao Li, Xiangang Li, Dongpeng Ma, Sharan Narang, Andrew Ng, Sherjil Ozair, Yiping Peng, Ryan Prenger, Sheng Qian, Zongfeng Quan, Jonathan Raiman, Vinay Rao, Sanjeev Satheesh, David Seetapun, Shubho Sengupta, Kavya Srinet, Anuroop Sriram, Haiyuan Tang, Liliang Tang, Chong Wang, Jidong Wang, Kaifu Wang, Yi Wang, Zhijian Wang, Zhiqian Wang, Shuang Wu, Likai Wei, Bo Xiao, Wen Xie, Yan Xie, Dani Yogatama, Bin Yuan, Jun Zhan, and Zhenyao Zhu. 2016. Deep Speech 2: End-to-end speech recognition in English and Mandarin. In *Proceedings of the 33rd International Conference on Machine Learning*, volume 48 of *Proceedings of Machine Learning Research*, pages 173–182, New York, New York, USA. PMLR.

Ebrahim Ansari, Amittai Axelrod, Nguyen Bach, Ondrej Bojar, Roldano Cattoni, Fahim Dalvi, Nadir Durrani, Marcello Federico, Christian Federmann, Jiatao Gu, Fei Huang, Kevin Knight, Xutai Ma, Ajay Nagesh, Matteo Negri, Jan Niehues, Juan Pino, Elizabeth Salesky, Xing Shi, Sebastian Stüker, Marco Turchi, and Changhan Wang. 2020. Findings of the IWSLT 2020 Evaluation Campaign. In *Proceedings of the 17th International Conference on Spoken Language Translation (IWSLT 2020)*, Seattle, USA.

Rosana Ardila, Megan Branson, Kelly Davis, Michael Henretty, Michael Kohler, Josh Meyer, Reuben Morais, Lindsay Saunders, Francis M. Tyers, and Gregor Weber. 2019. Common Voice: A massively-multilingual speech corpus.

Mikko Aulamo, Sami Virpioja, and Jörg Tiedemann. 2020. OpusFilter: A configurable parallel corpus filtering toolbox. Accepted to ACL 2020, System Demonstrations.

Dzmitry Bahdanau, Kyunghyun Cho, and Yoshua Bengio. 2015. Neural machine translation by jointly learning to align and translate. In *3rd International Conference on Learning Representations, ICLR 2015*, San Diego, California, USA. Conference Track.

Ondřej Cífka and Ondřej Bojar. 2018. Are BLEU and meaning representation in opposition? In *Proceedings of the 56th Annual Meeting of the Association for Computational Linguistics (Volume 1: Long Papers)*, pages 1362–1371, Melbourne, Australia. Association for Computational Linguistics.

Mattia A. Di Gangi, Roldano Cattoni, Luisa Bentivogli, Matteo Negri, and Marco Turchi. 2019a. MuST-C: a multilingual speech translation corpus. In *Proceedings of the 2019 Conference of the North American Chapter of the Association for Computational Linguistics: Human Language Technologies, Volume 2 (Short Papers)*, "Minneapolis, MN, USA".

Mattia A. Di Gangi, Matteo Negri, and Marco Turchi. 2019b. Adapting transformer to end-to-end spoken language translation. In *Proc. Interspeech 2019*, pages 1133–1137.

Daxiang Dong, Hua Wu, Wei He, Dianhai Yu, and Haifeng Wang. 2015. Multi-task learning for multiple language translation. In *Proceedings of the 53rd Annual Meeting of the Association for Computational Linguistics and the 7th International Joint Conference on Natural Language Processing (Volume 1: Long Papers)*, volume 1, pages 1723–1732, Beijing, China.

Orhan Firat, Kyunghyun Cho, Baskaran Sankaran, Fatos T Yarman Vural, and Yoshua Bengio. 2017. Multi-way, multilingual neural machine translation. *Computer Speech & Language*, 45:236–252.

Javier Iranzo-Sánchez, Joan Albert Silvestre-Cerdà, Javier Jorge, Nahuel Roselló, Adrià Giménez, Albert Sanchis, Jorge Civera, and Alfons Juan. Europarl-ST: A multilingual corpus for speech translation of parliamentary debates. Accepted to ICASSP2020.

Marcin Junczys-Dowmunt, Roman Grundkiewicz, Tomasz Dwojak, Hieu Hoang, Kenneth Heafield, Tom Neckermann, Frank Seide, Ulrich Germann, Alham Fikri Aji, Nikolay Bogoychev, André F. T. Martins, and Alexandra Birch. 2018. Marian: Fast neural machine translation in C++. In *Proceedings of ACL 2018, System Demonstrations*, pages 116–121, Melbourne, Australia. Association for Computational Linguistics.

Diederik P Kingma and Jimmy Ba. 2015. Adam: A method for stochastic optimization. *3rd International Conference for Learning Representations*.

Guillaume Klein, Yoon Kim, Yuntian Deng, Jean Senellart, and Alexander M. Rush. 2017. OpenNMT: Open-source toolkit for neural machine translation. In *Proceedings of ACL 2017, System Demonstrations*, Vancouver, Canada.

Philipp Koehn, Richard Zens, Chris Dyer, Ondřej Bojar, Alexandra Constantin, Evan Herbst, Hieu Hoang, Alexandra Birch, Chris Callison-Burch, Marcello Federico, Nicola Bertoldi, Brooke Cowan, Wade Shen, and Christine Moran. 2007. Moses: Open source toolkit for statistical machine translation. In *Proceedings of the 45th Annual Meeting of the ACL on Interactive Poster and Demonstration Sessions - ACL '07*, Prague, Czech Republic. Association for Computational Linguistics.

Taku Kudo and John Richardson. 2018. SentencePiece: A simple and language independent subword tokenizer and detokenizer for neural text processing. In *Proceedings of the 2018 Conference on Empirical Methods in Natural Language Processing: System Demonstrations*, pages 66–71, Brussels, Belgium. Association for Computational Linguistics.

Yichao Lu, Phillip Keung, Faisal Ladhak, Vikas Bhardwaj, Shaonan Zhang, and Jason Sun. 2018. A neural interlingua for multilingual machine translation. In *Proceedings of the Third Conference on Machine Translation: Research Papers*, pages 84–92, Belgium, Brussels. Association for Computational Linguistics.

Minh-Thang Luong, Quoc V Le, Ilya Sutskever, Oriol Vinyals, and Lukasz Kaiser. 2016. Multi-task sequence to sequence learning. In *4th International Conference on Learning Representations, ICLR 2016*, San Juan, Puerto Rico. Conference Track (Poster).

Graham Neubig, Matthias Sperber, Xinyi Wang, Matthieu Felix, Austin Matthews, Sarguna Padmanabhan, Ye Qi, Devendra Singh Sachan, Philip Arthur, Pierre Godard, John Hewitt, Rachid Riad, and Liming Wang. 2018. XNMT: The extensible neural machine translation toolkit. In *Conference of the Association for Machine Translation in the Americas (AMTA) Open Source Software Showcase*, Boston.

J. Niehues, R. Cattoni, S. Stüker, M. Negri, M. Turchi, E. Salesky, R. Sanabria, L. Barrault, L. Specia, and M. Federico. 2019. The IWSLT 2019 evaluation campaign. In *Proceedings of the 16th International Workshop on Spoken Language Translation (IWSLT 2019)*, Hong Kong, China.

Daniel S. Park, William Chan, Yu Zhang, Chung-Cheng Chiu, Barret Zoph, Ekin Dogus Cubuk, and Quoc V. Le. 2019. SpecAugment: A simple augmentation method for automatic speech recognition. In *INTERSPEECH*.

Ramon Sanabria, Ozan Caglayan, Shruti Palaskar, Desmond Elliott, Loïc Barrault, Lucia Specia, and Florian Metze. 2018. How2: A large-scale dataset for multimodal language understanding. In *Proceedings of the Workshop on Visually Grounded Interaction and Language (ViGIL)*. NeurIPS.

Holger Schwenk and Matthijs Douze. 2017. Learning joint multilingual sentence representations with neural machine translation. In *ACL workshop on Representation Learning for NLP*, pages 157–167, Vancouver, Canada.

Sandeep Subramanian, Adam Trischler, Yoshua Bengio, and Christopher J Pal. 2018. Learning general purpose distributed sentence representations via large scale multi-task learning. In *6th International Conference on Learning Representations, ICLR 2018*, Vancouver, Canada. Conference Track (Poster).

Umut Sulubacak, Jörg Tiedemann, Aku Rouhe, Stig-Arne Grönroos, and Mikko Kurimo. 2018. The memad submission to the iwslt 2018 speech translation task. In *Proceedings of the 16th International Workshop on Spoken Language Translation (IWSLT 2019)*, pages 89–94, Brussels, Belgium.

Mei Tu, Wei Liu, Lijie Wang, Xiao Chen, and Xue Wen. 2019. End-to-end speech translation system description of LIT for IWSLT 2019.

Ashish Vaswani, Noam Shazeer, Niki Parmar, Jakob Uszkoreit, Llion Jones, Aidan N Gomez, Łukasz Kaiser, and Illia Polosukhin. 2017. Attention is all you need. In *Advances in Neural Information*

Processing Systems, pages 5998–6008, Long Beach, California, USA.

Raúl Vázquez, Alessandro Raganato, Mathias Creutz, and Jörg Tiedemann. 2020. A systematic study of inner-attention-based sentence representations in multilingual neural machine translation. *Computational Linguistics*, 0(ja):1–53.

The AFRL IWSLT 2020 Systems: Work-From-Home Edition

Brian Ore, Eric Hansen, Timothy Anderson, Jeremy Gwinnup
Air Force Research Laboratory
{brian.ore.1,eric.hansen.5, timothy.anderson.20, jeremy.gwinnup.1}@us.af.mil

Abstract

This report summarizes the Air Force Research Laboratory (AFRL) submission to the offline spoken language translation (SLT) task as part of the IWSLT 2020 evaluation campaign. As in previous years, we chose to adopt the cascade approach of using separate systems to perform speech activity detection, automatic speech recognition, sentence segmentation, and machine translation. All systems were neural based, including a fully-connected neural network for speech activity detection, a Kaldi factorized time delay neural network with recurrent neural network (RNN) language model rescoring for speech recognition, a bidirectional RNN with attention mechanism for sentence segmentation, and transformer networks trained with OpenNMT and Marian for machine translation. Our primary submission yielded BLEU scores of 21.28 on tst2019 and 23.33 on tst2020.

1 Introduction

As part of the evaluation campaign for the 2020 International Workshop on Spoken Language Translation (IWSLT) (Ansari et al., 2020), the AFRL Human Language Technology team submitted an entry to the offline spoken language translation (SLT) task. The goal of this task is to automatically generate cased and punctuated German translations from English audio TED Talks using either a cascade of systems or the end-to-end approach. We chose to build upon our previous work (Ore et al., 2018; Kazi et al., 2016) and adopt the cascade approach of using separate systems to perform speech activity detection, automatic speech recognition (ASR), sentence segmentation, and machine translation (MT). Sections 2 and 3 describe our ASR and MT systems, respectively. Section 4 presents our results on the development set when the data is manually segmented into sentences, and Section 5 descibes our approach to SLT on unsegmented data.

Section 6 provides a post-evaluation analysis of our systems based on sentence length, and Section 7 presents our conclusions and future work.

2 Automatic Speech Recognition

This section describes the English ASR system that was developed for the offline speech translation task. First, we sequestered all talks from TEDLIUM-v3 (Hernandez et al., 2018) that were present in tst2014, tst2015, and tst2018. Next, language models (LMs) were estimated on TEDLIUM-v3 and the same subsets of News Crawl and News Discussions described in Ore et al. (2018). The text was formatted as follows:

- Numbers and special symbols were converted to words (*e.g.*, "%" converted to "percent", "&" converted to "and", "=" converted to "equals").

- Punctuation marks and any remaining symbols were removed.

- All text was converted to lowercase.

We used the SRILM select-vocab tool[1] to choose a 100,000 word vocabulary. An interpolated bigram language model (LM) was estimated using the SRILM toolkit, and a recurrent neural network (RNN) LM was trained using Kaldi (Povey et al., 2011).

Acoustic models were trained on TEDLIUM-v3 using Kaldi. In a preliminary experiment, we found that training on both TEDLIUM-v3 and CommonVoice did not lead to a reduction in word error rate (WER), so we decided to only use TEDLIUM-v3. The Kaldi system used in these experiments is a factorized time delay neural network (TDNN) with residual network style skip connections. Input Mel frequency cepstral coefficient

---

[1] Available at: http://www.speech.sri.com/projects/srilm

Proceedings of the 17th International Conference on Spoken Language Translation (IWSLT), pages 103–108
July 9-10, 2020. ©2020 Association for Computational Linguistics
https://doi.org/10.18653/v1/P17

(MFCC) features have standard speed perturbation applied (0.9 & 1.1 factor). The initial Kaldi finite state transducer (FST) was built with the bigram LM, and the resulting lattices were rescored using the pruned RNNLM lattice rescoring algorithm (Xu et al., 2018).

3 Machine Translation

In order to translate the ASR output from the previous section, we construct an English–German MT training corpus from allowable sources provided by the organizers[2]. We then prepare this corpus in a similar manner as described in Gwinnup et al. (2018) and Gwinnup et al. (2019), especially focusing on fastText (Joulin et al., 2016a,b) language-id filtering. As a contrast to Ore et al. (2018) we prepare data for additional systems on this same corpus where the source English text has been transformed to resemble output from our ASR systems. We then train transformer (Vaswani et al., 2017) based MT systems with the OpenNMT (Klein et al., 2018) and Marian (Junczys-Dowmunt et al., 2018) toolkits.

3.1 OpenNMT

The OpenNMT-tf system trained for this task used the default configuration for a transformer network. Two copies of the training data described above were concatenated together. One copy was lowercase and non-punctuated in order to resemble ASR output and an additional copy was cased and with punctuation. This combined corpus was processed with Sentencepiece (Kudo and Richardson, 2018) using a model trained only on the lowercase and non-punctuated corpus. The network was trained for 10 epochs of this training data using a batch size of 1562 with an effective batch size of 24992 using the lazy Adam (Kingma and Ba, 2015) optimizer. The final system was an average of the last 8 checkpoints of the training. Checkpoints were saved every 5000 steps. Results using this models for the punctuated test sets for the WMT news translation task are shown in Table 1 Column A. Column B is results with a model trained only on the cased and punctuated data. Column C is the results with a model trained only on the lowercased unpunctuated data.

Test Set	A	B	C
newstest2018	40.02	43.11	22.41
newstest2019	37.55	38.71	19.69

Table 1: OpenNMT system performance under different training corpus conditions.

Results using this model on tst2014, tst2015, and tst2018 with cased and punctuated input are shown in Table 2 Column A. Column B is the results with lowercase and non-punctuated input. Column C is with a model trained only on the cased and punctuated data, and Column D is the results with a model trained only on lowercase non-punctuated data.

Test Set	A	B	C	D
tst2014	27.67	26.99	28.43	26.48
tst2015	29.80	28.85	29.72	28.43
tst2018	27.46	25.53	27.81	25.81

Table 2: OpenNMT system performance under different training corpus conditions.

3.2 Marian

Our Marian systems also utilize the transformer (Vaswani et al., 2017) architecture. Network hyperparameters are the same as detailed in Gwinnup et al. (2018). We use the WMT16 newstest2016 as the validation set during training.

We used the following network configuration:

- 6 layer encoder

- 6 layer decoder

- 8 transformer heads

- Tied embeddings for source, target and output layers

- Layer normalization

- Label smoothing

- Learning rate warm-up and cool-down

A joint Sentencepiece vocabulary with 46k entries was employed, informed by experimentation performed for our WMT19 efforts. With lowercase non-punctuated input, this system yielded the following BLEU scores: 26.58 on tst2014, 28.47 on tst2015, and 26.57 on tst2018.

	Marian	OpenNMT
tst2014	24.80 (6.4)	24.67 (6.2)
tst2015	26.44 (6.6)	26.14 (6.5)
tst2018	23.91 (9.1)	23.09 (8.6)

Table 3: BLEU scores and WERs (in parentheses) on the manually segmented development sets. The MT systems were trained on lowercase non-punctuated English text.

	OpenNMT
tst2014	23.77 (6.2)
tst2015	24.26 (6.5)
tst2018	22.90 (8.6)

Table 4: BLEU scores and WERs (in parentheses) on the manually segmented development sets using the OpenNMT system trained on cased and punctuated English text.

4 Manual Segmentation

In order to evaluate the effect of automatic sentence segmentation on spoken language translation, we manually segmented the tst2014, tst2015, and tst2018 development sets into sentences using the provided reference files. This was done by automatically aligning the reference text using a Kaldi ASR system and then manually correcting any errors. The Kaldi system described in Section 2 was then used to generate ASR transcripts for each utterance. Note that for ASR tasks, a development set is typically used to select the LM scale that minimizes the WER; however, in this task our goal is to choose the best translation. We decided to generate 8 different hypotheses for each utterance by varying the ASR LM scale over 6, 8, 10, ..., 20, translating each utterance, and then selecting the ASR LM scale that yields the best overall BLEU score. Each ASR hypothesis was translated using the MT systems trained on lowercase non-punctuated English text. Compared to selecting the ASR LM scale to minimize WER, this method yields a very minor improvement with Marian (0.06 BLEU on tst2014 and tst2018, 0.17 BLEU on tst2015), but no improvement with OpenNMT. Table 3 shows the case-sensitive BLEU scores and corresponding WER in parentheses.

In a second set of experiments, an automatic punctuator and text recaser were applied to the English ASR text prior to performing translation. Compared to the previous approach, one advantage of this method is that we can train a single MT system to translate both ASR transcripts and text documents. The punctuator was a bidirectional RNN with attention mechanism that was trained on 4M words of English TED data using the Python fork of Ottokar Tilk's punctuator.[3] The punctuated text was recased using Moses and then translated

using the OpenNMT system that was trained on cased and punctuated English. Table 4 shows the BLEU scores and corresponding WER in parentheses. Comparing Tables 3 and 4, we can see that using the translation models trained on lowercase non-punctuated English text yields the best results; therefore, we decided to use these MT systems for all remaining experiments discussed in this paper.

5 Automatic Segmentation

In the previous section, we evaluated our ASR and MT systems on audio clips that were manually segmented into sentences. This section considers the task where we are given an audio stream that must be automatically segmented. First, we evaluated a speech activity detector (SAD) on each audio file. We used the same neural network based SAD as described in our IWSLT 2018 paper. Automatic segmentation of the test data was performed by evaluating the SAD, applying a dynamic programming algorithm to choose the best sequence of states, and defining utterance boundaries at the midpoint of each non-speech segment longer than 0.5 seconds. Next, the Kaldi ASR system was evaluated on each utterance using the same ASR LM scales found in the previous section. Two different methods were investigated for partitioning the time-aligned words into sentences. In the first method, we simply used the utterance boundaries from the SAD to define the sentence boundaries. For the second method, we evaluated the automatic punctuator from Section 4 on each utterance, and then defined additional sentence boundaries at words that ended with a period, exclamation, or question mark.

Table 5 shows the case-sensitive BLEU scores and corresponding WER obtained using each method. Comparing the two sentence segmentation methods, we can see that defining additional sentence boundaries with the punctuator led

---

[3] Available at: https://pypi.org/project/punctuator

	Marian		OpenNMT	
	SAD	SAD+punctuator	SAD	SAD+punctuator
tst2014	23.32 (7.0)	22.52 (7.0)	22.52 (6.6)	22.86 (6.6)
tst2015	23.93 (6.7)	23.59 (6.7)	23.69 (6.5)	23.90 (6.5)
tst2018	21.60 (9.4)	21.56 (9.4)	20.86 (9.0)	21.32 (9.0)

Table 5: BLEU scores and WERs (in parentheses) obtained on the automatically segmented development sets. Sentence boundaries were defined using (1) the SAD, or (2) a combination of the SAD marks and the automatic punctuator.

to an overall decrease in BLEU when translating with Marian, but an improvement with OpenNMT. Compared to the results obtained with the manual segments in Table 3, we find that the Marian BLEU score decreased by 1.48 on tst2014, 2.51 on tst2015, and 2.31 on tst2018; similarly, the OpenNMT BLEU score decreased by 1.81 on tst2014, 2.24 on tst2015, and 1.77 on tst2018. Lastly, if we compare the OpenNMT systems (which used the same ASR LM scale to minimize WER and maximize BLEU) in Tables 3 and 5, we can see that automatically segmenting the data yields no change in WER on tst2015, and an increase of 0.4% on tst2014 and tst2018.

Our primary submission to the IWSLT 2020 offline speech translation task can be summarized as follows. First, a neural network based SAD was used to segment each audio file into utterances. Next, ASR transcripts were generated using Kaldi and an automatic punctuator was applied to further split each utterance into sentences. Lastly, an OpenNMT system was used to translate the lowercase non-punctuated English into cased and punctuated German. As a contrasting system, we also submitted the translations obtained using Marian. The processing pipeline for the Marian system was identical to the OpenNMT system, except that we did not apply the automatic punctuator (*i.e.*, the sentence boundaries were defined solely on the pause durations from the SAD). The OpenNMT system yielded BLEU scores of 21.28 on tst2019 and 23.33 on tst2020; the Marian system yielded BLEU scores of 21.48 on tst2019 and 23.21 on tst2020.

6 Post-Evaluation Analysis

In Section 5 we found that defining additional sentence boundaries using an automatic punctuator led to a worse performance with Marian, but improved performance with OpenNMT. This led

#Words	#Sentences	Marian	OpenNMT
1-9	2266	30.62	28.12
10-19	2889	28.57	28.71
20-29	1456	28.16	28.39
30-39	665	26.55	26.88
40-49	275	25.78	25.34
50+	241	27.10	19.85

Table 6: BLEU scores on the reference text grouped by sentence length.

us to wonder if the automatic punctuator was actually helping to identify more correct sentence boundaries, or simply producing shorter sentences that were better translated with OpenNMT. Based on this idea, we decided to analyze how sentence length affects translation performance with each of our systems. First, the English reference text from dev2010, tst2010, tst2013, tst2014, tst2015, and tst2018 was processed using the same steps as described in Section 2 to match the expected MT input. Marian and OpenNMT were then used to translate each sentence, and the BLEU score was calculated for sentences where the English source included 1-9, 10-19, 20-29, 30-39, 40-49, and 50+ words. Table 6 shows the results obtained, including the number of sentences assigned to each group. These results show that for sentences longer than 50 words, the BLEU score drops substantially with the OpenNMT system.

As a final experiment, we re-evaluated our submitted OpenNMT system, but only inserted additional sentence boundaries if the English ASR utterance was longer than 50 words. This yielded the following BLEU scores: 23.21 on tst2014, 23.89 on tst2015, and 21.37 on tst2018. Compared with the OpenNMT SAD+punctuator results in Table 5, this represents a +0.35 BLEU improvement on tst2014 and similar results on tst2015 and tst2018.

7 Conclusion and Future Work

With our systems, we found that automatic sentence segmentation led to a decrease of up to -2.51 BLEU. The punctuator that we used provides functionality to specify the pause duration after each word when training the punctuator. This could be obtained by automatically aligning the original TED training transcripts; however, due to limited computational resources while working at home, we were not able to investigate this feature. In addition to text features and pause durations, other acoustic features might also prove useful for automatically identifying sentence boundaries. Alternatively, it may be interesting to resegment the MT training data to better match the ASR segmentation, although this would probably have to be done in an automatic fashion to take advantage of available text-only parallel corpora.

References

Ebrahim Ansari, Nguyen Bach, Ondrej Bojar, Roldano Cattoni, Marcello Federico, Christian Federmann, Jiatao Gu, Fei Huang, Ajay Nagesh, Matteo Negri, Jan Niehues, Elizabeth Salesky, Sebastian Stüker, and Marco Turchi. 2020. Findings of the IWSLT 2020 Evaluation Campaign. In *Proceedings of the 17th International Conference on Spoken Language Translation (IWSLT 2020)*, Seattle, USA.

Jeremy Gwinnup, Tim Anderson, Grant Erdmann, and Katherine Young. 2018. The AFRL WMT18 systems: Ensembling, continuation and combination. In *Proceedings of the Third Conference on Machine Translation: Shared Task Papers*, pages 394–398, Belgium, Brussels. Association for Computational Linguistics.

Jeremy Gwinnup, Grant Erdmann, and Tim Anderson. 2019. The AFRL WMT19 systems: Old favorites and new tricks. In *Proceedings of the Fourth Conference on Machine Translation (Volume 2: Shared Task Papers, Day 1)*, pages 203–208, Florence, Italy. Association for Computational Linguistics.

François Hernandez, Vincent Nguyen, Sahar Ghannay, Natalia A. Tomashenko, and Yannick Estève. 2018. TED-LIUM 3: twice as much data and corpus repartition for experiments on speaker adaptation. *CoRR*, abs/1805.04699.

Armand Joulin, Edouard Grave, Piotr Bojanowski, Matthijs Douze, Hérve Jégou, and Tomas Mikolov. 2016a. Fasttext.zip: Compressing text classification models. *arXiv preprint arXiv:1612.03651*.

Armand Joulin, Edouard Grave, Piotr Bojanowski, and Tomas Mikolov. 2016b. Bag of tricks for efficient text classification. *arXiv preprint arXiv:1607.01759*.

Marcin Junczys-Dowmunt, Roman Grundkiewicz, Tomasz Dwojak, Hieu Hoang, Kenneth Heafield, Tom Neckermann, Frank Seide, Ulrich Germann, Alham Fikri Aji, Nikolay Bogoychev, André F. T. Martins, and Alexandra Birch. 2018. Marian: Fast neural machine translation in C++. In *Proceedings of ACL 2018, System Demonstrations*, pages 116–121, Melbourne, Australia. Association for Computational Linguistics.

Michaeel Kazi, , Elizabeth Salesky, Brian Thompson, Jonathan Taylor, Jeremy Gwinnup, Tim Anderson, Grant Erdmann, Eric Hansen, Brian Ore, Katherine Young, and Michael Hutt. 2016. The MITLL-AFRL IWSLT-2016 systems. In *Proc. of the 13th International Workshop on Spoken Language Translation (IWSLT'16)*, Seattle, Washington.

Diederik P. Kingma and Jimmy Ba. 2015. Adam: A method for stochastic optimization. In *3rd International Conference on Learning Representations, ICLR 2015, San Diego, CA, USA, May 7-9, 2015, Conference Track Proceedings*.

Guillaume Klein, Yoon Kim, Yuntian Deng, Vincent Nguyen, Jean Senellart, and Alexander Rush. 2018. OpenNMT: Neural machine translation toolkit. In *Proceedings of the 13th Conference of the Association for Machine Translation in the Americas (Volume 1: Research Papers)*, pages 177–184. Association for Machine Translation in the Americas.

Taku Kudo and John Richardson. 2018. SentencePiece: A simple and language independent subword tokenizer and detokenizer for neural text processing. In *Proceedings of the 2018 Conference on Empirical Methods in Natural Language Processing: System Demonstrations*, pages 66–71, Brussels, Belgium. Association for Computational Linguistics.

Brian Ore, Eric Hansen, Timothy Anderson, and Jeremy Gwinnup. 2018. The AFRL IWSLT 2018 systems: What worked, what didn't. In *Proc. of the 15th International Workshop on Spoken Language Translation (IWSLT'18)*, Bruges, Belgium.

D. Povey, A. Ghoshal, G. Boulianne, L. Burget, O. Glembek, N. Goel, M. Hannemann, P. Motlicek, Y. Qian, P. Schwarz, J. Silovsky, G. Stemmer, and K. Vesely. 2011. The Kaldi Speech Recognition Toolkit. In *Proceedings of the Automatic Speech Recognition and Understanding Workshop*.

Ashish Vaswani, Noam Shazeer, Niki Parmar, Jakob Uszkoreit, Llion Jones, Aidan N Gomez, Łukasz Kaiser, and Illia Polosukhin. 2017. Attention is all you need. In *Advances in Neural Information Processing Systems*, pages 6000–6010.

Opinions, interpretations, conclusions and recommendations are those of the authors and are not necessarily endorsed by the United States Government. Cleared for public release on 08 May 2020. Originator reference number RH-20-121048. Case number 88ABW-2020-1696.

Hainan Xu, Tongfei Chen, Dongji Gao, Yiming Wang, Ke Li, Nagendra Goel, Yishay Carmiel, Daniel Povey, and Sanjeev Khudanpur. 2018. A pruned rnnlm lattice-rescoring algorithm for automatic speech recognition. In *2018 IEEE International Conference on Acoustics, Speech, and Signal Processing (ICASSP)*, Calgary, AB, Canada.

LIT Team's System Description for Japanese-Chinese Machine Translation Task in IWSLT 2020

Yimeng Zhuang, Yuan Zhang, Lijie Wang
Samsung Research China - Beijing (SRC-B)
{ym.zhuang, yuan.zhang, lijie.wang}@samsung.com

Abstract

This paper describes the LIT Team's submission to the IWSLT2020 open domain translation task, focusing primarily on Japanese-to-Chinese translation direction. Our system is based on the organizers' baseline system, but we do more works on improving the Transformer baseline system by elaborate data pre-processing. We manage to obtain significant improvements, and this paper aims to share some data processing experiences in this translation task. Large-scale back-translation on monolingual corpus is also investigated. In addition, we also try shared and exclusive word embeddings, compare different granularity of tokens like sub-word level. Our Japanese-to-Chinese translation system achieves a performance of BLEU=34.0 and ranks 2nd among all participating systems.

1 Introduction

In recent years, the neural machine translation (NMT) (Sun et al., 2019; Wu et al., 2016; Sennrich et al., 2015) has made great progress based on encoder-decoder architecture. We participate in the IWSLT 2020 open domain translation task: Japanese-to-Chinese. This paper describes the NMT systems for the IWSLT 2020 Japanese-to-Chinese machine translation task (Ansari et al., 2020).

Our main efforts are data pre-processing, specifically parallel data filter and sentence alignment. By elaborate data processing, we successfully improve the quality of the training set and thus boost the performance of our translation system. The back-translation mechanism (Edunov et al., 2018) is also investigated to extend the training corpus, we translate Chinese to Japanese to get the Japanese-to-Chinese training corpus, it is an effective approach to exploit the corresponding monolingual data sets.

The transformer model (Vaswani et al., 2017)

based on multi-head attention has achieved excellent performance in a variety of neural machine translation tasks in the last three years. This kind of NMT model surpasses the performance of the traditional statistical machine translation and the NMT performs particularly well especially with rich resource corpus. In our system, we adopt bigger transformer architecture, since the performance of the Transformer relies on model capacity, ex. the number of dimensions of the feed-forward network. To improve performance, we adopted the Relative Position Attention (Shaw et al., 2018). Also, we conduct experiments to compare the shared source and target word embeddings and exclusive word embeddings, and whether to adopt the shared embeddings relates to the translation direction. The Chinese-to-Japanese direction achieves higher scores when adopting shared word embeddings, however, the Japanese-to-Chinese direction produces opposite results.

The paper is structured as follows: Section 2 will present a detailed description of our data pre-processing, back-translation is introduced in Section 3, the model of our system will be introduced in Section 4, the main results of our experiment will be shown in Section 5. Section 6 will draw a brief conclusion of our work for the IWSLT 2020 open domain translation task.

2 Data and Pre-processing

On the whole, our system follows the standard Transformer-based translation pipeline, and our system implementation is based on the official baseline [1]. Most of our efforts in this competition are focused on data pre-processing and back-translation. We adopt the same strategies as the official baseline if we don't point out explicitly.

---

[1] https://github.com/didi/iwslt2020_
open_domain_translation

Proceedings of the 17th International Conference on Spoken Language Translation (IWSLT), pages 109–113
July 9-10, 2020. ©2020 Association for Computational Linguistics
https://doi.org/10.18653/v1/P17

Corpus	Original	Re-Filtered
Part A	2.0M	0.8M
Part B	19.0M	8.8M
Part C	161.5M	10.0M
Part D	-	2.7M
Monolingual	-	200M

Table 1: Statistics of the parallel sentence pairs used for training models in this paper. The monolingual data is used for back-translation.

2.1 Datasets

In Japanese-Chinese bidirectional machine translation competition(Ansari et al., 2020), the organizers provide a large, noisy set of Japanese-Chinese segment pairs built from web data. There are four parts:

Part A A small but relatively clean Japanese-Chinese parallel corpus, which is obtained from curating existing Japanese-Chinese parallel datasets.

Part B A pre-filtered dataset of the sentences that the organizers obtained from crawling the Web, aligning, and filtering.

Part C An unfiltered parallel web crawled corpus which is much noisier than previous datasets.

Part D A huge file of the unaligned scraped web pages with the document boundaries.

The following subsections detail how we handle these four parts of web data respectively. Besides, we conduct data augmentation by back-translation using extra monolingual data, which will be discussed in Section 3. Table 1 shows the statistics of the training data.

2.2 Parallel Data Filter

Although the organizers have filtered parts of the data, there are still many mismatched sentence pairs, i.e. the target sentence is not the corresponding translation of the source sentence. For the three aligned datasets, we re-filter them by the following rules.

- Remove empty or duplicated sentences.

- Remove sentence pairs when the source sentence and the target sentence are same.

- Convert all Chinese characters into simplified Chinese.

- Remove sentence pairs when there is no common Chinese character (Chu et al., 2014) between source sentence and target sentence.

- Remove sentences in which the number of non-English and non-punctuation characters is less than half of the length of the whole sentence.

- The maximum length ratio of sentence pairs is 1.8.

- Japanese (Chinese) sentence should be recognized as Japanese (Chinese) by fasttext's language identification model (Joulin et al., 2016b,a).

After that, we have a pre-processed bilingual training data consisting of 22.3 million parallel sentences. Note that we adjust filter rules many times, and finally adopt the above relatively strict rules, resulting in the training data is reduced significantly. Besides, the `fast_align` [2] toolkit is popular for computing the alignment score for parallel sentences, but the models trained on the training data filtered by `fast_align` become worse. We suspect that its scores may be highly related to the length of the sentences, this results in qualified long sentences are discarded. So we didn't use `fast_align` in this paper.

2.3 Web Crawled Sentence Alignment

The organizers provide us a huge corpus of more than 15 million unaligned bilingual document pairs. To extract the parallel sentences, we consider each sentence of a document as an element and adopt the longest common sub-sequence algorithm to find Ja-Zh sentence pairs with the highest character F1 similarity. Algorithm 1 shows the alignment process, in which we define the alignment score $score(C_i, J_j)$ between two sentences by the F1 value of their character overlap.

Unfortunately, this part of data is highly duplicated. After performing Algorithm 1 and filter algorithm mentioned in Section 2.2, we successfully obtained about 50 million parallel sentences pairs. But only 2.7 million sentence pairs are remained after deduplicating. Something is better than nothing, we still add the 2.7 million data into our training set.

3 Back-translation

In recent works, the back-translation mechanism (Edunov et al., 2018) has been proved as an effective method to improve machine translation systems by utilizing large-scale monolingual corpus.

---

[2] `https://github.com/clab/fast_align`

Algorithm 1 Align bilingual sentences from two documents.

Require: Chinese sentences $C_1, C_2, \cdots, C_N$; Japanese sentences $J_1, J_2, \cdots, J_M$;
Ensure: Aligned sentence pairs set A
1: Initialize all auxiliary variables s to zero;
2: **for** $i = 1 \to N$ **do**
3:    **for** $j = 1 \to M$ **do**
4:        **if** $s_{i-1,j} \geq s_{i,j}$ **then**
5:            $s_{i,j} \leftarrow s_{i-1,j}, trace(i,j) \leftarrow 0$
6:        **end if**
7:        **if** $s_{i,j-1} \geq s_{i,j}$ **then**
8:            $s_{i,j} \leftarrow s_{i,j-1}, trace(i,j) \leftarrow 1$
9:        **end if**
10:       **if** $s_{i-1,j-1} \geq s_{i,j}$ **then**
11:           $s_{i,j} \leftarrow s_{i-1,j-1}, trace(i,j) \leftarrow 2$
12:       **end if**
13:       **if** $s_{i-1,j-1}+score(C_i, J_j) > s_{i,j}$ **then**
14:           $s_{i,j} \leftarrow s_{i-1,j-1} + score(C_i, J_j)$
15:           $trace(i,j) \leftarrow 3$
16:       **end if**
17:    **end for**
18: **end for**
19: $i \leftarrow N, j \leftarrow M$
20: **while** $i > 0$ and $j > 0$ **do**
21:    **if** $trace(i,j) = 0$ **then**
22:       $i \leftarrow i - 1$
23:    **else if** $trace(i,j) = 1$ **then**
24:       $j \leftarrow j - 1$
25:    **else if** $trace(i,j) = 2$ **then**
26:       $i \leftarrow i - 1, j \leftarrow j - 1$
27:    **else if** $trace(i,j) = 3$ **then**
28:       add sentence pair (C_i, J_j) to set A
29:       $i \leftarrow i - 1, j \leftarrow j - 1$
30:    **end if**
31: **end while**

Model	Share	Truncate	BLEU
	$\times$	$\times$	32.4
ZH to JA	$\times$	$\checkmark$	32.6
	$\checkmark$	$\checkmark$	33.5

Table 2: Vocabulary strategy on Chinese-to-Japanese translation. The evaluation metric is 4-gram character BLEU score on the development set. In truncated version, the vocabulary is truncated to 40K BPE tokens.

In this paper, we follow the successful experiences in Edunov et al. (2018) to further extend our training data. Chinese monolingual data is extracted from the unaligned scraped web pages (Part D), and we select 200 million sentences to reduce training time.

3.1 Chinese-to-Japanese Translation

In order to generate a synthetic bilingual corpus, we trained a Chinese-to-Japanese transformer on the filtered parallel data mentioned in Section 2.2. Different from the Japanese-to-Chinese translation, we find that sharing BPE (Sennrich et al., 2015) tokens between Chinese and Japanese can produce better translation results. Besides, we can truncate the vocabulary size to accelerate model training. Table 2 shows the comparison of different vocabulary strategy. The number of BPE merge operations is 30k. In truncated version, the vocabulary is truncated to 40K BPE tokens.

3.2 Constructing Augmented Training Data

Following the work of Edunov et al. (2018), noise is added to the back-translation data. We delete a word with probability 10%, replace a word by a placeholder token with probability 10%, and swap words no further than three positions apart. Besides, we use bilingual data upsampling factor 4 to make the model pay more attention to the high-quality parallel data.

4 Model

We think the Transformer model is a strong model with excellent performance. So, we only take some small tricks on this model. In this section, we describe two different methods to enhance our model performance in this competition. All of them come from previous work (Sun et al., 2019; Shaw et al., 2018) and all of these methods help us to improve the baseline model. In the subsection, we will describe these methods briefly.

4.1 Bigger Transformer

In the work of (Sun et al., 2019), they proposed a method that increases the model capacity on the translation model and gets progress. Thus, we can think about if the model becomes wider, the performance may be better. We implement to increase the inner dimension of the feed-forward network in a big transformer model, from 4096 to 8192. Also, thinking about the overfitting problem, we increase the relu dropout value from 0.1 to 0.3.

4.2 Relative Position Representation

Recent empirical work shows that in the self-attention mechanism, it is better to use relative

System	Clean	Filtered	Re-Filtered	BT	Dev BLEU	Test BLEU
Baseline	√				20.0	22.0
	√	√			26.9	-
	√	√	√		28.6	-
	√	√	√	√	29.6	-
Bigger + RP*	√	√	√	√	30.3	34.0

Table 3: Results obtained by different data pre-processing methods and combinations. "Clean" denotes the data of Part A, "Filtered" denotes all training data filtered by the organizers, "Re-Filtered" denotes our re-filter method, "BT" is the abbreviation of back-translation, and "RP" means relative position. (* denotes our submitted system)

position (Shaw et al., 2018) to reflect the sequential relationship of words. In original ways, the Transformer only uses absolute position information in word embeddings. With the relative position feature, we compare the result and find it has better performance.

5 Submission to IWSLT 2020

5.1 Experiment

We compare the performance of our system on different data sets to show the effectiveness of data processing. In general, we adopt the default hyperparameters of `transformer_relative_big` in tensor2tensor [3]. Except that we set the inner dimension of the feed-forward network to 8192, and set relu dropout to 0.3. We conduct our experiments on a machine with 8 Nvidia P40 GPUs. The model is updated 500K times in 9 days. Model parameters are saved every 1000 steps, and the last three checkpoints are averaged to obtain the final model. In decoding, we search the best decoding configuration on the released development set and fix the beam size as 6, alpha as 0.8. It is regretful that because of limited computational resources, we only trained a single model and didn't conduct model ensemble experiments.

As for post-processing, we process the decoding results by removing "UNK" token and Japanese kana characters from translated Chinese texts.

5.2 Japanese-to-Chinese Translation Results

Table 3 lists results obtained by using different training data. We use the official baseline system to test the effects of data processing. In the table, data size increases from the left columns to the right columns, and the performance is also improved. This shows the importance of extending training data in this task and validates the necessity of data

pre-processing in boosting translation system accuracy. Also, the submitted system adopts a larger inner dimension and relative position, which shows the highest BLEU score in our systems.

6 Conclusion

We participated in the Japanese-to-Chinese translation direction in the IWSLT 2020 open domain translation task. We focus on improving the Transformer baseline system by doing elaborate data pre-processing, and we manage to obtain significant improvements. Experiments also show that increasing model capacity is beneficial on large training data. Finally, our submission of Japanese-to-Chinese translation achieves the 2nd highest BLEU score among all the submissions.

Acknowledgments

We thank the anonymous reviewers for their valuable comments, Mengxia Zhai for assisting processing data and Ajay Nagesh for evaluating our translation result on the secret mixed-genre test dataset.

References

Ebrahim Ansari, Amittai Axelrod, Nguyen Bach, Ondrej Bojar, Roldano Cattoni, Fahim Dalvi, Nadir Durrani, Marcello Federico, Christian Federmann, Jiatao Gu, Fei Huang, Kevin Knight, Xutai Ma, Ajay Nagesh, Matteo Negri, Jan Niehues, Juan Pino, Elizabeth Salesky, Xing Shi, Sebastian Stüker, Marco Turchi, and Changhan Wang. 2020. Findings of the IWSLT 2020 Evaluation Campaign. In *Proceedings of the 17th International Conference on Spoken Language Translation (IWSLT 2020)*, Seattle, USA.

Chenhui Chu, Toshiaki Nakazawa, and Sadao Kurohashi. 2014. Constructing a chinese—japanese parallel corpus from wikipedia. In *LREC*, pages 642–647.

Sergey Edunov, Myle Ott, Michael Auli, and David

---

[3] `https://github.com/tensorflow/tensor2tensor`

Grangier. 2018. Understanding back-translation at scale. *arXiv preprint arXiv:1808.09381*.

Armand Joulin, Edouard Grave, Piotr Bojanowski, Matthijs Douze, Hérve Jégou, and Tomas Mikolov. 2016a. Fasttext. zip: Compressing text classification models. *arXiv preprint arXiv:1612.03651*.

Armand Joulin, Edouard Grave, Piotr Bojanowski, and Tomas Mikolov. 2016b. Bag of tricks for efficient text classification. *arXiv preprint arXiv:1607.01759*.

Rico Sennrich, Barry Haddow, and Alexandra Birch. 2015. Neural machine translation of rare words with subword units. *arXiv preprint arXiv:1508.07909*.

Peter Shaw, Jakob Uszkoreit, and Ashish Vaswani. 2018. Self-attention with relative position representations. *arXiv preprint arXiv:1803.02155*.

Meng Sun, Bojian Jiang, Hao Xiong, Zhongjun He, Hua Wu, and Haifeng Wang. 2019. Baidu neural machine translation systems for wmt19. In *Proceedings of the Fourth Conference on Machine Translation (Volume 2: Shared Task Papers, Day 1)*, pages 374–381. Association for Computational Linguistics.

Ashish Vaswani, Noam Shazeer, Niki Parmar, Jakob Uszkoreit, Llion Jones, Aidan N Gomez, Łukasz Kaiser, and Illia Polosukhin. 2017. Attention is all you need. In *Advances in neural information processing systems*, pages 5998–6008.

Yonghui Wu, Mike Schuster, Zhifeng Chen, Quoc V Le, Mohammad Norouzi, Wolfgang Macherey, Maxim Krikun, Yuan Cao, Qin Gao, Klaus Macherey, et al. 2016. Google's neural machine translation system: Bridging the gap between human and machine translation. *arXiv preprint arXiv:1609.08144*.

OPPO's Machine Translation System for the IWSLT 2020 Open Domain Translation Task

Qian Zhang and **Tingxun Shi** and **Xiaopu Li** and **Dawei Dang** and
Di Ai and **Zhengshan Xue** and **Jie Hao**

{zhangqian666, shitingxun, lixiaopu, dangdawei
aidi1, xuezhengshan, haojie}@oppo.com
Manifold Lab, OPPO Research Institute

Abstract

In this paper, we demonstrate our machine translation system applied for the Chinese-Japanese bi-directional translation task (aka. open domain translation task) for the IWSLT 2020 (Ansari et al., 2020). Our model is based on Transformer (Vaswani et al., 2017), with the help of many popular, widely-proved effective data preprocessing and augmentation methods. Experiments show that these methods can improve the baseline model steadily and significantly.

1 Introduction

Machine translation, proposed even before the first computer was invented (Hutchins, 2007), has been always a famous research topic of computer science. In the recently years, with the renaissance of neural network and the emergence of attention mechanism (Sutskever et al., 2014) (Bahdanau et al., 2014), the old area has stepped into a new era. Furthermore, the Transformer architecture, after being published, has immediately attracted much attention nowadays and is dominating the whole field now.

Although Transformer has achieved many SOTA results, it has tremendous amount of parameters so is hard to be fit on small datasets, therefore it has a high demand on good and large data source. Despite of the lack of high quality data of parallel corpus, the document level comparable data is relatively easy to be crawled, so exploring an effective and accurate way of mining aligned sentence pairs from such large but noisy data, to enrich the small parallel corpus, could benefit the machine translation system a lot. Besides, currently, most open access big volume machine translation datasets are based on English, and many of them are translated to/from another European language – As many popular European languages are fusional languages, most corpus are composed by two fusional languages together. To understand whether the existing model architectures and training skills can be applied on the translation between Asian languages and other type of languages , such as between an analytic language like Chinese and an agglutinative language like Japanese, interest us.

In this paper, we demonstrate our system applied for the IWSLT 2020 open domain text translation task, which aims to translate Chinese from/to Japanese [1]. Besides describing how we trained the model that is used to generate the final result, this paper also introduces how do we mine extra parallel sentences from a large but noisy data released by the organizer, and several experiments inspired by the writing systems of Chinese and Japanese.

2 Data Preprocessing

Four pairs of parallel data are provided in the campaign, which are

- The very original file, which is crawled from various websites, and is very huge. According to the information of the campaign page, the corpus contains 15.7 million documents, which are composed by 941.3 million Japanese sentences and 928.7 million Chinese sentences — From the counts of sentences it can be immediately observed that the original corpus is not parallel, so cannot be directly used for the model. Mining parallel corpus from this mega size file is another work we have done during the campaign, which will be covered in another section of this report.

- A pre-filtered file, consists of 161.5 million "parallel" sentences. We tried to filter this

---

[1] In some cases later in the report, the two languages are noted by their ISO 639-1 codes, zh and ja respectively

114

Proceedings of the 17th International Conference on Spoken Language Translation (IWSLT), pages 114–121
July 9-10, 2020. ©2020 Association for Computational Linguistics
https://doi.org/10.18653/v1/P17

dataset to extract parallel lines, and this work will also be presented later.

- A filtered file, which has 19 million sentences, is aligned officially from the data described in the previous item. And,

- An existing parallel file, which contains 1.96 million pairs of sentences, is obtained by the provider from current existing Japanese-Chinese parallel datasets.

However, per our investigation, even the sentences in the existing parallel file are actually not fully aligned. For example, a sentence "*1994 年 2 月、ジャスコはつるまいの全株式を取得。*" (means "Jasco bought all shares in February, 1994") in the corpus is translated into "次年 6 月乌迪内斯买断了他的全部所有权。", which means "Udinese bought out all his ownership in June in the next year", so here is clearly a noise. Since deep neural network demands high quality input data, we combined the filtered file and the existing parallel file into a 20 million pairs dataset (noted as *combined dataset* afterwards) , and made a further data preprocessing, including two main steps:

2.1 Rule Based Preprocessing and Filtering

We first feed the combined dataset to a data preprocessing pipeline, including the following steps:

- Converting Latin letters to lower case. This step helps to decrease the size of the vocabularies, but since the evaluation is case-sensitive, we applied a further postprocessing step: Having generated the results from the model, we extract all Latin words from the sources and the hypotheses, and convert the words in the hypo side according to the case forms of their counterparts in the source side.

- For Chinese, converting traditional Chinese characters to simplified form; for Japanese, converting simplified Chinese characters to kanji.

- Converting full width characters to half width.

- Normalizing punctuations and other special characters, e.g. different forms of hyphen "-".

- Unescaping html characters.

- Removing html tags.

- Removing extra spaces around the dot symbol of float numbers

- Removing unnecessary spaces

Because both Chinese language and Japanese language don't use spaces to mark borders of words, we applied segmentation on each side (A branched experiment will be presented later in this report). For Chinese, we use *PKUSEG* (Luo et al., 2019) and for Japanese it is *mecab*[2]. After having observed the preprocessed data, sentence pairs are filtered out according to the following orders:

1. Sentences that contain too many non-sense symbols (including emojis ,kaomojis and emoticons, such as "(@ ˆ □ ˆ)". Although these symbols could bring semantic information, we don't consider they are important to machine translation system)

2. Sentence pairs that have abnormal length ratio, here "length" is the count of words of a sentence. As Chinese character is also an important constituent of Japanese writing system, we don't expect the Japanese sentences will be too much longer than the Chinese side; however in another hand, since Japanese is an agglutinative language, it always needs several additional (sub)words to express its own syntactical structure, so the Japanese sentences can neither be too short. We set the upper bound of words count ratio between Japanese and Chinese to 2.4 and the corresponding lower bound is 0.8.

3. Sentence pairs that occur more than once. We deduplicated and left only one single pair.

4. Sentence pairs that target is simply a replica of the source sentence.

5. Sentence pairs that target sentence shares the same beginning or ending 10 characters with source sentence.

6. Sentence pairs that the amount of Chinese words is less than 40% of the total word count in the Chinese side. Here "Chinese word" is defined as a word which is composed by Chinese characters only.

---

[2]https://taku910.github.io/mecab/

7. Sentence pairs that the amount of Japanese words is less than 40% of the total word count in the Japanese side. Here "Japanese word" is defined as a word which is composed by kanjis or kanas only. As Chinese language and Japanese language each has its own special "alphabets", this step together with the previous one can be seen as a way of language detection.

8. Sentence pairs that the count difference between numbers in Chinese side and numbers in Japanese side is greater than or equal to 3

9. Sentence pairs that cannot be aligned on numbers and Latin letters.

2.2 Alignment Information Based Filtering

Processing rules listed in the previous subsection can be applied to filter out sentence pairs that have obvious noises, but some pairs still have subtle noises that cannot be directly discovered. Therefore we use *fast_align* to align the source and target sentences, generate alignment score in the sentence level and word level [3], then further filter the combined dataset by the alignment results. For the sentence level alignment score, the threshold was set to -16 and for the word level it was -2.5. After multiple rounds cleaning, 75% of the data provided are swiped out, leaving about 5.4M sentence pairs as the foundation of our experiments described in the next section.

3 Main Task Experiments

Taking the 5.4M corpus in the hand, we further divided the words in the text into subwords (Sennrich et al., 2016b). BPE code is trained on the Chinese and Japanese corpus jointly, with 32,000 merging operations, but the vocabulary is extracted for each language individually, so for Chinese the size of its vocabulary is 31k and for Japanese it is 30k. Vocabularies for both two directions (ja-zh and zh-ja) are shared. We trained 8 heads Transformer Big models with Facebook FAIR's fairseq (Ott et al., 2019) using the following configuration:

- learning rate: 0.001

- learning rate schedule: inverse square root

- optimizer: Adam (Kingma and Ba, 2014)

- warmup steps: 4000

- dropout: 0.3

- clip-norm: 0.1

The first model trained on the filtered genuine parallel corpus (i.e. the 5.4M corpus) is not only seen as the baseline model of the consequent experiments, but also used as a scorer[4]. We re-scored the alignment scores of the sentences using this model, and again filtered away about one quarters data. The model trained on the refined data improved the BLEU score by 1.7 for zh-ja and 0.5 for ja-zh.

As many works proved, back-translation (BT) (Sennrich et al., 2016a) is a common data augmentation method in the machine translation research. Besides, (Edunov et al., 2018) also provides some other ways to back-translate. We applied both of them and in our experiments, top-10 sampling is effective on zh-ja direction and for ja-zh traditional argmax-based beam search is still better.

Firstly, 4M data in the original corpus is selected by the alignment score and translated by the models (models for the different directions) got in the previous step to build synthetic corpus, then for each direction a new model is trained on the augmented dataset (contains 5.4M + 4M + 4M = 13.4M pairs). To get a better translation result, we used ensemble model to augment the dataset. One more thing could be clarified that, in this augmentation step we not only introduced 4M back-translated data, but also generated 4M synthetic target sentences by applying knowledge distillation (KD) (Freitag et al., 2017).

On this genuine-BT-KD mixture dataset, we tried one more round of back-translation and knowledge distillation, but just saw a minor improvement. Afterwards we trained language model on the 5.4M parallel corpus for each language using kenlm (Heafield, 2011). With the help of the language model, 3M Chinese sentences and 4M Japanese sentences with the highest scores are selected from the unaligned monolingual corpus as the new input of BT models, augmented the mixture dataset to 20.4M pairs (noted as *final augmented dataset*, which will be referenced later

---

[3]To get a word level alignment score, we divide the sentence level score by the average length of source sentence and target sentence

[4]Many related works used to train a model in the very early stage, for example train from the rawest, uncleaned dataset. We did considered doing so at first but since the original dataset is too noisy, we decided to clean the corpus first to achieve a more meaningful baseline score.

in the report), and we did another round of back-translation and knowledge distillation. After these three rounds iterative BT (Hoang et al., 2018) and KD, several best single models are further composed together to an ensemble model. In the last step, following (Yee et al., 2019), we use both backward model (for zh-ja task, model from ja-zh is its backward model, and vice versa) and Transformer language model to rerank the n-best candidates of the output from the ensemble model, to generate the final results.

Detailed results on the dev dataset of each intermediate step is shown in table 1. We strictly followed the organizer's requirement to build a constrained system, means that we didn't add in any external data, nor made use of the test data in any other form besides of generating the final result.

4 Branched Task Experiments

Besides the main task experiments demonstrated in the previous section, as the *introduction* part says, we are also interested in how to mine or extract parallel data from such huge but noisy datasets, and explore some special skills on translating from Chinese to Japanese (and also vice versa). This section will mainly discuss our work on these two parts.

4.1 Filtering the Noisy Dataset

We first tried to extract parallel sentences from the pre-filtered, 161.5 million dataset. Since this dataset is "nearly aligned", it is assumed that for a given sentence pair, if the target side doesn't match the source, the whole pair can be safely dropped because the counterpart of the source doesn't exist in other places of the corpus. We first use *CLD* as the language detector to remove sentences that are neither Chinese nor Japanese — only in this step nearly 110 million pairs are filtered out. Next, we feed the data into the preprocessing pipeline which is the same as the one introduced in the *Preprocessing* section. The preprocessed corpus are then filtered in a similar way described in the *Preprocessing* section, with the following additional steps:

- We compared the url counts of each side and remove the inconsistent line pairs.

- We kept a set of common special characters as a white list, removed all other special characters

- We removed the sentence pairs that the source side is too similar to the target side. Con-

cretely, we compared the Levenshtein distance between the sentences, divided it by the average length (count of characters) of the text in the pair. If this ratio is above 0.9, we consider the source and the target are too similar.

After the filtering, 14.92 million sentence pairs are kept, and based on them we trained a model by Marian (Junczys-Dowmunt et al., 2018) using Transformer base model, see it as the baseline model for the current task. 36k BPE merge operations are applied on the remained sentence pairs, independently for each language, led to two vocabularies each contains 50k words. We use Adam optimizer with learning rate set to 3×10^{-4} and 16,000 warmup steps, clip-norm set to 0.5, dropout of attention set to 0.05, label smoothing set to 0.1. Decoder searches with a 6 beam-width and the length normalization is 0.8. [5]

To filter the noisy parallel corpora, We followed dual conditional cross-entropy filtering proposed by (Junczys-Dowmunt, 2018): for a parallel corpus D, in which the source language is noted as $\mathcal{X}$ and the target language is noted as $\mathcal{Y}$, two translation models can be trained: model A is trained from $\mathcal{X}$ to $\mathcal{Y}$ and model B is trained in the reversed direction. Given a sentence pair $(x, y) \in D$ and a translation model M, the conditional cross-entropy of the sentence pair normalized by target sentence length can be calculated:

$$H_M(y|x) = -\frac{1}{|y|} \log P_M(y|x)$$
$$= -\frac{1}{|y|} \sum_{t=1}^{|y|} \log P_M(y_t|y_{<t}, x)$$

As we have two models A and B, two scores achieved by each can be combined to calculate the maximal symmetric agreement (MSA) of the sentence pair, following:

$$\mathrm{MSA}(x, y) = |H_A(y|x) - H_B(x|y)| + \frac{1}{2}(H_A(y|x) + H_B(x|y))$$

---

[5] In the branched experiments, the machine translation framework and hyper-parameters applied are all different from those used in the main task. The reason is these experiments were taken concurrently by different team members, so they have each own hyperparameter settings.

	zh-ja **BLEU**	ja-zh **BLEU**
Baseline	34.6	32.6
+ Filtered by alignment information from baseline model	36.3 (+1.7, +1.7)	33.2 (+0.6, +0.6)
+ 1st round BT using genuine parallel corpus (13.4M pairs)	37.5 (+2.9, +1.2)	34.6 (+2.0, +1.4)
+ 2nd round BT using genuine parallel corpus (13.4M pairs)	37.6 (+3.0, +0.1)	34.6 (+2.0, +0.0)
+ BT using monolingual corpus (20.4M pairs)	38.8 (+4.2, +1.2)	35.4 (+2.8, +0.8)
+ 3rd round BT using both parallel and monolingual corpus (20.4M pairs)	39.2 (+4.6, +0.4)	36.0 (+3.4, +0.6)
+ Ensemble	40.1 (+5.5, +0.9)	36.6 (+4.0, +0.6)
+ Reranking	**40.8 (+6.2, +0.7)**	**37.2 (+4.6, +0.6)**

Table 1: Results of the main task experiments, evaluation is taken on the validation dataset provided officially. The improvement amount of each row is expressed in two forms: absolute improvement (current score - baseline score) and relative improvement (current score - previous step score). Note to get a more strict BLEU score, we used SacreBLEU (Post, 2018) to calculate the final BLEU score, and we didn't split words composed by Latin letters and numbers into characters, which differs from the official evaluation process. If the same splitting is applied, and evaluated by `multibleu` (https://github.com/moses-smt/mosesdecoder/blob/master/scripts/generic/multi-bleu-detok.perl) which is officially designated, the score could be higher by 1.x points

Since $\mathrm{MSA}(x, y) \in [0, +\infty)$, we can re-scale the score to $(0, 1]$, by

$$\mathrm{adq}(x, y) = \exp(-\mathrm{MSA}(x, y))$$

This method is noted as "adq" adapting the notation proposed in the original paper. We took a series of experiments on the direction zh-ja, but the results are not so good as we expected. Detailed information is listed in table 2. We also added dataset C mentioned in table 2 to the original dataset used for training baseline model of the main task, but still didn't see too much improvement. Using the configuration introduced in the *main task section*, the model's BLEU score is 34.7, only 0.1 points higher than the baseline score listed in table 1.

4.2 Mining the Unaligned Dataset

Besides the officially released pre-filtered dataset, we also paid our attention on the very original, huge but dirty dataset, tried some methods to clean it. As previously said, both Chinese and Japanese have its own closed characters set respectively, so we first simply remove the lines that don't contain any Chinese characters (for Chinese corpus), or those don't contain any katas or kanjis (for Japanese lines). This simple step directly removed about 400 million lines. We also applied the same preprocessing described before, like language detection, deduplication, and the cleaning pipeline. This preprocessing reserved 460 million lines.

For the remained data, as they are not aligned, we cannot follow the filtering process shown in the previous sub-section. However, we assumed that for a Chinese sentence, if we can find its Japanese counterpart, the corresponding line can only exist in the same document. As the dataset gives document boundary, we split the whole dataset into millions of documents, and use *hunalign* (Varga et al., 2007) to mine aligned pairs in each document (dictionaries are extracted from a cleaned version of the combined dataset). Although still hold the intra-document alignment assumption, we kept reading documents, didn't perform hunalign until the accumulated lines reached 100k (but we don't break the document), for the possible cross-document alignment. We kept all lines which have alignment scores higher than 0.8, and of which the words count ratio between source and target falls into $[0.5, 2]$. Then we removed all lines contains url, replaced numbers and English words which have more than 3 letters with tags, and deduplicated again, leaving only 5.5 million lines. We trained a Transformer base model using marian on the dataset which is utilized for training the baseline model in the *main task experiments*, applying the same configuration given in the previous sub-section, and ranked the results using *bleualign* (Sennrich and Volk, 2010) (Sennrich and Volk, 2011), finally kept 4 million lines. This dataset is patched to the original dataset which is used the main task, and a minor improvement (+0.6 BLEU) can be seen. However, due to the time limit this part of data were not further used in the whole main task experiments.

Filtering method	BLEU on dev set
Baseline	27.1
A. adq, 8M data with highest scores	**27.2 (+0.1)**
B. adq, 5M data with highest scores	26.2 (-0.9)
C. Filter A by fast_align scores and Japanese language models	26.8 (-0.3)

Table 2: `zh-ja` experiments using data filtered from the pre-filtered "parallel" corpus. BLEU is calculated by sacreBLEU in the same way depicted in the *main task experiments* section

4.3 Character Based Models and Some Variations

From the perspective of writing system research, Chinese characters system is a typical *logogram*, means a single character can also carry meaningful semantical information, which differs to phonologic writing systems widely used in the world. Previous research (Li et al., 2019) argues that for Chinese, character-based model even performs better than subword-based models. Moreover, For the Japanese language, its literacy "was introduced to Japan in the form of the Chinese writing system, by way of Baekje before the 5th century" [6], even today Chinese characters (Hanzi, in simplified Chinese 汉字, in traditional Chinese 漢字) are still important components of Japanese writing system (in Japanese called kanji, written as 漢字), so intuitively characters between two languages could have strong mapping relationship. (ngo, 2019) also shows that for Japanese-Vietnamese machine translation system, character-based model takes advantages to the traditional methods. As both Vietnamese and Japanese are impacted by Chinese language, it is reasonable to try character-based machine translation systems on Chinese ⇔ Japanese language pairs.

Inspired from the intuition and the previous related works, we further split the subwords in the *final augmented dataset* (presented in the main task experiments) into characters in three different ways, which are

- Split CJK characters (hanzi in Chinese and kanji in Japanese) only, since we assume that the characters are highly related between these two sets

- Split CJK characters and *katakana* (in kanji 片仮名). In Japanese writing system, besides kanji, another component is called *kana* (in kanji 仮名), which belongs to syllabic

system (one character is corresponding to a syllable). Kana further consists of a pair of syllabaries: *hiragana* (in kanji 平仮名) and katakana, the latter is generally used to transliterate loanword (including foreign names). Although a single katakana character doesn't carry semantical information, only imitates the pronunciation, the same situation exists in Chinese, too — when transliterating foreign names, a single Chinese character is only used to show the pronunciation, loses the means it could have. Therefore, katakanas can also be roughly mapped to Chinese characters.

- Split CJK characters and all kanas

For each direction, we trained four different Transformer Big models using the splitting methods described above (another one is subword-based model as baseline). In this series of experiments, we used FAIR's fairseq, set clipnorm to 0, max tokens to 12,200, update-freq to 8, dropout to 0.1, warmup-updates to 15,000. Length penalties are different among all models, we set the optimal value according to the results reported on the validation set. However, surprisingly, there is still no improvement can be observed, and for `zh-ja` direction models generally perform worse (detailed results are listed in table 3). It needs some extra work to find out the reason, one possible explanation is the big amount of back-translated synthesis corpus, which was generated by model based on subwords, changed the latent data distribution.

5 Final Results

From the evaluation results provided by the organizer officially, Our BLEU score for `jazh` direction is 32.9, for `zhja` is 30.1.

However, per our observation on the dev dataset, we found most of the numbers and Latin words are styled in full width characters, so we made an extra step in post-processing to convert all

---

[6]https://en.wikipedia.org/wiki/Japanese_language#Writing_system

Splitting method	zh-ja **BLEU**	ja-zh **BLEU**
zh-ja Baseline	**39.0**	35.1
Split cjk chars only	37.9 (-1.1)	**35.4 (+0.3)**
+ katakanas	37.9 (-1.1)	34.9 (-0.2)
+ hiraganas	38.2 (-0.8)	35.3 (+0.2)

Table 3: Experiments using character-based models. BLEU is calculated by sacreBLEU in the same way depicted in the *main task experiments* section. The "baseline" model here is trained on the 21M data after three rounds back-translation, compared to zh-ja 39.2/ja-zh 36.0 step in the *main task experiments* section, not to be confused with the baseline demonstrated in the previous section

jazh BLEU	zhja BLEU
55.8	43.0
34.0	**34.8**[*]
32.9	34.3
32.5	33.0
32.3	31.7
30.9	31.2
29.4	**30.1**
26.9	29.9
26.2	28.4
25.3	26.3
22.6	25.9
11.6	7.1
1.8	
0.1	

Table 4: Leaderboard released officially just after the submission. Scores shown in the table are character-level BLEU calculated by multibleu (https://github.com/moses-smt/mosesdecoder/blob/master/scripts/generic/multibleu-detok.perl). Our results are styled in bold and the contrastive one is marked with an additional asterisk symbol ∗. At the date of submitting the camera-ready version report, the leaderboard hasn't marked which system(s) is/are unconstrained

the numbers and Latin words in our final submission of zhja to full width characters. For example, "2008" was converted to " 2 0 0 8 "[7]. Our contrastive result, in which all the numbers and Latin words are composed by half width characters (and this is the only difference compared with the primary submission we made), was scored 34.8, gained an improvement of nearly 5 points. The contrastive result is generated by the same model we trained on the constrained dataset. All the results reported above is shown in table 4

---

[7]Whether a letter or a digit is styled in half width or full width doesn't change its meaning

6 Conclusion and Future Works

In this report, we demonstrate our work for the Chinese-Japanese and Japanese-Chinese open domain translation task. The system we submitted is a neural MT model based on Transformer architecture. During the experiments, many techniques, such as back-translation, ensemble, reranking are applied and are proved to be effective for the MT system. Parallel data extraction, noisy data filtering methods and character-based models are also experienced and discussed, although currently they are not integrated into our systems, there will be still a lot work on them to find out proper ways to optimize the procedure and models, or to prove their limitations.

References

2019. *How Transformer Revitalizes Character-based Neural Machine Translation: An Investigation on Japanese-Vietnamese Translation Systems*. Zenodo.

Ebrahim Ansari, Amittai Axelrod, Nguyen Bach, Ondrej Bojar, Roldano Cattoni, Fahim Dalvi, Nadir Durrani, Marcello Federico, Christian Federmann, Jiatao Gu, Fei Huang, Kevin Knight, Xutai Ma, Ajay Nagesh, Matteo Negri, Jan Niehues, Juan Pino, Elizabeth Salesky, Xing Shi, Sebastian Stüker, Marco Turchi, and Changhan Wang. 2020. Findings of the IWSLT 2020 Evaluation Campaign. In *Proceedings of the 17th International Conference on Spoken Language Translation (IWSLT 2020)*, Seattle, USA.

Dzmitry Bahdanau, Kyunghyun Cho, and Yoshua Bengio. 2014. Neural machine translation by jointly learning to align and translate. *arXiv preprint arXiv:1409.0473*.

Sergey Edunov, Myle Ott, Michael Auli, and David Grangier. 2018. Understanding back-translation at scale. In *Proceedings of the 2018 Conference on Empirical Methods in Natural Language Processing*, pages 489–500.

Markus Freitag, Yaser Al-Onaizan, and Baskaran Sankaran. 2017. Ensemble distillation for neural machine translation. *arXiv preprint arXiv:1702.01802*.

Kenneth Heafield. 2011. Kenlm: Faster and smaller language model queries. In *Proceedings of the sixth workshop on statistical machine translation*, pages 187–197. Association for Computational Linguistics.

Vu Cong Duy Hoang, Philipp Koehn, Gholamreza Haffari, and Trevor Cohn. 2018. Iterative back-translation for neural machine translation. In *Proceedings of the 2nd Workshop on Neural Machine Translation and Generation*, pages 18–24.

John Hutchins. 2007. Machine translation: A concise history. *Computer aided translation: Theory and practice*, 13(29-70):11.

Marcin Junczys-Dowmunt. 2018. Dual conditional cross-entropy filtering of noisy parallel corpora. In *Proceedings of the Third Conference on Machine Translation: Shared Task Papers*, pages 888–895.

Marcin Junczys-Dowmunt, Roman Grundkiewicz, Tomasz Dwojak, Hieu Hoang, Kenneth Heafield, Tom Neckermann, Frank Seide, Ulrich Germann, Alham Fikri Aji, Nikolay Bogoychev, André F. T. Martins, and Alexandra Birch. 2018. Marian: Fast neural machine translation in C++. In *Proceedings of ACL 2018, System Demonstrations*, pages 116–121, Melbourne, Australia. Association for Computational Linguistics.

Diederik P Kingma and Jimmy Ba. 2014. Adam: A method for stochastic optimization. *arXiv preprint arXiv:1412.6980*.

Xiaoya Li, Yuxian Meng, Xiaofei Sun, Qinghong Han, Arianna Yuan, and Jiwei Li. 2019. Is word segmentation necessary for deep learning of chinese representations? In *Proceedings of the 57th Annual Meeting of the Association for Computational Linguistics*, pages 3242–3252.

Ruixuan Luo, Jingjing Xu, Yi Zhang, Xuancheng Ren, and Xu Sun. 2019. Pkuseg: A toolkit for multi-domain chinese word segmentation. *CoRR*, abs/1906.11455.

Myle Ott, Sergey Edunov, Alexei Baevski, Angela Fan, Sam Gross, Nathan Ng, David Grangier, and Michael Auli. 2019. fairseq: A fast, extensible toolkit for sequence modeling. In *Proceedings of the 2019 Conference of the North American Chapter of the Association for Computational Linguistics (Demonstrations)*, pages 48–53.

Matt Post. 2018. A call for clarity in reporting BLEU scores. In *Proceedings of the Third Conference on Machine Translation: Research Papers*, pages 186–191, Belgium, Brussels. Association for Computational Linguistics.

Rico Sennrich, Barry Haddow, and Alexandra Birch. 2016a. Improving neural machine translation models with monolingual data. In *Proceedings of the 54th Annual Meeting of the Association for Computational Linguistics (Volume 1: Long Papers)*, pages 86–96.

Rico Sennrich, Barry Haddow, and Alexandra Birch. 2016b. Neural machine translation of rare words with subword units. In *Proceedings of the 54th Annual Meeting of the Association for Computational Linguistics (Volume 1: Long Papers)*, pages 1715–1725.

Rico Sennrich and Martin Volk. 2010. Mt-based sentence alignment for ocr-generated parallel texts.

Rico Sennrich and Martin Volk. 2011. Iterative, mt-based sentence alignment of parallel texts. In *Proceedings of the 18th Nordic Conference of Computational Linguistics (NODALIDA 2011)*, pages 175–182.

Ilya Sutskever, Oriol Vinyals, and Quoc V Le. 2014. Sequence to sequence learning with neural networks. In *Advances in neural information processing systems*, pages 3104–3112.

Dániel Varga, András Kornai, Viktor Nagy, László Németh, and Viktor Trón. 2007. Parallel corpora for medium density languages.

Ashish Vaswani, Noam Shazeer, Niki Parmar, Jakob Uszkoreit, Llion Jones, Aidan N Gomez, Łukasz Kaiser, and Illia Polosukhin. 2017. Attention is all you need. In *Advances in neural information processing systems*, pages 5998–6008.

Kyra Yee, Yann Dauphin, and Michael Auli. 2019. Simple and effective noisy channel modeling for neural machine translation. In *Proceedings of the 2019 Conference on Empirical Methods in Natural Language Processing and the 9th International Joint Conference on Natural Language Processing (EMNLP-IJCNLP)*, pages 5700–5705.

Character Mapping and Ad-hoc Adaptation:
Edinburgh's IWSLT 2020 Open Domain Translation System

Pinzhen Chen   **Nikolay Bogoychev**   **Ulrich Germann**

School of Informatics, University of Edinburgh

10 Crichton Street, Edinburgh EH8 9AB

`{pinzhen.chen, n.bogoych, ulrich.germann}@ed.ac.uk`

Abstract

This paper describes the University of Edinburgh's neural machine translation systems submitted to the IWSLT 2020 open domain Japanese↔Chinese translation task. On top of commonplace techniques like tokenisation and corpus cleaning, we explore character mapping and unsupervised decoding-time adaptation. Our techniques focus on leveraging the provided data, and we show the positive impact of each technique through the gradual improvement of BLEU.

1 Introduction

The University of Edinburgh presents its neural machine translation (NMT) systems for the IWSLT 2020 open domain translation task (Ansari et al., 2020). The task requires participants to submit systems to translate between Japanese (Ja) and Chinese (Zh), where the sentences come from mixed domains. For training purpose, 1.96 million existing sentence pairs and 59.49 million crawled sentence pairs[1] are provided, making the task a high-resource one. In our experiments, we focused on three aspects:

1. Corpus cleaning which consists of hand-crafted rules and cross-entropy based methods.

2. Japanese and Chinese character mapping to maximise vocabulary overlap and make embedding tying more intuitive.

3. Unsupervised ad-hoc adaptation during decoding time to translate a multi-domain test set, experimented at the sentence, cluster (sub-document) and document levels.

Our techniques are mostly data-centric and each technique improves translation in terms of BLEU on our development set. In the final automatic evaluation based on 4-gram character BLEU, our systems rank 6th out of 14 for Ja→Zh and 7th out of 11 for Zh→Ja.

2 Baseline with Rule-Based Cleaning

2.1 Preprocessing

We first tokenise our data at word-level, which is commonly done for the Japanese and Chinese (Barrault et al., 2019; Nakazawa et al., 2019). While it is unclear whether word-level or character-level models are superior (Bawden et al., 2019), word-level segmentation could resolve ambiguity and dramatically reduce sequence length. The tools we use are `KyTea` (Neubig et al., 2011) for Japanese and `Jieba_fast`[2] for Chinese.

2.2 Rule-based cleaning

We then apply a series of rule-based cleaning operations on both existing and crawled data to create baseline models. These steps are mostly inspired by submissions to the corpus filtering task at WMT 2018 (Koehn et al., 2018). The task shows that effective corpus filtering brings substantial gain in translation performance.

Language identification: One way of parallel corpus filtering is to restrict source sentences to be in the source language, and target sentences to be in the target language. However, distinguishing between Japanese and Chinese, particularly short sentences, is tricky because both share a set of common characters. Hence, we decide to relax this rule by keeping all sentences (pairs) which are identified as either Chinese or Japanese using `langid.py` (Lui and Baldwin, 2012). This inevitably leaves

---

[1] We mistakenly used an outdated dataset which is larger but noisier. The dataset was extracted from crawled texts with encoding issues and inconsistent handling of Japanese characters "ブ" and "で".

[2] https://github.com/deepcs233/jieba_fast, a faster implementation of `Jieba`

Proceedings of the 17th International Conference on Spoken Language Translation (IWSLT), pages 122–129

July 9-10, 2020. ©2020 Association for Computational Linguistics

https://doi.org/10.18653/v1/P17

some Chinese on the Japanese side and vice versa. It might have a beneficial copying effect (Currey et al., 2017), especially given the vocabulary overlap between the two languages.

Length ratio: We use the provided high-quality existing data to estimate the average Japanese and Chinese sentence lengths at character-level. We find the length ratio of Japanese to Chinese is about 1.4 to 1. We remove sentence pairs which have a length ratio outside the 3 standard deviations from this mean. This a lenient choice in order to keep short translations. This is applied to both existing and crawled data.

Sentence length: We remove sentence pairs with more than 70 tokens on the Chinese side or more than 100 tokens on the Japanese side, for both existing and crawled data.

Chinese simplification: The Chinese datasets contain both traditional and simplified characters, so we use `hanziconv`[3] to simplify them. This rule-based converter has a minor flaw that it sometimes confuses on characters that are in both traditional and simplified Chinese. An example is "著", the traditional form of "着", but also a simplified character on its own with a different meaning.

2.3 Model training

For the baseline model, we try out three combinations of data, namely existing only, crawled only and both. For Ja→Zh and Zh→Ja, this results in six models. As a comparison, we also train vanilla models without previously described cleaning steps.

All models are Transformer-Base with default configurations (Vaswani et al., 2017). We use `Marian` (Junczys-Dowmunt et al., 2018) to train our systems, with SentencePiece (Kudo and Richardson, 2018) applied on tokenised data. As stated previously, Chinese and Japanese share some characters, so it is intuitive to use a shared vocabulary between source and target, and to enable three-way weight-tying between source, target and output embeddings (Press and Wolf, 2017).

We report character-level BLEU on development set, using the evaluation script provided.[4] The baseline results are shown in Table 2 as "(1) vanilla" and "(2) rule-based cleaning". We see a significant improvement in BLEU after applying rule-based

---

[3]https://github.com/berniey/hanziconv
[4]https://github.com/didi/iwslt2020_open_domain_translation/tree/master/eval

cleaning. BLEU scores reported for the development set are based on tokenised output, but we perform de-tokenisation and normalisation of full-width numbers and punctuation symbols for our final submission to make the texts natural Chinese or Japanese.

3 Chinese and Japanese Mapping

In ancient times, Japanese borrowed (at that time, traditional) Chinese characters (Hanzi) to use as a written form (Kanji). After a long time of co- and separate evolution (e.g. Chinese simplification), the relationship between Hanzi and Kanji is complicated. Some Hanzi and Kanji stay unchanged, some develop different meanings, and some develop different written forms. A detailed description is given by Chu et al. (2012). More importantly, they released a Kanji to traditional and simplified Hanzi mapping table. With each Kanji being a key, there can be zero, one or many corresponding traditional and simplified Hanzi. In total, there are mapping entries for around 5700 Kanji to simplified Hanzi. Chu et al. (2013) use this character mapping to enhance word segmentation in statistical machine translation (SMT). Recently, Song et al. (2020) map characters in a Chinese corpus to Japanese, making it a pseudo-Japanese corpus for the purpose of pre-training Japanese↔English NMT.

In our work, we take a step forward to map Chinese and Japanese to each other for Chinese↔Japanese NMT directly. Without mapping as a data processing step, an NMT system needs to learn the mapping between Kanji and Hanzi implicitly. Therefore we hypothesise that mapping them before training a model will:

1. maximise character overlap percentage, reduce vocabulary size and make embedding-tying more effective, and

2. reduce the computation needed to learn to model the mapping.

Since we already simplified all Chinese characters, hereafter we refer to simplified Chinese as Hanzi. Mapping from Kanji to Hanzi is straightforward from the character mapping table. Next, according to the mapping table, we re-construct a mapping table indexed by Hanzi, but a minor difference is that each Hanzi will have at least one corresponding Kanji. It is not possible to get perfect one-to-one mappings due to the existing many-to-many

	Chinese→Japanese				Japanese→Chinese			
	Zh	**Ja**	**Total**	**Overlap**	**Zh**	**Ja**	**Total**	**Overlap**
no mapping	21168		24387	15283		18502	24387	15283
conservative	20958	18502	24117	15343	21168	16659	22891	14936
aggressive	20560		24086	14976		16341	22759	14750

Table 1: Character statistics of Chinese (Zh) and Japanese (Ja)

relationship between Hanzi and Kanji. In order to simplify post-processing. we only map source characters to target, so the target outputs are always in the genuine target language. Hence we map Chinese to Japanese or Japanese to Chinese depending on the translation direction. We design two simple mapping scheme variants:

1. **Conservative mapping**: apply one-to-one mapping and ignore all one-to-many cases. All target characters must be constrained to target corpus, in order not to introduce new characters.

2. **Aggressive mapping**: apply one-to-one mapping, and for the one-to-many mapping cases, pick the character that has the highest frequency in the target corpus. The target constraint applies too.

Table 1 shows the counts of characters before and after mapping in each language as well as the total counts, for Chinese→Japanese and Japanese→Chinese respectively, on all available data. We only map characters on the respective source side and leave the target side of the training data as it is.

We then train models on the mapped data for both directions, with results displayed in Table 2 as "(3) mapping". We observe that aggressive mapping is marginally better than conservative on Ja→Zh and much better on Zh→Ja. Thus, we pick aggressive mapping for our following experiments.

4 Filtering Based on Cross-Entropy

Our initial rule-based cleaning shows its effectiveness through improvement in BLEU scores. We further adopt two filtering steps based on cross-entropy proposed by Junczys-Dowmunt (2018):

4.1 Dual conditional cross-entropy

Dual conditional cross-entropy score is obtained from the absolute difference between cross-entropies of two translation models in inverse directions, weighted by the sum of cross-entropies

of the two models. The score of a sentence pair (x, y) is calculated according to Equation 1, where $H_{a \to b}(b|a)$ is the cross-entropy from a translation model that translates a to b. A lower score implies a better sentence pair.

$$\begin{aligned} \text{adequacy} = &\left| H_{x \to y}(y|x) - H_{y \to x}(x|y) \right| \\ &+ \frac{1}{2}(H_{x \to y}(y|x) + H_{y \to x}(x|y)) \end{aligned} \tag{1}$$

This step finds sentence pairs that are adequate, and more importantly, equally adequate in both directions. It effectively filters out non-parallel sentences, or even machine translations which have been optimised for just a single direction. We want to score sentence pairs with the best translation model we have, so we use the aggressive mapping models built in the previous section to score mapped corpus for both directions.

4.2 Language model cross-entropy difference

The previous step ensures the adequacy of sentence pairs, but it does not pick out unnatural sentences. For example, a concatenation of texts from a website's navigation bar, together with its translation, get a good score by fulfilling adequacy. To alleviate this issue, we apply cross-entropy difference scoring. The score for a single sentence a is calculated according to Equation 2, where $H_{desired}(a)$ is the cross-entropy from a language model trained on desired data (clean, in-domain) and $H_{undesired}(a)$ is the cross-entropy from a language model trained on undesired data (noisy, out-of-domain). It has an interpretation that, a high-quality sentence should be similar to the desired data but different from the undesired data. We used `KenLM` (Heafield et al., 2013) to build 4-gram language models on the existing and the crawled data respectively.

$$H_{\text{desired}}(x) - H_{\text{undesired}}(x) \tag{2}$$

Since our data serve both translation directions, we score both sides of a sentence pair and take the

Category	Data	Transformer size	BLEU		
			Ja→Zh	Zh→Ja	
(1) vanilla	existing	base	21.88	27.11	
(2) rule-based cleaning	existing	base	26.57	26.59	
	crawled		25.15	27.25	
	all		28.26	27.70	√
(3) mapping	conservative	base	29.09	24.37	
	aggressive		29.41	27.78	√
(4) cross-entropy filtering	best 50M	base	29.66	28.84	
	best 35M		30.45	28.92	
	best 20M		30.58	29.67	√
(5) deeper models	best 20M	big	30.91	30.13	
	best 10M		30.65	30.42	√ (a)
	best 10M		30.68	30.40	(b)
	best 5M		30.35	29.94	(c)
	best 5M		29.71	30.08	(d)
(6) ensembles	ensemble of (c) and (d)		30.63	30.55	
	ensemble of (a) and (b)		31.55	30.86	
	ensemble of (a), (b), (c) and (d)		31.61	30.90	

Table 2: Our models' 4-gram character-level BLEU on development set. A $\sqrt{}$ symbol denotes the best configuration in each category.

sum to get an overall fluency score:

$$\text{fluency} = H_{\text{existing\_ja}}(ja) - H_{\text{crawled\_ja}}(ja) \\ + H_{\text{existing\_zh}}(zh) - H_{\text{crawled\_zh}}(zh) \quad (3)$$

4.3 Ranking and cut-off

To combine both filtering methods, Junczys-Dowmunt (2018) negates the scores and exponentiate them. Furthermore, extreme cross-entropy difference scores are capped or cut to 0. Finally, a product of the two determines the quality of sentence pairs. After applying this procedure, we observe that the top-ranking sentences are dominated by the ones with perfect adequacy but not fluency (e.g. a translation of navigation bar). Thus we keep multiplication but omit capping and cutting to weight fluency more. Equation 4 shows how the final score of a sentence pair is calculated.

$$\text{score} = \exp(-\text{adequacy}) \times \exp(-\text{fluency}) \quad (4)$$

After we rank all sentences pairs by their scores, we empirically determine the data cut-off point. We test with top 50, 35 and 20 million sentence pairs with Transformer-Base architecture for both translation directions. We report BLEU scores in category "(4) cross-entropy filtering" in Table 2,

where we observe that translation performance improves as the size of training data drops. Thus we further experiment with 20, 10 and 5 million data on Transformer-Big. Results are displayed in the same table under category "(5) deeper models". In addition, we run ensemble decoding, combining the models trained on 10 million and 5 million sentences, and report results in the same table in category "(6) ensembles".

5 Ad-hoc Domain Adaptation

NMT is sensitive to domain mismatch (Koehn and Knowles, 2017), and there are numerous techniques for domain adaptation for NMT (Chu and Wang, 2018). Some model and training techniques require prior knowledge of the domain and cannot be easily applied. Nonetheless, one method that can be adopted during test sentence translation is retrieving samples that are similar to the input from the available training data, and fine-tuning a trained generic model on these samples. Such ad-hoc domain adaptation can be done at sentence level (Farajian et al., 2017; Li et al., 2018) or document level (Poncelas et al., 2018).

5.1 Similar sentence retrieval

A crucial factor for domain adaptation to work is to accurately retrieval representative sentences of test sentences. Farajian et al. (2017) store training data in the Lucene search engine and take the top-scoring outcomes ranked by sentence-level BLEU. Li et al. (2018) use word-based reverse indexing and explore three similarity measures: Levenshtein Distance, cosine similarity between average word embeddings, and cosine similarity between sentence embeddings from NMT. Additionally, they suggest an alternative approach, phrase coverage, inspired by phrase-based SMT, when no high-scoring match is found.

Sentence-level adaptation is computationally expensive because, for each sentence, a separate model needs to be fine-tuned. In contrast, Poncelas et al. (2018) synthesise data similar to the whole test set. They leverage a feature decay algorithm to select monolingual data in the target language that are similar to test sentences translated by a generic source-to-target model. Then, the selected sentences are back-translated to source language (Sennrich et al., 2016), forming synthetic parallel sentences for fine-tuning.

In our work, we adopt a pure phrase-coverage approach, which is compatible for both sentence and document level retrieval. As originally suggested for phrase-pair extraction in phrase-based SMT by Callison-Burch et al. (2005) and Zhang and Vogel (2005), we index the source side of the training data via a suffix array (Manber and Myers, 1990) for very fast identification of sentence pairs that contain a given phrase. Then we simply use the test data as a query to retrieval sentences based on n-gram overlapping. Figure 1 shows how efficiently our sentence retrieval method scales up.

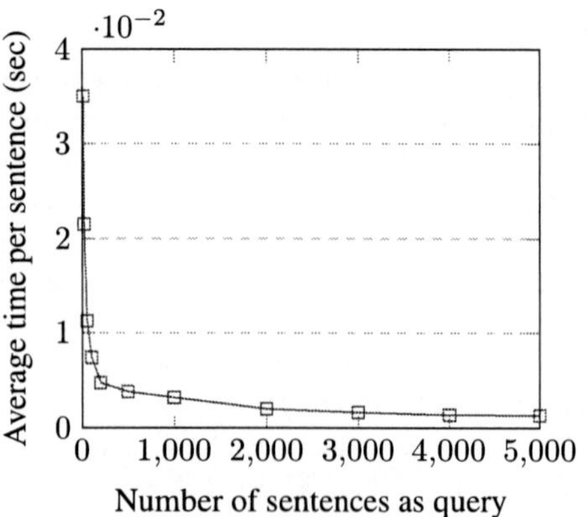

Figure 1: Average time to query one sentence against number of sentences in the query.

We set a threshold T, such that n-grams which occur more than T times in training data are disregarded, under the assumption that the generic model will already have learned to translate such phrases adequately. This is similar to Li et al. (2018)'s approach, but we try different T values. For other n-grams, we always include all matching sentences in the fine-tuning data.

5.2 Fine-tuning experiments

Due to time constraint, we only experiment our on-the-fly fine-tuning on Ja→Zh. We pick the generic baseline model to be the best-performing one trained on 10 million data. We test three different ways of doing the adaptation. First is the single-sentence adaptation, where the generic model is fine-tuned on selected training sentences for each sentence in development (dev) set. However, careful choice of hyperparameters is necessary to prevent overfitting because only a small number of sentences are retrieved. Next thing we try is to use 1 dev sentence and other 9 closet dev sentences together as a query. To form such a cluster of 10 dev sentences, we convert all dev sentences into n-gram TF-IDF vectors and score cosine similarity in a pairwise manner. This allows us to find the most similar sentences to any given one. For the above two choices, we set the threshold T to be 20, and fine-tune for 1 and 10 epochs separately. The results are reported in Table 3.

We observe that BLEU drops even we only fine-tune for a single epoch. Our intermediate conclusion is that there is overfitting or misfitting to out-of-domain sentences that have been incorrectly retrieved. Furthermore, sentence-level adaptation is fairly expensive, which prevents us from performing a grid search to find the most suitable configurations. Hence, we move on to document-level adaptation by using the whole dev set as a query to find similar sentences. As a comparison, we also use the whole test set, and a combination of dev and test as queries. This results in hundreds of thousands of sentences being retrieved, compared to hundreds to thousands for sentence-level retrieval. To prevent overfitting, we also raise threshold T to 120 and validate on dev set frequently instead of specifying an epoch budget.

As Table 3 shows, using a query of both dev and test data leads to the biggest improvement of 0.55. Surprisingly, using the whole test set as a query to retrieve sentence for dev set fine-tuning only leads to a small drop of 0.19 BLEU. This shows that our

Query	T	Epoch	BLEU
generic baseline			30.65
1 sentence	20	1	26.60
	20	10	26.25
a cluster of	20	1	25.81
10 sentences	20	10	27.24
dev set	120		31.09
test set	120	N/A	30.46
dev and test sets	120		31.20
ensemble	4 FT		32.12
	4 FT & 4 non-FT		32.06

Table 3: Character-level BLEU of ad-hoc fine-tuning experiments on Ja→Zh, at sentence, cluster and document levels. FT denotes fine-tuned models.

document adaptation is conservative, thanks to a large number of retrieved sentences. The considerations underlying adaptation over the entire dev and test sets (irrespective of the domain of individual sentences) are as follows: very frequent phrases including words, are the features of a language rather than a domain. For phrases that are frequent in some domains but not others, the generic model will probably have learned to translate them appropriately. What we are concerned about are the phrases seen rarely during generic model training, because of the bias in training data, or coming from niche domains. Sentences that share such phrases, we conjecture, are likely from the same or related domains anyway, so fine-tuning on them all is effective. For sentences with no overlap in such words and phrases, we are probably fine-tuning different areas in the overall parameter space, which can be harmless to each other.

6 Results and Conclusion

In our work, we explore a series of techniques which lead to improvements on Ja↔Zh NMT. Rule-based filtering brings a marginal increment in BLEU for Zh→Ja but a significant one for Ja→Zh. Character mapping, which increases source and target vocabulary overlap, has a tiny effect on Zh→Ja, but makes 1 BLEU improvement for Ja→Zh. Next, cross-entropy filtering adds 2.5 BLEU for Zh→Ja and 2 BLEU for Ja→Zh. Ad-hoc fine-tuning, aiming at enhancing open domain translation, delivers another 0.55 BLEU. Finally, an ensemble of 4 fine-tuned models boosts up 1 BLEU. Overall, our work has improved 10 and more than 3 BLEU for Ja→Zh and Zh→Ja respectively.

Character mapping between Japanese and Chinese may inspire two directions of research: applying character mapping on other tasks, and trying character mapping for other language pairs.

Due to time constraint, we could not perform exhaustive experiments to find the best configuration for sentence-level and cluster-level adaptation, which can be further investigated. We also propose to study further on cluster (sub-document) adaptation, where a system can group test sentences, and fine-tune before translating them. This can make adaptation more fine-grained compared to document adaptation, without the huge risk of overfitting at sentence-level.

Acknowledgments

This work has received funding from the European Union's Horizon 2020 research and innovation programme under grant agreements No 825303 (Bergamot) and 825627 (European Language Grid).

This research is based upon work supported in part by the Office of the Director of National Intelligence (ODNI), Intelligence Advanced Research Projects Activity (IARPA), via contract #FA8650-17-C-9117. The views and conclusions contained herein are those of the authors and should not be interpreted as necessarily representing the official policies, either expressed or implied, of ODNI, IARPA, or the U.S. Government. The U.S. Government is authorized to reproduce and distribute reprints for governmental purposes notwithstanding any copyright annotation therein.

This work was performed using resources provided by the Cambridge Service for Data Driven Discovery (CSD3) operated by the University of Cambridge Research Computing Service (www.csd3.cam.ac.uk), provided by Dell EMC and Intel using Tier-2 funding from the Engineering and Physical Sciences Research Council (capital grant EP/P020259/1), and DiRAC funding from the Science and Technology Facilities Council (www.dirac.ac.uk). We thank Kenneth Heafield for providing us with computing resources.

References

Ebrahim Ansari, Amittai Axelrod, Nguyen Bach, Ondrej Bojar, Roldano Cattoni, Fahim Dalvi, Nadir Durrani, Marcello Federico, Christian Federmann, Jiatao Gu, Fei Huang, Kevin Knight, Xutai Ma, Ajay

Nagesh, Matteo Negri, Jan Niehues, Juan Pino, Elizabeth Salesky, Xing Shi, Sebastian Stüker, Marco Turchi, and Changhan Wang. 2020. Findings of the IWSLT 2020 Evaluation Campaign. In *Proceedings of the 17th International Conference on Spoken Language Translation (IWSLT 2020)*, Seattle, USA.

Loïc Barrault, Ondřej Bojar, Marta R. Costa-jussà, Christian Federmann, Mark Fishel, Yvette Graham, Barry Haddow, Matthias Huck, Philipp Koehn, Shervin Malmasi, Christof Monz, Mathias Müller, Santanu Pal, Matt Post, and Marcos Zampieri. 2019. Findings of the 2019 conference on machine translation (WMT19). In *Proceedings of the Fourth Conference on Machine Translation (Volume 2: Shared Task Papers, Day 1)*, pages 1–61, Florence, Italy. Association for Computational Linguistics.

Rachel Bawden, Nikolay Bogoychev, Ulrich Germann, Roman Grundkiewicz, Faheem Kirefu, Antonio Valerio Miceli Barone, and Alexandra Birch. 2019. The university of Edinburgh's submissions to the WMT19 news translation task. In *Proceedings of the Fourth Conference on Machine Translation (Volume 2: Shared Task Papers, Day 1)*, pages 103–115, Florence, Italy. Association for Computational Linguistics.

Chris Callison-Burch, Colin Bannard, and Josh Schroeder. 2005. Scaling phrase-based statistical machine translation to larger corpora and longer phrases. In *Proceedings of the 43rd Annual Meeting of the Association for Computational Linguistics (ACL'05)*, pages 255–262, Ann Arbor, Michigan. Association for Computational Linguistics.

Chenhui Chu, Toshiaki Nakazawa, Daisuke Kawahara, and Sadao Kurohashi. 2013. Chinese-japanese machine translation exploiting chinese characters. *ACM Transactions on Asian Language Information Processing (TALIP)*, 12(4):1–25.

Chenhui Chu, Toshiaki Nakazawa, and Sadao Kurohashi. 2012. Chinese characters mapping table of Japanese, traditional Chinese and simplified Chinese. In *Proceedings of the Eighth International Conference on Language Resources and Evaluation (LREC-2012)*, pages 2149–2152, Istanbul, Turkey. European Languages Resources Association (ELRA).

Chenhui Chu and Rui Wang. 2018. A survey of domain adaptation for neural machine translation. In *Proceedings of the 27th International Conference on Computational Linguistics*, pages 1304–1319, Santa Fe, New Mexico, USA. Association for Computational Linguistics.

Anna Currey, Antonio Valerio Miceli Barone, and Kenneth Heafield. 2017. Copied monolingual data improves low-resource neural machine translation. In *Proceedings of the Second Conference on Machine Translation*, pages 148–156, Copenhagen, Denmark. Association for Computational Linguistics.

M. Amin Farajian, Marco Turchi, Matteo Negri, and Marcello Federico. 2017. Multi-domain neural machine translation through unsupervised adaptation. In *Proceedings of the Second Conference on Machine Translation*, pages 127–137, Copenhagen, Denmark. Association for Computational Linguistics.

Kenneth Heafield, Ivan Pouzyrevsky, Jonathan H. Clark, and Philipp Koehn. 2013. Scalable modified Kneser-Ney language model estimation. In *Proceedings of the 51st Annual Meeting of the Association for Computational Linguistics (Volume 2: Short Papers)*, pages 690–696, Sofia, Bulgaria. Association for Computational Linguistics.

Marcin Junczys-Dowmunt. 2018. Dual conditional cross-entropy filtering of noisy parallel corpora. In *Proceedings of the Third Conference on Machine Translation: Shared Task Papers*, pages 888–895, Belgium, Brussels. Association for Computational Linguistics.

Marcin Junczys-Dowmunt, Roman Grundkiewicz, Tomasz Dwojak, Hieu Hoang, Kenneth Heafield, Tom Neckermann, Frank Seide, Ulrich Germann, Alham Fikri Aji, Nikolay Bogoychev, André F. T. Martins, and Alexandra Birch. 2018. Marian: Fast neural machine translation in C++. In *Proceedings of ACL 2018, System Demonstrations*, pages 116–121, Melbourne, Australia. Association for Computational Linguistics.

Philipp Koehn, Huda Khayrallah, Kenneth Heafield, and Mikel L. Forcada. 2018. Findings of the WMT 2018 shared task on parallel corpus filtering. In *Proceedings of the Third Conference on Machine Translation: Shared Task Papers*, pages 726–739, Belgium, Brussels. Association for Computational Linguistics.

Philipp Koehn and Rebecca Knowles. 2017. Six challenges for neural machine translation. In *Proceedings of the First Workshop on Neural Machine Translation*, pages 28–39, Vancouver. Association for Computational Linguistics.

Taku Kudo and John Richardson. 2018. SentencePiece: A simple and language independent subword tokenizer and detokenizer for neural text processing. In *Proceedings of the 2018 Conference on Empirical Methods in Natural Language Processing: System Demonstrations*, pages 66–71, Brussels, Belgium. Association for Computational Linguistics.

Xiaoqing Li, Jiajun Zhang, and Chengqing Zong. 2018. One sentence one model for neural machine translation. In *Proceedings of the Eleventh International Conference on Language Resources and Evaluation (LREC-2018)*, Miyazaki, Japan. European Languages Resources Association (ELRA).

Marco Lui and Timothy Baldwin. 2012. langid.py: An off-the-shelf language identification tool. In *Proceedings of the ACL 2012 System Demonstrations*, pages 25–30, Jeju Island, Korea. Association for Computational Linguistics.

Udi Manber and Gene Myers. 1990. Suffix arrays: A new method for on-line string searches. In *Proceedings of the First Annual ACM-SIAM Symposium on Discrete Algorithms*, SODA '90, page 319–327, USA. Society for Industrial and Applied Mathematics.

Toshiaki Nakazawa, Nobushige Doi, Shohei Higashiyama, Chenchen Ding, Raj Dabre, Hideya Mino, Isao Goto, Win Pa Pa, Anoop Kunchukuttan, Shantipriya Parida, Ondřej Bojar, and Sadao Kurohashi. 2019. Overview of the 6th workshop on Asian translation. In *Proceedings of the 6th Workshop on Asian Translation*, pages 1–35, Hong Kong, China. Association for Computational Linguistics.

Graham Neubig, Yosuke Nakata, and Shinsuke Mori. 2011. Pointwise prediction for robust, adaptable Japanese morphological analysis. In *Proceedings of the 49th Annual Meeting of the Association for Computational Linguistics: Human Language Technologies*, pages 529–533, Portland, Oregon, USA. Association for Computational Linguistics.

Alberto Poncelas, Andy Way, and Kepa Sarasola. 2018. The ADAPT system description for the IWSLT 2018 Basque to English translation task. In *International Workshop on Spoken Language Translation*, pages 72–82, Bruges, Belgium.

Ofir Press and Lior Wolf. 2017. Using the output embedding to improve language models. In *Proceedings of the 15th Conference of the European Chapter of the Association for Computational Linguistics: Volume 2, Short Papers*, pages 157–163, Valencia, Spain. Association for Computational Linguistics.

Rico Sennrich, Barry Haddow, and Alexandra Birch. 2016. Improving neural machine translation models with monolingual data. In *Proceedings of the 54th Annual Meeting of the Association for Computational Linguistics (Volume 1: Long Papers)*, pages 86–96, Berlin, Germany. Association for Computational Linguistics.

Haiyue Song, Raj Dabre, Zhuoyuan Mao, Fei Cheng, Sadao Kurohashi, and Eiichiro Sumita. 2020. Pre-training via leveraging assisting languages and data selection for neural machine translation. In *Proceedings of the 58th Annual Meeting of the Association for Computational Linguistics: Student Research Workshop*. To appear.

Ashish Vaswani, Noam Shazeer, Niki Parmar, Jakob Uszkoreit, Llion Jones, Aidan N Gomez, Łukasz Kaiser, and Illia Polosukhin. 2017. Attention is all you need. In *Advances in Neural Information Processing Systems*, pages 5998–6008.

Ying Zhang and Stephan Vogel. 2005. An efficient phrase-to-phrase alignment model for arbitrarily long phrase and large corpora. In *In Proceed-*

ings of the 10th Conference of the European Association for Machine Translation (EAMT-05)*, pages 294–301.

CASIA's System for IWSLT 2020 Open Domain Translation

Qian Wang[1,2], **Yuchen Liu**[1,2], **Cong Ma**[1,2], **Yu Lu**[1,2], **Yining Wang**[1,2], **Long Zhou**[1,2]
Yang Zhao[1,2], **Jiajun Zhang**[1,2], **Chengqing Zong**[1,2]
[1]National Laboratory of Pattern Recognition, CASIA, Beijing, China
[2]School of Artificial Intelligence, University of Chinese Academy of Sciences, Beijing, China

Abstract

This paper describes the CASIA's system for the IWSLT 2020 open domain translation task. This year we participate in both Chinese→Japanese and Japanese→Chinese translation tasks. Our system is neural machine translation system based on Transformer model. We augment the training data with knowledge distillation and back translation to improve the translation performance. Domain data classification and weighted domain model ensemble are introduced to generate the final translation result. We compare and analyze the performance on development data with different model settings and different data processing techniques.

1 Introduction

Neural machine translation(NMT) has been introduced and made great success during the past few years (Sutskever et al., 2014; Bahdanau et al., 2015; Luong et al., 2015; Wu et al., 2016; Gehring et al., 2017; Zhou et al., 2017; Vaswani et al., 2017). Among those different neural network architectures, the Transformer, which is based on self-attention mechanism, has further improved the translation quality due to the ability of feature extraction and word sense disambiguation (Tang et al., 2018a,b). In this paper, we describe our Transformer based neural machine translation system submitted to the IWSLT 2020 Chinese→Japanese and Japanese→Chinese open domain translation task (Ansari et al., 2020).

Our system is built upon Transformer neural machine translation architecture. We also adopt Relative Position (Shaw et al., 2018) and Dynamic Convolutions (Wu et al., 2019) to investigate the performances of advanced model variations. For the implementation, we extend the latest release of Fairseq[1] (Ott et al., 2019).

---

[1]https://github.com/pytorch/fairseq

For data pre-processing, we use byte-pair encoding(BPE) segmentation (Sennrich et al., 2016b) for the source side and character level segmentation for the target side to improve the model performance on rare words. We also investigate the influence of different segmentation methods including word, BPE and character segmentation for both sides.

To further improve the translation quality, we utilize data augmentation techniques of back-translation with a sub-selected monolingual corpus to build additional pseudo parallel training data. Sentence level knowledge distillation is used to strengthen the performance of student model from multi-policy teacher models including left→right, right→left, source→target and target→source.

We also investigate the domain information of the large training data by using a Bert based domain classifier, which is a masked language model and has been shown effective in large scale text classification tasks (Devlin et al., 2019). With the in-domain data, we transfer the model of general domain to each specific domain, and use weighted domain model ensemble as decoding strategy.

2 System Description

Figure 1 depicts the whole process of our submission system, in which we pre-process the provided data and train our advanced Transformer models on the bilingual data together with synthetic corpora from back-translation and knowledge distillation. With domain classification and fine tuning techniques, we obtain multiple models for ensemble strategy and post-processing. In this section, we will introduce each process step in detail.

2.1 NMT Baseline

In this work, we build our model based on the powerful Transformer (Vaswani et al., 2017). The Transformer is a sequence-to-sequence neural

Proceedings of the 17th International Conference on Spoken Language Translation (IWSLT), pages 130–139
July 9-10, 2020. ©2020 Association for Computational Linguistics
https://doi.org/10.18653/v1/P17

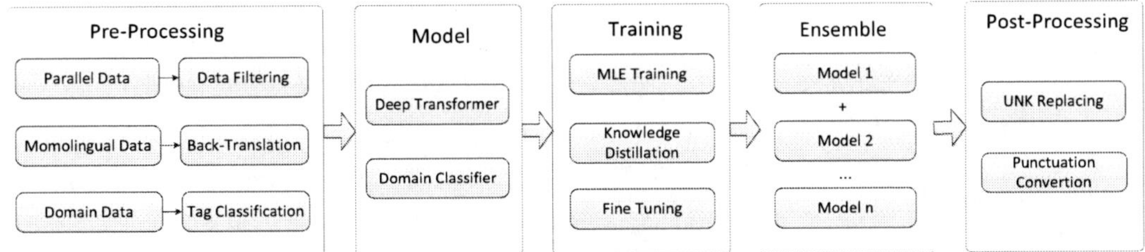

Figure 1: System process of our submissions.

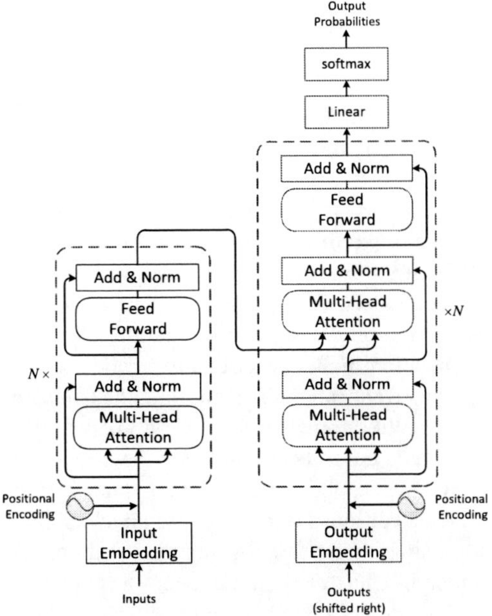

Figure 2: The Transformer model.

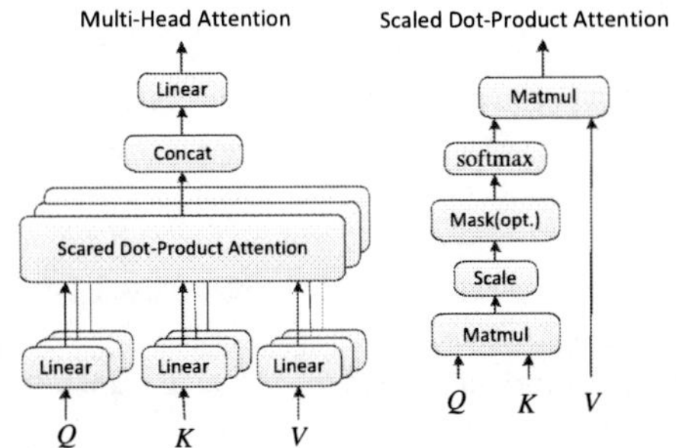

Figure 3: (left) Scaled Dot-Product Attention. (right) Multi-Head Attention.

model that consists of two components: the encoder and the decoder, as shown in Figure 2. The encoder network transforms an input sequence of symbols into a sequence of continues representations. The decoder, on the other hand, produces the target word sequence by predicting the words using a combination of the previously predicted word and relevant parts of the input sequence representations. Particularly, relying entirely on the multi-head attention mechanism, the Transformer with beam search algorithm achieves the state-of-the-art results for machine translation.

Multi-Head Attention We use the multi-head attention with h heads, which allow the model to jointly attend to information from different representation subspaces at different positions. Formally, multi-head attention first obtains h different representations of (Q_i, K_i, V_i). Specifically, for each attention head i, we project the hidden state matrix into distinct query, key and value representations $Q_i{=}QW_i^Q$, $K_i{=}KW_i^K$, $V_i{=}VW_i^V$ respectively. Then we perform **scaled dot-product attention** for each representation, concatenate the results, and project the concatenation with a feed-forward layer.

$$\text{MultiHead}(Q, K, V) = \text{Concat}_i(head_i)W^O$$
$$head_i = \text{Attention}(QW_i^Q, KW_i^K, VW_i^V)$$
$$(1)$$

where W_i^Q, W_i^K, W_i^V and W^O are parameter matrices .

Scaled Dot-Product Attention An attention function can be described as a mapping from a query and a set of key-value pairs to an output. Specifically, we can multiply query Q_i by key K_i to obtain an attention weight matrix, which is then multiplied by value V_i for each token to obtain the self-attention token representation. As shown in Figure 3, we compute the matrix of outputs as:

$$\text{Attention}(Q, K, V) = \text{Softmax}(\frac{QK^T}{\sqrt{d_k}})V \quad (2)$$

where d_k is the dimension of the key. For the sake of brevity, we refer the reader to Vaswani et al. (2017) for more details.

2.2 Back-Translation

Back-translation is an effective and commonly used data augmentation technique to incorporate monolingual data into a translation system (Sennrich et al., 2016a; Zhang and Zong, 2016). Especially for low-resource language tasks, it is indispensable to augment the training data by mixing the pseudo corpus with the parallel part. Back-translation first trains an intermediate target-to-source system that is used to translate monolingual target data into additional synthetic parallel data. This data is used in conjunction with human translated bitext data to train the desired source-to-target system.

How to select the appropriate sentences from the abundant monolingual data is a crucial issue due to the limitation of equipment and huge overhead time. We trained a n-gram based language model on the target side of bilingual data to score the monolingual sentences for each translation direction.

Recent work (Edunov et al., 2018) has shown that different methods of generating pseudo corpus made discrepant influence on translation performance. Edunov et al. (2018) indicated that sampling or noisy synthetic data gives a much stronger training signal than data generated by beam search or greedy search. We adopt the back-translation script from fairseq[2] and generate back-translated data with sampling for both translation directions.

2.3 Knowledge Distillation

The goal of knowledge distillation is to deliver a student model that matches the accuracy of a teacher model (Kim and Rush, 2016). Prior work (Yang et al., 2018) demonstrates that student model can surpass the accuracy of the teacher model. In our experiments, we adopt sequence-level knowledge distillation method and investigate four different teacher models to boost the translation quality of student model.

S2T+L2R Teacher Model: We translate the source sentences of the parallel data into target language using our source-to-target (briefly, S2T) system described in Section 2.1 with left-to-right (briefly, L2R) manner.

S2T+R2L Teacher Model: We translate the source sentences of the parallel data into target language using our S2T system with right-to-left (briefly, R2L) manner.

T2S+L2R Teacher Model: We translate the target sentences of the parallel data into source language using our target-to-source (briefly, T2S) system with L2R manner.

T2S+R2L Teacher Model: We translate the target sentences of the parallel data into source language using our T2S system with R2L manner.

In the final stage, we use the combination of the translated pseudo corpus to improve the student model. It is worth noting that we also mix the original bilingual sentences into these pseudo training corpus.

2.4 Model Ensemble and Reranking

Model ensemble is a method to integrate the probability distributions of multiple models before predicting next target word (Liu et al., 2018). We average the last 20 checkpoints for single model to avoid overfitting. One checkpoint is saved per 1000 steps. For model ensemble, we train six separate models. To achieve this, we fine-tune our student model described in Section 2.3 and back translation model described in Section 2.2 using corpus from three different domains (Spoken domain, Wiki domain and News domain). We use weighted ensemble to generate the translation result, in which the weights for each domain model is calculated from a Bert based domain classifier. The domain specific data for training the domain classifier and fine tuning the student translation model will be described in detail in Section 3.4.

For reranking, we rescore 50-best lists output from the ensemble model using a rescoring model, which includes the models we trained with different model sizes, different corpus portions and different token granularities.

3 Data Preparation

This section introduces the methods we employ to prepare the provided parallel data (18.9M *web_crawled* corpus and 1.9M *existing_parallel* sources) and monolingual sentences (*unaligned_web_crawled* data). We also describe how to prepare domain specific data to facilitate translation.

The provided parallel corpus *existing_parallel* for the two translation directions consists of around 1.9M sentence pairs with around 33.5M characters (Chinese side) in total. Furthermore, a large, noisy set of Japanese-Chinese segment pairs built from web data *web_crawled* is also provided, which con-

---

[2]https://github.com/pytorch/fairseq/
tree/master/examples/backtranslation

sists of around 18.9M sentence pairs with around 493.9M characters (Chinese side) in total. We use the provided development dataset as the validation set during training, which consists of 5,304 sentence pairs. The average length and length ratio of the provided parallel corpus and development dataset is shown as in Table 1.

3.1 Pre-processing and Post-processing

In the open domain translation task both on Chinese→Japanese and Japanese→Chinese translation directions, we first implement pre-processing on training corpus and then filter it.

Before pre-processing, We remove illegal sentences in the provided Japanese-Chinese parallel corpus which include duplicate sentences and sentences in different languages other than source or target (filtered by our language detector tools).

Pre-processing steps include escape character transformation, text normalization, language filtering and word segmentation. There are lots of escape characters in the *existing_parallel* and *web_crawled* which do not occur in development set. As a result, we transform all these escape characters into corresponding marks with a well designed rule-based method to make it consistent between the training and evaluation.

Text normalization step mainly focuses on normalization of numbers and punctuation. Based on analysis on development set, we found that in Chinese, most of the punctuation are double byte characters (DBC), while most of the numbers are single byte characters (SBC). However, most of the numbers and punctuation in Japanese are double byte characters (DBC). Hence we normalize the numbers and punctuation format to make it the same as development set.

In word segmentation step, we apply Jieba[3] as our Chinese word segmentation tool for segmenting Chinese parallel data and monolingual data. For Japanese text, word segmentation is used Mecab (Toshinori Sato and Okumura, 2017). After pre-processing, we filter the training corpus as mentioned in section 3.2.

Finally, we apply Byte Pair Encoding (BPE) (Sennrich et al., 2016b) on both Chinese and Japanese text. Separate BPE models are trained for Chinese and Japanese respectively. Based on the comparison of BPE operations from 30k, 35k, 40k, 45k, 50k, we determine to use 40k BPE operations

Length Statistic	Train		Dev	
	Ja	Zh	Ja	Zh
avg. length	17.56	14.52	10.12	7.82
avg. ratio	1.35		1.34	

Table 1: The average length and length ratio (Ja/Zh) of the provided parallel corpus and development dataset.

Filtering Methods	# of sentences
original	20,929,833
remove illegal	18,073,574
filter by length and ratio	15,708,757
filter by alignment	15,679,247

Table 2: The number of the remaining sentence pairs after each filtering operation.

in source language since it has the best performance on preliminary machine translation experiments. For target side, we determine to use character granular because character level decoder could perform better in our preliminary experiments.

Post-processing steps are similar to pre-processing without filtering. We apply escape character transformation, text normalization and unknown words (UNK) processing steps on machine translation results. The same methods are used to implement escape character transformation and text normalization as pre-processing. For UNK processing, we find some of the numbers can not be well translated by model and we replace these UNKs with the numbers in source sentence. Otherwise, we remove the UNK symbols.

3.2 Parallel Data Filtering

The following methods are applied to further filter the parallel sentence pairs.

We remove sentences longer than 50 and select the parallel sentences where the length ratio (Ja/Zh) is between 0.53 and 2.90. We then calculate word alignment of each sentence pair by using fast_align[4](Dyer et al., 2013). The percentage of aligned words and alignment perplexities are used as the metric where the thresholds are set as 0.4 and −30 respectively. Through the above filtering procedure, the number of the remaining data is reduced from 20.9M to 15.7M, as shown in Table 2.

3.3 Monolingual Data Filtering

It is proven that back-translation is a simple but effective approach to enhance the translation quality

---

[3]https://github.com/fxsjy/jieba

[4]https://github.com/clab/fast_align

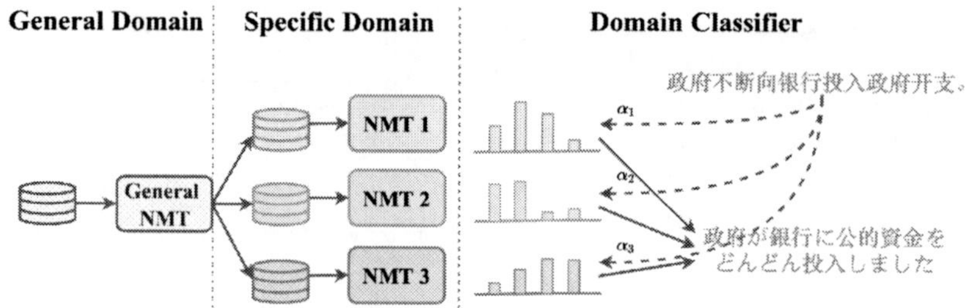

Figure 4: The domain data processing steps, including the NMT model trained on general domain data, the NMT models fine tuned on specific domain, the domain classification and weighted ensemble in the decoding stage.

Filtering Methods	Ja	Zh
original	941,297,925	928,670,666
remove illegal	10,078,827	32,644,917
filter by length	8,175,157	30,415,964
filter by LM	6,128,443	16,374,195

Table 3: The number of the remaining monolingual sentences for Japanese and Chinese after each filtering operation.

Domain	Existing	Web
Wiki	558,531	4,006,232
Spoken	1,290,796	9,534,754
News	21,661	2,444,884

Table 4: Statistics of domain data. Existing indicates *existing_parallel* which is used to train the domain classifier, while Web means *web_crawled_parallel* in which the domain labels are predicted by the classifier.

as described in Section 2.2. To achieve that, we extract the high-quality monolingual sentences from the provided *unaligned_web_crawled* data. After removing illegal sentences from *web_crawled* corpus, we limit the maximum sentence length as 50 and remove dirty data by a language model. Specially, we use KenLM[5] toolkit to train two language models with Japanese and Chinese monolingual data extracted from the provided parallel corpus *existing_parallel*. We then rank the sentences based on the perplexities calculated by the trained language models and filter by perplexity threshold of 4 for Chinese and 3 for Japanese. Note that the perplexities are normalized by sentence lengths. obtain 6.1M and 16.4M monolingual sentences for Japanese and Chinese separately. The filtering results are presented in Table 3.

The obtained monolingual sentences are fed to the trained model to generate pseudo parallel sentence pairs, which are employed to boost the performance of the model.

3.4 Domain Data Processing

Although the amount of provided training data is large enough, it is a noise set of web data built from multiple domain sources. Koehn and Knowles (2017) have demonstrated that the NMT model performs poorly when the test domain does not match

the training data. Only the same or similar corpora are typically able to improve translation performance. Therefore, we apply domain adaptation methods in this task.

Adaptation methods for neural machine translation have attracted much attention in the research community (Britz et al., 2017; Wang et al., 2017; Chu and Wang, 2018; Zhang and Xiong, 2018; Wang et al., 2020). They can be roughly classified into two categories, namely data selection and model adaptation. The former focuses on selecting the similar training data from out-of-domain parallel corpora, while the latter focuses on the internal model to improve model performance. Following these two categories, our domain data processing takes the following steps, as shown in Figure 4.

Domain Label In this task, there are two kinds of domain labels provided: domains in *existing_parallel* and domains in *web_crawled_parallel*. Since the later is mainly source document index for each sentence pair, the former is more meaningful for domain classification. We categorize the domain label of *existing_parallel* data into three commonly used classes, namely *Wiki, Spoken, and News*. The domain *Wiki* includes *wiki_facebook, wiki_zh_ja_tallip2015* and *wiktionary*. The label *Spoken* includes *ted* and *opensubtitles*. The label *News* includes *global-voices, newscommentary* and *tatoeba*.

<hr>

[5]https://github.com/kpu/kenlm

Domain classification Data selection can be conduct in supervised or unsupervised manners (Dou et al., 2019). Since there is a provided data source descriptive file in the *existing_parallel* data which can be regarded as domain labels, we choose the supervised way here. We use two BERT models pretrained on Chinese[6] and Japanese[7] data, respectively. Then the BERT models are fine tuned as a text classification task, based on the source and target side of *existing_parallel* with three domain label we defined. Since the domain data is uneven, we also adopt oversampling and use extra data to enlarge *News* domain For the remaining data in *web_crawled_parallel*, we use the classification model to classify the total data into the three different domains. The statistics of domain data we used is shown in Table 4.

Decoding Stage Considering the test set is also composed of a mixed-genre data, we first classify the domain of each sentence in the test set and obtain the probabilities corresponding to each domain. Then we apply a weighted ensemble method to integrate NMT models. Specifically, when computing the output probability of the next word, we multiply the output probability in each domain specific translation model with the corresponding domain probability of each sentence.

3.5 Other Data Resource

The task description says that the test data is a mixture of genres but the provided development set is mainly from spoken domain. Furthermore, we find that the domain distribution of the training data is severely unbalanced (as shown in Table 4). Especially, the data of *News* domain is quite limited. Due to above two reasons, we decided to crawl some data from other domains.

It is easy to find that *hujiangjp* [8] which is a website helping people to study foreign languages contains some parallel Chinese-Japanese sentences. Accordingly, we crawled all the available data in this website before test data release. The total amount of extra data consists of $12,665$ parallel sentences. We randomly select $4,877$ sentence pairs to build an extra development set. When training each domain model, all the extra data are used as part of *News* domain. We

find that 383 Chinese→Japanese pairs and 421 Japanese→Chinese pairs in the crawled data are overlapped with the final test set. We just used the originally trained model to decode the test set and decided not to retrain our model since it will take much time and the organizers remind that models cannot be changed after the test set is released. Anyway, we also suggest to test the translation quality on the remaining test set excluding the overlapped sentences.

4 Experiment Settings and Results

4.1 Experiment Setup

Our implementation of Transformer model is based on the latest release of Fairseq. We use Transformer-Big as basic setting, which contains layers of $N = 6$ for both encoder and decoder. Each layer consists of a multi-head attention sublayer with heads $h = 16$ and a feed-forward sublayer with inner dimension $d_{ff} = 4096$. The word embedding dimensions for source and target and the hidden state dimensions d_{model} are set to 1024. In the training phase, the dropout rate P_{drop} is set to 0.1. In the fine tuning phase, the dropout rate is changed to 0.3 to prevent over-fitting.

We use cross entropy as loss function and apply label smoothing of value $\epsilon_{ls} = 0.1$. For the optimizer, we use Adam (Kingma and Ba, 2015) with $\beta_1 = 0.9$, $\beta_2 = 0.98$ and $\epsilon = 10^{-8}$. The initial learning rate is set to 10^{-4} for training and 10^{-5} for fine tuning.

The models with complete training data are trained on 4 GPUs for 100,000 steps. For the dataset with knowledge distillation or back-translation, the models are trained for 150,000 steps. We validate the model every 1,000 mini-batches on the development data and perform early stop when the best loss is stable on validation set for 10,000 steps. At the end of training phase, we average last 20 checkpoints for each single model of general domain. In fine tuning phase, we use the averaged model of general domain as starting point for initializing the domain model, and continue training on 1 GPU with domain data for 50,000 steps without early stop. The batch sizes in training and fine tuning are set to 32768 and 8192 respectively.

4.2 Result

Table 5 shows the result on development data of both Chinese→Japanese (ZH→JA) and

---

[6]`https://github.com/ymcui/`
`Chinese-BERT-wwm`
[7]`https://github.com/cl-tohoku/`
`bert-japanese`
[8]`https://https://jp.hjenglish.com/new/`

Settings	ZH→JA	JA→ZH
Single System		
Baseline	28.07	22.19
Complete Parallel Data	27.38	27.41
+Parallel data Filtering	33.46	27.69
+Back Translation	34.42	28.08
+Knowledge Distillation	34.00	29.50
+Domain Classification	34.96	30.14
System Combination		
Ensemble Baseline	34.79	30.32
+ Weighted Ensemble	**35.41**	**30.55**
+ Reranking	34.92	30.41

Table 5: The BLEU scores of both directions on development data.

Japanese→Chinese (JA→ZH) translation directions. We report the character BLEU score calculated with *multi-bleu-detok.perl* script. As shown in the result, filtering with complete parallel data plays an important role in our system. Techniques of back translation and knowledge distillation consistently improve the BLEU score. When applying domain classification, we classify each sentence using the Bert-based domain classifier and decode each sentence with corresponding domain model.

As for combination methods, we build six separate models with three domain (*Wiki*, *Spoken* and *News*) fine tuned on two large synthetic data (back translation and knowledge distillation). In ensemble baseline, all of these models share the same weight in predicting word distributions. Weighted ensemble indicates we apply different weights for the ensemble models, in which the weights are obtained by the domain classifier. With weighted domain ensemble, our system achieves the best performance on development data in terms of BLEU, and surpass the single baseline systems by 7.34 BLEU for Chinese→Japanese and 8.36 BLEU for Japanese→Chinese.

We also find a performance drop with reranking. The reason may be that we train the reranking models on the complete parallel data, which is from general domain and may assign lower score for domain specific translations. As a result, our submission is based on the weighted ensemble system, which performs best in our experiments.

4.3 Analysis

We compare the performance of different model variations and token granularities on

Model Architecture	BLEU
Dynamic Convolutions (Big)	27.13
Transformer (Base)	27.16
Relative Position (Big)	27.41
Transformer (Big)	**27.89**

Table 6: The BLEU scores of Chinese→Japanese on development data with different model settings and variations.

Token Granularities	BLEU
Word→Word	25.45
Character→Character	26.92
BPE→BPE	27.89
BPE→Character	**28.07**

Table 7: The BLEU scores of Chinese→Japanese on development data with different token granularities.

Chinese→Japanese development data. The data we used to train the models is *existing parallel data*, which consists of 1.9M parallel sentences.

For the model variations, we compare Relative Position (Shaw et al., 2018), Dynamic Convolutions (Wu et al., 2019) and Transformer Base and Big settings (Vaswani et al., 2017). As shown in Table 6, The best result is produced by Transformer Big setting, which is used as default when training on large datasets.

For the token granularities, we report the result with four tokenization methods: Word→Word, Character→Character, BPE→BPE and BPE→Character. As shown in table 7, adopting BPE in source side and Character in target side performs better than other token granularities, which is used in our submission systems.

We notice that there exits a large divergence between the two translation directions when using complete parallel data and process with parallel data filtering. We have verified the result and the parallel data in depth. We find that the quality of Japanese data is lower. For example, there are sentences consist of punctuations only, which may harm the target side language model learned by the decoder. After parallel data filtering, the invalid sentences are removed and thus the translation quality of ZH-JA is improved.

We also find that the provided development data is mainly from spoken domain, and thus we use our collected data as extra development set from other domain to investigate the general performance of single model. The result is shown in table 8. We

Development data	ZH→JA	JA→ZH
Provided	34.00	29.50
Our collected	32.78	30.95

Table 8: The BLEU scores of best single model (with knowlegde distillation) on provided development data and our development data.

find there exists a small gap between provided development data and our collected data, which indicates that the domain information may further improve the translation quality, and thus leads us to utilize domain transfer and ensemble techniques. Note that the extra development set is only used in single models. When it comes to system combination, these data are added into News domain since the size of News domain data in parallel dataset is extremely smaller than other domains (Section 3.4).

5 Conclusion

We present the CASIA's neural machine translation system submitted to IWSLT 2020 Chinese→Japanese and Japanese→Chinese open domain translation task. Our system is built with Transformer architecture and incorporating the following techniques:

- Deliberate data pre-processing and filtering

- Back-translation of selected monolingual corpus

- Knowledge distillation from multi polity teacher models

- Domain classification and weighted domain model ensemble

As a result, our final system achieves substantial improvements over baseline system.

6 Acknowledgement

The research work described in this paper has been supported by the Natural Science Foundation of China under grant No.U1836221 and No.61673380.

References

Ebrahim Ansari, Amittai Axelrod, Nguyen Bach, Ondrej Bojar, Roldano Cattoni, Fahim Dalvi, Nadir Durrani, Marcello Federico, Christian Federmann, Jiatao Gu, Fei Huang, Kevin Knight, Xutai Ma, Ajay Nagesh, Matteo Negri, Jan Niehues, Juan Pino, Elizabeth Salesky, Xing Shi, Sebastian Stüker, Marco Turchi, and Changhan Wang. 2020. Findings of the IWSLT 2020 Evaluation Campaign. In *Proceedings of the 17th International Conference on Spoken Language Translation (IWSLT 2020)*, Seattle, USA.

Dzmitry Bahdanau, Kyunghyun Cho, and Yoshua Bengio. 2015. Neural machine translation by jointly learning to align and translate. In *3rd International Conference on Learning Representations, ICLR 2015, San Diego, CA, USA, May 7-9, 2015, Conference Track Proceedings*.

Denny Britz, Quoc Le, and Reid Pryzant. 2017. Effective domain mixing for neural machine translation. In *Proceedings of the Second Conference on Machine Translation*, pages 118–126.

Chenhui Chu and Rui Wang. 2018. A survey of domain adaptation for neural machine translation. In *Proceedings of the 27th International Conference on Computational Linguistics*, pages 1304–1319, Santa Fe, New Mexico, USA. Association for Computational Linguistics.

Jacob Devlin, Ming-Wei Chang, Kenton Lee, and Kristina Toutanova. 2019. BERT: pre-training of deep bidirectional transformers for language understanding. In *Proceedings of the 2019 Conference of the North American Chapter of the Association for Computational Linguistics: Human Language Technologies, NAACL-HLT 2019, Minneapolis, MN, USA, June 2-7, 2019, Volume 1 (Long and Short Papers)*, pages 4171–4186.

Zi-Yi Dou, Junjie Hu, Antonios Anastasopoulos, and Graham Neubig. 2019. Unsupervised domain adaptation for neural machine translation with domain-aware feature embeddings. In *2019 Conference on Empirical Methods in Natural Language Processing*, pages 1417–1422.

Chris Dyer, Victor Chahuneau, and Noah A. Smith. 2013. A simple, fast, and effective reparameterization of IBM model 2. In *Human Language Technologies: Conference of the North American Chapter of the Association of Computational Linguistics, Proceedings*, pages 644–648.

Sergey Edunov, Myle Ott, Michael Auli, and David Grangier. 2018. Understanding back-translation at scale. In *EMNLP*.

Jonas Gehring, Michael Auli, David Grangier, Denis Yarats, and Yann N Dauphin. 2017. Convolutional sequence to sequence learning. In *Proceedings of the 34th International Conference on Machine Learning-Volume 70*, pages 1243–1252. JMLR. org.

Yoon Kim and Alexander M Rush. 2016. Sequence-level knowledge distillation. pages 1317–1327. *Proceedings of the 2016 Conference on Empirical Methods in Natural Language Processing (EMNLP 2016)*.

Diederik P. Kingma and Jimmy Ba. 2015. Adam: A method for stochastic optimization. In *3rd International Conference on Learning Representations, ICLR 2015, San Diego, CA, USA, May 7-9, 2015, Conference Track Proceedings*.

Philipp Koehn and Rebecca Knowles. 2017. Six challenges for neural machine translation. In *Proceedings of the First Workshop on Neural Machine Translation*, pages 28–39, Vancouver. Association for Computational Linguistics.

Yuchen Liu, Long Zhou, Yining Wang, Yang Zhao, Jiajun Zhang, and Chengqing Zong. 2018. A comparable study on model averaging, ensembling and reranking in nmt. In *Natural Language Processing and Chinese Computing*, pages 299–308, Cham. Springer International Publishing.

Minh-Thang Luong, Hieu Pham, and Christopher D Manning. 2015. Effective approaches to attention-based neural machine translation. *arXiv preprint arXiv:1508.04025*.

Myle Ott, Sergey Edunov, Alexei Baevski, Angela Fan, Sam Gross, Nathan Ng, David Grangier, and Michael Auli. 2019. fairseq: A fast, extensible toolkit for sequence modeling. In *Proceedings of NAACL-HLT 2019: Demonstrations*.

Rico Sennrich, Barry Haddow, and Alexandra Birch. 2016a. Improving neural machine translation models with monolingual data. pages 86–96. *In Proceedings of the 54th Annual Meeting of the Association for Computational Linguistics (ACL 2016)*.

Rico Sennrich, Barry Haddow, and Alexandra Birch. 2016b. Neural machine translation of rare words with subword units. In *Proceedings of the 54th Annual Meeting of the Association for Computational Linguistics, ACL 2016, August 7-12, 2016, Berlin, Germany, Volume 1: Long Papers*.

Peter Shaw, Jakob Uszkoreit, and Ashish Vaswani. 2018. Self-attention with relative position representations. In *Proceedings of the 2018 Conference of the North American Chapter of the Association for Computational Linguistics: Human Language Technologies, NAACL-HLT, New Orleans, Louisiana, USA, June 1-6, 2018, Volume 2 (Short Papers)*, pages 464–468.

Ilya Sutskever, Oriol Vinyals, and Quoc V. Le. 2014. Sequence to sequence learning with neural networks. In *Advances in Neural Information Processing Systems 27: Annual Conference on Neural Information Processing Systems 2014, December 8-13 2014, Montreal, Quebec, Canada*, pages 3104–3112.

Gongbo Tang, Mathias Müller, Annette Rios, and Rico Sennrich. 2018a. Why self-attention? a targeted evaluation of neural machine translation architectures. In *Proceedings of the 2018 Conference on Empirical Methods in Natural Language Processing*, pages 4263–4272.

Gongbo Tang, Rico Sennrich, and Joakim Nivre. 2018b. An analysis of attention mechanism: The case of word sense disambiguation in neural machine translation. In *Third Conference on Machine Translation*, pages 26–35.

Taiichi Hashimoto Toshinori Sato and Manabu Okumura. 2017. Implementation of a word segmentation dictionary called mecab-ipadic-neologd and study on how to use it effectively for information retrieval (in japanese). In *Proceedings of the Twenty-three Annual Meeting of the Association for Natural Language Processing*, pages NLP2017–B6–1. The Association for Natural Language Processing.

Ashish Vaswani, Noam Shazeer, Niki Parmar, Jakob Uszkoreit, Llion Jones, Aidan N Gomez, Ł ukasz Kaiser, and Illia Polosukhin. 2017. Attention is all you need. In I. Guyon, U. V. Luxburg, S. Bengio, H. Wallach, R. Fergus, S. Vishwanathan, and R. Garnett, editors, *Advances in Neural Information Processing Systems 30*, pages 5998–6008. Curran Associates, Inc.

Rui Wang, Andrew Finch, Masao Utiyama, and Eiichiro Sumita. 2017. Sentence embedding for neural machine translation domain adaptation. In *Proceedings of the 55th Annual Meeting of the Association for Computational Linguistics (Volume 2: Short Papers)*, pages 560–566, Vancouver, Canada. Association for Computational Linguistics.

Yong Wang, Longyue Wang, Shuming Shi, Victor Li, and Zhaopeng Tu. 2020. Go from the general to the particular: Multi-domain translation with domain transformation networks. In *AAAI 2020 : The Thirty-Fourth AAAI Conference on Artificial Intelligence*.

Felix Wu, Angela Fan, Alexei Baevski, Yann N. Dauphin, and Michael Auli. 2019. Pay less attention with lightweight and dynamic convolutions. In *7th International Conference on Learning Representations, ICLR 2019, New Orleans, LA, USA, May 6-9, 2019*.

Yonghui Wu, Mike Schuster, Zhifeng Chen, Quoc V Le, Mohammad Norouzi, Wolfgang Macherey, Maxim Krikun, Yuan Cao, Qin Gao, Klaus Macherey, et al. 2016. Google's neural machine translation system: Bridging the gap between human and machine translation. *arXiv preprint arXiv:1609.08144*.

Chenglin Yang, Lingxi Xie, Siyuan Qiao, and Alan L. Yuille. 2018. Knowledge distillation in generations: More tolerant teachers educate better students. *arXiv preprint arXiv:1805.05551*.

Jiajun Zhang and Chengqing Zong. 2016. Exploiting source-side monolingual data in neural machine translation. page 1535–1545.

Shiqi Zhang and Deyi Xiong. 2018. Sentence weighting for neural machine translation domain adaptation. In *Proceedings of the 27th International Conference on Computational Linguistics*, pages 3181–3190, Santa Fe, New Mexico, USA. Association for Computational Linguistics.

Long Zhou, Wenpeng Hu, Jiajun Zhang, and Chengqing Zong. 2017. Neural system combination for machine translation. In *Proceedings of the 55th Annual Meeting of the Association for Computational Linguistics (Volume 2: Short Papers)*, volume 2, pages 378–384.

Deep Blue Sonics' Submission to IWSLT 2020 Open Domain Translation Task

Enmin Su
Deep Blue Sonics
enmin.su@pku.edu.cn

Yi Ren
Deep Blue Sonics
yi.ren@dbsonics.net

Abstract

We present in this report our submission to IWSLT 2020 Open Domain Translation Task(Ansari et al., 2020). We built a data pre-processing pipeline to efficiently handle large noisy web-crawled corpora, which boosts the BLEU score of a widely used transformer model in this translation task. To tackle the open-domain nature of this task, back-translation (Sennrich et al., 2016) is applied to further improve the translation performance.

1 Introduction

Neural machine translation (NMT) is a well-studied problem boosted in recent years by powerful transformer models (Vaswani et al., 2017), which find their ways to various sequence-to-sequence tasks, such as automatic speech recognition (ASR) (Dong et al., 2018), speech translation (Gangi et al., 2019), text-to-speech (Shin et al., 2019), to name a few. Nevertheless, many challenges remain in training an efficient transformer NMT model in practice, such as the following ones raised in IWSLT 2020 Open Domain Translation Task:

Handling noisy dataset Hassan et al. pointed out that machine translation models are vulnerable to noise even in small quantity. In practice, manual correction of a massive corpora is prohibitive, thus calling for an automatic data cleaning pipeline.

Leveraging monolingual data Compared to parallel corpora, monolingual data can be acquired at a much lower cost. Common ways of using monolingual data include language modeling (Çaglar Gülçehre et al., 2015), back-translation (Sennrich et al., 2016), and dual learning (He et al., 2016), all exhibiting promising results; furthermore, they could be adopted in a complementary way when carefully designed (Hassan et al., 2018).

Last but not least, massive pre-trained language models like BERT perform strongly in NLP tasks like question answering, reading comprehension and text classification (Devlin et al., 2019), motivating our attempts to incorporate them in our NMT system.

Domain mismatch NMT systems trained with data from specific domains may translate poorly in other domains (Freitag and Al-Onaizan, 2016). Training the model with all available corpora, and fine-tuning it on a specific domain generally achieves best results in this domain (Chu et al., 2017). In open domain cases, it's impractical to keep a dedicated model or to obtain enough training data for every single domain. Hence Multi-Domain NMT, where a single model generalizes to multiple domains, is gaining interest in recent research. For example, Tars and Fishel; Jiang et al.; Zeng et al. injected domain information into model input, leading to convincing and consistent improvements, in which domain information may be derived in both supervised and unsupervised manners.

Our work consists of establishing an efficient data pre-processing pipeline for large web-crawled corpora to train a transformer model for NMT and exploiting large amount of monolingual data with back-translation and language modeling.

This report is organized as follows: Section 2 depicts the different techniques applied to improve the official baseline model, whereas in Section 3 the experiments and results are described in greater details. Finally, we conclude our work and suggest a few future work directions in Section 4.

Proceedings of the 17th International Conference on Spoken Language Translation (IWSLT), pages 140–144
July 9-10, 2020. ©2020 Association for Computational Linguistics
https://doi.org/10.18653/v1/P17

2 System Overview

2.1 Noisy Data

According to Hassan et al., the common noises in web-crawled corpora can be categorized into the following groups:

- mis-aligned pairs,
- partially translated pairs,
- inaccurate or low-quality pairs,
- pairs in wrong languages, or as exact duplicates.

Meanwhile, in the context of training Transformer models with large-scale parallel data, Popel and Bojar found out while clean and smaller datasets help the model to converge faster, noisy and larger datasets help in converging to a better result. Our experiments indicate that with a pre-processing pipeline, training larger datasets is of great help in improving translation BLEU score.

2.2 NMT model

Our NMT model is identical to the baseline of IWSLT 2020 Open Domain Translation Task (Ansari et al., 2020), which is a common transformer architecture. The hyper-parameters of the model are listed in Table 1.

Hyper-parameters	
encoder layers	6
decoder layers	6
filter width	4096
attention width	1024
attention heads	16
token type	BPE
source vocabulary size	30k
target vocabulary size	30k
Total Parameters	270M

Table 1: Hyper-parameters for our NMT model.

2.3 Language Modeling

Çaglar Gülçehre et al. proposed language modeling as a way of leveraging monolingual corpora in the context of NMT. Given massive monolingual data, language modeling helps in decoding accuracy, thus ensuring improvements in iterative back-translation training. Among various ways of incorporating language models in an NMT system, we conduct experiments on shallow fusion and deep fusion, following the settings of Çaglar Gülçehre et al..

A rescoring method put forward by Shin et al. is also tested, where the translation candidates from beam search are reranked using a weighed combination of original scores and scores calculated by a pre-trained Japanese BERT model (Takeshi et al., 2019).

2.4 Back-translation

Back-translation (Hoang et al., 2018) has been proven to be an effective and highly applicable way to achieve consistent improvements by increasing both size and diversity of the training corpora (Edunov et al., 2018); we follow their back-translation setting in our experiments.

3 Experiments and Results

3.1 Data Acquisition and Pre-processing

All the datasets used in our experiments are listed in Table 2. While larger datasets boost model performance in general, we observe considerable amount of noises in all the datasets in Table 2 apart from the "clean parallel" set. As mentioned in Section 2.1, these noises are of various nature, and show negative impact in our primary experiments. To deal with them, several pre-processing steps have been applied as follows.

First, the noisy datasets turn out to contain a lot of rare or meaningless characters. In order to remove them, we define a valid Unicode range, consisting of basic Latin, Greek alphabet, Japanese alphabet and CJK symbols and punctuations. Then we discard sentence pairs including more than 20% of invalid characters, and delete the invalid symbols in the remaining pairs.

Second, we normalize these sentences with neologdn[1] to handle encoding issues and special punctuations.

Third, a naive de-duplicate algorithm is applied to get rid of redundancy in training data, which also eliminates invalid text containing only error messages.

Finally, the sentences in wrong languages in the datasets are filtered by a pre-trained Fasttext language classification model (Joulin et al., 2017), where sentences with wrong language labels or low confidence are removed.

The use of pre-processed noisy data results later in a notable increase of BLEU score (see Table 4).

---

[1] https://github.com/ikegami-yukino/neologdn

Dataset	Size	Source
training set		
clean parallel	2M	`existing_parallel`
noisy parallel	17M	pre-processed `web_crawled_parallel_filtered`
monolingual(Ja)	10M	`unaligned_documents`
monolingual(Zh)	10M	Large Scale Chinese Corpus for NLP (Xu, 2019)
validation set		
basic expressions	5304	JEC Basic Sentence Data (Kurohashi-Kawahara Lab.)

Table 2: Datasets used in our experiments. The size is in number of sentence pairs for parallel datasets, and number of sentences for monolingual ones.

3.2 Baseline Model

We train the transformer model in Section 2.2 on clean data as baseline. We use Jieba[2] and Mecab[3] to tokenize the Chinese and Japanese text respectively, and use subword-nmt[4] to perform BPE encoding/decoding (Gage, 1994), with vocabulary size approximately to 30k for each language. We use Tensor2Tensor (Vaswani et al., 2018) implementation of Transformer, with 4 GPU and accumulates gradient for 4 steps, resulting in an equivalent batch-size of 32768.

3.3 Language Modeling

Here we attempt to acquire some improvements utilizing unpaired data by means of language models (LM). The methods tested are:

- shallow fusion with language model (Çaglar Gülçehre et al., 2015)
- deep fusion with language model(Çaglar Gülçehre et al., 2015)
- BERT rescoring (Shin et al., 2019)

As summarized in Table 3, none of the LM-based methods leads to gain in BLEU score just yet, and further research needs to be conducted to beat the baseline with language models.

Methods	Zh2Ja
baseline model	27.48
shallow fusion	26.79
deep fusion	21.84
BERT rescoring	24.80

Table 3: BLEU scores after incorporating with language models.

[2]https://github.com/fxsjy/jieba
[3]https://taku910.github.io/mecab/
[4]https://github.com/rsennrich/subword-nmt

3.4 Back-translation

To generate a back-translation dataset, we first augment clean target sentences using the exact 'beam + noise' setting in (Edunov et al., 2018), with $p(deletion) = 0.1$, $p(substitution) = 0.1$ for each token in the sentence; for substitution, we randomly pick the ith token and draw a random number n from uniform distribution of {-3, 2, -1, 1, 2, 3}, and replace this token with the $(i + n)^{th}$ token. We generate noisy source sentences using a target-to-source NMT model trained from previous steps, and construct a dataset using noisy source sentences with their clean target counterparts. During training, parallel data and back-translated data are sampled at 1:1 ratio.

3.5 Final Results

As is shown in previous sections, using large normalized corpora and back-translation both improve the baseline system in two translation directions. The overall result on validation set is depicted in Table 4. The final result on test dataset is depicted in (Ansari et al., 2020).

To further confirm the effectiveness of our back-translation approach acorss different domains, we classify the validation set into 14 different topics using a validated pre-trained bag-of-words model, and compute the validation BLEU scores of each topic before and after back-translation. In Figure 1, an overall improvement is observed in all categories with a few exceptions, which is expected.

Methods	Ja2Zh	Zh2Ja
official baseline	20.28	26.57
clean parallel	20.37	27.48
+ noisy parallel	25.48	30.32
+ back-translation	27.79	35.87

Table 4: Overall BLEU Scores on Validation Set.

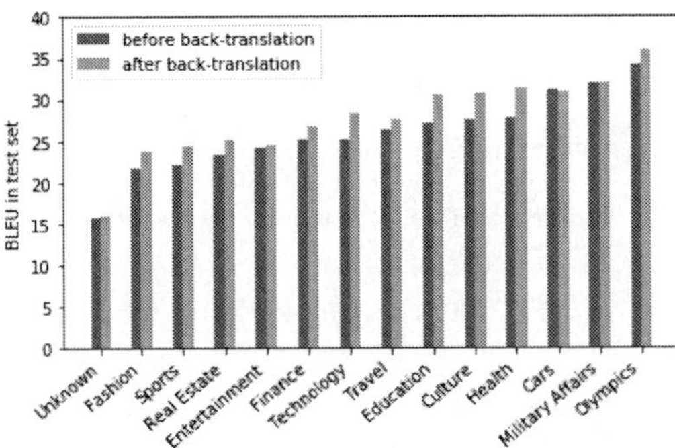

Figure 1: BLEU score in different domains in the validation set

4 Conclusion and Future Work

In this paper we described our submission to IWSLT 2020 open domain translation task. We improved the baseline model with a large amount of cleaned-up web-crawled data and the back-translation technique. Our final system achieved 27.79 and 35.87 BLEU scores on Ja2Zh and Zh2Ja tasks respectively, out running the official baseline by about 35%.

For future work, we first plan to improve the baseline model architecture, since it is left unchanged in our current experiments (e.g. by following (Sun et al., 2019)). Furthermore, loss masking (Rusiecki, 2019) would also be appealing, which ignores the samples of highest losses in each batch during training. Proven to be effective for noisy-label classification, loss masking may also be helpful to our NMT model trained with noisy sentence pairs. Another possibility is to filter noisy data with a learned representation in both languages (Hassan et al., 2018), which can further eliminate incomplete or mismatched translation pairs and help with model accuracy.

Initializing NMT decoder with a pre-trained BERT model is also stated to be useful; this technique is named 'cold fusion' in the context of ASR(Sriram et al., 2017), and we expect to see similar effects in the case of NMT. An alternative way of incorporating pre-trained BERT into NMT models is to merge hidden activations of these models together(Zhu et al., 2020). The results show that such a fusion is an effective way to utilize monolingual data as complementary to back-translation.

Finally, to tackle the multi-domain translation scenario, specific loss functions and model structures exhibit promising results (Zeng et al., 2018; Jiang et al., 2019); meanwhile, adding special domain tokens to source text may also achieve comparable results (Tars and Fishel, 2018).

References

Ebrahim Ansari, Amittai Axelroad, Nguyen Bach, Ondrej Bojar, Roldano Cattoni, Fahim Dalvi, Nadir Durrani, Marcello Federico, Christian Federmann, Jiatao Gu, Fei Huang, Kevin Knight, Xutai Ma, Ajay Nagesh, Matteo Negri, Jan Niehues, Juan Pino, Elizabeth Salesky, Xing Shi, Sebastian Stüker, Marco Turchi, and Changhan Wang. 2020. Findings of the IWSLT 2020 Evaluation Campaign. In *Proceedings of the 17th International Conference on Spoken Language Translation (IWSLT 2020)*, Seattle, USA.

Chenhui Chu, Raj Dabre, and Sadao Kurohashi. 2017. An empirical comparison of simple domain adaptation methods for neural machine translation. *ArXiv*, abs/1701.03214.

Jacob Devlin, Ming-Wei Chang, Kenton Lee, and Kristina Toutanova. 2019. Bert: Pre-training of deep bidirectional transformers for language understanding. In *NAACL-HLT*.

Linhao Dong, Shuang Xu, and Bo Xu. 2018. Speech-transformer: A no-recurrence sequence-to-sequence model for speech recognition. *2018 IEEE International Conference on Acoustics, Speech and Signal Processing (ICASSP)*, pages 5884–5888.

Sergey Edunov, Myle Ott, Michael Auli, and David Grangier. 2018. Understanding back-translation at scale. In *EMNLP*.

Markus Freitag and Yaser Al-Onaizan. 2016. Fast domain adaptation for neural machine translation. *ArXiv*, abs/1612.06897.

Philip J. Gage. 1994. A new algorithm for data compression. *The C Users Journal archive*, 12:23–38.

Mattia Antonino Di Gangi, Matteo Negri, Roldano Cattoni, Roberto Dessì, and Marco Turchi. 2019. Enhancing transformer for end-to-end speech-to-text translation. In *MTSummit*.

Çaglar Gülçehre, Orhan Firat, Kelvin Xu, Kyunghyun Cho, Loïc Barrault, Huei-Chi Lin, Fethi Bougares, Holger Schwenk, and Yoshua Bengio. 2015. On using monolingual corpora in neural machine translation. *ArXiv*, abs/1503.03535.

Hany Hassan, Anthony Aue, Chang Chen, Vishal Chowdhary, Jonathan Clark, Christian Federmann, Xuedong Huang, Marcin Junczys-Dowmunt, William Lewis, Mengnan Li, Shujie Liu, Tie-Yan Liu, Renqian Luo, Arul Menezes, Tao Qin, Frank Seide, Xu Tan, Fei Tian, Lijun Wu, Shuangzhi Wu, Yingce Xia, Dongdong Zhang, Zhirui Zhang, and Ming Zhou. 2018. Achieving human parity on automatic chinese to english news translation. *ArXiv*, abs/1803.05567.

Di He, Yingce Xia, Tao Qin, Liwei Wang, Nenghai Yu, Tie-Yan Liu, and Wei-Ying Ma. 2016. Dual learning for machine translation. In *NIPS*.

Cong Duy Vu Hoang, Philipp Koehn, Gholamreza Haffari, and Trevor Cohn. 2018. Iterative back-translation for neural machine translation. In *NMT@ACL*.

Haoming Jiang, Chen Liang, Chonggang Wang, and Tuo Zhao. 2019. Multi-domain neural machine translation with word-level adaptive layer-wise domain mixing. *ArXiv*, abs/1911.02692.

Armand Joulin, Edouard Grave, Piotr Bojanowski, and Tomas Mikolov. 2017. Bag of tricks for efficient text classification. In *Proceedings of the 15th Conference of the European Chapter of the Association for Computational Linguistics: Volume 2, Short Papers*, pages 427–431. Association for Computational Linguistics.

Martin Popel and Ondrej Bojar. 2018. Training tips for the transformer model. *The Prague Bulletin of Mathematical Linguistics*, 110:43 – 70.

Andrzej Rusiecki. 2019. Trimmed robust loss function for training deep neural networks with label noise. In *ICAISC*.

Rico Sennrich, Barry Haddow, and Alexandra Birch. 2016. Improving neural machine translation models with monolingual data. In *Proceedings of the 54th Annual Meeting of the Association for Computational Linguistics (Volume 1: Long Papers)*, pages 86–96, Berlin, Germany. Association for Computational Linguistics.

Joongbo Shin, Yoonhyung Lee, and Kyomin Jung. 2019. Effective sentence scoring method using bidirectional language model for speech recognition. *ArXiv*, abs/1905.06655.

Anuroop Sriram, Heewoo Jun, Sanjeev Satheesh, and Adam Coates. 2017. Cold fusion: Training seq2seq models together with language models. In *INTERSPEECH*.

Meng Sun, Bojian Jiang, Hao Xiong, Zhongjun He, Hua Wu, and Haifeng Wang. 2019. Baidu neural machine translation systems for WMT19. In *Proceedings of the Fourth Conference on Machine Translation (Volume 2: Shared Task Papers, Day 1)*, pages 374–381, Florence, Italy. Association for Computational Linguistics.

Sakaki Takeshi, Sakae Mizuki, and Naoyuki Gunji. 2019. Bert pre-trained model trained on large-scale japanese social media corpus.

Sander Tars and Mark Fishel. 2018. Multi-domain neural machine translation. *ArXiv*, abs/1805.02282.

Ashish Vaswani, Samy Bengio, Eugene Brevdo, Francois Chollet, Aidan N. Gomez, Stephan Gouws, Llion Jones, Łukasz Kaiser, Nal Kalchbrenner, Niki Parmar, Ryan Sepassi, Noam Shazeer, and Jakob Uszkoreit. 2018. Tensor2tensor for neural machine translation. *CoRR*, abs/1803.07416.

Ashish Vaswani, Noam Shazeer, Niki Parmar, Jakob Uszkoreit, Llion Jones, Aidan N. Gomez, Lukasz Kaiser, and Illia Polosukhin. 2017. Attention is all you need. In *NIPS*.

Bright Xu. 2019. Nlp chinese corpus: Large scale chinese corpus for nlp.

Jiali Zeng, Jinsong Su, Huating Wen, Yang Liu, Jun Xie, Yongjing Yin, and Jianqiang Zhao. 2018. Multi-domain neural machine translation with word-level domain context discrimination. In *EMNLP*.

Jinhua Zhu, Yingce Xia, Lijun Wu, Di He, Tao Qin, Wengang Zhou, Houqiang Li, and Tie-Yan Liu. 2020. Incorporating bert into neural machine translation. *ArXiv*, abs/2002.06823.

University of Tsukuba's Machine Translation System for IWSLT20 Open Domain Translation Task

Hongyi Cui⋆† **Yizhen Wei**⋆† **Shohei Iida**† **Masaaki Nagata**‡ **Takehito Utsuro**†
†Graduate School of Systems and Information Engineering, University of Tsukuba, Japan
‡NTT Communication Science Laboratories, NTT Corporation, Japan

Abstract

In this paper, we introduce University of Tsukuba's submission to the IWSLT20 Open Domain Translation Task. We participate in both Chinese→Japanese and Japanese→Chinese directions. For both directions, our machine translation systems are based on the Transformer architecture. Several techniques are integrated in order to boost the performance of our models: data filtering, large-scale noised training, model ensemble, reranking and postprocessing. Consequently, our efforts achieve 33.0 BLEU scores for Chinese→Japanese translation and 32.3 BLEU scores for Japanese→Chinese translation.

1 Introduction

In this paper, we introduce University of Tsukuba's submission to the IWSLT20 Open Domain Translation Task. The goal of this shared task is to promote: the research on translation between Asian languages, exploitation of noisy web corpora for machine translation, and smart processing of data and provenance. To have an overview look of the IWSLT20 Open Domain Translation Task, readers may refer to Ansari et al. (2020) for further details. We participated in both Chinese→Japanese and Japanese→Chinese directions.

It is widely acknowledged that a neural machine translation (NMT) system requires a large amount of training data. Meanwhile, the training process of NMT models may consume a long period of time and lots of computing resources. Considering the limitation of our computing power, our goal is to boost the performance of NMT systems with fewer and smaller components that require less time and computing resources. Our

models are based on the base Transformer as described in Vaswani et al. (2017) without special parameter fine-tuning. For data preprocessing, firstly, various orthodox methods including punctuation normalization, tokenization as well as byte pair encoding (Sennrich et al., 2016a) which have been widely used in recent researches are applied. Besides, we also apply manual rules, aiming to clean the provided parallel data, the monolingual data and the synthetic data which is generated by ourselves for data augmentation. For the sake of a better use of all provided data, we do a back-translation for either the source-side and the target-side monolingual data. Meanwhile, inspired by noised training method (Edunov et al., 2018; Wu et al., 2019; He et al., 2020), we add noise to the source sentences of the synthetic parallel corpus to make the translation models more robust and to improve its generalization ability. In addition, in inference phrase, we apply the model ensemble strategy while top n-best hypotheses are kept for further multi-features reranking process. At last, post-processing is applied to correct the inconsistent punctuation form.

This paper is organized as follows: in Section 2, we describe our data preprocessing and data filtering. Details of each component of our systems are described in Section 3. The results of the experiments for each component and language pair are summarized in Section 4.

2 Data

For all of our submissions, we only use datasets provided by the organizers. For training parallel data, we use the concatenation of **web_crawled_parallel_filtered** and **existing_parallel**. For data augmentation, since the unaligned data are extremely huge, we choose to use the separate side of the pre-filtered

---

⋆ Equal contribution.

Proceedings of the 17th International Conference on Spoken Language Translation (IWSLT), pages 145–148
July 9-10, 2020. ©2020 Association for Computational Linguistics
https://doi.org/10.18653/v1/P17

sentences (**web_crawled_parallel_unfiltered**) as monolingual data. Also, development dataset provided by the organizer is used for development and model evaluation.

2.1 Data Preprocessing

The provided parallel training data contains different forms of characters, for example, full-width form and half-width form. To get a normalized form, we remove all the spaces between characters and perform NFKC-based text normalization.

Chinese sentences are segmented with the default mode of Jieba[1] and Japanese sentences are segmented with Mecab[2] using mecab-ipadic-NEologd[3] dictionary. To limit the size of vocabularies of NMT models, we use byte pair encoding(BPE) (Sennrich et al., 2016b) with 32K split operations separately for both side.

2.2 Data Filtering

The provided datasets built from the web data are very noisy and can potentially decrease the performance of a system. To get a clean form, we filter the parallel training corpus with the following rules:

- Filter out duplicate sentence pairs.

- Filter out sentence pairs which have identical source-side and target-side sentences.

- Filter out sentence pairs with more than 10 punctuations or imbalanced punctuation ratio.

- Filter out sentence pairs which contains half or more tokens that are numbers or letters.

- Filter out sentence pairs which contain HTML tags or emoji.

- Filter out sentence pairs with wrong languages identified by langid.[4]

- Filter out sentence pairs exceeding length ratio 1.5.

- Filter out sentence pairs with less than 3 words or more than 100 word.

[1] https://github.com/fxsjy/jieba
[2] https://taku910.github.io/mecab
[3] https://github.com/neologd/
mecab-ipadic-neologd
[4] https://github.com/saffsd/langid.py

	Ja	Zh
Parallel data(in sents.)	20.9M	20.9M
+ Filtering(in sents.)	9.8M	9.8M
+ Filtering(in subwords.)	164.5M	128.1M
Monolingual data(in sents.)	161.5M	161.5M
+ Filtering(in sents)	17.8M	17.6M
+ Filtering(in subwords.)	308.3M	254.9M

Table 1: Statistics of the provided data. Notice that we treat two sides of the provided unfiltered dataset separately as monolingual data, therefore the number of monolingual data in terms of sentence pairs are identical as before data filtering.

The same data filtering strategies except those designed for sentence pairs are also employed on monolingual data. Details of the preprocessed dataset in terms of the amount of sentences and BPE subwords are listed out in millions in Table 1.

3 System

3.1 Baseline System

We adopt the base Transformer as our machine translation system following the settings as described in Vaswani et al. (2017), consisting of 6 encoder layers, 6 decoder layers, 8 heads, with an embedding dimension of 512 and feed-forward network dimension of 2048. The dropout probability is 0.2. For all experiments, we adopt the Adam optimizer (Kingma and Ba, 2014) using β_1 = 0.9, β_2 = 0.98, and ϵ = 1e-8. The learning rate is scheduled using inverse square root schedule with a maximum learning rate 0.0005 and 4000 warmup steps. We train all our models using fairseq[5] (Ott et al., 2019) on two NIVIDA 2080Ti GPUs with a batch size of around 4096 tokens. During training, we employ label smoothing of value 0.1. We average the last 5 model checkpoints and use it for decoding.

3.2 Large-scale Noised Training

It is widely known that the performance of a NMT system relies heavily on the amount of parallel training data. Back-translation (Sennrich et al., 2016a) and Self-training (Zhang and Zong, 2016) are effective and commonly used data augmentation techniques to leverage the monolingual data to augment the original parallel dataset.

In our case, we leverage both the source-side and target-side monolingual data to help the train-

[5] https://github.com/pytorch/fairseq

ing. Specifically, we train a baseline NMT model with the provided parallel corpus at first. Then, target-side monolingual sentences are translated by a target-to-source NMT model and source-side monolingual sentences are translated by a source-to-target NMT model.

Inspired by noised training method (Edunov et al., 2018; Wu et al., 2019; He et al., 2020), we add noise to the source sentences of the synthetic parallel corpus to make the translation models more robust and to improve its generalization ability. Specifically,

- We randomly replace a word by a special unknown token with probability 0.1.

- We randomly delete the words with probability 0.1.

- We randomly swap the words with constraint that no further than 3 words apart.

Then we add the synthetic parallel data to original parallel data and train a new NMT model.

3.3 Model Ensemble

Model ensemble is a common method to boost translation performance. However, due to the huge amount of training data and our limited computing power, we do not ensemble multiple strong models with different random seeds. Instead, we only combine three models trained on filtered data with different random seeds and one model trained through large-scale noised training. All individual models used for model ensemble are the average of the last 5 model checkpoints.

3.4 Reranking

Reranking is a method of improving translation quality by rescoring a list of n-best hypotheses. For our submissions, we generate n-best hypotheses through a source-to-target NMT model and then train a reranker using k-best MIRA (Cherry and Foster, 2012). The features we use for reranking are:

- **Left-to-right NMT Feature:** We keep the original perplexity by the original translation model as a L2R reranking feature.

- **Right-to-left NMT Feature:** In order to address exposure bias problem, we train a right-to-left (R2L) NMT model using the same

System	Ja→Zh	
	Dev	Test
Baseline	28.19	22.0
+ Data filtering	28.60	–
+ Noised training	29.42	–
+ Model ensemble	30.03	–
+ Reranking	30.29	–
+ Postprocessing	30.53	–
Our Submission	–	32.3

Table 2: BLEU scores on Japanese → Chinese.

System	Zh→Ja	
	Dev	Test
Baseline	27.29	26.3
+ Data filtering	32.37	–
+ Noised training	32.21	–
+ Model ensemble	32.82	–
+ Reranking	33.24	–
+ Postprocessing	33.26	–
Our Submission	–	33.0

Table 3: BLEU scores on Chinese → Japanese.

training data but with inverted target word order. We invert the hypothesis sequence and use the perplexity score given by the right-to-left NMT model as R2L feature.

- **Target-to-Source NMT Feature:** To reduce inadequate translation, we use the perplexity score given by the target-to-source NMT model as T2S feature. In addition, we also use the score generated by a target-to-source right-to-left model as a reranking feature.

- **Length Feature:** We also design a length feature that quantifies the difference between the ratio of each sentence pair and the optimal ratio. The optimal ratio is determined according to the training parallel corpus.

3.5 Postprocessing

Since we perform NFKC-based text normalization on the training corpus, we also employ a postprocessing algorithm on the generated hypothesis. To be more specific, we change half-width punctuations to full-width punctuations.

4 Results

Results and ablations for Ja→Zh and Zh→Ja are shown in Table 2 and Table 3 respectively. We report character-based BLEU calculated with the provided script. Reference for BLEU calculation on development dataset is in the raw form which has not been NFKC-normalized. Each line in the table represents for the result yielded from the model to which techniques declared in current line and all previous lines are added.

4.1 Japanese→Chinese

For Ja→Zh, data filtering improves our baseline performance on development data by + 0.41 BLEU scores. The addition of synthetic data and large-scale noised training further improves model performance by + 0.82 BLEU scores. We further gain + 0.61 BLEU scores and + 0.26 BLEU scores after applying model ensemble and reranking. Finally, applying postprocessing on top of generated hypothesis gives another improvement of 0.24 BLEU scores. The final BLEU score of our submission is 32.3.

4.2 Chinese→Japanese

For Zh→Ja, data filtering plays an important role and improves our baseline performance on development data by + 5.08 BLEU scores. The addition of synthetic data and large-scale noised training slightly hurt the performance.[6] After applying model ensemble and reranking, we further gain + 0.61 BLEU scores and + 0.42 BLEU scores respectively. Finally, applying postprocessing on top of the generated hypothesis gives another 0.02 BLEU scores. The final BLEU score of our submission is 33.0.

5 Conclusion

This paper describes University of Tsukuba's submission to IWSLT20 open domain translation task. We trained standard Transformer models and adopted various techniques for better performance, including data filtering, large-scale noised training, model ensemble, reranking and postprocessing. We demonstrated the effectiveness of our approach and achieved 33.0 BLEU scores for Chinese→Japanese translation and 32.3 BLEU scores for Japanese→Chinese translation.

---

[6]However, we also notice that, when BLEU is calculated with the NFKC-normalized reference it will be slightly improved if large-scale noised training is added (33.83 vs. 33.97). Therefore, we still adopt large-scale noised training for our final submission.

References

Ebrahim Ansari, Amittai Axelrod, Nguyen Bach, Ondrej Bojar, Roldano Cattoni, Fahim Dalvi, Nadir Durrani, Marcello Federico, Christian Federmann, Jiatao Gu, Fei Huang, Kevin Knight, Xutai Ma, Ajay Nagesh, Matteo Negri, Jan Niehues, Juan Pino, Elizabeth Salesky, Xing Shi, Sebastian Stüker, Marco Turchi, and Changhan Wang. 2020. Findings of the IWSLT 2020 Evaluation Campaign. In *Proceedings of the 17th International Conference on Spoken Language Translation (IWSLT 2020)*, Seattle, USA.

Colin Cherry and George Foster. 2012. Batch tuning strategies for statistical machine translation. In *NAACL*, pages 427–436.

Sergey Edunov, Myle Ott, Michael Auli, and David Grangier. 2018. Understanding back-translation at scale. In *EMNLP*, pages 489–500.

Junxian He, Jiatao Gu, Jiajun Shen, and Marc'Aurelio Ranzato. 2020. Revisiting self-training for neural sequence generation. In *ICLR*.

Diederik P. Kingma and Jimmy Ba. 2014. Adam: A method for stochastic optimization. In *ICLR*.

Myle Ott, Sergey Edunov, Alexei Baevski, Angela Fan, Sam Gross, Nathan Ng, David Grangier, and Michael Auli. 2019. fairseq: A fast, extensible toolkit for sequence modeling. In *NAACL*, pages 48–53.

Rico Sennrich, Barry Haddow, and Alexandra Birch. 2016a. Improving neural machine translation models with monolingual data. In *ACL*, pages 86–96.

Rico Sennrich, Barry Haddow, and Alexandra Birch. 2016b. Neural machine translation of rare words with subword units. In *ACL*, pages 1715–1725.

Ashish Vaswani, Noam Shazeer, Niki Parmar, Jakob Uszkoreit, Llion Jones, Aidan N Gomez, Ł ukasz Kaiser, and Illia Polosukhin. 2017. Attention is all you need. In *NIPS*.

Lijun Wu, Yiren Wang, Yingce Xia, Tao Qin, Jianhuang Lai, and Tie-Yan Liu. 2019. Exploiting monolingual data at scale for neural machine translation. In *EMNLP-IJCNLP*, pages 4207–4216.

Jiajun Zhang and Chengqing Zong. 2016. Exploiting source-side monolingual data in neural machine translation. In *EMNLP*, pages 1535–1545.

Xiaomi's Submissions for IWSLT 2020 Open Domain Translation Task

Yuhui Sun, Mengxue Guo, Xiang Li, Jianwei Cui, Bin Wang
AI Lab, Xiaomi Group
{sunyuhui1,guomengxue1,lixiang21,cuijianwei,wangbin11}@xiaomi.com

Abstract

This paper describes the Xiaomi's submissions to the IWSLT20 shared open domain translation task for Chinese↔Japanese language pair. We explore different model ensembling strategies based on recent Transformer variants. We also further strengthen our systems via some first-line techniques, such as data filtering, data selection, tagged back translation, domain adaptation, knowledge distillation, and re-ranking. Our resulting Chinese→Japanese primary system ranked second in terms of character-level BLEU score among all submissions. Our resulting Japanese→Chinese primary system also achieved a competitive performance.

1 Introduction

In this paper, we describe the Xiaomi's neural machine translation (NMT) systems evaluated at IWSLT 2020 (Ansari et al., 2020) shared open domain translation task in two directions, Chinese→Japanese (Zh→Ja) and Japanese→Chinese (Ja→Zh).

The accuracy of NMT systems relies on the quality of training data, we first consider careful pre-processing and discard the corrupted data from the existing bilingual sentences according to rule-based filtering and model-based scoring.

In the aspect of NMT architecture, we exploit some recent Transformer variants, including different Transformer models with deeper layers or wider inner dimension of feed-forward layers than the standard Transformer-Big model, Transformer with a dynamic linear combination of layers (DLCL) (Wang et al., 2019) and neural architecture search (NAS) based Transformer-Evolved (So et al., 2019), to increase the diversity of the system. We further strengthen our systems by diversifying the training data via some effective methods, including back-translation (BT) (Sennrich et al., 2016b),

knowledge distillation (KD) (Hinton et al., 2015) and right-to-left (R2L) NMT model. Finally, we also explore re-rank the n-best translation candidates generated by models ensembling with some effective features, including target-to-source (T2S) NMT model, left-to-right (L2R) NMT model, R2L NMT model (Liu et al., 2016), bilingual sentence BERT and language model (LM).

Through experiments, we evaluate how each system feature affects the accuracy of NMT. Our resulting Chinese→Japanese primary system ranked second in terms of character-level BLEU score among all submissions. Our resulting Japanese→Chinese primary system also achieved a competitive performance.

2 Data

2.1 Pre-processing

Our pre-processing pipeline begins by removing non-printable ASCII characters, lowercasing text, normalizing additional white-space, and control character and replacing any escaped characters with the corresponding symbol by our in-house script. All the data is further normalized so all full-width Roman characters and digits are normalized to half-width. All the traditional characters of Chinese data are converted to simplified characters using OpenCC[1]. For all corpora, Chinese sentences are segmented by our in-house Chinese word segmenter, and Japanese sentences are first segmented by the morphological analyzer Mecab (Kudo, 2006) and then tokenized only for the non-Japanese part by the Moses script[2].

---

[1] https://github.com/BYVoid/OpenCC
[2] https://github.com/moses-smt/
mosesdecoder/blob/master/scripts/
tokenizer/tokenizer.perl

Proceedings of the 17th International Conference on Spoken Language Translation (IWSLT), pages 149–157
July 9-10, 2020. ©2020 Association for Computational Linguistics
https://doi.org/10.18653/v1/P17

2.2 Parallel Data Filtering

Though the NMT performance is highly correlated to the huge amounts of training data, a robust body of studies (Carpuat et al., 2017; Khayrallah and Koehn, 2018; Wang et al., 2018; Koehn et al., 2018) has shown the bad impact of noisy data on general NMT translation accuracy. In addition to a small amount of Japanese-Chinese parallel data[3] from various public sources, the organizers also provide a large-scale but noisy parallel data[4] extracted from a non-parallel web-crawled data through some similarity measures for parallel data mining. We apply a two-stage process consisting of rule-based filtering and model-based scoring to further filter harmful sentence pairs that are bound to negatively affect the quality of NMT systems from the original parallel corpora as follows.

2.2.1 Rule-based Filtering

During the first stage, we remove some illegal parallel sentences by applying several rule-based heuristics. A sentence pair is deleted from the corpus if its source side or target side fails to obey any of the following wild rules reflecting what 'good data' should look like. Some of the heuristic filtering methods can deal with aspects that can not be captured with models.

- The token (i.e. character sequence between two spaces) length of every sentence is limited less than 50.

- Sentence pairs with a length ratio greater than 4 are removed.

- Chinese sentences with Chinese characters ratio less than 0.15 or any character of other than Chinese and English are removed. And Japanese sentences with Japanese characters ratio less than 0.25 or any character of other than Chinese, Japanese, and English are removed.

- Japanese sentences without any Hiragana or Katakana character are removed.

- Sentence pairs with mismatched numbers of length three or more digits or URLs are removed.

- Duplicated sentence pairs are discarded.

2.2.2 Model-based Scoring

In the second stage of our filtering pipeline, we utilize a variety of models to assign some scores to each sentence pair of the remaining rule-based filtered parallel corpus (RFPD). Afterward, we select better sentences according to these scores.

- Translation model: We construct parallel NMT systems based on the standard Transformer-big model in both directions using RFPD to obtain the target synthetic translation as the reference. BEER (Stanojević and Sima'an, 2014) is used as a sentence-level metric of sentence similarity. We prune the sentence pairs with the BEER score of lower than 0.2.

- SBERT model: Recently, contextualized word embeddings derived from large-scale pre-trained language models (Devlin et al., 2019; Liu et al., 2019; Yang et al., 2019) have achieved new state-of-the-arts in various monolingual NLP tasks. The success has also been extended to cross-lingual scenarios (Schwenk, 2018; Conneau and Lample, 2019; Mulcaire et al., 2019; Artetxe and Schwenk, 2019). Recently, Reimers and Gurevych (2019) proposed sentence BERT (SBERT) to derive semantically meaningful sentence embeddings. According to the training framework of SBERT, we use the multilingual pre-train BERT model[5] and finetune it on RFPD to yield useful Chinese and Japanese sentence embeddings in the same space. We reject sentence pairs with a cosine-similarity score below 0.2.

- Word alignment model: We perform a word alignment model on RFPD using *fast_align* (Dyer et al., 2013) to check whether the sentence pair has the same meaning. Sentence pairs with the alignment probability of being each other translation less than 0.1 are discarded.

- N-gram LM: It is beneficial to use fluent sentences for training NMT models. We train a 5-gram LM that is estimated with modified Kneser-Ney smoothing (Kneser and Ney,

---

1995) using KenLM (Heafield, 2011) on each
side of the parallel sentences to evaluate sentences' naturalness. We normalize the LM
perplexity (PPL) scores of all the sentences
to be between [0,1]. Sentences whose normalized PPL scores fall below the threshold
(0.45 and 0.53 for Chinese and Japanese data,
respectively) are removed.

It is worth noting that all the above thresholds
are determined experimentally.

2.3 Post-processing

All the outputs are post-processed by merging subwords, removing the space between the non-ASCII
characters, and rule-based de-truecasing. All halfwidth punctuation marks and digits are also converted back to their original full-width form in a
specific language when translating to Chinese and
Japanese.

3 Overview of System Features

3.1 Translation Models

NMT has gained rapid progress in recent
years (Sutskever et al., 2014; Bahdanau et al., 2015;
Vaswani et al., 2017). In addition to the standard
Transformer-Big (Vaswani et al., 2017) model, we
also apply recent Transformer variants for creating
better model ensembles.

- Wider model: Dimension is an important
  factor to enhance the Transformer model
  capacity and performance. Based on the
  standard Transformer-Big model, we train
  a Transformer-Wide model with a inner dimension of position-wise feed-forward layers
  8,192.

- Deeper model: Building deeper networks
  via stacking more encoder and decoder layers has been a trend in NMT (Bapna et al.,
  2018; Wu et al., 2019; Zhang et al., 2019).
  We also exploit three deeper Transformer
  models by simply increasing the layer size
  of Transformer-Big, including Transformer-
  Deep-12-12, Transformer-Deep-12-6, and
  Transformer-Deep-6-12 in which the first
  number represents the layer size of the encoder and the second number represents the
  layer size of the decoder. In addition to the
  standard Transformer in which the residual
  connection is applied between two adjacent

layers, we also implement two DLCL (Wang
et al., 2019)-based Transformer models which
can memorize the outputs from all preceding layers, including Transformer-DLCL-
Big based on the Transformer-Big model
and Transformer-DLCL-Deep based on the
Transformer-Deep-12-12 above.

- NAS-based model: Recently, NAS has begun to outperform human-designed models (Elsken et al., 2018). We use the computationally efficient Transformer-Evolved (So
  et al., 2019) model by NAS. The hyperparameters can be seen in Tensor2Tensor implementation[6].

3.2 Data Diversification

We employ an effective data augmentation strategy
to boost NMT accuracy by diversifying the training
data. We first use the following backward and forward models to generate a diverse set of synthetic
training data from both lingual sides of the original
training data or external monolingual data. Then,
we concatenate all the synthetic data with the original data to train the baseline models from scratch
in L2R, R2L, and T2S ways, respectively. Finally,
we conduct the aforementioned approach based on
ensemble models again to achieve better baseline
systems.

- T2S model: Back-translation has thus far
  been the most effective technique effective
  for NMT (Sennrich et al., 2016b). Instead of
  using the synthetic training data produced by
  translating monolingual data in the target language into the source language conventionally,
  we prepend a special tag to all the source sentences from the synthetic data to distinguish
  synthetic data from original data (Caswell
  et al., 2019).

- R2L model: Generally, most NMT systems
  produce translations in an L2R way, which suffers from the issue of exposure bias and consequent error propagation (Ranzato et al., 2016).
  It has been observed that the accuracy of the
  right part words in its translation results is
  usually worse than the left part words (Zhang
  et al., 2018; Zhou et al., 2019). We train all
  the baseline systems separately using L2R

---

⁶`https://github.com/tensorflow/`
`tensor2tensor/blob/master/tensor2tensor/`
`models/evolved_transformer.py`

and R2L decoding (Wang et al., 2017; Hassan et al., 2018).

- L2R model: Knowledge distillation has been widely applied to NMT (Kim and Rush, 2016; Freitag et al., 2017; Chen et al., 2017; Gu et al., 2018; Tan et al., 2019). Recent work (Furlanello et al., 2018) demonstrates that the student model can surpass the accuracy of the teacher model, even if the student model is identical to their teacher model. Following this work, the teacher and student models in our experiments keep the same architecture.

3.3 Model Ensembling

Ensemble decoding is an effective approach to boost the accuracy of NMT systems via averaging the word distributions output from multiple single models at each decoding step. We select the top 4 systems with the highest BLEU evaluated on the development dataset from all the available baseline systems of each direction for models ensembling.

3.4 Reranking

Reranking technique (Shen et al., 2004) has been applied in the recent years' WMT tasks (Sennrich et al., 2016a; Wang et al., 2017; Ng et al., 2019) and have provided significant improvements. We first use the S2T-L2R and S2T-R2L ensemble systems to generate more diverse translation hypotheses for a source sentence (Liu et al., 2016). Then we use ensemble models of S2T-L2R, S2T-R2L and T2S-L2R to calculate 3 different likelihood scores for each sentence pair. We obtain the perplexity score for the translation candidates with a neural LM based on the Transformer encoder. We also employ SBERT to calculate the similarity score for each sentence pair. Each model's score is treated as an individual feature. Considering the ranking problem as a classification problem, we employ the implementation of pairwise ranking in scikit-learn[7] RankSVM (Joachims, 2006) to learn the weights of all the features on the development data for reranking. We compute the relative distance between these two samples in the sentence-level BLEU metric by pairing up two translation candidates. In the training phase of the reranking model, we are only interested in whether the relative distance is positive or negative. For test data, we rescore the hypotheses in the list by the reranking model and select the hypothesis with the highest likelihood score as the final output.

4 Experiments and Results

In this section, we introduce the experimental and data setup used in our experiments and then evaluate each of the systems introduced in Section 3.

4.1 Experimental and Data Setup

Due to a large number of training parameters, our deeper Transformer models require larger GPU memory resources and more time to train. To avoid the out-of-memory issue when training models with adequate batch size, all models are optimized by the memory-efficient Adafactor (Shazeer and Stern, 2018) which has three times smaller models than Adam (Kingma and Ba, 2015). Furthermore, we also apply the mixed-precision training (Narang et al., 2018) without losing model accuracy to speed up the training significantly.

In the training stage, we batch sentence pairs by approximate length and limit the number of source and target tokens per batch to 2,048 for two deeper models and 4,096 for others per GPU. All models are trained on one machine with 8 NVIDIA V100 GPUs each of which has 16GB memory for a total of 200K steps. We optimize all models against BLEU using the development set provided by the organizer, stopping early if BLEU does not improve for 16 checkpoints of 2,000 updates each. We set dropout 0.1 for Chinese→Japanese and 0.2 is for Japanese→Chinese. We average the top 10 checkpoints evaluated against the development set as the final model for decoding. During decoding, the beam size is set to 4 for the single model and 10 for ensemble models. We report the 4-gram character BLEU (Papineni et al., 2002) evaluated by the provided automatic evaluation script[8].

The approach of two-stage parallel data filtering in Section 2.2 enables us to drastically reduce the training data from 19M to 12M. In order to enlarge the size of bilingual data, we also exploit to extract more high-quality sentence pairs from the provided pre-filtered parallel data[9]. We first pre-process the data and use the rules in Section 2.2 to remove

---

[7]https://scikit-learn.org/stable/ modules/generated/sklearn.svm.LinearSVC. html

[8]https://github.com/didi/iwslt2020_ open_domain_translation/blob/master/ scripts/multi-bleu-detok.perl

[9]https://iwslt.oss-cn-beijing.aliyuncs. com/web_crawled_parallel_1.1.tgz

Corpus	#Sentences	Zh→Ja	Ja→Zh
Original	21M	32.24	26.03
Filtered	12M	36.94	31.27
+augment($\mathcal{D}_1$)	16M	37.08	31.44

Table 1: Results for L2R Transformer-Big based Chinese↔Japanese systems on the development dataset with different training data.

illegal data. We then rank the remaining data according to the sum of S2T and T2S BEER scores of each sentence pair and select 4M sentence pairs with the highest score into the filtered training data. Finally, we obtain the augmented training data with 16M sentence pairs to train all models.

We learn BPE segmentation models (Sennrich et al., 2016c) with 30K merge operations and filter out sentence pairs consisting of rare subword units with a frequency threshold of less than 6 to speed up the training, in which 38.5K and 40K subword tokens are adopted as Chinese and Japanese vocabularies separately for each experiment.

We submit two systems per direction in constrained and unconstrained training data settings. In a constrained condition, we only use the training data provided by the organizer. And for unconstrained submission, we choose the large-scale amounts of Commoncrawl Chinese[10] and Japanese[11] dataset as additional monolingual data for training LMs and executing BT to enhance our NMT systems. We process these monolingual data as follows: (1)pre-process according to the pipeline described in Section 2.1; (2)sentence segmentation; (3) only keep sentences with token length between 5 and 100; (4) draw a random sample with 160M sentences as the final clean monolingual data for each language.

4.2 Results of Data Filtering and Augmentation

We first evaluate the effect of data filtering on the performance of the NMT system. We train the Transformer-Big model on (i) the original training data only, (ii) filtered training data, (iii) concatenating selected 4M training data from the provided pre-filtered parallel data (+augment). Table 1

shows that data filtering gives a significant improvement for NMT accuracy, up to 4.70 BLEU score for Zh→Ja and 5.24 BLEU score for Ja→Zh, and adding more high-quality data can further boost the performance for Zh↔Ja. The results shed light on the importance of effective data filtering for training a strong NMT system, particularly for the training data with much noise mined from the web. Finally, $\mathcal{D}_1$ with 16M sentence pairs is chosen as the starting training data for the task.

4.3 Results of Baseline Models

For each translation task, we compare the performance of all the baseline systems trained on $\mathcal{D}_1$ from L2R and R2L decoding directions on the official validation set.

For Zh→Ja task, Table 2a shows that the standard Transformer-Big model outperforms all the Transformer models with deeper layers or wider dimension by a small margin and achieves the best BLEU score for L2R direction. For R2L direction, however, the deeper Transformer model with 12 layers in both the encoder and the decoder provides a significant improvement as compared to the Transformer-Big model and obtains the best BLEU score.

For Ja→Zh task, Table 2b indicates that all deep Transformer models are superior to the shallow Transformer-Big model for both the L2R and R2L directions. For L2R direction, the Transformer-Deep-12-6 model obtains the best BLEU score. For R2L direction, the Transformer-DLCL-Deep outperforms other models, particularly up to 0.44 BLEU score as compared to the Transformer-Deep-12-12. The result also demonstrates that DLCL is useful for training deep models.

For both translation tasks, although with far fewer parameters than the Transformer-Big model, the Transformer-Evolved model still obtains a competitive performance among all the baseline systems. Table 2b shows that the performance of the R2L Transformer-Evolved model ranks second among all the models for Ja→Zh. It is interesting to note that L2R decoding behaves better than that of R2L decoding, and Ja→Zh has an opposite phenomenon. We suspect that the main reason is that Chinese is a subject–verb–object (SVO) language, while Japanese is a subject–object–verb (SOV) language.

---

[10]`http://web-language-models.`
`s3-website-us-east-1.amazonaws.com/`
`ngrams/zh/deduped/zh.deduped.xz`

[11]`http://web-language-models.`
`s3-website-us-east-1.amazonaws.com/`
`ngrams/ja/deduped/ja.deduped.xz`

System	Constrained						Unconstrained	
	$\mathcal{D}_1$		$\mathcal{D}_2$		$\mathcal{D}_3$		$\mathcal{D}_4$	
	L2R	R2L	L2R	R2L	L2R	R2L	L2R	R2L
Transformer-Big	**37.08**	36.28	37.98	37.59	37.88	37.88	39.08	39.35
Transformer-Wide	36.98	36.57	**38.20**	37.46	38.35	38.14	39.50	39.23
Transformer-Deep-6-12	36.84	36.71	37.73	37.60	37.77	38.04	38.98	39.28
Transformer-Deep-12-6	36.96	36.50	37.58	37.07	37.70	**38.32**	38.92	39.11
Transformer-Deep-12-12	37.00	**36.97**	38.06	**37.74**	**38.39**	38.17	39.42	39.27
Transformer-DLCL-Big	36.46	36.10	37.65	37.11	38.18	37.52	39.27	**39.49**
Transformer-DLCL-Deep	36.61	36.27	37.34	37.53	37.57	37.85	**39.59**	39.17
Transformer-Evolved	36.47	35.87	37.42	36.85	37.71	37.19	38.78	38.65
Ensemble	38.37	37.96	39.22	38.82	39.32	39.20	40.1	40.13
+Reranking	-		-		39.37$^{\#}$		41.54*	

(a) Chinese→Japanese

System	Constrained						Unconstrained	
	$\mathcal{D}_1$		$\mathcal{D}_2$		$\mathcal{D}_3$		$\mathcal{D}_4$	
	L2R	R2L	L2R	R2L	L2R	R2L	L2R	R2L
Transformer-Big	31.44	31.81	32.27	32.62	33.88	33.80	34.23	34.21
Transformer-Wide	31.25	31.98	32.11	32.84	33.58	34.07	34.02	34.25
Transformer-Deep-6-12	31.55	31.98	32.26	32.67	34.07	34.11	34.29	34.20
Transformer-Deep-12-6	**31.96**	32.22	32.15	32.94	33.59	34.07	33.98	**34.35**
Transformer-Deep-12-12	31.95	32.22	**32.49**	32.75	**34.22**	**34.15**	**34.31**	34.30
Transformer-DLCL-Big	31.82	32.07	32.31	32.64	34.09	34.03	34.29	34.18
Transformer-DLCL-Deep	31.64	**32.66**	32.46	33.18	34.11	34.12	34.17	34.21
Transformer-Evolved	31.44	32.46	31.99	**33.45**	32.95	33.91	33.97	33.99
Ensemble	32.57	33.17	33.30	33.79	34.73	34.52	34.82	34.85
+Reranking	-		-		34.78$^{\#}$		34.91*	

(b) Japanese→Chinese

Table 2: Results of various system trained on different training data evaluated on the Chinese↔Japanese validation sets. $\mathcal{D}_1$ (16M sentence pairs) is the starting training data. $\mathcal{D}_2$ (32M sentence pairs) is $\mathcal{D}_1$ concatenated with the pseudo-parallel data back-translated from the target side of $\mathcal{D}_1$ by the ensemble models based on the T2S single models trained on $\mathcal{D}_1$. $\mathcal{D}_3$ (64M sentence pairs) is $\mathcal{D}_2$ concatenated with two KD synthetic data, including translating the source side of $\mathcal{D}_1$ by the ensemble models from the S2T-L2R single models and the ensemble models from the S2T-R2L single models that are both trained on $\mathcal{D}_2$. Finally, for one S2T language pair, the external target monolingual data is translated by the T2S-L2R Transformer-Big model trained on $\mathcal{D}_3$. The generated synthetic corpus is splitted into eight parts equally. Each part (20M sentence pairs) is concatenated with $\mathcal{D}_3$ to generate the training data $\mathcal{D}_4$ (84M sentence pairs) that is applied to train one of all the eight baseline systems. For the given decoding direction and training data, result of the best single system is bold-faced. * denotes the submitted primary system in the unconstrained condition where only the provided training data is used. $^{\#}$ denotes the submitted contrastive system in the constrained condition where external public monolingual data is applied.

4.4 Results of Systems Features

In constrained condition, Table 2 shows that BT based on the target of bilingual data also brings large improvement to all baseline systems for both the Zh→Ja and Ja→Zh tasks. We observe a solid improvement of an average BLEU score of 0.95 for Zh→Ja and an average BLEU score of 0.67 for Ja→Zh. It is worth noting that the Transformer-Evolved model achieves the best BLEU score among all the R2L systems for Ja→Zh. The result suggests that the human-designed architectures may not be optimal. Therefore, it seems promising to replace the manual process of architecture design with NAS.

Table 2a shows that the improvement of KD is relatively slight for Zh→Ja. However, the translation quality of Ja→Zh strong models after BT is further largely improved using KD, up to an average BLEU score of 0.89. We attribute this finding to the quality gap between the provided Chinese and Japanese data.

Table 2a shows that adding large-scale synthetic parallel data back-translated from external monolingual data further boost the performance in different degree. Both the best baseline systems obtain a significant improvement by 1.32 1.32 BLEU score for Zh→Ja. However, it is currently not clear to us how to interpret on the marginal improvement for Ja→Zh. There is a reason to conjecture that we might be suffering from reference bias towards translationese and non-native data (Toral et al., 2018).

Unsurprisingly, utilizing diverse models with homogeneous architectures to the ensemble improves translation quality across both the tasks in different degrees. In constrained condition, the Zh→Ja ensemble models gain a substantial improvement compared to the baseline

From the Table 2a, our reranking model finally achieves a significant improvement of about 1.4 BLEU score for Zh→Ja, even when applied on top of an ensemble of very strong KD+BT models. However, the improvement of reranking is relatively inconsiderable for Ja→Zh, and we also attribute this to the issue of translationese reference above.

5 Conclusions

We present the Xiaomi's NMT systems for IWSLT 2020 Chinese↔Japanese open domain translation tasks. For both translation tasks, our final systems achieved substantial improvements up by about 9 BLEU score over baseline systems by integrating careful data filtering, data augmentation, and other effective NMT techniques. As a result, our submitted Chinese→Japanese system rank second to the official evaluation set in terms of character-level BLEU and Japanese→Chinese system also achieves a competitive performance.

References

Ebrahim Ansari, Amittai Axelrod, Nguyen Bach, Ondrej Bojar, Roldano Cattoni, Fahim Dalvi, Nadir Durrani, Marcello Federico, Christian Federmann, Jiatao Gu, Fei Huang, Kevin Knight, Xutai Ma, Ajay Nagesh, Matteo Negri, Jan Niehues, Juan Pino, Elizabeth Salesky, Xing Shi, Sebastian Stüker, Marco Turchi, and Changhan Wang. 2020. Findings of the IWSLT 2020 Evaluation Campaign. In *Proceedings of the 17th International Conference on Spoken Language Translation (IWSLT 2020)*, Seattle, USA.

Mikel Artetxe and Holger Schwenk. 2019. Margin-based parallel corpus mining with multilingual sentence embeddings. In *Proc. of ACL*, pages 3197–3203.

Dzmitry Bahdanau, Kyunghyun Cho, and Yoshua Bengio. 2015. Neural machine translation by jointly learning to align and translate. In *Proc. of ICLR*.

Ankur Bapna, Mia Chen, Orhan Firat, Yuan Cao, and Yonghui Wu. 2018. Training deeper neural machine translation models with transparent attention. In *Proc. of EMNLP*, pages 3028–3033.

Marine Carpuat, Yogarshi Vyas, and Xing Niu. 2017. Detecting cross-lingual semantic divergence for neural machine translation. In *Proc. of the First Workshop on Neural Machine Translation*, pages 69–79.

Isaac Caswell, Ciprian Chelba, and David Grangier. 2019. Tagged back-translation. In *Proc. of the Fourth Conference on Machine Translation*, pages 53–63.

Yun Chen, Yang Liu, Yong Cheng, and Victor O K Li. 2017. A teacher-student framework for zero-resource neural machine translation. In *Proc. of ACL*, pages 1925–1935.

Alexis Conneau and Guillaume Lample. 2019. Cross-lingual language model pretraining. In H. Wallach, H. Larochelle, A. Beygelzimer, F. d'Alché-Buc, E. Fox, and R. Garnett, editors, *Advances in Neural Information Processing Systems 32*, pages 7059–7069. Curran Associates, Inc.

Jacob Devlin, Ming-Wei Chang, Kenton Lee, and Kristina Toutanova. 2019. Bert: Pre-training of deep bidirectional transformers for language understanding. In *Proc. of NAACL*, pages 4171–4186.

Chris Dyer, Victor Chahuneau, and Noah A. Smith. 2013. A simple, fast, and effective reparameterization of IBM model 2. In *Proc. of NAACL*, pages 644–648.

Thomas Elsken, Jan Hendrik Metzen, and Frank Hutter. 2018. Neural architecture search: A survey. *arXiv preprint arXiv:1808.05377*.

Markus Freitag, Yaser Al-Onaizan, and Baskaran Sankaran. 2017. Ensemble distillation for neural machine translation. *arXiv preprint arXiv:1702.01802*.

Tommaso Furlanello, Zachary Lipton, Michael Tschannen, Laurent Itti, and Anima Anandkumar. 2018. Born again neural networks. In *Proc. of ICML*, pages 1607–1616.

Jiatao Gu, James Bradbury, Caiming Xiong, Victor O K Li, and Richard Socher. 2018. Non-autoregressive neural machine translation. In *Proc. of ICLR*.

Hany Hassan, Anthony Aue, Chang Chen, Vishal Chowdhary, Jonathan Clark, Christian Federmann, Xuedong Huang, Marcin Junczys-Dowmunt, William Lewis, Mu Li, et al. 2018. Achieving human parity on automatic chinese to english news translation. *arXiv preprint arXiv:1803.05567*.

Kenneth Heafield. 2011. Kenlm: Faster and smaller language model queries. In *Proc. of the Sixth Workshop on Statistical Machine Translation*, pages 187–197.

Geoffrey Hinton, Oriol Vinyals, and Jeffrey Dean. 2015. Distilling the knowledge in a neural network. In *NIPS Deep Learning and Representation Learning Workshop*.

Thorsten Joachims. 2006. Training linear svms in linear time. In *Proc. of SIGKDD*, pages 217–226.

Huda Khayrallah and Philipp Koehn. 2018. On the impact of various types of noise on neural machine translation. In *Proc. of the 2nd Workshop on Neural Machine Translation and Generation*, pages 74–83.

Yoon Kim and Alexander M Rush. 2016. Sequence-level knowledge distillation. In *Proc. of EMNLP*, pages 1317–1327.

Diederik P Kingma and Jimmy Ba. 2015. Adam: A method for stochastic optimization. In *Proc. of ICLR*.

Reinhard Kneser and Hermann Ney. 1995. Improved backing-off for m-gram language modeling. In *Proc. of ICASSP*, pages 181–184.

Philipp Koehn, Huda Khayrallah, Kenneth Heafield, and Mikel L Forcada. 2018. Findings of the wmt 2018 shared task on parallel corpus filtering. In *Proc. of the Third Conference on Machine Translation*, pages 726–739.

Taku Kudo. 2006. Mecab: Yet another part-of-speech and morphological analyzer. *http://mecab.sourceforge.jp*.

Lemao Liu, Masao Utiyama, Andrew Finch, and Eiichiro Sumita. 2016. Agreement on target-bidirectional neural machine translation. In *Proc. of NAACL*, pages 411–416.

Yinhan Liu, Myle Ott, Naman Goyal, Jingfei Du, Mandar Joshi, Danqi Chen, Omer Levy, Mike Lewis, Luke Zettlemoyer, and Veselin Stoyanov. 2019. Roberta: A robustly optimized bert pretraining approach. *arXiv preprint arXiv:1907.11692*.

Phoebe Mulcaire, Jungo Kasai, and Noah A Smith. 2019. Polyglot contextual representations improve crosslingual transfer. In *Proc. of NAACL*, pages 3912–3918.

Sharan Narang, Gregory Diamos, Erich Elsen, Paulius Micikevicius, Jonah Alben, David Garcia, Boris Ginsburg, Michael Houston, Oleksii Kuchaiev, Ganesh Venkatesh, et al. 2018. Mixed precision training. In *Proc. of ICLR*.

Nathan Ng, Kyra Yee, Alexei Baevski, Myle Ott, Michael Auli, and Sergey Edunov. 2019. Facebook FAIR's WMT19 news translation task submission. In *Proceedings of the Fourth Conference on Machine Translation*, pages 314–319.

Kishore Papineni, Salim Roukos, Todd Ward, and Wei-Jing Zhu. 2002. Bleu: a method for automatic evaluation of machine translation. In *Proc. of ACL*, pages 311–318.

Marc'Aurelio Ranzato, Sumit Chopra, Michael Auli, and Wojciech Zaremba. 2016. Sequence level training with recurrent neural networks. In *Proc. of ICLR*.

Nils Reimers and Iryna Gurevych. 2019. Sentence-BERT: Sentence embeddings using Siamese BERT-networks. In *Proc. of EMNLP*, pages 3982–3992.

Holger Schwenk. 2018. Filtering and mining parallel data in a joint multilingual space. In *Proc. of ACL*, pages 228–234.

Rico Sennrich, Barry Haddow, and Alexandra Birch. 2016a. Edinburgh neural machine translation systems for WMT 16. In *Proc. of the First Conference on Machine Translation*, pages 371–376.

Rico Sennrich, Barry Haddow, and Alexandra Birch. 2016b. Improving neural machine translation models with monolingual data. In *Proc. of ACL*, pages 86–96.

Rico Sennrich, Barry Haddow, and Alexandra Birch. 2016c. Neural machine translation of rare words with subword units. In *Proc. of ACL*, pages 1715–1725.

Noam Shazeer and Mitchell Stern. 2018. Adafactor: Adaptive learning rates with sublinear memory cost. *arXiv preprint arXiv:1804.04235*.

Libin Shen, Anoop Sarkar, and Franz Josef Och. 2004. Discriminative reranking for machine translation. In *Proc. of NAACL*, pages 177–184.

David R So, Chen Liang, and Quoc V Le. 2019. The evolved transformer. In *Proc. of ICML*.

Miloš Stanojević and Khalil Sima'an. 2014. BEER: BEtter evaluation as ranking. In *Proc. of the Ninth Workshop on Statistical Machine Translation*, pages 414–419.

Ilya Sutskever, Oriol Vinyals, and Quoc V Le. 2014. Sequence to sequence learning with neural networks. In *Proc. of NIPS*, pages 3104–3112.

Xu Tan, Yi Ren, Di He, Tao Qin, Zhou Zhao, and Tie-Yan Liu. 2019. Multilingual neural machine translation with knowledge distillation. In *Proc. of ICLR*.

Antonio Toral, Sheila Castilho, Ke Hu, and Andy Way. 2018. Attaining the unattainable? reassessing claims of human parity in neural machine translation. In *Proc. of the Third Conference on Machine Translation: Research Papers*, pages 113–123.

Ashish Vaswani, Noam Shazeer, Niki Parmar, Jakob Uszkoreit, Llion Jones, Aidan N Gomez, Ł ukasz Kaiser, and Illia Polosukhin. 2017. Attention is all you need. In I. Guyon, U. V. Luxburg, S. Bengio, H. Wallach, R. Fergus, S. Vishwanathan, and R. Garnett, editors, *Advances in Neural Information Processing Systems 30*, pages 5998–6008. Curran Associates, Inc.

Qiang Wang, Bei Li, Tong Xiao, Jingbo Zhu, Changliang Li, Derek F Wong, and Lidia S Chao. 2019. Learning deep transformer models for machine translation. In *Proc. of ACL*, pages 1810–1822.

Wei Wang, Taro Watanabe, Macduff Hughes, Tetsuji Nakagawa, and Ciprian Chelba. 2018. Denoising neural machine translation training with trusted data and online data selection. In *Proc. of WMT*.

Yuguang Wang, Xiang Li, Shanbo Cheng, Liyang Jiang, Jiajun Yang, Wei Chen, Lin Shi, Yanfeng Wang, and Hongtao Yang. 2017. Sogou neural machine translation systems for WMT17. In *Proc. of the Second Conference on Machine Translation*, pages 410–415.

Lijun Wu, Yiren Wang, Yingce Xia, Fei Tian, Fei Gao, Tao Qin, Jianhuang Lai, and Tie-Yan Liu. 2019. Depth growing for neural machine translation. In *Proc. of ACL*, pages 5558–5563.

Zhilin Yang, Zihang Dai, Yiming Yang, Jaime Carbonell, Russ R Salakhutdinov, and Quoc V Le. 2019. Xlnet: Generalized autoregressive pretraining for language understanding. In H. Wallach,

H. Larochelle, A. Beygelzimer, F. d'Alché-Buc, E. Fox, and R. Garnett, editors, *Advances in Neural Information Processing Systems 32*, pages 5753–5763. Curran Associates, Inc.

Biao Zhang, Ivan Titov, and Rico Sennrich. 2019. Improving deep transformer with depth-scaled initialization and merged attention. In *Proc. of EMNLP*, pages 897–908.

Xiangwen Zhang, Jinsong Su, Yue Qin, Yang Liu, Rongrong Ji, and Hongji Wang. 2018. Asynchronous bidirectional decoding for neural machine translation. In *Proc.s of AAAI*.

Long Zhou, Jiajun Zhang, and Chengqing Zong. 2019. Synchronous bidirectional neural machine translation. *Transactions of the Association for Computational Linguistics*, 7:91–105.

ISTIC's Neural Machine Translation System for IWSLT 2020

Jiaze Wei, Wenbin Liu, Zhenfeng Wu, You Pan, Yanqing He[1]

Institute of Scientific and Technical Information of China

No 15, Fuxing Road, Haidian District,Beijing, China, 100038

{weijz2018, liuwb2019, wuzf, pany, heyq}@istic.ac.cn

Abstract

This paper introduces technical details of machine translation system of Institute of Scientific and Technical Information of China (ISTIC) for the 17th International Conference on Spoken Language Translation (IWSLT 2020). ISTIC participated in both translation tasks of the Open Domain Translation track: Japanese-to-Chinese MT task and Chinese-to-Japanese MT task. The paper mainly elaborates on the model framework, data preprocessing methods and decoding strategies adopted in our system. In addition, the system performance on the development set are given under different settings.

1 Introduction

This paper describes the neural machine translation (NMT) system of the Institute of Scientific and Technical Information of China (ISTIC) for the 17th International Conference on Spoken Language Translation (IWSLT 2020) (Ebrahim et al., 2020). ISTIC participated in the Japanese-to-Chinese and Chinese-to-Japanese MT tasks of the Open Domain Translation track.

In this evaluation, we adopted the NMT Google Transformer (Vaswani et al., 2017) architecture as a part of our system. We use the data released by the organizer and adopted general and specific preprocessing methods to the training and development data. Several filtering methods of corpus are explored to improve the quality of the training data. A corpus filtering method based on Elasticsearch is used to select the development data similar to test data. We adopted a model averaging strategy in the decoding phase and different results are combined in post-processing stage to obtain the final translation. The performance of the system is compared under different settings in the two translation directions, and further analyzed.

2 System Architecture

Figure 1 shows the flow chart of ISTIC's NMT system in this evaluation. Our model architecture, data processing and decoding strategy are given below.

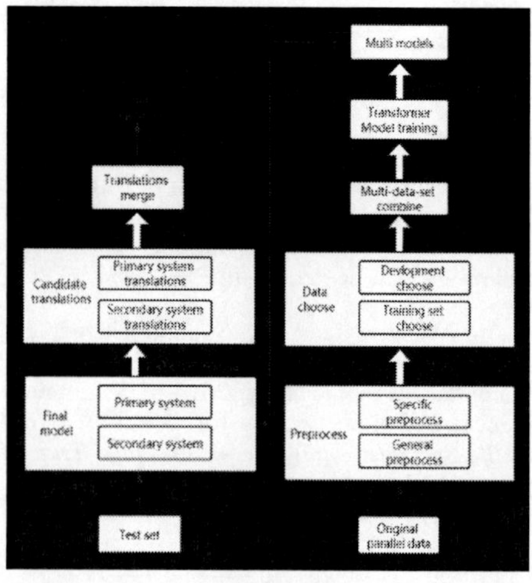

Figure 1. Overall flow chart of evaluation

[1] Responsible author, heyq@istic.ac.cn. This research has been partially supported by ISTIC research foundation projects ZD2019-20, ZD2020-10.

Proceedings of the 17th International Conference on Spoken Language Translation (IWSLT), pages 158–165

July 9-10, 2020. ©2020 Association for Computational Linguistics

https://doi.org/10.18653/v1/P17

Our baseline system used in this evaluation is the Transformer (Vaswani et al., 2017) based on a full attention mechanism, which includes an encoder and a decoder, as shown in Figure 2. Transformer does not use a recurrent neural network (Cho et al., 2014) or a convolutional neural network (Gehring et al., 2017), but is completely based on attention mechanism. It can achieve algorithm parallelism, speed up model training, further alleviate long-distance dependence and improve translation quality.

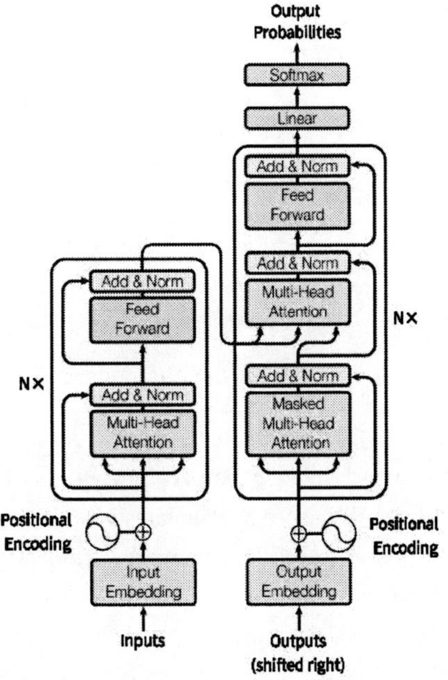

Figure 2. Transformer model (Vaswani et al., 2017)

The encoder and decoder are formed by stacking N layer blocks. Each layer of encoder contains two sub-modules, namely a multi-head self-attention module and a feed-forward neural network module. The multi-head self-attention module divides the dimension of hidden state into multiple parts，and each part is separately calculated by using self-attention function, furthermore, these output vectors are concatenated together. Multi-head mechanism enables the model to pay more attention to the feature information of different positions and different sub-spaces. The multi-head attention

method includes two steps: 1) dot product attention calculation; 2) multi-head attention calculation. The calculation method of dot product attention can be expressed as:

$$\text{Attention}(Q, K, V) = \text{softmax}(\frac{QK^{\mathrm{T}}}{\sqrt{d_k}})V$$

where Q is the query vector, K is the key vector, V is the value vector, and d_k is the dimension of the hidden layer state. On the basis of dot product attention, the calculation method of the multi-head attention mechanism can be expressed as:

$$\text{MultiHead}(Q,K,V) = \text{Concat}(\text{head}_1, \ldots, \text{head}_h)W^O$$

where W^O is the matrix parameter. The attention value of each head is:

$$\text{head} = \text{Attention}(QW_i^Q, KW_i^K, VW_i^V)$$

Each layer of the decoder is composed of three sub-modules. In addition to the two modules similar to the encoder, an decoder-encoder attention module is added between them and can focus attention on source language information in decoding process. In order to avoid the problem that too many layers cause the model to be difficult to converge, both the encoder and the decoder use residual connection and hierarchical regularization techniques. To make the model obtain the position information of the input sentence, additional position encoding vectors are added to the input layer of the encoder and decoder.

After the encoder obtains a hidden state, Transformer model inputs the hidden state into the softmax layer and scores with candidate vocabulary to obtain the final translation result.

3 Data processing

3.1 Corpus preprocessing

In this evaluation we use data of the open domain translation track released by the evaluation organizer of IWSLT 2020, as shown in Table 1. It contains existing

Data1	web_crawled_parallel_filtered.tar.gz
Data2	existing_parallel.tar.gz
Data3	web_crawled_parallel_unfiltered.tar.gz
Data4	web_crawled_unaligned.tar.gz

Table 1. Data provided by reviewer

Japanese-Chinese parallel data (Data 2) and web crawl data (Data 1, Data 3, Data 4)

The quality of Data 2 is much better than other web crawling data. Therefore, a two-stage preprocessing method is designed as a general preprocessing stage and a specific preprocessing stage.

General preprocessing stage: Due to time limitation, we did not have a chance to use Data 4, only the following preprocessing operations were performed on Data 1, Data 2 and Data 3:

- Traditional Chinese to Simplified Chinese
- Word segmentation
- Filtering of adjacent similar sentences
- Sentence length filtering, sentence length ratio filtering
- Language token ratio filtering
- Special character filtering

Among them, the filtering of adjacent similar sentences calculates the Dice similarity (Dice, 1945) of the current sentence with the previous sentence in the corpus of source language side or target language side, and remove the current sentence pair if the Dice similarity exceeds 0.9. Sentence length filtering removes sentence pairs which source sentence length or target sentence length is 0 or exceeds 50, and sentence length ratio filtering excludes the sentence pairs whose ratio of source sentence length and target sentence length exceeds the range of [0.2, 5]. Since a certain percentage of sentence pairs in the corpus use the same language as the source and target sentences. The language token ratio method (Lu et al., 2018) is used to eliminate sentence pairs where the proportion of Japanese or Chinese words is smaller than a certain threshold，here set to 0.1. Both Japanese and

Chinese word segmentation are implemented using the lexical tool Urheen[2].

Specific preprocessing stage: The quality of training corpus has a great influence on the performance of machine translation model. The web crawling data is large in scale but has a great amount of noise, thus, the following specific preprocessing operations are performed on Data 1 and Data 3:

GIZA++[3] tool is used on Data 2 to obtain an alignment dictionary, and each word only retains the top ten translations in their probability ranking. According to the alignment dictionary, the alignment scores for each sentence pair in Data 1 and Data 3 are calculated and the threshold is set as 0.4 as the alignment ratio:

$$alignment_{ratio(X,Y)} = \frac{\sum_x \sum_y p(x,y)}{length(X)} + \frac{\sum_y \sum_x p(y,x)}{length(Y)}$$

where X is a source sentence, Y is a target sentence; $alignment_{ratio(X,Y)}$ is the alignment ratio of sentence pair(X,Y); x is the word in sentence X, y is the word in sentence Y; p(x, y) is the probabilities that word x translates into word y, p(y, x) is the probabilities that word y translates into word x; and $length(X)$ is the length of sentence X; $length(Y)$ is the length of sentence Y.

The filtering results after general preprocessing and specific preprocessing are shown in Table 2.

Data	Original sents number	After filtering
Data1	18966595	8531325
Data2	1963238	1726668
Data3	160M+	44557281

Table 2. Data filtering results

3.2 Elasticsearch similar corpus filtering

In order to further improve the consistency of the development set and test set，and further

---

[2] https://www.nlpr.ia.ac.cn/cip/software.html
[3] https://github.com/moses-smt/giza-pp

optimize the machine translation performance, we choose similar sentence pairs from Data 1 and Data 2 for each sentence in test set to build a new development set and a new test set. We define them as ES development set, ES test set. ES development set is used for early stopping and fit the model to the test set. ES test set is used to compare the performance of the original development set and ES development set.

Specifically, for $q_i, 1 \leq i \leq 875$, in each test set sentence, we create an index base D of Data 1 and Data 2 to retrieve similar sentences from D with the Elasticsearch[4] retrieval tool (version number: v6.1.0). Elasticsearch returns a similarity score between q_i and each sentence $d_j, 1 \leq j \leq |D|$ in D:

$$score(q_i, d_j) = coord(q_i, d_j) * queryNorm(q_i)$$
$$* \sum_{t \ in \ q_i} \left(tf(t \ in \ d_j) * idf(t)^2 * boost(t) * norm(t, d_j) \right)$$

where, $score(q_i, d_j)$ is the similarity score of the test set sentence q_i with the sentence d_j of Data 1 and Data 2; $1 \leq i \leq 875$, $1 \leq j \leq |D|$, $|D|$ represents the total number of sentences of Data 1 and Data 2; $coord(q_i, d_j)$ is the coordination factor between sentence q_i and sentence d_j; $queryNorm(q_i)$ is the normalization factor of query sentence q_i; $tf(t \ in \ d_j)$ is the frequency of word t in sentence d_j; $idf(t)$ is the inverse document-word frequency of word t; $boost(t)$ is the weight used to query the word t; $norm(t, d_j)$ is the length norm of the sentence d_j when querying word t. We select rank first and third sentence pairs in similarity in D to build a new development set -- ES development set, and rank second sentence pairs in similarity to a new test set -- ES test set. After filtering out duplicate sentence pairs and low-quality sentence pairs, the development sets and test sets for Zh-Ja and Ja-Zh eventually obtained as shown in Table 3.

The Data	Original	ES	
		Zh - Ja	Ja - Zh
Development set	5304	1609	1557
Test set	875	904	869

Table 3. selection of similar data

4 Decoding strategy

4.1 Model average

In order to reduce model parameter instability and improve model robustness, the model averaging technique was applied on the parameters stored in the same model at different training moments. We average the parameters of the last N epochs when the model is converged. N is set to 5 for this evaluation.

4.2 Candidate translations merge

Data 1 and Data 2 are included in training set. However, Data 1 contains a great amount of noise and results in some untranslated sentences in the Zh-Ja translations task, some of which take the source sentences directly as the target translations. This rarely happens in the translation model which was trained only with Data 2. Therefore, the former system is taken as primary system and the latter as secondary

---

[4] https://www.elastic.co/guide/cn/elasticsearch/guide/current/practical-scoring-function.html

system. The final translations are obtained by combining two systems' translations. For each source sentence in the test set of the Zh-Ja task, primary system translations and secondary system translations are checked by the following standards: 1) the primary system translation are exactly the same as the source sentence; 2) the primary system translation are judged as non-Japanese words by the language detection tool. If one of the two checks is satisfied and the secondary system translation is also judged to be Japanese, then the secondary system translation will replace the primary system translation as final translation.

5 Experimental results

5.1 Parameters setting

The open source project tensor2tensor[5] is chosen for this evaluation system. The main parameters are set as follows. Each model uses 1-3 GPUs for training, and the batch size is 2048. We use six self-attention layers for both encoder and decoder, and the multi-head self-attention mechanism has 16 heads. The embedding size and hidden size are set to 1024, the dimension of the feed-forward layer is 4096 and ReLU (Krizhevsky et al., 2012) is used as the activation function. The dropout mechanism (Gal and Ghahramani, 2015) was adopted, and dropout probabilities are set to 0.1. BPE (Sennrich et al., 2015) is used in all experiments, where the merge operation is set to 30K. The initial learning rate is 0.2, and the warm-up steps are set to 8000.

To choose the method of word segmentation, we use Data 2 as training data and score on the development set provided by evaluation organizer, as shown in Figures 3 and 4 where the horizontal axis is the different settings of model parameter alpha, and vertical axis as the

character-based bleu4. Zh_ja_b and ja_zh_b means Jieba[6] word segmentation in Chinese (Zh) and Mecab[7] word segmentation in Japanese (Ja). Zh_ja_u and ja_zh_u use the lexical tool Urheen (Zh,Ja) in both the two language.

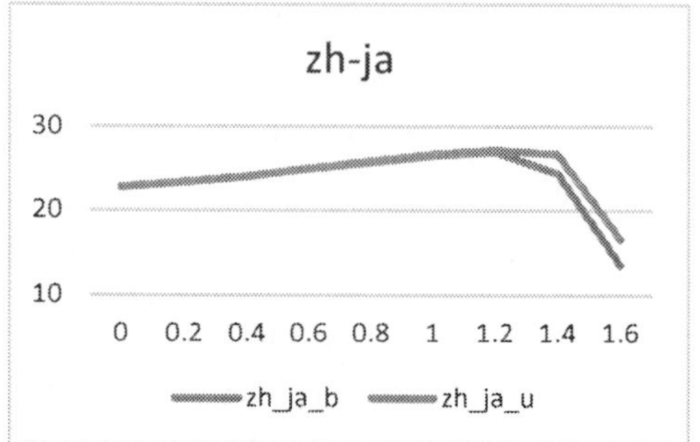

Figure 3. Comparison of word segmentation in Chinese-to-Japanese task

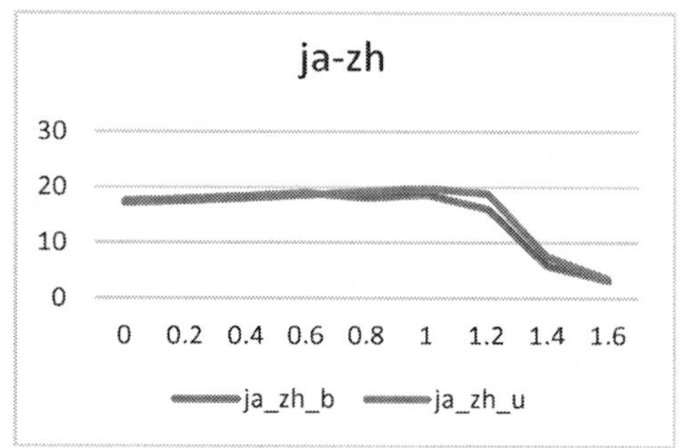

Figure 4. Comparison of word segmentation in Japanese-to-Chinese task

5.2 Experimental results

Training data comparison: In order to choose training data, we use baseline system and score on the original development set, shown in Tables 4-5. It can be seen that increasing the scale of training corpus helps to improve the translation ability. Although Bleu (token) score decreased after Data 1 was added to Chinese-to-Japanese task, we still decided to adopt Data1 + Data2 for training data on the both translation tasks.

---

[5] https://github.com/tensorflow/tensor2tensor

[6] https://github.com/fxsjy/jieba
[7] https://github.com/SamuraiT/mecab-python3

The direction	Data	Number of sentences	Number of words
Zh-JA	Training data	54M	ZH-613M; JA-753M
	Original + Es Development set	6913	ZH-64K; JA-79K
JA-Zh	Training data	54M	Zh-613M; Ja-753M
	Original + Es Development set	6861	ZH-68K; JA-84K

Table 8. The statistics of data

Data	Bleu (token)	Bleu (character)
Data2	16.76	26.14
Data1 + Data2	15.83	27.01
Data1,2,3	17.64	28.9

Table 4. Training data comparison in Chinese-to-Japanese task

Data	Bleu (token)	Bleu (character)
Data2	11.67	19.95
Data1 + Data2	14.79	26
Data1,2,3	13.97	24.75

Table 5. Training data comparison in Japanese -to-Chinese task

Development data	Bleu (token)	Bleu (character)
Original development set	20.79	28.72
Es development set	21.15	29.6
Original development set + Es development set	21.28	28.96

Table 6. Development set comparison in Chinese-to-Japanese task

Development data	Bleu (token)	Bleu (character)
Original development set	13.91	25.79
Es development set	14.34	25.86
Original development set + Es development set	13.94	25.97

Table 7. Development set comparison in Japanese -to-Chinese task

ES development set: In order to verify the effect of ES development set, we use Data2 as training data, and to train baseline system on different combinations of development sets, and score on ES test set, as shown in Tables 6-7. The experimental results show that ES

System	Bleu (token)	Bleu (character)
Data2	18.86	28.82
Data1 + Data2	23.82	35.95
Data1+Data2+ Data3	22.87	35.14
Data2 + avg	19.59	29.81
Data1+Data2+avg	24.51	36.70

Table 9. System comparison inChinese-to-Japan task

System	Bleu (token)	Bleu (character)
Data2	12.00	23.25
Data1 + Data2	20.04	32.09
Data1+Data2+ Data3	16.34	27.72
Data1+Data2+avg	20.98	33.27

Table 10. System comparison in Japanese-to-Chinese task

development set alone or together with the original development set is better than the original development set alone to train machine translation system.

The statistics of training data and development set that are used in this evaluation can be found in Table 8.

System comparison: In order to choose machine translation system, we designed different combinations of training data, and further trying model average strategy on original development set + ES-development set, and score on them, as shown in Tables 9-10. It can be seen that the larger training set Data2+Data1 leads to the result improvement, but no further effect to the growth of training set. Since Data3 was captured from public network, its quality is still limited even though we have

Source-Zh	Data2+avg Translation	Data2+Data1+avg Translation
<sent1>2月13日，日本东京一改前几日的寒凉，迎来一个拨云见日的好天气。(On February 13, Tokyo, Japan ushered in a good weather to see the sun as soon as it changed the cold of the previous days.)	2月13日（2月13日）、日本の東京で少し前の寒さにより、晴れた日を迎える。(February 13 (February 13) greets a sunny day with the recent cold in Tokyo in Japan.)	2月13日，日本东京一改前几日的寒凉，迎来一个拨云见日的好天气。(It's just a copy of Chinese.)
<sent2>阿部知事对中国疫情致以慰问，介绍了长野县为中方抗击疫情提供支持情况，表示当前日本国内正全力阻止疫情扩散，愿同中方继续加强配合，早日战胜疫情。(Abe extended condolences to China on the epidemic and introduced nagano prefecture's support for China's fight against the epidemic. Abe said that Japan is doing its best to prevent the spread of the epidemic and is ready to strengthen cooperation with China to overcome the epidemic at an early date.)	阿部知事は中国の疫病に対する哀悼の意を表明し、長野県を中国側が積極的に支持していることを紹介し、現在の日本国内では流行を阻止しつつあると述べた。(Governor Abe expressed his condolences to the plague of China and introduced the fact that the Chinese side actively supported Nagano Prefecture, and said it was blocking the epidemic in present Japan.)	阿部知事は中国の流行を慰問し、長野県の中で流行に対抗するための支援を紹介し、日本国内では流行の拡散を全面的に阻止していることを明らかにした。(Governor Abe extended condolences to the epidemic in China, introduced support for combating the epidemic in Nagano Prefecture, and made clear that it was completely stopping the spread of the epidemic in Japan.)

Table 11. Translation results merge in Chinses-to-Japanese

adopted a few strategies to filter it. Meanwhile, Data 3 has open domains yet we did not carry out consistency analysis on the data domain. In addition, the model average strategy also brings some improvement to the translation effect.

Therefore, we adopted model average strategy and train on data1+data2 for the two translation tasks. Table 11 shows some translation results of Chinese-to-Japanese translation task. It can be seen that for <sent2>, the translation quality of Data2+Data1+avg model is better than that of Data2+avg model. But due to the noise in Data 1, some translations of the sentences are completely the same as source text. But the situation for Data2+avg model is rare, thus we take the post-processing strategy to merge them. Data1+Data2+avg model is looked as primary system, Data2+avg model as secondary system. Take <sent1> as an example, primary system translation is judged to be in Chinese and is just a copy of Chinese. The secondary translation was checked to be in Japanese, and successfully express the meaning of the source sentence.

Our final system: 1) data filtering; 2) a transformer system trained with Data2+Data1; 3) decoding: model average, candidate translations merge.

6 Conclusions

This paper introduces the main techniques and methods used by the Institute of Scientific and Technical Information of China on the task of two-directions translation of Japanese and Chinese in IWSLT 2020 Open Domain Translation track. We use the architecture of transformer model based on a full attention mechanism. Several filtering methods were explored in data preprocessing, and the model average strategy is adopted in decoding. Similar development set is chosen based on ES and the results are merged by post-processing. Experimental results show that these methods can effectively improve the quality of translation.

Due to limited time, many methods are not able to execute during this evaluation. Our adopted translation model still has a lot room to improve. We expect to learn more advanced techniques and construct a better machine translation system in a short future.

Acknowledgments

We thank the reviewers for their detailed and constructed comments. Yanqing He is the corresponding author. The research work is partially supported by ISTIC research foundation projects ZD2019-20, ZD2020-10.

References

Cho, K., Van Merrienboer, B., Gulcehre, C., et al. (2014). Learning Phrase Representations using RNN Encoder-Decoder for Statistical Machine Translation. arXiv: Computation and Language.

Dice, L. R. (1945). Measures of the Amount of Ecologic Association Between Species. Ecology, 26(3), 297-302.

Ebrahim Ansari , Amittai Axelrod, Nguyen Bach et al. (2020). Findings of the IWSLT 2020 Evaluation Campaign. Proceedings of the 17th International Conference on Spoken Language Translation (IWSLT 2020), Seattle, USA.

Gal. Y., and Ghahramani. Z. (2015). A Theoretically Grounded Application of Dropout in Recurrent Neural Networks. arXiv: Machine Learning.

Gehring. J., Auli. M., Grangier. D.,et al. (2017). Convolutional Sequence to Sequence Learning. arXiv: Computation and Language.

Krizhevsky. A., Sutskever. I., and Hinton. G. E. (2012). ImageNet Classification with Deep Convolutional Neural Networks. Neural Information Processing Systems.

Lu. J., Lv. X., Shi. Y., et al. (2018). Alibaba Submission to the WMT18 Parallel Corpus Filtering Task. Proceedings of the Third Conference on Machine Translation: Shared Task Papers.

Vaswani, A., Shazeer, N., Parmar, N., et al. (2017). Attention is all you need. Neural Information Processing Systems.

Sennrich. R., Haddow. B., and Birch. A. (2015). Neural Machine Translation of Rare Words with Subword Units. arXiv: Computation and Language.

Octanove Labs' Japanese-Chinese Open Domain Translation System

Masato Hagiwara

Octanove Labs LLC

Seattle, WA

masato@octanove.com

Abstract

This paper describes Octanove Labs' submission to the IWSLT 2020 open domain translation challenge. In order to build a high-quality Japanese-Chinese neural machine translation (NMT) system, we use a combination of 1) parallel corpus filtering and 2) back translation. We have shown that, by using heuristic rules and learned classifiers, the size of the parallel data can be reduced by 70% to 90% without much impact on the final MT performance. We have also shown that including the artificially generated parallel data through back-translation further boosts the metric by 17% to 27%, while self-training contributes little. Aside from a small number of parallel sentences annotated for filtering, no external resources have been used to build our system.

1 Introduction

Building a robust, open domain machine translation (MT) system for non-English, Asian languages remains a challenge since many MT research efforts have focused mainly on European languages (such as English and German) and/or on particular domains (such as news). This is especially the case when there is lack of high-quality, human-curated parallel corpora and one needs to bootstrap an MT system from noisy parallel data crawled from the Web.

This is the exact setting of the IWSLT 2020 open domain translation challenge (Ansari et al., 2020), where the organizers provide large, noisy parallel datasets crawled from the Web and the participants build open-domain machine translation systems between Japanese (JA) and Chinese (ZH). The participants are also encouraged to only use the provided datasets to train their models. Therefore, the key to building high-quality MT systems seems to be in how to filter and make the most of the provided, noisy datasets.

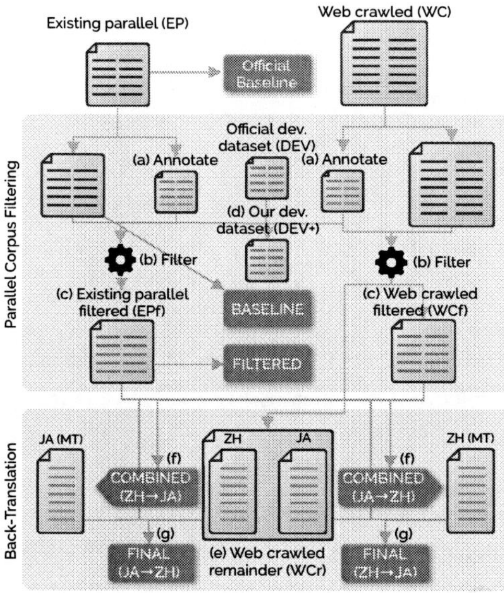

Figure 1: Overview of the data/training pipeline

Based on these insights, we used a combination of 1) parallel corpus filtering (Koehn et al., 2018, 2019) and 2) back-translation (Sennrich et al., 2016; Edunov et al., 2018) techniques as our main strategy. For 1), we showed that we can reduce the size of the parallel corpora by 70% to even 90% without much impact on the final MT performance. As demonstrated in (Chen et al., 2019), we also verified that artificially generated parallel data through back-translation can further help improve the performance by 17% to 27% depending on the direction. We used the vanilla Transformer (Vaswani et al., 2017) as our NMT model.

In the following sections, we describe the data and training pipeline for building our NMT system. We start with the two datasets provided by the shared task organizers—the existing parallel (EP)

Proceedings of the 17th International Conference on Spoken Language Translation (IWSLT), pages 166–171

July 9-10, 2020. ©2020 Association for Computational Linguistics

https://doi.org/10.18653/v1/P17

dataset that includes public, parallel sentences, as well as the Web crawled (WC) dataset created by crawling, aligning, and filtering JA-ZH parallel sentences from the Web. Aside from a small number of parallel sentences annotated for filtering, no external resources besides these two have been used to build our NMT system. The entire data and training pipeline is illustrated in Figure 1.

2 Parallel Corpus Filtering

Our data processing pipeline consists of two main strategies–parallel corpus filtering and back-translation, which are shown as two main blocks in Figure 1. This section describes the first.

2.1 Sentence Pair Quality Analysis

The first observation we make is that many of the sentence pairs, even from the existing parallel (EP) dataset, are not high quality. In order to investigate the quality of the datasets, we first extracted roughly 1,000 sentence pairs from each dataset ((a) in Figure 1) and had two fluent speakers of both languages annotate each pair with a label indicating whether the pair is an accurate translation of each other, and if not, the reason why. We used the following tags to indicate the reasons:

- INVALID: text is garbled or contains few natural language words

- MT: text is suspected to be generated by MT. We made sure at least one native speaker of each language double checks this label.

- MISSING: information is missing from either side

- MISALIGNED: information is missing from both sides

- NOT TRANSLATED: both sides are identical except minor variations (e.g., simplified vs traditional Chinese)

- THIRD LANGUAGE: text is written in a language that is neither Japanese nor Chinese

Table 1 shows the breakdown of the labels and reasons annotated to sentence pairs, both for the existing parallel (EP) and the Web crawled (WC) datasets. Only 38% and 29% of the sentence pairs were deemed suitable for EP and WC, respectively. The most common error was MIS-ALIGNED, meaning the sentences contain similar

Label	Reason	EP	WC
NG	BOTH INVALID	0	2
	BOTH MT	0	92
	BOTH ZH	0	60
	JA INVALID	1	1
	JA MISSING	149	33
	JA MT	3	49
	ZH INVALID	8	0
	ZH MISSING	80	21
	ZH MT	9	24
	MISALIGNED	366	371
	NOT TRANSLATED	2	50
	THIRD LANGUAGE	4	11
OK		380	287
Total		1002	1001

Table 1: Result of sentence pair quality analysis

information but have some degree of mismatch that disqualifies the pair as a quality translation of each other. This can happen when the both segments are crawled from the same source (e.g., a webpage) but mis-aligned due to the way the text is segmented.

2.2 Training Sentence Pair Classifiers

These results led us to decide to use heuristic rules and build learned classifiers to filter out low quality sentence pairs from both datasets, illustrated as (b) in Figure 1. There is a large body of research on parallel corpus filtering (Koehn et al., 2018, 2019). We used a combination of heuristics rules as well as classifiers learned from the annotated data mentioned above.

First, we filter out sentence pairs that violate any one of the following criteria:

- both sides are 512 or fewer Unicode characters.

- $L_{JA}/L_{ZH} < 9$ and $L_{ZH}/L_{JA} < 9$ where L_{JA} and L_{ZH} are the lengths of the Japanese and the Chinese side, respectively.

- the detected languages match the expected ones (Japanese and Simplified Chinese). We used a neural language detector NanigoNet[1] to automatically detect the language of text.

---

[1] `https://github.com/mhagiwara/nanigonet`

	EP	WC
Before	1,963,238	18,966,595
After	627,811	1,973,068

Table 2: Size of the datasets before and after filtering

Second, we trained a binary logistic regression classifier from the annotated sentence pairs mentioned above, and applied it to the rest of the dataset to filter out low-quality sentence pair candidates. The classifier uses only three features. We built one classifier per each dataset (EP and WC) only using the annotated portion of the dataset and applied to the rest.

- log length of the Japanese text (in Unicode characters)

- log length of the Chinese text (in Unicode characters)

- cosine similarity between the sentence embeddings computed using the Universal Sentence Encoder (USE) (Cer et al., 2018)

As a result, we were able to reduce datasets to 31.9% (EP) and 10.4% (WC) of their original size (Table 2). We call the resulting filtered datasets the existing parallel filtered (EPf) and the Web crawled filtered (WCf), respectively, as shown as (c) in Figure 1. We achieved this with little impact on the translation quality. See the experiment section for more details.

Finally, we note that the official development dataset (DEV), which is created from the JEC Basic Sentence Data[2], might not be the best choice for evaluating an open domain machine translation system. Due to the way the the dataset is created (by first mining "typical" Japanese sentence structures from a large text corpus, then by translating these sentences to Chinese), it may not be well suited to evaluate ZH-to-JA MT systems. We augmented this dataset by adding sentence pairs that were tagged "OK" in the annotation process. This increased the size of the development dataset from 5,304 to 5,970 pairs. All the subsequent experiments were validated using this dataset, which we call DEV+ hereafter ((d) in Figure 1).

[2]http://nlp.ist.i.kyoto-u.ac.jp/EN/
index.php?JEC%20Basic%20Sentence%20Data

3 Back-Translation

One of the effective techniques, especially for low-resource settings, is the use of back-translation (Sennrich et al., 2016; Edunov et al., 2018). The idea is to first train a target-to-source MT system to translate a large, monolingual dataset in the target language into the source language, and add the resulting, artificial parallel dataset to existing ones and retrain a source-to-target MT system.

We decided to reuse the "leftover" from the filtering process, that is, the set of sentence pairs that deemed low-quality in the parallel corpus filtering phase described in the previous section. Specifically, after running sentence pairs through the set of heuristic rules described above, we break them into the source side (Japanese) and the target side (Chinese) and treat each as an independent monolingual corpus. We call this corpus the Web crawled remainder (WCr) dataset ((e) in Figure 1).

We then trained ZH-to-JA and JA-to-ZH NMT systems from a combination of EPf and WCf datasets and used the systems to generate artificial source sides for both directions ((f) in Figure 1). When generating artificial source sides, we used top-k sampling (versus beam search) based on the findings of Edunov et al. (2018). The final models, shown as (g) in Figure 1, were trained from the combination of EPf, WCf, as well as WCr and its machine translated version.

4 Experiments

4.1 Experimental Settings

We used the vanilla Transformer (Vaswani et al., 2017) as our neural MT model. All the experiments were conducted using the fairseq library (Ott et al., 2019) with half precision floating point (fp16). The training objective is the label smoothed cross entropy, which was optimized by the Adam optimizer (Kingma and Ba, 2014) with $\beta_1 = 0.9$, $\beta_2 = 0.997$, and $\varepsilon = 1.0 \times 10^{-9}$. We ran each experiment for 40 epochs and chose the best checkpoint based on the development set loss. The beam width was 20.

We tokenized both Japanese and Chinese with the SentencePiece library (Kudo and Richardson, 2018) with a shared vocabulary. The translation quality was evaluated with the character 4-gram BLEU (Papineni et al., 2002).

At the test time, we resolved unknown words (which often arise when there are rare unknown characters on the source side) using word alignment obtained by fast_align (Dyer et al., 2013)[3].

4.2 Hyperparameters

Before we experiment with parallel corpus filtering and back-translation, we ran random parameter search with the baseline dataset (EP) to find the optimal set of hyperparameters. The type and the range of hyperparameters we considered are as follows:

- Size of SentencePiece vocabulary: **10k**, 15k, 20k, 25k, 30k

- Frequency threshold for including tokens (both sides): **3**, 5, 10

- Number of encoder/decoder layers: 4, 5, **6**

- Embedding dimension: 256, 512, 768, **1024**

- Feedforward dimension: 256, 512, 1024, 2048, 4096, **8192**

- Number of attention heads: 1, 2, 4, 8, **16**

- Gradient clipping: 0.0, 10.0, **25.0**, 50.0

- Learning rate: 1e-6, 2.5e-6, 5e-6, 1e-5, 2.5e-5, 5e-5, **1e-4**, 2.5e-4, 5e-4

- Number of warmup steps: 2000, 4000, 8000, **16000**, 32000

- Dropout: **0.1**, 0.2, 0.3, 0.4, 0.5

- Weight decay: 0.0, 1.0e-4, **2.5e-4**, 5.0e-4

- Label smoothing: 0.1, **0.2**, 0.3

- Batch size in tokens: 2048, 4096, **6144**

We ran about 20 rounds of random parameter search and settled with the hyperparameter setting shown by the bold face in the list above. The final models were an ensemble of 6, 8, and 10-layer Transformers with all other hyperparameters being identical.

4.3 Results

Here is the list of all the models trained from different combinations of datasets:

	JA→ZH	ZH→JA
Official baseline	20.03	27.03
BASELINE	24.02	27.68
FILTERED	23.15	27.11
COMBINED	26.19	29.68
BT w/ 500k pairs	28.39	30.68
BT w/ 1M pairs	28.47	31.29
BT w/ 2.6M pairs	29.24	32.66
BT w/ 13M pairs	30.67	33.46
FINAL	31.21	33.81

Table 3: BLEU scores for different models

- Official baseline: the baseline BLEU scores provided by the organizer. Note that the these scores are not comparable to other models below since the development set is different. We also note that the official baseline model is very similar to our model in terms of the neural architectures as well as the number of parameters.

- BASELINE: baseline model trained with EP

- FILTERED: same as BASELINE but trained with EPf

- COMBINED: model trained with EPf and WCf

- BT: model trained with EPf, WCf, and back-translated WCr with varying size

- FINAL: BT trained on the entire WCr with ensemble

Table 3 shows the BLEU scores of these models computed against the DEV+ dataset. By comparing BASELINE and FILTERED, you see that filtering had little impact on the final BLEU scores. By comparing COMBINED and BT with different sizes, you see that adding back-translation helped the performance—the larger the amount of back-translation, the larger the increase was. These results confirm that our strategy—parallel corpus filtering and back-translation—was effective.

5 Discussion

5.1 Negative Results

Finally, here we include the list of things we tried but didn't contribute to the improvement of the MT quality:

---

[3]https://github.com/clab/fast_align

- Filtering by provenance: upon cursory review, we found that the quality of parallel sentences varies a lot by their provenance. We included the source of each pair as an extra set of indicator features, although doing so ended up removing too many pairs and hurt the final performance.

- Self-training (Ueffing, 2006; Zhang and Zong, 2016; He et al., 2019): we also tried using forward-direction MT models to generate the target side from WCr. Including artificially generated parallel data this way didn't improve the final BLEU score.

- Beam search: when generating back-translation, using beam search instead of top-k sampling didn't improve the metrics as much.

- Normalizing to Simplified Chinese: we tried normalizing the Chinese side to the simlified script using the OpenCC toolkit[4] to ensure the consistency. We observed that doing so inadvertently normalized many traditional characters that should be preserved between Japanese and Chinese and didn't improve the final performance.

We note that increasing the size of the Transformer beyond 6 layers did not necessarily lead to improved quality, while ensembling multiple large models did. We also considered leveraging the unaligned version of the Web crawled dataset provided by the organizers, although the dataset contains a large amount of low-quality text that appears to be generated by templates (such as updates on currency exchange rates) and we believe it would add little value as an extra data source.

5.2 Use of External Data

Finally, we ran a follow-up experiment in order to explore the extent to which our model can be improved by adding external data. Specifically, we obtained parallel sentences from HiNative[5], a community-driven language learning QA service, by collecting Japanese-Chinese question-answer pairs in the form of "How do you say X in Japanese/Chinese?" Both the questions and the answers are written by the user community and the resulting dataset is fairly noisy. In addition to the heuristic rules, we trained a logistic regression

	JA→ZH	ZH→JA
BASELINE	24.02	27.68
BASELINE w/ HiNative data	25.32	29.20

Table 4: BLEU scores for models with external data

classifier in a similar way to the ones described in Section 2, except that we trained only one classifier using a combined held-out data from both EP and WC. After filtering, the HiNative dataset has been reduced to around 80k sentence pairs, which we added to EP to explore its impact on the NMT performance.

As Table 4 shows, even though the amount of the added data is a fraction of the original size (80k vs 1.9M), BLEU scores improved by more than 5%. This result suggests that our filtering method is very effective in only retaining high-quality pairs and the newly added data from HiNative provides new perspectives and genres that were not covered by the existing parallel dataset.

As future work, we wish to explore other external datasets for Japanese-Chinese translation, namely, JParaCrawl (Morishita et al., 2019) and WikiMatrix (Schwenk et al., 2019).

6 Conclusion

This paper describes Octanove Labs' submission to the IWSLT 2020 open domain translation challenge. We combined parallel corpus filtering and back-translation to build a Japanese-Chinese open domain NMT system. Through a series of experiments, we verified that our filtering method is effective in preserving the translation accuracy while greatly reducing the size of parallel data required to train the NMT model. We also found that use of artificially generated parallel data from the remainder of the filtered corpus through back-translation improved the final performance of the system.

Acknowledgments

We would like to thank the team at Lang-8, Inc. for providing the HiNative data.

---

[4]https://opencc.byvoid.com/
[5]https://hinative.com/

References

Ebrahim Ansari, Amittai Axelrod, Nguyen Bach, Ondrej Bojar, Roldano Cattoni, Fahim Dalvi, Nadir Durrani, Marcello Federico, Christian Federmann, Jiatao Gu, Fei Huang, Kevin Knight, Xutai Ma, Ajay Nagesh, Matteo Negri, Jan Niehues, Juan Pino, Elizabeth Salesky, Xing Shi, Sebastian Stüker, Marco Turchi, and Changhan Wang. 2020. Findings of the IWSLT 2020 Evaluation Campaign. In *Proceedings of the 17th International Conference on Spoken Language Translation (IWSLT 2020)*, Seattle, USA.

Daniel Cer, Yinfei Yang, Sheng-yi Kong, Nan Hua, Nicole Limtiaco, Rhomni St. John, Noah Constant, Mario Guajardo-Cespedes, Steve Yuan, Chris Tar, Brian Strope, and Ray Kurzweil. 2018. Universal sentence encoder for English. In *Proceedings of the 2018 Conference on Empirical Methods in Natural Language Processing: System Demonstrations*, pages 169–174.

Peng-Jen Chen, Jiajun Shen, Matt Le, Vishrav Chaudhary, Ahmed El-Kishky, Guillaume Wenzek, Myle Ott, and Marc'Aurelio Ranzato. 2019. Facebook AI's WAT19 Myanmar-English translation task submission. In *Proceedings of the 6th Workshop on Asian Translation*, pages 112–122.

Chris Dyer, Victor Chahuneau, and Noah A. Smith. 2013. A simple, fast, and effective reparameterization of IBM model 2. In *Proceedings of the 2013 Conference of the North American Chapter of the Association for Computational Linguistics: Human Language Technologies*, pages 644–648.

Sergey Edunov, Myle Ott, Michael Auli, and David Grangier. 2018. Understanding back-translation at scale. In *Proceedings of the 2018 Conference on Empirical Methods in Natural Language Processing*, pages 489–500.

Junxian He, Jiatao Gu, Jiajun Shen, and Marc'Aurelio Ranzato. 2019. Revisiting self-training for neural sequence generation.

Diederik P. Kingma and Jimmy Ba. 2014. Adam: A method for stochastic optimization.

Philipp Koehn, Francisco Guzmán, Vishrav Chaudhary, and Juan Pino. 2019. Findings of the WMT 2019 shared task on parallel corpus filtering for low-resource conditions. In *Proceedings of the Fourth Conference on Machine Translation (Volume 3: Shared Task Papers, Day 2)*, pages 54–72.

Philipp Koehn, Huda Khayrallah, Kenneth Heafield, and Mikel L. Forcada. 2018. Findings of the WMT 2018 shared task on parallel corpus filtering. In *Proceedings of the Third Conference on Machine Translation: Shared Task Papers*, pages 726–739.

Taku Kudo and John Richardson. 2018. SentencePiece: A simple and language independent subword tokenizer and detokenizer for neural text processing. In *Proceedings of the 2018 Conference on Empirical Methods in Natural Language Processing: System Demonstrations*, pages 66–71.

Makoto Morishita, Jun Suzuki, and Masaaki Nagata. 2019. JParaCrawl: A large scale web-based japanese-english parallel corpus. *arXiv preprint arXiv:1911.10668*.

Myle Ott, Sergey Edunov, Alexei Baevski, Angela Fan, Sam Gross, Nathan Ng, David Grangier, and Michael Auli. 2019. fairseq: A fast, extensible toolkit for sequence modeling. In *Proceedings of the 2019 Conference of the North American Chapter of the Association for Computational Linguistics (Demonstrations)*, pages 48–53.

Kishore Papineni, Salim Roukos, Todd Ward, and Wei-Jing Zhu. 2002. Bleu: a method for automatic evaluation of machine translation. In *Proceedings of the 40th Annual Meeting of the Association for Computational Linguistics*, pages 311–318.

Holger Schwenk, Vishrav Chaudhary, Shuo Sun, Hongyu Gong, and Francisco Guzmán. 2019. WikiMatrix: Mining 135m parallel sentences in 1620 language pairs from Wikipedia. *ArXiv*, abs/1907.05791.

Rico Sennrich, Barry Haddow, and Alexandra Birch. 2016. Improving neural machine translation models with monolingual data. In *Proceedings of the 54th Annual Meeting of the Association for Computational Linguistics (Volume 1: Long Papers)*, pages 86–96.

Nicola Ueffing. 2006. Using monolingual source-language data to improve mt performance. In *IWSLT*.

Ashish Vaswani, Noam Shazeer, Niki Parmar, Jakob Uszkoreit, Llion Jones, Aidan N. Gomez, Lukasz Kaiser, and Illia Polosukhin. 2017. Attention is all you need.

Jiajun Zhang and Chengqing Zong. 2016. Exploiting source-side monolingual data in neural machine translation. In *Proceedings of the 2016 Conference on Empirical Methods in Natural Language Processing*, pages 1535–1545.

NAIST's Machine Translation Systems for IWSLT 2020 Conversational Speech Translation Task

Ryo Fukuda[1], Katsuhito Sudoh[1], Satoshi Nakamura[1,2]

[1]Nara Institute of Science and Technology
[2]AIP Center, RIKEN, Japan
`{fukuda.ryo.fo3, sudoh, s-nakamura}@is.naist.jp`

Abstract

This paper describes NAIST's NMT system submitted to the IWSLT 2020 conversational speech translation task. We focus on the translation disfluent speech transcripts that include ASR errors and non-grammatical utterances. We tried a domain adaptation method by transferring the styles of out-of-domain data (United Nations Parallel Corpus) to be like in-domain data (Fisher transcripts). Our system results showed that the NMT model with domain adaptation outperformed a baseline. In addition, slight improvement by the style transfer was observed.

1 Introduction

Neural Machine Translation (NMT) has significantly improved the quality of Machine Translation (MT) (Bahdanau et al., 2014; Sutskever et al., 2014; Luong et al., 2015). However, domain-specific translation is still difficult in low-resource scenarios, although high performance can be achieved in resource-rich scenarios (Chu and Wang, 2018). Another major problem is the difficulty in translating noisy input sentences including filler, hesitation, etc. Belinkov and Bisk (2017) suggests the difficulty in learning to translate noisy sentences compared to clean ones. The translation of noisy sentences is very important for spoken language translation. In the IWSLT 2020 Conversational Speech Translation Task, we are going to tackle these two problems.

The task includes speech-to-text and text-to-text translation from disfluent Spanish speeches/transcripts to fluent English text. We chose the text-to-text subtask for our challenge task participation. The data for this task consists of about 130K bilingual pairs, would not be enough to learn a highly accurate NMT (Koehn and Knowles, 2017). In such a low-resource scenario, one promising way is domain adaptation using out-of-domain parallel corpora and in-domain monolingual corpora (Wang et al., 2016; Chu et al., 2017).

In domain adaptation, the "similarity" between in-domain and out-of-domain data affects the translation accuracy significantly (Koehn and Knowles, 2017). A domain can be defined by any property of the training data such as topic and style. We expect that the domain similarity comes from these properties.

Let us return to the task description. In the task, the inputs are conversational speech transcripts by Automatic Speech Recognition (ASR). They can include ASR errors as well as disfluent and non-grammatical utterances in spontaneous speech. In contrast, the outputs are fluent sequences. In other words, the purpose of this task is to translate disfluent transcripts into fluent sentences. As mentioned before, domain adaptation is a common practice in a low-resource scenario. However, it is difficult to prepare external parallel data in a disfluent source language and a fluent target language. Although fluent written parallel data are widely available, the effects of training with them are limited because the style of the input sentences differs from the in-domain data. We need a new strategy for training that can effectively use out-of-domain data with low similarity to in-domain data.

In this paper, we propose a novel domain adaptation method through style transfer of out-of-domain data using unsupervised machine translation. We increase the similarity between out-of-domain and in-domain data by transferring out-of-domain fluent input sentences into disfluent styles. This enables effective domain adaptive training and provides a robust NMT system for noisy input sentences.

Proceedings of the 17th International Conference on Spoken Language Translation (IWSLT), pages 172–177
July 9-10, 2020. ©2020 Association for Computational Linguistics
https://doi.org/10.18653/v1/P17

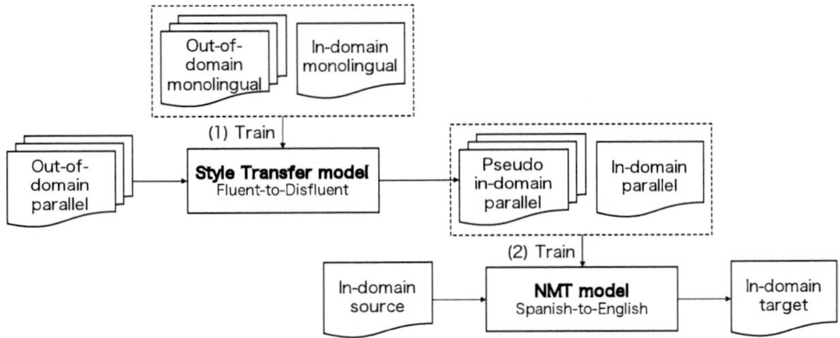

Figure 1: Overview of the proposed method.

2 System Details

Our method consists of two components: (1) Style Transfer model from fluent to disfluent Spanish. (2) Translation model from disfluent Spanish to fluent English, as illustrated in Figure 1. First, we transferred fluent Spanish in out-of-domain data into disfluent Spanish (Section 2.1). Then we trained the NMT model leveraging both out-of-domain parallel data as well as in-domain parallel data (Section 2.2).

2.1 Unsupervised Style Transfer

We employed an unsupervised learning method for the style transfer of Spanish of out-of-domain data. This is because there is no parallel corpus of fluent and disfluent Spanish and it is not possible to adapt supervised learning methods. Artetxe et al. (2018); Lample et al. (2018a,b) proposed Unsupervised Neural Machine Translation (UNMT) that learns the translation using monolingual corpora of two languages. In this system, we built a fluent-to-disfluent style transfer model based on UNMT with out-of-domain fluent data and in-domain disfluent data.

2.2 Domain Adaptation

For the challenge task, we apply fine-tuning, which is one of the conventional domain adaptation methods of MT (Sennrich et al., 2016a). The fine-tuning can result in significant improvements compared to both only in-domain training or only out-of-domain training (Dakwale and Monz, 2017). In this method, an NMT is pre-trained on a resource rich out-of-domain data until convergence, and then its parameters are fine-tuned on a low-resource in-domain data.

In this study, we pre-trained the NMT model on the pseudo in-domain data generated in 2.1, and

Table 1: The number of sentence pairs of the data.

	# sentences
Fisher/Train	138,720
Dev	3,977
Test	3,641
UNCorpus/Train	1,000,000
Dev	4,000
Test	4,000

then fine-tuned on true in-domain data.

3 Results

3.1 Datasets

We used the LDC Fisher Spanish speech (disfluent) with new English translations (fluent) (Post et al., 2013; Salesky et al., 2018) as parallel in-domain data and the United Nations Parallel Corpus (UNCorpus) (Ziemski et al., 2016) as parallel out-of-domain data.

Fisher has the following multi-way parallel data distributed by the task organizer:

1. Spanish disfluent speech

2. Spanish disfluent transcripts (gold)

3. Spanish disfluent transcripts (ASR output)

4. English disfluent translations

5. English fluent translations

When training, we used (3) as input and (4) or (5) as output. UNCorpus consists of manually translated UN documents of the 25 years (1990 to 2014) for the six official UN languages, Arabic, Chinese, English, French, Russian, and Spanish. For our submission, one million Spanish-English bilingual sentence pairs were chosen randomly and used as out-of-domain data. Data statistics are shown in Table 1.

3.2 Spanish Style Transfer

3.2.1 Experimental Settings

Data   We trained the style transfer from fluent to disfluent sentences using both Fisher and UNCorpus Spanish data. We preprocessed the data with Byte Pair Encoding (Sennrich et al., 2016b) to split sentences into subwords. The vocabulary size was set to 32,000 and sentences longer than 175 subwords were excluded from the training. We apply lowercasing and punctuation removal to UNCorpus same as Fisher corpus.

Model   We used the implementation of UNMT[1] by Lample et al. (2018b). UNMT model was based on Transformer (Vaswani et al., 2017). Our models follow the suggested parameters from implementation of UNMT. We used three-layer shared encoder and shared decoder. We set the word embedding dimensions, hidden state dimensions, feed-forward dimensions to 512, 512, and 2048, respectively. We employed eight attention heads for both the encoder and the decoder. We chose Adam (Kingma and Ba, 2014) with a learning rate of 0.0001, $\beta_1 = 0.9$, $\beta_2 = 0.999$ as the optimizer. Each mini-batch contained 16 sentences.

In order to gain robustness to the content of the sentence, we first pre-trained the model using only UNCorpus/Train. During pre-training, early stopping was applied on the BLEU score between source sentences and back-translated sentences of the UNCorpus/Dev with a patience of 10 iterations, and the model with the highest score was stored. After that, additional training of 1 iteration using the Fisher/Train was performed.

Evaluation   Axelrod et al. (2011) used a language model of in-domain data for out-of-domain data selection in domain adaptation. Following this study, we estimated the similarity between domains by measuring the perplexity (PPL) of the training set W of the out-of-domain data using a 3-gram language model M made from the in-domain data (Equation 1).

$$PPL = 10^{H(W|M)} \tag{1}$$

$H(W|M)$ is the entropy, defined as the average of the negative log-likelihood per token, as shown in the following equation:

$$H(W|M) = \frac{1}{|W|} \sum_{s \in W} -\log_{10} P(s|M) \tag{2}$$

Table 2: Perplexity and the number of unknown words (# UNK) for Fisher/train in the 3-gram language model.

Training data	perplexity	# UNK
Fisher	72.46	0
UNCorpus	589.81	5,173,539
Fisher-like UNCorpus	474.47	4,217,819

$P(s|M)$ is the probability of sentence s in the language model M. We used the SRI Language Modeling Toolkit to build the language model[2].

3.2.2 Results

Table 2 shows the perplexity of the language model for the Fisher/train. By transferring the fluent UNCorpus into the disfluent Fisher tone (Fisher-like UNCorpus) reduced the perplexity and number of unknown words.

3.3 NMT with Domain Adaptation

We trained the NMT models which translate from disfluent Spanish to fluent English.

3.3.1 Experimental Settings

Data   For training data, we used Fisher/train as in-domain data and UNCorpus/Train and Fisher-like UNCorpus/Train as out-domain data. Fisher-like UNCorpus has the same number of sizes as UNCorpus. During training, we used Fisher/Dev as a validation set. Fisher/Test was used for evaluation. We preprocessed the data in the same way as in the previous experiment. However, for practical use, lowercasing and punctuation removal were applied only to the source language.

Model   We used OpenNMT-py[3]. The NMT model was based on Transformer. The hyper-parameters of the model almost follow the *transformer_base* settings (Vaswani et al., 2017). Note that in the Fisher-only experiment without domain adaptation, the batch size was halved to 2048 tokens. The model was trained for 20,000 iterations using out-of-domain data, and then fine-tuned for 1,000 iterations using in-domain data. The model parameters saved every 100 iterations.

Evaluation   To evaluate the performance, we calculated the BLEU scores (Papineni et al., 2002) with sacreBLEU[4].

---

[1]https://github.com/facebookresearch/UnsupervisedMT

[2]http://www.speech.sri.com/projects/srilm/
[3]https://github.com/OpenNMT/OpenNMT-py
[4]https://github.com/mjpost/sacreBLEU

Table 3: BLEU scores of trained NMT models for Disfluent Spanish to Fluent English.

System	Fisher/Test
Fisher	14.8
UNCorpus	7.8
Fisher-like UNCorpus	6.7
UNCorpus + Fisher	18.3
Fisher-like UNCorpus + Fisher	**18.5**

Table 4: BLEU scores for Disfluent Spanish to Fluent English. NMT models used Fisher's disfluent references for training.

System	Fisher/Test
Fisher	11.6
UNCorpus + Fisher	15.2
Fisher-like UNCorpus + Fisher	**15.6**

3.3.2 Results

Tables 3 and 4 show the BLEU scores of the systems evaluated with single fluent references. In Table 3, "Fisher", "UNCorpus" and "Fisher-like UNCorpus" are models trained on a single training data. "UNCorpus + Fisher" and "Fisher-like UNCorpus + Fisher" are models that were pre-trained on UNCorpus and Fisher-like UNCorpus and then fine-tuned on Fisher/Train, respectively. The models in Table 4 did not use Fisher's fluent references when training but instead used disfluent references.

Both with and without Fisher's fluent references, domain adaptation training outperformed the baseline. Furthermore, when the pseudo-disfluent Spanish generated by the style transfer was used for training, the score was better than the use of the original UNCorpus without the style transfer. We submitted six systems in total: "Fisher", "UNCorpus + Fisher" and "Fisher-like UNCorpus + Fisher" in Table 3, and all of Table 4.

4 Discussion

Effect of Style Transfer In domain adaptation training, the accuracy was slightly improved by transferring the style of out-of-domain data to be like in-domain data. This shows that there is some significance in increasing the similarity between domains through style transfer.

However, when we did not perform domain adaptation and only trained with out-of-domain data, the accuracy for in-domain data was reduced by style transfer. The following is an example of style transferred sentence:

nueva york 1 a 12 de junio de 2015 (original)
nueva york oh a mi eh de de de de (generated)

As shown above, some generated sentences lost the meaning of the sentence due to missing phrases. As a result, the quality of the parallel data decreased and the final translation performance was also degraded. One of the causes of this problem is style transfer constraints are too strong. Thus, it may be mitigated by a model that could control the trade-off between style transfer and content preservation (Niu et al., 2017; Agrawal and Carpuat, 2019; Lample et al., 2019).

Further improvement can be expected by preventing changes in the meaning of sentences and converting only the style.

Fluent vs Disfluent references The model trained using Fisher's original disfluent data had a BLEU score of about three points lower than the model trained using the fluent data. In other words, in this task, we found that removing the disfluency of reference sentences improves the BLEU by about three points for all the learning strategies we tried. In domain adaptation, we expected this problem to be mitigated by training on large out-of-domain data with fluent reference sentences, but the desired results were not obtained.

5 Conclusion

In this paper, we presented NAIST's submission to the IWSLT2020 Conversational Speech Translation task. We experimentally show that domain adaptation can improve the translation accuracy of disfluent sentences. Moreover, the translation accuracy was improved by increasing the similarity between domains through style transfer, but the effect was limited due to the parallel data quality degradation.

Furthermore, The loss of accuracy caused by not using clean reference sentences of in-domain data could not be resolved by domain adaptation either.

In future work, we will pursue a style transfer system that does not reduce the quality of the parallel data and use it to improve the translation accuracy of NMT. High-quality style transfer may allow us to acquire robustness to the disfluency of input sentences and to learn fluent outputs by removing the disfluency of output sentences.

References

Sweta Agrawal and Marine Carpuat. 2019. Controlling text complexity in neural machine translation. In *Proceedings of the 2019 Conference on Empirical Methods in Natural Language Processing and the 9th International Joint Conference on Natural Language Processing (EMNLP-IJCNLP)*, pages 1549–1564, Hong Kong, China. Association for Computational Linguistics.

Mikel Artetxe, Gorka Labaka, Eneko Agirre, and Kyunghyun Cho. 2018. Unsupervised neural machine translation. In *International Conference on Learning Representations*.

Amittai Axelrod, Xiaodong He, and Jianfeng Gao. 2011. Domain adaptation via pseudo in-domain data selection. In *Proceedings of the 2011 Conference on Empirical Methods in Natural Language Processing*, pages 355–362, Edinburgh, Scotland, UK. Association for Computational Linguistics.

Dzmitry Bahdanau, Kyunghyun Cho, and Yoshua Bengio. 2014. Neural machine translation by jointly learning to align and translate.

Yonatan Belinkov and Yonatan Bisk. 2017. Synthetic and natural noise both break neural machine translation.

Chenhui Chu, Raj Dabre, and Sadao Kurohashi. 2017. An empirical comparison of domain adaptation methods for neural machine translation. In *Proceedings of the 55th Annual Meeting of the Association for Computational Linguistics (Volume 2: Short Papers)*, pages 385–391, Vancouver, Canada. Association for Computational Linguistics.

Chenhui Chu and Rui Wang. 2018. A survey of domain adaptation for neural machine translation. In *Proceedings of the 27th International Conference on Computational Linguistics*, pages 1304–1319, Santa Fe, New Mexico, USA. Association for Computational Linguistics.

Praveen Dakwale and Christof Monz. 2017. Finetuning for neural machine translation with limited degradation across in-and out-of-domain data. In *the 16th Machine Translation Summit*, pages 156–169.

Diederik P. Kingma and Jimmy Ba. 2014. Adam: A method for stochastic optimization. Cite arxiv:1412.6980Comment: Published as a conference paper at the 3rd International Conference for Learning Representations, San Diego, 2015.

Philipp Koehn and Rebecca Knowles. 2017. Six challenges for neural machine translation. In *Proceedings of the First Workshop on Neural Machine Translation*, pages 28–39, Vancouver. Association for Computational Linguistics.

Guillaume Lample, Alexis Conneau, Ludovic Denoyer, and Marc'Aurelio Ranzato. 2018a. Unsupervised machine translation using monolingual corpora only. In *International Conference on Learning Representations*.

Guillaume Lample, Myle Ott, Alexis Conneau, Ludovic Denoyer, and Marc'Aurelio Ranzato. 2018b. Phrase-based & neural unsupervised machine translation. In *Proceedings of the 2018 Conference on Empirical Methods in Natural Language Processing*, pages 5039–5049, Brussels, Belgium. Association for Computational Linguistics.

Guillaume Lample, Sandeep Subramanian, Eric Smith, Ludovic Denoyer, Marc'Aurelio Ranzato, and Y-Lan Boureau. 2019. Multiple-attribute text rewriting. In *International Conference on Learning Representations*.

Thang Luong, Hieu Pham, and Christopher D. Manning. 2015. Effective approaches to attention-based neural machine translation. In *Proceedings of the 2015 Conference on Empirical Methods in Natural Language Processing*, pages 1412–1421, Lisbon, Portugal. Association for Computational Linguistics.

Xing Niu, Marianna Martindale, and Marine Carpuat. 2017. A study of style in machine translation: Controlling the formality of machine translation output. In *Proceedings of the 2017 Conference on Empirical Methods in Natural Language Processing*, pages 2814–2819, Copenhagen, Denmark. Association for Computational Linguistics.

Kishore Papineni, Salim Roukos, Todd Ward, and Wei-Jing Zhu. 2002. Bleu: a method for automatic evaluation of machine translation. In *Proceedings of the 40th Annual Meeting of the Association for Computational Linguistics*, pages 311–318, Philadelphia, Pennsylvania, USA. Association for Computational Linguistics.

Matt Post, Gaurav Kumar, Adam Lopez, Damianos Karakos, Chris Callison-Burch, and Sanjeev Khudanpur. 2013. Improved speech-to-text translation with the fisher and callhome spanish–english speech translation corpus. In *International Workshop on Spoken Language Translation*.

Elizabeth Salesky, Susanne Burger, Jan Niehues, and Alex Waibel. 2018. Towards fluent translations from disfluent speech. *2018 IEEE Spoken Language Technology Workshop (SLT)*.

Rico Sennrich, Barry Haddow, and Alexandra Birch. 2016a. Improving neural machine translation models with monolingual data. In *Proceedings of the 54th Annual Meeting of the Association for Computational Linguistics (Volume 1: Long Papers)*, pages 86–96, Berlin, Germany. Association for Computational Linguistics.

Rico Sennrich, Barry Haddow, and Alexandra Birch. 2016b. Neural machine translation of rare words with subword units. In *Proceedings of the 54th Annual Meeting of the Association for Computational Linguistics (Volume 1: Long Papers)*, pages 1715–1725, Berlin, Germany. Association for Computational Linguistics.

Ilya Sutskever, Oriol Vinyals, and Quoc V Le. 2014. Sequence to sequence learning with neural networks. In Z. Ghahramani, M. Welling, C. Cortes, N. D. Lawrence, and K. Q. Weinberger, editors, *Advances in Neural Information Processing Systems 27*, pages 3104–3112. Curran Associates, Inc.

Ashish Vaswani, Noam Shazeer, Niki Parmar, Jakob Uszkoreit, Llion Jones, Aidan N Gomez, Lukasz Kaiser, and Illia Polosukhin. 2017. Attention is all you need. In I. Guyon, U. V. Luxburg, S. Bengio, H. Wallach, R. Fergus, S. Vishwanathan, and R. Garnett, editors, *Advances in Neural Information Processing Systems 30*, pages 5998–6008. Curran Associates, Inc.

Rui Wang, Hai Zhao, Bao-Liang Lu, Masao Utiyama, and Eiichiro Sumita. 2016. Connecting phrase based statistical machine translation adaptation. In *Proceedings of COLING 2016, the 26th International Conference on Computational Linguistics: Technical Papers*, pages 3135–3145, Osaka, Japan. The COLING 2016 Organizing Committee.

Michał Ziemski, Marcin Junczys-Dowmunt, and Bruno Pouliquen. 2016. The united nations parallel corpus v1.0. In *Proceedings of the Tenth International Conference on*

Language Resources and Evaluation (LREC 2016), pages
3530–3534, Portorož, Slovenia. European Language Resources Association (ELRA).

Generating Fluent Translations from Disfluent Text
Without Access to Fluent References: IIT Bombay@IWSLT2020

Nikhil Saini, Jyotsana Khatri, Preethi Jyothi, Pushpak Bhattacharyya
Department of Computer Science and Engineering
Indian Institute of Technology Bombay
Mumbai, India
{nikhilra, jyotsanak, pjyothi, pb}@cse.iitb.ac.in

Abstract

Machine translation systems perform reasonably well when the input is well-formed speech or text. Conversational speech is spontaneous and inherently consists of many disfluencies. Producing fluent translations of disfluent source text would typically require parallel disfluent to fluent training data. However, fluent translations of spontaneous speech are an additional resource that is tedious to obtain. This work describes the submission of IIT Bombay to the Conversational Speech Translation challenge at IWSLT 2020. We specifically tackle the problem of disfluency removal in disfluent-to-fluent text-to-text translation assuming no access to fluent references during training. Common patterns of disfluency are extracted from disfluent references and a noise induction model is used to simulate them starting from a clean monolingual corpus. This synthetically constructed dataset is then considered as a proxy for labeled data during training. We also make use of additional fluent text in the target language to help generate fluent translations. This work uses no fluent references during training and beats a baseline model by a margin of 4.21 and 3.11 BLEU points where the baseline uses disfluent and fluent references, respectively.

Index Terms- disfluency removal, machine translation, noise induction, leveraging monolingual data, denoising for disfluency removal.

1 Introduction and Related Work

Spoken language translation often suffers due to the presence of disfluencies. In conversational speech, speakers often use disfluencies such as filler words, repetitions of fillers, repetitions of fluent phrases, false starts, and corrections which do not occur in the text. Standard machine translation and spoken translation systems perform competitively when the input is well-formed text or rehearsed speech as in TED talks or broadcast news (Cho et al., 2014; Wang et al., 2010; Honal and Schultz, 2005; Zayats et al., 2016). With the increasing popularity of end-to-end speech translation systems (Weiss et al., 2017; Bansal et al., 2018), one may not want disfluency removal to be treated as an intermediate step between ASR and MT. It might be more desirable for disfluency removal to be handled within the model itself, or as a separate post-processing step.

To produce fluent translations from disfluent text, one would typically require access to disfluent speech (or text) and its corresponding fluent translations during training. While some corpora with labeled disfluencies exist (Cho et al., 2014; Burger et al., 2002), only subsets have been translated and/or released. (Salesky et al., 2018) introduced a set of fluent references for the Fisher Spanish-English conversational speech corpus (David Graff and Cieri.). This has enabled a new task of end-to-end training and evaluation on fluent references. (Salesky et al., 2019) reports results using a speech-to-text model trained on this corpus using both fluent and disfluent translations. However, fluent translations of disfluent speech or text are a scarce resource. It would be highly desirable to build a system for disfluency removal that does not rely on fluent references.

In this work, we propose a framework for disfluency removal that utilizes a simple noise induction technique for data augmentation using fluent monolingual text in the target language. During denoising, such disfluent text is trained jointly with parallel disfluent-to-disfluent textual translation data, thus simultaneously optimizing the objectives of disfluency removal and translation. This work describes the submission of IIT Bombay to the Conversational Speech Translation challenge at IWSLT 2020 (Ansari et al., 2020). We release code for our

Proceedings of the 17th International Conference on Spoken Language Translation (IWSLT), pages 178–186
July 9-10, 2020. ©2020 Association for Computational Linguistics
https://doi.org/10.18653/v1/P17

proposed approach at the following URL.[1]

Section 2 describes the details of the data used and the proposed noise induction technique to leverage monolingual data. Section 3 describes our proposed architecture. We then present experimental details in Section 4, followed by our main results in Section 4.2. Finally, we analyze our model outputs in Section 5 and present our conclusions in Section 6.

2 Data

2.1 Fisher Corpus

For our experiments, we use the Fisher Spanish dataset (David Graff and Cieri.), comprising telephone conversations between mostly native Spanish speakers. The dataset contains speech utterances (disfluent Spanish), their corresponding ASR outputs (disfluent Spanish), and two sets of English translations (both fluent and disfluent) (Salesky et al., 2018; Post et al., 2013). The Fisher dataset has disfluent Spanish ASR output *(text)* which we use as input to our model. Additionally, two sets of English translations *(disfluent & fluent)* are also available in *(text)* form. For training, we only make use of disfluent English sentences. i.e. we train a *text-to-text* model. We explicitly note here that no fluent English reference text was used during training. The corpus consists of 819 transcribed conversations on predetermined topics between strangers, yielding $\approx$ 160 hours of speech and 150k utterances. We used one reference during training and evaluation with the validation (dev) and test data sets.[2]

2.1.1 Disfluencies

Disfluencies can be filler words and hesitations, discourse markers *(you know, well, umm)*, phrase repetitions, filler word repetitions, corrections, and false starts, among others. There can be different and often overlapping disfluencies in a single sentence. Fluent words like *so, oh, yes, no, etc.* could either be categorized as fluent or disfluent depending on the context in which they appear. We selected the most commonly occurring filler words in English, namely *hmm, hm, em, eh, uh, um, umm, ah, aha, mm, oh, wow, yes, ok* from the Fisher English corpus. These filler words either occur alone as a single unit or with self-repetitions up to a maximal length of 5 or 6. We extracted the frequencies

of each one of them and their repetitions. Table 1 shows the counts for the *aha* token along with its successive repetitions. We repeat this for all filler words and store them in a comma-separated value file.

Filler phrase	Frequency
ah	9572
ah ah	233
ah ah ah	29
ah ah ah ah	5
ah ah ah ah ah	1
ah ah ah ah ah ah	0

Table 1: Filler phrase frequencies in the Fisher English training corpus.

2.2 Parallel Corpus for Translation

We extract monolingual fluent textual data from the news-commentary parallel corpus in Spanish-English from the shared task on machine translation in 2013.[3] The corpus consists of 174,441 parallel sentences. We divide the dataset into two halves. We consider the first half of 87220 sentences to be our fluent monolingual corpus. The other half wasn't used to account for resource constraints. Future work can incorporate the whole corpus for training. This corpus is modified and turned into a parallel disfluent to fluent corpus in the same language i.e. EN-disfluent to EN-fluent. This process is described in more detail in the next section.

2.3 Data Augmentation via Noise Induction

Most disfluent sentences could be loosely thought of as a composition of a fluent part and an additive noise characterizing the underlying disfluency type. We aimed to generate a parallel EN-disfluent to EN-fluent dataset, starting with fluent English text and adding disfluencies that we extract from real disfluent text. We stress here that we do not make use of any parallel disfluent-fluent text to extract patterns of disfluencies; the latter was generated by solely examining disfluent text. Three levels of disfluency induction have been implemented where disfluencies are incrementally added. We have tested with 10%, 30%, 50% disfluency induction. Section 2.3.1, 2.3.2, 2.3.3, 2.3.4 will describe the techniques used to introduce disfluencies within a fluent corpus to create a parallel corpus.

---

[1] https://github.com/niksarrow/cst
[2] We do not make use of dev2 during training.

[3] https://www.statmt.org/wmt13/translation-task.html

2.3.1 Pronoun Phrase Repetition

The English language has seven pronouns, namely, *"i, we, you, he, she, it, they"*. In the conversational speech, many times an utterance that starts with a pronoun repeats itself. Here is an example:

i am i am fond of paintings ...
it is cold it is cold and windy outside ...

Our algorithm iterates through all 87220 sentences in the English news-commentary corpus and treats every sentence which starts with a pronoun as a candidate. With hyperparameter value $\alpha = 0.1, 0.3, 0.5$, we either select or reject the candidate for disfluency induction. Here, α is the probability of selecting the candidate and $1 - \alpha$ is the rejection probability. If a candidate is selected, we select the length (l) of the phrase starting from the first word (which is the pronoun itself) which will be repeated. The length is uniformly sampled from four length values i.e. $1, 2, 3, 4$. The phrase up to length (l) is repeated in the sentence just after it ends. The following examples show how disfluencies are introduced for two different values of l:

Original fluent sentence: *i was saying that we should go for a movie*
Disfluent sentence ($l = 1$): *i i was saying that we should go for a movie*
Disfluent sentence ($l = 2$): *i was i was saying that we should go for a movie*

2.3.2 Fluent Phrase Repetition

Many disfluencies are just repetitions of meaningful phrases where the speaker intentionally or unintentionally repeats a phrase. We iterate through all the sentences and every sentence with length greater than 5 becomes a candidate with hyperparameter $\alpha = 0.1, 0.3, 0.5$ (as we did with pronoun phrase repetition). We randomly selected a length(l) in the range $[1, 3]$ and carefully selected an index i in the fluent sentence starting from which a phrase of length l is repeated and a disfluent sentence is formed. Here is an example:

Original fluent sentence: *easier to trade and speculate in gold*
Disfluent sentence ($l = 1, i = 5$): *easier to trade and speculate in in gold*
Disfluent sentence ($l = 2, i = 3$): *easier to trade and speculate and speculate in gold*

2.3.3 Insertion of filler words/phrases

The filler word/phrase frequency count which is described in Section 2.1.1 and table 1 is used as a guide to introduce them within clean text. We iterate through all sentences in the English corpus and uniformly select a (phrase, frequency) pair such that the frequency is greater than 0. If the sentence becomes a candidate according to the sampling probability $\alpha = 0.1, 0.3, 0.5$ (as we did with pronoun phrase repetition), an index i is uniformly selected from the range $[0, l]$, and the phrase is inserted at index i along with a decrement of one in the frequency of the phrase. As before, l is the length of the candidate. Example:

Before: (filler, frequency) $= (ah\ ah, 233)$
Original sentence: *the new year is looking grim*
Disfluent sentence ($i = 0$): *ah ah the new year is looking grim*
After: (filler, frequency) $= (ah\ ah, 232)$

2.3.4 False Start

In disfluent English, an utterance can start with an affirmation (i.e. beginning with a *yes* or *yeah*) and suddenly turn into negation or denial. For example: *yes, no we can't increase the price*. Here, the speaker first uttered *yes* and then shifted to negation with *no*. Similarly, a negative utterance can suddenly shift to an affirmative one.

We iterate through all the sentences in the Fisher English corpus which begins with an affirmation *yes, yeah* or a negation *no, nah* and prepend *yes or no* of length($l = 1 or 2$) to make it a false starting sentence (if the sentence is chosen with a sampling probability of $\alpha = 0.1, 0.3, 0.5$). An example:

Original sentence: *yes the price will go up*
Disfluent sentence ($l = 2$): *no no yes the price will go up*

2.3.5 Other Possible Noise Induction Techniques

Synonym insertion can be done by examining the synset of the language in question (say English), picking a word from a candidate sentence, and attaching its synonym next to it. A denoising step is expected to retain only one of the meanings which is fluent as per the language model. We also introduce singleton utterances which only contain a single filler word and its corresponding fluent version is labeled as *None*. We leave the exploration of more techniques that are relevant to introducing disfluencies within fluent text as future work.

2.4 Data Statistics

Table 2 shows utterance counts from the parallel disfluent Spanish to disfluent English corpus. Apart from this dataset, we also make use of three parallel disfluent-to-fluent English texts which were synthetically created using the techniques described in Section 2.3, corresponding to α values of 0.1, 0.3 and 0.5, respectively. Each of these three parallel datasets contains 87220 sentences each.

Fisher Data		
Train	138720 (DFLT)	138720 (DFLT)
Validation	3977 (DFLT)	3977 (FLT)
Test	3641 (DFLT)	3641 (FLT)

Table 2: DFLT: Disfluent and FLT: Fluent. Disfluent Spanish source and disfluent English target utterances in training. For validation and test set evaluations, we use fluent translations. Numbers indicate the count of utterances in the train, validation and test sets, respectively.

3 Model

This section describes the proposed architecture for disfluency removal and translation. Since our objective is two-fold, which is disfluency removal and translation, Section 3.2.1 first presents our denoising module which is aimed at achieving the task of disfluency removal and Section 3.2.2 describes how translation is achieved by our model.

3.1 System Architecture

As shown in Figure 1, the proposed system follows a fairly standard encoder-decoder architecture. More concretely, we use a four-layer transformer encoder and another four-layer transformer decoder (Vaswani et al., 2017). There are 8 attention heads in both the encoder and decoder. We pretrain joint token embeddings of 512 dimensionalities on concatenated Fisher Spanish (disfluent) and English (disfluent) and News-commentary English data using fastext (Bojanowski et al., 2016). We use byte-pair encoding (Sennrich et al., 2015) with 50K BPE units to effectively handle out-of-vocabulary words at test time. We share language embeddings in the encoder. We set dropout (Gal and Ghahramani, 2016) and label-smoothing (Szegedy et al., 2016) to 0.3 and 0.1, respectively. In addition to the disfluency induction, we use word-shuffle,

word-dropout, and word-blank with probabilities 3, 0.1, 0.2 (Lample et al., 2017) respectively when training the denoising encoder.

3.1.1 Shared Encoder

Our system makes use of two encoders with three out of four layers shared by the two input languages. This is inspired from (Artetxe et al., 2017; Lample et al., 2017). The first three layers are shared across both tasks i.e. denoising from disfluent English to fluent English and translating from Spanish to English. The fourth layer is language-dependent to allow the encoder to learn language-specific information. The shared layers of the encoder encourage the output representations of Spanish and English to use a common subspace shared across both languages, which is further transformed into fluent English using a common decoder. In this manner, our model jointly achieves disfluency removal along with translation.

3.1.2 Fixed Language Embeddings in the Encoder

While many machine translation systems randomly initialize their embeddings and update them during training, we use pretrained sub-word level embeddings and keep them fixed during training (Artetxe et al., 2017). We share the vocabulary for Spanish and English as their alphabet size is 27 and 26 respectively. The additional letter in Spanish is a $\tilde{n}$ to indicate the palatal nasal; the remaining letters are the same as in English.

3.2 Training

The encoder & decoder are trained using Adam (Kingma and Ba, 2015) with a learning rate of 0.001 and a mini-batch size of 32. The training alternates evenly between denoising and translation procedures.

3.2.1 Denoising

C(x) is a randomly sampled noisy version of sentence x similar to the noise model by (Lample et al., 2017). The denoising done here is a mixture of standard denoising as done in (Lample et al., 2017) and a supervised training step using the parallel disfluent-fluent English text that we created using the techniques described in Section 2.3. The loss for the latter training phase is the sum of cross-entropy losses between pred_{EN} and its fluent counterpart.

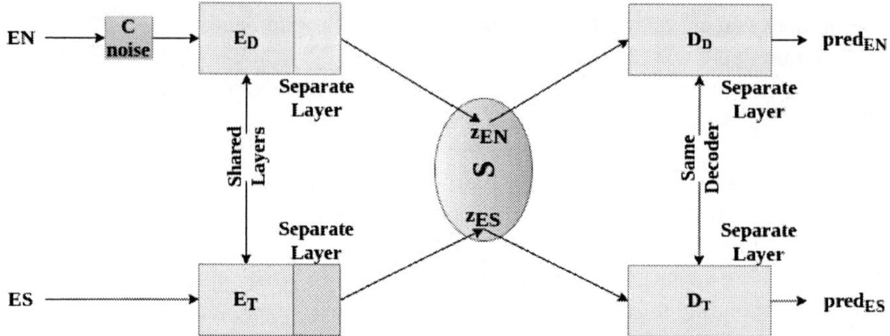

Figure 1: Illustration of proposed architecture. EN: noise-augmented input in English language (text), ES: disfluent Spanish input (text), E_D: Denoising encoder for English language, D_D: Denoising decoder for English language, E_T: Translation encoder whose input is Spanish, D_T: Translation decoder whose output is English, $pred_{EN}$: fluent output of denoising decoder, $pred_{EN}$: Translated output of translation decoder in English language. C_{noise} is the noise model used in (Lample et al., 2017) i.e. word-dropout, word-shuffle, S: Shared latent space, z_{EN} and z_{ES}: latent representation of top and bottom encoders, respectively.

3.2.2 Translation

The translation is done using the parallel Fisher dataset, where disfluent Spanish is used as input and disfluent English is generated as output. The sum of token level cross-entropy is used as the loss function between $pred_{EN}$ (predicted English output) and reference disfluent English.

4 Experiments

4.1 Experimental Setup

We have used lowercased, tokenized, normalized data with all punctuations (except apostrophe) removed. This is the same setting as used by (Salesky et al., 2019) allowing for a comparison with the baseline proposed. The system is evaluated using BLEU[4] and METEOR[5] scoring metrics. BLEU assesses how well predicted translations match a set of reference translations using modified n-gram precision, weighted by a brevity penalty in place of recall to penalize short hypothesis translations without full coverage. In our task of disfluency removal, the generated tokens should contain much of the same content but with certain tokens removed, thereby creating shorter hypotheses. When scoring *fluent output* with *disfluent references*, the difference in BLEU score will come from two sources: shorter n-gram matches, and the brevity penalty. METEOR, on

the other hand, is a semantic evaluation metric. It uses the harmonic mean of precision and recall, with more weight assigned to recall. It also takes into account stem, synonym, paraphrase, and exact matches. In our task, semantic meaning should be retained while disfluencies are removed. Similar METEOR scores are expected when scored with fluent references and disfluent references. METEOR will indicate that meaning is maintained, but not assess disfluency removal, while BLEU will indicate whether disfluencies have been removed.

The parallel Fisher data remains constant in all settings. We have tested with three increasing levels of disfluency induction in the synthetic data. This is denoted using three different values, 0.1, 0.3, and 0.5, for the hyperparameter α. We use a batch size of 32 and epoch size 50000. All other hyperparameters are similar to (Lample et al., 2017)'s implementation.

4.2 Results and Discussion

Table 3 compares the baseline BLEU scores of (Salesky et al., 2019) with our implementation. Our proposed model operates in a mismatched setting i.e. training using disfluent-to-disfluent text data, and evaluating on fluent references for the validation and test sets. We show two baseline scores in Table 3. "BaselineD" refers to the use of disfluent reference text during training and "BaselineF" refers to the use of fluent reference text during training. It should be noted that the reported baseline from (Salesky et al., 2019) is a speech-to-text

---

[4]BLEU scores computed using multi-bleu.pl from the Moses toolkit (Koehn et al., 2007).

[5]METEOR is computed using the script from http://www.cs.cmu.edu/~alavie/METEOR/ (Denkowski and Lavie, 2014).

Model	α	dev		test	
		1Ref	2Ref	1Ref	2Ref
BaselineD	-	13	16.2	13.5	17.0
BaselineF	-	14.6	18.1	14.6	18.1
Our Impl.D	0.5	**17.27**	**17.54**	17.36	20.47
Our Impl.D	0.3	17.2	17.46	**17.71**	**20.93**
Our Impl.D	0.1	16.96	17.22	17.08	20.15

Table 3: BLEU on development and test set with single vs multiple references. End-to-end model performance evaluated with new fluent references. D: Disfluent reference, F: Fluent reference as used in training. Our implementation is trained using disfluent references only.

Model	α	dev		test	
		1Ref	2Ref	1Ref	2Ref
BaselineD	-	22.2	23.9	23.1	24.8
BaselineF	-	22.3	24.0	23.1	24.9
Our Impl.D	0.5	24.9	24.7	25.8	27.2
Our Impl.D	0.3	**25.7**	**25.4**	**26.5**	**28.0**
Our Impl.D	0.1	24.9	24.7	25.7	27.1

Table 4: METEOR on development and test set with single vs multiple references. End-to-end model performance evaluated with new fluent references. D: Disfluent reference, F: Fluent reference as used in training. Our implementation is trained using disfluent references only.

model, while our implementation is a text-to-text model. Scores on the development set and test set using both single and multiple references are shown. We demonstrate that our implementation with three levels of disfluency induction and trained only on disfluent references outperforms the baseline score by a margin of 4.21 BLEU when the baseline uses disfluent references and by a margin of 3.11 BLEU even when the baseline system uses fluent references during training.

Table 4 shows the METEOR score evaluated on all three disfluency induction levels, using both single and multiple references. When comparing METEOR on single and multiple references of the same setting, the precision is the same up to two decimal digits, while there is a slight drop of 0.01 in recall in 2Ref when compared to 1Ref. The comparable METEOR values indicate that semantic meaning is retained in the output.

On comparing METEOR scores of our implementation with that of both baseline models, we observe that our model retains more semantic meaning than the baseline models. Using a single reference, we obtain an absolute difference of 3.4 and 3.6 METEOR scores on the dev and test sets respectively, between the best baseline system and our proposed model. This shows that while doing disfluency removal, the output also manages to

successfully retain semantic meaning.

5   Analysis

In this section, we discuss different types of examples that were generated by our model and how they differ from the disfluent reference and the fluent reference. *Output* is the generated translation from our implementation, *disfluent Ref* and *Fluent Ref* are the disfluent and fluent references, respectively. It should be noted that fluent references were not used during training and are only being shown here for the sake of comparison[6]. Segment Comparison: Deletion, **Insertion**, **Shift**.

Figure 2 shows that the filler word *oh* has been omitted in the generated output.

Figure 2: Removing filler words.

---

[6]The figures used for comparison are created with Char-Cut (Lardilleux and Lepage, 2017)

In Figure 3, we observe that the repetition of the fluent phrase *peruvian peruvian* is handled correctly, but not the repetition of *yes*.

Spanish Input

```
sí sí sí ella es peruana hermana sí
```

Output

```
yes yes yes she's peruvian yes
```

Disfluent Ref

```
yes yes yes she's peruvian peruvian yes
```

Output

```
yes yes yes she's peruvian yes
```

Fluent Ref

```
yes she's peruvian
```

Figure 3: Repetitions (I)

In Figures 4, the output carefully rejects *um*, along with legitimately paraphrasing the sentence as a result of the language model that it has learned from the corpus.

Spanish Input

```
am el tema de hoy es la música
```

Output

```
today's subject is music
```

Disfluent Ref

```
um the topic for today is the music
```

Output

```
today's subject is music
```

Fluent Ref

```
the topic for today is the music
```

Figure 4: Removing filled pause + paraphrasing (II)

In Figures 5, the disfluency *right yes yes* has been completely removed. Instead of choosing *yes*, it replaced it with *well sure*, but the disfluency has been removed.

Spanish Input

```
bueno claro sí sí vas a la cierra este
```

Output

```
well sure you pass by this mountain
```

Disfluent Ref

```
well right yea yes if you go to the mountains
```

Output

```
well sure you pass by this mountain
```

Fluent Ref

```
yes if you go to the mountains
```

Figure 5: Disfluency removal + paraphrasing (II)

6 Conclusion

In this work, we propose a model for generating fluent translations from disfluent text without any access to fluent references during training. We rely on having access to monolingual fluent text in the target language, which is largely available for most languages. We extract disfluency patterns by examining the disfluent text and inject disfluencies to create a parallel disfluent-to-fluent text corpus in the target language. We compare our results at different levels of disfluency induction and show significant improvements over a competitive baseline.

For future work, we aim at building more sophisticated and rich disfluency induction models. In this work, we focused on the text-to-text setting. We will look at extending this approach to a speech-to-text spoken translation task, with disfluency removal being an auxiliary task and investigate how to meaningfully tie parameters across an audio encoder and a text encoder. Furthermore, we only report standard quantitative metrics like BLEU and METEOR here. More detailed human evaluations may better highlight the benefits and limitations of our approach. We also believe that our proposed approach can be easily applied to other language pairs and hope to verify this as part of future work.

7 Acknowledgements

The authors thank the anonymous reviewers for their helpful feedback and comments. The last two authors gratefully acknowledge support from IBM Research (specifically the IBM AI Horizon Networks-IIT Bombay initiative).

References

Ebrahim Ansari, Amittai Axelrod, Nguyen Bach, Ondrej Bojar, Roldano Cattoni, Fahim Dalvi, Nadir Durrani, Marcello Federico, Christian Federmann, Jiatao Gu, Fei Huang, Kevin Knight, Xutai Ma, Ajay Nagesh, Matteo Negri, Jan Niehues, Juan Pino, Elizabeth Salesky, Xing Shi, Sebastian Stüker, Marco Turchi, and Changhan Wang. 2020. Findings of the IWSLT 2020 Evaluation Campaign. In *Proceedings of the 17th International Conference on Spoken Language Translation (IWSLT 2020)*, Seattle, USA.

Mikel Artetxe, Gorka Labaka, Eneko Agirre, and Kyunghyun Cho. 2017. Unsupervised neural machine translation. *CoRR*, abs/1710.11041.

Sameer Bansal, Herman Kamper, Karen Livescu, Adam Lopez, and Sharon Goldwater. 2018. Low-resource speech-to-text translation. *CoRR*, abs/1803.09164.

Piotr Bojanowski, Edouard Grave, Armand Joulin, and Tomas Mikolov. 2016. Enriching word vectors with subword information. *arXiv preprint arXiv:1607.04606*.

Susanne Burger, Victoria MacLaren, and Hua Yu. 2002. The isl meeting corpus: The impact of meeting type on speech style.

Eunah Cho, Sarah Fünfer, Sebastian Stüker, and Alex Waibel. 2014. A corpus of spontaneous speech in lectures: The KIT lecture corpus for spoken language processing and translation. In *Proceedings of the Ninth International Conference on Language Resources and Evaluation (LREC'14)*, pages 1554–1559, Reykjavik, Iceland. European Language Resources Association (ELRA).

Ingrid Cartagena Kevin Walker David Graff, Shudong Huang and Christopher Cieri. Fisher spanish speech (ldc2010s01).

Michael Denkowski and Alon Lavie. 2014. Meteor universal: Language specific translation evaluation for any target language. In *Proceedings of the Ninth Workshop on Statistical Machine Translation*, pages 376–380, Baltimore, Maryland, USA. Association for Computational Linguistics.

Yarin Gal and Zoubin Ghahramani. 2016. A theoretically grounded application of dropout in recurrent neural networks. In *Proceedings of the 30th International Conference on Neural Information Processing Systems*, NIPS'16, page 1027–1035, Red Hook, NY, USA. Curran Associates Inc.

Matthias Honal and Tanja Schultz. 2005. Automatic disfluency removal on recognized spontaneous speech - rapid adaptation to speaker-dependent disfluencies. In *Proceedings of the IEEE International Conference on Acoustics, Speech, and Signal Processing*.

Diederik P. Kingma and Jimmy Ba. 2015. Adam: A method for stochastic optimization. *CoRR*, abs/1412.6980.

Philipp Koehn, Hieu Hoang, Alexandra Birch, Chris Callison-Burch, Marcello Federico, Nicola Bertoldi, Brooke Cowan, Wade Shen, Christine Moran, Richard Zens, Chris Dyer, Ondřej Bojar, Alexandra Constantin, and Evan Herbst. 2007. Moses: Open source toolkit for statistical machine translation. In *Proceedings of the 45th Annual Meeting of the Association for Computational Linguistics Companion Volume Proceedings of the Demo and Poster Sessions*, pages 177–180, Prague, Czech Republic. Association for Computational Linguistics.

Guillaume Lample, Ludovic Denoyer, and Marc'Aurelio Ranzato. 2017. Unsupervised machine translation using monolingual corpora only. *CoRR*, abs/1711.00043.

Adrien Lardilleux and Yves Lepage. 2017. CHARCUT: Human-Targeted Character-Based MT Evaluation with Loose Differences. In *Proceedings of IWSLT 2017*, Tokyo, Japan.

Matt Post, Gaurav Kumar, Adam Lopez, Damianos Karakos, Chris Callison-Burch, and Sanjeev Khudanpur. 2013. Improved speech-to-text translation with the fisher and callhome spanish–english speech translation corpus. In *International Workshop on Spoken Language Translation (IWSLT 2013)*.

Elizabeth Salesky, Susanne Burger, Jan Niehues, and Alex Waibel. 2018. Towards fluent translations from disfluent speech. *CoRR*, abs/1811.03189.

Elizabeth Salesky, Matthias Sperber, and Alex Waibel. 2019. Fluent translations from disfluent speech in end-to-end speech translation. *CoRR*, abs/1906.00556.

Rico Sennrich, Barry Haddow, and Alexandra Birch. 2015. Neural machine translation of rare words with subword units. *CoRR*, abs/1508.07909.

Christian Szegedy, Vincent Vanhoucke, Sergey Ioffe, Jon Shlens, and ZB Wojna. 2016. Rethinking the inception architecture for computer vision.

Ashish Vaswani, Noam Shazeer, Niki Parmar, Jakob Uszkoreit, Llion Jones, Aidan N Gomez, Ł ukasz Kaiser, and Illia Polosukhin. 2017. Attention is all you need. In I. Guyon, U. V. Luxburg, S. Bengio, H. Wallach, R. Fergus, S. Vishwanathan, and R. Garnett, editors, *Advances in Neural Information Processing Systems 30*, pages 5998–6008. Curran Associates, Inc.

W. Wang, G. Tur, J. Zheng, and N. F. Ayan. 2010. Automatic disfluency removal for improving spoken language translation. In *2010 IEEE International Conference on Acoustics, Speech and Signal Processing*, pages 5214–5217.

Ron J. Weiss, Jan Chorowski, Navdeep Jaitly, Yonghui Wu, and Zhifeng Chen. 2017. Sequence-to-sequence models can directly transcribe foreign speech. *CoRR*, abs/1703.08581.

Vicky Zayats, Mari Ostendorf, and Hannaneh Hajishirzi. 2016. Disfluency detection using a bidirectional LSTM. *CoRR*, abs/1604.03209.

The HW-TSC Video Speech Translation system at IWSLT 2020

Minghan Wang, Hao Yang, Yao Deng, Ying Qin, Lizhi Lei,
Daimeng Wei, Hengchao Shang, Jiaxin Guo, Ning Xie, Xiaochun Li
Huawei Translation Service Center, Beijing, China
{wangminghan,yanghao30,dengyao3,qinying,leilizhi
weidaimeng,shanghengchao,guojiaxin1,
nicolas.xie,carol.lixiaochun}@huawei.com

Abstract

In this paper, we present details of our system in the IWSLT Video Speech Translation evaluation. The system works in a cascade form, which contains three modules: 1) A proprietary ASR system. 2) A disfluency correction system aims to remove interregnums or other disfluent expressions with a fine-tuned BERT and a series of rule based algorithms. 3) An NMT System based on the Transformer and trained with massive publicly available corpus is used for translation.

1 Introduction

There has been great advances in Neural Machine Translations (NMT) in recent years which also promotes Multimodal translation including image (Specia et al., 2016), speech and video translation (Wang et al., 2020; Imankulova et al., 2020; Wu et al., 2019). For speech and video translation, there are basically two types of systems (i.e. cascade and end-to-end). Cascade systems are often composed of several independent modules, where each one can be trained with intermediate inputs and labels. End-to-end systems can be fully differentiable and trained with original multimodality data.

In the IWSLT 2020 Video Speech Translation task (Ansari et al., 2020), participants are required to develop systems to translate speeches in the video from source language into target language. However, we consider that visual contexts are not necessarily important for a translation task, therefore we only use audio as contexts, and treat it as a offline speech translation task, in addition, our system is built mainly for Chinese to English translation.

We choose to build our system in a cascade manner because training an end-to-end system requires massive aligned audio and text data, which is hard

to find. On the other hand, a cascade system allows us to train each part separately, which is more feasible.

Our system is composed with three modules. 1) A proprietary ASR system. 2) A disfluency correction system (Wang et al., 2019). 3) An NMT model based on the Transformer (Vaswani et al., 2017).

2 System Architecture

2.1 ASR

For the task, we simply extract the sound tracks from videos, then feed them to our proprietary ASR system and proceed transcripts to downstream modules.

2.2 Disfluency Correction

A major flaw of the cascade system is the error propagation from the ASR to the NMT system. For example, interregnums like "uh", "you know" should not be translated, or repeated words like "I wanna wanna ..." due to disfluency (Shriberg, 1994; Wang et al., 2018). To deal with this problem, we developed the disfluency correction system to de-noise the ASR outputs so that the NMT model could generate more fluent translations. The disfluency correction system is based on fine-tuning BERT for sequence tagging and incorrect N-gram mining. BERT is fine-tuned to predict whether a token generated by the ASR system should be kept or deleted. The N-gram model is able to mine high-frequency mistakes, e.g. "a i"(AI), "r and d"(R&D).

2.2.1 Data

The dataset used to train the disfluency detection model is collected from internal meeting recordings, which are transcribed by human. We create the golden set based on these transcripts. It con-

Proceedings of the 17th International Conference on Spoken Language Translation (IWSLT), pages 187–190
July 9-10, 2020. ©2020 Association for Computational Linguistics
https://doi.org/10.18653/v1/P17

Strategy	Train	Dev	Test
Baseline	35.2	36.3	33.1
+ Domain rule	31.8 (-3.4)	31.9 (-4.4)	30.1 (-3.0)
+ BERT model	28.3 (-3.5)	28.3 (-3.6)	26.7 (-3.4)
+ N-gram mining	26.4 (-1.9)	25.9 (-2.4)	24.9 (-1.8)

Table 1: The performance of each strategy evaluated on our own dataset

tains approximately 200,000 tokens and are split into train/dev/test set with the proportion of 7:1:2.

We use sclite from SCTK to score the ASR outputs, the sclite is able to output four types of actions for tokens and gaps in the ASR outputs. Then, those actions will be used to automatically label the ASR outputs with following rules:

- Tokens are scored as C (correct) by the sclite means that the ASR system outputs a correct token, compared to the ground truth sequence. These tokens will be labeled as **OK** and should be preserved in post-processing.

- Tokens are scored as S (substitute) by the sclite means the ASR system outputs an incorrect (substituted) token at current position, compared to the ground truth sequence. These tokens are labeled as **BAD** and will be deleted. Note that we don't consider predicting the correct token because of the complexity.

- Tokens are scored as I (insertion) means the ASR system inserts an unnecessary token at current position. These tokens will be labeled as **BAD** and should be deleted.

- Gaps are scored as D (deletion) means the ASR fails to output a necessary token at the gap. This situation also involves predicting the missing token therefore is not considered.

Based on these rules, the ASR outputs are labeled with OK and BAD for each token, which will be used to fine-tune the BERT model.

2.2.2 BERT based Disfluency Detection

BERT is widely used in many NLP tasks thanks to its flexible architecture and pre-trained weights contributed by the community. As described previously, we formulate the task as a sequential labelling problem so that the pre-trained BERT can be fine-tuned easily. In the post-processing, we simply remove tokens which are predicted as BAD. The model used for fine-tuning is provided by transformers' (Wolf et al., 2019) BERT-base.

2.2.3 N-Gram Disfluency Mining

Except from training a detection model, we also create a mistake table with n-grams (where n=1,2,3,4), aiming to correct high-frequency mistakes. The table statistics the frequency of incorrect transcripts, and top 10 mistakes are used as a rule based mapping. We mainly use it to solve some situations where the pronunciation and text are not the same, this situation mainly appears in terminologies.

2.2.4 Disfluency Correction Experiments

We preform several experiments on the created dataset with the combination of methods mentioned above to evaluate the effectiveness. We use WER as the evaluation metric. Detailed results are presented in Table 1.

2.3 NMT

The NMT model is based on a Transformer (Vaswani et al., 2017) model with some modifications that will be introduced later. The model is trained with approximately 26M publicly available parallel corpora.

2.3.1 Data

There is no officially published in-domain text data to train and evaluate the model, therefore, we use the WMT 2019 Chinese to English news translation corpora which is composed with 6.5M CWMT and 20M UN sentence pairs. The test set of CCMT 2018 news translation is used as our test set for the experiment.

First of all, we clean up the dataset as follows:

- Remove duplicated sentences.

- Sentences that are too short (e.g. less than two tokens) are removed.

- Sentences that are too long (e.g. greater than 300 tokens) are removed.

- Parallel sentence pairs with abnormal length ratio (e.g. greater than 3 times standard deviation) are removed.

Strategy	BLEU
Transformer-big	36.27
+ Domain Classification	37.63
+ Ensemble	39.25

Table 2: The performance of the nmt model evaluated on CCMT dataset.

- Sentences with abnormal characters are considered as HTML entities, e.g. , are removed.

Subword-nmt (Sennrich et al., 2016) is used to tokenize English sentences, while character based tokenization is used for Chinese sentences.

2.3.2 Model

Transformer Big (Vaswani et al., 2017) is used in our NMT system, which has same number layers compared to Transformer base but with wider embedding and FFN layers, additional normalization and dropout layers are also added.

As we mentioned in Section 2.3.1, we mix the CWMT and UN corpus in which sentences may draw from different distributions and thus may have significant differences in the quality, domain as well as the style. These differences may degrade the performance of a NMT model. To deal with such problem, inspired by (Britz et al., 2017), we add a domain discrimination tag (token) at the start of the sentence for target sentences, here, we use [CWMT] and [UN] to represent two domains (data sources). The initial tag will be used to calculate a discrimination loss thus makes the model trained in a multi-task setting. In the inference phase, the generated tag will be removed in the post-processing.

2.3.3 NMT experiments

We perform experiments with three strategies: Transformer-big with and without domain classification as well as an ensemble model. We use BLEU (Papineni et al., 2002) as the evaluation metric. Details are shown in Table 2.

3 Conclusion

In this paper, we introduce our system for IWSLT 2020 Video Speech Translation evaluation. Our cascade system is developed and evaluated separately, we select the best strategy for each module to integrate a pipeline system which finally makes predictions for our submission.

References

Ebrahim Ansari, Amittai Axelrod, Nguyen Bach, Ondrej Bojar, Roldano Cattoni, Fahim Dalvi, Nadir Durrani, Marcello Federico, Christian Federmann, Jiatao Gu, Fei Huang, Kevin Knight, Xutai Ma, Ajay Nagesh, Matteo Negri, Jan Niehues, Juan Pino, Elizabeth Salesky, Xing Shi, Sebastian Stüker, Marco Turchi, and Changhan Wang. 2020. Findings of the IWSLT 2020 Evaluation Campaign. In *Proceedings of the 17th International Conference on Spoken Language Translation (IWSLT 2020)*, Seattle, USA.

Denny Britz, Quoc V. Le, and Reid Pryzant. 2017. Effective domain mixing for neural machine translation. In *Proceedings of the Second Conference on Machine Translation, WMT 2017, Copenhagen, Denmark, September 7-8, 2017*, pages 118–126.

Aizhan Imankulova, Masahiro Kaneko, Tosho Hirasawa, and Mamoru Komachi. 2020. Towards multimodal simultaneous neural machine translation. *CoRR*, abs/2004.03180.

Kishore Papineni, Salim Roukos, Todd Ward, and Wei-Jing Zhu. 2002. Bleu: a method for automatic evaluation of machine translation. In *Proceedings of the 40th Annual Meeting of the Association for Computational Linguistics, July 6-12, 2002, Philadelphia, PA, USA*, pages 311–318.

Rico Sennrich, Barry Haddow, and Alexandra Birch. 2016. Neural machine translation of rare words with subword units. In *Proceedings of the 54th Annual Meeting of the Association for Computational Linguistics, ACL 2016, August 7-12, 2016, Berlin, Germany, Volume 1: Long Papers*.

Elizabeth Shriberg. 1994. Preliminaries to a theory of speech disfluencies. phd, University of California, Berkeley.

Lucia Specia, Stella Frank, Khalil Sima'an, and Desmond Elliott. 2016. A shared task on multimodal machine translation and crosslingual image description. In *Proceedings of the First Conference on Machine Translation, WMT 2016, colocated with ACL 2016, August 11-12, Berlin, Germany*, pages 543–553.

Ashish Vaswani, Noam Shazeer, Niki Parmar, Jakob Uszkoreit, Llion Jones, Aidan N. Gomez, Lukasz Kaiser, and Illia Polosukhin. 2017. Attention is all you need. In *Advances in Neural Information Processing Systems 30: Annual Conference on Neural Information Processing Systems 2017, 4-9 December 2017, Long Beach, CA, USA*, pages 5998–6008.

Chengyi Wang, Yu Wu, Shujie Liu, Ming Zhou, and Zhenglu Yang. 2020. Curriculum pretraining for end-to-end speech translation. *CoRR*, abs/2004.10093.

Feng Wang, Wei Chen, Zhen Yang, Qianqian Dong, Shuang Xu, and Bo Xu. 2018. Semi-supervised disfluency detection. In *Proceedings of the 27th International Conference on Computational Linguistics,*

COLING 2018, Santa Fe, New Mexico, USA, August 20-26, 2018, pages 3529–3538.

Shaolei Wang, Wanxiang Che, Qi Liu, Pengda Qin, Ting Liu, and William Yang Wang. 2019. Multi-task self-supervised learning for disfluency detection. *CoRR*, abs/1908.05378.

Thomas Wolf, Lysandre Debut, Victor Sanh, Julien Chaumond, Clement Delangue, Anthony Moi, Pierric Cistac, Tim Rault, R'emi Louf, Morgan Funtowicz, and Jamie Brew. 2019. Huggingface's transformers: State-of-the-art natural language processing. *ArXiv*, abs/1910.03771.

Zixiu Wu, Ozan Caglayan, Julia Ive, Josiah Wang, and Lucia Specia. 2019. Transformer-based cascaded multimodal speech translation. *CoRR*, abs/1910.13215.

CUNI Neural ASR with Phoneme-Level Intermediate Step
for Non-Native SLT at IWSLT 2020

Peter Polák and **Sangeet Sagar** and **Dominik Macháček** and **Ondřej Bojar**

Charles University

Faculty of Mathematics and Physics

Institute of Formal and Applied Linguistics

`{polak,sagar,machacek,bojar}@ufal.mff.cuni.cz`

Abstract

In this paper, we present our submission to the Non-Native Speech Translation Task for IWSLT 2020. Our main contribution is a proposed speech recognition pipeline that consists of an acoustic model and a phoneme-to-grapheme model. As an intermediate representation, we utilize phonemes. We demonstrate that the proposed pipeline surpasses commercially used automatic speech recognition (ASR) and submit it into the ASR track. We complement this ASR with off-the-shelf MT systems to take part also in the speech translation track.

1 Introduction

This paper describes our submission to Non-Native Speech Translation Task in IWSLT 2020 (Ansari et al., 2020). We participate in two sub-tracks: offline speech recognition and offline speech translation from English into Czech and German.

We focus on the speech recognition, proposing a robust pipeline consisting of two components — an acoustic model recognizing phonemes, and a phoneme-to-grapheme translation model, see Figure 1. We decided to use phonemes as the intermediate representation between the acoustic and the translation model because we believe that conventional grapheme representation is too constrained with complicated rules of mapping speech to a transcript. This issue becomes immense when dealing with dialects and non-native speakers.

Both models used in our pipeline are end-to-end deep neural networks, Jasper (Li et al., 2019) for the acoustic model and Transformer (Vaswani et al., 2017) for the phoneme-to-grapheme translation model.

For punctuating, truecasing, segmenting and translation into Czech and German, we use off-the-shelf systems provided by ELITR project.

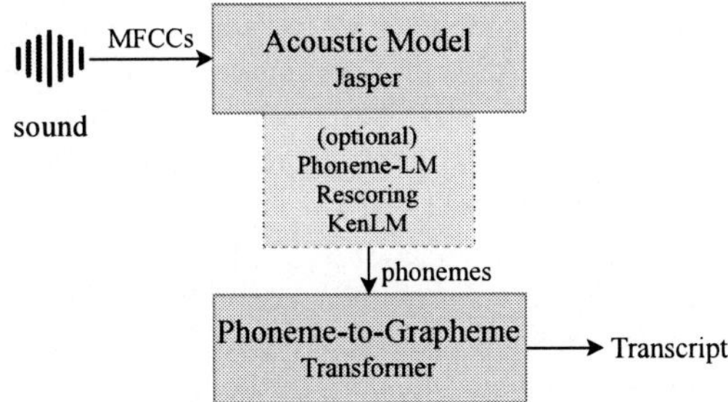

Figure 1: The architecture of proposed model.

The paper is organized as follows: Section 2 reviews related work. In Sections 3 and 4 we describe models for our speech recognition pipeline and their training. In Section 5, we describe the punctuator, truecasor and segmenter, and machine translation into Czech and German in Section 6. We summarize our submissions in Section 7 and conclude in Section 8.

2 Related Work

This section reviews the related work.

2.1 Phonemes and Acoustic Models

Phones and phonemes are well-established modelling units in ASR. They have been used since the beginning of the technology in 1950s (Juang and Rabiner, 2005), for an empirical comparison of different linguistic units for sound representation, see Riley and Ljolje (1992).

An important work popularizing neural networks in ASR to phonemes is Waibel et al. (1989). This work proposes using a time-delayed neural network (TDNN) to model acoustic-phonetic features and the temporal relationship between them. The authors demonstrate that the proposed TDNN can learn shift-invariant internal abstraction of speech and use it to make a robust final decision.

Proceedings of the 17th International Conference on Spoken Language Translation (IWSLT), pages 191–199

July 9-10, 2020. ©2020 Association for Computational Linguistics

https://doi.org/10.18653/v1/P17

Salesky et al. (2019) suggest using of phoneme-based ASR in speech translation. Their end-to-end speech translation pipeline first obtains phoneme alignment using the deep neural network hidden Markov models (DNN-HMM) system and then averages feature vectors with the same phoneme for consecutive frames. Phonemes outputted by DNN-HMM then serve as input features for speech translation.

2.2 Phoneme-to-Grapheme Models

In most past studies that included a separate phoneme-to-grapheme (P2G) translation component into the ASR, the phoneme representation was used only for out-of-vocabulary (OOV) words, see, e.g. Decadt et al. (2001); Horndasch et al. (2006); Basson and Davel (2013).

Decadt et al. (2001) apply phoneme-to-grapheme to enhance the readability of OOV output in Dutch speech recognition. In their setup, the ASR outputs standard (orthographic) text for known words. For OOVs, phonemes are outputted. Because the phonemes are unreadable for most users, the authors translate phonemes using memory-based learning. The word error rate of this improved setup of Dutch ASR was actually higher than the baseline, on the other hand, the output was better readable for an untrained person. They report that 41 % of words were transcribed with at most one error, and 62 % have only two errors. Furthermore, most of the incorrectly transcribed words do not exist in Dutch.

Horndasch et al. (2006) introduce a data-driven approach called MASSIVE. Their main objective is to find appropriate orthographic representations for dictated Internet search queries. Their system iteratively refines sequences of symbol pairs in different alphabets. In the first step, they find the best phoneme-grapheme alignment using the expectation-maximization algorithm. In the second step, they cluster neighbouring symbols together to account for insertions. Finally, n-gram probabilities of symbol pairs are learned. During the inference, the input string is split into individual symbols. All possible symbol pairs are generated for each symbol, and the best sequences are selected in a beam search.

2.3 Error Correction in ASR

Hrinchuk et al. (2019) deal with the correction of errors in ASR by introducing Transformer post-processing. The authors first train an ensemble of 10 ASR models. Using these models, they collect "ASR corrupted" data. Subsequently, they train a Transformer on this data where the "ASR corrupted" text serves as the source and the original true transcripts as the target. In their best setup, they utilize transfer learning. They use BERT (Devlin et al., 2018), a masked language model consisting only of Transformer encoder, and initialize both encoder and decoder of their Transformer correction model with BERT's weights.

2.4 Online ASR Services

We compare our work with Google Cloud Speech-to-Text API[1] and Microsoft Azure Speech to Text.[2] Both of these services provide publicly available APIs for transcribing audio recordings.

3 Neural ASR with Phoneme-Level Intermediate Step

Our main idea is to couple an end-to-end acoustic model with a specialized "translation" model, which translates phonemes to graphemes and corrects the ASR errors.

The motivation for the translation step is that the translation model can exploit larger context than a basic convolutional acoustic model. Furthermore, we can utilize considerably larger non-speech corpora to train this part of the pipeline.

3.1 Acoustic Model

For our acoustic model, we use the Jasper (Li et al., 2019) convolutional neural architecture in the variant of Jasper DR 10x5 variant, as described in the original paper. It is implemented within the NeMo library (Kuchaiev et al., 2019).

For training, we use approximatelly 1 000 hours of speech data from LibriSpeech (Panayotov et al., 2015) and 1 000 hours of Common Voice[3]. Because we want the model to produce phonemes and not graphemes, which are available in the training corpora, we converted the transcript to IPA phonemes using the `phonemizer`[4] tool.

To speed-up the training process, we initialize our English sound-to-phoneme Jasper model with

---

[1] `https://cloud.google.com/speech-to-text`

[2] `https://azure.microsoft.com/en-us/services/cognitive-services/speech-to-text/`

[3] `https://voice.mozilla.org/en`

[4] `https://github.com/bootphon/phonemizer`

Type	Corpus	Adapt.	Full training
dev	LS Clean	46.07	3.84
	CV	54.69	11.86
test	LS Clean	-	4.18 / 4.48† / 3.58‡
	LS Other	-	11.48 / 11.67† / 8.57‡
	CV	-	10.21 / 10.47† / 6.46‡

Table 1: Results in % of *Phoneme* Word Error Rate (PWER) using greedy decoding (no mark), beam search (†) and beam search with language model (‡). The language model is trained on phonemized ASR training data. Note, PWER is not directly comparable to WER. "LS" LibriSpeech. "CV" Common Voice.

the available checkpoint of the standard sound-to-grapheme model.[5]. This seed model was trained on LibriSpeech, Mozilla Common Voice, WSJ, Fisher, and Switchboard corpora, which is beyond the set of corpora allowed for a constrained submission. The model yields word error rate (WER) of 3.69 % on LibriSpeech test-clean, and 10.49 % on test-other using greedy decoding.

For a smooth transition from the Latin alphabet to IPA, we start our training with an adaptation phase of 2,000 training steps. As the model's memory footprint is smaller during this phase, we increase the batch size to 64 (global batch size is 640). One thousand steps are warm-up; the maximal learning rate is 0.004.

The full training takes ten epochs. The model memory requirements increase, therefore we reduce the batch size to 16 (global batch size is 160). We also reduce the learning rate to 0.001.

Optionally, we include a phoneme-level language model, which re-scores the output of the acoustic model before the phoneme-to-grapheme translation, to achieve higher quality. Setups that use this component are further in this paper marked with "_lm".

Results of training after the Adaptation phase (the "Adaptation" column) and the Full training are in Table 1. Note that these scores are calculated on the reference transcript converted to phonemes using phonemizer. Token ambiguities thus change, and these scores are not comparable to standard grapheme WER.

The training is executed on 10 NVIDIA GTX 1080 Ti GPUs with 11 GB VRAM.

---

[5] `https://ngc.nvidia.com/catalog/`
`models/nvidia:multidataset_jasper10x5dr`

4 Phoneme-to-Grapheme Model

We seek a model for translating transcripts written in phonemes into graphemes in the same language. Unlike the most studies reviewed in Section 2, we propose to use Transformer (Vaswani et al., 2017) architecture for phoneme-to-grapheme translation. We believe that Transformer is the best option for these tasks. Transformer has shown its potential in many NLP tasks. Most importantly, we consider its ability to learn the structure of a sentence, see e.g. Pham et al. (2019).

4.1 Text Encoding Considerations

We use Byte Pair Encoding (BPE) (Sennrich et al., 2016) for text encoding in our experiments. We use the implementation in YouTokenToMe[6] library. It is fast and offers BPE-dropout (Provilkov et al., 2019) regularization technique.

First, we decided to use separate vocabularies for source and target sentences, because the source and target representations, IPA phonemes and English graphemes, have no substantial overlap.

There has been a quite intensive discussion about vocabulary size in neural machine translation (NMT) (Denkowski and Neubig, 2017; Gupta et al., 2019; Ding et al., 2019). All works agree that for low-resource translation tasks, it is better to apply smaller vocabulary sizes. For a high-resource task, it is convenient to use larger vocabulary. Our task, translation of phonemes into graphemes in the same language, differs from the previous works. Hence, we decided to experiment with vocabulary sizes. We also want to know whether we should train the sub-word units for source on clean data (phonemes without errors), or we should introduce ASR-like errors to these data.

We design the experiment as follows: we test character-level encoding and BPE vocabulary sizes of 128, 512, 2 000, 8 000 and 32 000. Further, we test a clean data configuration, "corrupted" data (we collect transcripts from an ensemble of 10 ASR systems) and a "mixed" data — combination of the two previous.

Because of the data scarcity, we use Transformer Base configuration. We alter maximum sequence length to 1024 because for character-level, 128, and 512 BPE configurations, many sentences do not fit into the model. We train all models for 70 000 steps on one GPU using the same batch size for all configurations: 12 000 tokens. We set the learning rate

---

[6] `https://github.com/VKCOM/YouTokenToMe`

to 0.04. As training data, we use "corrupted" ASR transcripts paired with true transcripts. We collect the data from an ensemble of 10 ASR models, yielding approximately 7 million sentence pairs. For the collection of ASR corrupted data, we used LibriSpeech and Common Voice datasets.

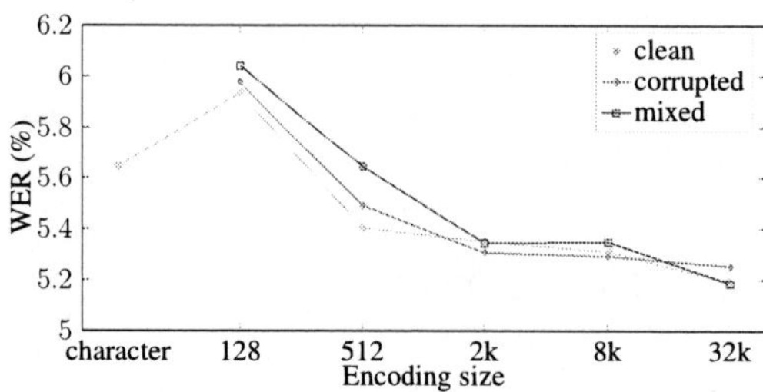

Figure 2: Results in % of word error rate on the Common Voice test set.

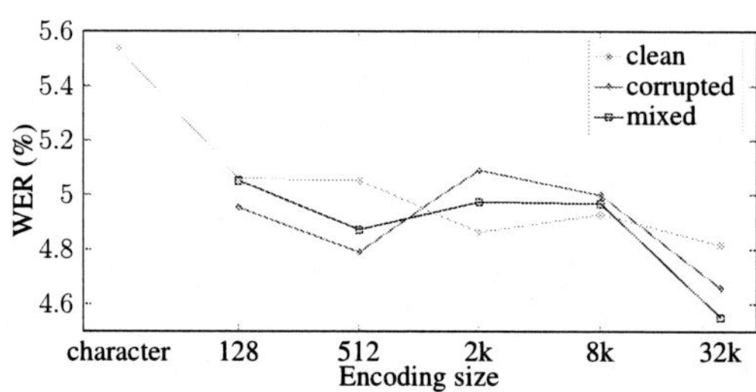

Figure 3: Results in % of word error rate on the LibriSpeech test clean.

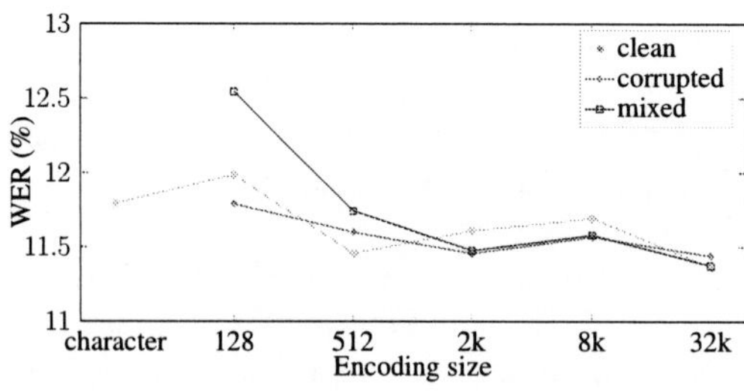

Figure 4: Results in % of word error rate on the LibriSpeech test other.

Graphical comparison is in Figures 2 to 4.

BPE size Character-level encoding seems to be the worst or second-worst possible representation. For the Common Voice test set, it scores almost one percentage point of WER more compared to the best result (5.53 vs 4.55). Also, all other encodings performed almost half a percentage point better.

For both LibriSpeech test sets, it performed a bit better than BPE 128.

Generally, the results suggest a the larger the vocabulary, the lower WER. Among the different BPE sizes, we can recognize the 32 000 vocabulary size has the best results systematically on all test sets.

Finally, we consider the following: a model can better learn from larger vocabulary sizes. First, a model does not have to learn low-level orthography extensively. Rather than memorizing characters (or other smaller units), it can focus on the whole sentence and how individual words interact. Second, a larger model can detect errors because of anomalies in the input encoding. Larger vocabularies produce a shorter representation. Corrupted word is more likely to be broken down to smaller pieces. When a model detects such a situation, it can, for example, decide the right target word based on context, rather than the suspicious word. Such anomaly will most likely not occur in the text encoded with small BPE.

Source of BPE training data For Common Voice, we observe some variation in performance. Best seems to be the "mixed" configuration. Somewhat worse is "corrupted" and the worst is "clean" version. In this case, we think the "mixed" is best as it has frequent enough "corrupted" words. This enables a model to learn to translate these corrupted words into the correct ones. Also, it knows enough other words, so it can adequately work with correct phonemes.

For other test sets, we observe almost no differences. Only "corrupted" configuration has slightly worse performance.

We conclude that the source of training data for BPE has almost no impact on the final result.

4.2 Baseline Phoneme-to-Grapheme Model ("asr" Configuration)

We decided to use Transformer Big configuration (as opposed to the initial experiment with BPE vocabularies). As we concluded in the previous part, we select BPE vocabulary size of 32 000, and the BPE encoding is trained on "clean" phonemized English part of Czeng 1.7 (Bojar et al., 2016) corpus.

First, we train a randomly initialized Transformer model. The source of the "translation" is the phonemized English Czeng and the target is the original English.

We use six 16 GB GPUs for the training. We set the batch size to 6 000 tokens, learning rate to 0.02, warm-up steps to 16 000 and total steps to 600 000. We manually abort the training after the convergence is reached (140 000 steps in our case).

4.3 Transfer from SLT ("asr_slt" Configuration)

In standard NMT, the source text usually does not suffer from so many errors as in our setup. We address this "correction" need by training on artificially corrupted source side.

We initialize the Transformer encoder from our in-house speech translation model trained from English phonemes to Czech graphemes (described in Polák (2020)) and the decoder from a model for the opposite direction. Both of these initial models were trained on CzEng, with one side converted to phonemes using `phonemizer`.

These pre-trained parts of the model, the encoder and decoder need joint training to learn to operate with each other. We employ this training also to inject the capacity of correcting ASR output.

Specifically, we apply the jack-knife scheme to our ASR training data (LibriSpeech and Common Voice), training ten different ASR models, always leaving one-tenth of the training data aside. This one-tenth is recognized with the model, leading to the full speech corpus equipped not only with golden transcripts but also with ASR outputs. We call this an "ASR-corrupted" corpus.

Based on our experience from the experiment with BPE vocabularies, where the model easily over-fit to the sentences from ASR transcripts from speech corpora, we mix the corrupted and clean data with a 1:1 ratio. This is different from Hrinchuk et al. (2019) who use only the ASR-corrupted data to train. We then train the complete Transformer model from English phonemes to English graphemes with the same hyper-parameters as the baseline.

4.4 Transfer from BERT ("asr_bert" Configuration)

Finally, we use the pre-trained BERT (Devlin et al., 2018). Unlike Hrinchuk et al. (2019), we do not initialize both the encoder and decoder with the BERT. We initialize the encoder from the English-to-Czech speech translation model (as in Section 4.3) because we need the model to process phonemes, not graphemes on the source side. The decoder is initialized from the BERT "large" to match the dimension of the Transformer encoder.

For this setup, we tried the same training procedure on half-noisy data as above. However, we were unable to obtain any reasonable performance (we got WER of 28 % on LibriSpeech dev-other). We hypothesize this is due to the vast amount of weights that must be randomly initialized in the decoder: BERT is a Transformer encoder only. Hence it does not have the Encoder-Decoder attention layer which must be trained from scratch. During the training of the whole model with many randomly initialized weights, the initially trained weights from the BERT might depart too far from the optimum.

To overcome this issue, we use an analogous adaptation trick as for the training of the acoustic model. We freeze all weights initialized from seed models and train only the randomly initialized weights until convergence (the criterion was the loss on the validation dataset). This adaptation takes 13 500 steps in our case. Subsequently, the training continues as in the previous case with one exception — we used only ASR corrupted data from LibriSpeech.

4.5 ASR Results

	CV	LS clean	LS other
asr (primary)	9.72	4.87	11.67
asr_lm	7.00	4.63	10.25
asr_slt	**3.26**	5.10	11.75
asr_slt_lm	3.97	5.00	10.63
bert	12.93	4.13	10.21
bert_lm†	11.25	**4.04**	**9.69**

Table 2: Performance of the submitted models in terms of % WER on the Common Voice test set (CV), and LibriSpeech (LS) clean and other test set. † not submitted due to time constraints. Best results in bold.

Table 2 reports the performance of our proposed systems on Common Voice test set and LibriSpeech test-clean and test-other.

The performance of "slt"-pretrained models is very good on Common Voice (CV), reaching WER of 3.26 %. However, we suspect that the model overfitted to CV texts. The corpus contains many speakers, but the set of underlying sentences is very limited, and our models can memorize them. The more realistic evaluation on the independent LibriSpeech other indicates that "asr_slt" is actually rather poor.

For the general domain, assessed by LibriSpeech

	AMIa	AMIb	AMIc	AMId	Teddy	Autocentrum	Audit	Weightened		
								AMI	Rest	Total
asr (primary)	**35.89**	**32.76**	35.60	39.90	57.43	11.62	9.83	**35.05**	19.67	**33.99**
asr_lm†	37.58	33.66	**35.32**	40.60	56.65	14.01	11.00	35.70	20.54	34.65
asr_slt	36.73	33.22	35.70	39.69	56.87	**10.93**	10.22	35.37	19.66	34.28
asr_slt_lm†	37.71	33.83	35.67	40.45	56.31	12.87	10.71	35.88	20.07	34.78
asr_bert	36.69	33.82	36.50	**39.63**	56.76	12.87	**9.60**	35.85	**19.64**	34.72
asr_lm‡	35.95	32.94	35.57	40.43	**56.20**	13.10	10.67	35.20	20.22	34.17
asr_slt_lm‡	37.72	33.86	35.59	40.59	56.42	13.10	10.71	35.88	20.29	34.80
Microsoft	53.72	52.62	56.67	58.58	87.82	39.64	24.22	54.80	39.75	53.76
Google	51.52	49.47	53.11	56.88	61.01	14.12	17.47	51.87	25.33	50.03

Table 3: Results in % WER on IWSLT ASR development set. † submitted without punctuation and segmentation.
‡ submitted with punctuation and segmentation after the deadline.

	AMIa	Teddy	Autocentrum	Audit
asr	4.79	1.41	21.66	5.59
asr_lm†	2.80	1.57	12.53	1.84
asr_lm†*	2.86	1.57	12.79	1.93
asr_slt	4.52	1.48	**22.02**	5.56
asr_slt_lm†	3.19	1.55	8.85	1.81
asr_slt_lm†*	3.26	1.55	9.32	1.88
asr_bert	**6.08**	1.41	19.01	**5.79**
asr_lm‡	3.92	5.65	21.65	5.24
asr_slt_lm‡	4.01	**6.08**	21.50	5.02
Gold	21.09	54.77	42.52	9.03

Table 4: Czech BLEU scores on the IWSLT development set. † submitted without punctuation and segmentation. ‡ submitted with punctuation and segmentation after the deadline. * lower case BLEU.

	AMIa	Teddy	Autocentrum	Audit
asr	8.87	**5.20**	15.94	22.40
asr_lm†	3.45	2.02	4.16	6.15
asr_lm†*	5.30	4.33	8.64	18.16
asr_slt	9.77	4.35	16.40	22.91
asr_slt_lm†	3.45	2.21	4.00	6.54
asr_slt_lm†*	5.34	4.20	6.92	20.07
asr_bert	10.22	3.99	13.38	24.76
asr_lm‡	10.79	4.36	17.24	25.09
asr_slt_lm‡	**10.88**	3.60	**17.34**	**26.64**
Gold	34.95	45.57	36.56	38.97

Table 5: German BLEU scores on the IWSLT development set. † submitted without punctuation and segmentation. ‡ submitted with punctuation and segmentation after the deadline. * lower case BLEU.

clean, we would choose the BERT-pretrained model with phoneme LM rescoring. This model was unfortunately trained too late, so we did not include it in our submission.

The Non-Native Task setting is very specific, and we carefully examine the performance on the IWSLT development (Table 3). The performance varies considerably, but the baseline setup (**"asr"**) perform well on average, and it is also not much worse than the best system on the particular files, e.g. 9.83 on the Audit file compared to "asr_bert" which wins there with 9.60. Based on these results, we selected **"asr"** as our primary submission for speech recognition track.

It the particular domain of non-native speech recognition, the usefulness of the phoneme language model seems to be minor, unlike on the CV and LS test sets in Table 2. However, this result could be unreliable because the IWSLT development set is very small.

We note that all proposed systems outperform publicly available Google and Microsoft ASR on all files in the development set, see the last two rows of Table 3.

5 Punctuation, Truecasing and Segmentation

Our ASR system produces lowercased, unpunctuated text, but the machine translation works on capitalized, punctuated text, segmented to individual sentences. We use the same biRNN punctuator, truecaser and segmenter as Macháček et al. (2020). The punctuator is a bidirectional recurrent neural network by Tilk and Alumäe (2016) trained on the English side of CzEng (Bojar et al., 2016). The truecaser uses tri-grams (Lita et al., 2003). We use a rule-based Moses Sentence Splitter (Koehn et al., 2007). More details are in Macháček et al. (2020), Section 4.2.

6 Machine Translation

Our submission to the SLT track relies on the MT systems, which are used also by ELITR project and are described in their submission to this task (Macháček et al., 2020). We do not rely on their validation for this task. As our primary MT systems, we select "WMT18 T2T" for Czech and "de T2T" for German, because they were easily accessible

Name	Initialization		LM rescoring
	Encoder	Decoder	
asr (primary)	random	random	no
asr_lm	random	random	yes
asr_slt	EN CS	CS EN	no
asr_slt_lm	EN CS	CS EN	yes
bert	EN CS	BERT	no

Table 6: Submitted English ASR configurations. "EN CS" means the Transformer encoder was initialized with the encoder weights from a translation model trained from English phonemes to Czech graphemes. "CS EN" means the decoder was initialized from an MT model translating Czech phonemes to English graphemes.

through Lindat service[7].

"WMT18 T2T" was originally trained for English-Czech WMT18 news translation task (Popel, 2018), and was also between the top systems in WMT19 (Popel et al., 2019). It is a single-sentence Transformer Big model in Tensor2Tensor framework (Vaswani et al., 2018). "de T2T" is a similar system, but trained on the data for English-German WMT news translation. Tables 4 and 5 present BLEU scores of our primary systems for Czech and German, respectively. Note that the files Teddy, Autocentrum and Audit are very short.

We submit also all other machine translation systems for Czech and German by ELITR with our "asr" source for contrastive evaluation. See Macháček et al. (2020) for more details.

7 Submission Summary

We participate in two tracks of the non-native speech translation task: speech recognition, and speech translation into both Czech and German. In both cases, our submissions are off-line.

The acoustic model was initialized from a checkpoint trained on other data than allowed for the task. Therefore, our systems are unconstrained.

For the speech recognition track, we utilize our speech recognition pipeline in various configurations. We first obtain the phoneme transcripts using the acoustic model. For configurations marked with "_lm", we additionally use a phoneme language model during the acoustic model inference. Subsequently, we feed these phonetic transcripts to the phoneme-to-grapheme translation model. We have three variants of this model: plain ("asr"), with pre-trained weights from SLT ("slt"), and with pre-

trained weights from SLT for encoder and BERT for decoder ("bert"). In this manner, we yield five different configurations for submission (see Table 6). The transcripts are then punctuated and truecased. Based on the punctuation, we further segment the transcripts. Our primary submission for the ASR track is the "asr" system.

We do not have our own translation model. To participate in the translation track, we utilize the MT systems of the ELITR project, which are mostly Transformer neural models. We select as our primary submission the "asr" system.

8 Conclusion

We presented our submissions to the Non-Native Speech Translation Task for IWSLT 2020.

For the non-native speech recognition, we proposed a pipeline that consists of an acoustic model and a phoneme-to-grapheme model. We demonstrated that the proposed pipeline surpasses commercially used ASR on the development set.

To participate in the non-native speech translation track, we use off-the-shelf translation model on our ASR transcripts.

Acknowledgments

The research was partially supported by the grants 19-26934X (NEUREM3) of the Czech Science Foundation, H2020-ICT-2018-2-825460 (ELITR) of the EU, 98120 of the Grant Agency of Charles University and by SVV project number 260 575.

References

Ebrahim Ansari, Amittai Axelrod, Nguyen Bach, Ondrej Bojar, Roldano Cattoni, Fahim Dalvi, Nadir Durrani, Marcello Federico, Christian Federmann, Jiatao Gu, Fei Huang, Kevin Knight, Xutai Ma, Ajay Nagesh, Matteo Negri, Jan Niehues, Juan Pino, Elizabeth Salesky, Xing Shi, Sebastian Stüker, Marco Turchi, and Changhan Wang. 2020. Findings of the IWSLT 2020 Evaluation Campaign. In *Proceedings of the 17th International Conference on Spoken Language Translation (IWSLT 2020)*, Seattle, USA.

Willem D Basson and Marelie H Davel. 2013. Category-based phoneme-to-grapheme transliteration.

Ondřej Bojar, Ondřej Dušek, Tom Kocmi, Jindřich Libovický, Michal Novák, Martin Popel, Roman Sudarikov, and Dušan Variš. 2016. CzEng 1.6: Enlarged Czech-English Parallel Corpus with Processing Tools Dockered. In *Text, Speech, and Dialogue: 19th International Conference, TSD 2016*, number

---

[7]`https://lindat.mff.cuni.cz/services/translation/`

9924 in Lecture Notes in Computer Science, pages 231–238, Cham / Heidelberg / New York / Dordrecht / London. Masaryk University, Springer International Publishing.

B. Decadt, J. Duchateau, W. Daelemans, and P. Wambacq. 2001. Phoneme-to-grapheme conversion for out-of-vocabulary words in large vocabulary speech recognition. In *IEEE Workshop on Automatic Speech Recognition and Understanding, 2001. ASRU '01.*, pages 413–416.

Michael Denkowski and Graham Neubig. 2017. Stronger baselines for trustable results in neural machine translation. In *Proceedings of the First Workshop on Neural Machine Translation*, pages 18–27.

Jacob Devlin, Ming-Wei Chang, Kenton Lee, and Kristina Toutanova. 2018. Bert: Pre-training of deep bidirectional transformers for language understanding. *arXiv preprint arXiv:1810.04805*.

Shuoyang Ding, Adithya Renduchintala, and Kevin Duh. 2019. A call for prudent choice of subword merge operations in neural machine translation. In *Proceedings of Machine Translation Summit XVII Volume 1: Research Track*, pages 204–213.

Rohit Gupta, Laurent Besacier, Marc Dymetman, and Matthias Gallé. 2019. Character-based nmt with transformer. *arXiv preprint arXiv:1911.04997*.

Axel Horndasch, Elmar Nöth, Anton Batliner, and Volker Warnke. 2006. Phoneme-to-grapheme mapping for spoken inquiries to the semantic web. In *Ninth International Conference on Spoken Language Processing*.

Oleksii Hrinchuk, Mariya Popova, and Boris Ginsburg. 2019. Correction of automatic speech recognition with transformer sequence-to-sequence model. *arXiv preprint arXiv:1910.10697*.

Biing-Hwang Juang and Lawrence R Rabiner. 2005. Automatic speech recognition–a brief history of the technology development. *Georgia Institute of Technology. Atlanta Rutgers University and the University of California. Santa Barbara*, 1:67.

Philipp Koehn et al. 2007. Moses: Open Source Toolkit for Statistical Machine Translation. In *ACL Interactive Poster and Demonstration Sessions*, page 177–180, USA. Association for Computational Linguistics.

Oleksii Kuchaiev, Jason Li, Huyen Nguyen, Oleksii Hrinchuk, Ryan Leary, Boris Ginsburg, Samuel Kriman, Stanislav Beliaev, Vitaly Lavrukhin, Jack Cook, Patrice Castonguay, Mariya Popova, Jocelyn Huang, and Jonathan M. Cohen. 2019. Nemo: a toolkit for building ai applications using neural modules.

Jason Li, Vitaly Lavrukhin, Boris Ginsburg, Ryan Leary, Oleksii Kuchaiev, Jonathan M. Cohen, Huyen Nguyen, and Ravi Teja Gadde. 2019. Jasper: An End-to-End Convolutional Neural Acoustic Model. In *Proc. Interspeech 2019*, pages 71–75.

Lucian Vlad Lita, Abe Ittycheriah, Salim Roukos, and Nanda Kambhatla. 2003. Truecasing. In *Proceedings of the 41st Annual Meeting on Association for Computational Linguistics - Volume 1*, ACL '03, page 152–159, USA. Association for Computational Linguistics.

Dominik Macháček, Jonáš Kratochvíl, Sangeet Sagar, Matúš Žilinec, Ondřej Bojar, Thai-Son Nguyen, Felix Schneider, Philip Williams, and Yuekun Yao. 2020. ELITR Non-Native Speech Translation at IWSLT 2020. In *Proceedings of the 17th International Conference on Spoken Language Translation (IWSLT 2020)*, Seattle, USA.

Vassil Panayotov, Guoguo Chen, Daniel Povey, and Sanjeev Khudanpur. 2015. Librispeech: an asr corpus based on public domain audio books. In *2015 IEEE International Conference on Acoustics, Speech and Signal Processing (ICASSP)*, pages 5206–5210. IEEE.

Thuong-Hai Pham, Dominik Macháček, and Ondřej Bojar. 2019. Promoting the knowledge of source syntax in transformer nmt is not needed. *Computación y Sistemas*, 23(3):923–934.

Peter Polák. 2020. Spoken language translation via phoneme representation of the source language. Master's thesis, Charles University.

Martin Popel. 2018. CUNI transformer neural MT system for WMT18. In *Proceedings of the Third Conference on Machine Translation: Shared Task Papers*, pages 482–487, Belgium, Brussels. Association for Computational Linguistics.

Martin Popel, Dominik Macháček, Michal Auersperger, Ondřej Bojar, and Pavel Pecina. 2019. English-czech systems in wmt19: Document-level transformer. In *WMT*.

Ivan Provilkov, Dmitrii Emelianenko, and Elena Voita. 2019. Bpe-dropout: Simple and effective subword regularization. *arXiv preprint arXiv:1910.13267*.

Michael D Riley and Andrej Ljolje. 1992. Recognizing phonemes vs. recognizing phones: a comparison. In *Second International Conference on Spoken Language Processing*.

Elizabeth Salesky, Matthias Sperber, and Alan W Black. 2019. Exploring phoneme-level speech representations for end-to-end speech translation. In *Proceedings of the 57th Annual Meeting of the Association for Computational Linguistics*, pages 1835–1841, Florence, Italy. Association for Computational Linguistics.

Rico Sennrich, Barry Haddow, and Alexandra Birch. 2016. Neural machine translation of rare words with subword units. In *Proceedings of the 54th Annual Meeting of the Association for Computational*

Linguistics (Volume 1: Long Papers), pages 1715–1725.

Ottokar Tilk and Tanel Alumäe. 2016. Bidirectional recurrent neural network with attention mechanism for punctuation restoration. pages 3047–3051.

Ashish Vaswani, Samy Bengio, Eugene Brevdo, Francois Chollet, Aidan N. Gomez, Stephan Gouws, Llion Jones, Łukasz Kaiser, Nal Kalchbrenner, Niki Parmar, Ryan Sepassi, Noam Shazeer, and Jakob Uszkoreit. 2018. Tensor2tensor for neural machine translation. *CoRR*, abs/1803.07416.

Ashish Vaswani, Noam Shazeer, Niki Parmar, Jakob Uszkoreit, Llion Jones, Aidan N Gomez, Łukasz Kaiser, and Illia Polosukhin. 2017. Attention is all you need. In *Advances in neural information processing systems*, pages 5998–6008.

Alex Waibel, Toshiyuki Hanazawa, Geoffrey Hinton, Kiyohiro Shikano, and Kevin J Lang. 1989. Phoneme recognition using time-delay neural networks. *IEEE transactions on acoustics, speech, and signal processing*, 37(3):328–339.

ELITR Non-Native Speech Translation at IWSLT 2020

Dominik Macháček[†] and **Jonáš Kratochvíl**[†] and **Sangeet Sagar**[†] and
Matúš Žilinec[†] and **Ondřej Bojar**[†] and **Thai-Son Nguyen**[‡] and **Felix Schneider**[‡] and
Philip Williams[*] and **Yuekun Yao**[*]

[†]Charles University, [‡]Karlsruhe Institute of Technology, [*]University of Edinburgh

[†]{surname}@ufal.mff.cuni.cz, except jkratochvil@ufal.mff.cuni.cz,
[‡]{firstname.lastname}@kit.edu,
[*]pwillia4@inf.ed.ac.uk,yyao2@exseed.ed.ac.uk

Abstract

This paper is an ELITR system submission for the non-native speech translation task at IWSLT 2020. We describe systems for offline ASR, real-time ASR, and our cascaded approach to offline SLT and real-time SLT. We select our primary candidates from a pool of pre-existing systems, develop a new end-to-end general ASR system, and a hybrid ASR trained on non-native speech. The provided small validation set prevents us from carrying out a complex validation, but we submit all the unselected candidates for contrastive evaluation on the test set.

1 Introduction

This paper describes the submission of the EU project ELITR (European Live Translator)[1] to the non-native speech translation task at IWSLT 2020 (Ansari et al., 2020). It is a result of a collaboration of project partners Charles University (CUNI), Karlsruhe Institute of Technology (KIT), and University of Edinburgh (UEDIN), relying on the infrastructure provided to the project by PerVoice company.

The non-native speech translation shared task at IWSLT 2020 complements other IWSLT tasks by new challenges. Source speech is non-native English. It is spontaneous, sometimes disfluent, and some of the recordings come from a particularly noisy environment. The speakers often have a significant non-native accent. In-domain training data are not available. They consist only of native out-domain speech and non-spoken parallel corpora. The validation data are limited to 6 manually transcribed documents, from which only 4 have reference translations. The target languages are Czech and German.

The task objectives are quality and simultaneity, unlike the previous tasks, which focused only on

the quality. Despite the complexity, the resulting systems can be potentially appreciated by many users attending an event in a language they do not speak or having difficulties understanding due to unfamiliar non-native accents or unusual vocabulary.

We build on our experience from the past IWSLT and WMT tasks, see e.g. Pham et al. (2019); Nguyen et al. (2017); Pham et al. (2017); Wetesko et al. (2019); Bawden et al. (2019); Popel et al. (2019). Each of the participating institutions has offered independent ASR and MT systems trained for various purposes and previous shared tasks. We also create some new systems for this task and deployment for the purposes of the ELITR project. Our short-term motivation for this work is to connect the existing systems into a working cascade for SLT and evaluate it empirically, end-to-end. In the long-term, we want to advance state of the art in non-native speech translation.

2 Overview of Our Submissions

This paper is a joint report for two primary submissions, for online and offline sub-track of the non-native simultaneous speech translation task.

First, we collected all ASR systems that were available for us (Section 3.1) and evaluated them on the validation set (Section 3.2). We selected the best candidate for offline ASR to serve as the source for offline SLT. Then, from the ASR systems, which are usable in online mode, we selected the best candidate for online ASR and as a source for online SLT.

In the next step (Section 4), we punctuated and truecased the online ASR outputs of the validation set, segmented them to individual sentences, and translated them by all the MT systems we had available (Section 5.1). We integrated the online ASRs and MTs into our platform for online SLT

---

[1]http://elitr.eu

Proceedings of the 17th International Conference on Spoken Language Translation (IWSLT), pages 200–208
July 9-10, 2020. ©2020 Association for Computational Linguistics
https://doi.org/10.18653/v1/P17

(Sections 5.2 and 5.3). We compared them using automatic MT quality measures and by simple human decision, to compensate for the very limited and thus unreliable validation set (Section 5.4). We selected the best candidate systems for each target language, for Czech and German.

Both best candidate MT systems are very fast (see Section 5.5). Therefore, we use them both for the online SLT, where the low translation time is critical, and for offline SLT.

In addition to the primary submissions, we included all the other candidate systems and some public services as contrastive submissions.

3 Automatic Speech Recognition

This section describes our automatic speech recognition systems and their selection.

3.1 ASR Systems

We use three groups of ASR systems. They are described in the following sections.

3.1.1 KIT ASR

KIT has provided three hybrid HMM/ANN ASR systems and an end-to-end sequence-to-sequence ASR system.

The hybrid systems, called KIT-h-large-lm1, KIT-h-large-lm2 and KIT-hybrid, were developed to run on the online low-latency condition, and differ in the use of the language models.

The KIT-h-large-lm adopted a 4-gram language model which was trained on a large text corpus (Nguyen et al., 2017), while the KIT-hybrid employed only the manual transcripts of the speech training data. We would refer the readers to the system paper by Nguyen et al. (2017) for more information on the training data and the studies by Nguyen et al. (2020); Niehues et al. (2018) for more information about the online setup.

The end-to-end ASR, so-called KIT-seq2seq, followed the architecture and the optimizations described by Nguyen et al. (2019). It was trained on a large speech corpus, which is the combination of Switchboard, Fisher, LibriSpeech, TED-LIUM, and Mozilla Common Voice datasets. It was used solely without an external language model.

All KIT ASR systems are unconstrained because they use more training data than allowed for the task.

3.1.2 Kaldi ASR Systems

We used three systems trained in the Kaldi ASR toolkit (Povey et al., 2011). These systems were trained on Mozilla Common Voice, TED-LIUM, and AMI datasets together with additional textual data for language modeling.

Kaldi-Mozilla For Kaldi-Mozilla, we used the Mozilla Common Voice baseline Kaldi recipe.[2] The training data consist of 260 hours of audio. The number of unique words in the lexicon is 7996, and the number of sentences used for the baseline language model is 6994, i.e., the corpus is very repetitive. We first train the GMM-HMM part of the model, where the final number of hidden states for the HMM is 2500, and the number of GMM components is 15000. We then train the chain model, which uses the Time delay neural network (TDNN) architecture (Peddinti et al., 2015) together with the Batch normalization regularization and ReLU activation. We use MFCC features to represent audio frames, and we concatenate them with the 100-dimensional I-vector features for the neural network training. We recompile the final chain model with CMU lexicon to increase the model capacity to 127384 words and 4-gram language model trained with SRILM (Stolcke, 2002) on 18M sentences taken from English news articles.

Kaldi-TedLium serves as another baseline, trained on 130 hours of TED-LIUM data (Rousseau et al., 2012) collected before the year 2012. The Kaldi-TedLium model was developed by the University of Edinburgh and was fully described by Klejch et al. (2019). This model was primarily developed for discriminative acoustic adaptation to domains distinct from the original training domain. It is achieved by reusing the decoded lattices from the first decoding pass and by finetuning for TED-LIUM development and test set. The setup follows the Kaldi 1f TED-LIUM recipe. The architecture is similar to Kaldi-Mozilla and uses a combination of TDNN layers with batch normalization and ReLU activation. The input features are MFCC and I-vectors.

Kaldi-AMI was trained on the 100 hours of the AMI data, which comprise of staged meeting recordings (Mccowan et al., 2005). These data

---

[2]`https://github.com/kaldi-asr/kaldi/tree/master/egs/commonvoice/s5`

| domain | AMI | | | | Antrecorp | | Auditing |
document	AMIa	AMIb	AMIc	AMId	Teddy	Autocentrum	Auditing
KIT-h-large-lm1	50.71	47.96	53.11	50.43	65.92	19.25	18.54
KIT-h-large-lm2	47.82	41.71	42.10	45.77	75.87	28.59	19.81
KIT-hybrid	40.72	38.45	41.09	43.28	58.99	21.04	21.44
KIT-seq2seq	33.73	28.54	34.45	42.24	42.57	9.91	10.45
Kaldi-TedLium	42.44	38.56	41.83	44.36	61.12	18.68	22.81
Kaldi-Mozilla	52.89	56.37	58.50	58.90	68.72	45.41	34.36
Kaldi-AMI	~~28.01~~	~~23.04~~	~~26.87~~	~~29.34~~	59.66	20.62	28.39
Microsoft	53.72	52.62	56.67	58.58	87.82	39.64	24.22
Google	51.52	49.47	53.11	56.88	61.01	14.12	17.47

Table 1: WER rates of individual documents in the development set. Kaldi-AMI scores on AMI domain are striked through because they are unreliable due to an overlap with the training data.

domain	document	sents.	tokens	duration	references
Antrecorp	Teddy	11	171	1:15	2
Antrecorp	Autocentrum	12	174	1:06	2
Auditing	Auditing	25	528	5:38	1
AMI	AMIa	220	1788	15:09	1
AMI	AMIb	614	4868	35:17	0
AMI	AMIc	401	3454	24:06	0
AMI	AMId	281	1614	13:01	0

Table 2: The size of the development set `iwslt2020-nonnative-minidevset-v2`. The duration is in minutes and seconds. As "references" we mean the number of independent referential translations into Czech and German.

| | WER weighted average | | | avg |
	AMI	Antrecorp	Auditing	domain
KIT-seq2seq[1]	**32.96**	**26.10**	**10.45**	**23.17**
Kaldi-TedLium	40.91	39.72	22.81	34.48
Kaldi-Mozilla	56.82	56.96	34.36	49.38
Kaldi-AMI	~~25.79~~	39.97	28.39	31.38
Microsoft	54.80	63.52	24.22	47.51
Google	51.88	37.36	17.47	35.57
KIT-h-large-lm1	50.24	42.38	**18.54**[2]	37.05
KIT-h-large-lm2	43.32	52.02	19.81	38.38
KIT-hybrid	**40.24**[1]	**39.85**[1]	21.44	**33.84**

Table 3: Weighted average WER for the domains in validation set, and their average. The top line-separated group are offline ASR systems, the bottom are online. Bold numbers are the lowest considerable WER in the group. Kaldi-AMI score on AMI is not considered due to overlap with training data. Bold names are the primary (marked with [1]) and secondary (marked with [2]) candidates.

were recorded mostly by non-native English speakers with a different microphone and acoustic environment conditions. The model setup used follows the Kaldi 1i ami recipe. Kaldi-AMI cannot be reliably assessed on the AMI part of the development due to the overlap of training and development data. We have decided not to exclude this overlap so that we do not limit the amount of available training data for our model.

3.1.3 Public ASR Services

As part of our baseline models, we have used Google Cloud Speech-to-Text API[3] and Microsoft Azure Speech to Text.[4] Both of these services provide an API for transcription of audio files in WAV format, and they use neural network acoustic models. We kept the default settings of these systems.

The Google Cloud system supports over 100 languages and several types of English dialects (such as Canada, Ireland, Ghana, or the United Kingdom). For decoding of the development and test set, we have used the United Kingdom English

dialect option. The system can be run either in real-time or offline mode. We have used the offline option for this experiment.

The Microsoft Azure Bing Speech API supports fewer languages than Google Cloud ASR but adds more customization options of the final model. It can be also run both in real-time or offline mode. For the evaluation, we have used the offline mode and the United Kingdom English (en-GB) dialect.

3.2 Selection of ASR Candidates

We processed the validation set with all the ASR systems, evaluated WER, and summarized them in Table 1. The validation set (Table 2) contains three different domains with various document sizes, and the distribution does not fully correspond to the test set. The AMI domain is not present in the test set at all, but it is a part of Kaldi-AMI training data. Therefore, a simple selection by an average WER on the whole validation set could favor the systems which perform well on the AMI domain, but they

---

[3] `https://cloud.google.com/speech-to-text`

[4] `https://azure.microsoft.com/en-us/services/cognitive-services/speech-to-text/`

could not be good candidates for the other domains.

In Table 3, we present the weighted average of WER in the validation domains. We weight it by the number of gold transcription words in each of the documents. We observe that Kaldi-AMI has a good performance on the AMI domain, but it is worse on the others. We assume it is overfitted for this domain, and therefore we do not use it as the primary system.

For offline ASR, we use KIT-seq2seq as the primary system because it showed the lowest error rate on the averaged domain.

The online ASR systems can exhibit somewhat lower performance than offline systems. We select KIT-h-large-lm1 as the primary online ASR candidate for Auditing, and KIT-hybrid as primary for the other domains.

Our second primary offline ASR is Kaldi-AMI.

4 Punctuation and Segmentation

All our ASR systems output unpunctuated, often all lowercased text. The MT systems are designed mostly for individual sentences with proper casing and punctuation. To overcome this, we first insert punctuation and casing to the ASR output. Then, we split it into individual sentences by the punctuation marks by a rule-based language-dependent Moses sentence splitter (Koehn et al., 2007).

Depending on the ASR system, we use one of two possible punctuators. Both of them are usable in online mode.

4.1 KIT Punctuator

The KIT ASR systems use an NMT-based model to insert punctuation and capitalization in an otherwise unsegmented lowercase input stream (Cho et al., 2012, 2015). The system is a monolingual translation system that translates from raw ASR output to well-formed text by converting words to upper case, inserting punctuation marks, and dropping words that belong to disfluency phenomena. It does not use the typical sequence-to-sequence approach of machine translation. However, it considers a sliding window of recent (uncased) words and classifying each one according to the punctuation that should be inserted and whether the word should be dropped for being a part of disfluency. This gives the system a constant input and output size, removing the need for a sequence-to-sequence model.

While inserting punctuation is strictly necessary for MT to function at all, inserting capitalization and removing disfluencies improves MT performance by making the test case more similar to the MT training conditions (Cho et al., 2017).

4.2 BiRNN Punctuator

For other systems, we use a bidirectional recurrent neural network with an attention-based mechanism by Tilk and Alumäe (2016) to restore punctuation in the raw stream of ASR output. The model was trained on 4M English sentences from CzEng 1.6 (Bojar et al., 2016) data and a vocabulary of 100K most frequently occurring words. We use CzEng because it is a mixture of domains, both originally spoken, which is close to the target domain, and written, which has richer vocabulary, and both original English texts and translations, which we also expect in the target domain. The punctuated transcript is then capitalized using an English tri-gram truecaser by Lita et al. (2003). The truecaser was trained on 2M English sentences from CzEng.

5 Machine Translation

This section describes the translation part of SLT.

5.1 MT Systems

See Table 4 for the summary of the MT systems. All except de-LSTM are Transformer-based neural models using Marian (Junczys-Dowmunt et al., 2018) or Tensor2Tensor (Vaswani et al., 2018) back-end. All of them, except de-T2T, are unconstrained because they are trained not only on the data sets allowed in the task description, but all the used data are publicly available.

5.1.1 WMT Models

WMT19 Marian and WMT18 T2T models are Marian and T2T single-sentence models from Popel et al. (2019) and Popel (2018). WMT18 T2T was originally trained for the English-Czech WMT18 news translation task, and reused in WMT19. WMT19 Marian is its reimplementation in Marian for WMT19. The T2T model has a slightly higher quality on the news text domain than the Marian model. The Marian model translates faster, as we show in Section 5.5.

5.1.2 IWSLT19 Model

The IWSLT19 system is an ensemble of two English-to-Czech Transformer Big models trained using the Marian toolkit. The models were originally trained on WMT19 data and then finetuned

system	back-end	source-target	constrained	reference
WMT19 Marian	Marian	en→cs	no	Popel et al. (2019), Section 5.1.1
WMT18 T2T	T2T	en→cs	no	Popel et al. (2019), Section 5.1.1
IWSLT19	Marian	en→cs	no	Wetesko et al. (2019), Section 5.1.2
OPUS-A	Marian	en↔{cs,de+5 l.}	no	Section 5.1.3
OPUS-B	Marian	en↔{cs,de+39 l.}	no	Section 5.1.3
T2T-multi	T2T	en↔{cs,de,en+39 l.}	no	Section 5.1.4
T2T-multi-big	T2T	en↔{cs,de,en+39 l.}	no	Section 5.1.4
de-LSTM	NMTGMinor	en→de	no	Dessloch et al. (2018), Section 5.1.6
de-T2T	T2T	en→de	yes	Section 5.1.5

Table 4: The summary of our MT systems.

on MuST-C TED data. The ensemble was a component of Edinburgh and Samsung's submission to the IWSLT19 Text Translation task. See Section 4 of Wetesko et al. (2019) for further details of the system.

5.1.3 OPUS Multi-Lingual Models

The OPUS multilingual systems are one-to-many systems developed within the ELITR project. Both were trained on data randomly sampled from the OPUS collection (Tiedemann, 2012), although they use distinct datasets. OPUS-A is a Transformer Base model trained on 1M sentence pairs each for 7 European target languages: Czech, Dutch, French, German, Hungarian, Polish, and Romanian. OPUS-B is a Transformer Big model trained on a total of 231M sentence pairs covering 41 target languages that are of particular interest to the project[5] After initial training, OPUS-B was finetuned on an augmented version of the dataset that includes partial sentence pairs, artificially generated by truncating the original sentence pairs (similar to Niehues et al., 2018). We produce up to 10 truncated sentence pairs for every one original pair.

5.1.4 T2T Multi-Lingual Models

T2T-multi and T2T-multi-big are respectively Transformer and Transformer Big models trained on a Cloud TPU based on the default T2T hyper-parameters, with the addition of target language tokens as in Johnson et al. (2017). The models were trained with a shared vocabulary on a dataset of English-to-many and many-to-English sentence pairs from OPUS-B containing 42 languages in total, making them suitable for pivoting. The models do not use finetuning.

5.1.5 de-T2T

de-T2T translation model is based on a Tensor2Tensor translation model model using training hyper-parameters similar to Popel and Bojar (2018). The model is trained using all the parallel corpora provided for the English-German WMT19 News Translation Task, without back-translation. We use the last training checkpoint during model inference. To reduce the decoding time, we apply greedy decoding instead of a beam search.

5.1.6 KIT Model

KIT's translation model is based on an LSTM encoder-decoder framework with attention (Pham et al., 2017). As it is developed for our lecture translation framework (Müller et al., 2016), it is finetuned for lecture content. In order to optimize for a low-latency translation task, the model is also trained on partial sentences in order to provide more stable translations (Niehues et al., 2016).

5.2 ELITR SLT Platform

We use a server called Mediator for the integration of independent ASR and MT systems into a cascade for online SLT. It is a part of the ELITR platform for simultaneous multilingual speech translation (Franceschini et al., 2020). The workers, which can generally be any audio-to-text or text-to-text processors, such as ASR and MT systems, run inside of their specific software and hardware environments located physically in their home labs around Europe. They connect to Mediator and offer a service. A client, often located in another lab, requests Mediator for a cascade of services, and Mediator connects them. This platform simplifies the cross-institutional collaboration when one institution offers ASR, the other MT, and the third tests them as a client. The platform enables using the SLT pipeline easily in real-time.

---

[5]The 41 target languages include all EU languages (other than English) and 18 languages that are official languages of EUROSAI member countries. Specifically, these are Albanian, Arabic, Armenian, Azerbaijani, Belorussian, Bosnian, Georgian, Hebrew, Icelandic, Kazakh, Luxembourgish, Macedonian, Montenegrin, Norwegian, Russian, Serbian, Turkish, and Ukrainian.

5.3 MT Wrapper

The simultaneous ASR incrementally produces the recognition hypotheses and gradually improves them. The machine translation system translates one batch of segments from the ASR output at a time. If the translation is not instant, then some ASR hypotheses may be outdated during the translation and can be skipped. We use a program called MT Wrapper for connecting the output of self-updating ASR with non-instant NMT systems.

MT Wrapper has two threads. The receiving thread segments the input for our MTs into individual sentences, saves the input into a buffer, and continuously updates it. The translating thread is a loop that retrieves the new content from the buffer. If a segment has been translated earlier in the current process, it is outputted immediately. Otherwise, the new segments are sent in one batch to the NMT system, stored to a cache and outputted.

For reproducibility, the translation cache is empty at the beginning of a process, but in theory it could be populated by a translation memory. The cache significantly reduces the latency because the punctuator often oscillates between two variants of casing or punctuation marks within a short time.

MT Wrapper has a parameter to control the stability and latency. It can mask the last k words of incomplete sentences from the ASR output, as in Ma et al. (2019) and Arivazhagan et al. (2019), considering only the currently completed sentences, or only the "stable" sentences, which are beyond the ASR and punctuator processing window and never change. We do not tune these parameters in the validation. We do not mask any words or segments in our primary submission, but we submit multiple non-primary systems differing in these parameters.

5.4 Quality Validation

For comparing the MT candidates for SLT, we processed the validation set by three online ASR systems, translated them by the candidates, aligned them with reference by mwerSegmenter (Matusov et al., 2005) and evaluated the BLEU score (Post, 2018; Papineni et al., 2002) of the individual documents. However, we were aware that the size of the validation set is extremely limited (see Table 2) and that the automatic metrics as the BLEU score estimate the human judgment of the MT quality reliably only if there is a sufficient number of sentences or references. It is not the case of this

validation set.

Therefore, we examined them by a simple comparison with source and reference. We realized that the high BLEU score in the Autocentrum document is induced by the fact that one of the translated sentences matches exactly matches a reference because it is a single word "thanks". This sentence increases the average score of the whole document, although the rest is unusable due to mistranslated words. The ASR quality of the two Antrecorp documents is very low, and the documents are short. Therefore we decided to omit them in comparison of the MT candidates.

We examined the differences between the candidate translations on the Auditing document, and we have not seen significant differences, because this document is very short. The AMIa document is longer, but it contains long pauses and many isolated single-word sentences, which are challenging for ASR. The part with a coherent speech is very short.

Finally, we selected the MT candidate, which showed the highest average BLEU score on the three KIT online ASR systems both on Auditing and AMIa document because we believe that averaging the three ASR sources shows robustness against ASR imperfections. See Table 5 and Table 6 for the BLEU scores on Czech and German. The selected candidates are IWSLT19 for Czech and OPUS-B for German. However, we also submit all other candidates as non-primary systems to test them on a significantly larger test set. We use these candidates both for online and offline SLT.

5.5 Translation Time

We measured the average time, in which the MT systems process a batch of segments of the validation set (Table 7). If the ASR updates are distributed uniformly in time, than the average batch translation time is also the expected delay of machine translation. The shortest delay is almost zero; in cases when the translation is cached or for very short segments. The longest delay happens when an ASR update arrives while the machine is busy with processing the previous batch. The delay is time for translating two subsequent batches, waiting and translating.

We suppose that the translation time of our primary candidates is sufficient for real-time translation, as we verified in on online SLT test sessions.

We observe differences between the MT systems.

MT	document	gold	KIT-hybrid	KIT-h-large-lm1	KIT-h-large-lm2	avg KIT
OPUS-B	Teddy	42.8463	2.418	2.697	1.360	2.158
IWSLT19	Teddy	51.397	1.379	2.451	1.679	1.836
WMT19 Marian	Teddy	49.328	1.831	1.271	1.649	1.584
WMT18 T2T	Teddy	54.778	1.881	1.197	1.051	1.376
OPUS-A	Teddy	25.197	1.394	1.117	1.070	1.194
T2T-multi	Teddy	36.759	1.775	0.876	0.561	1.071
WMT18 T2T	Autocentrum	42.520	12.134	13.220	14.249	13.201
WMT19 Marian	Autocentrum	39.885	10.899	10.695	12.475	11.356
OPUS-B	Autocentrum	29.690	12.050	10.873	9.818	10.914
IWSLT19	Autocentrum	37.217	9.901	8.996	8.900	9.266
OPUS-A	Autocentrum	30.552	9.201	9.277	8.483	8.987
T2T-multi	Autocentrum	20.011	6.221	2.701	3.812	4.245
IWSLT19	AMIa	**22.878**	5.377	2.531	3.480	**3.796**
WMT18 T2T	AMIa	21.091	5.487	2.286	3.411	3.728
WMT19 Marian	AMIa	22.036	4.646	2.780	3.739	3.722
OPUS-B	AMIa	19.224	4.382	3.424	2.672	3.493
OPUS-A	AMIa	15.432	3.131	2.431	2.500	2.687
T2T-multi	AMIa	13.340	2.546	2.061	1.847	2.151
IWSLT19	Auditing	**9.231**	1.096	3.861	2.656	**2.538**
OPUS-B	Auditing	6.449	1.282	3.607	2.274	2.388
OPUS-A	Auditing	8.032	1.930	4.079	0.900	2.303
WMT19 Marian	Auditing	8.537	1.087	3.571	1.417	2.025
WMT18 T2T	Auditing	9.033	1.201	2.935	1.576	1.904
T2T-multi	Auditing	3.923	1.039	1.318	1.110	1.156

Table 5: Validation BLEU scores in percents (range 0-100) for SLT into Czech from ASR sources. The column "gold" is translation from the gold transript. It shows the differences between MT systems, but was not used in validation.

The size and the model type of WMT19 Marian and WMT18 T2T are the same (see Popel et al., 2019), but they differ in implementation.

WMT19 Marian is slightly faster than IWSLT19 model because the latter is an ensemble of two models. OPUS-B is slower than OPUS-A because the former is bigger. Both are slower than WMT19 Marian due to multi-targeting and different preprocessing. WMT19 Marian uses embedded SentencePiece (Kudo and Richardson, 2018), while the multi-target models use an external Python process for BPE (Sennrich et al., 2016). The timing may be affected also by different hardware.

At the validation time, T2T-multi and T2T-multi-big used suboptimal setup.

6 Conclusion

We presented ELITR submission for non-native SLT at IWSLT 2020. We observe a significant qualitative difference between the end-to-end offline ASR methods and hybrid online methods. The component that constrains the offline SLT from real-time processing is the ASR, not the MT.

We selected the best candidates from a pool of pre-existing and newly developed components, and submitted our primary submissions, although the size of the development set limits us from a reliable validation. Therefore, we submitted all our unselected candidates for contrastive evaluation on the test set. For the results, we refer to Ansari et al. (2020).

Acknowledgments

The research was partially supported by the grants 19-26934X (NEUREM3) of the Czech Science Foundation, H2020-ICT-2018-2-825460 (ELITR) of the EU, 398120 of the Grant Agency of Charles University, and by SVV project number 260 575.

References

Ebrahim Ansari, Amittai Axelroad, Nguyen Bach, Ondrej Bojar, Roldano Cattoni, Fahim Dalvi, Nadir Durrani, Marcello Federico, Christian Federmann, Jiatao Gu, Fei Huang, Kevin Knight, Xutai Ma, Ajay Nagesh, Matteo Negri, Jan Niehues, Juan Pino, Elizabeth Salesky, Xing Shi, Sebastian Stüker, Marco Turchi, and Changhan Wang. 2020. Findings of the IWSLT 2020 Evaluation Campaign. In *Proceedings of the 17th International Conference on Spoken Language Translation (IWSLT 2020)*, Seattle, USA.

Naveen Arivazhagan, Colin Cherry, Isabelle Te, Wolfgang Macherey, Pallavi Baljekar, and George Foster. 2019. Re-translation strategies for long form, simultaneous, spoken language translation. *ArXiv*, abs/1912.03393.

MT	document	gold	KIT-hybrid	KIT-h-large-lm1	KIT-h-large-lm2	avg KIT
de-T2T	Teddy	45.578	2.847	3.181	1.411	2.480
OPUS-A	Teddy	29.868	1.873	1.664	1.139	1.559
de-LSTM	Teddy	3.133	2.368	2.089	1.254	1.904
OPUS-B	Teddy	41.547	2.352	1.878	1.454	1.895
T2T-multi	Teddy	31.939	1.792	3.497	1.661	2.317
de-T2T	Autocentrum	36.564	9.031	6.229	3.167	6.142
OPUS-A	Autocentrum	26.647	8.898	13.004	2.324	8.075
de-LSTM	Autocentrum	19.573	10.395	13.026	2.322	8.581
OPUS-B	Autocentrum	28.841	10.153	12.134	9.060	10.449
T2T-multi	Autocentrum	22.631	8.327	8.708	6.651	7.895
de-T2T	AMIa	34.958	8.048	5.654	7.467	7.056
OPUS-A	AMIa	30.203	7.653	5.705	5.899	6.419
de-LSTM	AMIa	31.762	7.635	6.642	1.843	5.373
OPUS-B	AMIa	38.315	8.960	7.613	6.837	7.803
T2T-multi	AMIa	28.279	6.202	3.382	3.869	4.484
de-T2T	Auditing	38.973	11.589	17.377	18.841	15.936
OPUS-A	Auditing	38.866	10.355	19.414	18.540	16.103
de-LSTM	Auditing	21.780	10.590	12.633	11.098	11.440
OPUS-B	Auditing	38.173	10.523	18.237	17.644	15.468
T2T-multi	Auditing	22.442	7.896	8.664	11.269	9.276

Table 6: Validation BLEU scores in percents (range 0-100) for MT translations into German from ASR outputs and from the gold transcript.

MT	avg ± std dev
T2T-multi	2876.52 ±1804.63
T2T-multi-big	5531.30 ±3256.81
IWSLT19	275.51 ± 119.44
WMT19 Marian	184.08 ± 89.17
WMT18 T2T	421.11 ± 201.64
OPUS-B	287.52 ± 141.28
OPUS-A	263.31 ± 124.75

Table 7: Average and standard deviation time for translating one batch in validation set, in milliseconds. Bold are the candidate systems for online SLT.

Rachel Bawden, Nikolay Bogoychev, Ulrich Germann, Roman Grundkiewicz, Faheem Kirefu, Antonio Valerio Miceli Barone, and Alexandra Birch. 2019. The university of edinburgh's submissions to the wmt19 news translation task. In *WMT*.

Ondřej Bojar, Ondřej Dušek, Tom Kocmi, Jindřich Libovický, Michal Novák, Martin Popel, Roman Sudarikov, and Dušan Variš. 2016. CzEng 1.6: Enlarged Czech-English Parallel Corpus with Processing Tools Dockered. In *TSD*.

Eunah Cho, Jan Niehues, Kevin Kilgour, and Alex Waibel. 2015. Punctuation insertion for real-time spoken language translation. In *IWSLT*.

Eunah Cho, Jan Niehues, and Alex Waibel. 2012. Segmentation and punctuation prediction in speech language translation using a monolingual translation system. In *IWSLT*.

Eunah Cho, Jan Niehues, and Alex Waibel. 2017. Nmt-based segmentation and punctuation insertion for real-time spoken language translation. In *INTERSPEECH*.

Florian Dessloch, Thanh-Le Ha, Markus Müller, Jan Niehues, Thai-Son Nguyen, Ngoc-Quan Pham, Elizabeth Salesky, Matthias Sperber, Sebastian Stüker, Thomas Zenkel, and Alexander Waibel. 2018. KIT lecture translator: Multilingual speech translation with one-shot learning. In *COLING: System Demonstrations*.

Dario Franceschini et al. 2020. Removing european language barriers with innovative machine translation technology. In *LREC IWLTP*. In print.

Melvin Johnson, Mike Schuster, Quoc V. Le, Maxim Krikun, Yonghui Wu, Zhifeng Chen, Nikhil Thorat, Fernanda Viégas, Martin Wattenberg, Greg Corrado, Macduff Hughes, and Jeffrey Dean. 2017. Google's multilingual neural machine translation system: Enabling zero-shot translation. *Transactions of the Association for Computational Linguistics*, 5:339–351.

Marcin Junczys-Dowmunt et al. 2018. Marian: Fast neural machine translation in C++. In *ACL System Demonstrations*.

Ondrej Klejch, Joachim Fainberg, Peter Bell, and Steve Renals. 2019. Lattice-based unsupervised test-time adaptation of neural networkacoustic models. *CoRR*, abs/1906.11521.

Philipp Koehn et al. 2007. Moses: Open Source Toolkit for Statistical Machine Translation. In *ACL Interactive Poster and Demonstration Sessions*.

Taku Kudo and John Richardson. 2018. SentencePiece: A simple and language independent subword tokenizer and detokenizer for neural text processing. In *EMNLP: System Demonstrations*.

Lucian Vlad Lita, Abe Ittycheriah, Salim Roukos, and Nanda Kambhatla. 2003. TRuEcasIng. In *ACL*.

Mingbo Ma, Liang Huang, Hao Xiong, Renjie Zheng, Kaibo Liu, Baigong Zheng, Chuanqiang Zhang, Zhongjun He, Hairong Liu, Xing Li, Hua Wu, and Haifeng Wang. 2019. STACL: Simultaneous translation with implicit anticipation and controllable latency using prefix-to-prefix framework. In *ACL*.

Evgeny Matusov, Gregor Leusch, Oliver Bender, and Hermann Ney. 2005. Evaluating machine translation output with automatic sentence segmentation. In *International Workshop on Spoken Language Translation*, pages 148–154, Pittsburgh, PA, USA.

Iain Mccowan, J Carletta, Wessel Kraaij, Simone Ashby, S Bourban, M Flynn, M Guillemot, Thomas Hain, J Kadlec, Vasilis Karaiskos, M Kronenthal, Guillaume Lathoud, Mike Lincoln, Agnes Lisowska Masson, Wilfried Post, Dennis Reidsma, and P Wellner. 2005. The ami meeting corpus. *Int'l. Conf. on Methods and Techniques in Behavioral Research*.

Markus Müller, Thai Son Nguyen, Jan Niehues, Eunah Cho, Bastian Krüger, Thanh-Le Ha, Kevin Kilgour, Matthias Sperber, Mohammed Mediani, Sebastian Stüker, et al. 2016. Lecture translator-speech translation framework for simultaneous lecture translation. In *NAACL: Demonstrations*.

Thai-Son Nguyen, Markus Müller, Sebastian Sperber, Thomas Zenkel, Sebastian Stüker, and Alex Waibel. 2017. The 2017 KIT IWSLT Speech-to-Text Systems for English and German. In *IWSLT*.

Thai Son Nguyen, Jan Niehues, Eunah Cho, Thanh-Le Ha, Kevin Kilgour, Markus Muller, Matthias Sperber, Sebastian Stueker, and Alex Waibel. 2020. Low latency asr for simultaneous speech translation.

Thai-Son Nguyen, Sebastian Stueker, Jan Niehues, and Alex Waibel. 2019. Improving sequence-to-sequence speech recognition training with on-the-fly data augmentation. *arXiv preprint arXiv:1910.13296*.

Jan Niehues, Thai Son Nguyen, Eunah Cho, Thanh-Le Ha, Kevin Kilgour, Markus Müller, Matthias Sperber, Sebastian Stüker, and Alex Waibel. 2016. Dynamic transcription for low-latency speech translation. In *Interspeech*.

Jan Niehues, Ngoc-Quan Pham, Thanh-Le Ha, Matthias Sperber, and Alex Waibel. 2018. Low-latency neural speech translation. In *Proc. Interspeech 2018*.

Kishore Papineni, Salim Roukos, Todd Ward, and Wei-Jing Zhu. 2002. Bleu: a method for automatic evaluation of machine translation. In *ACL*.

Vijayaditya Peddinti, Daniel Povey, and Sanjeev Khudanpur. 2015. A time delay neural network architecture for efficient modeling of long temporal contexts. In *INTERSPEECH*.

Ngoc-Quan Pham, Thai-Son Nguyen, Thanh-Le Ha, Juan Hussain, Felix Schneider, Jan Niehues, Sebastian Stüker, and Alexander Waibel. 2019. The iwslt 2019 kit speech translation system. In *Proceedings of the 16th International Workshop on Spoken Language Translation (IWSLT 2019)*.

Ngoc-Quan Pham, Matthias Sperber, Elizabeth Salesky, Thanh-Le Ha, Jan Niehues, and Alexander Waibel. 2017. Kit's multilingual neural machine translation systems for iwslt 2017. In *The International Workshop on Spoken Language Translation (IWSLT)*, Tokyo, Japan.

Martin Popel. 2018. CUNI transformer neural MT system for WMT18. In *Proceedings of the Third Conference on Machine Translation: Shared Task Papers*, pages 482–487, Belgium, Brussels. Association for Computational Linguistics.

Martin Popel and Ondrej Bojar. 2018. Training Tips for the Transformer Model. *PBML*, 110.

Martin Popel, Dominik Macháček, Michal Auersperger, Ondřej Bojar, and Pavel Pecina. 2019. English-czech systems in wmt19: Document-level transformer. In *WMT*.

Matt Post. 2018. A call for clarity in reporting BLEU scores. In *WMT*.

Daniel Povey et al. 2011. The kaldi speech recognition toolkit. In *IEEE Workshop on Automatic Speech Recognition and Understanding*.

Anthony Rousseau, Paul Deléglise, and Yannick Esteve. 2012. Ted-lium: an automatic speech recognition dedicated corpus. In *LREC*.

Rico Sennrich, Barry Haddow, and Alexandra Birch. 2016. Neural machine translation of rare words with subword units. *ArXiv*, abs/1508.07909.

Andreas Stolcke. 2002. Srilm-an extensible language modeling toolkit. In *ICLSP*.

Jörg Tiedemann. 2012. Parallel data, tools and interfaces in OPUS. In *LREC*.

Ottokar Tilk and Tanel Alumäe. 2016. Bidirectional recurrent neural network with attention mechanism for punctuation restoration.

Ashish Vaswani, Samy Bengio, Eugene Brevdo, Francois Chollet, Aidan N. Gomez, Stephan Gouws, Llion Jones, Łukasz Kaiser, Nal Kalchbrenner, Niki Parmar, Ryan Sepassi, Noam Shazeer, and Jakob Uszkoreit. 2018. Tensor2tensor for neural machine translation. *CoRR*, abs/1803.07416.

Joanna Wetesko, Marcin Chochowski, Pawel Przybysz, Philip Williams, Roman Grundkiewicz, Rico Sennrich, Barry Haddow, Antonio Valerio Miceli Barone, and Alexandra Birch. 2019. Samsung and University of Edinburgh's System for the IWSLT 2019. In *IWSLT*.

Is 42 the Answer to Everything
in Subtitling-oriented Speech Translation?

Alina Karakanta
Fondazione Bruno Kessler
University of Trento
Trento - Italy
akarakanta@fbk.eu

Matteo Negri
Fondazione Bruno Kessler
Trento - Italy
negri@fbk.eu

Marco Turchi
Fondazione Bruno Kessler
Trento - Italy
turchi@fbk.eu

Abstract

Subtitling is becoming increasingly important for disseminating information, given the enormous amounts of audiovisual content becoming available daily. Although Neural Machine Translation (NMT) can speed up the process of translating audiovisual content, large manual effort is still required for transcribing the source language, and for spotting and segmenting the text into proper subtitles. Creating proper subtitles in terms of timing and segmentation highly depends on information present in the audio (utterance duration, natural pauses). In this work, we explore two methods for applying Speech Translation (ST) to subtitling: a) a direct end-to-end and b) a classical cascade approach. We discuss the benefit of having access to the source language speech for improving the conformity of the generated subtitles to the spatial and temporal subtitling constraints and show that length[1] is not the answer to everything in the case of subtitling-oriented ST.

1   Introduction

Vast amounts of audiovisual content are becoming available every minute. From films and TV series, informative and marketing video material, to home-made videos, audiovisual content is reaching viewers with various needs and expectations, speaking different languages, all across the globe. This unprecedented access to information through audiovisual content is made possible mainly thanks to subtitling. Subtitles, despite being the fastest and most wide-spread way of translating audiovisual

content, still rely heavily on human effort. In a typical multilingual subtitling workflow, a subtitler first creates a subtitle template (Georgakopoulou, 2019) by transcribing the source language audio, timing and adapting the text to create proper subtitles in the source language. These source language subtitles (also called captions) are already compressed and segmented to respect the subtitling constraints of length, reading speed and proper segmentation (Cintas and Remael, 2007; Karakanta et al., 2019). In this way, the work of an NMT system is already simplified, since it only needs to translate matching the length of the source text (Matusov et al., 2019; Lakew et al., 2019). However, the essence of a good subtitle goes beyond matching a predetermined length (as, for instance, 42 characters per line in the case of TED talks). Apart from this spatial dimension, subtitling relies heavily on the temporal dimension, which is incorporated in the subtitle templates in the form of timestamps. However, templates are expensive and slow to create and as so, not a viable solution for short turn-around times and individual content creators. Therefore, skipping the template creation process would greatly extend the application of NMT in the subtitling process, leading to massive reductions in costs and time and making multilingual subtitling more accessible to all types of content creators.

In this work, we propose Speech Translation as an alternative to the template creation process. We experiment with cascade systems, i.e. pipelined ASR+MT architectures, and direct, end-to-end ST systems. While the MT system in the pipelined approach receives a raw textual transcription as input, the direct speech translation receives temporal and prosodic information from the source language input signal. Given that several decisions about the form of subtitles depend on the audio (e.g. subtitle segmentation at natural pauses, length based on utterance duration), in this work we ask the question

---

[1]Speaking of subtitles and their optimum length of 42 characters per line, we could not help but alluding to the book and series *The Hitchhiker's Guide to the Galaxy* by Douglas Adams, where the number 42 is the "Answer to the Ultimate Question of Life, the Universe, and Everything", calculated by a massive supercomputer named Deep Thought for over 7.5 million years.

Proceedings of the 17th International Conference on Spoken Language Translation (IWSLT), pages 209–219
July 9-10, 2020. ©2020 Association for Computational Linguistics
https://doi.org/10.18653/v1/P17

whether end-to-end ST systems can take advantage of this information to better model the subtitling constraints and subtitle segmentation. In other words, we investigate whether, in contrast to text translation (where one mainly focuses on returning subtitles of a maximum length of 42 characters), in speech translation additional information can help to develop a more advanced approach that goes beyond merely matching the source text length.

Our contributions can be summarised as follows:

- We present the first end-to-end solution for subtitling, completely eliminating the need of a source language transcription and any extra segmenting component;

- We conduct a thorough analysis of cascade vs. end-to-end systems both in terms of translation quality and conformity to the subtitling contraints, showing that end-to-end systems have large potential for subtitling.

2 Background

2.1 Subtitling

Subtitling involves translating the audio (speech) in a video into text in another language (in the case of interlingual subtitling). Subtitling is therefore a multi-modal phenomenon, incorporating visual images, gestures,[2] sound and language (Taylor, 2016), but also an intersemiotic process, in the sense that it involves a change of channel, medium and code from speech to writing, from spoken verbal language to written verbal language (Assis, 2001).

The temporal dimension of subtitles and the relation between audio and text has been stressed also in professional subtitling guidelines. In their subtitling guidelines, Carroll and Ivarsson (1998) mention that: *"The in and out times of subtitles must follow the speech rhythm of the dialogue, taking cuts and sound bridges into consideration"* and that: *"There must be a close correlation between film dialogue and subtitle content; source language and target language should be synchronized as far as possible"*. Therefore, a subtitler's decisions are guided not only by attempting to transfer the source language content, but also by achieving a high correlation between the source language speech and target language text.

In addition, subtitles have specific properties in the sense that they have to conform to spatial and temporal constraints in order to ensure comprehension and a pleasant user experience. For example, due to limited space on screen, a subtitle cannot be longer than a fixed number of characters per line, ranging between 35-43 (Cintas and Remael, 2007). When it comes to the temporal constraints, a comfortable reading speed (about 21 chars/second) is key to a positive user experience. It should be ensured that viewers have enough time to read and assimilate the content, while at the same time their attention is not monopolised by the subtitles. Lastly, the segmentation of subtitles should be performed in a way that facilitates comprehension, by keeping linguistic units (e.g. phrases) in the same line. For the reasons mentioned above, subtitlers should ideally always have access to the source video when translating. However, working directly from the video can have several drawbacks. The subtitler needs to make sense of what is said on the screen, deal with regional accents, noise, unintelligible speech etc.

One way to automatise this labour-intensive process, especially in settings where several target languages are involved, is creating a subtitle template of the source language (Georgakopoulou, 2019). A subtitle template is an enriched transcript of the source language speech where the text is already compressed, timed and segmented into proper subtitles. This template can serve as a basis for translation into other languages, whether the translation is performed by a human or an MT system.

In the case of templates, optimal duration, length and proper segmentation are ensured, since the change of code between oral and written in the source language has already been curated by an expert. Due to the high costs and time required, creating a subtitle template is not a feasible solution both for small content creators and in the case of high volumes and fast turn-around times.

In the absence of a subtitle template, an automatic transcription of the source language audio could seem an efficient alternative. However, Automatic Speech Recognition (ASR) systems produce word-for-word transcriptions of the source speech, not adapted to the subtitling constraints, and where all information coming from the speech is discarded. This purely textual transcription is then translated by the MT system. Therefore, it is highly probable that a higher post-editing effort is

---

[2]While we recognise the importance of the visual dimension in the process of subtitling, incorporating visual cues in the NMT system is beyond the scope of this work.

required not only in terms of translation errors, but chiefly for repairing the form of the subtitles.

Direct, end-to-end speech translation receives audio as input. Therefore, the model receives two types of information from the spectrogram: 1) information about the temporal dimension of the speech, e.g. duration, and 2) information related to the frequency, such as pitch, power and other prosodic elements. While intonation and stress are mostly related to semantic properties, speech tempo directly affects the compression rate of subtitles, and pauses often correspond to prosodic chunks which can determine the subtitle segmentation. Given that, it is worth asking the question whether access to this information can lead to better modelling of the subtitling constraints and subtitle segmentation.

2.2 Speech translation

Traditionally, the task of Speech-to-Text Translation has been addressed with cascade systems consisting of two components: an ASR system, which transcribes the speech into text, and an MT system, which translates the transcribed text into the target language (Eck and Hori, 2005). This approach has the benefit that it can take advantage of state-of-the-art technology for both components and leverage the large amount of data available for both tasks. On the other hand, it suffers from error propagation from the ASR to the MT, since transcription errors are impossible to recover because the MT component typically does not have access to the audio. Several works have attempted to make MT robust to ASR errors (Di Gangi et al., 2019b; Sperber et al., 2017) by working on noisy transcripts.

One further drawback of the cascaded approach, particularly relevant for the task of subtitling, is that any transcript, no matter how accurate, is subject to information loss in the semiotic shift from the richer audio representation to the poorer text representation. This limitation has been addressed in the past in speech-to-speech translation cascades chiefly for improving the naturalness of the synthesised speech and for resolving ambiguities. This has been performed through acoustic feature vectors related to different prosodic elements, such as duration and power (Kano et al., 2013), emphasis (Do et al., 2015, 2016) and intonation (Aguero et al., 2006; Anumanchipalli et al., 2012).

By avoiding intermediate textual representations, end-to-end speech translation (Bérard et al., 2016)

can cope with the above limitations. However, its performance and suitability for reliable applications has been impeded by the limited amount of training data available. In spite of this data scarcity problem, it has been recently shown that the gap between the two approaches is closing (Niehues et al., 2018, 2019), especially with specially-tailored architectures (Di Gangi et al., 2019c; Dong et al., 2018) and via effective data augmentation strategies (Jia et al., 2019). Despite an increasing amount of works attempting to improve the performance of ST for general translation, there has been almost no work on comparing the two technologies on specific problems and applications, which is among the focus points of this work.

2.3 Machine Translation for subtitling

Despite the relevance of developing automatic solutions for subtitling both for the industry and academia, there have been very limited attempts to customise MT for subtitling. Previous works based on Statistical MT (SMT) used mostly proprietary data and led to completely opposite outcomes. Volk et al. (2010) developed SMT systems for the Scandinavian TV industry and reported very good results in this practical application. Aziz et al. (2012) reported significant reductions in post-editing effort compared to translating from scratch for DVD subtitles for English-Portuguese. On the other hand, the SUMAT project (Bywood et al., 2013, 2017), involving seven European language pairs, concluded that subtitling poses particular challenges for MT and therefore a lot of work is still required before MT can lead to real improvements in audiovisual translation workflows (Burchardt et al., 2016).

Recently, after the advent of the neural machine translation paradigm, Matusov et al. (2019) presented an NMT system customised to subtitling. The main contribution of the paper is a segmenter module trained on human segmentation decisions, which splits the resulting translation into subtitles. The authors reported reductions in post-editing effort, especially regarding subtitle segmentation. On a different strand of research, Lakew et al. (2019) proposed two methods for controlling the output length in NMT. The first one is based on adding a token, as in Multilingual NMT (Johnson et al., 2017; Ha et al., 2016), which in this setting represents the length ratio between source and target, and the second inserts length information in the positional encoding of the Transformer.

The application of MT (either SMT or NMT) in the works described above is possible only because of the presence of a "perfect" source language transcript, either for the translation itself or for computing the length ratio. To our knowledge today, no work so far has experimented with direct end-to-end ST in the domain of subtitling.

3 Experimental Setup

3.1 Data

For the experiments we use the MuST-Cinema corpus (Karakanta et al., 2020),[3] which contains (*audio*, *transcription*, *translation*) triplets where the breaks between subtitles have been annotated with special symbols. The symbol <eol> corresponds to a line break inside a subtitle block, while the symbol <eob> to a subtitle block break (the next subtitle comes on a different screen), as seen in the following example from the MuST-Cinema test set:

This kind of harassment keeps women <eol>
from accessing the internet – <eob>
essentially, knowledge. <eob>

We experiment with 2 language pairs, English→French and English→German, as languages with different syntax and word order. The training data consist of 229K and 275K sentences (408 and 492 hours) for German and French respectively, while the development sets contain 1088/1079 sentences and the test sets 542/544 sentences.

3.2 MT and ST systems

The **Cascade** system consists of an ASR and an MT component. The ASR component is based on the KALDI toolkit (Povey et al., 2011), featuring a time-delay neural network and lattice-free maximum mutual information discriminative sequence-training (Povey et al., 2016). The audio data for acoustic modelling include the clean portion of LibriSpeech (Panayotov et al., 2015) (∼460h) and a variable subset of the MuST-Cinema training set (∼450h), from which 40 MFCCs per time frame were extracted. A MaxEnt language model (Alumäe and Kurimo, 2010) is estimated from the corresponding transcripts (∼7M words). The MT component is based on the Transformer architecture (big) (Vaswani et al., 2017) with similar settings to the original paper. The system is first

trained on the OPUS data, with 120M sentences for EN→FR and 50M for EN→DE and then fine-tuned on MuST-Cinema. Considering that the ASR output is lower-cased and without punctuation, we lowercase and remove the punctuation from the source side of the parallel data used in pre-training the MT system. To mitigate the error propagation between the ASR and the MT, for fine-tuning, we use a version of MuST-Cinema where the source audio has been transcribed by the tuned ASR.

For the **End-to-End** system, we experiment with two data conditions, one where we only use the MuST-Cinema training data (**E2E-small**) and a second one where we pre-train on a larger amount of data and fine-tune on MuST-Cinema (**E2E**). This will allow us to detect whether there is any trade-off between translation quality and conformity to constraints when increasing the amount of training data that are not representative of the target application (subtitling). The architecture used is S-Transformer, (Di Gangi et al., 2019c), an ST-oriented adaptation of Transformer, which has been shown to achieve high performance on different speech translation benchmarks. We remove the 2D self-attention layers and increase the size of the encoder to 11 layers, while for the decoder we use 4 layers. This choice was motivated by preliminary experiments, where we noted that replacing the 2D self-attention layers with normal self-attention layers and adding more layers in the encoder increased the final score, while removing a few decoder layers did not negatively affect the performance. As distance penalty, we choose the logarithmic distance penalty. We use the encoder of the ASR model to initialise the weights of the ST encoder and achieve faster convergence (Bansal et al., 2019).

Since the E2E-small system, trained only on MuST-Cinema, is disadvantaged in terms of the amount of training data compared to the cascade, we utilise synthetic data to boost the performance of the ST system (E2E). To this aim, we automatically translate into German and into French the English transcriptions of the data available for the IWSLT2020 offline speech translation task[4] (whenever the translation is not available in the respective target language). To this aim, we use an MT Transformer model achieving 43.2 BLEU points on the WMT'14 test set (Ott et al., 2018) for EN→FR.

---

[3]Must-Cinema has been derived from the MuST-C corpus (Di Gangi et al., 2019a), which currently represents the largest multilingual corpus for ST.

[4]http://iwslt.org/doku.php?id=offline_speech_translation

Our EN→DE Transformer model using similar settings achieves 25.3 BLEU points on the WMT'14 test set. The resulting training data (both real and synthetic) amount to 1.5M sentences on the target side. We use a different tag to separate the real from the synthetic data. We further use SpecAugment (Park et al., 2019), a technique for online data augmentation, with augment rate of 0.5. Finally, we fine-tune on MuST-Cinema.

For comparison, we also report MT results when starting from a "subtitle template" (**Template**). In this setting, we use the textual source side of MuST-Cinema, which contains the human transcriptions of the source language audio and its segmentation into subtitles. In this way, the input to the MT system is already split in subtitles using the special symbols, respecting the subtitling constraints and with proper segmentation. This will allow us to have an upper-bound of the performance that NMT can achieve when provided with input already in the form of subtitles. We pre-train large models with the OPUS data used in the cascade but without lowercasing or removing punctuation and then fine-tune them on the full training set of MuST-Cinema. It should be noted that only the MuST-Cinema data contain break symbols. We use the same Transformer architecture as in the cascade system. For all the experiments we use the fairseq toolkit (Gehring et al., 2017). Models are trained until convergence. Byte-Pair Encoding (BPE) (Sennrich et al., 2016) is set to 8K operations for the E2E-small and E2E systems while to 50K joint operations for the Cascade and the Template systems.

3.3 Evaluation

To evaluate translation quality we use BLEU (Papineni et al., 2002) against the MuST-Cinema test set, both with the break symbols and after removing them (BLEU-nob). For BLEU, an incorrect break symbol would account for an extra n-gram error in the score computation, while BLEU-nob allows us to evaluate only the translation quality without taking into account the subtitle segmentation.

For evaluating the conformity to the constraint of length, we calculate the percentage of subtitles with a maximum length of 42 characters per line (CPL), while for reading speed the percentage of sentences with maximum 21 characters per second (CPS). Since the MuST-Cinema data come from TED talks, these values were chosen according to

the TED subtitling guidelines[5].

Finally, for judging the goodness of the segmentation, i.e. the position of the breaks in the translation, we mask all words except for the break symbols and compute Translation Edit Rate (Snover et al., 2006) only for the breaks against the reference translation (TER-br). This will allow us to determine the effort required by a human subtitler to manually correct the segmentation.

4 Results

4.1 Translation quality

The results are shown Table 1. As far as translation quality is concerned, the best performance is reached, as expected, in the Template setting, where the MT system is provided with "perfect" source language transcriptions. On the MuST-Cinema test set, this leads to BLEU scores of 30.62 and 22.08 respectively for French and German. The Cascade setting follows with a BLEU score reduction of 8 points for French and 4 points for German, which can be attributed to error propagation from the ASR component to the MT.

The E2E-small model (trained solely on MuST-Cinema) achieves 18.76 and 11.92 BLEU points for French and German respectively, which is a relatively low performance compared to the rest of the systems. This "low-resource" setting is a didactic experiment aimed at exploring how far the data-hungry neural approach can go with the limited amount of data available in the domain of ST for subtitling (280K and 234K sentences). It should be also noted that MuST-Cinema is the only Speech Translation corpus of the subtitle genre, both respecting the subtitling constraints and containing break symbols. Consequently, the interference of other data may hurt the conformity to the subtitling constraints, despite improving the translation performance. On the other hand, pretraining has evolved in a standard procedure for coping with the data-demanding nature of NMT. Therefore, pre-training also in the case of end-to-end speech translation offers a comparable setting with the template and the cascade experiments. Indeed, after fine-tuning the pre-trained model on MuST-Cinema, E2E reaches 22.22 and 17.28 BLEU points for French and German. The difference in translation quality is not statistically significant between the Cascade and the E2E, with the

[5] https://translations.ted.com/TED_Translator_Resources:_Main_guide

		BLEU↑	BLEU-nob↑	CPL↑	CPS↑	TER-br↓
FR	Template	30.62	28.86	91%	68%	18
	Cascade	22.41†	22.06	93%	72%	22
	E2E-small	18.76	18.03	95%	70%	23
	E2E	22.22†	21.9	95%	70%	20
DE	Template	22.08	21.10	90%	56%	17
	Cascade	17.81†	17.82	90%	56%	21
	E2E-small	11.92	11.38	93%	55%	24
	E2E	17.28†	16.90	92%	56%	20

Table 1: Results for translation quality (BLEU, BLEU-nob), for conformity to the subtitling constraints (CPL, CPS) and for subtitle segmentation (TER-br) for the four systems. Results marked with † are not statistically significant.

Cascade scoring higher with 0.2/0.6 BLEU points for French/German respectively. This shows that when increasing the size of the training data for the E2E the gap between the cascade and the end-to-end approach is closed and that end-to-end approaches may have finally found a steady ground for flourishing in different applications.

4.2 Conformity to the subtitling constraints and subtitle segmentation

When it comes to the conformity to the subtitling constraints, the results show a different picture (see CPS and CPL of Table 1). E2E exceeds all models at achieving proper length of subtitles, with 95% and 93% of the subtitles having length of maximum 42 characters. E2E achieves higher conformity with length even compared to the Template, for which the segmentation is already provided to the system in the form of break symbols, while the cascade is behind by 2%. The same tendency is observed in the TER-br results computed to measure the proper placement of the break symbols. While the Template benefits from the source language segmentation and therefore requires less edits to properly segment the subtitles, the Cascade is disadvantaged in guessing the correct position of the break symbols, as shown by a 22 and 21 TER score. For E2E-small TER-br is higher, possibly due to the low translation quality. However, E2E outperforms the Cascade by 1 TER point in this respect, showing that less effort would be required to segment the sentences into subtitles. This suggests that the E2E system receives information compared to the Cascade, which allows for better guessing the positions of the break symbols in the translation. This is another indication that subtitle segmentation decisions are not solely determined by reaching a maximum length of 42 characters, but a combination of multiple (possibly intersemiotic) factors can offer a better answer to automatic subtitling.

5 Analysis

The higher scores for CPL and TER-br in Section 4 suggest that the E2E system is better at modelling the subtitling constraints of length and proper segmentation. In this section we shed more light into this aspect by analysing factors which might be determining the system's behaviour in relation to the insertion of the break symbols <eol> and <eob>.

One question quickly arising is how the system can determine whether to insert a subtitle break symbol <eob> (which means that the next subtitle will follow on a new screen) or a line break symbol <eol> (which means that the next line of the subtitle will appear on the same screen). Since the maximum number of lines allowed per subtitle block is 2, a simple answer would be to alternate between <eob> and <eol> such that all subtitles would consist of two lines (two-liners). However, anyone having watched a film with subtitles is aware that subtitles can be two-liners or one-liners. Coming back to the example in Section 3.1, depending on the choice of break symbols (except for the last symbol which should always be an <eob>), there are two possible renderings of the subtitle:

```
10
00:00:31,066 --> 00:00:34,390
This kind of harassment keeps women
from accessing the internet --
11
00:00:34,414 --> 00:00:36,191
essentially, knowledge.
```

and

```
10
00:00:31,066 --> 00:00:34,390
This kind of harassment keeps women
11
00:00:34,414 --> 00:00:36,191
from accessing the internet --
essentially, knowledge.
```

Only the first rendering is acceptable because it satisfies the reading speed constraint but also corresponds to the speech rhythm, since the speaker makes a pause after uttering the word "internet". In this case, how can the MT system determine which type of break symbol to insert?

We have mentioned in Section 2.1 that the *in* and *out* times of a subtitle should follow the rhythm of speech. Therefore, we expect that the end of a subtitle block, which in our setting is signalled by the break symbol <eob>, should correspond to the end of a speech act, a pause or a terminal juncture. On the other hand, line breaks inside the same subtitle block, which in our work correspond to the break symbol <eol>, have a different role. While line breaks can still overlap with pauses or signal the change of speaker, their function is to split a long subtitle into two smaller parts in order to fit the screen. The decision of where to insert a line break inside a subtitle block is determined by two factors: achieving a more or less equal length of the upper and the lower subtitle line and inserting the break in a position such that syntactic units are kept together. Consequently, the insertion of <eol> is determined more by the length and the syntactic properties of the subtitle and less by the natural rhythm of the speech.

If the hypothesis above holds, the choice of whether to insert an <eob> or an <eol> symbol is defined by prosodic properties and not solely by reaching the maximum length of 42 characters. As a consequence, it is not a simple alternating procedure.

To test this hypothesis, we compute the duration of the pause coming after each word in the source side of the MuST-Cinema test set. To achieve this, we perform forced alignment of the transcript against the audio and subtract the end time of each word from the start time of the next word:

$$pause_{w1w2} = start\_time_{w2} - end\_time_{w1} \quad (1)$$

Then we separate the pauses in 3 groups: *i)* pauses corresponding to positions where <eob> is present, *ii)* pauses corresponding to positions where <eol> is present and *iii)* pauses after which there is no break symbol (*None*). In Table 2 we report average and standard deviation of the pause duration for each category.

Pauses corresponding to the positions where <eob> symbols are present are more than x10 longer than the pauses in positions without any break symbols (None). Even if we take the most extreme cases (based on standard deviation), any

Pause type	Avg	Stdev
None	0.039	0.022
<eob>	0.551	0.181
<eol>	0.074	0.027

Table 2: Average pause duration and standard deviation (in seconds) for the category without breaks (None), and for the categories with the two types of break symbols <eob> and <eol>.

pause above 0,37 seconds requires the insertion of <eob>. Pauses corresponding to <eol> symbols are on average x2 longer, but there is an overlap between the possible durations of the *None* and the <eol> category. This confirms our hypothesis about the different roles of the two subtitle breaks. Therefore, prosodic information is an important factor which can help the ST system determine the subtitling segmentation according to the speech rhythm. This finding provides strong evidence towards a clear limitation of the cascade setting, where the raw textual transcription from the ASR does not provide any prosodic information to the MT system. The MT system in the cascade setting is disadvantaged by the inability to: *i)* recover from possible ASR errors, and *ii)* make decisions determined by factors other than text.

With this knowledge, we analyse the breaks in the results of the two systems. In order to control for differences in translation, we select all sentences with at least 2 breaks and with the same number of break symbols (regardless of whether <eob> or <eol>) between the reference, the output of the Cascade and of the E2E. The resulting sentences are 137 for French and 158 for German. We calculate the accuracy of the type of break symbols for the two systems. For French the accuracy is 89% for the Cascade and 93% for the E2E. For German the accuracy is 85% for the Cascade and 88% for the E2E. This difference in accuracy suggests that the E2E is aided by the acoustic information and specifically by the pause duration in determining the correct break symbol.

Table 3 presents some examples, evaluated also against the video. In the first example, the decision of which type of break to insert between the two sentences can only be determined by the duration of the pause that comes between them. Indeed, the speaker in the video asks the question and then leaves some time to the audience before giving the answer. The pause between the two sentences is about 2 seconds. In this case, the first sentence

EN	"Who do you report to?" <eob> "It depends".
CS	Wen melden Sie an? <eol> Es hängt davon ab.
E2E	Wen berichten Sie? <eob> Es kommt darauf an.
REF	"An wen schickst du deine Berichte?" <eob> "Das kommt darauf an".

One executive at another company <eob> likes to explain how he used to be <eol> a master of milestone-tracking.
Un cadre d'une autre entreprise aime expliquer <eob> comment il était jadis un maître <eol> du trek capital.
Un dirigeant d'une autre entreprise <eob> aime expliquer comment il était <eol> un maître de traçage en pierre.
Un cadre d'une autre entreprise <eob> aime raconter comme il était passé maître <eol> dans la surveillance des étapes.

But you know how they say <eol> that information is a source of power?
Vous savez comment dire que l'information <eol> est une source de pouvoir.
Saviez-vous comment dire <eol> que l'information est une source de pouvoir ?
Mais vous savez qu'on dit que <eol> l'information est source de pouvoir ?

Table 3: Examples of translations by the cascade (CS) and the end-to-end model (E2E) compared to the source sentence (EN) and the reference (REF). The sentence-final <eob> has been removed.

should be in one subtitle block, then disappear, and the second sentence should come in the next subtitle block in order not to reveal the answer before it was spoken by the speaker. This information is only available to the E2E system.

In the second example, although both systems have chosen the right type of break, there are differences in the actual positions of the breaks. The E2E inserts the first break symbol in the same position as in the source and reference (*entreprise*), while the Cascade inserts it at a later position (*expliquer*), resulting in a subtitle of 46 characters, which is above the 42-character length limit. The Cascade correctly inserts the second break (*maître*), as in the reference. Here, the E2E copies the break position from the source sentence, which is in a different position compared to the reference (after the word *be* instead of the word *master* as in the reference). The E2E is faithful to the segmentation of the source language when it corresponds to the pauses of the speaker. The positions chosen by the Cascade to insert the break symbols are before a conjunction (*comment*) and a preposition (*du*). Contrary to the E2E, the Cascade's decisions are based more on syntactic patterns, learned from the existing human segmentation decisions in the training data.

The third example shows that prosody is important also for other factors related to the translation. The Cascade, not receiving any punctuation, was not able to reproduce the question in the translation, while the intonation might have helped the E2E to render the sentence as a question despite using the wrong tense (*saviez* instead of *savez*).

All in all, these examples confirm our analysis and once again indicate the importance of considering the intersemiotic nature of subtitling when developing MT systems for this task.

6 Conclusion

We have presented the first Speech Translation systems specifically tailored for subtitling. The first system is an ASR-MT cascade, while the second a direct, end-to-end ST system. These systems allow, for the first time, to create satisfactory subtitles both in terms of translation quality and conformity to the subtitling constraints in the absence of a human transcription of the source language speech (template). We have shown that while the two systems have similar translation quality performance, the E2E seems to be modelling the subtitle constraints better. We show that this could be attributed to acoustic features, such as natural pauses, becoming available to the E2E system through the audio input. This leads to a segmentation closer to the speech rhythm, which is key to a pleasant user experience. Our work takes into account the intersemiotic nature of subtitling by avoiding conditioning the translation on the textual source language length, as in previous approaches to NMT for subtitling, arriving to the conclusion that 42 is not the answer to everything in the case of NMT for subtitling. Rather, key elements for good automatic subtitling are prosodic elements such as intonation, speech tempo and natural pauses. We hope that this work will pave the way for developing more comprehensive approaches to NMT for subtitling.

Acknowledgments

This work is part of the "End-to-end Spoken Language Translation in Rich Data Conditions" project,[6] which is financially supported by an Amazon AWS ML Grant.

---

[6] `https://ict.fbk.eu/ units-hlt-mt-e2eslt/`

References

Pablo Daniel Aguero, Jordi Adell, and Antonio Bonafonte. 2006. Prosody generation in the speech-to-speech translation framework. In *Acoustics, Speech and Signal Processing, ICASSP 2006*, volume 1. IEEE International Conference.

Tanel Alumäe and Mikko Kurimo. 2010. Efficient estimation of maximum entropy language models with n-gram features: an SRILM extension. In *INTERSPEECH 2010, 11th Annual Conference of the International Speech Communication Association, Makuhari, Chiba, Japan, September 26-30, 2010*, pages 1820–1823.

G. K. Anumanchipalli, L. C. Oliveira, and A. W. Black. 2012. Intent transfer in speech-to-speech machine translation. In *2012 IEEE Spoken Language Technology Workshop (SLT)*, pages 153–158.

Rosa Alexandra Assis. 2001. Features of oral and written communication in subtitling. *(Multi)Media Translation. Concepts, Practices and Research*, pages 213–221.

Wilker Aziz, Sheila Castilho Monteiro de Sousa, and Lucia Specia. 2012. Cross-lingual sentence compression for subtitles. In *16th Annual Conference of the European Association for Machine Translation, EAMT*, pages 103–110, Trento, Italy.

Sameer Bansal, Herman Kamper, Karen Livescu, Adam Lopez, and Sharon Goldwater. 2019. Pretraining on high-resource speech recognition improves low-resource speech-to-text translation. In *Proceedings of the 2019 Conference of the North American Chapter of the Association for Computational Linguistics: Human Language Technologies, Volume 1 (Long and Short Papers)*, pages 58–68, Minneapolis, Minnesota. Association for Computational Linguistics.

Alexandre Bérard, Olivier Pietquin, Laurent Besacier, and Christophe Servan. 2016. Listen and translate: A proof of concept for end-to-end speech-to-text translation. In *NIPS Workshop on end-to-end learning for speech and audio processing*, Barcelona, Spain.

Aljoscha Burchardt, Arle Lommel, Lindsay Bywood, Kim Harris, and Maja Popović. 2016. Machine translation quality in an audiovisual context. *Target*, 28(2):206–221.

Lindsay Bywood, Panayota Georgakopoulou, and Thierry Etchegoyhen. 2017. Embracing the threat: machine translation as a solution for subtitling. *Perspectives*, 25(3):492–508.

Lindsay Bywood, Martin Volk, Mark Fishel, and Panayota Georgakopoulou. 2013. Parallel subtitle corpora and their applications in machine translation and translatology. *Perspectives*, 21(4):595–610.

Mary Carroll and Jan Ivarsson. 1998. *Code of Good Subtitling Practice*. Simrishamn: TransEdit.

Jorge Diaz Cintas and Aline Remael. 2007. *Audiovisual Translation: Subtitling*. Translation practices explained. Routledge.

Mattia Antonino Di Gangi, Roldano Cattoni, Luisa Bentivogli, Matteo Negri, and Marco Turchi. 2019a. MuST-C: a Multilingual Speech Translation Corpus. In *Proceedings of the 2019 Conference of the North American Chapter of the Association for Computational Linguistics: Human Language Technologies, Volume 1 (Long and Short Papers)*, pages 2012–2017, Minneapolis, Minnesota.

Mattia Antonino Di Gangi, Robert Enyedi, Alessandra Brusadin, and Marcello Federico. 2019b. Robust neural machine translation for clean and noisy speech transcripts. In *16th International Workshop on Spoken Language Translation (IWSLT)*.

Mattia Antonino Di Gangi, Matteo Negri, and Marco Turchi. 2019c. Adapting transformer to end-to-end spoken language translation. In *INTERSPEECH*, pages 1133–1137.

Quoc Truong Do, Sakriani Sakti, Graham Neubig, and Satoshi Nakamura. 2016. Transferring emphasis in speech translation using hard-attentional neural network models. In *17th Annual Conference of the International Speech Communication Association (InterSpeech 2016)*, San Francisco, California, USA.

Quoc Truong Do, Sakriani Sakti, Graham Neubig, Tomoki Toda, and Satoshi Nakamura. 2015. Improving translation of emphasis with pause prediction in speech-to-speech translation systems. In *12th International Workshop on Spoken Language Translation (IWSLT)*, Da Nang, Vietnam.

Linhao Dong, Shuang Xu, and Bo Xu. 2018. Speech-Transformer: A No-Recurrence Sequence-to-Sequence Model for Speech Recognition. In *IEEE International Conference on Acoustics, Speech and Signal Processing (ICASSP)*. IEEE.

Matthias Eck and Chiori Hori. 2005. Overview of the IWSLT 2005 Evaluation Campaign. In *International Workshop on Spoken Language Translation (IWSLT)*.

Jonas Gehring, Michael Auli, David Grangier, and Yann Dauphin. 2017. A convolutional encoder model for neural machine translation. In *Proceedings of the 55th Annual Meeting of the Association for Computational Linguistics (Volume 1: Long Papers)*, pages 123–135, Vancouver, Canada. Association for Computational Linguistics.

Panayota Georgakopoulou. 2019. Template files: The holy grail of subtitling. *Journal of Audiovisual Translation*, 2(2):137–160.

Thanh-Le Ha, Jan Niehues, and Alexander H. Waibel. 2016. Toward Multilingual Neural Machine Translation with Universal Encoder and Decoder. In *International Workshop on Spoken Language Translation (IWSLT*.

Ye Jia, Melvin Johnson, Wolfgang Macherey, Ron J. Weiss, Yuan Cao, Chung-Cheng Chiu, Naveen Ari, Stella Laurenzo, and Yonghui Wu. 2019. Leveraging weakly supervised data to improve end-to-end speech-to-text translation. In *ICASSP*.

Melvin Johnson, Mike Schuster, Quoc V. Le, Maxim Krikun, Yonghui Wu, Zhifeng Chen, Nikhil Thorat, Fernanda Viégas, Martin Wattenberg, Greg Corrado, Macduff Hughes, and Jeffrey Dean. 2017. Google's multilingual neural machine translation system: Enabling zero-shot translation. *Transactions of the Association for Computational Linguistics*, 5:339–351.

Takatomo Kano, Shinnosuke Takamichi, Sakriani Sakti, Graham Neubig, Tomoki Toda, and Satoshi Nakamura. 2013. Generalizing continuous-space translation of paralinguistic information. In *14th Annual Conference of the International Speech Communication Association (InterSpeech 2013)*, Lyon, France.

Alina Karakanta, Matteo Negri, and Marco Turchi. 2019. Are Subtitling Corpora really Subtitle-like? In *Sixth Italian Conference on Computational Linguistics, CLiC-It*.

Alina Karakanta, Matteo Negri, and Marco Turchi. 2020. MuST-Cinema: a Speech-to-Subtitles Corpus. In *Proceedings of the 12th International Conference on Language Resources and Evaluation (LREC 2020)*, Marseille, France.

Surafel Melaku Lakew, Mattia Di Gangi, and Marcello Federico. 2019. Controlling the Output Length of Neural Machine Translation. In *Proceedings of the 16th International Workshop on Spoken Language Translation, (IWSLT)*.

Evgeny Matusov, Patrick Wilken, and Yota Georgakopoulou. 2019. Customizing neural machine translation for subtitling. In *Proceedings of the Fourth Conference on Machine Translation (Volume 1: Research Papers)*, pages 82–93, Florence, Italy. Association for Computational Linguistics.

Jan Niehues, Roldano Cattoni, Sebastian Stüker, Matteo Negri, Marcho Turchi, and Marcello Federico. 2018. The IWSLT 2018 Evaluation Campaign. In *Proceedings of the 15th International Workshop on Spoken Language Translation, (IWSLT)*, Bruges, Belgium.

Jan Niehues, Roldano Cattoni, Sebastian Stüker, Matteo Negri, Marcho Turchi, Elizabeth Salesky, Ramon Sanabria, Loic Barrault, Lucia Specia, and Marcello Federico. 2019. The IWSLT 2019 Evaluation Campaign. In *Proceedings of the 16th International Workshop on Spoken Language Translation, (IWSLT)*.

Myle Ott, Sergey Edunov, David Grangier, and Michael Auli. 2018. Scaling neural machine translation. In *Proceedings of the Third Conference on Machine Translation: Research Papers*, pages 1–9,

Belgium, Brussels. Association for Computational Linguistics.

Vassil Panayotov, Guoguo Chen, Daniel Povey, and Sanjeev Khudanpur. 2015. Librispeech: an ASR corpus based on public domain audio books. In *2015 IEEE International Conference on Acoustics, Speech and Signal Processing (ICASSP)*, pages 5206–5210. IEEE.

Kishore Papineni, Salim Roukos, Todd Ward, and Wei-Jing Zhu. 2002. Bleu: a method for automatic evaluation of machine translation. In *Proceedings of the 40th Annual Meeting of the Association for Computational Linguistics*, pages 311–318, Philadelphia, Pennsylvania, USA. Association for Computational Linguistics.

Daniel S. Park, William Chan, Yu Zhang, Chung-Cheng Chiu, Barret Zoph, Ekin D. Cubuk, and Quoc V. Le. 2019. SpecAugment: A Simple Data Augmentation Method for Automatic Speech Recognition. *Interspeech 2019*.

Daniel Povey, Arnab Ghoshal, Gilles Boulianne, Lukas Burget, Ondrej Glembek, Nagendra Goel, Mirko Hannemann, Petr Motlicek, Yanmin Qian, Petr Schwarz, et al. 2011. The Kaldi speech recognition toolkit. In *IEEE 2011 workshop on automatic speech recognition and understanding*, CONF. IEEE Signal Processing Society.

Daniel Povey, Vijayaditya Peddinti, Daniel Galvez, Pegah Ghahremani, Vimal Manohar, Xingyu Na, Yiming Wang, and Sanjeev Khudanpur. 2016. Purely Sequence-Trained Neural Networks for ASR Based on Lattice-Free MMI. In *Proc. of Interspeech*, pages 2751–2755.

Rico Sennrich, Barry Haddow, and Alexandra Birch. 2016. Neural machine translation of rare words with subword units. In *Proceedings of the 54th Annual Meeting of the Association for Computational Linguistics (Volume 1: Long Papers)*, pages 1715–1725, Berlin, Germany. Association for Computational Linguistics.

Matthew Snover, Bonnie Dorr, Richard Schwartz, Linnea Micciulla, and John Makhoul. 2006. A study of Translation Edit Rate with targeted human annotation. In *In Proceedings of Association for Machine Translation in the Americas*, pages 223–231.

Matthias Sperber, Jan Niehues, and Alex Waibel. 2017. Toward robust neural machine translation for noisy input sequences. In *International Workshop on Spoken Language Translation (IWSLT)*.

Christopher Taylor. 2016. The multimodal approach in audiovisual translation. *Target*, 2(28).

Ashish Vaswani, Noam Shazeer, Niki Parmar, Jakob Uszkoreit, Llion Jones, Aidan N Gomez, Łukasz Kaiser, and Illia Polosukhin. 2017. Attention is all you need. In *Advances in Neural Information Processing Systems*, pages 6000–6010.

Martin Volk, Rico Sennrich, Christian Hardmeier, and
Frida Tidström. 2010. Machine Translation of TV
Subtitles for Large Scale Production. In *Proceedings of the Second Joint EM+/CNGL Workshop
"Bringing MT to the User: Research on Integrating
MT in the Translation Industry (JEC'10)*, pages 53–
62, Denver, CO.

Re-translation versus Streaming for Simultaneous Translation

Naveen Arivazhagan,[*] Colin Cherry,[*] Wolfgang Macherey and George Foster
Google Research
{navari,colincherry,wmach,fosterg}@google.com

Abstract

There has been great progress in improving streaming machine translation, a simultaneous paradigm where the system appends to a growing hypothesis as more source content becomes available. We study a related problem in which revisions to the hypothesis beyond strictly appending words are permitted. This is suitable for applications such as live captioning an audio feed. In this setting, we compare custom streaming approaches to re-translation, a straightforward strategy where each new source token triggers a distinct translation from scratch. We find re-translation to be as good or better than state-of-the-art streaming systems, even when operating under constraints that allow very few revisions. We attribute much of this success to a previously proposed data-augmentation technique that adds prefix-pairs to the training data, which alongside wait-k inference forms a strong baseline for streaming translation. We also highlight re-translation's ability to wrap arbitrarily powerful MT systems with an experiment showing large improvements from an upgrade to its base model.

1 Introduction

In simultaneous machine translation, the goal is to translate an incoming stream of source words with as low latency as possible. A typical application is speech translation, where we often assume the eventual output modality to also be speech. In a speech-to-speech scenario, target words must be appended to existing output with no possibility for revision. The corresponding translation task, which we refer to as *streaming translation*, has received considerable recent attention, generating custom approaches designed to maximize quality and minimize latency (Cho and Esipova, 2016; Gu et al.,

2017; Dalvi et al., 2018; Ma et al., 2019a). However, for applications where the output modality is text, such as live captioning, the prohibition against revising output is overly stringent.

The ability to revise previous partial translations makes simply re-translating each successive source prefix a viable strategy. Compared to streaming models, re-translation has the advantage of low latency, since it always attempts a translation of the complete source prefix, and high final-translation quality, since it is not restricted to preserving previous output. It has the disadvantages of higher computational cost, and a high revision rate, visible as textual *instability* in an online translation display. When revisions are an option, it is unclear whether one should prefer a specialized streaming model or a re-translation strategy.

In light of this, we make the following contributions: (1) We evaluate a combination of re-translation techniques that have not previously been studied together. (2) We provide the first empirical comparison of re-translation and streaming models, demonstrating that re-translation operating in a very low-revision regime can match or beat the quality-latency trade-offs of streaming models. (3) We test a 0-revision configuration of re-translation, and show that it is surprisingly competitive, due to the effectiveness of data augmentation with prefix pairs.

2 Related Work

Cho and Esipova (2016) propose the first streaming techniques for NMT, using heuristic agents based on model scores, while Gu et al. (2017) extend their work with agents learned using reinforcement learning. Ma et al. (2019a) recently broke new ground by integrating their read-write agent directly into NMT training. Similar to Dalvi et al. (2018), they employ a simple agent that first reads k source to-

---

[*]Equal contributions

Proceedings of the 17th International Conference on Spoken Language Translation (IWSLT), pages 220–227
July 9-10, 2020. ©2020 Association for Computational Linguistics
https://doi.org/10.18653/v1/P17

kens, and then proceeds to alternate between writes and reads until the source sentence has finished. This agent is easily integrated into NMT training, which allows the NMT engine to learn to anticipate occasionally-missing source context. We employ their wait-k training as a baseline, and use their wait-k inference to improve re-translation. Our second and strongest streaming baseline is the MILk approach of Arivazhagan et al. (2019b), who improve upon wait-k training with an attention that can adapt how it will wait based on the current context. Both wait-k training and MILk attention provide hyper-parameters to control their quality-latency trade-offs: k for wait-k, and latency weight for MILk.

Re-translation was originally investigated by Niehues et al. (2016, 2018), and more recently extended by Arivazhagan et al. (2019a), who propose a suitable evaluation framework, and use it to assess inference-time re-translation strategies for speech translation. We adopt their inference-time heuristics to stabilize re-translation, and extend them with prefix training from Niehues et al. (2018). Where they experiment on TED talks, compare only to vanilla re-translation and use proprietary NMT, we follow recent work on streaming by using WMT training and test data, and provide a novel comparison to streaming approaches.

3 Metrics

We adapt the evaluation framework from Arivazhagan et al. (2019a), which includes metrics for latency, stability, and quality. Where they measure latency with a temporal lag, we adopt an established token lag that does not rely on machine speed.

Our evaluation is built around a *prefix translation list* (PTL), which can be generated for any streaming or re-translation system. For each token in the source sentence (after merging subwords), this list stores the tokenized system output. Table 1 shows an example. We use I for the final number of source tokens, and J for the final number of target tokens.

3.1 Quality

Translation quality is measured by calculating BLEU (Papineni et al., 2002) on the final output of each PTL; that is, standard corpus-level BLEU on complete translations. Specifically, we report tokenized, cased BLEU calculated by an internal tool. We make no attempt to directly measure the quality

of intermediate outputs; instead, their quality is captured indirectly through final output quality and stability.

3.2 Latency

Latency is the amount of time the target listener spends waiting for their translation. Most latency metrics are based on a delay vector g, where g_j reports how many source tokens were read before writing the jth target token (Cho and Esipova, 2016). This delay is trivial to determine for streaming systems, but to address the scenario where target content can change, we introduce the notion of *content delay*, which is closely related to the finalization event index used to calculate time delay in Arivazhagan et al. (2019a).

We take the pessimistic view that content in flux is useless; for example, in Table 1, the 4th target token first appears in step 4, but only becomes useful in step 7, when it shifts from *be* to *slow*. Therefore, we calculate delay with respect to when a token *finalizes*. Let $o_{i,j}$ be the jth token of the ith output in a PTL; $1 \leq i \leq I$ and $1 \leq j \leq J$. For each position j in the final output, we define g_j as:

$$g_j = \min_i \text{ s.t. } o_{i',j'} = o_{I,j'} \ \forall i' \geq i \text{ and } \forall j' \leq j$$

that is, the number of source tokens read before the prefix ending in j took on its final value. The *Content Delay* row in Table 1 shows delays for our running example. Note that content delay is identical to standard delay for streaming systems, which always have stable prefixes.

With this refined g, we can make several latency metrics content-aware, including average proportion (Cho and Esipova, 2016), consecutive wait (Gu et al., 2017), average lagging (Ma et al., 2019a), and differentiable average lagging (Arivazhagan et al., 2019b). We opt for differentiable average lagging (DAL) because of its interpretability and because it sidesteps some problems with average lagging (Cherry and Foster, 2019). It can be thought of as the average number of source tokens a system lags behind a perfectly simultaneous translator:

$$\text{DAL} = \frac{1}{J} \sum_{j=1}^{J} \left[g'_j - \frac{j-1}{\gamma} \right]$$

where $\gamma = J/I$ accounts for the source and target having different lengths, and g' adjusts g to incorporate a minimal time cost of $\frac{1}{\gamma}$ for each token:

$$g'_j = \begin{cases} g_j & j = 1 \\ \max \left[g_j, g'_{j-1} + \frac{1}{\gamma} \right] & j > 1 \end{cases}$$

Source	Output								Erasure
1: Neue	New								-
2: Arzneimittel	New	Medicines							0
3: könnten	New	Medicines							0
4: Lungen-	New	drugs	may	be	lung				1
5: und	New	drugs	could	be	lung	and			3
6: Eierstockkrebs	New	drugs	may	be	lung	and	ovarian	cancer	4
7: verlangsamen	New	drugs	may	slow	lung	and	ovarian	cancer	5
Content Delay	1	4	6	7	7	7	7	7	

Table 1: An example prefix translation list for the tokenized German sentence, "Neue Arzneimittel könnten Lungen- und Eierstockkrebs verlangsamen", with reference, "New drugs may slow lung , ovarian cancer".

Note that DAL sums over the final number of target tokens (J), but it is possible for intermediate hypotheses to have more than J tokens. Any such tokens are ignored by DAL.

3.3 Stability

Following Niehues et al. (2016, 2018) and Arivazhagan et al. (2019a), we measure stability with *erasure*, which measures the length of the suffix that is deleted to produce the next revision. Let o_i be the ith output of a PTL. The normalized erasure (NE) for PTL is defined as:

$$\text{NE} = \frac{1}{J} \sum_{i=2}^{I} \big[|o_{i-1}| - |\text{LCP}(o_i, o_{i-1})| \big]$$

where the $|\cdot|$ operator returns the length of a token sequence, and LCP calculates the longest common prefix of two sequences. Table 1 shows pointwise erasures for each output; its NE would be $13/8 = 1.625$, interpretable as the number of intermediate tokens deleted for each final token.

4 Re-translation Methods

To evaluate re-translation, we build up the source sentence one token at a time, translating each resulting source prefix from scratch to construct the PTL for evaluation.

4.1 Prefix Training

Standard models trained on full sentences are unlikely to perform well when applied to prefixes. We alleviate this problem by generating prefix pairs from our parallel training corpus, and subsequently training on a 1:1 mix of full-sentence and prefix pairs (Niehues et al., 2018; Dalvi et al., 2018). Following Niehues et al. (2018), we augment our training data with prefix pairs created by selecting a source prefix length uniformly at random, then selecting a target length either proportionally according to sentence length, or based on self-contained word alignments. For the latter, for each source prefix, we attempt to find a target prefix such that all tokens in the source prefix align only to words in the target prefix and vice versa. In preliminary experiments, we confirmed a finding by Niehues et al. (2018) that word-alignment-based prefix selection is no better than proportional selection, so we report results only for the proportional method.[1] An example of proportional prefix training is given in Table 2. With prefix training, we expect intermediate translations of source prefixes to be shorter, and to look more like partial target prefixes than complete target sentences (Niehues et al., 2018).

4.2 Inference-time Heuristics

To improve stability, Arivazhagan et al. (2019a) propose a combination of biased search and delayed predictions. Biased search encourages the system to respect its previous predictions by modifying search to interpolate between the distribution from the NMT model (with weight $1 - \beta$) and the one-hot distribution formed by the system's translation of the previous prefix (with weight β). We only bias a hypothesis for as long as it strictly follows the previous translation. No bias is applied after the first point of divergence.

To delay predictions until more source context is available, we adopt Ma et al. (2019a)'s wait-k approach at inference time. We implement this by truncating the target to $\max(i - k, 0)$ tokens, where i is the current source prefix length and k is a constant inference-time hyper-parameter. To

---

[1] Word-alignment-based prefix selection may become more important when working on more distant language pairs such as English-Japanese.

Full	Source	Die Führungskräfte der Republikaner rechtfertigen ihre Politik mit der Notwendigkeit , den Wahlbetrug zu bekämpfen [*15 tokens*]
	Target	Republican leaders justified their policy by the need to combat electoral fraud [*12 tokens*]
Prefix	Source	Die Führungskräfte der Republikaner rechtfertigen [*5 tokens*]
	Target	Republican leaders justified their [*4 tokens*]

Table 2: An example of proportional prefix training. Each example in the minibatch has a 50% chance to be truncated, in which case, we truncate its source and target to a randomly-selected fraction of their original lengths, 1/3 in this example. No effort is made to ensure that the two halves of the prefix pair are semantically equivalent.

avoid confusion with Ma et al. (2019a)'s *wait-k training*, we refer to wait-k used for re-translation as *wait-k inference*.[2]

5 Experiments

We use standard WMT14 English-to-French (EnFr; 36.3M sentences) and WMT15 German-to-English (DeEn; 4.5M sentences) data. For EnFr, we use newstest 2012+2013 for development, and newstest 2014 for test. For DeEn, we validate on newstest 2013 and report results on newstest 2015. We use BPE (Sennrich et al., 2016) on the training data to construct a 32K-type vocabulary that is shared between the source and target languages.

5.1 Models

Our streaming and re-translation models are implemented in Lingvo (Shen et al., 2019), sharing architecture and hyper-parameters wherever possible. Our RNMT+ architecture (Chen et al., 2018) consists of a 6 layer LSTM encoder and an 8 layer LSTM decoder with additive attention (Bahdanau et al., 2014). Both encoder and decoder LSTMs have 512 hidden units, apply per-gate layer normalization (Ba et al., 2016), and use residual skip connections after the second layer.

The models are regularized using a dropout of 0.2 and label smoothing of 0.1 (Szegedy et al., 2016). Models are optimized using 32-way data parallelism with Google Cloud's TPUv3, using Adam (Kingma and Ba, 2015) with the learning rate schedule described in Chen et al. (2018) and a batch size of 4,096 sentence-pairs. Checkpoints for the base models are selected based on development perplexity.

Streaming We train several wait-k training and MILk models to obtain a range of quality-latency trade-offs. Five wait-k training models are trained with sub-word level waits of 2, 4, 6, 8, and 10. Five MILk models are trained with latency weights of 0.1, 0.2, 0.3, 0.4, 0.5 and 0.75; weights lower than 0.1 tend to increase lag without improving BLEU. All streaming models use unidirectional encoders and greedy search.

Re-translation We test two NMT architectures with re-translation: a *Base* system with unidirectional encoding and greedy search, designed for fair comparisons to our streaming baselines above; and a more powerful *Bidi+Beam* system using bidirectional encoding and beam search of size 20, designed to test the impact of an improved base model. Training data is augmented through the proportional prefix training method unless stated otherwise (§ 4.1). Beam-search bias β is varied in the range 0.0 to 1.0 in increments of 0.2. When wait-k inference is enabled, k is varied in 1, 2, 4, 6, 8, 10, 15, 20, 30. Note that we do not need to re-train to test different values of β or k.

5.2 Translation with few revisions

Biased search and wait-k inference used together can reduce re-translation's revisions, as measured by normalized erasure (NE in § 3.3), to negligible levels (Arivazhagan et al., 2019a). But how does re-translation compare to competing approaches? To answer this, we compare the quality-latency trade-offs achieved by re-translation in a low-revision regime to those of our streaming baselines.

First, we need a clear definition of low-revision re-translation. By manual inspection on the DeEn development set, we observe that systems with an NE of 0.2 or lower display many different latency-quality trade-offs. But is NE stable across evaluation sets? When we compare development and

---

[2]When wait-k truncation is combined with beam search, its behavior is similar to that of Zheng et al. (2019b): sequences are scored accounting for "future" tokens that will not be shown to the user.

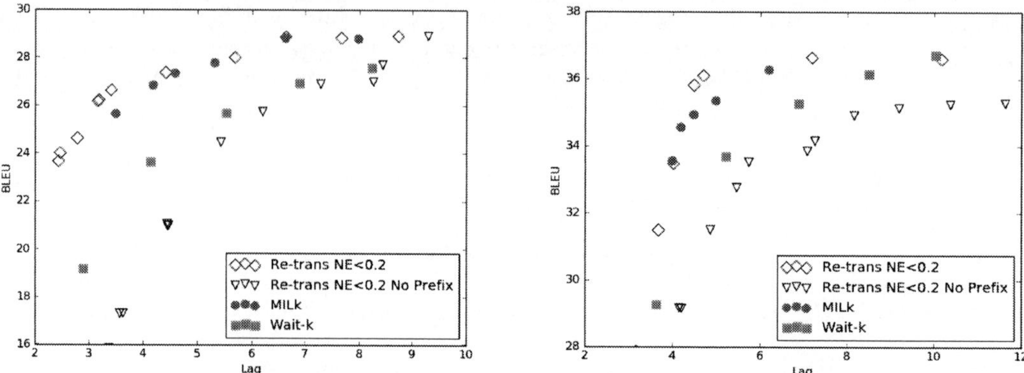

Figure 1: BLEU vs lag (DAL) curves for translation with low erasure for DeEn (left) and EnFr (right) test sets.

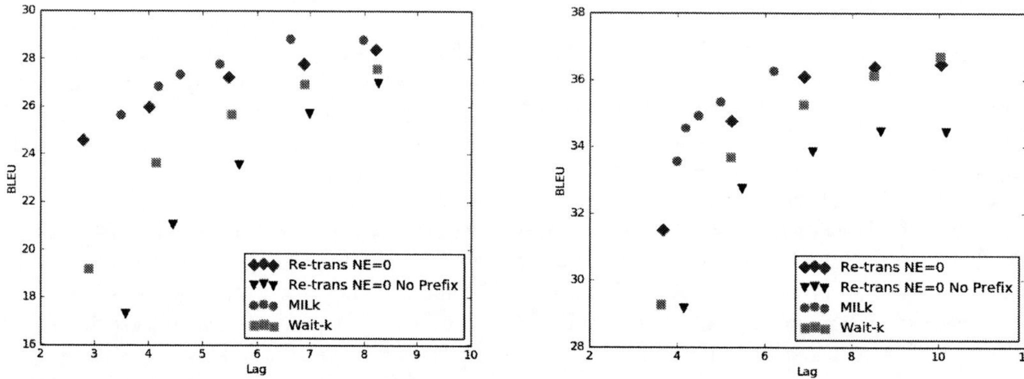

Figure 2: BLEU vs lag (DAL) curves for translation with no erasure for DeEn (left) and EnFr (right) test sets.

test NE for all 50 non-zero-erasure combinations of β and k, the average absolute difference is 0.005 for DeEn, and 0.004 for EnFr, indicating that development NE is very predictive of test NE. This gives us an operational definition of low-revision re-translation as any configuration with a dev NE < 0.2, allowing on average less than 1 token to be revised for every 5 tokens in the system output.

Since we need to vary both β and k for our re-translation systems, we plot BLEU versus DAL curves by finding the Pareto frontier on the dev set, and then projecting to the test set. To ensure a fair comparison to our baselines, we test only the *Base* system here. As an ablation, we include a variant that does not use proportional prefixes, and instead trains only on full sentences.

Figure 1 shows our results. Re-translation is nicely separated from wait-k, and intertwined with the adaptive MILk. In fact, it is noticeably better than MILk at several latency levels for EnFr. Since re-translation is not adaptive, this indicates that

being able to make a small number of revisions is quite advantageous for finding good quality-latency trade-offs. On the other hand, the ablation curve, "Re-trans NE < 0.2 No Prefix" is much worse, indicating that proportional prefix training is very valuable in this setting. We probe its value further in the next experiment.

5.3 Translation with no revisions

Motivated by the strong performance of re-translation with few revisions, we now evaluate it with no revisions, by setting β to 1, which guarantees NE $= 0$. Since β is locked at 1, we can build a curve by varying k from 2 to 10 in increments of 2. In this setting, re-translation becomes equivalent to wait-k inference without wait-k training, which is studied as an ablation to wait-k training by Ma et al. (2019a).[3] However, where they tested

---

[3]Re-translation with beam search and with $\beta = 1$ is similar to wait-k inference with speculative beam search (Zheng et al., 2019b), due to effective look-ahead from implementing wait-k

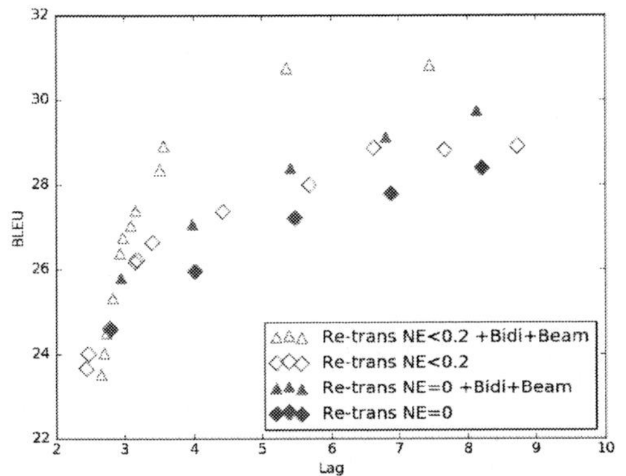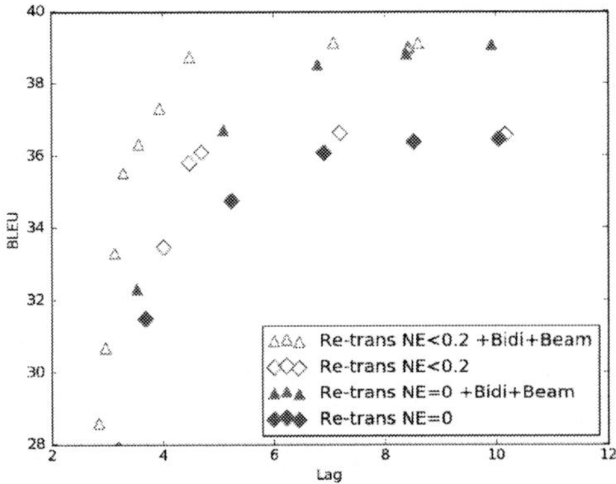

Figure 3: BLEU vs lag (DAL) curves for re-translation with improved models for DeEn (left) and EnFr (right) test sets.

wait-k inference on a system with full-sentence training, we do so for a system with proportional prefix training (§ 4.1). As before, we compare to our streaming baselines, test only our *Base* system, and include a no-prefix ablation corresponding to full-sentence training.

Results are shown in Figure 2. First, re-translation outperforms wait-k training at almost all latency levels. This is startling, because each wait-k training point is trained specifically for its k, while the re-translation points reflect a single training run, reconfigured for different latencies by adjusting k at test time. We suspect that this improvement stems from prefix-training introducing stochasticity to the amount of source context used to predict target words, making the model more robust. Second, without prefix training, re-translation is consistently below wait-k training, confirming earlier experiments by Ma et al. (2019a) on the ineffectiveness of wait-k inference without specialized training, and confirming our earlier observations on the surprising effectiveness of prefix training. Finally, we see that even without revisions, re-translation is very close to MILk, suggesting that this combination of prefix training and wait-k inference is an extremely strong baseline, even for a 0-revision regime.

5.4 Extendability of re-translation

Re-translation's primary strengths lie in its ability to revise and its ability to apply to any MT system. With some effort, streaming systems can be fitted with enhancements such as bidirectional en-

coding (Ma et al., 2019a),[4] beam search (Zheng et al., 2019b) and multihead attention (Ma et al., 2019b). Conversely, re-translation can wrap any auto-regressive NMT system and immediately benefit from its improvements. Furthermore, re-translation's latency-quality trade-off can be manipulated without retraining the base system. It is not the only solution to have these properties; most policies that are not trained jointly with NMT can make the same claims (Cho and Esipova, 2016; Gu et al., 2017; Zheng et al., 2019a). We conduct an experiment to demonstrate the value of this flexibility, by comparing our *Base* system to the upgraded *Bidi+Beam*.[5] We carry out this test with few revisions (NE < 0.2) and without revisions (NE = 0), projecting Pareto curves from dev to test where necessary. The results are shown in Figure 3.

Comparing the few-revision (NE < 0.2) curves, we see large improvements, some more than 2 BLEU points, from using better models. Looking at the no-revision (NE = 0) curves, we see that this configuration also benefits from modeling improvements, but for DeEn, the deltas are noticeably smaller than those of the few-revision curves.

5.5 On computational complexity

Re-translation is conceptually simple and easy to implement, but also incurs an increase in asymptotic time complexity. If the base model can translate a sentence in time $O(x)$, then re-translation

---

with truncation. However, we only evaluate greedy search in this comparison, where their equivalence is exact.

[4] Any streaming model with a bidirectional encoder requires re-encoding for each source prefix, resulting in higher compute and memory costs.

[5] We could just as easily upgrade to a different base architecture, such as the Transformer (Vaswani et al., 2017), which could potentially to lead to further improvements.

takes $O(nx)$ where n is the number of times we request re-translation for that sentence. n is capped at the length of the sentence, as we never revise translations of earlier sentences in the transcript.[6]

For many settings, this increase in complexity can be easily ignored. We are not concerned with the total time to translate a sentence, but instead with the latency between a new source word being uttered and its translation's appearance on the screen. Modern accelerators can translate a complete sentence in the range of 100 milliseconds,[7] meaning that the time required to update the screen by translating an updated source prefix is small enough to be imperceptible. As in all simultaneous systems, the largest source of latency is waiting for new source content to arrive.[8]

6 Conclusion

We have presented the first comparison of re-translation and streaming strategies for simultaneous translation. We have shown re-translation with low levels of erasure ($\text{NE} < 0.2$) to be as good or better than the state of the art in streaming translation. Also, re-translation easily embraces arbitrary improvements to NMT, which we have highlighted with large gains from an upgraded base model.

In our setting, re-translation with no erasure reduces to wait-k inference, which we have shown to be much more effective than previously reported, so long as the underlying NMT system's training data has been augmented with prefix pairs. Due to its simplicity and its effectiveness, we suggest re-translation as a strong baseline for future research on simultaneous translation.

References

Naveen Arivazhagan, Colin Cherry, Te I, Wolfgang Macherey, Pallavi Baljekar, and George Foster. 2019a. Re-translation strategies for long form, simultaneous, spoken language translation. *CoRR*, abs/1912.03393.

Naveen Arivazhagan, Colin Cherry, Wolfgang Macherey, Chung-Cheng Chiu, Semih Yavuz, Ruoming Pang, Wei Li, and Colin Raffel. 2019b. Monotonic infinite lookback attention for simultaneous machine translation. In *Proceedings of the 57th Annual Meeting of the Association for Computational Linguistics*, pages 1313–1323, Florence, Italy. Association for Computational Linguistics.

Jimmy Lei Ba, Jamie Ryan Kiros, and Geoffrey E. Hinton. 2016. Layer Normalization. *arXiv e-prints*, page arXiv:1607.06450.

Dzmitry Bahdanau, Kyunghyun Cho, and Yoshua Bengio. 2014. Neural machine translation by jointly learning to align and translate. *arXiv preprint arXiv:1409.0473*.

Mia Xu Chen, Orhan Firat, Ankur Bapna, Melvin Johnson, Wolfgang Macherey, George Foster, Llion Jones, Mike Schuster, Noam Shazeer, Niki Parmar, Ashish Vaswani, Jakob Uszkoreit, Lukasz Kaiser, Zhifeng Chen, Yonghui Wu, and Macduff Hughes. 2018. The best of both worlds: Combining recent advances in neural machine translation. In *Proceedings of the 56th Annual Meeting of the Association for Computational Linguistics (Volume 1: Long Papers)*, pages 76–86. Association for Computational Linguistics.

Colin Cherry and George Foster. 2019. Thinking slow about latency evaluation for simultaneous machine translation. *CoRR*, abs/1906.00048.

Kyunghyun Cho and Masha Esipova. 2016. Can neural machine translation do simultaneous translation? *CoRR*, abs/1606.02012.

Fahim Dalvi, Nadir Durrani, Hassan Sajjad, and Stephan Vogel. 2018. Incremental decoding and training methods for simultaneous translation in neural machine translation. In *Proceedings of the 2018 Conference of the North American Chapter of the Association for Computational Linguistics: Human Language Technologies, Volume 2 (Short Papers)*, pages 493–499. Association for Computational Linguistics.

Jiatao Gu, Graham Neubig, Kyunghyun Cho, and Victor O.K. Li. 2017. Learning to translate in real-time with neural machine translation. In *Proceedings of the 15th Conference of the European Chapter of the Association for Computational Linguistics: Volume 1, Long Papers*, pages 1053–1062. Association for Computational Linguistics.

Diederik P. Kingma and Jimmy Ba. 2015. Adam: A method for stochastic optimization. In *International Conference on Learning Representations*.

---

[6]Though our experiments in this paper are sentence-level for the sake of continuity with earlier work on streaming translation, in practice, source sentence boundaries can be provided by speech-recognition endpointing or unspoken punctuation prediction (Arivazhagan et al., 2019a).

[7]24.43 milliseconds per sentence is achievable on a NVIDIA TITAN RTX, according to MLPerf v0.5 Inference Closed NMT Stream. Retrieved from www.mlperf.org November 6th, 2019, entry Inf-0.5-27. MLPerf name and logo are trademarks. See www.mlperf.org for more information.

[8]We acknowledge the desirability of low computational complexity, both for reducing the cumulative burden alongside other sources of latency, such as network delays, and for reducing power consumption for mobile or green computing. Finding a lower-cost solution that preserves the flexibility of re-translation is a worthy goal for future research.

Mingbo Ma, Liang Huang, Hao Xiong, Renjie Zheng, Kaibo Liu, Baigong Zheng, Chuanqiang Zhang, Zhongjun He, Hairong Liu, Xing Li, Hua Wu, and Haifeng Wang. 2019a. STACL: Simultaneous translation with implicit anticipation and controllable latency using prefix-to-prefix framework. In *Proceedings of the 57th Annual Meeting of the Association for Computational Linguistics*, pages 3025–3036, Florence, Italy. Association for Computational Linguistics.

Xutai Ma, Juan Pino, James Cross, Liezl Puzon, and Jiatao Gu. 2019b. Monotonic multihead attention. *CoRR*, abs/1909.12406.

Jan Niehues, Thai Son Nguyen, Eunah Cho, Thanh-Le Ha, Kevin Kilgour, Markus Müller, Matthias Sperber, Sebastian Stüker, and Alex Waibel. 2016. Dynamic transcription for low-latency speech translation. In *Interspeech*, pages 2513–2517.

Jan Niehues, Ngoc-Quan Pham, Thanh-Le Ha, Matthias Sperber, and Alex Waibel. 2018. Low-latency neural speech translation. In *Proc. Interspeech 2018*, pages 1293–1297.

Kishore Papineni, Salim Roukos, Todd Ward, and Wei-Jing Zhu. 2002. Bleu: a method for automatic evaluation of machine translation. In *Proceedings of the 40th Annual Meeting of the Association for Computational Linguistics*.

Rico Sennrich, Barry Haddow, and Alexandra Birch. 2016. Neural machine translation of rare words with subword units. In *Proceedings of the 54th Annual Meeting of the Association for Computational Linguistics (Volume 1: Long Papers)*, pages 1715–1725. Association for Computational Linguistics.

Jonathan Shen, Patrick Nguyen, Yonghui Wu, et al. 2019. Lingvo: a modular and scalable framework for sequence-to-sequence modeling. *CoRR*, abs/1902.08295.

Christian Szegedy, Vincent Vanhoucke, Sergey Ioffe, Jonathon Shlens, and Zbigniew Wojna. 2016. Rethinking the inception architecture for computer vision. *2016 IEEE Conference on Computer Vision and Pattern Recognition (CVPR)*, pages 2818–2826.

Ashish Vaswani, Noam Shazeer, Niki Parmar, Jakob Uszkoreit, Llion Jones, Aidan N Gomez, Łukasz Kaiser, and Illia Polosukhin. 2017. Attention is all you need. In *Advances in neural information processing systems*, pages 5998–6008.

Baigong Zheng, Renjie Zheng, Mingbo Ma, and Liang Huang. 2019a. Simpler and faster learning of adaptive policies for simultaneous translation. In *Proceedings of the 2019 Conference on Empirical Methods in Natural Language Processing and the 9th International Joint Conference on Natural Language Processing (EMNLP-IJCNLP)*, pages 1349–1354, Hong Kong, China. Association for Computational Linguistics.

Renjie Zheng, Mingbo Ma, Baigong Zheng, and Liang Huang. 2019b. Speculative beam search for simultaneous translation. In *Proceedings of the 2019 Conference on Empirical Methods in Natural Language Processing and the 9th International Joint Conference on Natural Language Processing (EMNLP-IJCNLP)*, pages 1395–1402, Hong Kong, China. Association for Computational Linguistics.

Towards Stream Translation: Adaptive Computation Time for Simultaneous Machine Translation

Felix Schneider
Karlsruhe Institute of Technology
`felix.schneider@kit.edu`

Alexander Waibel
Karlsruhe Institute of Technology
`alexander.waibel@kit.edu`

Abstract

Simultaneous machine translation systems rely on a policy to schedule read and write operations in order to begin translating a source sentence before it is complete. In this paper, we demonstrate the use of Adaptive Computation Time (ACT) as an adaptive, learned policy for simultaneous machine translation using the transformer model and as a more numerically stable alternative to Monotonic Infinite Lookback Attention (MILk). We achieve state-of-the-art results in terms of latency-quality tradeoffs. We also propose a method to use our model on unsegmented input, i. e. without sentence boundaries, simulating the condition of translating output from automatic speech recognition. We present first benchmark results on this task.

1 Introduction

Simultaneous machine translation (MT) must accomplish two tasks: First, it must deliver correct translations on incomplete input as early as possible, i. e. before the source sentence is completely spoken. Second, in a realistic usage scenario, it must deal with unsegmented input, either speech directly or automatic transcriptions without punctuation or sentence boundaries. Until now, staged models (Niehues et al., 2016), which have a separate component to insert punctuation (Cho et al., 2012) achieved the best results in this task. In this paper, we will present the first step towards an end-to-end approach.

In recent years, a number of approaches for neural simultaneous machine translation have been proposed. They generally build on the common encoder-decoder framework (Sutskever et al., 2014), with the decoder deciding at each step whether to output a target language token based on the currently available information (WRITE) or to wait for one more encoder step in order to have more information available (READ).

In order to do this, the decoder relies on a *wait policy*. The published policies can be broadly divided into two categories:

- Fixed policies, which rely on pre-programmed rules to schedule the read and write operations, such as wait-k (Ma et al., 2019a) and wait-if (Cho and Esipova, 2016).

- Learned policies, which are trained either jointly with the translation model or separately. Examples include MILk (Arivazhagan et al., 2019) and the models of Satija and Pineau (2016) and Alinejad et al. (2018)

However, all of the above approaches train and evaluate their models on individual sentences. We want to work towards a translation system that can work on a continuous stream of input, such as text without punctuation and sentence segmentation. In a realistic usage scenario, segmentation information is not available and an end-to-end solution without a separate segmentation component is desirable. We therefore propose the use of Adaptive Computation Time (Graves, 2016) for simultaneous machine translation. This method achieves a better latency-quality trade-off than the previous best model, MILk, on segmented WMT 2014 German-to-English data. By extending this model with Transformer-XL-style memory (Dai et al., 2019), we are able to apply it directly to unsegmented text.

2 Background

As Arivazhagan et al. (2019) point out, most previous work in simultaneous machine translation focuses on segmenting continuous input into parts that can be translated, whether it is utterances speech or sentences for text (Cho et al., 2012, 2017;

Proceedings of the 17th International Conference on Spoken Language Translation (IWSLT), pages 228–236
July 9-10, 2020. ©2020 Association for Computational Linguistics
https://doi.org/10.18653/v1/P17

Fügen et al., 2007; Oda et al., 2014; Yarmohammadi et al., 2013). For statistical machine translations, some approaches for stream translation without segmentation were known (Kolss et al., 2008). The more recent neural simultaneous MT approaches simply take this segmentation as given and focus on translating simultaneously within a sentence.

Several approaches (Grissom II et al., 2014; Niehues et al., 2018; Alinejad et al., 2018) try to predict the whole target sentence in advance, before the input is complete. It may be possible to extend such approaches to work on an input stream, but they have the undesirable property of overriding their old output, which can make reading the translation difficult to follow for a human.

Satija and Pineau (2016) train the wait policy as an agent with reinforcement learning, considering the pre-trained and fixed MT system as part of the environment. Such an agent could learn to also predict the end of sentences and thus extend to stream translation, but it would be effectively the same as an explicit segmentation.

Cho and Esipova (2016) and Ma et al. (2019a) each define their own fixed policy for simultaneous MT. Wait-k in particular is attractive because of its simplicity and ease of training. However, we believe that for very long input streams, an adaptive policy is necessary to make sure that the decoder never "falls behind" the input stream.

Most recently, the best results are produced by monotonic attention approaches (Raffel et al., 2017; Chiu and Raffel, 2017), in particular Arivazhagan et al. (2019). Their approach uses RNNs, whereas we would like to use the state-of-the-art Transformer architecture (Vaswani et al., 2017). Unfortunately, we were unable to transfer their results to the Transformer, largely due to numerical instability problems. Ma et al. (2019b) claim to have done this, but we were unable to reproduce their results either. We therefore propose our own, more stable, architecture based on Adaptive Computation Time (ACT, Graves (2016))

3 Model

A machine translation model transforms a source sequence $x = \{x_1, x_2, \ldots x_{|x|}\}$ into a target sequence $y = \{y_1, y_2, \ldots y_{|y|}\}$, where, generally, $|x| \neq |y|$. Our model is based on the Transformer model (Vaswani et al., 2017), consisting of an encoder and a decoder. The encoder produces a vector representation for each input token, the decoder autoregressively produces the target sequence. The decoder makes use of the source information via an attention mechanism (Bahdanau et al., 2015), which calculates a context vector from the encoder hidden states.

$$h_{1\ldots|x|} = \text{ENCODER}(x_{1\ldots|x|}) \tag{1}$$
$$c_i = \text{ATTENTION}(y_{i-1}, h_{1\ldots|x|}) \tag{2}$$
$$y_i = \text{DECODER}(y_{i-1}, c_i) \tag{3}$$

In the offline case, the encoder has access to all inputs at once and the attention has access to all encoder hidden states. The standard soft attention calculates the context vector as a linear combination of all hidden states:

$$e_i^n = \text{ENERGY}(y_{i-1}, h_n) \tag{4}$$
$$w_i^n = \frac{\exp(e_i^n)}{\sum_{k=1}^{|x|} \exp(e_i^k)} \tag{5}$$
$$c_i = \sum_{n=1}^{|x|} w_i^k h_n \tag{6}$$

Here, Energy could be a multi-layer perceptron or, in the case of Transformer, a projection followed by a dot product.

In the simultaneous case, there are additional constraints: Each encoder state must only depend on the representations before it and the inputs up to the current one as input becomes available incrementally. In addition, we require a *wait policy* which decides in each step whether to READ another encoder state or to WRITE a decoder output. Each READ incurs a delay, but gives the decoder more information to work with. We denote the encoder step at which the policy decides to WRITE in decoder step i as $N(i)$.

$$h_j = \text{ENCODER}(h_{j-1}, x_j) \tag{7}$$
$$a_i^n = \text{POLICY}(y_{i-1}, h_n) \tag{8}$$
$$N(i) = \min\{n : a_i^n = \text{WRITE}\} \tag{9}$$
$$c_i = \text{ATTENTION}(y_{i-1}, h_{1\ldots N(i)}) \tag{10}$$
$$y_i = \text{DECODER}(y_{i-1}, c_i) \tag{11}$$

Note that this kind of discrete decision-making process is not differentiable. Some approaches using reinforcement learning have been proposed

(Grissom II et al., 2014; Satija and Pineau, 2016), but we will focus on the monotonic attention approaches.

3.1 Monotonic Attention

In monotonic attention (Raffel et al., 2017), the context is exactly the encoder state at $N(i)$. Additionally, $N(i)$ increases monotonically. For each encoder and decoder step, the policy predicts p_i^n, the probability that we will WRITE at encoder step n. During inference, we simply follow this (non-differentiable) stochastic process[1]. During training, we instead train with the expected value of c_i. To that end, we calculate α_i^n, the probability that decoder step i will attend to encoder step n.

$$p_i^n = \sigma(\text{ENERGY}(s_{i-1}, h_n)) \tag{12}$$

$$a_i^n \sim \text{Bernoulli}(p_i^n) \quad \text{Inference only} \tag{13}$$

$$\alpha_i^n = p_i^n \left((1 - p_i^{n-1}) \frac{\alpha_i^{n-1}}{p_i^{n-1}} + \alpha_{i-1}^n \right) \tag{14}$$

$$c_i = \sum_{n=1}^{|\mathbf{x}|} \alpha_i^n h_n \tag{15}$$

This model needs no additional loss function besides the translation loss. It is not incentivised to READ any further than it has to because the model can only attend to one token at a time. At the same time, this is a weakness of the model, as it has access to only a very narrow portion of the input at a time.

To address this, two extensions to monotonic attention have been proposed: Monotonic Chunkwise Attention (MoChA, Chiu and Raffel (2017)) and Monotonic Infinite Lookback Attention (MILk, Arivazhagan et al. (2019)), which we will look at in more detail here.

3.2 Monotonic Infinite Lookback Attention

Monotonic Infinite Lookback Attention (MILk) combines soft and monotonic attention. The attention can look at all hidden states from the start of the input up to $N(i)$, which is determined by a monotonic attention module. The model is once again trained in expectation, with p_i^n and α_i^n calculated as in eqs. (12) and (14). The attention energies e_i^n are calculated as in equation (4).

<hr>

$$\beta_i^n = \sum_{k=n}^{|\mathbf{x}|} \left(\frac{\alpha_i^k \exp(e_i^n)}{\sum_{l=1}^{k} \exp(e_i^l)} \right) \tag{16}$$

$$c_i = \sum_{n=1}^{|\mathbf{x}|} \beta_i^n h_n \tag{17}$$

This method does however introduce the need for a second loss function, as the monotonic attention head can simply always decide to advance to the end of the input where the soft attention can attend to the whole sequence. Therefore, in addition to the typical log-likelihood loss, the authors introduce a loss derived from $\mathbf{n} = \{N(1), \ldots N(|\mathbf{y}|)\}$, weighted by a hyperparameter λ:

$$L(\theta) = -\sum_{(\mathbf{x},\mathbf{y})} \log p(\mathbf{y}|\mathbf{x}; \theta) + \lambda \mathcal{C}(\mathbf{n}) \tag{18}$$

Unfortunately, despite following all advice from Raffel et al. (2017), applying gradient clipping and different energy functions from Arivazhagan et al. (2019), we were not able to adapt MILk for use with the transformer model, largely due to the numerical instability of calculating α_i^n (see Raffel et al. (2017) for more details on this problem). We therefore turn to a different method which has so far not been applied to simultaneous machine translation, namely Adaptive Computation Time (ACT, (Graves, 2016)).

3.3 Adaptive Computation Time

Originally formulated for RNNs without the encoder-decoder framework, Adaptive Computation Time is a method that allows the RNN to "ponder" the same input for several timesteps, effectively creating sub-timesteps. We will first go over the original use-case, although we intentionally match the notation above. At each timestep i, we determine $N(i)$, the number of timesteps spent pondering the current input. We do so by predicting a probability at each sub-timestep s_i^n. We stop once the sum of these probabilities exceeds a threshold. We also calculate a *remainder* $R(i)$. Eqns. (19) through (22) are adapted from Graves (2016) and apply to RNNs:

$$p_i^n = \sigma(\text{ENERGY}(s_i^n)) \tag{19}$$

$$N(i) = \min\{n' : \sum_{n=1}^{n'} p_i^n \geq 1 - \epsilon\} \tag{20}$$

$$R(i) = 1 - \sum_{n=1}^{N(i)-1} p_i^n \tag{21}$$

$$\alpha_i^n = \begin{cases} R(i) & \text{if } n = N(i) \\ p_i^n & \text{otherwise} \end{cases} \tag{22}$$

It follows directly from the definition that α_i is a valid probability distribution. Compared to monotonic attention, ACT directly predicts the expected value for the amount of steps that the model takes, rather than calculating it from stopping probabilites. As-is, the model has no incentive to keep the ponder times short, so we introduce an additional loss:

$$\mathcal{C} = \sum_{i=1}^{|x|} N(i) + R(i) \tag{23}$$

Note that the computation for $N(i)$ is not differentiable so it is treated as a constant and the loss is equivalent to just summing the remainders.

We now go on to transfer ACT to the encoder-decoder domain. Now, instead of pondering the input to an RNN, like in original ACT, the decoder ponders over zero or more encoder steps. The encoder still works as in eq. (7) and does not use ACT. Instead, we apply the ACT ponder mechanism to the monotonic encoder-decoder attention. Let $N(i)$ denote the last encoder step to which we can attend. We make sure that $N(i)$ advances monotonically:

$$p_i^n = \sigma(\text{ENERGY}(y_{i-1}, h_n)) \tag{24}$$

$$N(i) = \min\{n' : \sum_{n=N(i-1)}^{n'} p_i^n \geq 1 - \epsilon\} \tag{25}$$

$$\alpha_i^n = \begin{cases} R(i) & \text{if } n = N(i) \\ p_i^n & \text{if } N(i-1) \leq n < N(i) \\ 0 & \text{otherwise} \end{cases}$$
$$\tag{26}$$

Then we proceed as in equations (16) and (17). Note that in this formulation, it is possible that $N(i) = N(i-1)$ (i.e. the model pondering for zero steps), indicating consecutive WRITEs. In original ACT, it is not possible to ponder the input for zero steps. Also, similar to MILk, we consider $p_i^{|x|}$ to be 1 always. See figure 2 for a visualisation of α_i^n on a concrete example.

3.4 Transformer XL

Finally, we introduce two aspects of the Transformer XL language model (Dai et al., 2019) into our model: Relative attention and memory.

We replace the Transformer self-attention in both encoder and decoder with relative attention. In relative self-attention, we calculate ENERGY as follows:

$$\begin{aligned} \text{ENERGY}(x_i, x_j) = {} & x_i^\top W_q^\top W_E\, x_j \\ & + x_i^\top W_q^\top W_R\, R_{i-j} \\ & + u^\top W_E\, x_j \\ & + v^\top W_R\, R_{i-j} \end{aligned} \tag{27}$$

Where W_q, W_e, W_R, u, v are learnable parameters and R are relative position encodings. Afterwards, we proceed as in equation (16) and (17) for simultaneous models or eqautions (5) and (6) for offline models.

For our streaming model, we also use Transformer XL-style memory during training. This means that we keep the hidden states of both encoder and decoder from the previous training step during training. Both self-attention and encoder-decoder attention are able to attend to these states as well as the current input sentence. However, no gradients can flow through the old states to the model parameters.

3.5 Stream Translation

Our stream translation model should not rely on any segmentation information of the input and must be able to translate a test set as a single, continuous sequence. To achieve this, we extend the standard transformer model in the following ways:

- We use ACT monotonic attention to constrain the encoder-decoder attention. The position of the monotonic attention head also gives us a pointer to the model's current read position in the input stream that advances token by token, and not sentence by sentence and therefore requires no sentence segmentation.

- We change all self-attentions to relative attention, as well as removing absolute position encodings. We could encode positions as absolute since the beginning of the stream. However, Neishi and Yoshinaga (2019) showed that Transformer with absolute position encodings generalizes poorly to unseen sequence lengths. In a continuous stream, relative encodings are the more logical choice.

- We add Transformer XL-style history to the model so that even the first positions of a sample have a history buffer for self-attention. This simulates the evaluation condition where we don't restart the model each sentence.

- During inference, we cannot cut off the history at sentence boundaries (such as keeping exactly the last sentence) because this information is not available. Instead, we adopt a rolling history buffer approach, keeping n_h previous positions for the self-attention. To simulate this condition in training, we apply a mask to the self-attention, masking out positions more than n_h positions in the past.

- During training, we concatenate multiple samples to a length of at least n_h tokens. This is to allow the model to READ past the end of an input sentence into the next one. Normally, this is prevented by setting $p_i^{|x|} = 1$. However during inference, $|x|$ is not available and therefore the model should learn to stop READing at appropriate times even across sentence boundaries.

- We use the ponder loss of equation (23) in addition to the cross-entropy translation loss with a weighting parameter λ as in equation (18).

4 Experiments

4.1 Segmented Translation

In our first set of experiments, we demonstrate the ability of ACT to produce state-of-the art results in sentence-based simultaneous machine translation. For comparison to Arivazhagan et al. (2019), we choose the same dataset: WMT2014 German-to-English (4.5M sentences). As they report their delay metrics on tokenized data, we also use the same tokenization and vocabulary.

All models follow the Transformer "base" configuration (Vaswani et al., 2017) and are implemented in fairseq (Ott et al., 2019). In addition to the simultaneous models, we train a baseline Transformer model. All models except the baseline use relative self-attention. We pre-train an offline model with future-masking in the encoder as a common basis for all simultaneous models.

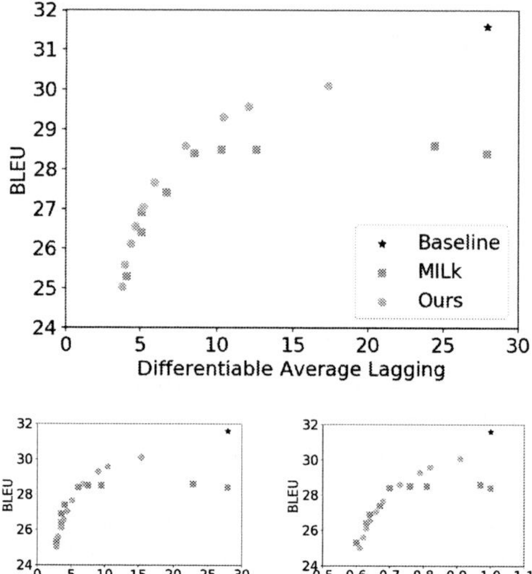

Figure 1: Quality-Latency comparison for German-to-English `newstest2015` in tokenized DAL (top), AL (bottom left) and AP (bottom right)

For the simultaneous models, we vary the value of λ and initialize the parameters from the pre-trained model. We found that training from the start with the latency loss can cause extreme latency behaviour, where the model either reads no input from the source at all or always waits until the end. We theorize that the best strategy would be to introduce the latency loss gradually during training, but leave that experiment for future work.

All models are trained using the Adam Optimizer (Kingma and Ba, 2015). For the pre-training model, we vary the learning rate using a cosine schedule from $2.5 \cdot 10^{-4}$ to 0 over 200k steps. For the ACT model, we start the learning rate at $4 \cdot 10^{-5}$ and use inverse square root decay (Vaswani et al., 2017) for 1000 steps.

We measure translation quality in detokenized, cased BLEU using `sacrebleu`[2] (Post, 2018). We measure latency in Average Lagging (Ma et al., 2019a), Differentiable Average Lagging (Arivazhagan et al., 2019) and Average Proportion (Cho and Esipova, 2016). For direct comparison, we report the tokenized latency metrics, but we provide the detokenized metrics in the appendix.

Figure 1 shows our results for this task. We generally achieve a better quality-latency tradeoff

[2]BLEU+case.mixed+lang.de-en+numrefs.1
+smooth.exp+test.wmt15+tok.13a
+version.1.4.3

as measured by DAL, and a comparable one as measured by AP and AL. We note also that the ceiling for quality of ACT is higher than that of MILk. Whereas MILk loses two BLEU points to their baseline model even when given full attention ($\lambda = 0.0$), our model would seem to get closer to the performance of the baseline with decreasing λ.

4.2 Stream Translation

In this set of experiments, we demonstrate our model's ability to translate continuous streams of input with no sentence segmentation. For training, we use the IWSLT 2020 simultaneous translation data (which includes all WMT2019 data) with 37.6M sentences total. We choose this dataset because of a larger amount of document-level data (3.8M sentences). Because we will use Transformer XL-style memory, we depend on as much contextual data as possible. We evaluate on the IWSLT tst2010 test set in German to English. On the source side, we convert to lower case and remove all punctuation.

In addition to the baseline normal Transformer model, we train our model in three steps: First an offline, sentence-based relative self-attention Transformer, then the Transformer XL and finally the ACT+XL model, each one initializing its parameters on the last one. Both the relative model and the Transformer XL use the cosine schedule starting at $2.5 \cdot 10^{-4}$ and training for 200k and 40k steps, respectively. The ACT+XL model uses inverse square root decay, starting at $4 \cdot 10^{-5}$ as above and trains for 1000 steps. We also experiment with training ACT+XL directly from the relative model.

We evaluate as before[3], treating the test set as a single sequence. BLEU scores are calculated by re-segmenting the output according to the original reference based on Word Error Rate (Matusov et al., 2005). All reported metrics are detokenized. The baseline and relative models use beam search, the others use greedy decoding.

Unfortunately, the range of the λ parameter that produces sensible results is much more restricted than for the sentence-based model (see "Analysis", below). We report results with $\lambda = 0.25$ and 0.3.

Table 1 shows our results. There is a drop of 4 BLEU points when moving to simultaneous translation, which is similar to our experiments on segmented text. While there is room for improvement,

Model	AP	AL	DAL	BLEU
Baseline	—	—	—	32.0
Relative	—	—	—	33.1
XL	—	—	—	34.4
ACT+XL				
$\lambda = 0.25$	0.5	206	329	30.2
$\lambda = 0.3$	0.5	107	180	30.3
ACT+XL	*directly from relative*			
$\lambda = 0.25$	0.5	222	394	26.4

Table 1: Results for the stream translation experiment

these are promising results, and, to the best of our knowledge, the first demonstration of unsegmented end-to-end stream translation.

4.3 Analysis

For the segmented translation, we compare two different latency schedules in figure 2. Both schedules advance relatively homogenously. This may indicate that the ACT attention layer needs to be expanded to extract more grammatical information and make more informed decisions on waiting. Nevertheless, the model produces good results and we even observe implicit verb prediction as in Ma et al. (2019a). We also note that the high latency models' latency graph tends to describe a curve, whereas the low latency models tend to uniformly advance by one token per output token.

This behaviour can be explained by the properties of Differentiable Average Lagging. The ponder loss objective that ACT is trained on may seem very different, but actually produces somewhat similar gradients to DAL [4], so the model incidentally also learns a behaviour that optimizes DAL.

DAL is monotonically increasing, i.e. the model can never "catch up" any delay by WRITing multiple tokens without READing (assuming $|y| = |x|$). It achieves the same DAL but with better translation by always READing one token when it WRITEs. Therefore, to achieve DAL $= k$ for a given k, the ideal waiting strategy is wait-k.

In the case of stream translation, we make two important observations: First, that systems with $\lambda < 0.25$ do not produce acceptable results (BLEU scores < 10). This is because they fall behind the input by waiting too much and have to skip sentences to catch back up. Once an input word is more than n_h tokens behind, it is removed from

---

[3] BLEU+case.mixed+lang.de-en+numrefs.1
+smooth.exp+iwslt17+tst2010+tok.13a
+version.1.4.3

[4] $\frac{\partial \text{DAL}}{\partial \alpha_i^n} = i - N(i) - 1$, $\frac{\partial \text{ACT}}{\partial \alpha_i^n} = -1$ for $N(i-1) \leq i \leq N(i)$, else 0

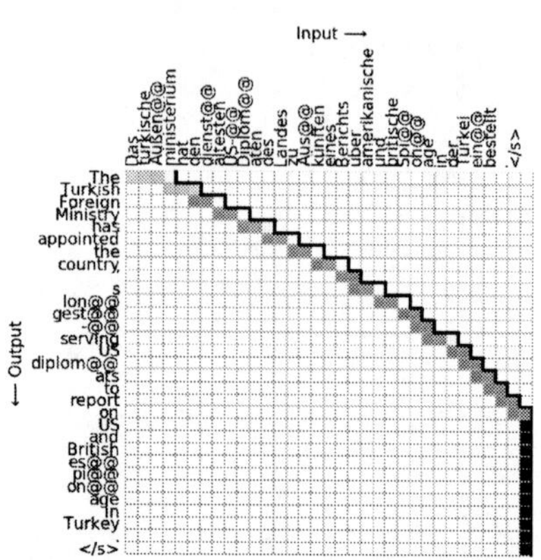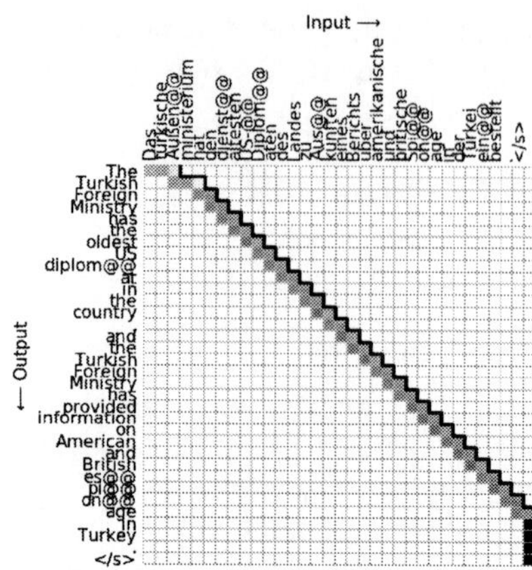

Figure 2: The same sentence from `newstest2015` translated by an ACT system with $\lambda = 0.1$ (left) and $\lambda = 0.4$ (right). The shading indicates the α_i^n as predicted by the ACT attention module (darker = higher probability), the black line indicates the hard attention cutoff. The low-latency model approaches the behaviour of a wait-4 model. Note the (incorrect) attempt of the left model to predict the verb "einbestellt" = "summons", whereas the right model takes the first half of the sentence as complete, leaving out the verb.

the memory and if it is not translated by then, it may be forgotten. Therefore, we found it essential to train more aggressive latency regimes. On the other hand, systems with $\lambda > 0.3$ sometimes read too little source information or stop reading new source words altogether.

Second, that the established latency metrics do not perform well on the very long sequence (with our tokenization, the source is 29 317 tokens long). While on single sentences, an AL score of 4 might indicate quite consistently a lag of around 4 tokens, a manual analysis of the output of our $\lambda = 0.3$ system shows a delay of between 40 and 60 words, quite far away from the automatic metrics of AL=107 and DAL=180. Average proportion in particular breaks down under these conditions and always reports 0.5.[5]

5   Conclusion and Future work

We have presented Adaptive Compuation Time (ACT) for simultaneous machine translation and demonstrated its ability to translate continuous, unsegmented streams of input text. To the best of our knowledge, this is the first end-to-end NMT model to do so. While stream translation model still loses a lot of performance compared to the sentence-based models, we see this as an important step towards end-to-end simultaneous stream

translation.

We see several possibilites for future work on this model: Training the whole model in one training rather than the multiple rounds of pre-training may be possible by gradually introducing the latency loss during training. Perhaps the latency decisions can be improved by adding extra layers to the ACT attention module.

But most importantly, we believe the model must be adapted to the speech domain. Recently (see e. g. Di Gangi et al. (2019)), the Transformer has shown promising results for speech translation. For a realistic application we believe that a simultaneous translation model must work with speech input.

Acknowledgments

The work leading to these results has received funding from the European Union under grant agreement № 825460.

References

Ashkan Alinejad, Maryam Siahbani, and Anoop Sarkar. 2018. Prediction improves simultaneous neural machine translation. In *Proceedings of the 2018 Conference on Empirical Methods in Natural Language Processing*, pages 3022–3027.

Naveen Arivazhagan, Colin Cherry, Wolfgang Macherey, Chung-Cheng Chiu, Semih Yavuz, Ruoming Pang, Wei Li, and Colin Raffel. 2019. Monotonic infinite lookback attention for simultaneous machine translation. In *Proceedings of*

---

[5]The full output of the $\lambda = 0.3$ model can be found here: `https://gist.github.com/felix-schneider/1462d855808e582aa19307f6b0d576e1`

the 57th Annual Meeting of the Association for Computational Linguistics, pages 1313–1323.

Dzmitry Bahdanau, Kyunghyun Cho, and Yoshua Bengio. 2015. Neural machine translation by jointly learning to align and translate. In *3rd International Conference on Learning Representations, ICLR 2015*.

Chung-Cheng Chiu and Colin Raffel. 2017. Monotonic chunkwise attention. *arXiv preprint arXiv:1712.05382*.

Eunah Cho, Jan Niehues, and Alex Waibel. 2012. Segmentation and punctuation prediction in speech language translation using a monolingual translation system. In *International Workshop on Spoken Language Translation (IWSLT) 2012*.

Eunah Cho, Jan Niehues, and Alex Waibel. 2017. Nmt-based segmentation and punctuation insertion for real-time spoken language translation. In *INTERSPEECH*, pages 2645–2649.

Kyunghyun Cho and Masha Esipova. 2016. Can neural machine translation do simultaneous translation? *arXiv preprint arXiv:1606.02012*.

Zihang Dai, Zhilin Yang, Yiming Yang, Jaime G Carbonell, Quoc Le, and Ruslan Salakhutdinov. 2019. Transformer-xl: Attentive language models beyond a fixed-length context. In *Proceedings of the 57th Annual Meeting of the Association for Computational Linguistics*, pages 2978–2988.

Mattia A Di Gangi, Matteo Negri, and Marco Turchi. 2019. Adapting transformer to end-to-end spoken language translation. In *INTERSPEECH 2019*, pages 1133–1137. International Speech Communication Association (ISCA).

Christian Fügen, Alex Waibel, and Muntsin Kolss. 2007. Simultaneous translation of lectures and speeches. *Machine translation*, 21(4):209–252.

Alex Graves. 2016. Adaptive computation time for recurrent neural networks. *arXiv preprint arXiv:1603.08983*.

Alvin Grissom II, He He, Jordan Boyd-Graber, John Morgan, and Hal Daumé III. 2014. Don't until the final verb wait: Reinforcement learning for simultaneous machine translation. In *Proceedings of the 2014 Conference on empirical methods in natural language processing (EMNLP)*, pages 1342–1352.

Diederik P. Kingma and Jimmy Ba. 2015. Adam: A method for stochastic optimization. In *3rd International Conference on Learning Representations, ICLR 2015, San Diego, CA, USA, May 7-9, 2015, Conference Track Proceedings*.

Muntsin Kolss, Stephan Vogel, and Alex Waibel. 2008. Stream decoding for simultaneous spoken language translation. In *Ninth Annual Conference of the International Speech Communication Association*.

Mingbo Ma, Liang Huang, Hao Xiong, Renjie Zheng, Kaibo Liu, Baigong Zheng, Chuanqiang Zhang, Zhongjun He, Hairong Liu, Xing Li, et al. 2019a. Stacl: Simultaneous translation with implicit anticipation and controllable latency using prefix-to-prefix framework. In *Proceedings of the 57th Annual Meeting of the Association for Computational Linguistics*, pages 3025–3036.

Xutai Ma, Juan Pino, James Cross, Liezl Puzon, and Jiatao Gu. 2019b. Monotonic multihead attention. *arXiv preprint arXiv:1909.12406*.

Evgeny Matusov, Gregor Leusch, Oliver Bender, and Hermann Ney. 2005. Evaluating machine translation output with automatic sentence segmentation. In *International Workshop on Spoken Language Translation (IWSLT) 2005*.

Masato Neishi and Naoki Yoshinaga. 2019. On the relation between position information and sentence length in neural machine translation. In *Proceedings of the 23rd Conference on Computational Natural Language Learning (CoNLL)*, pages 328–338.

Jan Niehues, Thai Son Nguyen, Eunah Cho, Thanh-Le Ha, Kevin Kilgour, Markus Müller, Matthias Sperber, Sebastian Stüker, and Alex Waibel. 2016. Dynamic transcription for low-latency speech translation. In *Interspeech*, pages 2513–2517.

Jan Niehues, Ngoc-Quan Pham, Thanh-Le Ha, Matthias Sperber, and Alex Waibel. 2018. Low-latency neural speech translation. In *Proc. Interspeech 2018*, pages 1293–1297.

Yusuke Oda, Graham Neubig, Sakriani Sakti, Tomoki Toda, and Satoshi Nakamura. 2014. Optimizing segmentation strategies for simultaneous speech translation. In *Proceedings of the 52nd Annual Meeting of the Association for Computational Linguistics (Volume 2: Short Papers)*, pages 551–556.

Myle Ott, Sergey Edunov, Alexei Baevski, Angela Fan, Sam Gross, Nathan Ng, David Grangier, and Michael Auli. 2019. fairseq: A fast, extensible toolkit for sequence modeling. In *Proceedings of NAACL-HLT 2019: Demonstrations*.

Matt Post. 2018. A call for clarity in reporting bleu scores. In *Proceedings of the Third Conference on Machine Translation: Research Papers*, pages 186–191.

Colin Raffel, Minh-Thang Luong, Peter J Liu, Ron J Weiss, and Douglas Eck. 2017. Online and linear-time attention by enforcing monotonic alignments. In *Proceedings of the 34th International Conference on Machine Learning-Volume 70*, pages 2837–2846. JMLR. org.

Harsh Satija and Joelle Pineau. 2016. Simultaneous machine translation using deep reinforcement learning. In *ICML 2016 Workshop on Abstraction in Reinforcement Learning*.

Ilya Sutskever, Oriol Vinyals, and Quoc V Le. 2014. Sequence to sequence learning with neural networks. In *Advances in neural information processing systems*, pages 3104–3112.

Ashish Vaswani, Noam Shazeer, Niki Parmar, Jakob Uszkoreit, Llion Jones, Aidan N Gomez, Łukasz Kaiser, and Illia Polosukhin. 2017. Attention is all you need. In *Advances in neural information processing systems*, pages 5998–6008.

Mahsa Yarmohammadi, Vivek Kumar Rangarajan Sridhar, Srinivas Bangalore, and Baskaran Sankaran. 2013. Incremental segmentation and decoding strategies for simultaneous translation. In *Proceedings of the Sixth International Joint Conference on Natural Language Processing*, pages 1032–1036.

A   Segmented Translation Results

λ	Tokenized		
	AP	**AL**	**DAL**
Baseline	1.0	27.9	27.9
0.0	0.91	15.4	17.3
0.01	0.82	10.4	12.1
0.05	0.79	9.0	10.4
0.1	0.73	6.8	7.9
0.15	0.68	5.1	5.9
0.2	0.66	4.4	5.2
0.25	0.64	3.8	4.7
0.3	0.63	3.5	4.4
0.4	0.62	3.0	4.0
0.5	0.61	2.8	3.8

Table 2: Tokenized metrics for `newstest2015` backing figure 1

λ	Detokenized			
	AP	**AL**	**DAL**	**BLEU**
Baseline	1.0	18.6	18.6	31.6
0.0	0.93	10.4	11.7	30.1
0.01	0.84	7.2	8.5	29.6
0.05	0.81	6.3	7.5	29.3
0.1	0.76	4.9	6.0	28.6
0.15	0.71	3.8	4.8	27.7
0.2	0.69	3.4	4.4	27.0
0.25	0.68	3.0	4.1	26.6
0.3	0.67	2.9	3.9	26.1
0.4	0.66	2.6	3.7	25.6
0.5	0.65	2.4	3.6	25.0

Table 3: Detokenized metrics for `newstest2015`

Neural Simultaneous Speech Translation
Using Alignment-Based Chunking

Patrick Wilken, Tamer Alkhouli, Evgeny Matusov, Pavel Golik

Applications Technology (AppTek), Aachen, Germany

`{pwilken,talkhouli,ematusov,pgolik}@apptek.com`

Abstract

In simultaneous machine translation, the objective is to determine when to produce a partial translation given a continuous stream of source words, with a trade-off between latency and quality. We propose a neural machine translation (NMT) model that makes dynamic decisions when to continue feeding on input or generate output words. The model is composed of two main components: one to dynamically decide on ending a source chunk, and another that translates the consumed chunk. We train the components jointly and in a manner consistent with the inference conditions. To generate chunked training data, we propose a method that utilizes word alignment while also preserving enough context. We compare models with bidirectional and unidirectional encoders of different depths, both on real speech and text input. Our results on the IWSLT[1] 2020 English-to-German task outperform a wait-k baseline by 2.6 to 3.7% BLEU absolute.

1 Introduction

Simultaneous machine translation is the task of generating partial translations before observing the entire source sentence. The task fits scenarios such as live captioning and speech-to-speech translation, where the user expects a translation before the speaker finishes the sentence. Simultaneous MT has to balance between latency and translation quality. If more input is consumed before translation, quality is likely to improve due to increased context, but latency also increases. On the other hand, consuming limited input decreases latency, but degrades quality.

There have been several approaches to solve simultaneous machine translation. In (Dalvi et al., 2018; Ma et al., 2019), a fixed policy is introduced

to delay translation by a fixed number of words. Alternatively, Satija and Pineau (2016); Gu et al. (2017); Alinejad et al. (2018) use reinforcement learning to learn a dynamic policy to determine whether to read or output words. Cho and Esipova (2016) adapt the decoding algorithm without relying on additional components. However, these methods do not modify the training of the underlying NMT model. Instead, it is trained on full sentences. Arivazhagan et al. (2019) introduce a holistic framework that relaxes the hard notion of read/write decisions at training time, allowing it to be trained jointly with the rest of the NMT model.

In this paper, we integrate a source chunk boundary detection component into a bidirectional recurrent NMT model. This component corresponds to segmentation or read/write decisions in the literature. It is however trained jointly with the rest of the NMT model. We propose an algorithm to chunk the training data based on automatically learned word alignment. The chunk boundaries are used as a training signal along with the parallel corpus. The main contributions of this work are as follows:

- We introduce a source chunk boundary detection component and train it jointly with the NMT model. Unlike in (Arivazhagan et al., 2019), our component is trained using hard decisions, which is consistent with inference.

- We propose a method based on word alignment to generate the source and target chunk boundaries, which are needed for training.

- We study the use of bidirectional vs unidirectional encoder layers for simultaneous machine translation. Previous work focuses mostly on the use of unidirectional encoders.

- We provide results using text and speech input. This is in contrast to previous work that only simulates simultaneous NMT on text input.

---

[1]The International Conference on Spoken Language Translation, `http://iwslt.org`.

Proceedings of the 17th International Conference on Spoken Language Translation (IWSLT), pages 237–246
July 9-10, 2020. ©2020 Association for Computational Linguistics
https://doi.org/10.18653/v1/P17

2 Related Work

Oda et al. (2014) formulate segmentation as an optimization problem solved using dynamic programming to optimize translation quality. The approach is applied to phrase-based machine translation. Our chunking approach is conceptually simpler, and we explore its use with neural machine translation. Cho and Esipova (2016) devise a greedy decoding algorithm for simultaneous neural machine translation. They use a model that is trained on full sentences. In contrast, we train our models on chunked sentences to be consistent with the decoding condition. Satija and Pineau (2016), Alinejad et al. (2018), and Gu et al. (2017) follow a reinforcement learning approach to make decisions as to when to read source words or to write target words. Zheng et al. (2019) propose the simpler approach to use the position of the reference target word in the beam of an existing MT system to generate training examples of read/write decisions. We extract such decisions from statistical word alignment instead.

In Ma et al. (2019); Dalvi et al. (2018), a wait-k policy is proposed to delay the first target word until k source words are read. The model alternates between generating s target words and reading s source words, until the source words are exhausted. Afterwards, the rest of the target words are generated. In addition, Dalvi et al. (2018) convert the training data into chunks of predetermined fixed size. In contrast, we train models that learn to produce dynamic context-dependent chunk lengths.

The idea of exploiting word alignments to decide for necessary translation context can be found in several recent papers. Arthur et al. (2020) train an agent to imitate read/write decisions derived from word alignments. In our architecture such a separate agent model is replaced by a simple additional output of the encoder. Xiong et al. (2019) use word alignments to tune a pretrained language representation model to perform word sequence chunking. In contrast, our approach integrates alignment-based chunking into the translation model itself, avoiding the overhead of having a separate component and the need for a pretrained model. Moreover, in this work we improve on pure alignment-based chunks using language models (Section 6.3) to avoid leaving relevant future source words out of the chunk. Press and Smith (2018) insert ϵ-tokens into the target using word alignments to develop an NMT model without an attention mechanism.

Those tokens fulfill a similar purpose to *wait* decisions in simultaneous MT policies.

Arivazhagan et al. (2019) propose an attention-based model that integrates an additional monotonic attention component. While the motivation is to use hard attention to select the encoder state at the end of the source chunk, they avoid using discrete attention to keep the model differentiable, and use soft probabilities instead. The hard mode is only used during decoding. We do not have to work around discrete decisions in this work, since the chunk boundaries are computed offline before training, resulting in a simpler model architecture.

3 Simultaneous Machine Translation

The problem of offline machine translation is focused on finding the target sequence $e_1^I = e_1...e_I$ of length I given the source sequence f_1^J of length J. In contrast, simultaneous MT does not necessarily require the full source input to generate the target output. In this work, we formulate the problem by assuming latent monotonic chunking underlying the source and target sequences.

Formally, let $s_1^K = s_1...s_k...s_K$ denote the chunking sequence of K chunks, such that $s_k = (i_k, j_k)$, where i_k denotes the target position of last target word in the k-th chunk, and j_k denotes the source position of the last source word in the chunk. Since the source and target chunks are monotonic, the beginnings of the source and target chunks do not have to be defined explicitly. The chunk positions are subject to the following constraints:

$$i_0 = j_0 = 0, \quad i_K = I, \quad j_K = J,$$
$$i_{k-1} < i_k, \quad j_{k-1} < j_k. \tag{1}$$

We use $\tilde{e}_k = e_{i_{k-1}+1}...e_{i_k}$ to denote the k-th target chunk, and $\tilde{f}_k = f_{j_{k-1}+1}...f_{j_k}$ to denote its corresponding source chunk. The target sequence e_1^I can be rewritten as $\tilde{e}_1^K$, similarly, the source sequence can be rewritten as $f_1^J = \tilde{f}_1^K$.

We introduce the chunk sequence s_1^K as a latent variable as follows:

$$p(e_1^I|f_1^J) = \sum_{K,s_1^K} p(e_1^I, s_1^K|f_1^J) \tag{2}$$

$$= \sum_{K,s_1^K} p(\tilde{e}_1^K, s_1^K|\tilde{f}_1^K) \tag{3}$$

$$= \sum_{K,s_1^K} \prod_{k=1}^K p(\tilde{e}_k, s_k|\tilde{e}_1^{k-1}, s_1^{k-1}, \tilde{f}_1^K) \tag{4}$$

$$= \sum_{K,s_1^K} \prod_{k=1}^{K} p(i_k|\tilde{e}_1^k, s_1^{k-1}, j_k, \tilde{f}_1^K)$$

$$\cdot \, p(\tilde{e}_k|\tilde{e}_1^{k-1}, s_1^{k-1}, j_k, \tilde{f}_1^K)$$

$$\cdot \, p(j_k|\tilde{e}_1^{k-1}, s_1^{k-1}, \tilde{f}_1^K), \qquad (5)$$

where Equation 2 introduces the latent sequence s_1^K with a marginalization sum over all possible chunk sequences and all possible number of chunks K. In Equation 3 we rewrite the source and target sequences using the chunk notation, and we apply the chain rule of probability in Equation 4. We use the chain rule again in Equation 5 to decompose the probability further into a *target chunk boundary probability* $p(i_k|\tilde{e}_1^k, s_1^{k-1}, j_k, \tilde{f}_1^K)$, a *target chunk translation probability* $p(\tilde{e}_k|\tilde{e}_1^{k-1}, s_1^{k-1}, j_k, \tilde{f}_1^K)$, and a *source chunk boundary probability* $p(j_k|\tilde{e}_1^{k-1}, s_1^{k-1}, \tilde{f}_1^K)$. This creates a generative story, where the source chunk boundary is determined first, followed by the translation of the chunk, and finally by the target chunk boundary. The translation probability can be further decomposed to reach the word level:

$$p(\tilde{e}_k, |\tilde{e}_1^{k-1}, s_1^{k-1}, j_k, \tilde{f}_1^K)$$

$$= \prod_{i=i_{k-1}+1}^{i_k} p(e_i|\underbrace{e_{i_{k-1}+1}^{i-1}, \tilde{e}_1^{k-1}}_{=e_1^{i-1}}, s_1^{k-1}, j_k, \tilde{f}_1^K)$$

$$\approx \prod_{i=i_{k-1}+1}^{i_k} p(e_i|e_1^{i-1}, f_1^{j_k}, k). \qquad (6)$$

In this work, we drop the marginalization sum over chunk sequences and use fixed chunks during training. The chunk sequences are generated as described in Section 6.

4 Model

4.1 Source Chunk Boundary Detection

We simplify the chunk boundary probability, dropping the dependence on the target sequence and previous target boundary decisions

$$p(j_k|\tilde{e}_1^{k-1}, s_1^{k-1}, \tilde{f}_1^K) \approx p(j_k|f_1^{j_k}, j_1^{k-1}), \qquad (7)$$

where the distribution is conditioned on the source sequence up to the last word of the k-th chunk. It is also conditioned on the previous source boundary decisions $j_1...j_{k-1}$. Instead of computing a distribution over the source positions, we introduce a binary random variable b_j such that for each source

position we estimate the probability of a chunk boundary:

$$b_{j,k} = \begin{cases} 1 & \text{if } j \in \{j_1, j_2...j_k\} \\ 0 & \text{otherwise.} \end{cases} \qquad (8)$$

For this, we use a forward stacked RNN encoder. The l-th forward encoder layer is given by

$$\overrightarrow{h}_{j,k}^{(l)} = \begin{cases} LSTM([\hat{f}_j; \hat{b}_{j-1,k}], \overrightarrow{h}_{j-1,k}^{(l)}) & l = 1 \\ LSTM(\overrightarrow{h}_{j,k}^{(l-1)}, \overrightarrow{h}_{j-1,k}^{(l)}) & 1 < l < L_{enc}, \end{cases} \qquad (9)$$

where $\hat{f}_j$ is the word embedding of the word f_j, which is concatenated to the embedding of the boundary decision at the previous source position $\hat{b}_{j-1,k}$. L_{enc} is the number of encoder layers. On top of the last layer a softmax estimates $p(b_{j,k})$:

$$p(b_{j,k}) = \text{softmax}(g([\overrightarrow{h}_{j,k}^{(L_{enc})}; \hat{f}_j; \hat{b}_{j-1,k}])), \qquad (10)$$

where $g(\cdot)$ denotes a non-linear function.

4.2 Translation Model

We use an RNN attention model based on (Bahdanau et al., 2015) for $p(e_i|e_1^{i-1}, f_1^{j_k})$. The model shares the forward encoder with the chunk boundary detection model. In addition, we extend the encoder with a stacked backward RNN encoder. The l-th backward layer is given by

$$\overleftarrow{h}_{j,k}^{(l)} = \begin{cases} 0 & j > j_k, \forall l \\ LSTM([\hat{f}_j; b_{j,k}], \overleftarrow{h}_{j+1,k}^{(l)}) & l = 1 \\ LSTM(\overleftarrow{h}_{j,k}^{(l-1)}, \overleftarrow{h}_{j+1,k}^{(l)}) & 1 < l < L_{enc}, \end{cases} \qquad (11)$$

where the backward layer is computed within a chunk starting at the last position of the chunk $j = j_k$. $\mathbf{0}$ indicates a vector of zeros for positions beyond the current chunk. The source representation is given by the concatenation of the last forward and backward layer

$$h_{j,k} = [\overrightarrow{h}_{j,k}^{(L_{enc})}; \overleftarrow{h}_{j,k}^{(L_{enc})}]. \qquad (12)$$

We also stack L_{dec} LSTM layers in the decoder

$$u_{i,k}^{(l)} = \begin{cases} LSTM(u_{i,k}^{(l-1)}, u_{i-1,\hat{k}}^{(l)}) & 1 < l < L_{dec} \\ LSTM([\hat{e}_i; d_{i,k}], u_{i-1,\hat{k}}^{(l)}) & l = 1, \end{cases} \qquad (13)$$

where $\hat{e}_i$ is the target word embedding of the word e_i, $\hat{k} = k$ unless the previous decoder state belongs to the previous chunk, then $\hat{k} = k - 1$. The vector $d_{i,k}$ is the context vector computed over source positions up to the last source position j_k in the k-th chunk

$$d_{i,k} = \sum_{j=1}^{j_k} \alpha_{i,j,k} h_{j,k} \tag{14}$$

$$\alpha_{i,j,k} = \text{softmax}(r_{i,1,k}...r_{i,j_k,k})|_j \tag{15}$$

$$r_{i,j,k} = f(h_{j,k}, u_{i-1,\hat{k}}^{(L_{dec})}), \tag{16}$$

where $\alpha_{i,j,k}$ is the attention weight normalized over the source positions $1 \leq j \leq j_k$, and $r_{i,j,k}$ is the energy computed via the function f which uses tanh of the previous top-most decoder layer and the source representation at position j. Note the difference to the attention component used in offline MT, where the attention weights are computed considering the complete source sentence f_1^J. The output distribution is computed using a softmax function of energies from the top-most decoder layer $u_{i-1,k}^{(L_{dec})}$, the target embedding of the previous word $\hat{e}_{i-1}$, and the context vector $d_{i-1,k}$

$$p(e_i|e_1^{i-1}, f_1^{j_k}, k) =$$
$$\text{softmax}\big(g([u_{i-1,k}^{(L_{dec})}; \hat{e}_{i-1}; d_{i-1,k}])\big). \tag{17}$$

4.3 Target Chunk Boundary Factor

Traditionally, the translation model is trained to produce a sentence end token to know when to stop the decoding process. In our approach, this decision has to be made for each chunk (see next section). Hence, we have to train the model to predict the end positions of the chunks on the target side. For this, we use a target factor (García-Martínez et al., 2016; Wilken and Matusov, 2019), i.e. a second output of the decoder in each step:

$$p(b_i|e_1^i, f_1^{j_k}, k) =$$
$$\text{softmax}(g(u_{i-1,k}^{(L_{dec})}, \hat{e}_i, \hat{e}_{i-1}, d_{i-1,k})) \tag{18}$$

where b_i is a binary random variable representing target chunk boundaries analogous to b_j on the source side. This probability corresponds to the first term in Equation 5, making the same model assumptions as for the translation probability. Note however, that we make the boundary decision dependent on the embedding $\hat{e}_i$ of the target word produced in the current decoding step.

5 Search

Decoding in simultaneous MT can be seen as an asynchronous process that takes a stream of source words as input and produces a stream of target words as output. In our approach, we segment the incoming source stream into chunks and output a translation for each chunk individually, however always keeping the full source and target context.

Algorithm 1: Simultaneous Decoding

lists in bold, [] is the empty list, += appends to a list

---

  input : source word stream f_1^J
  output : target word stream e_1^I

  $\hat{\boldsymbol{f}}_k = []$, $\overrightarrow{\boldsymbol{h}} = []$, $\overleftarrow{\boldsymbol{h}} = []$
  for f_j **in** f_1^J **do**
    $\hat{f}_j = \text{Embedding}(f_j)$
    $\overrightarrow{h}_j, p(b_j) = \text{runForwardEncoder}(\hat{f}_j)$
    $\hat{\boldsymbol{f}}_k \mathrel{+}= \hat{f}_j$
    $\overrightarrow{\boldsymbol{h}} \mathrel{+}= \overrightarrow{h}_j$
    if $p(b_i) > t_b$ **or** $j = J$ **then**
      $\overleftarrow{\boldsymbol{h}}_k = \text{runBackwardEncoder}(\hat{\boldsymbol{f}}_k)$
      $\overleftarrow{\boldsymbol{h}} \mathrel{+}= \overleftarrow{\boldsymbol{h}}_k$
      $\tilde{e}_k = \text{runDecoder}(\overrightarrow{\boldsymbol{h}}, \overleftarrow{\boldsymbol{h}})$
      $e_1^I \mathrel{+}= \tilde{e}_k$
      $\hat{\boldsymbol{f}}_k = []$

Algorithm 1 explains the simultaneous decoding process. One source word f_j (i.e. its embedding $\hat{f}_j$) is read at a time. We calculate the next step of the shared forward encoder (Equation 9), including source boundary detection (Equation 10). If the boundary probability $p(b_j)$ is below a certain threshold t_b, we continue reading the next source word f_{j+1}. If, however, a chunk boundary is detected, we first feed all word embeddings $\hat{f}_k$ of the current chunk into the backward encoder (Equation 11), resulting in representations $\overleftarrow{h}_k$ for each of the words in the current chunk. After that, the decoder is run according to Equations 12–18. Note, that it attends to representations $\overrightarrow{h}$ and $\overleftarrow{h}$ of all source words read so far, not only the current chunk. Here, we perform beam search such that in each decoding step those combinations of target words and target chunk boundary decisions are kept that have the highest joint probability. A hypothesis is considered final as soon as it reaches a position i where a chunk boundary $b_i = 1$ is predicted. Note that the length of a chunk translation is not restricted and hypotheses of different lengths compete. When all hypotheses in the beam are final, the first-best hypothesis is declared as the translation $\tilde{e}_k$ of the current chunk and all its words are flushed into the output stream at once.

During search, the internal states of the forward encoder and the decoder are saved between consecutive different calls while the backward decoder is initialized with a zero state for each chunk.

6 Alignment-Based Chunking

6.1 Baseline Approach

We aimed at a meaningful segmentation of sentence pairs into bilingual chunks which could then be translated in monotonic sequence and each chunk is – in terms of aligned words – translatable without consuming source words from succeeding chunks. We extract such a segmentation from unsupervised word alignments in source-to-target and target-to-source directions that we trained using the Eflomal toolkit (Östling and Tiedemann, 2016) and combined using the *grow-diag-final-and* heuristic (Koehn et al., 2003). Then, for each training sentence pair, we extract a sequence of "minimal-length" monotonic phrase pairs, i.e. a sequence of the smallest possible bilingual chunks which do not violate the alignment constraints[2] and at the same time are conform with the segmentation constraints in Equation 1. By this we allow word reordering between the two languages to happen only within the chunk boundaries. The method roughly follows the approach of (Mariño et al., 2005), who extracted similar chunks as units for n-gram based statistical MT.

For fully monotonic word alignments, only chunks of length 1 either on the source or the target side are extracted (corresponding to 1-to-1, 1-to-M, M-to-1 alignments). For non-monotonic alignments larger chunks are obtained, in the extreme case the whole sentence pair is one chunk. Any unaligned source or target words are attached to the chunk directly preceding them, also any non-aligned words that may start the source/target sentence are attached to the first chunk. We perform the word alignment and chunk boundary extraction on the word level, and then convert words to subword units for the subsequent use in NMT.

---

[2]This means that all source words within a bilingual chunk are aligned only to the target words within this chunk and vice versa.

6.2 Delayed Source Chunk Boundaries

We observed that the accuracy of source boundary detection can be improved significantly by including the words immediately following the source chunk boundary into the context. Take e.g. the source word sequence `I have seen it`. It can be translated into German as soon as the word `it` was read: `Ich habe es gesehen`. Therefore the model is likely to predict a chunk boundary after `it`. However, if the next read source word is `coming`, it becomes clear that we should have waited because the correct German translation is now `Ich habe es kommen gesehen`. There is a reordering which invalidates the previous partial translation.

To be able to resolve such cases, we shift the source chunks by a constant delay D such that $j_1, ..., j_k, ..., j_K$ becomes $j_1 + D, ..., j_k + D, ..., j_K + D$.[3] Note that the target chunks remain unchanged, thus the extra source words also provide an expanded context for translation. In preliminary experiments we saw large improvements in translation quality when using a delay of 2 or more words, therefore we use it in all further experiments.

6.3 Improved Chunks for More Context

The baseline chunking method (Section 6.1) considers word reordering to determine necessary context for translation. However, future context is often necessary for correct translation. Consider the translation `The beautiful woman` → `Die schöne Frau`. Here, despite of the monotonic alignment, we need the context of the third English word `woman` to translate the first two words as we have to decide on the gender and number of the German article `Die` and adjective `schöne`.

In part, this problem is already addressed by adding future source words into the context as described in Section 6.2. However, this method causes a general increase in latency by D source positions and yet covers only short-range dependencies. A better approach is to remove any chunk boundary for which the words following it are important for a correct translation of the words preceding it. To this end, we introduce a heuristic that uses two bigram target language models (LMs). The first language model yields the probability $p(e_{i_k}|e_{i_k-1})$ for the last word e_{i_k} of chunk s_k,

---

[3]If $j_K + D > J$, we shift the boundary to J, allowing empty source chunks at sentence end.

```
EN:  And | along came | a | brilliant | inventor, | a | scientist, |
     who | came up with a partial cure for that disease
DE:  Dann | kam | ein | brillanter | Erfinder des Wegs, | ein | Wissenschaftler, |
     der | eine teilweise Heilung für diese Krankheit fand

EN:  And | along came | a brilliant inventor, | a scientist, |
     who | came up with a partial cure for that disease
DE:  Dann | kam | ein brillanter Erfinder des Wegs, | ein Wissenschaftler, |
     der | eine teilweise Heilung für diese Krankheit fand
```

Figure 1: Examples of the baseline and the improved approach of extracting chunk boundaries. Note how in the improved approach noun phrases were merged into single bigger chunks. Also note the long last chunk that corresponds to the non-monotonic alignment of the English and German subordinate clause.

whereas the second one computes the probability $p(e_{i_k}|e_{i_k+1})$ for the last word in the chunk given the first word e_{i_k+1} of the next chunk s_{k+1} that follows the word e_{i_k}. The chunk boundary after e_{i_k} is removed if the probability of the latter reverse bigram LM is higher than the probability of the first one by a factor $l = \sqrt{i_k - i_{k-1}}$, i.e. dependent on the length of the current chunk. The motivation for this factor is that shorter chunks should be merged with the context to the right more often than chunks which are already long, provided that the right context word has been frequently observed in training to follow the last word of such a chunk candidate. The two bigram LMs are estimated on the target side of the bilingual data, with the second one trained on sentences printed in reverse order.

Examples of the chunks extracted with the baseline and the improved approach for a given training sentence pair are shown in Figure 1.

7   Streaming Speech Recognition

To translate directly from speech signal, we use a cascaded approach. The proposed simultaneous NMT system consumes words from a streaming automatic speech recognition (ASR) system. This system is based on a hybrid LSTM/HMM acoustic model (Bourlard and Wellekens, 1989; Hochreiter and Schmidhuber, 1997), trained on a total of approx. 2300 hours of transcribed English speech from the corpora allowed by IWSLT 2020 evaluation, including MUST-C, TED-LIUM, and LibriSpeech. The acoustic model takes 80-dim. MFCC features as input and estimates state posterior probabilities for 5000 tied triphone states. It consists of 4 bidirectional layers with 512 LSTM units for each direction. Frame-level alignment and state tying were bootstrapped with a Gaussian mixtures acoustic model. The LM of the streaming recognizer is a 4-gram count model trained with Kneser-

Ney smoothing on English text data (approx. 2.8B running words) allowed by the IWSLT 2020 evaluation. The vocabulary consists of 152K words and the out-of-vocabulary rate is below 1%. Acoustic training and the HMM decoding were performed with the RWTH ASR toolkit (Wiesler et al., 2014).

The streaming recognizer implements a version of chunked processing (Chen and Huo, 2016; Zeyer et al., 2016) which allows for the same BLSTM-based acoustic model to be used in both offline and online applications. By default, the recognizer updates the current first-best hypothesis by Viterbi decoding starting from the most recent frame and returns the resulting word sequence to the client. This makes the first-best hypothesis "unstable", i.e. past words can change depending on the newly received evidence due to the global optimization of the Viterbi decoding. To make the output more stable, we made the decoder delay the recognition results until all active word sequences share a common prefix. This prefix is then guaranteed to remain unchanged independent of the rest of the utterance and thus can be sent out to the MT model.

8   Experiments

We conduct experiments on the IWSLT simultaneous translation task for speech translation of TED talks from English to German.

8.1   Setup

For training the baseline NMT system, we utilize the parallel data allowed for the IWSLT 2020 evaluation. We divide it into 3 parts: in-domain, clean, and out-of-domain. We consider data from the TED and MUST-C corpora (Di Gangi et al., 2019) as in-domain and use it for subsequent fine-tuning experiments, as well as the "ground truth" for filtering the out-of-domain data based on sentence embedding similarity with the in-domain data; details are given in (Bahar et al., 2020). As "clean" we consider the News-Commentary, Europarl, and WikiTitles corpora and use their full versions in training. As out-of-domain data, we consider Open-Subtitles, ParaCrawl, CommonCrawl, and *rapid* corpora, which we reduce to 40% of their total size, or to 23.2M parallel lines, with similarity-based filtering. Thus, in total, we use almost 26M lines of parallel data to train our systems, which amounts to ca. 327M running words on the English side. Furthermore, we added 7.9M sentence pairs or ca. 145M running words of similarity-filtered back-translated[4] German monolingual data allowed by the IWSLT 2020 evaluation.

In training, the in-domain and clean parallel data had a weight of 5. All models were implemented and trained with the RETURNN toolkit (Zeyer et al., 2018). We used an embedding size of 620 and LSTM state sizes of 1000.

As heldout tuning set, we use a combination of IWSLT dev2010, tst2014, and MUST-C-dev corpora. To obtain bilingual chunks as described in Section 6, we word-align all of the filtered parallel/back-translated and tuning data in portions of up to 1M sentence pairs, each of them combined with all of the in-domain and clean parallel data. As heldout evaluation sets, we use IWSLT tst2015, as well as MUST-C HE and COMMON test data.

For the text input condition, we applied almost no preprocessing, tokenization was handled as part of the subword segmentation with the sentence-piece toolkit (Kudo and Richardson, 2018). The vocabularies for both the source and the target sub-word models had a size of 30K. For the speech input condition, the additional preprocessing applied to the English side of the parallel data had the goal to make it look like speech transcripts. We lowercased the text, removed all punctuation marks, expanded common abbreviations, especially for measurement units, and converted numbers, dates, and other entities expressed with digits into their spoken form. For the cases of multiple readings of a given number (e.g. one oh one, one hundred and one), we selected one randomly, so that the system could learn to convert alternative readings in English to the same number expressed with digits in German. Because of this preprocessing, our system for the speech condition learned to insert punctuation marks, restore word case, and

convert spoken number and entity forms to digits as part of the translation process.

The proposed chunking method (Section 6) is applied to the training corpus as a data preparation step. We measured average chunk lengths of 2.9 source words and 2.7 target words. 40% of both the source and target chunks consist of a single word, about 20% are longer than 3 words.

We compute case-sensitive BLEU (Papineni et al., 2002) and TER (Snover et al., 2006) scores as well as the average lagging (AL) metric (Ma et al., 2019).

8.2 Results

Table 1 shows results for the proposed simultaneous MT system. For reference, we first provide the translation quality of an offline system that is trained on full sentences. It is a transformer "base" model (Vaswani et al., 2017) that we trained on the same data as the online systems. Row 1 shows BLEU and TER scores for translation of the human reference transcription of the speech input (converted to lower-case, punctuation removed), whereas row 2 uses the automatic transcription generated by our streaming ASR system (Section 7). The ASR system has a word error rate (WER) of 8.7 to 11.2% on the three test sets, causing a drop of 4-6% BLEU absolute.

All following systems are cascaded streaming ASR + MT online systems that produce translations from audio input in real-time. Those systems have an overall AL of 4.1 to 4.5 seconds, depending on D. We compare between two categories of models: unidirectional and bidirectional. For the unidirectional models the backwards decoder (Equation 11) was removed from the architecture. We show results for different values of source boundary delay D (see Section 6.2). For the number of layers we choose $L_{enc} = 6$ and $L_{dec} = 2$ for the unidirectional models, and $L_{enc} = 4$ (both directions) and $L_{dec} = 1$ for the bidirectional models, such that the number of parameters is comparable. Contradicting our initial assumption, bidirectional models do not outperform unidirectional models. This might indicate be due to the fact that the majority of chunks are too short to benefit from a backwards encoding. Also, the model is not sensitive to the delay D. This *confirms* our assumption that the additional context of future source words is primarily useful for making the source boundary decision, and for this a context of 2 following (sub-)words

---

[4]The German-to-English system that we used to translate these data into English is an off-line system trained using the Transformer Base architecture (Vaswani et al., 2017) on the in-domain and clean parallel data.

System	Delay	tst2015		must-c-HE		must-c-COMMON	
		BLEU	**TER**	**BLEU**	**TER**	**BLEU**	**TER**
Offline baseline, Transformer							
using reference transcript	n/a	32.7	50.9	30.1	54.3	32.6	48.9
using streaming ASR	n/a	28.6	56.3	26.0	59.2	26.4	57.3
Proposed simultaneous NMT	2	24.8	60.2	21.7	63.0	21.9	60.2
unidirectional,	3	24.6	60.2	22.6	62.7	21.8	60.8
(6 enc. 2 dec.)	4	24.6	61.1	22.8	62.8	21.7	61.5
Proposed simultaneous NMT	2	24.6	60.0	21.4	62.8	21.9	60.6
bidirectional,	3	24.4	60.5	22.0	62.7	21.7	61.1
(2x4 enc. 1 dec.)	4	24.6	61.0	21.8	63.1	21.9	61.4

Table 1: Experimental results (in %) for simultaneous NMT of speech, IWSLT 2020 English→German.

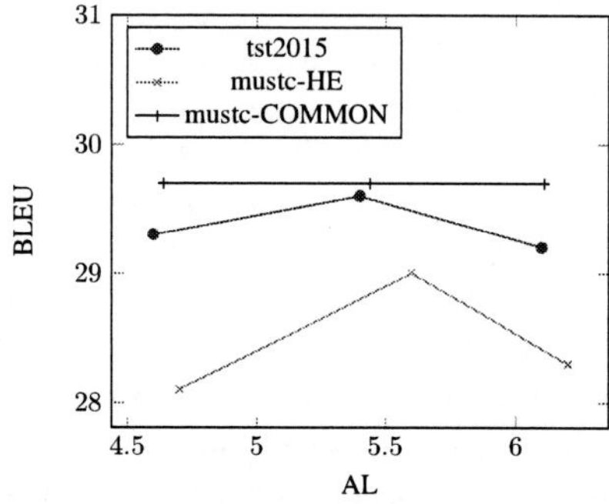

Figure 2: BLEU vs. AL for bidirectional systems from Table 2, generated using a delay D of 2, 3, and 4.

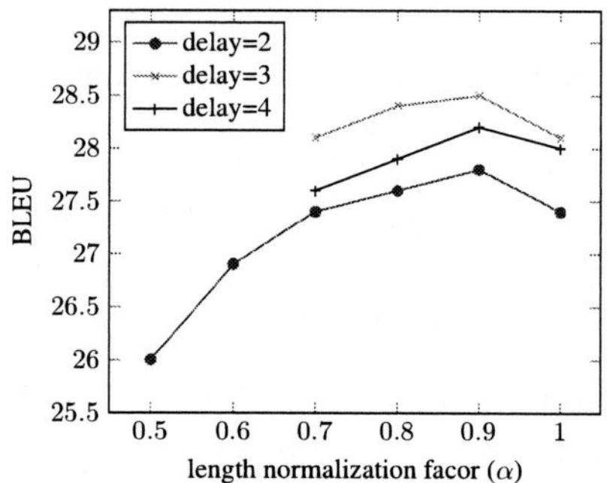

Figure 3: BLEU vs. the length normalization factor (α) on the tuning set (dev2010 + tst2014 + MUST-C-dev).

is sufficient. For translation, the model does not depend on this "extra" context but instead is able to make sufficiently good chunking decisions.

Table 2 shows results for the case of streamed text input (cased and with punctuation marks). We compare our results to a 4-layer unidirectional system that was trained using the wait-k policy (Ma et al., 2019). For this, we chunk the training data into single words, except for a first chunk of size $k = 9$ on the source side, and set the delay to $D = 0$. All of our systems outperform this wait-k system by large margins. We conclude that the alignment-based chunking proposed in Section 6 is able to provide better source context than a fixed policy and that the source boundary detection component described in Section 4.1 successfully learns to reproduce this chunking at inference time. Also for the text condition, we do not observe large differences between uni- and bidirectional models and between different delays.

For all systems, we report AL scores averaged over all test sets. Figure 2 breaks down the scores to the individual test sets for the bidirectional models.

For a source boundary delay $D = 2$ we observe an AL of 4.6 to 4.7 words. When increasing D, we increase the average lagging score by roughly the same amount, which is expected, since the additional source context for the boundary decision is not translated in the same step where it is added. As discussed before, translation quality does not consistently improve from increasing D.

We found tuning of length normalization to be important, as the average decoding length for chunks is much shorter than in offline translation. For optimal results, we divided the model scores by I^α, I being the target length, and tuned the parameter α. Figure 3 shows that $\alpha = 0.9$ works best in our experiments, independent of the source boundary delay D. This value is used in all experiments.

Furthermore, we found the model to be very sensitive to a source boundary probability threshold t_b different than 0.5 regarding translation quality. This means the "translating" part of the network strongly adapts to the chunking component.

System	Delay	Avg. AL	tst2015		must-c-HE		must-c-COMMON	
			BLEU	**TER**	**BLEU**	**TER**	**BLEU**	**TER**
Baseline wait-k (k=9)	-		27.4	55.8	25.1	59.5	27.4	54.2
Proposed simultaneous MT	2	4.72	30.2	52.6	28.8	55.0	30.0	50.8
unidirectional	3	5.26	30.3	53.2	28.8	55.2	29.7	50.8
(6 enc. 2 dec.)	4	6.17	29.9	53.1	28.6	55.1	29.6	50.8
Proposed simultaneous MT	2	4.65	29.3	53.4	28.1	55.4	29.7	50.9
bidirectional	3	5.46	29.6	53.7	29.0	54.8	29.7	51.6
(2x4 enc. 1 dec.)	4	6.15	29.2	54.0	28.3	55.3	29.7	51.5

Table 2: Experimental results (in %) for simultaneous NMT of text input, IWSLT 2020 English→German.

9 Conclusion

We proposed a novel neural model architecture for simultaneous MT that incorporates a component for splitting the incoming source stream into translatable chunks. We presented how we generate training examples for such chunks from statistical word alignment and how those can be improved via language models. Experiments on the IWSLT 2020 English-to-German task proved that the proposed learned source chunking outperforms a fixed wait-k strategy by a large margin. We also investigated the value of backwards source encoding in the context of simultaneous MT by comparing uni- and bidirectional versions of our architecture.

Acknowledgements

We would like to thank our colleague Albert Zeyer for fruitful discussions and RETURNN implementation support.

References

Ashkan Alinejad, Maryam Siahbani, and Anoop Sarkar. 2018. Prediction improves simultaneous neural machine translation. In *Proceedings of the 2018 Conference on Empirical Methods in Natural Language Processing*, pages 3022–3027, Brussels, Belgium. Association for Computational Linguistics.

Naveen Arivazhagan, Colin Cherry, Wolfgang Macherey, Chung-Cheng Chiu, Semih Yavuz, Ruoming Pang, Wei Li, and Colin Raffel. 2019. Monotonic infinite lookback attention for simultaneous machine translation. In *Proceedings of the 57th Annual Meeting of the Association for Computational Linguistics*, pages 1313–1323, Florence, Italy. Association for Computational Linguistics.

Philip Arthur, Trevor Cohn, and Gholamreza Haffari. 2020. Learning coupled policies for simultaneous machine translation. *arXiv preprint arXiv:2002.04306*.

Parnia Bahar, Patrick Wilken, Tamer Alkhouli, Andreas Guta, Pavel Golik, Evgeny Matusov, and Christian Herold. 2020. Start-before-end and end-to-end: Neural speech translation by apptek and rwth aachen university. In *International Workshop on Spoken Language Translation*.

Dzmitry Bahdanau, Kyunghyun Cho, and Yoshua Bengio. 2015. Neural machine translation by jointly learning to align and translate. In *Proceedings of the International Conference on Learning Representations (ICLR)*.

Hervé Bourlard and Christian J. Wellekens. 1989. Links between Markov models and multilayer perceptrons. In D.S. Touretzky, editor, *Advances in Neural Information Processing Systems 1*, pages 502–510. Morgan Kaufmann, San Mateo, CA, USA.

Kai Chen and Qiang Huo. 2016. Training deep bidirectional LSTM acoustic model for LVCSR by a context-sensitive-chunk BPTT approach. *IEEE/ACM Transactions on Audio, Speech, and Language Processing*, 24(7):1185–1193.

Kyunghyun Cho and Masha Esipova. 2016. Can neural machine translation do simultaneous translation? *arXiv preprint arXiv:1606.02012*.

Fahim Dalvi, Nadir Durrani, Hassan Sajjad, and Stephan Vogel. 2018. Incremental decoding and training methods for simultaneous translation in neural machine translation. In *Proceedings of the 2018 Conference of the North American Chapter of the Association for Computational Linguistics: Human Language Technologies, Volume 2 (Short Papers)*, pages 493–499, New Orleans, Louisiana. Association for Computational Linguistics.

Mattia Antonino Di Gangi, Roldano Cattoni, Luisa Bentivogli, Matteo Negri, and Marco Turchi. 2019. MuST-C: a Multilingual Speech Translation Corpus. In *Proceedings of the 2019 Conference of the North American Chapter of the Association for Computational Linguistics: Human Language Technologies, Volume 2 (Short Papers)*, Minneapolis, MN, USA.

Mercedes García-Martínez, Loïc Barrault, and Fethi Bougares. 2016. Factored neural machine translation architectures. In *International Workshop on Spoken Language Translation (IWSLT'16)*.

Jiatao Gu, Graham Neubig, Kyunghyun Cho, and Victor O.K. Li. 2017. Learning to translate in real-time with neural machine translation. In *Proceedings of the 15th Conference of the European Chapter of the Association for Computational Linguistics: Volume 1, Long Papers*, pages 1053–1062, Valencia, Spain. Association for Computational Linguistics.

Sepp Hochreiter and Jürgen Schmidhuber. 1997. Long short-term memory. *Neural Computation*, 9(8):1735–1780.

Philipp Koehn, Franz Joseph Och, and Daniel Marcu. 2003. Statistical Phrase-Based Translation. In *Proc. of the Human Language Technology Conf. (HLT-NAACL)*, pages 127–133, Edmonton, Canada.

Taku Kudo and John Richardson. 2018. Sentencepiece: A simple and language independent subword tokenizer and detokenizer for neural text processing. In *Proceedings of the 2018 Conference on Empirical Methods in Natural Language Processing: System Demonstrations*, pages 66–71.

Mingbo Ma, Liang Huang, Hao Xiong, Renjie Zheng, Kaibo Liu, Baigong Zheng, Chuanqiang Zhang, Zhongjun He, Hairong Liu, Xing Li, Hua Wu, and Haifeng Wang. 2019. STACL: Simultaneous translation with implicit anticipation and controllable latency using prefix-to-prefix framework. In *Proceedings of the 57th Annual Meeting of the Association for Computational Linguistics*, pages 3025–3036, Florence, Italy. Association for Computational Linguistics.

J.B. Mariño, R. Banchs, JM Crego, A. de Gispert, P. Lambert, José Adrián Fonollosa, and M. Ruiz. 2005. Bilingual N-gram Statistical Machine Translation. In *The 10th Machine Translation Summit*, pages 275–282, Phuket, Thailand. Asia-Pacific Association for Machine Translation (AAMT).

Yusuke Oda, Graham Neubig, Sakriani Sakti, Tomoki Toda, and Satoshi Nakamura. 2014. Optimizing segmentation strategies for simultaneous speech translation. In *Proceedings of the 52nd Annual Meeting of the Association for Computational Linguistics (Volume 2: Short Papers)*, pages 551–556, Baltimore, Maryland. Association for Computational Linguistics.

Robert Östling and Jörg Tiedemann. 2016. Efficient word alignment with Markov Chain Monte Carlo. *Prague Bulletin of Mathematical Linguistics*, 106:125–146.

Kishore Papineni, Salim Roukos, Todd Ward, and Wei-Jing Zhu. 2002. BLEU: a Method for Automatic Evaluation of Machine Translation. In *Proceedings of the 41st Annual Meeting of the Association for Computational Linguistics*, pages 311–318, Philadelphia, Pennsylvania, USA.

Ofir Press and Noah A Smith. 2018. You may not need attention. *arXiv preprint arXiv:1810.13409*.

Harsh Satija and Joelle Pineau. 2016. Simultaneous machine translation using deep reinforcement learning. In *ICML 2016 Workshop on Abstraction in Reinforcement Learning*.

Matthew Snover, Bonnie Dorr, Richard Schwartz, Linnea Micciulla, and John Makhoul. 2006. A Study of Translation Edit Rate with Targeted Human Annotation. In *Proceedings of the 7th Conference of the Association for Machine Translation in the Americas*, pages 223–231, Cambridge, Massachusetts, USA.

Ashish Vaswani, Noam Shazeer, Niki Parmar, Jakob Uszkoreit, Llion Jones, Aidan N Gomez, Łukasz Kaiser, and Illia Polosukhin. 2017. Attention is all you need. In *Advances in Neural Information Processing Systems*, pages 5998–6008.

Simon Wiesler, Alexander Richard, Pavel Golik, Ralf Schlüter, and Hermann Ney. 2014. RASR/NN: The RWTH neural network toolkit for speech recognition. In *IEEE International Conference on Acoustics, Speech, and Signal Processing*, pages 3313–3317, Florence, Italy.

Patrick Wilken and Evgeny Matusov. 2019. Novel applications of factored neural machine translation. *arXiv preprint arXiv:1910.03912*.

Hao Xiong, Ruiqing Zhang, Chuanqiang Zhang, Zhongjun He, Hua Wu, and Haifeng Wang. 2019. Dutongchuan: Context-aware translation model for simultaneous interpreting. *ArXiv*, abs/1907.12984.

Albert Zeyer, Tamer Alkhouli, and Hermann Ney. 2018. RETURNN as a generic flexible neural toolkit with application to translation and speech recognition. In *Proceedings of ACL 2018, Melbourne, Australia, July 15-20, 2018, System Demonstrations*, pages 128–133.

Albert Zeyer, Ralf Schlüter, and Hermann Ney. 2016. Towards online-recognition with deep bidirectional LSTM acoustic models. In *Interspeech*, pages 3424–3428, San Francisco, CA, USA.

Baigong Zheng, Renjie Zheng, Mingbo Ma, and Liang Huang. 2019. Simpler and faster learning of adaptive policies for simultaneous translation. In *EMNLP/IJCNLP*.

Adapting End-to-End Speech Recognition for Readable Subtitles

Danni Liu, Jan Niehues, Gerasimos Spanakis
Department of Data Science and Knowledge Engineering,
Maastricht University
{danni.liu, jan.niehues, jerry.spanakis}@maastrichtuniversity.nl

Abstract

Automatic speech recognition (ASR) systems are primarily evaluated on transcription accuracy. However, in some use cases such as subtitling, verbatim transcription would reduce output readability given limited screen size and reading time. Therefore, this work focuses on ASR with output compression, a task challenging for supervised approaches due to the scarcity of training data. We first investigate a cascaded system, where an unsupervised compression model is used to post-edit the transcribed speech. We then compare several methods of end-to-end speech recognition under output length constraints. The experiments show that with limited data far less than needed for training a model from scratch, we can adapt a Transformer-based ASR model to incorporate both transcription and compression capabilities. Furthermore, the best performance in terms of WER and ROUGE scores is achieved by explicitly modeling the length constraints within the end-to-end ASR system.

1 Introduction

Automatic speech recognition (ASR) has become ubiquitous in human interaction with digital devices, such as keyboard voice inputs (He et al., 2019) and virtual home assistants (Li et al., 2017). While transcription accuracy is often the primary goal when designing ASR systems, in some use cases the readability of outputs is crucial to user experience. A prominent example is subtitling for TV. In this case, the audience need to multitask, i.e. simultaneously watch video contents, listen to speech utterances, and read subtitles. To avoid a visual overload, not every spoken word needs to be displayed. Meanwhile, the shortened subtitles must still retain the meaning of the spoken content. Moreover, large deviations from the original utterance are also undesirable, as the disagreement with auditory input would create a distraction.

To compress the subtitles, one straightforward approach is to post-process ASR transcriptions. The task of sentence compression has been well-studied (Knight and Marcu, 2002; Clarke and Lapata, 2006; Rush et al., 2015). In extractive compression (Filippova et al., 2015; Angerbauer et al., 2019), only deletion operations are performed on the input. Despite the simplicity, this approach tends to produce outputs that are less grammatical (Knight and Marcu, 2002). On the other hand, abstractive compression (Cohn and Lapata, 2008; Rush et al., 2015; Chopra et al., 2016; Yu et al., 2018) involves more sophisticated input reformulation, such as word reordering and paraphrasing (Clarke and Lapata, 2006). For the task of compressing subtitles, however, the extent of rewriting must be controlled in order to retain consistency with spoken utterances.

From a practical point of view, building a sentence compression system typically requires training corpora where the target sequences are summarized. For most languages and domains, there exists scarcely any resource suitable for supervised training. This low-resource condition is even more severe for audio inputs. To the best of our knowledge, currently there is no publicly available spoken language compression corpora.

Given the challenges outlined above, this work investigates ASR with output compression. We test our approaches on German TV subtitles. The combination of this task and the use case is to the extent of our knowledge previously unexplored.

The first contribution of this work is a comparison of cascaded and end-to-end approaches to generating compressed ASR transcriptions, where the former consists of separate ASR and compression modules, and the latter integrates transcription and compression. The experiments show that our sentence compression module trained in an unsupervised fashion tends to excessively paraphrase,

Proceedings of the 17th International Conference on Spoken Language Translation (IWSLT), pages 247–256
July 9-10, 2020. ©2020 Association for Computational Linguistics
https://doi.org/10.18653/v1/P17

whereas the end-to-end model can be better adapted to the task of interest. Secondly, we show that, after fine-tuning on a small adaption corpus, an ASR model can perform transcription and compression simultaneously. Without being given explicit length constraints, the adapted model shows increased recognition accuracy on rare words as well as paraphrasing capabilities to produce shorter outputs. Furthermore, by explicitly encoding the length constraints, we achieve further performance gains in addition to those brought by adaptation.

2 Task

The task of creating readable subtitles for video contents has several unique properties. First, due to limited screen size and reading time, not every spoken word needs to be transcribed, especially when utterances are spoken fast. A full transcription could even hamper user experience due to poor readability. Second, although output shortening is typically realized by deleting non-essential words, the output is not only deletion-based. A real-life example from the German TV program Tagesschau[1] shown in Table 1 contain rephrasing (from "freed from" to "without") in addition to word removal (dropping the word "ethically"). A further requirement is that the subtitles should stay reasonably authentic to the spoken contents, only modifying them when necessary. Otherwise, the disagreement with audio contents could become distracting to the audience.

Within the framework of common NLP tasks, the task of generating readable subtitles combines ASR and abstractive compression, while being subjected to the additional requirements as outlined above.

Spoken: <u>Befreit vom</u> fraktionszwang soll das Parlament wohl nach der Sommerpause die <u>ethisch</u> schwierige Frage debattieren. (<u>Freed from</u> pressure from the coalition party, the parliamentary should debate the ethically difficult question after the summer break.)
Subtitle: <u>Ohne</u> Fraktionszwang soll das Parlament wohl nach der Sommerpause die schwierige Frage debattieren. (<u>Without</u> pressure from the coalition party, the parliamentary should debate the difficult question after the summer break.)

Table 1: Examples of TV subtitles compared to actual spoken words. Underlined words are the differences between the spoken words and the subtitles.

---

3 ASR with Output Length Constraints

3.1 Baseline ASR Model with Adaptation

For the baseline ASR model, we use the Transfomer architecture (Vaswani et al., 2017) similar to that by Pham et al. (2019). As there is no spoken language compression corpus available to us that is large enough for training an end-to-end model from scratch, we first train an ASR model without output compression, and then adapt it to our task of interest using a small web-scraped corpus. In the first training stage, the model is solely trained for transcribing speech. In the fine-tuning stage, we let the model continue training at a reduced learning rate on the adaptation corpus with shortened transcriptions. The intended goal of adaptation is to let the model learn the compression task on the basis of the transcription capability acquired before.

3.2 End-to-End Length-Constrained ASR

With the baseline introduced above, the ASR model is not aware of the compression task until the adaptation step. If the model already has a sense of output length constraints earlier, i.e. when training for the ASR task, it could better utilize the abundance of training data. Motivated by this hypothesis, we inject information about the allowable output lengths using a count-down at each decoding step, as illustrated in Figure 1. In a vanilla decoder, the hidden state at position i would ingest an embedding of the previously generated token. With the count-down for target length t, decoder state $\mathbf{y}_i$ additionally ingests a representation of the number of allowed output tokens, $t - i$.

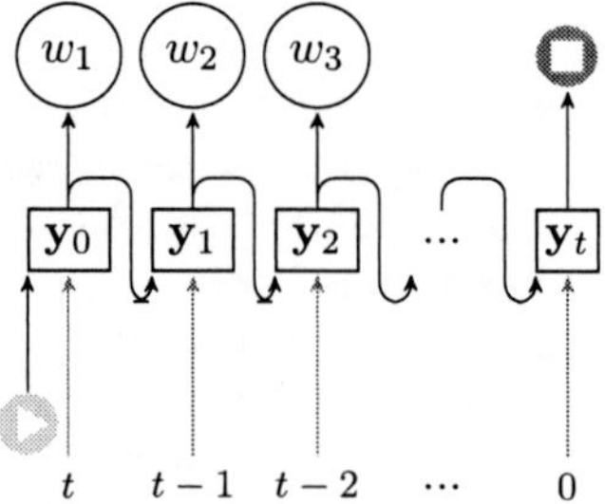

Figure 1: An illustration of the length countdown during decoding. The values are represented with learned embeddings or trigonometric encoding.

We explore two ways to represent the length count-down. The first one utilizes length embeddings learned during training, motivated by the approach Kikuchi et al. (2016) proposed. Given a target sequence of length t, at decoding time step i, the input to decoder hidden state $\mathbf{y}_i$ is based on a concatenation of the previous state $\mathbf{y}_{i-1}$ and an embedding of the remaining length

$$\mathbf{y}_{i-1} \oplus \text{emb}(t - i), \tag{1}$$

where $\text{emb}(t - i)$ is an embedding of the number of allowed tokens. To keep the same dimensionality as that of the original word embedding, the output from Equation 1 further undergoes a linear transformation followed by the ReLU activation.

With the length embedding approach, the model learns representations of different length values during training. Therefore, learning to represent rarely-encountered lengths may be difficult.

The second method modifies the trigonometric positional encoding from the Transformer (Vaswani et al., 2017) to represent the remaining length rather than the current position. This method has been applied in summarization (Takase and Okazaki, 2019) and machine translation (Lakew et al., 2019; Niehues, 2020) to limit output lengths. Motivated by these examples from related sequence generation tasks, we explore the "backward" positional encoding in ASR models.

With the original positional encoding, for input dimension $d \in \{0, 1, \ldots, D - 1\}$, the encoding at position i is defined as

$$\begin{cases} \sin(i/10000^{d/D}), & \text{if } d \text{ is even} \\ \cos(i/10000^{(d-1)/D}), & \text{if } d \text{ is odd.} \end{cases} \tag{2}$$

The backward positional encoding is the same as Equation (2), except that the current position i is replaced by the remaining length $t - i$. Given a target sequence of length t, the length encoding at decoding step i becomes

$$\begin{cases} \sin((t - i)/10000^{d/D}), & \text{if } d \text{ is even} \\ \cos((t - i)/10000^{(d-1)/D}), & \text{if } d \text{ is odd.} \end{cases} \tag{3}$$

Like the positional encoding, the length encoding is also summed together with the input embedding to decoder hidden states. Moreover, since the encoding is based on sinusoids, it can be easily extrapolated to lengths unseen during training. This is a potential advantage over the learned length embeddings.

3.3 Unsupervised Sentence Compression

Compared to training ASR models to jointly perform transcription and compression, a more straightforward approach is to post-edit ASR outputs using a compression model. However, training such a model in a supervised fashion requires reliable target sequences. Due to the scarcity of suitable training corpora, we choose an unsupervised approach inspired by multilingual translation (Ha et al., 2017; Johnson et al., 2017).

Similar to in Niehues (2020), this approach relies on a multilingual translation system that is trained on several language pairs. At training time, language tokens are embedded together with the source and target sentences. At test time, the model is given the same source and target language token, which is a translation direction unseen in training. Since the multilingual training enables zero-shot translation, the model is able to reformulate the input in the same language. To achieve output compression, the length constraints introduced in Section 3.2 are applied in the decoder.

4 Experiment Setup

4.1 Datasets

Table 2 provides an overview of audio corpora we use. The baseline ASR model is trained on the German part of LibriVoxDeEn (Beilharz et al., 2020), a recently released corpus consisting of open-domain German audio books. Since the corpus creators did not suggest a train-dev-test partition, we split the dataset ourselves. The test set contains the following books: *Jonathan Frock*[2], *Jolanthes Hochzeit* and *Kammmacher*.

For the spoken language compression adaptation corpus, we collect spoken utterances and subtitles from the German news program Tagesschau from 1 January to 15 August 2019. To control for recording condition and disfluency, we exclude interviews or press conferences and only keep utterances from the news anchors. The utterances are segmented based on the start and end time of subtitles. Since the timestamps do not always precisely correspond to utterance boundaries, we manually verify the test set and edit when necessary.

For the unsupervised compression system, we use the multilingual translation corpus from the IWSLT 2017 evaluation campaign (Cettolo et al., 2017). It consists of English, German, Dutch, Italian and Romanian parallel sentences based on TED

---

[2]In the recordings of *Jonathan Frock*, we found some sections with misaligned utterances therefore incorrect transcriptions. The following sections are excluded from our test set: 00006_jonathanfrock, 00007_jonathanfrock.

Dataset	Total length (h:m)	Total utterances	Average length (s)	Total words
LibriVoxDeEn (train)	469:21	206,490	8.18	3,622,560
LibriVoxDeEn (test)	5:17	2,446	7.78	51,314
Tagesschau (adapt)	37:28	11,559	11.67	243,728
Tagesschau (test)	46	213	13.01	4,864

Table 2: Corpus statistics.

talks. All 10×2 translation directions are used in training. At test time, the model is given the same source and target language tag (German in our case) in order to generate summarization in the same language. We use the positional embedding introduced in Section 3.2 for length control.

4.2 Preprocessing

We use the Kaldi toolkit (Povey et al., 2011) to preprocess the raw audio utterances into 23-dimensional filter banks. We choose not to apply any utterance-level normalization to allow for future work towards online processing. For text materials, i.e. audio transcriptions and the translation source and target sentences, we use byte-pair encoding (BPE) (Sennrich et al., 2016) to create subword-based dictionaries.

4.3 Hyperparameters

For the ASR model, we adopt many reported values in the work of Pham et al. (2019), including the optimizer choice, learning rate, warmup steps, dropout rate, label smoothing rate, and embedding dimension. There are several parameters that we choose differently. The size of the inner feed forward layer is 2048. Moreover, we use 32 encoder and 12 decoder layers, and BPE of size 10,000. For the compression model, we use a Transformer with 8 encoder and decoder layers each.[3]

5 Experiments

5.1 Post-Editing with Compression Model

To gain an initial understanding of the task, we start with a more controlled setup, where the test utterances are transcribed by a commercial off-the-shelf ASR system. The transcriptions are then post-processed with our compression model.

First, we analyze the level of desired output compression by contrasting the lengths of the off-the-shelf transcriptions against those of the references.

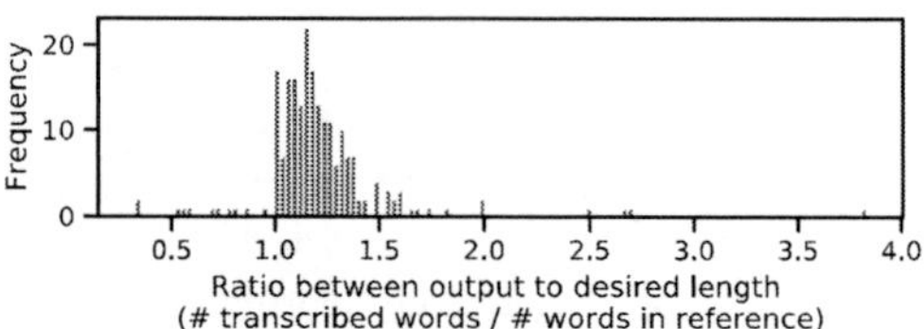

Figure 2: Histogram of compression rate on the test set. Ratios lower than 1 are outliers where the off-the-shelf ASR model terminates decoding prematurely.

Ground-truth: (17 words) Allerdings können Ausnahmeanträge gestellt werden, von Pendlern und von Stuttgartern, was Tausende auch bereits getan haben. (However, commuters and Stuttgarter can apply for exception-permits, which thousands have already done.)
Reference: (6 words) Es können aber Ausnahmeantrge gestellt werden. (However, exception-permits can be applied for.)

Ground-truth: (13 words) In der Debatte über neue Regeln für Organspenden gibt es einen ersten Gesetzentwurf. (There is a first draft law in the debate about new rules for organ donation.)
Reference: (12 words) In der Debatte über neue Regeln für Organspenden gibt es einen Gesetzentwurf. (There is a draft law in the debate about new rules for organ donation.)

Table 3: Two examples of various levels of compression, where the first shortens from 17 to 6 words, and the second only removes one word.

In Figure 2, we plot the distribution of the ratio between transcription lengths and target lengths over the test set. The first observation is that most of the transcriptions require shortening, as shown by the high frequencies of ratios over 1.

Moreover, the compression ratio varies across different utterances. Table 3 shows two examples, where the first compressed from 17 to 6 words, while the second only deletes one word. When inspecting the original videos, we notice that the first example contains many other visual contents, some also in text form, whereas the second example only involves the new anchorwoman speaking. The examples showcase that the level of desired compression depends on various factors, such as

---

[3]The code is available at `https://github.com/quanpn90/NMTGMinor/tree/DbMajor`.

Model	Ratio (output to desired length)	WER	R-1	R-2	R-L
Off-the-shelf ASR	1.09	41.5	75.9	58.9	72.6
+ compression	0.95	69.1	55.7	29.5	51.6
Baseline ASR	1.21	57.7	65.2	43.6	61.9
+ compression	1.00	74.3	48.5	23.3	44.7

Table 4: Word error rate and summarization quality on the test set by cascading two separate models for ASR and sentence compression.

Ground-truth	Es ist kurz nach Mitternacht, als plötzlich ein Auto in eine Gruppe von Menschen steuert, die ausgelassen ins neue Jahr feiern. It is just after midnight, when a car suddenly drives into a group of people who joyfully celebrate the new year.
Reference	Kurz nach Mitternacht steuert ein Auto in eine Gruppe von Menschen, die ins neue Jahr feiern. Just after midnight a car drives into a group of people who celebrate the new year.
Unsupervised compression	Kurz nach Mitternacht <u>fährt</u> ein Auto plötzlich in eine Gruppe von <u>Leuten</u>, die das <u>nächste</u> Jahr feiern. Just after midnight a car suddenly drives into a group of people who celebrate the <u>next</u> year.
Ground-truth	Unter dem Eindruck der Massenproteste hatten sich zuletzt auch hochrangige Militärs von ihm abgewandt. Under the impression of mass protests, senior military officials have finally also turned away from him.
Reference	Unter dem Eindruck der Proteste wandten sich zuletzt auch hochrangige Militärs ab. Under the impression of protests, senior military officials finally also turned away.
Unsupervised compression	Unter dem Eindruck <u>von</u> Massenprotest<u>ieren</u> <u>waren</u> auch hochrangige Militärs von ihm <u>entfernt</u>. Under the impression of mass protesting, senior military officials <u>were</u> also <u>distanced</u> from him.

Table 5: Examples outputs of the unsupervised compression model, where undesired paraphrasing is underlined. English translations are in gray.

the amount of visual information simultaneously shown on the screen. Therefore, a globally fixed compression rate would not be suitable.

To comply with length constraints, the ASR outputs are shortened by the unsupervised sentence compression model. As the system is trained based on subwords, we use the number of BPE-tokens in the reference as target length. The first two rows in Table 4 contrast the output quality before and after compression, as measured in case-insensitive word error rate (WER), and ROUGE scores (Lin, 2004).[4] To our surprise, compression has a large negative impact on the outputs in all four metrics, creating a gap of over 20% absolute. Via an exhaustive manual inspection over the test set, we find that the unsupervised compression model tends to paraphrase much more frequently than the references. While

the paraphrased output is often valid both grammatically and semantically, the deviation from the references leads to higher WER and lower ROUGE scores. Two examples are given in Table 5, where several synonym replacements appear in the compression outputs, e.g. "fährt" for "steuert" (both "drives"), "Leute" for "Menschen" (both "people"), "nächste Jahr" for "neue Jahr" ("next year" for "new year"). In all these places, the references keep the original spoken words unchanged. Given the nature of our task, it is indeed undesirable to paraphrase excessively, as subtitles that are too different from the original spoken utterances could create a cognitive overload to users.

Considering these downsides, an ASR system is trained from scratch to provide more flexibility of structural modification. On our self-partitioned LibriVoxDeEn test set, we achieve a WER of 9.2%. The compression performance is reported in the lower section of Table 4. As this model is only

---

[4]Ideally, these metrics should be accompanied by an independent human evaluation, which we could not perform due to resource constraints.

Model	Ratio (output to desired length)	WER	R-1	R-2	R-L
Baseline ASR	1.12	57.7	65.2	43.6	61.9
+adapt	1.05	38.5	76.8	58.7	74.4
+adapt+stop decoding	0.96	39.9	74.6	57.0	72.6

Table 6: Word error rate and summarization quality on the test set by the baseline ASR model. Fine-tuning on in-domain data is beneficial for both shortening outputs and increasing transcription quality.

Reference	In Brasilien ist Präsident Bolsonaro vereidigt worden.
	In Brazil new president Bolsonaro has been inaugurated.
Before adaptation	In Brasilien <u>ist</u> der neue Präsident *voll zu Narro* vereidigt worden.
	In Brazil the new president "voll zu Narro" has been inaugurated.
After adaptation	In Brasilien <u>wurde</u> der neue Präsident *Bolsonaro* vereidigt.
	In Brazil the new president Bolsonaro was inaugurated.

Table 7: Example outputs of the ASR model before and after adapting to the compression task. After adaptation, the model can perform shortening by changing tense, and correctly recognize the proper noun "Bolsonaro". English translations are below each sentence in gray.

trained on LibriVoxDeEn audio books, its performance suffers from the train-test domain mismatch. This is exhibited by the gap of nearly 10% to the off-the-shelf system, which is trained on larger volume of data from various domains. Moreover, the transcription errors by the ASR system carry over as the input of the compression model, which is further disadvantageous to the final output quality. Lastly, similar to previous observations, post-processing by the compression model has a negative effect in terms of the evaluation metrics.

Overall, the performance of the unsupervised compression model suffers from paraphrasing. As an anonymous reviewer suggested, the aggressive paraphrasing can be remedied during decoding. For example, given a large beam size, we can select candidates that contain less paraphrasing. Otherwise, training with a paraphrasing penalty could also alleviate the problem. While we have not explored these methods here, they would indeed provide a more complete picture when comparing the cascaded and end-to-end approach.

5.2 Fine-Tuning ASR Model for Compression

Our baseline ASR model is trained on a different domain than the test set, and only for the transcription task. To improve performance on our task of interest, we apply fine-tuning on the adaptation corpus. The results are in Table 6. For easy visual comparison, the pre-adaptation performance in the first row is repeated from Table 4. Contrasting the performance before and after adaptation, we see no-

ticeable gains brought by adaptation in terms of all four quality metrics. Moreover, as evidenced by the reduced ratio of output to desired length, the model already performs shortening, despite not having received explicit length constraints. Table 7 shows an example where the adapted model changes verb tense to reduce output length. Specifically, by using the simple past ("wurde vereidigt / was inaugurated") instead of the present perfect tense ("ist vereidigt worden / has been inaugurated"), the output becomes shorter. Meanwhile, we also observe the correct transcription of the proper noun "Bolsonaro", which was mistakenly transcribed to the phonetically-similar "voll zu Narro" before adaption. This illustrates that the adaptation step enables the model to improve recognition quality and compress its outputs simultaneously.

Despite the positive observations, the desired length constraints are not yet fully satisfied, as shown by the ratio of 1.05 between output to desired lengths. To examine the scenario of fully obeying the length constraints, we stop decoding once the number of allowed tokens runs out. The result is reported in the last row of Table 6. The ratio of 0.96 is lower than 1 because of a few instances where decoding stops before the countdown reaches zero. As the same output sequence can be constructed by different BPE-units, choosing longer subword units earlier on can lead to reaching the end-of-sequence token before depleting the number of allowed tokens. Lastly, from the quality metrics in the last row of Table 6, we see

Model	Ratio (output to desired length)	WER	R-1	R-2	R-L
(1): Baseline (satisfy length)	0.97	55.1	62.5	41.5	60.4
(2): + adapt	0.96	39.9	74.6	**57.0**	72.6
(3): Length embedding	1.00	57.8	61.9	40.5	59.8
(4): + adapt	0.96	39.3	74.3	55.2	72.5
(5): Length encoding	1.00	57.4	62.6	40.7	60.1
(6): + adapt	0.96	**38.6**	**75.1**	56.4	**73.2**

Table 8: Word error rate and summarization quality by the models with length count-down. Adaptation results in large gains. The model with length encoding outperforms the baseline and the one with length embedding.

Reference	[... 75 tokens] Sea-Watch spricht von einer politisch motivierten Blockade, um Rettungsaktionen zu verhindern. Sea-Watch speaks of a politically motivated blockade to prevent bailouts.
Len. Encoding	[... 83 tokens] Die Hilfsorganisation Sea-Watch spricht von einer politisch motivierten Blockade. The aid organization Sea-Watch speaks of a politically motivated blockade.
Len. Embedding	[... 82 tokens] Die Hilfsorganisation Sea-Watch spricht von einer politisch motivierten Blockade zu verhinder. The aid organization Sea-Watch speaks of a politically motivated blockade to prevent.

Table 9: Comparison of length encoding and length embedding models (after adaptation). When facing exceptionally long outputs, the length embedding model tends to stop abruptly, producing non-grammatical half-sentences.

that the forced termination of decoding comes with higher WER and lower ROUGE scores, indicating reduced output quality when fully satisfying the target length constraints.

5.3 Models with Explicit Length Constraints

While the baseline ASR model achieves some degree of compression after adaptation, it cannot fully comply with length constraints. Therefore, the following experiments examine the effects of training with explicit length count-downs. In Table 8, we report the performance of the ASR models with length embedding or encoding, as introduced in Section 3.2. For a complete comparison, in the first two rows of Table 8, we also include the baseline performance with forced termination of decoding.

Rows (3) and (5) show the performance of the two length count-down methods before adaptation. As the ratios of output to desired length are equal to 1, the models are always faithful to the given length constraints. This shows the effectiveness of injecting allowable length in training. However, we also observe that there is no quality gain over the baseline in row (1). To investigate the reason for this, we experimented by decoding one sample sequence with different allowable lengths. As

we gradually reduce the target length, the models first shorten their outputs by removing punctuation marks. Afterwards, instead of shortening the outputs by summarization, they stop decoding when running out of allowed number of tokens. Indeed, during training, the models are only incentivized to accurately transcribe the spoken utterance and to stop decoding when the count-down reaches zero. The same behavior therefore carries over to test time. Contrary to abstractive summarization (Takase and Okazaki, 2019) and machine translation (Lakew et al., 2019), in ASR, an input sequence has one single ground-truth transcription rather than multiple viable outputs. This could lead to a different level of abstraction than required in summarization or translation models. These observations with the unadapted model also highlight the importance of the subsequent fine-tuning step.

The results after adaptation are reported in rows (4) and (6). The large improvement in WER and ROUGE scores is in line with the previous finding when adapting the baseline. When decoding with length count-down, we define the target output length as the minimum of the baseline output length and the reference length. This ensures the same output-to-desired length ratio as the baseline in row (1). Here, the first observation is that the length encoding model in row (5) outperforms the baseline in three of the four evaluation metrics. This suggests that it is beneficial to represent the constraints explicitly during training. Moreover, the length encoding model also consistently outperforms its embedding-based counterpart. This could be because the length encoding can extrapolate to any length values, and is equipped with a sense of relative differences between numerical values at initialization. On the other hand, the length embedding would need to learn the representation for different lengths during training. When inspecting the outputs for long utterances, we found that the embedding model is more likely to abruptly stop, such as the example shown in Table 9.

6   Related Work

6.1   Length-Controlled Text Generation

Controlling output length of natural language generation systems has been studied for several tasks.

For abstractive summarization, Kikuchi et al. (2016) proposed two methods to incorporate length constraints into LSTM-based encoder-decoder models. The first method uses length embedding at every decoding step, while the second adds the desired length in the first decoder state. For convolutional models, Fan et al. (2018) used special tokens to represent quantized length ranges, and provides the desired token to the decoder before output generation. Liu et al. (2018) adopted a more general approach, where the decoder directly ingests the desired length. More recently, Takase and Okazaki (2019) modified the positional encoding from the Transformer (Vaswani et al., 2017) to encode allowable lengths. Makino et al. (2019) proposed a loss function that encourages summaries within desired lengths. Saito et al. (2020) introduced a model that controls both output length and informativeness.

For machine translation, Lakew et al. (2019) used both the length range token and reverse length encoding. Niehues (2020) used the length embedding, encoding, as well as a combination of the original positional encoding and length count-down.

6.2   Sentence Compression

Our task of length-controlled ASR outputs is related to sentence compression, as the transcriptions can be compressed in post-processing. An early approach of supervised extractive sentence compression was by Filippova et al. (2015), who proposed to predict the delete-or-keep choice for each output symbol. Angerbauer et al. (2019) extended this approach by integrating the desired compression ratio as part of the prediction label. Yu et al. (2018) proposed to combine the merits of extractive and abstractive approaches by first deleting on non-essential words and then generating new words. For unsupervised compression, Fevry and Phang (2018) trained a denoising auto-encoder to reconstruct original sentences, and in this way circumvented the need for supervised corpora.

7   Conclusion

In this work, we explored the task of compressing ASR outputs to enhance subtitle readability. This task has several unique properties. First, the compression is not solely deletion-based. Moreover, unnecessary paraphrasing must be limited to maintain a consistent user experience between hearing and reading.

We first investigated cascading an ASR module with a sentence compression model. Due to the absence of supervised corpora, the compression model is trained in an unsupervised fashion. Experiments showed that the outputs generated this way do not suit our task requirements because of unnecessary paraphrasing. We then adapted an end-to-end ASR model on a small corpus with compressed transcriptions. Via adaptation, the model learned to both shorten its outputs and improve transcription quality. Nevertheless, the given length constraints were not fully satisfied. Lastly, by explicitly injecting length constraints via reverse positional encoding, we achieved further performance gain, while completely adhering to length constraints.

A direction for future work is to incorporate more diverse measurements of output length as well as complexity. In this work, we measured length by the number of BPE-tokens. While this typically corresponds to the output length perceived visually, a more direct metric would be the number of characters. Moreover, output complexity, such as the proportion of long words, is also important for readability and therefore worth exploring. In a broader scope, as an anonymous reviewer suggested, a way to alleviate the resource scarcity for end-to-end ASR compression is to augment the training data with synthesized utterances from summarization corpora. We expect the augmentation to be complementary to our approaches in this work.

References

Katrin Angerbauer, Heike Adel, and Ngoc Thang Vu. 2019. Automatic compression of subtitles with neural networks and its effect on user experience. In Proceedings of Interspeech'2019, pages 594–598.

Benjamin Beilharz, Xin Sun, Sariya Karimova, and Stefan Riezler. 2020. LibriVoxDeEn: A corpus for German-to-English speech translation and speech recognition. In Proceedings of LREC'2020.

Mauro Cettolo, Marcello Federico, Luisa Bentivogli, Jan Niehues, Sebastian Stüker, Katsuitho Sudoh, Koichiro Yoshino, and Christian Federmann. 2017. Overview of the IWSLT 2017 evaluation campaign. In Proceedings of IWSLT'2017, pages 2–14.

Sumit Chopra, Michael Auli, and Alexander M. Rush. 2016. Abstractive sentence summarization with attentive recurrent neural networks. In Proceedings of NAACL-HLT'2016, pages 93–98.

James Clarke and Mirella Lapata. 2006. Models for sentence compression: A comparison across domains, training requirements and evaluation measures. In Proceedings of COLING/ACL'2006, pages 377–384.

Trevor Cohn and Mirella Lapata. 2008. Sentence compression beyond word deletion. In Proceedings of COLING'2008, pages 137–144.

Angela Fan, David Grangier, and Michael Auli. 2018. Controllable abstractive summarization. In Proceedings of WNMT'2018, pages 45–54, Melbourne, Australia. Association for Computational Linguistics.

Thibault Fevry and Jason Phang. 2018. Unsupervised sentence compression using denoising autoencoders. In Proceedings of CoNLL'2018, pages 413–422.

Katja Filippova, Enrique Alfonseca, Carlos A. Colmenares, Lukasz Kaiser, and Oriol Vinyals. 2015. Sentence compression by deletion with LSTMs. In Proceedings of EMNLP'2015, pages 360–368.

Thanh-Le Ha, Jan Niehues, and Alexander Waibel. 2017. Toward multilingual neural machine translation with universal encoder and decoder. In Proceedings of IWSLT'2016.

Y. He, T. N. Sainath, R. Prabhavalkar, I. McGraw, R. Alvarez, D. Zhao, D. Rybach, A. Kannan, Y. Wu, R. Pang, Q. Liang, D. Bhatia, Y. Shangguan, B. Li, G. Pundak, K. C. Sim, T. Bagby, S. Chang, K. Rao, and A. Gruenstein. 2019. Streaming end-to-end speech recognition for mobile devices. In Proceedings of ICASSP'2019, pages 6381–6385.

Melvin Johnson, Mike Schuster, Quoc V. Le, Maxim Krikun, Yonghui Wu, Zhifeng Chen, Nikhil Thorat, Fernanda Viégas, Martin Wattenberg, Greg Corrado, Macduff Hughes, and Jeffrey Dean. 2017. Google's multilingual neural machine translation system: Enabling zero-shot translation. Transactions of the Association for Computational Linguistics, 5:339–351.

Yuta Kikuchi, Graham Neubig, Ryohei Sasano, Hiroya Takamura, and Manabu Okumura. 2016. Controlling output length in neural encoder-decoders. In Proceedings of EMNLP'2016, pages 1328–1338.

Kevin Knight and Daniel Marcu. 2002. Summarization beyond sentence extraction: A probabilistic approach to sentence compression. Artificial Intelligence, 139(1):91–107.

Surafel Melaku Lakew, Mattia Di Gangi, and Marcello Federico. 2019. Controlling the output length of neural machine translation. In Proceedings of IWSLT'2019.

Bo Li, Tara N Sainath, Arun Narayanan, Joe Caroselli, Michiel Bacchiani, Ananya Misra, Izhak Shafran, Hasim Sak, Golan Pundak, Kean K Chin, et al. 2017. Acoustic modeling for google home. In Proceedings of Interspeech'2017, pages 399–403.

Chin-Yew Lin. 2004. ROUGE: A package for automatic evaluation of summaries. In Text Summarization Branches Out, pages 74–81, Barcelona, Spain. Association for Computational Linguistics.

Yizhu Liu, Zhiyi Luo, and Kenny Zhu. 2018. Controlling length in abstractive summarization using a convolutional neural network. In Proceedings of EMNLP'2018, pages 4110–4119.

Takuya Makino, Tomoya Iwakura, Hiroya Takamura, and Manabu Okumura. 2019. Global optimization under length constraint for neural text summarization. In Proceedings of ACL'2019, pages 1039–1048.

Jan Niehues. 2020. Machine translation with unsupervised length-constraints. arXiv preprint arXiv:2004.03176.

Ngoc-Quan Pham, Thai-Son Nguyen, Jan Niehues, Markus Müller, and Alex Waibel. 2019. Very deep self-attention networks for end-to-end speech recognition. In Proceedings of Interspeech'2019, pages 66–70.

Daniel Povey, Arnab Ghoshal, Gilles Boulianne, Lukas Burget, Ondrej Glembek, Nagendra Goel, Mirko Hannemann, Petr Motlicek, Yanmin Qian, Petr Schwarz, Jan Silovsky, Georg Stemmer, and Karel Vesely. 2011. The Kaldi speech recognition toolkit. In Proceedings of ASRU'2011.

Alexander M. Rush, Sumit Chopra, and Jason Weston. 2015. A neural attention model for abstractive sentence summarization. In Proceedings EMNLP'2015, pages 379–389.

Itsumi Saito, Kyosuke Nishida, Kosuke Nishida, Atsushi Otsuka, Hisako Asano, Junji Tomita, Hiroyuki Shindo, and Yuji Matsumoto. 2020. Length-controllable abstractive summarization by guiding with summary prototype. arXiv preprint arXiv:2001.07331.

Rico Sennrich, Barry Haddow, and Alexandra Birch. 2016. Neural machine translation of rare words with subword units. In Proceedings of ACL'2016, pages 1715–1725.

Sho Takase and Naoaki Okazaki. 2019. Positional encoding to control output sequence length. In Proceedings NAACL-HLT'2019, pages 3999–4004.

Ashish Vaswani, Noam Shazeer, Niki Parmar, Jakob Uszkoreit, Llion Jones, Aidan N. Gomez, undefinedukasz Kaiser, and Illia Polosukhin. 2017. Attention is all you need. In Proceedings of NIPS'2017, pages 6000–6010.

Naitong Yu, Jie Zhang, Minlie Huang, and Xiaoyan Zhu. 2018. An operation network for abstractive sentence compression. In Proceedings of COLING'2018, pages 1065–1076.

From Speech-to-Speech Translation to Automatic Dubbing

Marcello Federico   Robert Enyedi   Roberto Barra-Chicote   Ritwik Giri

Umut Isik   Arvindh Krishnaswamy   Hassan Sawaf[*]

Amazon

Abstract

We present enhancements to a speech-to-speech translation pipeline in order to perform automatic dubbing. Our architecture features neural machine translation generating output of preferred length, prosodic alignment of the translation with the original speech segments, neural text-to-speech with fine tuning of the duration of each utterance, and, finally, audio rendering to enriches text-to-speech output with background noise and reverberation extracted from the original audio. We report and discuss results of a first subjective evaluation of automatic dubbing of excerpts of TED Talks from English into Italian, which measures the perceived naturalness of automatic dubbing and the relative importance of each proposed enhancement.

1 Introduction

Automatic dubbing can be regarded as an extension of the speech-to-speech translation (STST) task (Wahlster, 2013), which is generally seen as the combination of three sub-tasks: (i) transcribing speech to text in a source language (ASR), (ii) translating text from a source to a target language (MT) and (iii) generating speech from text in a target language (TTS). Independently from the implementation approach (Weiss et al., 2017; Waibel, 1996; Vidal, 1997; Metze et al., 2002; Nakamura et al., 2006; Casacuberta et al., 2008), the main goal of STST is producing an output that reflects the linguistic content of the original sentence. On the other hand, automatic dubbing aims to replace all speech contained in a video document with speech in a different language, so that the result sounds and looks as natural as the original. Hence, in addition to conveying the same content of the original utterance, dubbing should also match the

original timbre, emotion, duration, prosody, background noise, and reverberation.

While STST has been addressed for long time and by several research labs (Waibel, 1996; Vidal, 1997; Metze et al., 2002; Nakamura et al., 2006; Wahlster, 2013), relatively less and more sparse efforts have been devoted to automatic dubbing (Matoušek et al., 2010; Matoušek and Vít, 2012; Furukawa et al., 2016; Öktem et al., 2019), although the potential demand of such technology could be huge. In fact, multimedia content created and put online has been growing at exponential rate, in the last decade, while availability and cost of human skills for subtitling and dubbing still remains a barrier for its diffusion worldwide.[1] Professional dubbing (Martínez, 2004) of a video file is a very labor intensive process that involves many steps: (i) extracting speech segments from the audio track and annotating these with speaker information; (ii) transcribing the speech segments, (iii) translating the transcript in the target language, (iv) adapting the translation for timing, (v) casting the voice talents, (vi) performing the dubbing sessions, (vii) fine-aligning the dubbed speech segments, (viii) mixing the new voice tracks within the original soundtrack.

Automatic dubbing has been addressed both in monolingual cross-lingual settings. In (Verhelst, 1997), synchronization of two speech signals with the same content was tackled with time-alignment via dynamic time warping. In (Hanzlìček et al., 2008) automatic monolingual dubbing for TV users with special needs was generated from subtitles. However, due to the poor correlation between length and timing of the subtitles, TTS output fre-

---

[*] Contribution while the author was with Amazon.

[1]Actually, there is still a divide between countries/languages where either subtitling or dubbing are the preferred translation modes (Kilborn, 1993; Koolstra et al., 2002). The reasons for this are mainly economical and historical (Danan, 1991).

Proceedings of the 17th International Conference on Spoken Language Translation (IWSLT), pages 257–264
July 9-10, 2020. ©2020 Association for Computational Linguistics
https://doi.org/10.18653/v1/P17

quently broke the timing boundaries. To avoid unnatural time compression of TTS's voice when fitting its duration to the duration of the original speech, (Matoušek et al., 2010) proposed phone-dependent time compression and text simplification to shorten the subtitles, while (Matoušek and Vít, 2012) leveraged scene-change detection to relax the subtitle time boundaries. Regarding cross-lingual dubbing, lip movements synchronization was tackled in (Furukawa et al., 2016) by directly modifying the actor's mouth motion via shuffling of the actor's video frames. While the method does not use any prior linguistic or phonetic knowledge, it has been only demonstrated on very simple and controlled conditions. Finally, mostly related to our contribution is (Öktem et al., 2019), which discusses speech synchronization at the phrase level (prosodic alignment) for English-to-Spanish automatic dubbing.

In this paper we present research work to enhance a STST pipeline in order to comply with the timing and rendering requirements posed by cross-lingual automatic dubbing of TED Talk videos. Similarly to (Matoušek et al., 2010), we also shorten the TTS script by directly modifying the MT engine rather than via text simplification. As in (Öktem et al., 2019), we synchronize phrases across languages, but follow a fluency-based rather than content-based criterion and replace generation and rescoring of hypotheses in (Öktem et al., 2019) with a more efficient dynamic programming solution. Moreover, we extend (Öktem et al., 2019) by enhancing neural MT and neural TTS to improve speech synchronization, and by performing audio rendering on the dubbed speech to make it sound more real inside the video.

In the following sections, we introduce the overall architecture (Section 2) and the proposed enhancements (Sections 3-6). Then, we present results (Section 7) of experiments evaluating the naturalness of automatic dubbing of TED Talk clips from English into Italian. To our knowledge, this is the first work on automatic dubbing that integrates enhanced deep learning models for MT, TTS and audio rendering, and evaluates them on real-world videos.

2 Automatic Dubbing

With some approximation, we consider here automatic dubbing of the audio track of a video as the

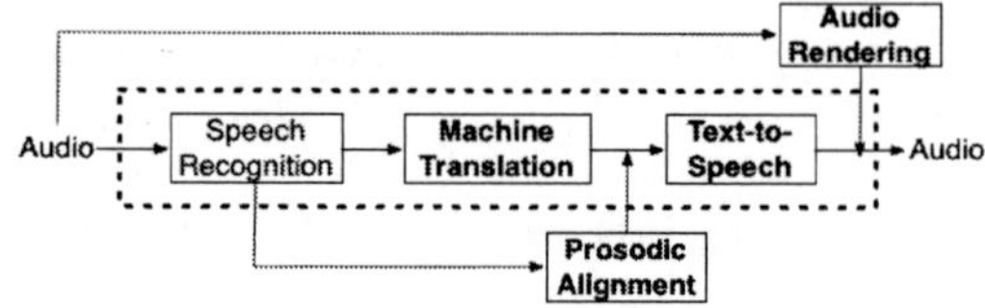

Figure 1: Speech-to-speech translation pipeline (dotted box) with enhancements to perform automatic dubbing (in bold).

task of STST, i.e. ASR + MT + TTS, with the additional requirement that the output must be temporally, prosodically and acoustically close to the original audio. We investigate an architecture (see Figure 1) that enhances the STST pipeline with (i) enhanced MT able to generate translations of variable lengths, (ii) a prosodic alignment module that temporally aligns the MT output with the speech segments in the original audio, (iii) enhanced TTS to accurately control the duration of each produce utterance, and, finally, (iv) audio rendering that adds to the TTS output background noise and reverberation extracted from the original audio. In the following, we describe each component in detail, with the exception of ASR, for which we use (Di Gangi et al., 2019a) an of-the-shelf online service[2].

3 Machine Translation

Our approach to control the length of MT output is inspired by *target forcing* in multilingual neural MT (Johnson et al., 2017; Ha et al., 2016). We partition the training sentence pairs into three groups (short, normal, long) according to the target/source string-length ratio. In practice, we select two thresholds t_1 and t_2, and partition training data according to the length-ratio intervals $[0, t_1)$, $[t_1, t_2)$ and $[t_2, \infty]$. At training time a *length token* is prepended to each source sentence according to its group, in order to let the neural MT model discriminate between the groups. At inference time, the length token is instead prepended to bias the model to generate a translation of the desired length type. We trained a Transformer model (Vaswani et al., 2017) with output length control on web crawled and proprietary data amounting to 150 million English-Italian sentence pairs (with no overlap with the test data). The model has encoder and decoder with 6 layers, layer size of 1024, hidden size of 4096 on feed forward layers, and 16

---

[2]Amazon Transcribe: https://aws.amazon.com/transcribe.

heads in the multi-head attention. For the reported experiments, we trained the models with thresholds $t_1 = 0.95$ and $t_2 = 1.05$ and generated at inference time translations of the shortest type, resulting, on our test set, in an average length ratio of 0.97. A reason for the length exceeding the threshold could be that for part of test data the model did not learn ways to keep the output short. A detailed account of the approach, the followed training procedure and experimental results on the same task of this paper, but using slightly different thresholds, can be found in (Lakew et al., 2019). The paper also shows that human evaluation conducted on the short translations resulted in a minor loss in quality with respect to the model without output length control. Finally, as baseline MT system for our evaluation experiments we used an online service [3]

4 Prosodic Alignment

Prosodic alignment (Öktem et al., 2019) is the problem of segmenting the target sentence to optimally match the distribution of words and pauses[4]. Let $\mathbf{e} = e_1, e_2, \ldots, e_n$ be a source sentence of n words which is segmented according to k breakpoints $1 \le i_1 < i_2 < \ldots i_k = n$, shortly denoted with $\mathbf{i}$. Given a target sentence $\mathbf{f} = f_1, f_2, \ldots, f_m$ of m words, the goal is to find within it k corresponding breakpoints $1 \le j_1 < j_2 < \ldots j_k = m$ (shortly denoted with $\mathbf{j}$) that maximize the probability:

$$\max_{\mathbf{j}} \log \Pr(\mathbf{j} \mid \mathbf{i}, \mathbf{e}, \mathbf{f}) \tag{1}$$

By assuming a Markovian dependency on $\mathbf{j}$, i.e.:

$$\Pr(\mathbf{j} \mid \mathbf{i}, \mathbf{e}, \mathbf{f}) = \sum_{t=1}^{k} \log \Pr(j_t \mid j_{t-1}; t, \mathbf{i}, \mathbf{e}, \mathbf{f}) \tag{2}$$

and omitting from the notation the constant terms $\mathbf{i}, \mathbf{e}, \mathbf{f}$, we can derive the following recurrent quantity:

$$Q(j, t) = \max_{j' < j} \log \Pr(j \mid j'; t) + Q(j', t - 1) \tag{3}$$

where $Q(j, t)$ denotes the log-probability of the optimal segmentation of $\mathbf{f}$ up to position j with t break points. It is easy to show that the solution of (1) corresponds to $Q(m, k)$ and that optimal segmentation can be efficiently computed via

dynamic-programming. Let $\tilde{f}_t = f_{j_{t-1}+1}, \ldots, f_{j_t}$ and $\tilde{e}_t = e_{i_{t-1}+1}, \ldots, e_{i_t}$ indicate the t-th segments of $\mathbf{f}$ and $\mathbf{e}$, respectively, we define the conditional probability of the t-th break point in $\mathbf{f}$ by:

$$\Pr(j_t \mid j_{t-1}, t) \;\propto\; \exp\left(1 - \frac{|d(\tilde{e}_t) - d(\tilde{f}_t)|}{d(\tilde{e}_t)}\right)$$
$$\times \Pr(\text{br} \mid j_t, \mathbf{f}) \tag{4}$$

The first term computes the relative match in duration between the corresponding t-th segments[5], while the second term measure the linguistic plausibility of a placing a break after the j_t in $\mathbf{f}$. For this, we simply compute the following ratio of normalized language model probabilities of text windows centered on the break point, by assuming or not the presence of a pause (br) in the middle:

$$\Pr(\text{br} \mid j, \mathbf{f}) = \frac{\Pr(f_j, \text{br}, f_{j+1})^{1/3}}{\Pr(f_j, \text{br}, f_{j+1})^{1/3} + \Pr(f_j, f_{j+1})^{1/2}}$$

The rational of our model is that we want to favor split points were also TTS was trained to produce pauses. TTS was in fact trained on read speech that generally introduces pauses in correspondence of punctuation marks such as period, comma, semicolon, colon, etc. Notice that our interest, at the moment, is to produce fluent TTS speech, not to closely match the speaking style of the original speaker. In our implementation, we use a larger text window (last and first two words), we replace words with parts-of speech, and estimate the language model with KenLM (Heafield, 2011) on the training portion of the MUST-C corpus tagged with parts-of-speech using an online service[6].

5 Text To Speech

Our neural TTS system consists of two modules: a Context Generation module, which generates a context sequence from the input text, and a Neural Vocoder module, which converts the context sequence into a speech waveform. The first one is an attention-based sequence-to-sequence network (Prateek et al., 2019; Latorre et al., 2019) that predicts a Mel-spectrogram given an input text. A grapheme-to-phoneme module converts the sequence of words into a sequence of phonemes

---

[3]Amazon Translate: https://aws.amazon.com/translate.

[4]In this work the minimum pause interval is set to $300ms$. Pauses are detected from the time stamps produce by force-aligning audio with the transcript (Ochshorn and Hawkins, 2017).

[5]We approximate the duration $d(\cdot)$ of a segment with the sum of the lengths of its words. We plan to use better approximations in the future, e.g. the number of syllables (Öktem et al., 2019).

[6]Amazon Comprehend:https://aws.amazon.com/comprehend.

plus augmented features like punctuation marks and prosody related features derived from the text (e.g. lexical stress). For the Context Generation module, we trained speaker-dependent models on two Italian voices, male and female, with 10 and 37 hours of high quality recordings, respectively. We use the Universal Neural Vocoder introduced in (Lorenzo-Trueba et al., 2019), pre-trained with 2000 utterances per each of the 74 voices from a proprietary database.

To ensure close matching of the duration of Italian TTS output with timing information extracted from the original English audio, for each utterance we re-size the generated Mel spectrogram using spline interpolation prior to running the Neural Vocoder. We empirically observed that this method produces speech of better quality than traditional time-stretching.

6 Audio Rendering

6.1 Foreground-Background Separation

The input audio can be seen as a mixture of foreground (speech) and background (everything else) and our goal is to extract the background and add it to the dubbed speech to make it sound more real and similar to the original. Notice that in the case of TED talks, background noise is mainly coming from the audience (claps and laughs) but sometime also from the speaker, e.g. when she is explaining some functioning equipment. For the foreground-background separation task, we adapted (Giri et al., 2019; Tolooshams et al., 2020) the popular U-Net (Ronneberger et al., 2015) architecture, which is described in detail in (Jansson et al., 2017) for a music-vocal separation task. It consists of a series of down-sampling blocks, followed by one bottom convolutional layer, followed by a series of up-sampling blocks with skip connections from the down-sampling to the up-sampling blocks. Because of the down-sampling blocks, the model can compute a number of high-level features on coarser time scales, which are concatenated with the local, high-resolution features computed from the same-level up-sampling block. This concatenation results into multi-scale features for prediction. The model operates on a time-frequency representation (spectrograms) of the audio mixture and it outputs two soft ratio masks corresponding to foreground and background, respectively, which are multiplied element-wise with the mixed spectrogram, to ob-

tain the final estimates of the two sources. Finally, the estimated spectrograms go through an inverse short-term Fourier transform block to produce raw time domain signals. The loss function used to train the model is the sum of the L_1 losses between the target and the masked input spectrograms, for the foreground and the background (Jansson et al., 2017), respectively. The model is trained with the Adam optimizer on mixed audio provided with foreground and background ground truths. Training data was created from 360 hours of clean speech from Librispeech (foreground) and 120 hours of recording taken from audioset (Gemmeke et al., 2017) (background), from which speech was filtered out using a Voice Activity Detector (VAD). Foreground and background are mixed for different signal-to-noise ratio (SNR), to generate the audio mixtures.

6.2 Re-reverberation

In this step, we estimate the environment reverberation from the original audio and apply it to the dubbed audio. Unfortunately, estimating the room impulse response (RIR) from a reverberated signal requires solving an ill-posed blind deconvolution problem. Hence, instead of estimating the RIR, we do a blind estimation of the reverberation time (RT), which is commonly used to assess the amount of room reverberation or its effects. The RT is defined as the time interval in which the energy of a steady-state sound field decays 60 dB below its initial level after switching off the excitation source. In this work we use a Maximum Likelihood Estimation (MLE) based RT estimate (see details of the method in (Löllmann et al., 2010)). Estimated RT is then used to generate a synthetic RIR using a publicly available RIR generator (Habets, 2006). This synthetic RIR is finally applied to the dubbed audio.

7 Experimental Evaluation

We evaluated our automatic dubbing architecture (Figure 1), by running perceptual evaluations in which users are asked to grade the naturalness of video clips dubbed with three configurations (see Table 1): (A) speech-to-speech translation baseline, (B) the baseline with enhanced MT and prosodic alignment, (C) the former system enhanced with audio rendering.[7] Our evaluation fo-

---

[7]Notice that after preliminary experiments, we decided to not evaluate the configuration *A with Prosodic Alignment*,

System	Condition
R	Original recording (reference)
A	Speech-to-speech translation (baseline)
B	A with Enhanced MT and Pros. Align.
C	B with Audio Rendering

Table 1: Evaluated dubbing conditions.

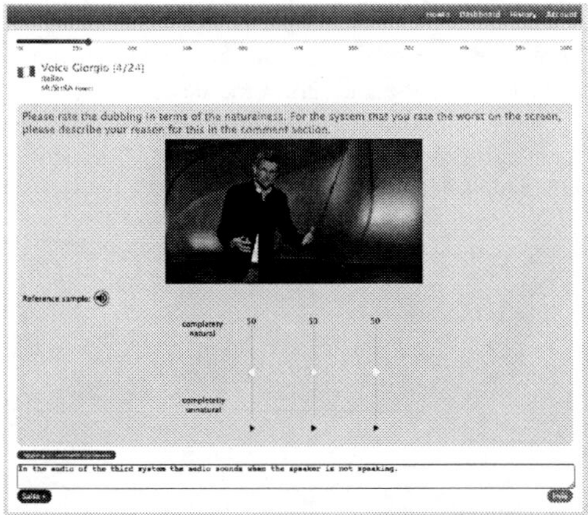

Figure 2: MUSHRA perceptual evaluation interface

cuses on two questions:

- What is the overall naturalness of automatic dubbing?

- How does each introduced enhancement contribute to the naturalness of automatic dubbing?

We adopt the MUSHRA (MUlti Stimulus test with Hidden Reference and Anchor) methodology (MUSHRA, 2014), originally designed to evaluate audio codecs and later also TTS. We asked listeners to evaluate the naturalness of each versions of a video clip on a 0-100 scale. Figure 2 shows the user interface. In absence of a human dubbed version of each clip, we decided to use, for calibration purposes, the clip in the original language as hidden reference. The clip versions to evaluate are not labeled and randomly ordered. The observer has to play each version at least once before moving forward and can leave a comment about the worse version.

In order to limit randomness introduced by ASR and TTS across the clips and by MT across ver-

sions of the same clip, we decided to run the experiments using manual speech transcripts,[8] one TTS voice per gender, and MT output by the baseline (A) and enhanced MT system (B-C) of quality judged at least acceptable by an expert.[9] With these criteria in mind, we selected 24 video clips from 6 TED Talks (3 female and 3 male speakers, 5 clips per talk) from the official test set of the MUST-C corpus (Di Gangi et al., 2019b) with the following criteria: duration of around 10-15 seconds, only one speaker talking, at least two sentences, speaker face mostly visible.

We involved in the experiment both Italian and non Italian listeners. We recommended all participants to disregard the content and only focus on the naturalness of the output. Our goal is to measure both language independent and language dependent naturalness, i.e. to verify how speech in the video resembles human speech with respect to acoustics and synchronization, and how intelligible it is to native listeners.

7.1 Results

We collected a total of 657 ratings by 14 volunteers, 5 Italian and 9 non-Italian listeners, spread over the 24 clips and three testing conditions. We conducted a statistical analysis of the data with linear mixed-effects models using the `lme4` package for R (Bates et al., 2015). We analyzed the naturalness score (response variable) against the following two-level fixed effects: dubbing system A vs. B, system A vs. C, and system B vs. C. We run separate analysis for Italian and non-Italian listeners. In our mixed models, listeners and video clips are random effects, as they represent a tiny sample of the respective true populations(Bates et al., 2015). We keep models maximal, i.e. with intercepts and slopes for each random effect, end remove terms required to avoid singularities. Each model is fitted by maximum likelihood and significance of intercepts and slopes are computed via t-test.

Table 2 summarized our results. In the first comparison, baseline (A) versus the system with enhanced MT and prosody alignment (B), we see that both non-Italian and Italian listeners perceive a similar naturalness of system A (46.81 vs.

---

given its very poor quality, as also reported in (Öktem et al., 2019). Other intermediate configurations were not explored to limit the workload of the subjects participating in the experiment.

[8]We would clearly expect significant drop in dubbing quality due to the propagation of ASR errors.

[9]We use the scale: 1 - Not acceptable: not fluent or not correct; 2 - Acceptable: almost fluent and almost correct; 3 - Good: fluent and correct.

47.22). When moving to system B, non-Italian listeners perceive a small improvement (+1.14), although not statistically significant, while Italian speaker perceive a statistically significant degradation (-10.93).

In the comparison between B and C (i.e. B enhanced with audio rendering), we see that non-Italian listeners observe a significant increase in naturalness (+10.34), statistically significant, while Italian listeners perceive a smaller and not statistical significant improvement (+1.05).

The final comparison between A and C gives almost consistent results with the previous two evaluations: non-Italian listeners perceive better quality in condition C (+11.01), while Italian listeners perceive lower quality (-9.60). Both variations are however not statistically significant due to the higher standard errors of the slope estimates ΔC. Notice in fact that each mixed-effects model is trained on distinct data sets and with different random effect variables. A closer look at the random effects parameters indeed shows that for the B vs. C comparison, the standard deviation estimate of the listener intercept is 3.70, while for the A vs. C one it is 11.02. In other words, much higher variability across user scores is observed in the A vs. C case rather than in the B vs. C case. A much smaller increase is instead observed across the video-clip random intercepts, i.e. from 11.80 to 12.66. The comments left by the Italian listeners tell that the main problem of system B is the unnaturalness of the speaking rate, i.e. is is either too slow, too fast, or too uneven.

The distributions of the MUSHRA scores presented at the top of Figure 3 confirm our analysis. What is more relevant, the distribution of the rank order (bottom) strengths our previous analysis. Italian listeners tend to rank system A the best system (median 1.0) and vary their preference between systems B and C (both with median 2.0). In contrast, non-Italian rank system A as the worse system (median 2.5), system B as the second (median 2.0), and statistically significantly prefer system C as the best system (median 1.0).

Hence, while our preliminary evaluation found that shorter MT output can potentially enable better synchronization, the combination of MT and prosodic alignment appears to be still problematic and prone to generate unnatural speech. In other words, while non-Italian listeners seem to value synchronicity achieved through prosodic align-

Fixed effects	Non Italian		Italian	
	Estim	SE	Estim.	SE
A intercept	46.81•	4.03	47.22•	6.81
ΔB slope	+1.14	4.02	-10.93*	4.70
B intercept	47.74•	3.21	35.19•	7.22
ΔC slope	+10.34[+]	3.53	+1.05	2.30
A intercept	46.92•	4.95	45.29•	7.42
ΔC slope	+11.01	6.51	-9.60	4.89

Table 2: Summary of the analysis of the evaluation with mixed-effects models. From top down: A vs. B, B vs. C, A vs. C. For each fixed effect, we report the estimate and standard error. Symbols •, *, [+] indicate significance levels of 0.001, 0.01, and 0.05, respectively.

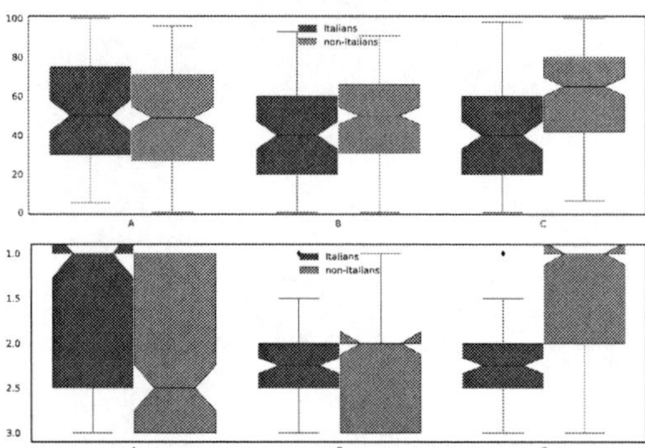

Figure 3: Boxplots with the MUSHRA scores (top) and Rank Order (bottom) per system and mother language (Italian vs Non-Italian).

ment, Italian listeners seem to prefer trading synchronicity for more fluent speech. We think that more work is needed to get MT closer to the script adaptation (Chaume, 2004) style used for dubbing, and to improve the accuracy of prosodic alignment.

The incorporation of audio rendering (system C) significantly improves the experience of the non-Italian listeners (66 in median) respect to systems B and C. This points out the relevance of including para-linguist aspects (i.e. applause's, audience laughs in jokes,etc.) and acoustic conditions (i.e. reverberation, ambient noise, etc.). For the target (Italian) listeners this improvement appears instead masked by the disfluencies introduced by the prosodic alignment step. If we try to directly measure the relative gains given by audio rendering, we see that Italian listeners score system B better than system A 27% of the times and system C better than A 31% of the times, which is a 15% relative gain. On the contrary non-Italian speakers score B better than A 52% of the times, and C better than A 66% of the times, which is a 27% relative gain.

8 Conclusions

We have perceptually evaluated the naturalness of automatic speech dubbing after enhancing a baseline speech-to-speech translation system with the possibility to control the verbosity of the translation output, to segment and synchronize the target words with the speech-pause structure of the source utterances, and to enrich TTS speech with ambient noise and reverberation extracted from the original audio. We tested our system with both Italian and non-Italian listeners in order to evaluate both language independent and language dependent naturalness of dubbed videos. Results show that while we succeeded at achieving synchronization at the phrasal level, our prosodic alignment step negatively impacts on the fluency and prosody of the generated language. The impact of these disfluencies on native listeners seems to partially mask the effect of the audio rendering with background noise and reverberation, which instead results in a major increase of naturalness for non-Italian listeners. Future work will be devoted to better adapt machine translation to the style used in dubbing and to improve the quality of prosodic alignment, by generating more accurate sentence segmentation and by introducing more flexible synchronization.

9 Acknowledgements

The authors would like to thank the Amazon Polly, Translate and Transcribe research teams; Adam Michalski, Alessandra Brusadin, Mattia Di Gangi and Surafel Melaku for contributions to the project, and all colleagues at Amazon AWS who helped with the evaluation.

References

Douglas Bates, Martin Mchler, Ben Bolker, and Steve Walker. 2015. Fitting Linear Mixed-Effects Models Using lme4. *Journal of Statistical Software*, 67(1):1–48.

F. Casacuberta, M. Federico, H. Ney, and E. Vidal. 2008. Recent efforts in spoken language translation. *IEEE Signal Processing Magazine*, 25(3):80–88.

Frederic Chaume. 2004. Synchronization in dubbing: A translation approach. In *Topics in Audiovisual Translation*, pages 35–52. John Benjamins B.V.

Martine Danan. 1991. Dubbing as an Expression of Nationalism. *Meta: Translators' Journal*, 36(4):606–614.

Mattia Di Gangi, Robert Enyedi, Alessndra Brusadin, and Marcello Federico. 2019a. Robust neural machine translation for clean and noisy speech translation. In *Proc. IWSLT*.

Mattia A. Di Gangi, Roldano Cattoni, Luisa Bentivogli, Matteo Negri, and Marco Turchi. 2019b. MuST-C: a Multilingual Speech Translation Corpus. In *Proc. NAACL*, pages 2012–2017.

Shoichi Furukawa, Takuya Kato, Pavel Savkin, and Shigeo Morishima. 2016. Video reshuffling: automatic video dubbing without prior knowledge. In *Proc. ACM SIGGRAPH*.

Jort F Gemmeke, Daniel PW Ellis, Dylan Freedman, Aren Jansen, Wade Lawrence, R Channing Moore, Manoj Plakal, and Marvin Ritter. 2017. Audio set: An ontology and human-labeled dataset for audio events. In *Proc. ICASSP*, pages 776–780.

Ritwik Giri, Umut Isik, and Arvindh Krishnaswamy. 2019. Attention Wave-U-Net for Speech Enhancement. In *Proc. IEEE Workshop on Applications of Signal Processing to Audio and Acoustics (WASPAA)*, pages 249–253, New Paltz, NY, USA. IEEE.

Thanh-Le Ha, Jan Niehues, and Alexander Waibel. 2016. Toward multilingual neural machine translation with universal encoder and decoder. *Proc. IWSLT*.

Emanuel AP Habets. 2006. Room impulse response generator. Technical Report 2.4, Technische Universiteit Eindhoven.

Z. Hanzlíček, J. Matoušek, and D. Tihelka. 2008. Towards automatic audio track generation for Czech TV broadcasting: Initial experiments with subtitles-to-speech synthesis. In *Proc. Int. Conf. on Signal Processing*, pages 2721–2724.

Kenneth Heafield. 2011. KenLM: Faster and smaller language model queries. In *Proceedings of the Sixth Workshop on Statistical Machine Translation*, pages 187–197.

Andreas Jansson, Eric Humphrey, Nicola Montecchio, Rachel Bittner, Aparna Kumar, and Tillman Weyde. 2017. Singing voice separation with deep u-net convolutional networks. In *Proc. ISMIR*.

Melvin Johnson, Mike Schuster, Quoc V Le, Maxim Krikun, Yonghui Wu, Zhifeng Chen, Nikhil Thorat, Fernanda Viégas, Martin Wattenberg, Greg Corrado, et al. 2017. Google's multilingual neural machine translation system: Enabling zero-shot translation. *Trans. of the ACL*, 5:339–351.

Richard Kilborn. 1993. 'Speak my language': current attitudes to television subtitling and dubbing. *Media, Culture & Society*, 15(4):641–660.

Cees M. Koolstra, Allerd L. Peeters, and Herman Spinhof. 2002. The Pros and Cons of Dubbing and Subtitling. *European Journal of Communication*, 17(3):325–354.

Surafel Melaku Lakew, Mattia Di Gangi, and Marcello Federico. 2019. Controlling the output length of neural machine translation. In *Proc. IWSLT*.

Javier Latorre, Jakub Lachowicz, Jaime Lorenzo-Trueba, Thomas Merritt, Thomas Drugman, Srikanth Ronanki, and Klimkov Viacheslav. 2019. Effect of data reduction on sequence-to-sequence neural TTS. In *Proc. ICASSP*, pages 7075–7079.

Heiner Löllmann, Emre Yilmaz, Marco Jeub, and Peter Vary. 2010. An improved algorithm for blind reverberation time estimation. In *Proc. IWAENC*, pages 1–4.

Jaime Lorenzo-Trueba, Thomas Drugman, Javier Latorre, Thomas Merritt, Bartosz Putrycz, Roberto Barra-Chicote, Alexis Moinet, and Vatsal Aggarwal. 2019. Towards Achieving Robust Universal Neural Vocoding. In *Proc. Interspeech*, pages 181–185.

Xènia Martínez. 2004. Film dubbing, its process and translation. In *Topics in Audiovisual Translation*, pages 3–8. John Benjamins B.V.

J. Matoušek, Z. Hanzlíček, D. Tihelka, and M. Měner. 2010. Automatic dubbing of TV programmes for the hearing impaired. In *Proc. IEEE Signal Processing*, pages 589–592.

J. Matoušek and J. Vít. 2012. Improving automatic dubbing with subtitle timing optimisation using video cut detection. In *Proc. ICASSP*, pages 2385–2388.

F. Metze, J. McDonough, H. Soltau, A. Waibel, A. Lavie, S. Burger, C. Langley, K. Laskowski, L. Levin, T. Schultz, F. Pianesi, R. Cattoni, G. Lazzari, N. Mana, and E. Pianta. 2002. The NE-SPOLE! Speech-to-speech Translation System. In *Proc. HLT*, pages 378–383.

MUSHRA. 2014. *Method for the subjective assessment of intermediate quality level of coding systems*. International Communication Union. Recommendation ITU-R BS.1534-2.

S. Nakamura, K. Markov, H. Nakaiwa, G. Kikui, H. Kawai, T. Jitsuhiro, J. Zhang, H. Yamamoto, E. Sumita, and S. Yamamoto. 2006. The ATR Multilingual Speech-to-Speech Translation System. *IEEE Trans. on Audio, Speech, and Language Processing*, 14(2):365–376.

R. M. Ochshorn and M. Hawkins. 2017. Gentle Forced Aligner. Https://lowerquality.com/gentle/.

Alp Öktem, Mireia Farrùs, and Antonio Bonafonte. 2019. Prosodic Phrase Alignment for Machine Dubbing. In *Proc. Interspeech*.

Nishant Prateek, Mateusz Lajszczak, Roberto Barra-Chicote, Thomas Drugman, Jaime Lorenzo-Trueba, Thomas Merritt, Srikanth Ronanki, and Trevor Wood. 2019. In other news: A bi-style text-to-speech model for synthesizing newscaster voice with limited data. In *Proc. NAACL*, pages 205–213.

Olaf Ronneberger, Philipp Fischer, and Thomas Brox. 2015. U-net: Convolutional networks for biomedical image segmentation. In *Proc. ICMAI*, pages 234–241. Springer.

Bahareh Tolooshams, Ritwik Giri, Andrew H. Song, Umut Isik, and Arvindh Krishnaswamy. 2020. Channel-Attention Dense U-Net for Multichannel Speech Enhancement. In *Proc. IEEE International Conference on Acoustics, Speech and Signal Processing (ICASSP)*, pages 836–840, Barcelona, Spain.

Ashish Vaswani, Noam Shazeer, Niki Parmar, Jakob Uszkoreit, Llion Jones, Aidan N Gomez, Lukasz Kaiser, and Illia Polosukhin. 2017. Attention is all you need. In *Proc. NIPS*, pages 5998–6008.

Werner Verhelst. 1997. Automatic Post-Synchronization of Speech Utterances. In *Proc. Eurospeech*, pages 899–902.

E. Vidal. 1997. Finite-state speech-to-speech translation. In *Proc. ICASSP*, volume 1, pages 111–114 vol.1.

Wolfgang Wahlster. 2013. *Verbmobil: Foundations of Speech-to-Speech Translation*. Springer Science & Business Media. Google-Books-ID: NoqrCAAAQBAJ.

A. Waibel. 1996. Interactive translation of conversational speech. *Computer*, 29(7):41–48.

Ron J. Weiss, Jan Chorowski, Navdeep Jaitly, Yonghui Wu, and Zhifeng Chen. 2017. Sequence-to-Sequence Models Can Directly Translate Foreign Speech. In *Proc. Interspeech 2017*, pages 2625–2629. ISCA.

Joint translation and unit conversion for end-to-end localization

Georgiana Dinu   Prashant Mathur   Marcello Federico   Stanislas Lauly   Yaser Al-Onaizan

Amazon AWS AI

{gddinu,pramathu,marcfede,laulysl,onaizan}@amazon.com

Abstract

A variety of natural language tasks require processing of textual data which contains a mix of natural language and formal languages such as mathematical expressions. In this paper, we take unit conversions as an example and propose a data augmentation technique which lead to models learning both translation and conversion tasks as well as how to adequately switch between them for end-to-end localization.

1   Introduction

Neural networks trained on large amounts of data have been shown to achieve state-of-the art solutions on most NLP tasks such as textual entailment, question answering, translation, etc. In particular, these solutions show that one can successfully model the ambiguity of language by making very few assumptions about its structure and by avoiding any formalization of language. However, unambiguous, formal languages such as numbers, mathematical expressions or even programming languages (e.g. markup) are abundant in text and require the ability to model the symbolic, "procedural" behaviour governing them. (Ravichander et al., 2019; Dua et al., 2019).

An example of an application where such examples are frequent is the extension of machine translation to localization. Localization is the task of combining translation with "culture adaptation", which involves, for instance, adapting dates (*12/21/2004* to *21.12.2004*), calendar conversions (*March 30, 2019* to *Rajab 23, 1441* in Hijri Calendar) or conversions of currencies or of units of measure (*10 kgs* to *22 pounds*).

Current approaches in machine translation handle the processing of such sub-languages in one of two ways: The sub-language does not receive any special treatment but it may be learned jointly with the main task if it is represented enough in the data. Alternatively, the sub-language is decoupled from the natural text through pre/post processing techniques: e.g. a *miles* expression is converted into *kilometers* in a separate step after translation.

Arguably the first approach can successfully deal with some of these phenomena: e.g. a neural network may learn to invoke a simple conversion rule for dates, if enough examples are seen training. However, at the other end of the spectrum, correctly converting distance units, which itself is a simple algorithm, requires knowledge of numbers, basic arithmetic and the specific conversion function to apply. It is unrealistic to assume a model could learn such conversions from limited amounts of parallel running text alone. Furthermore, this is an unrealistic task even for distributional, unsupervised pre-training (Turney and Pantel, 2010; Baroni and Lenci, 2010; Peters et al., 2018), despite the success of such methods in capturing other non-linguistic phenomena such as world knowledge or cultural biases (Bolukbasi et al., 2016; Vanmassenhove et al., 2018).[1]

While the second approach is currently the preferred one in translation technology, such decoupling methods do not bring us closer to end-to-end solutions and they ignore the often tight interplay of the two types of language: taking unit conversion as an example, *approximately 500 miles*, should be translated into *ungefähr 800 km* (approx. 800km) and not *ungefähr 804 km* (approx. 804km).

In this paper we highlight several of such language mixing phenomena related to the task of localization for translation and focus on two distance (miles to kilometers) and temperature (Fahrenheit to Celsius) conversion tasks. Specifically, we per-

---

[1](Wallace et al., 2019) show that numeracy is encoded in pre-trained embeddings. While promising, this does not show that more complex and varied manipulation of numerical expressions can be learned in a solely unsupervised fashion.

Proceedings of the 17th International Conference on Spoken Language Translation (IWSLT), pages 265–271
July 9-10, 2020. ©2020 Association for Computational Linguistics
https://doi.org/10.18653/v1/P17

form experiments using the popular MT transformer architecture and show that the model is successful at learning these functions from symbolically represented examples. Furthermore, we show that data augmentation techniques together with small changes in the input representation produce models which can both translate and appropriately convert units of measure in context.

2   Related work

Several theoretical and empirical works have addressed the computational capabilities end expressiveness of deep learning models. Theoretical studies on language modeling have mostly targeted simple grammars from the Chomsky hierarchy. In particular, Hahn (2019) proves that Transformer networks suffer limitations in modeling regular periodic languages (such as $a^n b^n$) as well as hierarchical (context-free) structures, unless their depth or self-attention heads increase with the input length. On the other hand, Merrill (2019) proves that LSTM networks can recognize a subset of periodic languages. Also experimental papers analyzed the capability of LSTMs to recognize these two language classes (Weiss et al., 2018; Suzgun et al., 2019; Sennhauser and Berwick, 2018; Skachkova et al., 2018; Bernardy, 2018), as well as natural language hierarchical structures (Linzen et al., 2016; Gulordava et al., 2018).   It is worth noticing, however, that differently from formal language recognition tasks, state of the art machine translation systems (Barrault et al., 2019; Niehues et al., 2019) are still based on the Transformer architecture .

Other related work addresses specialized neural architectures capable to process and reason with numerical expressions for binary addition, evaluating arithmetic expressions or other number manipulation tasks (Joulin and Mikolov, 2015; Saxton et al., 2019; Trask et al., 2018; Chen et al., 2018). While this line of work is very relevant, we focus on the natural intersection of formal and everyday language. The types of generalization that these studies address, such as testing with numbers orders of magnitude larger than those in seen in training, are less relevant to our task.

The task of solving verbal math problems (Mitra and Baral, 2016; Wang et al., 2017; Koncel-Kedziorski et al., 2016; Saxton et al., 2019) specifically addresses natural language mixed with formal language. Similarly, (Ravichander et al., 2019) introduces a benchmark for evaluating quantitative

reasoning in natural language inference and (Dua et al., 2019) one for symbolic operations such as addition or sorting in reading comprehension. However these papers show the best results with two-step approaches, which extract the mathematical or symbolic information from the text and further manipulate it analytically. We are not aware of any other work successfully addressing both machine translation and mathematical problems, or any of the benchmarks above, in an end-to-end fashion.

3   Unit conversion in MT localization

The goal of localization is to enhance plain content translation so that the final result looks and feels as being created for a specific target audience.

Parallel corpora in general include localization of formats numeric expressions (e.g. from *1,000,000.00* (en-us) to *1.000.000,00* (de-de)). Format conversions in most of the cases reduce to operations such as reordering of elements and replacement of symbols, which quite naturally fit inside the general task of machine translation. In this paper, we are interested in evaluating the capability of neural MT models to learn less natural operations, which are typically involved in the conversion of time expressions (e.g. 3:30pm $\rightarrow$ 15:30) and units of measure, such as lengths (10ft to 3m) and temperatures (55F to 12.8C).

We choose two measure unit conversion tasks that are very prevalent in localization: Fahrenheit to Celsius temperature conversion and miles to kilometers. We address the following questions: 1) Can a standard NMT architecture, the transformer, be used to learn the functions associated with these two conversion tasks (Section 3.1) and 2) Can the same architecture be used to train a model that can do both MT and unit conversion? (Section 3.2)

3.1   Unit conversion

Network architecture   We use the state-of-the-art transformer architecture (Vaswani et al., 2017) and the Sockeye Toolkit (Hieber et al., 2017) to train a network with 4 encoder layers and 2 decoder layers for a maximum of 3000 epochs (See Appendix A for details). As the vocabulary size is small the training is still very efficient. For the experiments training several tasks jointly we facilitate the context-switching between the different tasks with an additional token-level parallel stream (source factors) (Sennrich and Haddow, 2016). We use two values for the digits in numerical expres-

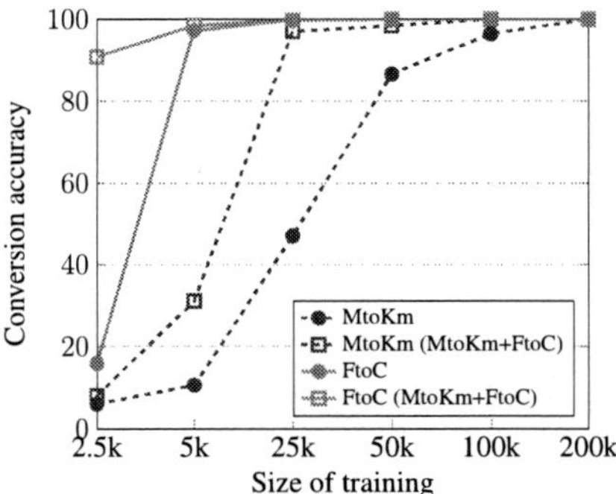

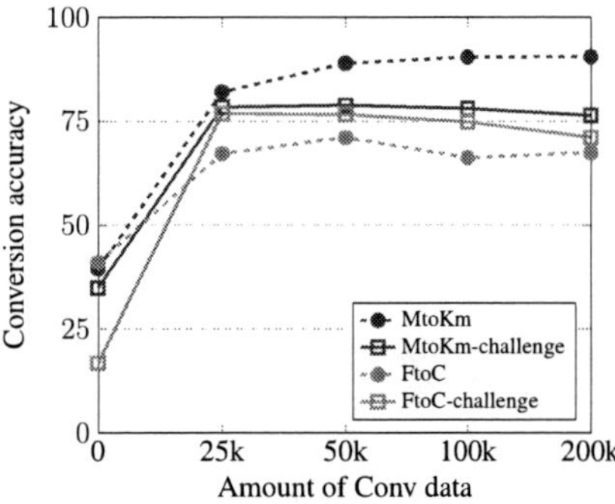

Figure 1: Conversion accuracy with $\pm 10^{-4}$ tolerance on relative error, as a function of the number of the target conversion examples in the train data. Functions are learned both in isolation and in a joint setting (MtoKm + FtoC) which adds to training an equal amount of data for the other function.

Figure 2: Accuracy of localization conversion (tolerance 0.01%) on regular and *challenge* sets. All models use source factors and are trained using: 2.2M MT data + 15k Loc data + varying amounts of Conv data.

sions (distance/temperature) and a third value for all other tokens. These are concatenated to each token as 8-dimensional embeddings.

Data The models are trained with parallel examples of the two functions, one affine: $°F \to °C(x) = (x - 32) \times \frac{5}{9}$ and one linear: $mi \to km(x) = x \times 1.60934$. For each task, we generate training data of various input lengths ranging from 1 to 6 digits in the input. The input is distributed uniformly w.r.t 1) integer versus single digit precision (with the output truncated to same precision as the input) and 2) the length of the input in digits. We over-sample when there are not enough distinct data points, such as in the case of double- or single-digit numbers. The numerical input is tokenized into digits (e.g. *5 2 1 miles*) and we train individual models for the two functions, as well as joint models, using held-out data for validation and testing. Note that unlike previous work, we are interested only in interpolation generalization: test numbers are unseen, but the *range* of test numbers does not increase.

Results Results as a function of the amount of training data are given in Figure 1. Test sets are synthetic and contain numbers in $[10^3 - 10^6]$ range.

The results show that the transformer architecture can learn the two functions perfectly, however, interestingly enough, the two functions are learned differently. While the degree conversion is learned with a high accuracy with as little as several thousand examples, the distance conversion is learned gradually, with more data leading to better and better numerical approximations: in this case the model reaches high precision in conversion only with data two orders of magnitude larger. Both

functions are learned with less data when training is done jointly and source factors are used - this suggests that, despite the fact that the functions are very different, joint training may facilitate the learning of numbers as a general concept and helps learn additional functions more efficiently.

3.2 Joint MT and unit conversion

In a second set of experiments we investigate if the transformer model is able to perform both the translation and the unit conversion tasks and learns to adequately switch from one to the other in context. We use the same architecture as in the previous section, with minor modifications: we use subword embeddings with a shared vocabulary of size 32000 and a maximum number of epochs of 30.

Data As standard MT parallel data we use a collection containing Europarl (Koehn, 2005) and news commentary data from WMT En$\to$De shared task 2019 totalling 2.2 million sentences.[2] Standard translation test sets do not have, however, enough examples of unit conversions and in fact corpora such as CommonCrawl show inconsistent treatment of units. For this reason, we create a unit conversion (Localization) data set. We extract sentences containing Fahrenheit/Celsius and miles/km from a mix of open source data sets namely, ParaCrawl, DGT (Translation Memories), Wikipedia and OpenSubtitles, TED talks from OPUS (Tiedemann, 2012). Regular expressions are used to extract the sentences containing the units and modify the source or the reference by

---

[2]We opt for a smaller experiment in order to speed up computations and to prioritize efficiency in our experiments (Strubell et al., 2019). We have no reason to assume any dependency on the data size.

	Example	
Conv	5 2 1 miles	8 3 9 km
MT	We do not know what is happening.	Wir wissen nicht, was passiert.
Loc.	The venue is within 3 . 8 miles from the city center	Die Unterkunft ist 6 km vom Stadtzentrum entfernt

Table 1: The three types of data used in training the joint model: unit conversion data, standard MT data and localization (Loc) data containing unit conversions in context.

		news17	Loc-dist		Loc-temp	
S.f.	#Loc	Bleu	Bleu	Acc.	Bleu	Acc.
-	0	22.7	20.6	0%	16.1	0%
-	5k	22.7	56.7	52.3%	44.1	48.3%
-	15k	23.0	61.7	76.2%	48.5	80.3%
-	30k	23.0	65.0	90.3%	48.9	81.3%
✓	0	22.9	19.5	1%	16.6	3.4%
✓	5k	22.9	58.7	69.4%	46.8	64.8%
✓	15k	23.2	63.0	88.0%	48.6	77.8%
✓	30k	22.6	64.0	88.3%	48.8	79.4%

Table 2: Bleu scores and accuracy on conversion of degrees (temp) and miles (dist) expressions in Loc test sets. Conversion accuracy is computed with a tolerance of 0.01%. All models are trained using: 2.2M MT+ 100k Conv + #Loc data (col 2) for each function, with and without Source factors (column 1).

converting the matched units. For example, if *5 km* is matched in the reference, we modify the source expression to *3.1 miles*.[3] We are able to extract a total of 7k examples for each of the two conversion tasks and use 5k for training and 2k for testing, making sure the train/test numerical expressions are distinct.

Results In the experimental setting, we distinguish the following three types of data: translation (**MT**), conversion (**Conv**) and localization data (conversion in context) (**Loc**), and measure performance when varying amounts of Conv and Loc are used in training. Examples of these data types are given in Table 1. The first set of experiments (Table 2) uses MT and Conv data and tests the models' performance with varying amounts of Loc data. We observe that for localization performance, Loc data in training is crucial: accuracy jumps from 2% when no Loc data is used to 66% for 5k Loc and to 82%, on average, with 15k localization examples for each function (w. source factors). However, the 15k data points are obtained by up-sampling the linguistic context and replacing the unit conversions with new unit conversions, and therefore no "real" new data is added. We observe no further improvements when more Loc data is added. Regarding the use of source factors, they help when the localization data is non-existent or very limited,

however their benefits are smaller otherwise.

The Bleu scores measured on a news data set as well as on the localization data sets show no degradation from a baseline setting, indicating that the additional data does not affect translation quality. The exception is the #Loc-0 setting, in which the model wrongly learns to end all localization sentences with *km* and *C* tokens respectively, as seen in the Conv data. Similarly to the previous results, temp conversions are learned either correctly or not at all while the distance ones show numerical approximation errors: When measuring exact match in conversion (0.0 tolerance), the temperature accuracy remains largely the same while the distance accuracy drops by up to 30%.

Given the observation that Loc data is crucial, we perform another set of experiments to investigate if the Conv data is needed at all. Results are shown in Figure 2. In light of the limited amount of real distinct conversions that we see in testing, we create two additional challenge sets which use the same linguistic data and replace the original conversions with additional ones uniformly distributed w.r.t the length in digits from 1 to 6. The results indicate that conversion data is equally critical, and that the conversion cannot be learned from the localization data provided alone. The localization data rather acts as a "bridge" allowing the network to combine the two tasks it has learned independently.

4 Conclusions

We have outlined natural/formal language mixing phenomena in the context of end-to-end localization for MT and have proposed a data augmentation method for learning unit conversions in context. Surprisingly, the results show not only that a single architecture can learn both translation and unit conversions, but can also appropriately switch between them when a small amount of localization data is used in training. For future work we plan to create a diverse localization test suite and investigate if implicit learning of low-level concepts such as natural numbers takes place and if unsupervised pre-training facilitates such learning.

---

[3]Scripts to create this data will be released, however the data used itself does not grant us re-distribution rights.

References

Marco Baroni and Alessandro Lenci. 2010. Distributional memory: A general framework for corpus-based semantics. *American Journal of Computational Linguistics*, 36(4):673–721.

Loïc Barrault, Ondřej Bojar, Marta R. Costa-jussà, Christian Federmann, Mark Fishel, Yvette Graham, Barry Haddow, Matthias Huck, Philipp Koehn, Shervin Malmasi, Christof Monz, Mathias Müller, Santanu Pal, Matt Post, and Marcos Zampieri. 2019. Findings of the 2019 conference on machine translation (WMT19). In *Proceedings of the Fourth Conference on Machine Translation (Volume 2: Shared Task Papers, Day 1)*, pages 1–61, Florence, Italy. Association for Computational Linguistics.

Jean-Philippe Bernardy. 2018. Can Recurrent Neural Networks Learn Nested Recursion. In *Linguistic Issues in Language Technology*, volume 16.

Tolga Bolukbasi, Kai-Wei Chang, James Y. Zou, Venkatesh Saligrama, and Adam Kalai. 2016. Man is to computer programmer as woman is to homemaker? debiasing word embeddings. *CoRR*, abs/1607.06520.

Kaiyu Chen, Yihan Dong, Xipeng Qiu, and Zitian Chen. 2018. Neural arithmetic expression calculator. *CoRR*, abs/1809.08590.

Dheeru Dua, Yizhong Wang, Pradeep Dasigi, Gabriel Stanovsky, Sameer Singh, and Matt Gardner. 2019. DROP: A reading comprehension benchmark requiring discrete reasoning over paragraphs. In *Proceedings of the 2019 Conference of the North American Chapter of the Association for Computational Linguistics: Human Language Technologies, Volume 1 (Long and Short Papers)*, pages 2368–2378, Minneapolis, Minnesota. Association for Computational Linguistics.

Kristina Gulordava, Piotr Bojanowski, Edouard Grave, Tal Linzen, and Marco Baroni. 2018. Colorless Green Recurrent Networks Dream Hierarchically. In *Proceedings of the 2018 Conference of the North American Chapter of the Association for Computational Linguistics: Human Language Technologies, Volume 1 (Long Papers)*, pages 1195–1205, New Orleans, Louisiana. Association for Computational Linguistics.

Michael Hahn. 2019. Theoretical Limitations of Self-Attention in Neural Sequence Models. *arXiv:1906.06755 [cs]*. ArXiv: 1906.06755.

Felix Hieber, Tobias Domhan, Michael Denkowski, David Vilar, Artem Sokolov, Ann Clifton, and Matt Post. 2017. Sockeye: A toolkit for neural machine translation. *CoRR*, abs/1712.05690.

Armand Joulin and Tomas Mikolov. 2015. Inferring algorithmic patterns with stack-augmented recurrent nets. In *Proceedings of the 28th International Conference on Neural Information Processing Systems - Volume 1*, NIPS'15, pages 190–198, Cambridge, MA, USA. MIT Press.

Philipp Koehn. 2005. Europarl: A Parallel Corpus for Statistical Machine Translation. In *Conference Proceedings: the tenth Machine Translation Summit*, pages 79–86, Phuket, Thailand. AAMT, AAMT.

Rik Koncel-Kedziorski, Subhro Roy, Aida Amini, Nate Kushman, and Hannaneh Hajishirzi. 2016. MAWPS: A math word problem repository. In *Proceedings of the 2016 Conference of the North American Chapter of the Association for Computational Linguistics: Human Language Technologies*, pages 1152–1157, San Diego, California. Association for Computational Linguistics.

Tal Linzen, Emmanuel Dupoux, and Yoav Goldberg. 2016. Assessing the Ability of LSTMs to Learn Syntax-Sensitive Dependencies. *Transactions of the Association for Computational Linguistics*, 4:521–535.

William Merrill. 2019. Sequential neural networks as automata. In *Proceedings of the Workshop on Deep Learning and Formal Languages: Building Bridges*, pages 1–13, Florence. Association for Computational Linguistics.

Arindam Mitra and Chitta Baral. 2016. Learning to use formulas to solve simple arithmetic problems. In *Proceedings of the 54th Annual Meeting of the Association for Computational Linguistics (Volume 1: Long Papers)*, pages 2144–2153, Berlin, Germany. Association for Computational Linguistics.

Jan Niehues, Cattoni Roldano, Sebastian Stüker, Matteo Negri, Marco Turchi, Elizabeth Salesky, R. Sanabria, Loïc Barrault, Lucia Specia, and Marcello Federico. 2019. The iwslt 2019 evaluation campaign. In *Proceedings of IWSLT*.

Matthew Peters, Mark Neumann, Mohit Iyyer, Matt Gardner, Christopher Clark, Kenton Lee, and Luke Zettlemoyer. 2018. Deep contextualized word representations. In *Proceedings of the 2018 Conference of the North American Chapter of the Association for Computational Linguistics: Human Language Technologies, Volume 1 (Long Papers)*, pages 2227–2237, New Orleans, Louisiana. Association for Computational Linguistics.

Abhilasha Ravichander, Aakanksha Naik, Carolyn Penstein Rosé, and Eduard H. Hovy. 2019. EQUATE: A benchmark evaluation framework for quantitative reasoning in natural language inference. *CoRR*, abs/1901.03735.

David Saxton, Edward Grefenstette, Felix Hill, and Pushmeet Kohli. 2019. Analysing mathematical reasoning abilities of neural models. *CoRR*, abs/1904.01557.

Luzi Sennhauser and Robert Berwick. 2018. Evaluating the Ability of LSTMs to Learn Context-Free Grammars. In *Proceedings of the 2018 EMNLP*

Workshop BlackboxNLP: Analyzing and Interpreting Neural Networks for NLP, pages 115–124, Brussels, Belgium. Association for Computational Linguistics.

Rico Sennrich and Barry Haddow. 2016. Linguistic input features improve neural machine translation. In *Proceedings of the First Conference on Machine Translation: Volume 1, Research Papers*, pages 83–91, Berlin, Germany. Association for Computational Linguistics.

Natalia Skachkova, Thomas Trost, and Dietrich Klakow. 2018. Closing Brackets with Recurrent Neural Networks. In *Proceedings of the 2018 EMNLP Workshop BlackboxNLP: Analyzing and Interpreting Neural Networks for NLP*, pages 232–239, Brussels, Belgium. Association for Computational Linguistics.

Emma Strubell, Ananya Ganesh, and Andrew McCallum. 2019. Energy and policy considerations for deep learning in NLP. In *Proceedings of the 57th Annual Meeting of the Association for Computational Linguistics*, pages 3645–3650, Florence, Italy. Association for Computational Linguistics.

Mirac Suzgun, Yonatan Belinkov, and Stuart M. Shieber. 2019. On Evaluating the Generalization of LSTM Models in Formal Languages. In *Proceedings of the Society for Computation in Linguistics (SCiL) 2019*, pages 277–286.

Jörg Tiedemann. 2012. Parallel data, tools and interfaces in opus. In *Proceedings of the Eight International Conference on Language Resources and Evaluation (LREC'12)*, Istanbul, Turkey. European Language Resources Association (ELRA).

Andrew Trask, Felix Hill, Scott E Reed, Jack Rae, Chris Dyer, and Phil Blunsom. 2018. Neural arithmetic logic units. In S. Bengio, H. Wallach, H. Larochelle, K. Grauman, N. Cesa-Bianchi, and R. Garnett, editors, *Advances in Neural Information Processing Systems 31*, pages 8035–8044. Curran Associates, Inc.

Peter D. Turney and Patrick Pantel. 2010. From frequency to meaning: Vector space models of semantics. *J. Artif. Int. Res.*, 37(1):141–188.

Eva Vanmassenhove, Christian Hardmeier, and Andy Way. 2018. Getting gender right in neural machine translation. In *Proceedings of the 2018 Conference on Empirical Methods in Natural Language Processing*, pages 3003–3008, Brussels, Belgium. Association for Computational Linguistics.

Ashish Vaswani, Noam Shazeer, Niki Parmar, Jakob Uszkoreit, Llion Jones, Aidan N. Gomez, Lukasz Kaiser, and Illia Polosukhin. 2017. Attention is all you need. In *NIPS*, pages 6000–6010.

Eric Wallace, Yizhong Wang, Sujian Li, Sameer Singh, and Matt Gardner. 2019. Do NLP models know numbers? probing numeracy in embeddings. In *Proceedings of the 2019 Conference on Empirical Methods in Natural Language Processing and the 9th International Joint Conference on Natural Language Processing (EMNLP-IJCNLP)*, pages 5306–5314, Hong Kong, China. Association for Computational Linguistics.

Yan Wang, Xiaojiang Liu, and Shuming Shi. 2017. Deep neural solver for math word problems. In *Proceedings of the 2017 Conference on Empirical Methods in Natural Language Processing*, pages 845–854, Copenhagen, Denmark. Association for Computational Linguistics.

Gail Weiss, Yoav Goldberg, and Eran Yahav. 2018. On the Practical Computational Power of Finite Precision RNNs for Language Recognition. In *Proceedings of the 56th Annual Meeting of the Association for Computational Linguistics (Volume 2: Short Papers)*, pages 740–745, Melbourne, Australia. Association for Computational Linguistics.

A Appendix

```
encoder-config:
  act_type: relu
  attention_heads: 8
  conv_config: null
  dropout_act: 0.1
  dropout_attention: 0.1
  dropout_prepost: 0.1
  dtype: float32
  feed_forward_num_hidden: 2048
  lhuc: false
  max_seq_len_source: 101
  max_seq_len_target: 101
  model_size: 512
  num_layers: 4
  positional_embedding_type:
      fixed
  postprocess_sequence: dr
  preprocess_sequence: n
  use_lhuc: false

decoder config:
  act_type: relu
  attention_heads: 8
  conv_config: null
  dropout_act: 0.1
  dropout_attention: 0.1
  dropout_prepost: 0.1
  dtype: float32
  feed_forward_num_hidden: 2048
  max_seq_len_source: 101
  max_seq_len_target: 101
  model_size: 512
  num_layers: 2
  positional_embedding_type:
      fixed
  postprocess_sequence: dr
  preprocess_sequence: n

config_loss: !LossConfig
  label_smoothing: 0.1
  name: cross-entropy
  normalization_type: valid
  vocab_size: 32302

config_embed_source: !
  EmbeddingConfig
  dropout: 0.0
  dtype: float32
  factor_configs: null
  num_embed: 512
  num_factors: 1
  vocab_size: 32302

config_embed_target: !
  EmbeddingConfig
  dropout: 0.0
  dtype: float32
  factor_configs: null
  num_embed: 512
  num_factors: 1
  vocab_size: 32302
```

Efficient Automatic Punctuation Restoration Using Bidirectional Transformers with Robust Inference

Maury Courtland, Adam Faulkner, Gayle McElvain
Capital One, Vision and Language Technologies

{maury.courtland, adam.faulkner, gayle.mcelvain}
@capitalone.com

Abstract

Though people rarely speak in complete sentences, punctuation confers many benefits to the readers of transcribed speech. Unfortunately, most ASR systems do not produce punctuated output. To address this, we propose a solution for automatic punctuation that is both cost efficient and easy to train. Our solution benefits from the recent trend in fine-tuning transformer-based language models. We also modify the typical framing of this task by predicting punctuation for sequences rather than individual tokens, which makes for more efficient training and inference. Finally, we find that aggregating predictions across multiple context windows improves accuracy even further. Our best model achieves a new state of the art on benchmark data (TED Talks) with a combined F1 of 83.9, representing a 48.7% relative improvement (15.3 absolute) over the previous state of the art.

1 Introduction

Enabling computers to use speech as input has long been an aspirational goal in the field of human computer interaction. Recent advances have had dramatic impact across multiple domains (e.g. relieving medical professionals from having to transcribe medical dictation (Edwards et al., 2017), improving real-time spoken language translation (Gu et al., 2017), and affording convenience through conversational interfaces like those in virtual personal assistants (McTear et al., 2016)). For use cases that require reading transcribed speech, however, it is often still a challenge to recover meaningful clause boundaries from disfluent, errorful utterances.

Humans rely on punctuation for readability, perhaps because it lessens the burden of ambiguous phrasing. Studies have found that removing punctuation from manual transcriptions can be even more detrimental to understanding than a word error rate

of 15% or 20% (Tündik et al., 2018). Reading comprehension is also significantly slower without punctuation (Jones et al., 2003). For downstream NLP models, the lack of clausal boundaries can significantly decrease accuracy (e.g. a 4.6% BLEU decrease in NMT; Vandeghinste et al. 2018). This likely reflects the discrepancy between well-segmented training corpora and ASR output.

To solve the lack of punctuation in ASR output, we propose an automatic punctuation model, which leverages the recent trend in unsupervised pre-training (Devlin et al., 2019) and the parallel architecture of transformer networks (Vaswani et al., 2017). Unsupervised pre-training dramatically reduces the amount of labeled data required for superior performance on this task. Additionally, the model's departure from a recurrent architecture allows direct connections between all input tokens. This enables the network to more easily model long-distance dependencies (e.g. *on one hand, ... on the other, ...*) for improved punctuation performance. The departure from a recurrent architecture also allows computations to be performed in parallel for each layer with the speed of computations limited by the number of layers rather than the number of time steps (usually fewer). In addition to the parallel nature of the hidden layers, our network also predicts in parallel for all tokens in the input simultaneously. This helps significantly speed up inference compared with individual predictions for each token. During training, the parallel prediction task provides a richer signal compared with a sequential task, thereby making more efficient use of each example. Furthermore, advancing the prediction window less than the window's width (e.g. steps of 20 with a window of 50) allows aggregating multiple windows of context to predict a token's label. This allows the network to effectively become its own prediction ensemble and boosts accuracy further. Given that the aggregate predictions

Proceedings of the 17th International Conference on Spoken Language Translation (IWSLT), pages 272–279
July 9-10, 2020. ©2020 Association for Computational Linguistics
https://doi.org/10.18653/v1/P17

are independently obtained, these calculations too can be performed in parallel.

2 Related Work

Our biggest departure from previous approaches lies in the parallel nature of inference and the deep bidirectional information flow of our model (for more detail, see Devlin et al. 2019). This is in contrast with the vast majority of previous approaches which use a variant of Recurrent Neural Network architecture (Tundik et al., 2017; Vandeghinste et al., 2018; Ballesteros and Wanner, 2016; Alumäe et al., 2019; Szaszák, 2019; Öktem, 2018; Xu et al., 2016; Pahuja et al., 2017; Tundik and Szaszak, 2018; Tündik et al., 2017; Tilk and Alumae, 2015; Żelasko et al., 2018; Treviso and Aluísio, 2018). This includes those that incorporate acoustic information (B. Garg and Anika, 2018; Moro and Szaszak, 2017; Szaszák and Tündik, 2019; Nanchen and Garner, 2019; Moró and Szaszák, 2017; Klejch et al., 2016, 2017) and those that apply attention on top (Tilk and Alumäe, 2016; Salloum et al., 2017; Öktem et al., 2017; Kim, 2019; Juin et al., 2017).

Though non-sequential, several previous approaches use simpler network architectures (e.g. DNNs (Yi et al., 2017; Che et al., 2016) or CNNs (B. Garg and Anika, 2018; Che et al., 2016; Żelasko et al., 2018)), which have less predictive power. The handful of approaches that make use of Transformer architectures are not bidirectional (Chen et al., 2020; Nguyen et al., 2019; Vāravs and Salimbajevs, 2018; Wang et al., 2018). Our model also differs from the above in that it leverages pre-training to reduce training time and increase accuracy. The one previous work that uses a pre-trained bidirectional transformer (Cai and Wang, 2019) only predicts punctuation one token at a time, which significantly increases both training and inference time. It is also unable to aggregate predictions across multiple contexts, limiting performance.

3 Method

Architecture The network architecture can be seen in Figure 1. The first component of our network is a pre-trained language model (RoBERTa$_{base}$; Liu et al. 2019) employing the recent deep bidirectional Transformer architecture (Devlin et al., 2019; Vaswani et al., 2017). The network's input is a sequence of unpunctuated lowercased words tokenized using RoBERTa's tokeniza-

tion scheme (see Liu et al. 2019 for more details). We then add two additional linear layers after the pre-trained network with each layer preserving the fully-connected nature of the entire network. The first linear layer maps from the masked language model output space to a hidden state space for each input token with parameters shared across tokens. The second linear layer concatenates the hidden state representations into a vector for the prediction window which allows the tokens to interact arbitrarily within the window. We then apply batch normalization (Ioffe and Szegedy, 2015) and dropout (best results obtained with a rate of 0.2; Hinton et al. 2012) prior to predicting punctuation marks for all tokens in the window.

When aggregating predictions across contexts, activations at the sequence layer are added for each token prior to classification (see Figure 1 for visualization). Prediction is performed in parallel during both training and inference with the output size of the final classifier being $|classes| * length_{window}$.

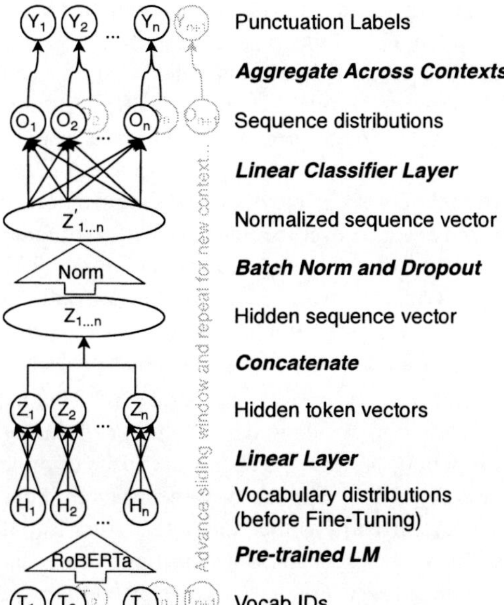

Figure 1: The punctuation network takes as input a sequence of unpunctuated words tokenized in the same manner as RoBERTa. It outputs predictions for these sequences individually during training (layer O_n). For validation and testing, however, these labels are aggregated across overlapping context windows to obtain the final punctuation predictions (layer Y_n). Note that while the pre-trained LM's output begins as vocabulary distributions, they cease to be so once the entire network undergoes fine-tuning.

Models	Comma			Period			Question			Overall		
	P	R	F	P	R	F	P	R	F	P	R	F
DNN-A (Che et al., 2016)	48.6	42.4	45.3	59.7	68.3	63.7	—	—	—	54.8	53.6	54.2
CNN-2A (Che et al., 2016)	48.1	44.5	46.2	57.6	69.0	62.8	—	—	—	53.4	55.0	54.2
T-LSTM (Tilk and Alumae, 2015)	49.6	41.4	45.1	60.2	53.4	56.6	57.1	43.5	49.4	55.0	47.2	50.8
T-BRNN (Tilk and Alumäe, 2016)	64.4	45.2	53.1	72.3	71.5	71.9	67.5	58.7	62.8	68.9	58.1	63.1
T-BRNN-pre (Tilk and Alumäe, 2016)	65.5	47.1	54.8	73.3	72.5	72.9	70.7	63.0	66.7	70.0	59.7	64.4
Single-BiRNN (Pahuja et al., 2017)	62.2	47.7	54.0	74.6	72.1	73.4	67.5	52.9	59.3	69.2	59.8	64.2
Corr-BiRNN (Pahuja et al., 2017)	60.9	52.4	56.4	75.3	70.8	73.0	70.7	56.9	63.0	68.6	61.6	64.9
DRNN-LWMA (Kim, 2019)	63.4	55.7	59.3	76.0	73.5	74.7	75.0	71.7	73.3	70.0	64.6	67.2
DRNN-LWMA-pre (Kim, 2019)	62.9	60.8	61.9	77.3	73.7	75.5	69.6	69.6	69.6	69.9	67.2	68.6
RoBERTa$_{base}$	**76.9**	75.4	**76.2**	**86.1**	89.3	87.7	**88.9**	87.0	**87.9**	**84.0**	83.9	**83.9**
Different Pre-trained Language Models												
RoBERTa$_{large}$	74.3	76.9	75.5	85.8	**91.6**	**88.6**	83.7	89.1	86.3	81.3	**85.9**	83.5
XLNet$_{base}$	76.6	74.9	75.8	84.6	90.6	87.5	82.0	89.1	85.4	81.1	84.9	82.9
T5$_{base}$	70.5	**77.2**	73.7	85.6	85.5	85.6	83.7	89.1	86.3	79.9	84.0	81.9
BERT$_{base}$	72.8	70.8	71.8	81.9	86.6	84.2	80.8	**91.3**	85.7	78.5	82.9	80.6
ALBERT$_{base}$	69.4	69.3	69.4	80.9	84.5	82.7	76.7	71.7	74.2	75.7	75.2	75.4
DistilRoBERTa	70.0	64.5	67.1	78.2	83.5	80.8	75.0	71.7	73.3	74.4	73.2	73.7

Table 1: Compared to previous approaches, our model achieves state of the art performance on the reference transcripts of the TED Talks dataset as measured by precision (P), recall (R), and F-1 score (F). Experimental results with different pre-trained language models are included below for comparison with the best RoBERTa$_{base}$ model.

Training Schedule It is worth noting that we use only the TED Talks dataset described below for training but enjoy significant benefits from a sizable pre-training corpus (Liu et al., 2019). Although prediction is performed on multiple tokens at once, the same number of training samples are generated from the corpus by moving the sliding window one token at a time over the input. To perform gradient descent, we use LookAhead (Zhang et al., 2019) with RAdam (Liu et al., 2020) as the base optimizer. We use a simple cross-entropy function to calculate the loss for each token's classification prediction.

Our best performing model (see Table 1) uses a prediction window size of 100, a final-layer dropout of 0.2, and a hidden-state space of dimensionality 1500. The top two linear layers (henceforth referred to as the "top layers") are initially trained from scratch while the transformer core remains frozen. Then, having selected the model version with the lowest validation loss from training the top layers, the transformer core is unfrozen, and we fine-tune the parameters of the entire network. We then select the model version with the lowest validation loss to prevent overfitting.

We train the top layers for nine epochs with a mini-batch size of 1000 (using 100-token sequences) while the transformer is frozen. The lowest validation loss for the top layers is usually achieved around the sixth epoch. We then unfreeze the transformer and fine-tune the entire network for three more epochs with a mini-batch size of 250. We typically observe the lowest validation loss midway through the first epoch while fine-tuning. It is worth noting that a highly competitive model (82.6 overall F1) can be trained with just 1 epoch each for the top layers and fine-tuning. This training can be completed in slightly less than 1 hour on a p3.16xlarge AWS instance (with 8x Tesla V100 GPUs).

For the LookAhead optimizer, we use a sync rate of 0.5, and a sync period of 6. The RAdam optimizer—used as the model's base optimizer—has its learning rate set to 10^{-5}, $\beta_1 = 0.9$, $\beta_2 = 0.999$, $\epsilon = 10^{-8}$. We do not use weight decay.

Data To train the network and evaluate its performance (both at test and validation time), we use the IWSLT 2012 TED Talks dataset (Cettolo et al., 2012). This dataset is a common benchmark in automatic punctuation (e.g. Kim 2019) and consists of a 2.1M word training set, a 296k word validation set, and a 12.6k word test set (for reference transcription, 12.8k for ASR output). Each word is labeled with the punctuation mark that follows it, yielding a 4-class classification problem: comma, period, question mark, or no punctuation. The class balance of the training dataset is as follows: 85.7% no punctuation, 7.53% comma, 6.3% period, 0.47% question mark.

4 Results

The results of our best performing model relative to previous results published on this benchmark can be found in Table 1. Additionally, we conducted a number of ablation experiments manipulating various aspects of the architecture and training routine. In providing accuracy comparisons, all results in this section are reported in terms of the absolute change in the overall F1 measure.

In place of the pre-trained RoBERTa$_{base}$ language model, which provided the best result, we also evaluated (in order of decreasing performance relative to RoBERTa as implemented by Wolf et al. (2020)[1]): XLNet$_{base}$ (-1.0%; Yang et al. 2020), T5$_{base}$ (-2.1%; Raffel et al. 2019), BERT$_{base}$ (-3.4%; Devlin et al. 2019), and ALBERT$_{base}$ (-8.5%; Lan et al. 2020). Full results from these models can be seen at the bottom of Table 1. The performance benefit of RoBERTa$_{base}$ over BERT$_{base}$ is likely due to the significant increase in pre-training corpus size. The lower performance of ALBERT$_{base}$ may be due to the sharing of parameters across layers. It is interesting to note that XLNet$_{base}$ provides higher recall for periods and question marks and T5$_{base}$ for commas and question marks, but both sacrifice significant precision to achieve this.

In addition to the LookAhead optimizer using RAdam as its base, we also evaluated: LookAhead with Adam (-1.5%), RAdam alone (-1.6%), and Adam alone (-2.9%; Kingma and Ba 2017). Given the class imbalance inherent in the dataset between the no punctuation class and all the punctuation marks, we tested focal loss (Lin et al., 2018), class weighting, and their combination, but found that none outperformed simple cross-entropy loss.

Perhaps the most noteworthy result is the comparison between parallel prediction (described above) and sequential prediction, wherein the forward pass predicts punctuation for one token at a time using a context window centered on that token. Sequential prediction requires longer inference times (>15x) yet yields only a marginal performance benefit (2.2%) relative to a parallel prediction without aggregation across multiple contexts. Ensembling predictions over multiple contexts overcomes the performance gap, while retaining an advantage with respect to inference time. Compared to the self-ensemble approach, sequential prediction is >4x slower and 5.4% less accu-

[1]Available from https://github.com/huggingface/transformers

Predictions per token	F1 Overall	CPU Runtime	GPU Runtime
1	76.3	1x	1x
2	79.4	1.8x	1.1x
3	81.8	2.6x	1.2x
6	83.2	5.2x	1.5x
9	83.9	7.7x	1.9x
Processor	—	18x Intel Xeon (c5.18xlarge)	8x Tesla V100 (p3.16xlarge)

Table 2: Aggregating multiple parallel predictions exhibits a tradeoff between runtime and accuracy. Runtime results on the TED test set are presented relative to single predictions separately on CPU and GPU for ease of reading. To relate the two, the CPU single predictions are 9.4x slower than GPU. All runtime estimates are obtained from the mean of 10 runs.

rate.

A less obvious choice must be made between a single parallel prediction and multiple aggregated predictions, given the additional runtime of multiple predictions (see Table 2 for details). For our purposes, the 7.6% improvement is worth the increase in inference time, which is sub-linear given GPU parallelization but still appreciable. While our best method sums activations from different contexts to obtain the aggregate predictions, we also tested adding normalized probabilities across classes and then renormalizing, but we found it resulted in slightly worse performance (-0.3%).

In addition to the RoBERTa$_{base}$ model whose results are reported here, we also trained with a RoBERTa$_{large}$ model. There was no appreciable performance difference between the two sizes (the large being -0.4% worse) however the large model incurred a significant slowdown ($\approx$1.5x). This may imply that the base model size is adequately powered for punctuation tasks, at least on manually transcribed English datasets similar to the benchmark. This is supported by the findings of Kovaleva et al. (2019), who found BERT$_{base}$ to be overparameterized for most downstream tasks, implying RoBERTa$_{large}$ would be extremely overparameterized. A smaller pre-trained language model option is DistilRoBERTa, a knowledge distilled version of RoBERTa (analogous to DistilBERT: Sanh et al. 2020). The DistilRoBERTa network is 12% smaller and performs inference $\approx$1.2x faster, but sacrifices 9.1% in accuracy on the benchmark.

The previous state of the art approach was a multi-headed attention network on top of multiple stacked bidirectional GRU layers (Kim, 2019).

Given the recurrent nature of the GRU layers, the network is subject to the shortcomings of sequential computation discussed in the Introduction. Our findings illustrate yet another language task where transformers outperform previous recurrent neural network approaches.

Our approach enjoys a 48.7% relative improvement (15.3 absolute) over the previous state of the art (Kim, 2019). Given the ablation results presented above, we attribute the performance gains to the deeply bi-directional transformer architecture, the benefit of leveraging RoBERTa's pre-trained language model trained on $\approx$ 33B words, and the aggregation of multiple prediction contexts for robust inference. Some performance gain may also be attributed to the addition of an encoding layer trained solely on the punctuation task.

One of the more notable findings is that the non-recurrent nature of the entire network allows for a large degree of parallelization resulting in a more competitive runtime compared to previous recurrent approaches. While source code was not openly available for benchmarking runtime against Kim (2019), we did compare against a similar approach from Tilk and Alumäe (2016)[2], which was roughly 78.8x slower on GPUs and 1.2x slower on a CPU, when evaluating the TED Talks test set.

The results presented here have not benefited from any rigorous hyperparameter tuning (e.g. grid search or Bayesian optimization). We leave that to future work given that a rigorous systematic approach may yield appreciable improvements in accuracy.

5 Conclusion

We have presented a state of the art automatic punctuation system which aggregates multiple prediction contexts for robust inference on transcribed speech. The use of multiple prediction contexts, unsupervised pre-training, and increased parallelism makes it possible to achieve significant performance gains without increased runtime or cost.

On a different dataset, Boháč et al. (2017) reported human agreement of around 76% for punctuation location and 70% for use of the same punctuation mark. Although we have yet to make a direct comparison, it's possible our model is already competitive with human performance on this task. Future work will explore how this performance

translates in terms of readability and whether it is sufficient to compensate for some amount of word error, as suggested by Tündik et al. (2018).

References

Tanel Alumäe, Ottokar Tilk, and Asadullah. 2019. Advanced Rich Transcription System for Estonian Speech. *arXiv:1901.03601 [cs].* ArXiv: 1901.03601.

B. Garg and Anika. 2018. Analysis of Punctuation Prediction Models for Automated Transcript Generation in MOOC Videos. In *2018 IEEE 6th International Conference on MOOCs, Innovation and Technology in Education (MITE)*, pages 19–26. Journal Abbreviation: 2018 IEEE 6th International Conference on MOOCs, Innovation and Technology in Education (MITE).

Miguel Ballesteros and Leo Wanner. 2016. A Neural Network Architecture for Multilingual Punctuation Generation. In *Proceedings of the 2016 Conference on Empirical Methods in Natural Language Processing*, pages 1048–1053, Austin, Texas. Association for Computational Linguistics.

Marek Boháč, Michal Rott, and Vojtěch Kovář. 2017. Text Punctuation: An Inter-annotator Agreement Study. In Kamil Ekštein and Václav Matoušek, editors, *Text, Speech, and Dialogue*, volume 10415, pages 120–128. Springer International Publishing, Cham. Series Title: Lecture Notes in Computer Science.

Yunqi Cai and Dong Wang. 2019. Question Mark Prediction By Bert. In *2019 Asia-Pacific Signal and Information Processing Association Annual Summit and Conference (APSIPA ASC)*, pages 363–367, Lanzhou, China. IEEE.

M Federico M Cettolo, L Bentivogli, M Paul, and S Stuker. 2012. Overview of the IWSLT 2012 Evaluation Campaign. page 22.

Xiaoyin Che, Cheng Wang, Haojin Yang, and Christoph Meinel. 2016. Punctuation Prediction for Unsegmented Transcript Based on Word Vector. In *Proceedings of the Tenth International Conference on Language Resources and Evaluation (LREC'16)*, pages 654–658, Portorož, Slovenia. European Language Resources Association (ELRA).

Qian Chen, Mengzhe Chen, Bo Li, and Wen Wang. 2020. Controllable Time-Delay Transformer for Real-Time Punctuation Prediction and Disfluency Detection. *arXiv:2003.01309 [cs, eess].* ArXiv: 2003.01309.

Jacob Devlin, Ming-Wei Chang, Kenton Lee, and Kristina Toutanova. 2019. BERT: Pre-training of Deep Bidirectional Transformers for Language Understanding. *arXiv:1810.04805 [cs].* ArXiv: 1810.04805.

---

[2]The source code is available from `https://github.com/ottokart/punctuator2`

Erik Edwards, Wael Salloum, Greg P. Finley, James Fone, Greg Cardiff, Mark Miller, and David Suendermann-Oeft. 2017. Medical Speech Recognition: Reaching Parity with Humans. In *Speech and Computer*, pages 512–524, Cham. Springer International Publishing.

Jiatao Gu, Graham Neubig, Kyunghyun Cho, and Victor O. K. Li. 2017. Learning to Translate in Real-time with Neural Machine Translation. *arXiv:1610.00388 [cs]*. ArXiv: 1610.00388.

Geoffrey E. Hinton, Nitish Srivastava, Alex Krizhevsky, Ilya Sutskever, and Ruslan R. Salakhutdinov. 2012. Improving neural networks by preventing co-adaptation of feature detectors. *arXiv:1207.0580 [cs]*. ArXiv: 1207.0580.

Sergey Ioffe and Christian Szegedy. 2015. Batch Normalization: Accelerating Deep Network Training by Reducing Internal Covariate Shift. *arXiv:1502.03167 [cs]*. ArXiv: 1502.03167.

Douglas Jones, Florian Wolf, Edward Gibson, Elliott Williams, Evelina Fedorenko, Douglas Reynolds, and Marc Zissman. 2003. Measuring the readability of automatic speech-to-text transcripts. In *In EUROSPEECH*, pages 1585–1588.

Chin Char Juin, Richard Xiong Jun Wei, Luis Fernando D'Haro, and Rafael E. Banchs. 2017. Punctuation prediction using a bidirectional recurrent neural network with part-of-speech tagging. In *TENCON 2017 - 2017 IEEE Region 10 Conference*, pages 1806–1811, Penang. IEEE.

Seokhwan Kim. 2019. Deep Recurrent Neural Networks with Layer-wise Multi-head Attentions for Punctuation Restoration. In *ICASSP 2019 - 2019 IEEE International Conference on Acoustics, Speech and Signal Processing (ICASSP)*, pages 7280–7284, Brighton, United Kingdom. IEEE.

Diederik P. Kingma and Jimmy Ba. 2017. Adam: A Method for Stochastic Optimization. *arXiv:1412.6980 [cs]*. ArXiv: 1412.6980.

Ondrej Klejch, Peter Bell, and Steve Renals. 2016. Punctuated transcription of multi-genre broadcasts using acoustic and lexical approaches. In *2016 IEEE Spoken Language Technology Workshop (SLT)*, pages 433–440, San Diego, CA. IEEE.

Ondrej Klejch, Peter Bell, and Steve Renals. 2017. Sequence-to-sequence models for punctuated transcription combining lexical and acoustic features. In *2017 IEEE International Conference on Acoustics, Speech and Signal Processing (ICASSP)*, pages 5700–5704, New Orleans, LA. IEEE.

Olga Kovaleva, Alexey Romanov, Anna Rogers, and Anna Rumshisky. 2019. Revealing the Dark Secrets of BERT. In *Proceedings of the 2019 Conference on Empirical Methods in Natural Language Processing and the 9th International Joint Conference on Natural Language Processing (EMNLP-IJCNLP)*, pages

4364–4373, Hong Kong, China. Association for Computational Linguistics.

Zhenzhong Lan, Mingda Chen, Sebastian Goodman, Kevin Gimpel, Piyush Sharma, and Radu Soricut. 2020. ALBERT: A Lite BERT for Self-supervised Learning of Language Representations. *arXiv:1909.11942 [cs]*. ArXiv: 1909.11942.

Tsung-Yi Lin, Priya Goyal, Ross Girshick, Kaiming He, and Piotr Dollár. 2018. Focal Loss for Dense Object Detection. *arXiv:1708.02002 [cs]*. ArXiv: 1708.02002.

Liyuan Liu, Haoming Jiang, Pengcheng He, Weizhu Chen, Xiaodong Liu, Jianfeng Gao, and Jiawei Han. 2020. On the Variance of the Adaptive Learning Rate and Beyond. *arXiv:1908.03265 [cs, stat]*. ArXiv: 1908.03265.

Yinhan Liu, Myle Ott, Naman Goyal, Jingfei Du, Mandar Joshi, Danqi Chen, Omer Levy, Mike Lewis, Luke Zettlemoyer, and Veselin Stoyanov. 2019. RoBERTa: A Robustly Optimized BERT Pretraining Approach. *arXiv:1907.11692 [cs]*. ArXiv: 1907.11692.

Michael McTear, Zoraida Callejas, and David Griol. 2016. *The conversational interface: talking to smart devices*. Electrical engineering. Springer, Cham. OCLC: 953421937.

Anna Moro and Gyorgy Szaszak. 2017. A prosody inspired RNN approach for punctuation of machine produced speech transcripts to improve human readability. In *2017 8th IEEE International Conference on Cognitive Infocommunications (CogInfoCom)*, pages 000219–000224, Debrecen. IEEE.

Anna Moró and György Szaszák. 2017. A Phonological Phrase Sequence Modelling Approach for Resource Efficient and Robust Real-Time Punctuation Recovery. In *Interspeech 2017*, pages 558–562. ISCA.

Alexandre Nanchen and Philip N. Garner. 2019. Empirical Evaluation and Combination of Punctuation Prediction Models Applied to Broadcast News. In *ICASSP 2019 - 2019 IEEE International Conference on Acoustics, Speech and Signal Processing (ICASSP)*, pages 7275–7279, Brighton, United Kingdom. IEEE.

Binh Nguyen, Vu Bao Hung Nguyen, Hien Nguyen, Pham Ngoc Phuong, The-Loc Nguyen, Quoc Truong Do, and Luong Chi Mai. 2019. Fast and Accurate Capitalization and Punctuation for Automatic Speech Recognition Using Transformer and Chunk Merging. *arXiv:1908.02404 [cs]*. ArXiv: 1908.02404.

Vardaan Pahuja, Anirban Laha, Shachar Mirkin, Vikas Raykar, Lili Kotlerman, and Guy Lev. 2017. Joint Learning of Correlated Sequence Labelling Tasks Using Bidirectional Recurrent Neural Networks. *arXiv:1703.04650 [cs]*. ArXiv: 1703.04650.

Colin Raffel, Noam Shazeer, Adam Roberts, Katherine Lee, Sharan Narang, Michael Matena, Yanqi Zhou, Wei Li, and Peter J. Liu. 2019. Exploring the Limits of Transfer Learning with a Unified Text-to-Text Transformer. *arXiv:1910.10683 [cs, stat]*. ArXiv: 1910.10683.

Wael Salloum, Greg Finley, Erik Edwards, Mark Miller, and David Suendermann-Oeft. 2017. Deep Learning for Punctuation Restoration in Medical Reports. In *BioNLP 2017*, pages 159–164, Vancouver, Canada,. Association for Computational Linguistics.

Victor Sanh, Lysandre Debut, Julien Chaumond, and Thomas Wolf. 2020. DistilBERT, a distilled version of BERT: smaller, faster, cheaper and lighter. *arXiv:1910.01108 [cs]*. ArXiv: 1910.01108.

György Szaszák. 2019. An Audio-based Sequential Punctuation Model for ASR and its Effect on Human Readability. *Acta Polytechnica Hungarica*, 16(2).

György Szaszák and Máté Ákos Tündik. 2019. Leveraging a Character, Word and Prosody Triplet for an ASR Error Robust and Agglutination Friendly Punctuation Approach. In *Interspeech 2019*, pages 2988–2992. ISCA.

Ottokar Tilk and Tanel Alumae. 2015. LSTM for Punctuation Restoration in Speech Transcripts. In *INTERSPEECH*, page 6.

Ottokar Tilk and Tanel Alumäe. 2016. Bidirectional Recurrent Neural Network with Attention Mechanism for Punctuation Restoration. pages 3047–3051.

Marcos Vinícius Treviso and Sandra Maria Aluísio. 2018. Sentence Segmentation and Disfluency Detection in Narrative Transcripts from Neuropsychological Tests. In Aline Villavicencio, Viviane Moreira, Alberto Abad, Helena Caseli, Pablo Gamallo, Carlos Ramisch, Hugo Gonçalo Oliveira, and Gustavo Henrique Paetzold, editors, *Computational Processing of the Portuguese Language*, volume 11122, pages 409–418. Springer International Publishing, Cham. Series Title: Lecture Notes in Computer Science.

Mate Akos Tundik and Gyorgy Szaszak. 2018. Joint Word- and Character-level Embedding CNN-RNN Models for Punctuation Restoration. In *2018 9th IEEE International Conference on Cognitive Infocommunications (CogInfoCom)*, pages 000135–000140, Budapest, Hungary. IEEE.

Mate Akos Tundik, Balazs Tarjan, and Gyorgy Szaszak. 2017. Á bilingual comparison of MaxEnt- and RNN-based punctuation restoration in speech transcripts. In *2017 8th IEEE International Conference on Cognitive Infocommunications (CogInfoCom)*, pages 000121–000126, Debrecen. IEEE.

Máté Ákos Tündik, György Szaszák, Gábor Gosztolya, and András Beke. 2018. User-centric Evaluation of Automatic Punctuation in ASR Closed Captioning. In *Interspeech 2018*, pages 2628–2632. ISCA.

Máté Ákos Tündik, Balázs Tarján, and György Szaszák. 2017. Low Latency MaxEnt- and RNN-Based Word Sequence Models for Punctuation Restoration of Closed Caption Data. In Nathalie Camelin, Yannick Estève, and Carlos Martín-Vide, editors, *Statistical Language and Speech Processing*, volume 10583, pages 155–166. Springer International Publishing, Cham. Series Title: Lecture Notes in Computer Science.

Vincent Vandeghinste, Lyan Verwimp, Joris Pelemans, and Patrick Wambacq. 2018. A Comparison of Different Punctuation Prediction Approaches in a Translation Context. In *Proceedings of the 21st Annual Conference of the European Association for Machine Translation*, pages 269–278.

Ashish Vaswani, Noam Shazeer, Niki Parmar, Jakob Uszkoreit, Llion Jones, Aidan N. Gomez, Lukasz Kaiser, and Illia Polosukhin. 2017. Attention Is All You Need. *arXiv:1706.03762 [cs]*. ArXiv: 1706.03762.

Andris Vāravs and Askars Salimbajevs. 2018. Restoring Punctuation and Capitalization Using Transformer Models. In Thierry Dutoit, Carlos Martín-Vide, and Gueorgui Pironkov, editors, *Statistical Language and Speech Processing*, volume 11171, pages 91–102. Springer International Publishing, Cham. Series Title: Lecture Notes in Computer Science.

Feng Wang, Wei Chen, Zhen Yang, and Bo Xu. 2018. Self-Attention Based Network for Punctuation Restoration. In *2018 24th International Conference on Pattern Recognition (ICPR)*, pages 2803–2808, Beijing. IEEE.

Thomas Wolf, Lysandre Debut, Victor Sanh, Julien Chaumond, Clement Delangue, Anthony Moi, Pierric Cistac, Tim Rault, Rémi Louf, Morgan Funtowicz, and Jamie Brew. 2020. HuggingFace's Transformers: State-of-the-art Natural Language Processing. *arXiv:1910.03771 [cs]*. ArXiv: 1910.03771.

Kaituo Xu, Lei Xie, and Kaisheng Yao. 2016. Investigating LSTM for Punctuation Prediction. In *2016 10th International Symposium on Chinese Spoken Language Processing (ISCSLP)*, pages 1–5.

Zhilin Yang, Zihang Dai, Yiming Yang, Jaime Carbonell, Ruslan Salakhutdinov, and Quoc V. Le. 2020. XLNet: Generalized Autoregressive Pretraining for Language Understanding. *arXiv:1906.08237 [cs]*. ArXiv: 1906.08237.

Jiangyan Yi, Jianhua Tao, Zhengqi Wen, and Ya Li. 2017. Distilling Knowledge from an Ensemble of Models for Punctuation Prediction. In *Interspeech 2017*, pages 2779–2783. ISCA.

Michael R. Zhang, James Lucas, Geoffrey Hinton, and Jimmy Ba. 2019. Lookahead Optimizer: k steps forward, 1 step back. *arXiv:1907.08610 [cs, stat]*. ArXiv: 1907.08610.

Alp Öktem. 2018. *Incorporating Prosody into Neural Speech Processing Pipelines*. Ph.D. thesis.

Alp Öktem, Mireia Farrús, and Leo Wanner. 2017. Attentional Parallel RNNs for Generating Punctuation in Transcribed Speech. In Nathalie Camelin, Yannick Estève, and Carlos Martín-Vide, editors, *Statistical Language and Speech Processing*, volume 10583, pages 131–142. Springer International Publishing, Cham. Series Title: Lecture Notes in Computer Science.

Piotr Żelasko, Piotr Szymański, Jan Mizgajski, Adrian Szymczak, Yishay Carmiel, and Najim Dehak. 2018. Punctuation Prediction Model for Conversational Speech. In *Interspeech 2018*, pages 2633–2637. ISCA.

How Human is Machine Translationese?
Comparing Human and Machine Translations of Text and Speech

Yuri Bizzoni[1], **Tom S Juzek**[1], **Cristina España-Bonet**[2], **Koel Dutta Chowdhury**[1],
Josef van Genabith[1,2], and **Elke Teich**[1]

[1] Department of Language, Science and Technology, Saarland University, Germany
[2] DFKI GmbH, Saarbrücken, Germany
{yuri.bizzoni,tom.juzek,koel.duttachowdhury}@uni-saarland.de
{cristinae,Josef.Van_Genabith}@dfki.de,{e.teich}@mx.uni-saarland.de

Abstract

Translationese is a phenomenon present in human translations, simultaneous interpreting, and even machine translations. Some translationese features tend to appear in simultaneous interpreting with higher frequency than in human text translation, but the reasons for this are unclear. This study analyzes translationese patterns in translation, interpreting, and machine translation outputs in order to explore possible reasons. In our analysis we (*i*) detail two non-invasive ways of detecting translationese and (*ii*) compare translationese across human and machine translations from text and speech. We find that machine translation shows traces of translationese, but does not reproduce the patterns found in human translation, offering support to the hypothesis that such patterns are due to the model (human vs. machine) rather than to the data (written vs. spoken).

1 Introduction

In recent years, a growing body of work has pointed to the presence, across different genres and domains, of a set of relevant linguistic patterns with respect to syntax, semantics and discourse of human translations. Such patterns make translations more similar to each other than to texts in the same genre and style originally authored in the target language. These patterns are together called "translationese" (Teich, 2003; Volansky et al., 2015).

Linguists classify translationese in two main categories: (i) source's interference, or *shining-though* as put forward by Teich (2003). For example, a translation replicating a syntactic pattern which is typical of the source language, and rare in the target language, displays a typical form of shining-through; (ii) aherence or over-adherence to the target language's standards, that is *normalisation*. For example, translating a sentence displaying marked

order in the source with a sentence displaying standard order in the target it a typical example of over-normalization. Nonetheless, translationese's main causes remain unclear (Koppel and Ordan, 2011; Schmied and Schäffler, 1996).

Translationese displays different patterns depending on the translation's mode and register: a typical example is simultaneous interpreting, which shows translationese patterns distinct from those observed in written translations (Bernardini et al., 2016). We can interpret differences as either (*i*) an effect of the limitations of the human language apparatus that constrain translations, (*ii*) an inevitable effect of the structural and semantic differences between languages; or (*iii*) a combination of the two. To test these hypotheses, it is common to compare human translations (HT) produced under different circumstances, e.g. written translation versus simultaneous interpreting, following the assumption that, if translationese is a product of human cognitive limitations, translations produced under higher cognitive constrains should present more evident translationese symptoms. Machine translation (MT) does not have any human cognitive limitation, but current state-of-the-art systems learn to translate using human data, which is affected by translationese. On the other hand, unlike human translators, most standard modern MT systems still work at the level of individual sentences (rather than document or dialog) unaware of the surrounding co-text and context. Taking these observations into account, this paper explores the following research questions:

Q1. *Does machine translation replicate the translationese differences observed between text and speech in human translation?*

Q2. *Do different machine translation architectures learn differently enough to display distinctive translationese patterns?*

We study translationese in speech and writ-

Proceedings of the 17th International Conference on Spoken Language Translation (IWSLT), pages 280–290
July 9-10, 2020. ©2020 Association for Computational Linguistics
https://doi.org/10.18653/v1/P17

ten text by comparing human and machine translations to original documents. Specifically, we present a comparison between three MT architectures and the human translation of spoken and written language in German and English, exploring the question of whether MT replicates the differences observed in human data between text-based and interpreting-based translationese.

While some aspects of translationese tend to appear in simultaneous translation of speech with higher frequency than in translation of text, it is unclear whether such patterns are data- or model-dependent. Since machine translation does not have the cognitive limitations humans have (in terms of memory, online processing, etc.), MT systems should fail to replicate the differences between text and speech translationese observed in human translations, if such differences are due to the limits of human cognitive capacities.

Assuming that MT engines are trained only on translated texts and *not* on simultaneous interpreting, so that they cannot simply learn to mimic interpreting's translationese signal, the differences between text and speech translationese observed in human translation vs. interpreting are not expected to the same extent in MT if they are an effect of human cognitive limitations. If, on the other hand, translationese patterns in text and speech are due to characteristics inherent in the two modes of expression, MT systems' translationese patterns should mimic human translationese patterns.

The paper is organized as follows. Section 2 presents related work. Section 3 introduces the translationese measures and Section 4 the data and translation systems used in our study. Section 5 presents our results, comparing human with machine translations and comparing MT architectures among themselves. Section 6 concludes the paper.

2   Related Work

Translationese seems to affect the semantic as well as the structural level of text, but much of its effects can be seen in syntax and grammar (Santos, 1995; Puurtinen, 2003). An interesting aspect of translationese is that, while it is somewhat difficult to detect for the human eye (Tirkkonen-Condit, 2002), it can be machine learned with high accuracy (Baroni and Bernardini, 2006; Rubino et al., 2016). Many ways to automatically detect translationese have been devised, both with respect to textual translations and simultaneous interpreting (Baroni

and Bernardini, 2006; Ilisei et al., 2010; Popescu, 2011). Simultaneous interpreting has shown specific forms of translationese distinct from those of textual translation (He et al., 2016; Shlesinger, 1995), with a tendency of going in the direction of simplification and explicitation (Gumul, 2006). Due to the particularly harsh constraints imposed on human interpreters, such particularities can be useful to better understand the nature and causes of translationese in general (Shlesinger and Ordan, 2012).

The features of machine translated text depend on the nature of both training and test data; and possibly also on the approach to machine translation, i.e. statistical, neural or rule-based. The best translation quality is achieved when the training parallel corpus is in the same direction as the test translation, i.e. original-to-translationese when one wants to translate originals (Lembersky et al., 2013). In this case, more human translationese features are expected, as systems tend to learn to reproduce human features. The effects of translationese in machine translation test sets is also studied in Zhang and Toral (2019a). In fact, texts displaying translationese features seems to be much easier to translate than originals, and recent studies advise to use only translations from original texts in order to (automatically) evaluate translation quality (Graham et al., 2019; Zhang and Toral, 2019b). By contrast, Freitag et al. (2019) show a slight preference of human evaluators to outputs closer to originals; in this case the translation is done from translationese input, because, as noted by Riley et al. (2019), the best of the two worlds is not possible: one cannot create original-to-original corpora to train bias-free systems. Aranberri (2020) analyzed translationese characteristics on translations obtained by five state-of-the-art Spanish-to-Basque translation systems, neural and rule-based. The author quantifies translationese by measuring lexical variety, lexical density, length ratio and perplexity with part of speech (PoS) language models and finds no clear correlation with automatic translation quality across different test sets. The results are not conclusive but translation quality seems not to correlate with translationese. Similar results are obtained by Kunilovskaya and Lapshinova-Koltunski (2019) when using 45 morpho-syntactic features to analyze English-to-Russian translations. Vanmassenhove et al. (2019) noted that statistical systems reproduce human lexical diversity better than neural systems, for English–Spanish and English–French even if transformer models, i.e. neural, are those with the highest BLEU score. However, their transformer model did not use subword segmentation putting a limit on the plausible lexical diversity it can achieve.

In our study, we focus on English (*en*) and German (*de*) texts and compare the presence of translationese in human translations and interpreting, and in machine translations obtained by in-house MT engines. Differently to Aranberri (2020), we develop the MT engines to have control on the training data, since the aim of this work is not to study how translationese features correlate with translation quality, but the presence of translationese features themselves. To measure them, we use two metrics: part-of-speech (PoS) perplexity and dependency parsing distances. We use them as complementary measures, perplexity to model PoS sequences of linguistics objects in sentences (linear dimension), and dependency distance to model their syntactic depth (hierarchical dimension).

3 Translationese Measures

3.1 Part-of-Speech Perplexity

Our first measure to detect translationese is based on the assumption that a language model is able to capture the characteristic PoS sequences of a given language . Since grammatical structures between languages differ, a language model trained on Universal Part of Speech sequences of English will on average display less perplexity if exposed to an English text than if exposed to a German text. Following the same logic, if two models, one trained on English and one on German, were to progress through the PoS sequences of an English translation showing strong German interference, we could expect the English model's perplexity scores to rise, while the German model's perplexity would stay relatively low (Toral, 2019). On the other hand, if the English translation were displaying normalisation, we would expect the English model to display a lower perplexity than the German one. Perplexity is defined as the exponentiation of the entropy $H(p)$:

$$2^{H(p)} = 2^{-\sum_x p(x) \log_2 p(x)} \tag{1}$$

where $p(x)$ is the probability of a token x (possibly given its context), and $-\log_2 p(x)$ is the surprisal of x. While surprisal measures in bits the uncertainty in a random variable taking a certain value

x, entropy measures the weighted average surprisal of the variable.

3.2 Universal Dependencies

A syntactic analysis examines how the elements of a linguistic sequence relate to each other; for our purposes, those elements are words of a sentence. We employ the framework of Universal Dependencies (UD), which expresses syntactic relations through dependencies: each element depends on another element, its head (Nivre et al., 2019). In UD, in contrast to most other dependency frameworks, the head is the semantically more salient element and the dependent modifies the head. The top-level head is the root of a sequence, which is typically the main verb of the matrix clause. For instance, in the sentence *The great sailor is waiving, the* and *great* modify and depend on *sailor*, while *sailor* and *is* modify and depend on *waiving*, which is the root of the sentence. Figure 1 illustrates a dependency analysis of this example. The UD framework aims to be universal, i.e. suitable for all of the world's languages, and there are a large number of resources and tools available.[1]

An analysis of dependency lengths could help to identify translation artifacts. If a source language is shining-through, the translation's dependency lengths will be closer to the source language's average; and vice versa for normalisation. Explicitation will lead to longer, and simplification to shorter distances compared to originals.

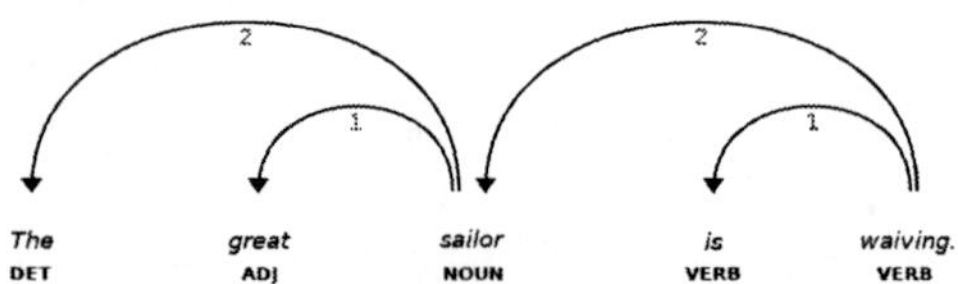

Figure 1: Visualizing a simple sequence in the Universal Dependencies framework, incl. dependency distances (red numerals below a dependency arch/edge).

We use spaCy's parser[2] to parse our corpora. An evaluation of 2000 head tags taken from randomly sampled sentences gives an accuracy rate of 91.2% and 93.6% for the German spoken and written originals, respectively, and 95.0% and 95.8% for English, as evaluated by a senior linguist. Sentences shorter than 3 tokens were excluded, as such sequences typically lack a verb and thus a root.

---

[1]See https://universaldependencies.org/ for details.

[2]https://spacy.io

We then use those parses for a macro-analysis of the syntactic structures, viz. an analysis of *average summed distances*. This analysis measures for each word the distance in words to its head. In Figure 1, the distance from *the* to its head is 2, from *great* to its head, it is 1. The sum of distances for the example is 6. In the following, we average the summed distances per sentence length. The measure can be interpreted as a proxy of (cumulative) processing difficulty/complexity of a sequence, where long distance structures are regarded as more complex than structures with shorter distances. Particle verbs illustrate this. In *Mary picked the guy that we met the other day up*, the particle *up* has a long distance to its head and the sequence is relatively hard to process. This contrasts to *Mary picked up the guy that we met the other day*, where the distance between particle and verb is short, which reduces the cognitive load. This dependency-based measure is taken from Gibson et al. (2019) and Futrell et al. (2015) and builds on work by Liu (2008).

4 Experimental Settings

4.1 Corpora

Originals and Human Translations. We used human written texts and speech transcriptions to train and test our language models and to extract part of our syntactic distance measures. We use datasets that belong to the same genre and register but to different modalities: transcriptions of European Parliament speeches by native speakers and their interpreted renditions (EPIC-UdS, spoken), the written speeches and their official translations (Europarl-UdS, written) (Karakanta et al., 2018). Table 1 summarizes the number of sentences and words for each of the six categories:

1. Original written English
2. Original written German
3. Original spoken English (transcript)
4. Original spoken German (transcript)
5. English to German translations
6. English to German interpreting (transcript)

For each corpus, we train the PoS models on 3000 random sentences and evaluate on the remaining data. We tokenized our data using NLTK (Bird and Loper, 2004) and performed universal PoS tagging via spaCy. We train our language models using a one-layer LSTM with 50 units (Chollet et al., 2015). Due to the small dimensions of the

vocabulary (17 PoS), 5 iterations over 3000 sentences suffice to converge. In our experiments, we measure the average perplexity of each model on *unseen* human data from of each category, and on the translations produced by three MT architectures in two different settings (see Section 4.2).

MT Training Data. In order to adapt our machine translation engines to the previous modalities as much as possible, we gather two different corpora from OPUS (Tiedemann, 2012), one of them text-oriented (C_t) and the other speech-oriented (C_s). The distribution of their sub-corpora is shown in Table 2. Note that we do not include Europarl data here so that there is no overlap between MT training and our analysis data.

Note also that our speech data (TED talks and subtitles) is still made up from translations and not simultaneous interpreting. This is important since it prevents MT systems from simply mimicking interpreting's pronounced translationese.

All datasets are normalised, tokenized and true-cased using standard Moses scripts (Koehn et al., 2007) and cleaned for low quality pairs. Duplicates are removed and sentences shorter than 4 tokens or with a length ratio greater than 9 are discarded. We also eliminate sentence pairs which are not identified as English/German by *langdetect*[3] and apply basic cleaning procedures. With this, we reduce the corpus size by more than half of the sentences. In order to build balanced corpora we limit the number of sentences we used from ParaCrawl to 5 million and from Open Subtitles to 10 million. With this, both C_t and C_s contain around 200 million tokens per language. Finally, a byte-pair-encoding (BPE) (Sennrich et al., 2016) with 32 k merge operations trained jointly on *en–de* data is applied before training neural systems. After shuffling, 1,000 sentences are set aside for tuning/validation.

4.2 Machine Translation Engines

We train three different architectures, one statistical and two neural, on the corpora above.

Phrase-Based Statistical Machine Translation (SMT). SMT systems are trained using standard freely available software. We estimate a 5-gram language model using interpolated Kneser–Ney discounting with SRILM (Stolcke, 2002). Word alignment is done with GIZA++ (Och and Ney, 2003)

---

[3]https://pypi.org/project/langdetect/

Europarl-UdS	lines	tokens	EPIC-UdS	lines	tokens
German Translation	137,813	3,100,647	German Interpreting	4,080	58,371
Written German	427,779	7,869,289	Spoken German	3,408	57,227
Written English	372,547	8,693,135	Spoken English	3,623	68,712

Table 1: Corpus collections used to train our language models: Europarl-UdS (written) and EPIC-UdS (spoken). German translation and interpreting are both from English.

	lines	de tokens	en tokens	C_t	C_s
CommonCrawl	2,212,292	49,870,179	54,140,396	✓	✓
MultiUN	108,387	4,494,608	4,924,596	✓	✓
NewsCommentary	324,388	8,316,081	46,222,416	✓	✓
academia career limiting moves Rapid	1,039,918	24,563,476	148,360,866	✓	✓
ParaCrawl-5M	5,000,000	96,262,081	103,287,049	✓	✗
TED	198,583	3,833,653	20,141,669	✗	✓
OpenSubtitles-10M	10,000,000	85,773,795	93,287,837	✗	✓
Total clean Speech	13,379,441	187,551,444	197,175,542	✗	✓
Total clean Text	9,121,710	198,340,602	207,434,038	✓	✗

Table 2: Text-oriented (C_t) and speech-oriented (C_s) corpora used for training the MT systems.

and both phrase extraction and decoding are done with the `Moses` package (Koehn et al., 2007). The optimization of the feature weights of the model is done with Minimum Error Rate Training (MERT) (Och, 2003) against the BLEU (Papineni et al., 2002) evaluation metric. As features, we use the language model, direct and inverse phrase probabilities, direct and inverse lexical probabilities, phrase and word penalties, and lexicalized reordering.

The neural systems are trained using the `Marian` toolkit (Junczys-Dowmunt et al., 2018) in a bidirectional setting $\{en,de\} \leftrightarrow \{de,en\}$:

RNN-Based Neural Machine Translation (RNN). The architecture consists of a 1-layer bidirectional encoder with complex GRU units (4 layers) and a decoder also with complex GRUs (8 layers). The tied embeddings have a dimension of 512 and hidden states with a size of 1024, using the Adam optimizer (Kingma and Ba, 2015) with β_1=0.9, β_2=0.98 and ϵ=1e-09 and a growing learning rate from 0 to 0.0003. Label (0.1) and exponential smoothing, dropout of 0.1 and layer normalisation are also applied.

Transformer Base Neural Machine Translation (TRF). We use a base transformer architecture as defined in Vaswani et al. (2017), that is, a 6-layer encoder–decoder with 8-head self-attention, a 2048-dim hidden feed-forward, and 512-dim word vectors. Optimization algorithm, dropout, smoothings and learning rate (with warmup till update 16,000) are the same as for RNN.

5 Experimental Results

Below we present the translationese characteristics in the different modalities found in our study.

5.1 Human Translationese

5.1.1 Perplexity

The PoS perplexity scores of our language models on human data shows that, as expected, each model's perplexity is at its lowest when confronted with data from the same category. Since the amount of data differs among modalities, we checked that 10 independent partitions of the data lead to the same results. Translation and interpreting models are least perplexed by unseen instances of their own categories, and are not confused by original written or spoken data: translation and interpreting display indeed detectable and idiosyncratic patterns.

Figure 2 shows perplexity scores in a matrix where the x-axis reflects the data on which the language models have been trained, and the y-axis reflects the partition of data on which the PoS mod-

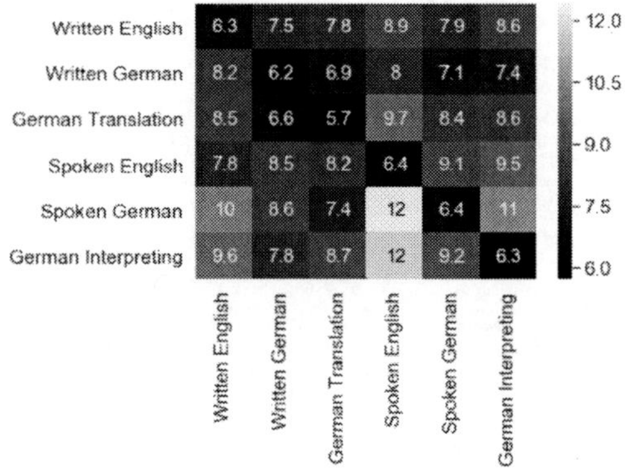

Figure 2: Perplexity of each universal PoS language model (x-axis) on unseen data from each category (y-axis).

els are tested. The diagonal corresponds to training and testing in the same modality and language and, consequently, shows the lowest perplexities as said before. Leaving the diagonal of the matrix aside, we see that German translations are least perplexing for the model trained on written German, and vice-versa, written German sequences are least perplexing for the model trained on German translation. The German translation model displays its highest perplexity on English, and the written English model is more perplexed by German translations than by German originals. These observations seem to point away from shining-through, and to point instead towards the presence of normalization in German translation and interpreting.

Interpreting differs from translation. While German translation sequences are of low-perplexity for the written German model, German interpreting sequences are quite perplexing for the spoken German model, and in general present higher levels of perplexity than translation for all German models. Unlike German translation, the interpreting model returns high perplexity on all datasets except its own. This particularity of interpreting data was previously noted (Bizzoni et al., 2019) and ascribed to structural over-simplification, as a possible effect of the cognitive pressure on interpreters.

5.1.2 Syntax: Dependency Length

The corresponding analysis for our syntax measure is presented in Figure 3, the top left and top center plots. For written spoken data in both German and English, the summed dependency distances increase as sentence lengths increase, as one would

expect. Translations from English into German are slightly less complex than German originals. The same applies to English–German interpreting. This is in contrast with translations from German into English, that are somewhat more complex than the English originals. For German–English interpreting, there is no difference to the originals. Arguably, the fact that English-to-German translations are less complex than German originals and that German-to-English translations are more complex than English originals is an artifact of source language shining-through. Notice that discrepancies between curves are more evident for long sentences, and that sentences in spoken texts are systematically shorter than in written text.

5.2 Human vs. Machine Translationese

Effects of translationese are expected in MT outputs as long as the systems are trained with human data which is rich in translationese artifacts. In this section, we compare the translationese effects present in human translations with those present in TRF translations, the state-of-the-art MT architecture. For comparison, our bidirectional TRF trained with text-oriented data achieves a BLEU score of 35.5 into English and 38.1 into German on Newstest 2018, and 33.0 and 36.2 respectively when trained with speech-oriented data. MT systems have been trained using the corpora described in Table 2. Data has not been classified according to translationese, but one can assume[4] that most of the corpora will be original English. This would create a bias towards human-like translationese in German translations.

The single translationese feature that seems to be most characteristic of the output of our MT model is structural shining-through, a characteristic present in human translations, but that appears to become particularly relevant in various MT outputs, specially the ones translating German written modality into English. Figure 4 shows low perplexities when the written German language model is used on the translated text into English (5.9 vs. 7.3 for the English model on the English translation). According to the MT training data distribution, this feature cannot be due to data biases but to the MT architecture itself. At the same time,

---

[4]Riley et al. (2019) quantified the amount of original German texts in the WMT18 data with a 22%. Their corpora only differ from ours by lacking Europarl and by including in addition TED talks and OpenSubtitles. The authors report an F_1=0.85 for their classification.

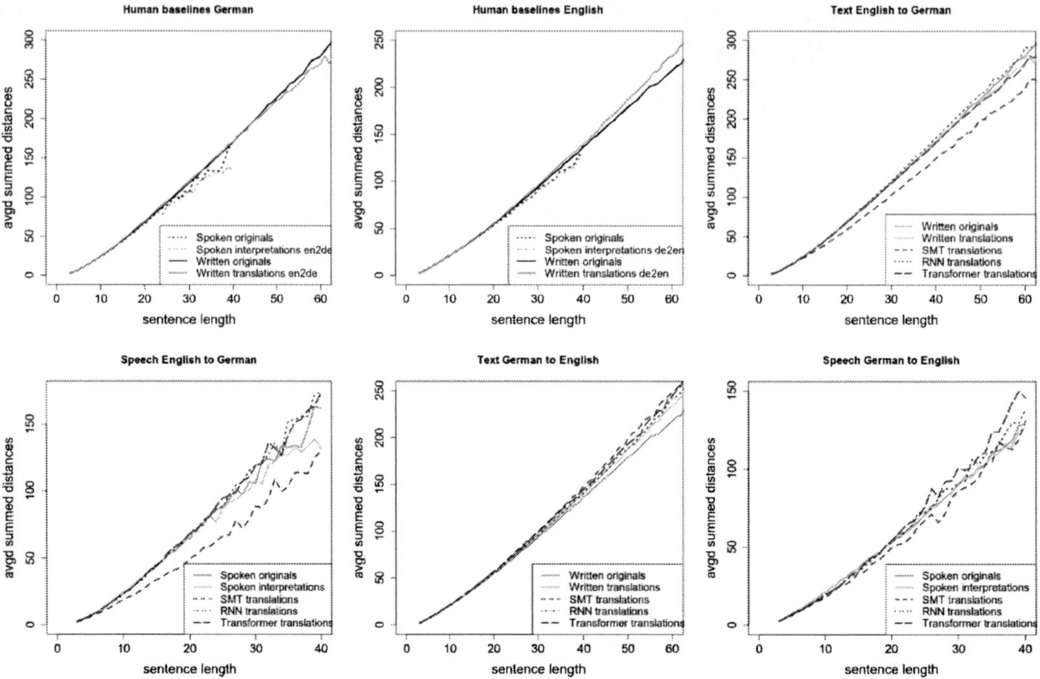

Figure 3: Averaged summed dependency distances, y-axis, per sentence length, x-axis, for German HTs (top left) and for English HTs (top center). The same incl. HTs and MTs for translations of written English to German (top right), spoken English to German (bottom left), written German to English (bottom center), and for spoken German to English (bottom right).

target language normalisation, which is a prominent translationese feature in human translations, appears less evident in our MT output. In this case, normalisation is only slightly more prominent in translations into German with a perplexity of 6.9 in translated text and 7.0 in translated speech, where translations into English score 7.3 and 6.9 respectively. We also checked if the content of the MT training data is relevant for the conclusions and might bias the comparison with interpretings and translations for instance. To this end, we use the text-oriented MT engine to translate speech, and the speech-oriented MT engine to translate text. In our experiments, we reach equivalent perplexities for written text data whichever engine we use but, for speech, perplexities are in general higher when the text-oriented MT is used. This could be expected, but we attribute the noticeable effect only on spoken data due to its completely different nature.[5]

Possibly due to the larger presence of shining-through, machine translations from English to German appear to behave quite differently from machine translations from German to English. While differences due to the source and target language naturally exist in human translations, the MT output appears more sensitive to such variations. Summed parse tree distance Figure 3 show how TRF outputs are more complex than English originals and translations/interpretings but have a similar degree in the German counterparts. We found that machine translation seems to *over-correct* translationese effects, again not following the characteristics of training data.

5.3 Translationese across MT Architectures

The previous section summarizes the differences between a state-of-the-art MT system and human translations/interpretings, but one could expect different behaviors for other architectures. In the following, we present a detailed analysis of each ar-

<hr>

[5]Whereas clean transcriptions as TED talks are used to train our speech-oriented engines, Europarl data include many speech-distinctive elements such as hesitations, broken sentences and repetitions: *but / is / euh what/ what's most difficulty*

bringing in prisoners from Guantánamo because we see them to be a security euh risk.

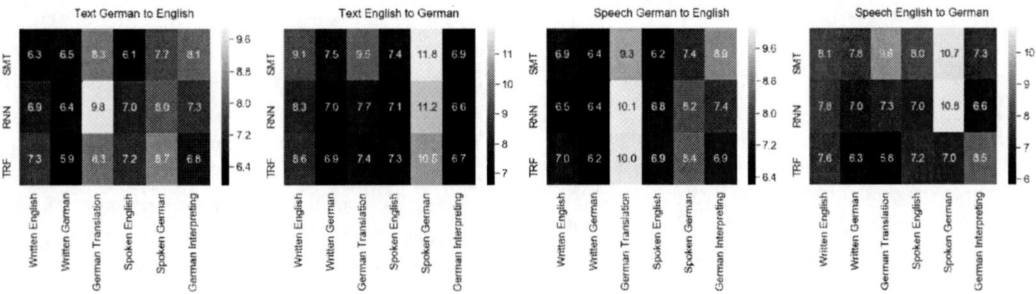

Figure 4: Perplexity per language and mode. Language: German to English and English to German. Mode: written and spoken.

chitecture for our two measures independently.

5.3.1 Perplexity

The results for PoS perplexities are illustrated in Figure 4.

Results on SMT. German language models return on average higher perplexities on SMT than English models, and translations into English are on average less perplexing than translations into German, which hints at English to German shining-through. The observed absence of shining-through in the human data confirms this hypothesis, since our German translation and interpreting models are highly perplexed by SMT data, indicating that this kind of translation presents structural patterns that differ from human translationese. It also differs from neural systems in the sense that SMT seems to better reproduce the structure of the MT training corpus. SMT is acknowledged to translate more literally, while NMT tends to be more inspirational, and this trend is observed in our setting too.

Results on RNN. English models show higher perplexities when tested on any translated German than when tested on translated English, and German models show more perplexity for German translations than for English ones. German translation and interpreting models reverse the pattern, showing lower perplexity on German translations than on English translations. This seems to point to a more complex phenomenon, possibly a mix of shining-through and normalization, but it seems to be less perplexing for the models trained on translation and interpreting. RNN's translation patterns are clearly closer to human translationese than SMTs.

Results on TRF. While RNN data attains the lowest *average* perplexity, our Transformer man-

ages to attain the lowest single scores —reaching in some cases lower perplexities than the ones elicited by human equivalents. Consistently, the highest TRF perplexities are lower than the highest perplexities of the other systems. The single model displaying the lowest perplexity on this data is German Translation, followed by written German, while spoken German shows the highest perplexity, followed by German Interpreting. Written German shows low-level perplexities on German translations, in accordance with the German translation model; but also lower perplexities on English translations, which instead spark significant perplexities in the German translation model. This behavior seems to point to a "stronger than human" shining-through of German into English, which makes English translations less surprising for German than for English but perplexes a model trained on the patterns of human translations. Models trained on spoken data also appear more perplexed than models trained on written data, hinting at a presence of "written patterns" in speech translation that does not appear in human data.

5.3.2 Syntax: Dependency Length

The results for the syntactic macro-analysis of dependency lengths are illustrated in Figure 3 (top right and all bottom plots).

Results on SMT. Similarly to the trends observed with perplexities, the SMT translations diverge the most of all models. Translations into German of English speech and text lack the complexity of the German originals and are even considerably less complex than human interpreting/translation. Translations into English of German speech are also less complex than the HTs, in contrast to other models. The model is only in line with human translations and other models when it comes to translations of German text.

Results on RNN. Overall, RNN translations come out really well for this measure, meaning that they are able to mimic human outputs. Translations of English texts into German are in line with German originals, translation of English speech is slightly more complex than the HTs. Translations of German speech and texts into English are very close to the HTs.

Results on TRF. The TRF translations of English texts into German come out really well, i.e. close to the HTs – the TRF comes closest of all models here. Translations of English speech also comes close to the HTs. However, TRF translations of German speech into English is overly complex in comparison to the HTs. Translations of German texts are slightly more complex than the HTs.

6 Conclusions

Crossing PoS perplexity scores and syntactic dependency lengths, we draw some conclusions about the difference between human and machine structural translationese in text and speech. We summarize our findings as preliminary answers to the questions posed in the Introduction.

Q1. The structural particularity displayed by human interpreting is not replicated by MT models: machine translation of spoken language is not as marked as human interpreting. Human written translations are similar to comparable originals, while interpreting transcripts appear different from all other datasets, at least based on our measures. This feature fails to appear in any of the machine translations. If we look at MT models' outputs going from SMT to TRF, we see that written language perplexity for the target decreases, without getting smaller than the human "lower bound". For spoken language, perplexity in MT seems to outdo human levels with ease: for example, TRF reaches 7.2 where human perplexity is 12 (English to German Interpreting). This apparent improvement on speech-based data could confirm the idea that the special features of interpreting depend on the cognitive overload of human translators rather than to a systematic difficulty of translating speech.

Q2. Overall, we see a decrease of perplexity and an increase in syntactic complexity when moving from SMT to RNN to TRF, hinting at a tendency for SMT to produce over-simplified structures, while neural systems seem able to deal better with the complexity of their source. Figures 3 and 4 show these trends. With respect to the syntactic measures, we see clear tendencies in the human translations. The MTs, however, are more heterogeneous: translations by the SMT often over-simplify in contrast to the HTs, translations by the neural systems come out reasonably close to the HTs, i.e. close to originals, but they are sometimes more complex. In general the statistical engines show more evident signs of syntactic simplification than both human and neural translations. This can be the result of having a phrase-based translation (SMT) in contrast to sentence-based translations (humans and neural systems). The difference between architectures is less strong for the grammatical perplexities, where machine translation displays in general higher levels of structural shining-through than human translation, and lower levels of normalization, presenting more sensibility to the source language than human translation.

In general, while we find evident differences in translationese between human and machine translations of text and speech, our results are complex to analyze and it would be wise not to over-interpret our findings. In future work, the impact of the difference in the amount of available data and languages involved for written and spoken texts should also be analysed. Machine translations do present symptoms of structural translationese, but such symptoms only in part resemble those displayed by human translators and interpreters, and often follow independent patterns that we still have to understand in depth. This understanding can help in improving machine translation itself with simple techniques such as reranking of translation options, or more complex ones such as guiding the decoder to follow the desired patterns or rewarding their presence. For this, a complementary study on the correlation of translation quality with our translationese measures is needed.

Acknowledgments

This research was funded by the German Research Foundation (DFG) as part of SFB 1102 Information Density and Linguistic Encoding.

References

Nora Aranberri. 2020. Can translationese features help users select an MT system for post-editing? *Proce-

samiento del Lenguaje Natural, 64:93–100.

Marco Baroni and Silvia Bernardini. 2006. A new approach to the study of translationese: Machine-learning the difference between original and translated text. *Literary and Linguistic Computing*, 21(3):259–274.

Silvia Bernardini, Adriano Ferraresi, and Maja Miličević. 2016. From EPIC to EPTICExploring simplification in interpreting and translation from an intermodal perspective. *Target. International Journal of Translation Studies*, 28(1):61–86.

Steven Bird and Edward Loper. 2004. NLTK: The natural language toolkit. In *Proceedings of the ACL Interactive Poster and Demonstration Sessions*, pages 214–217, Barcelona, Spain. Association for Computational Linguistics.

Yuri Bizzoni, Elke Teich, Tom S Juzek, Katherine Menzel, and Heike Przybyl. 2019. Found in Interpreting: Detection and analysis of translationese using computational language models. Poster at SFB Colloquium, Saarbrücken.

François Chollet et al. 2015. Keras. `https://keras.io`.

Markus Freitag, Isaac Caswell, and Scott Roy. 2019. APE at scale and its implications on MT evaluation biases. In *Proceedings of the Fourth Conference on Machine Translation (Volume 1: Research Papers)*, pages 34–44, Florence, Italy. Association for Computational Linguistics.

Richard Futrell, Kyle Mahowald, and Edward Gibson. 2015. Large-Scale Evidence of Dependency Length Minimization in 37 Languages. In *Proceedings of the National Academy of Sciences*, volume 112, pages 10336–10341.

Edward Gibson, Richard Futrell, Steven Piantadosi, Isabelle Dautriche, Kyle Mahowald, Leon Bergen, and Roger Levy. 2019. How Efficiency Shapes Human Language. *Trends in Cognitive Sciences*, 23(5):389–407.

Yvette Graham, Barry Haddow, and Philipp Koehn. 2019. Translationese in Machine Translation Evaluation. *ArXiv*, abs/1906.09833.

Ewa Gumul. 2006. Explicitation in simultaneous interpreting: A strategy or a by-product of language mediation? *Across Languages and Cultures*, 7(2):171–190.

He He, Jordan Boyd-Graber, and Hal Daumé III. 2016. Interpretese vs. translationese: The uniqueness of human strategies in simultaneous interpretation. In *Proceedings of the 2016 Conference of the North American Chapter of the Association for Computational Linguistics: Human Language Technologies*, pages 971–976.

Iustina Ilisei, Diana Inkpen, Gloria Corpas Pastor, and Ruslan Mitkov. 2010. Identification of translationese: A machine learning approach. In *International Conference on Intelligent Text Processing and Computational Linguistics*, pages 503–511. Springer.

Marcin Junczys-Dowmunt, Roman Grundkiewicz, Tomasz Dwojak, Hieu Hoang, Kenneth Heafield, Tom Neckermann, Frank Seide, Ulrich Germann, Alham Fikri Aji, Nikolay Bogoychev, André F. T. Martins, and Alexandra Birch. 2018. Marian: Fast Neural Machine Translation in C++. In *Proceedings of ACL 2018, System Demonstrations*, pages 116–121, Melbourne, Australia. Association for Computational Linguistics.

Alina Karakanta, Mihaela Vela, and Elke Teich. 2018. EuroParl-UdS: Preserving and Extending Metadata in Parliamentary Debates. *ParlaCLARIN: Creating and Using Parliamentary Corpora*.

Diederik P. Kingma and Jimmy Ba. 2015. Adam: A method for stochastic optimization. In *3rd International Conference on Learning Representations, ICLR 2015, San Diego, CA, USA, May 7-9, 2015, Conference Track Proceedings*.

Philipp Koehn, Hieu Hoang, Alexandra Birch, Chris Callison-Burch, Marcello Federico, Nicola Bertoldi, Brooke Cowan, Wade Shen, Christine Moran, Richard Zens, Chris Dyer, Ondrej Bojar, Alexandra Constantin, and Evan Herbst. 2007. Moses: Open source toolkit for statistical machine translation. In *Proceedings of the 45th Annual Meeting of the Association for Computational Linguistics Companion Volume Proceedings of the Demo and Poster Sessions*, pages 177–180. Association for Computational Linguistics.

Moshe Koppel and Noam Ordan. 2011. Translationese and its dialects. In *Proceedings of the 49th Annual Meeting of the Association for Computational Linguistics: Human Language Technologies*, pages 1318–1326, Portland, Oregon, USA. Association for Computational Linguistics.

Maria Kunilovskaya and Ekaterina Lapshinova-Koltunski. 2019. Translationese features as indicators of quality in English-Russian human translation. In *Proceedings of the Human-Informed Translation and Interpreting Technology Workshop (HiT-IT 2019)*, pages 47–56, Varna, Bulgaria. Incoma Ltd., Shoumen, Bulgaria.

Gennadi Lembersky, Noam Ordan, and Shuly Wintner. 2013. Improving statistical machine translation by adapting translation models to translationese. *Computational Linguistics*, 39(4):999–1023.

Haitao Liu. 2008. Dependency Distance as a Metric of Language Comprehension Difficulty. *Journal of Cognitive Science*, 9:159–191.

Joakim Nivre, Mitchell Abrams, Zeljko Agić, and et al. 2019. Universal Dependencies 2.4.

Franz Josef Och. 2003. Minimum error rate training in statistical machine translation. In *Proceedings of the 41st Annual Meeting on Association for Computational Linguistics - Volume 1*, pages 160–167, Stroudsburg, PA, USA. Association for Computational Linguistics.

Franz Josef Och and Hermann Ney. 2003. A Systematic Comparison of Various Statistical Alignment Models. *Computational Linguistics*, 29(1):19–51.

Kishore Papineni, Salim Roukos, Todd Ward, and Wei-Jing Zhu. 2002. BLEU: a Method for Automatic Evaluation of Machine Translation. In *Proceedings of the Association of Computational Linguistics*, pages 311–318.

Marius Popescu. 2011. Studying translationese at the character level. In *Proceedings of the International Conference Recent Advances in Natural Language Processing 2011*, pages 634–639, Hissar, Bulgaria. Association for Computational Linguistics.

Tiina Puurtinen. 2003. Features of translationese contradicting translation universals? *Corpus-based approaches to contrastive linguistics and translation studies*, 20:141.

Parker Riley, Isaac Caswell, Markus Freitag, and David Grangier. 2019. Translationese as a Language in "Multilingual" NMT. *ArXiv*, abs/1911.03823.

Raphael Rubino, Ekaterina Lapshinova-Koltunski, and Josef van Genabith. 2016. Information density and quality estimation features as translationese indicators for human translation classification. In *Proceedings of the 2016 Conference of the North American Chapter of the Association for Computational Linguistics: Human Language Technologies*, pages 960–970, San Diego, California. Association for Computational Linguistics.

Diana Santos. 1995. On grammatical translationese. In *Short papers presented at the Tenth Scandinavian Conference on Computational Linguistics*, pages 59–66.

Josef Schmied and Hildegard Schäffler. 1996. Approaching translationese through parallel and translation corpora. *Language and Computers*, 16:41–58.

Rico Sennrich, Barry Haddow, and Alexandra Birch. 2016. Neural Machine Translation of Rare Words with Subword Units. In *Proceedings of the 54th Annual Meeting of the Association for Computational Linguistics, (ACL 2016), Volume 1: Long Papers*, pages 1715–1725, Berlin, Germany.

Miriam Shlesinger. 1995. Shifts in cohesion in simultaneous interpreting. *The translator*, 1(2):193–214.

Miriam Shlesinger and Noam Ordan. 2012. More spoken or more translated?: Exploring a known unknown of simultaneous interpreting. *Target. International Journal of Translation Studies*, 24(1):43–60.

Andreas Stolcke. 2002. SRILM – An extensible language modeling toolkit. In *Proceedings of the 7th International Conference on Spoken Language Processing*, pages 901–904.

Elke Teich. 2003. *Cross-Linguistic Variation in System and Text. A Methodology for the Investigation of Translations and Comparable Texts.* Mouton de Gruyter, Berlin.

Jörg Tiedemann. 2012. Parallel data, tools and interfaces in OPUS. In *Proceedings of the Eighth International Conference on Language Resources and Evaluation (LREC'12)*, pages 2214–2218, Istanbul, Turkey. European Language Resources Association (ELRA).

Sonja Tirkkonen-Condit. 2002. Translationese –a myth or an empirical fact?: A study into the linguistic identifiability of translated language. *Target. International Journal of Translation Studies*, 14(2):207–220.

Antonio Toral. 2019. Post-editese: an exacerbated translationese. In *Proceedings of Machine Translation Summit XVII Volume 1: Research Track*, pages 273–281, Dublin, Ireland. European Association for Machine Translation.

Eva Vanmassenhove, Dimitar Shterionov, and Andy Way. 2019. Lost in translation: Loss and decay of linguistic richness in machine translation. In *Proceedings of Machine Translation Summit XVII Volume 1: Research Track*, pages 222–232, Dublin, Ireland. European Association for Machine Translation.

Ashish Vaswani, Noam Shazeer, Niki Parmar, Jakob Uszkoreit, Llion Jones, Aidan N Gomez, Ł ukasz Kaiser, and Illia Polosukhin. 2017. Attention is All you Need. In *Advances in Neural Information Processing Systems 30*, pages 5998–6008. Curran Associates, Inc.

Vered Volansky, Noam Ordan, and Shuly Wintner. 2015. On the features of translationese. *Digital Scholarship in the Humanities*, 30(1):98–118.

Mike Zhang and Antonio Toral. 2019a. The effect of translationese in machine translation test sets. *arXiv preprint arXiv:1906.08069*.

Mike Zhang and Antonio Toral. 2019b. The effect of translationese in machine translation test sets. In *Proceedings of the Fourth Conference on Machine Translation (Volume 1: Research Papers)*, pages 73–81, Florence, Italy. Association for Computational Linguistics.

Association for Computational Linguistics
209 N. Eighth Street
Stroudsburg, Pennsylvania 18360

ISBN 978-1-7138-1388-0